Amsterdam

timeout.com/amsterdam

Published by Time Out Guides Ltd, a wholly owned subsidiary of Time Out Group Ltd.
Time Out and the Time Out logo are trademarks of Time Out Group Ltd.

© Time Out Group Ltd 2005
Previous editions 1991, 1993, 1995, 1996, 1998, 2000, 2002, 2004

10 9 8 7 6 5 4 3 2 1

This edition first published in Great Britain in 2005 by Ebury
Ebury is a division of The Random House Group Ltd,
20 Vauxhall Bridge Road, London SW1V 2SA

Random House Australia Pty Limited, 20 Alfred Street, Milsons Point, Sydney, New South Wales 2061, Australia
Random House New Zealand Limited, 18 Poland Road, Glenfield, Auckland 10, New Zealand
Random House South Africa (Pty) Limited, Endulini, 5A Jubilee Road, Parktown 2193, South Africa

Random House UK Limited Reg. No. 954009

Distributed in USA by Publishers Group West
1700 Fourth Street, Berkeley, California 94710

Distributed in Canada by Penguin Canada Ltd
10 Alcorn Avenue, Toronto, Ontario, Canada M4V 3B2

For further distribution details, see www.timeout.com

ISBN 1-904978-36-3

A CIP catalogue record for this book is available from the British Library

Colour reprographics by Icon, Crowne House, 56-58 Southwark Street, London SE1 1UN

Printed and bound in Germany by Appl
Papers used by Ebury Press are natural, recyclable products made from wood grown in sustainable forests

Time Out Guides Limited
Universal House
251 Tottenham Court Road
London W1T 7AB
Tel + 44 (0)20 7813 3000
Fax + 44 (0)20 7813 6001
Email guides@timeout.com
www.timeout.com

Contents

Introduction

'Oh, man, I'm goin', that's all there is to it. I'm fuckin' goin'!' exclaims Jules (Samuel L Jackson) in *Pulp Fiction* after having Amsterdam's singular drugs policy explained to him by fellow hitman Vincent Vega (John Travolta). No doubt this was not the first time such a conversation inspired future holiday plans. But while the city is often painted as a colder and wetter version of Babylon, awash with sex and drugs, there are different visions of the town too. Like many other European cities, Amsterdam had its 'Golden Age', but in this case the appellation was deserved: during the first six decades of the 17th century it was the richest city in the world and the money that poured into the muddy port on the Amstel was used to build the image-defining girdle of canals. The lessons learned then and in the subsequent centuries, when the Dutch battled to claim and reclaim land from the sea, have found applications in many different arenas, from Piet Mondriaan's playful use of line and form to Johan Cruijff's almost miraculous ability to change the available space on an apparently fixed football field.

So, what has made this city unique? There's a clue in another of the adjectives often applied to Amsterdam: relaxed. Every visitor comes away, having seen rows of sun-starved Amsterdammers lying out throughout a summer's day, muttering something about whether anyone here actually has a job. But the locals in fact balance relaxation with a crafty business acumen. They are very much aware, after centuries of accumulated experience, that openness and tolerance are efficient ways of doing business. And, while you'll have no problem chilling out in this most global of villages, be wary of going with the flow too much, otherwise you might find yourself endlessly looping back to Amsterdam's near geographic centre, the Red Light District. The way the city radiates out from this – certainly not charmless – ancient inner pit and its flesh-squeegeed windows, led a visiting Albert Camus to observe that the circumscribing canals resemble the circles of Hell.

The chaotic tendencies of the centre soon give way to rarefied wandering opportunities in the Canal Ring, which in turn give way to the down-to-earth street vibe of less-visited neighbourhoods like the Jordaan and the Pijp, or the art-as-metropolitan-religion splendours of the Museum Quarter. But you will also note during your travels that Amsterdam is more askew than usual. Many of the major museums are in the middle of being redeveloped, as are the eastern docklands. As if this was not enough, a Metro line is being dug from north to south through the heart of the city. Add to that the emotional fallout from the murder of Theo Van Gogh, and you have a city in an intense state of flux. But hey, fluxing is what this city does best.

ABOUT THE TIME OUT CITY GUIDES

Time Out Amsterdam is one of an expanding series of Time Out City Guides, now numbering 50, produced by the people behind London and New York's successful listings magazines. Our guides are all written and updated by resident experts who have striven to provide you with all the most up-to-date information you'll need to explore the city or read up on its background, whether you're a local or a first-time visitor.

THE LOWDOWN ON THE LISTINGS

Above all, we've tried to make this book as useful as possible. Addresses, telephone numbers, websites, transport information, opening times, admission prices and credit card details have all been included in the listings. And, as far as possible, we've given details of facilities, services and events, all checked and correct as we went to press. However, owners and managers can change their arrangements at any time, and they often do. Before you go out of your way, we'd advise you to telephone and check opening times, ticket prices and other particulars. While every effort has been made to ensure the accuracy of the information contained in this guide, the publishers cannot accept responsibility for any errors it may contain.

PRICES AND PAYMENT

We have noted where venues such as shops, hotels, restaurants, museums, attractions and the like accept the following credit cards: American Express (AmEx), Diners Club (DC), MasterCard (MC) and Visa (V). Many will also accept travellers' cheques, along with other, less widely held credit cards.

After some wild fluctuations following the introduction of the Euro as the national currency, costs have generally settled down

in the Netherlands, but the prices we've
supplied should be treated as guidelines, not
gospel. However, if they vary greatly from
those we've quoted, please write and let us
know. We aim to give the best and most
up-to-date advice, so we always want to know
if you've been badly treated or overcharged.

THE LIE OF THE LAND
Central Amsterdam divides fairly neatly into
separate neighbourhoods. The Old Centre is
split down the middle into the Old Side and the
New Side, and is bordered by a ring of canals
known as the *grachtengordel*. Outside these
canals lie a number of smaller, primarily
residential neighbourhoods, such as the Pijp,
the Museum Quarter and the Jordaan. Each
of these areas has its own section within
the Sightseeing chapter, and these area
designations have been used consistently
throughout the book.

TELEPHONE NUMBERS
The area code for Amsterdam is 020. All
phone numbers in this guide, when dialled from
outside the city, take this code unless otherwise
stated. Dialling from abroad you'll need to

preface them with the country code for the
Netherlands, 31, and then the 20 city code
(but first dropping the initial zero). We have
stipulated where phone numbers are charged
at non- standard rates – such as 0800 numbers,
which are free, and 0900, which are billed at
premium rate. For more details on telephone
codes and charges, *see p294*.

ESSENTIAL INFORMATION
For all the practical information you might
need when visiting Amsterdam – on such
topics as visas, facilities and access for the
disabled, emergency telephone numbers,
Dutch vocabulary and the local transport
system – turn to the Directory chapter at
the back of the guide. It starts on page 279.

MAPS
Wherever possible, map references have
been provided for every venue in the guide,
indicating the page and grid reference at which
it can be found on our street maps of Amsterdam.
There are also overview maps of the city and
of the Netherlands, and a map of Amsterdam's
tram network. The maps start on page 305.

LET US KNOW WHAT YOU THINK
We hope you enjoy *Time Out Amsterdam* and
we'd like to know what you think of it. We
welcome tips for places that you consider we
should include in future editions and take note
of your criticism of our choices. You can email
us at guides@timeout.com.

There is an online version of this book,
along with guides to over 45 other
international cities, at **www.timeout.com**.

In Context

History

From streaking Anabaptists to hectares full of hippies:
Amsterdam's history was never dull.

According to legend, Amsterdam was founded by two lost fishermen who vowed they'd build a town where they made landfall. They reached terra firma, and their seasick dog anointed the chosen patch with his vomit.

The reality is even more mundane. Although the Romans occupied other parts of Holland, they didn't reach the north. Soggy bog was not the stuff on which empires were built, so the legions moved on. Archaeologists have found no evidence of settlement before AD 1000, though there are prehistoric remains further east in Drenthe. Amsterdam's site, in fact, was partially under water for years, and the River Amstel had no fixed course until enterprising farmers from around Utrecht built dykes during the 11th century. Once the peasants had done the work, the nobility took over.

During the 13th century the most important place in the newly reclaimed area was the tiny hamlet of Oudekerk aan de Amstel. In 1204 the Lord of Amstel built a castle nearby on what is

now the outskirts of Amsterdam. After the Amstel was dammed in about 1270, a village grew up on the site of what is now Dam Square, acquiring the name Aemstelledamme.

The Lord of Amstel at this time was Gijsbrecht, a pugnacious man often in trouble with his liege lord, the Bishop of Utrecht, and with his nearest neighbour, Count Floris V of Holland. Tension increased when Floris bestowed toll rights – and some independence – on the young town in 1275. (Medieval gossip also whispers of cuckolding amongst the counts.) Events culminated with Gijsbrecht murdering Floris at Muiden (where Floris's castle, Muiderslot, can be seen to this day). Gijsbrecht's estates were confiscated by the Bishop of Utrecht and given to the Counts of Holland, and Amsterdam has remained part of the province of North Holland ever since.

In 1323 the Count of Holland, Floris VI, made Amsterdam one of only two toll points in the province for the import of brews. This was no trivial matter at a time when most people drank beer; drinking the local water, in fact, was practically suicidal. Hamburg had the largest brewing capacity in northern Europe and within 50 years a third of that city's production was flowing through Amsterdam. Thanks to its position between the Atlantic and Hanseatic ports, and by pouring its beer profits into other ventures, the city increased its trade in an assortment of essential goods.

Yet Amsterdam remained small. As late as 1425 the 'city' consisted of a few blocks of houses with kitchen gardens and two churches, arranged along the final 1,000-metre (0.62-mile) stretch of the River Amstel and bordered by what are now known as Geldersekade, Singel and Kloveniersburgwal. Virtually all these old buildings – such as the Houtenhuis, still standing in the Begijnhof – were wooden, so fire was a constant threat; in the great fire of May 1452, three quarters of the town was razed. One of the few examples of medieval architecture left standing is the Munttoren (Mint Tower) at Muntplein. Structures built after the fire had to be faced with stone and roofed with tiles and slates. These new developments coincided with urban expansion, as – most notably – foreign commerce led to improvements in shipbuilding.

WAR AND REFORMATION
None of the wealth and glory of Amsterdam's Golden Age would have been possible without the turbulence that preceded it. During the 16th century, Amsterdam's population increased from 10,000 (low even by medieval standards) to 50,000 by 1600. The city's first big expansion accommodated this growth, but people coming to the city found poverty, disease and squalor in the workers' quarters. Local merchants, however, weren't complaining: during the 1500s, the city started to emerge as one of the world's major trading powers.

Amsterdam may have been almost autonomous as a chartered city, but on paper it was still under the thumbs of absentee rulers. Through the intricate marriage bureau and shallow genetic pool known as the European aristocracy, the Low Countries (the Netherlands and Belgium) had passed into the hands of the Catholic Austro-Spanish House of Habsburg. The Habsburgs were the mightiest monarchs in Europe and Amsterdam was a comparative backwater among their European possessions, but events soon brought the city to prominence.

Amsterdam's status as a trade centre attracted all kinds of radical religious ideas that were flourishing across northern Europe, encouraged by Martin Luther's condemnation of the Catholic Church in 1517. Though Luther's beliefs failed to catch on with locals, many were

drawn to the austere creeds of the Anabaptists and, later, John Calvin. When they first arrived from Germany in about 1530, the Catholic city fathers tolerated the Anabaptists. But when they started to run around naked and even seized the Town Hall in 1534 during an attempt to establish a 'New Jerusalem' on the River Amstel, the leaders were arrested, forced to dress, and then executed, signalling an unparalleled period of religious repression: 'heretics' were burned at the stake on the Dam.

After the Anabaptists were culled, Calvinist preachers arrived from Geneva, where the movement started, and via France. Their coming caused a transformation. In 1566 religious discontent erupted into what became known as the Iconoclastic Fury. Churches and monasteries were sacked and Philip II of Spain sent an army to suppress the heresy.

ALTERED STATES
The Eighty Years' War (1568-1648) between the Habsburgs and the Dutch is often seen as a struggle for religious freedom, but there was more to it than that. The Dutch were, after all, looking for political autonomy from an absentee king who represented a continual drain on their coffers. By the last quarter of the 16th century Philip II of Spain was fighting wars against England and France, in the East against the Ottoman Turks, and in the New World for control of his colonies. The last thing he needed was a revolt in the Low Countries.

Amsterdam toed the Catholic line during the revolt, supporting Philip II until it became clear he was losing. Only in 1578 did the city patricians side with the Calvinist rebels, led by the first William of Orange. The city and William then combined to expel the Catholics and dismantle their institutions in what came to be called the Alteration. A year later, the Protestant states of the Low Countries united in opposition to Philip when the first modern-day European Republic was born at the Union of Utrecht. The Republic of Seven United Provinces was made up of Friesland, Gelderland, Groningen, Overijssel, Utrecht, Zeeland and Holland. Though lauded as the forerunner of the modern Netherlands, it wasn't the unitary state that William of Orange wanted, but rather a loose federation with an impotent States General assembly.

Each province appointed a Stadhouder (or viceroy), who commanded the Republic's armed forces and had the right to appoint some of the cities' regents or governors. The Stadhouder of each province sent delegates to the assembly, held at the Binnenhof in the Hague. While fitted with clauses to hinder Catholicism from ever suppressing the Reformed religion again, the

Where they once made a mint. The **Munttoren**. *See p11.*

Union of Utrecht also enshrined freedom of conscience and religion (at least until the Republic's demise in 1795), thus providing the blueprint that made Amsterdam a safe haven for future political and religious refugees.

CALVIN CLEAN

From its earliest beginnings, Amsterdam had been governed by four Burgomasters – mayors, basically – and a council representing citizens' interests. By 1500, though, city government had become an incestuous business: the city council's 36 members were appointed for life, 'electing' the mayors from their own ranks. Selective intermarriage meant that the city was, in effect, governed by a handful of families. When Amsterdam joined the rebels in 1578, the only change in civic administration was that the Catholic elite was replaced by a Calvinist faction of equally wealthy families. The city, now home to 225,000, remained the third city of Europe, after London and Paris.

However, social welfare was transformed. Formerly the concern of the Catholic Church, welfare under the Calvinists was incorporated into government. The Regents, as the Calvinist elite became known, took over the convents and monasteries, starting charitable organisations such as orphanages. But the Regents' work ethic and abstemious way of life would not tolerate any kind of excess: crime, drunkenness and immorality were all punishable offences.

During the two centuries before the Eighty Years' War, Amsterdam had developed a powerful maritime force. Even so, it remained overshadowed by Antwerp until 1589, when that city fell to those darned Spaniards. In Belgium, the Habsburg Spanish had adopted siege tactics, leaving Amsterdam unaffected by the hostilities and free to benefit from the blockades suffered by rival ports. Thousands of refugees fled north, among them some of Antwerp's most prosperous merchants, who were mostly Protestant and Jewish (specifically Sephardic Jews who had earlier fled their original homes in Spain and Portugal to escape the Inquisition). These refugees brought the skills, the gold and, famously, the diamond industry that would soon help make the city one of the greatest trading centres in the world.

THE GOLDEN AGE

European history seems to be littered with Golden Ages, but in Amsterdam's case the first six decades of the 17th century genuinely deserve the label. It's a remarkable story how such a small and isolated city on the Amstel could come to dominate world trade and set up major colonies, resulting in a local population explosion and a frenzy of urban expansion. Its girdle of canals was one of the great engineering feats of the time. This all happened while the country was at war with Spain and presided over not by kings, but businessmen.

The East India Company doesn't have much of a ring to it, but Verenigde Oost Indische

Verenigde Oost Indische Compagnie (VOC) ships set sail for the east.

Compagnie (VOC), the world's first transnational, loses something in translation. The VOC was created by a States General charter in 1602 to finance the wildly expensive and hellishly dangerous voyages to the East. Drawn by the potential fortunes to be made out of trade in spices and silk, the shrewd Dutch saw sense in sending out merchant fleets, but they also knew that one disaster could leave an individual investor penniless. As a result, the main cities set up trading 'chambers', which evaluated the feasibility (and profitability) of ventures, then sent ships eastwards. The power of the VOC was far-reaching: it had the capacity to found colonies, establish its own army, declare war and sign treaties. With 1,450 ships, the VOC made over 4,700 profitable journeys.

'Oranges were not popular with everyone.'

While the VOC concentrated on the spice trade, a new company received its charter from the Dutch Republic in 1621. The Dutch West India Company (West Indische Compagnie), while not as successful as its sister, dominated trade with Spanish and Portuguese territories in Africa and America, and in 1623 began to colonise Manhattan Island. The settlement was laid out on a grid similar to Amsterdam's, and adopted the Dutch city's name. But although it flourished to begin with, New Amsterdam

didn't last. After the Duke of York's invasion in 1664, the peace treaty between England and the Netherlands determined that New Amsterdam would change its name to New York and come under British control. The Dutch got Surinam as a feeble consolation prize.

Though commerce with the Indies became extensive, it never surpassed Amsterdam's European business: the city had become the major European centre for distribution and trade. Grain from Russia, Poland and Prussia, salt and wine from France, cloth from Leiden and tiles from Delft all passed through the port. Whales were hunted by Amsterdam's fleets, generating a flourishing soap trade, and sugar and spices from Dutch colonies were distributed throughout Scandinavia and the north of Europe. All this activity was financed by the Bank of Amsterdam, which had been set up in the cellars of the City Hall by the municipal council as early as 1609. It was a unique initiative and led to the city being considered the money vault of Europe, its notes readily exchangeable throughout the trading world.

A QUESTION OF WILL POWER

The political structure of the young Dutch Republic was complex. When the Union of Utrecht was signed in 1579, no suitable monarch or head of state was found, so the existing system was adapted to fit new needs. The seven provinces were represented by a 'national' council, the States General. In addition, the provinces appointed a Stadhouder. The obvious choice for Stadhouder after the union was William of Orange, the wealthy Dutchman who had led the rebellion against Philip II of Spain. William was then succeeded by his son, Maurits of Nassau, who was as successful against the Spanish as his father had been, eventually securing the Twelve Years' Truce (1609-21). Though each province could, in theory, elect a different Stadhouder, in practice they usually chose the same person. After William's popular tenure, it became a tradition to elect an Orange as Stadhouder. By 1641 the family had become sufficiently powerful for William II to marry a British princess, Mary Stuart. It was their son, William III, who set sail in 1688 to accept the throne of England in the so-called Glorious Revolution.

But the Oranges were not popular with everyone. The provinces' representatives at the States General were known as regents, and Holland's – and so Amsterdam's – regent was in a powerful enough position to challenge the authority and decisions of the Stadhouder. This power was exercised in 1650, in a crisis caused by Holland's decision to disband its militia after the Eighty Years' War against Spain. Stadhouder William II wanted the militia to be maintained – and, importantly, paid for – by Holland, and in response to the disbandment, he had kinsman William Frederick launch a surprise attack on Amsterdam.

When William II died three months later, the leaders of the States of Holland called a Great Assembly of the provinces. Even though there was no outward resistance to the Williams' earlier attack on the city, the provinces – with the exception of Friesland and Groningen, which remained loyal to William Frederick – decided that there should be no Stadhouders, and Johan de Witt, Holland's powerful regent, swore no prince of Orange would ever become Stadhouder again. This became law in the Act of Seclusion of 1653.

The hose master

Jan van der Heyden (1637-1712) was truly a Jan-of-all-trades, but he will go down in history as the ultimate hose-*meester*. Beginning as a mirror framer, he one day started to paint canvases – portraits, cityscapes and even 'architectural fantasies'. He soon went on to embrace life as an inventor in a workplace on Koestraat, where a gable stone still commemorates him. With his brother Nicolaas, he invented a fire hose that would end up saving countless lives and buildings. Until then fire-fighting was about people with buckets running around like headless chickens, but this system employed a specially designed pump that drew canal water to an elevated supply bag that then discharged the water via hoses. Since this system used gravity, the hoses no longer needed to be hard and rigid and could instead be soft and limp and thereby much easier to roll up and transport to the next fire. With this innovation, the city had the best fire brigade in Europe until the early 19th century.

Meanwhile, Jan not only found time to illustrate many of the fires he fought, but he also went on to design a new street lantern – copies of which grace the 'Skinny Bridge' (*see p99*) – that proved so effective that Amsterdam also held the title of 'Best lit city on earth' for centuries. It's only appropriate that not one, but two, streets are named after him in Amsterdam's Old South.

During this era, Amsterdam's ruling assembly, the Heren XLVIII (a sheriff, four mayors, a 36-member council and seven jurists), kept a firm grip on all that went on both within and without the city walls. Though this system was self-perpetuating, with the mayors and the council coming from a handful of prominent families, these people were merchants rather than aristocrats, and anyone who made enough money could, in theory, become a member.

The less elevated folk – the craftsmen, artisans and shopkeepers – were equally active in maintaining their position. A guild system had developed in earlier centuries, linked to the Catholic Church, but under the new order, guilds were independent organisations run by their members. The original Amsterdammers – known as *poorters* from the Dutch for 'gate', as they originally lived within the gated walls of the city – began to see their livelihoods being threatened by an influx of newcomers who were prepared to work for lower wages.

Things came to a head when the shipwrights began to lose their trade to competitors in the nearby Zaan region and protested. The shipwrights' lobby was so strong that the city regents decreed Amsterdam ships had to be repaired in Amsterdam yards. This kind of protectionism extended to almost all industrial sectors in the city and effectively meant most crafts became closed shops. Only *poorters*, or those who had married *poorters*' daughters, were allowed to join a guild, thereby protecting Amsterdammers' livelihoods and, essentially, barring outsiders from joining their trades.

GROWING PAINS

Though Amsterdam's population had grown to 50,000 by 1600, this was nothing compared with the next 50 years, when it ballooned fourfold. Naturally, the city was obliged to expand. The most elegant of the major canals circling the city centre was Herengracht (Lords' Canal): begun in 1613, this was where many of the Heren XLVIII had their homes. So there would be no misunderstanding about relative status, Herengracht was followed further out by Keizersgracht (Emperors' Canal) and Prinsengracht (Princes' Canal). Immigrants were housed in the Jordaan.

For all the city's wealth, famine hit Amsterdam with dreary regularity in the 17th century. Guilds had benevolent funds set aside for their members in times of need, but social welfare was primarily in the hands of the ruling merchant class. Amsterdam's elite was noted for its philanthropy, but only *poorters* were eligible for assistance: even they had to fall into a specific category, described as 'deserving poor'. Those seen as undeserving were sent to

Eel-advised?

In 1886 something happened that helped gel the Jordaan's fierce sense of community. When Lindengracht was still a canal it was the city's premier venue for the sport of eel-pulling. The trick to this most peculiar of games was to yank a live eel off the rope from which it dangled over the canal, while standing in a tipsy – an adjective that could also probably be applied to the participants – boat. The sport was banned, and on the fateful day a passing policeman elected to cut the rope from which the eel hung. This was, perhaps, not the wisest idea: the residents of the Jordaan had long felt hard done by, and the cop's interference was the final straw. The Eel Riot of 1886, as the incident came to be known, escalated so quickly that the army had to be called in. After a few days, it was announced that 26 Jordaansers had died and 136 were wounded. And the eel? Astonishingly, it survived the event, and its dry husk was auctioned in 1913 for the sum of ƒ1.75 (less than €1 in today's money). So why not visit a fish stall (*see p128*) and pay tribute to a working-class eel-ro by ordering one of his smoked brethren? It might just make for a perfect Amster-moment!

houses of correction. The initial philosophy behind these had been idealistic: hard work would produce useful citizens. But soon, the institutions became little more than prisons.

Religious freedom was still not what it might have been, either. As a result of the Alteration of 1578, open Catholic worship was banned in the city during the 17th century, and Catholics were forced to practise in secret. Some Catholics started attic churches, which are exactly what their name suggests: of those set up during the 1600s, the Museum Amstelkring has preserved Amsterdam's only surviving example – Our Lord in the Attic – in its entirety (*see p87*).

DECLINE AND FALL

Though Amsterdam remained one of the wealthiest cities in Europe until the early 19th century, its dominant trading position was lost to England and France after 1660. The United Provinces then spent a couple of centuries bickering about trade and politics with Britain and the other main powers. Wars were frequent: major sea conflicts included battles against the Swedes and no fewer than four Anglo-Dutch wars, from which the Dutch came off worse. It wasn't that they didn't win any battles; more that they ran out of men and money.

Despite – or perhaps because of – its history with the Orange family, Amsterdam became the most vocal opponent of the family's attempt to acquire kingdoms, though it supported William III when he crossed the sea to become King of England in 1688. The city fathers believed a Dutchman on their rival's throne could only be an advantage, and for a while they were proved right. However, William was soon back in Amsterdam looking for more money to fight more battles, this time against France.

'The French moved over the land like locusts.'

The naval officers who led the wars against Britain are Dutch heroes, and the Nieuwe Kerk has monuments to admirals Van Kinsbergen (1735-1819), Bentinck (1745-1831) and, most celebrated of all, Michiel de Ruyter (1607-76). The most famous incident, although not prominent in British history books, occurred during the Second English War (1664-7), when de Ruyter sailed up the rivers Thames and Medway to Chatham, stormed the dockyards and burnt the *Royal Charles*, the British flagship, as it lay at anchor. The *Royal Charles*'s

coat of arms was stolen, and is now displayed in the Rijksmuseum. The Dutch certainly put fear into the English, as reflected in the propaganda of the time: from one-liners like 'a Dutchman is a lusty, fat, two-legged cheese worm' and the still-common 'Dutch courage', to pamphlets entitled *The Dutch-men's Pedigree as a Relation, Showing how They Were First Bred and Descended from a Horse-Turd which Was Enclosed in a Butter-Box*.

Despite diminished maritime prowess, Amsterdam retained the highest standard of living in Europe until well into the 18th century. The Plantage was a direct result of the city's wealth, and tradesmen and artisans flourished.

But the Dutch Republic began to lag behind the major European powers in the 18th century. The Agricultural and Industrial Revolutions didn't get off the ground in the Netherlands until later: Amsterdam was nudged out of the shipbuilding market by England, and its lucrative textile industry was lost to other provinces. However, the city managed to exploit its position as the financial centre of the world until the final, devastating Anglo-Dutch War (1780-84). The British hammered the Dutch merchant and naval fleets, crippling the profitable trade with their Far Eastern colonies.

The closest the Dutch came to the Republican movements of France and the United States was with the Patriots. During the 1780s, the Patriots

The **Amsterdam School**. *See p19.*

managed to shake off the influence of the Stadhouders in many smaller towns, but in 1787 they were foiled in Amsterdam by the intervention of the Prince of Orange and his brother-in-law, Frederick William II, King of Prussia. Hundreds of Patriots then fled to exile in France, where their welcome convinced them that Napoleon's intentions towards the Dutch Republic were benign. In 1795, they returned, backed by a French army of 'advisers'. With massive support from Amsterdam, they celebrated the new Batavian Republic.

It sounded too good to be true, and it was. According to one contemporary, 'the French moved over the land like locusts'. Over ƒ100 million (about €50 million today) was extracted from the Dutch, and the French also sent an army, 25,000 of whom had to be fed, equipped and housed by their Dutch 'hosts'. Republican ideals seemed hollow when Napoleon installed his brother, Louis, as King of the Netherlands in 1806, and the symbol of Amsterdam's mercantile ascendancy and civic pride, the City Hall of the Dam, was requisitioned as the royal palace. Even Louis was disturbed by the impoverishment of a nation that had been Europe's most prosperous. However, after Louis had allowed Dutch smugglers to break Napoleon's blockade of Britain, he was forced to abdicate in 1810 and the Low Countries were absorbed into the French Empire.

Even so, government by the French wasn't an unmitigated disaster for the Dutch. The foundations of the modern state were laid in the Napoleonic period, and a civil code introduced – not to mention a broadening of culinary possibilities. However, trade with Britain ceased, and the cost of Napoleon's wars prompted the Dutch to join the revolt against France. After Napoleon's defeat, Amsterdam became the capital of a constitutional monarchy, incorporating what is now Belgium; William VI of Orange was crowned King William I in 1815. But though the Oranges still reigned in the northern provinces, the United Kingdom of the Netherlands, as it then existed, lasted only until 1830.

BETWEEN THE OCCUPATIONS

When the French were finally defeated and left Dutch soil in 1813, Amsterdam emerged as the capital of the new kingdom of the Netherlands but very little else. With its coffers depleted and its colonies occupied by the British, Amsterdam faced a hard fight for recovery.

The fight was made tougher by two huge obstacles. For a start, Dutch colonial assets had been reduced to present-day Indonesia, Surinam and the odd island in the Caribbean. Just as important, though, was the fact that the Dutch

were slow to join the Industrial Revolution. The Netherlands had few natural resources to exploit, and business preferred sail power to steam. Add to this the fact that Amsterdam's opening to the sea, the Zuider Zee, was too shallow for the new steamships, and it's easy to see why the Dutch were forced to struggle.

Prosperity, though, returned to Amsterdam after the 1860s. The city adjusted its economy, and its trading position was improved by the building of two canals. The opening of the Suez Canal in 1869 sped up the passage to the Orient and led to an increase in commerce, while the discovery of diamonds in South Africa revitalised the diamond industry. But what the city needed most was easy access to the major shipping lanes of northern Europe. When it was opened in 1876, the Noordzee Kanaal (North Sea Canal) let Amsterdam take advantage of German industrial trade and it became the Netherlands' greatest shipbuilding port again, at least temporarily. Industrial machinery was introduced late to Amsterdam. However, by the late 19th century, the city had begun to modernise production of the luxury goods for which it would become famous: beer, chocolates, cigars and cut diamonds.

Of course, not all of Amsterdam's trade was conducted on water, and the city finally got a major rail link in 1889. Centraal Station was designed by PJH Cuypers in 1876 and worked counterproductively to a degree by separating the city from the lifeblood of its seafront. Meanwhile Cuyper's Rijksmuseum on the other fringe of the city became, like Centraal Station, uniquely eclectic and was even derided as a 'cathedral of the arts'. Still, Amsterdam consolidated its position at the forefront of Europe with the building of a number of other landmarks such as the Stadsschouwburg (in 1894), the Stedelijk Museum (1895) and the Tropen Institute (1926). The city's international standing had soon improved to such a point that, in 1928, it hosted the Olympics.

NEW DEVELOPMENTS

Amsterdam's population had stagnated at 250,000 for two centuries after the Golden Age, but between 1850 and 1900 it more than doubled. Extra labour was needed to meet the demands of a revitalised economy, but the major problem was how to house the new workers. Today the old inner-city quarters are desirable addresses, but they used to be the homes of Amsterdam's poor. The picturesque Jordaan, where regular riots broke out at the turn of the century (see p15 **Eel-advised?**), was occupied primarily by the lowest-paid workers, its canals were used as cesspits and the mortality rate was high. Around the centre,

Hongerwinter. See p20.

new developments – the Pijp, Dapper and Staatslieden quarters – were built: they weren't luxurious, but at least they had simple lavatory facilities, while the Amsterdam School of architects, inspired by their socialist beliefs, designed now classic housing for the poor. Wealthier city-dwellers, meanwhile, found elegance and space in homes constructed around Vondelpark and further south.

The city didn't fare badly in the first two decades of the 20th century, but Dutch neutrality during World War I brought problems to parts of the population. While the elite lined their pockets selling arms, the poor were confronted with food shortages. In 1917, with food riots erupting, the city had to open soup kitchens and introduce rationing. The army was called in to suppress another outbreak of civil unrest in the Jordaan in 1934. This time the cause was unemployment, endemic throughout the industrialised world after the Wall Street Crash of 1929.

Unfortunately, the humiliation of means testing for unemployment benefit meant that many families suffered in hungry silence. Many Dutch workers moved to Germany, where National Socialism was creating jobs. The city was just emerging from the Depression when the Nazis invaded in May 1940.

WORLD WAR II

Amsterdam endured World War II without being flattened by bombs, but nonetheless its buildings, infrastructure, inhabitants and morale were reduced to a terrible state by the occupying Nazi forces. The Holocaust also left an indelible scar on a city whose population in 1940 was ten per cent Jewish.

Early in the morning of 10 May 1940, German bombers mounted a surprise attack on Dutch airfields and military barracks. The government and people had hoped that the Netherlands could remain neutral, as it had in World War I, so the armed forces were unprepared for war. Though the Dutch aimed to hold off the Germans until the British and French could come to their assistance, their plan failed. Queen Wilhelmina fled to London to form a government in exile, leaving Supreme Commander Winkelman in charge. After Rotterdam was destroyed by bombing and the Germans threatened other cities with the same treatment, Winkelman surrendered on 14 May. The Dutch colonies of Indonesia and New Guinea were invaded by the Japanese in January 1942. After their capitulation on 8 March, Dutch colonials were imprisoned in Japanese concentration camps.

During the war, Hitler appointed Austrian Nazi Arthur Seyss-Inquart as Rijkskommissaris (State Commissioner) of the Netherlands, and asked him to tie the Dutch economy to the German one and to Nazify Dutch society. Though it won less than five per cent of the votes in the 1939 elections, the National Socialist Movement (NSB) was the largest fascist political party in the Netherlands, and was the only Dutch party not prohibited during the occupation. Its doctrine resembled German Nazism, but the NSB wanted to maintain Dutch autonomy under the direction of Germany.

During the first years of the war, the Nazis let most people live relatively unmolested. Rationing, however, made the Dutch vulnerable to the black market, while cinemas and theatres eventually closed because of curfews and censorship. Later, the Nazis adopted more aggressive measures: Dutch men were forced to work in German industry, and economic exploitation assumed appalling forms. In April 1943, all Dutch soldiers, who had been captured during the invasion and then released in the summer of 1940, were ordered to give themselves up as prisoners of war. In an atmosphere of deep shock and outrage, strikes broke out, but were violently suppressed.

To begin with, ordinary citizens, as well as the political and economic elite, had no real reason to make a choice between collaboration and resistance. But as Nazi policies became more virulent, opposition to them swelled, and a growing minority of people were confronted with the difficult choice of whether to obey German measures or to resist. There were several patterns of collaboration. Some people joined the NSB, while others intimidated Jews, got involved in economic collaboration or betrayed people in hiding or members of the Resistance. Amazingly, a small number even signed up for German military service. But in general there was a small resistance, a small group of collaborators, and a very large majority of 'grey' in between.

The most shocking institutional collaboration involved the police, who dragged Jews out of their houses for deportation, and Dutch Railways, which was paid for transporting Jews to their deaths. When the war was over, 450,000 people were arrested for collaborating – although most were quickly released. Mitigating circumstances – NSB members who helped the Resistance, for example – made judgments complicated. Of 14,500 convicted and sentenced, only 39 were executed.

'I see how the world is slowly becoming a desert.'

The Resistance was made up chiefly of Communists and, to a lesser extent, Calvinists. Anti-Nazi activities took several forms, with illegal newspapers keeping the population informed and urging them to resist the Nazi dictators. Underground groups took many shapes and sizes. Some spied for the Allies, others fought an armed struggle against the Germans through assassination and sabotage, and others falsified identity cards and food vouchers. A national organisation took care of people who wanted to hide, and aided the railway strikers, Dutch soldiers and illegal workers being sought by the Germans, with other groups helping Jews into hiding. By 1945, more than 300,000 people had gone underground in the Netherlands.

Worse was to follow towards the end of the war. In 1944, the Netherlands plunged into Hongerwinter – the Hunger Winter. Supplies of coal vanished after the liberation of the south and a railway strike, called by the Dutch government in exile in order to hasten German defeat, was disastrous for the supply of food. In retaliation, the Germans damaged Schiphol Airport and the harbours of Rotterdam and Amsterdam – foiling any attempts to bring in supplies – and grabbed everything they could. Walking became the only means of transport, domestic refuse was no longer collected, sewers overflowed and the population fell to disease. To survive, people stole fuel: more than 20,000 trees were cut down and 4,600 buildings were demolished. Floors, staircases, joists and rafters were plundered, causing the collapse of

many houses, particularly those left by deported Jews. Supplies were scarce and many couldn't afford to buy their rationing allowance, let alone the expensive produce on the black market. By the end of the winter 20,000 people had died of starvation and disease, and much of the city was seriously damaged.

But hope was around the corner. The Allies liberated the south of the Netherlands on 5 September 1944, Dolle Dinsdag (Mad Tuesday), and complete liberation came on 5 May 1945, when it became apparent that the Netherlands was the worst-hit country in western Europe.

In spite of the destruction and the loss of so many lives, there were effusive celebrations. But more blood was shed on 7 May, when German soldiers opened fire on a crowd who had gathered in Dam Square to welcome their Canadian liberators: 22 people were killed.

THE HOLOCAUST

'I see how the world is slowly becoming a desert, I hear more and more clearly the approaching thunder that will kill us,' wrote Anne Frank in her diary on 15 July 1944. Though her words obviously applied to the Jews, they were relevant to all those who were persecuted during the war. Granted, anti-Semitism in Holland had not been as virulent as in Germany, France or Austria. But even so, most – though not all – of the Dutch population closed its eyes to the persecution, and there's still a feeling of national guilt as a result.

The Holocaust happened in three stages. First came measures to enforce the isolation of the Jews: the ritual slaughter of animals was prohibited, Jewish government employees were dismissed, Jews were banned from public places and, eventually, all Jews were forced to wear a yellow Star of David. (Some non-Jews wore the badge as a mark of solidarity.) Concentration was the second stage. From early 1942, all Dutch Jews were obliged to move to three areas in Amsterdam, isolated by signs, drawbridges and barbed wire. The final stage was deportation. Between July 1942 and September 1943, most of the 140,000 Dutch Jews were deported, via Kamp Westerbork. Public outrage at the deportations was foreshadowed by the one and only protest, organised by dock workers, against the anti-Semitic terror, the February Strike of 1941.

The Nazis also wanted to eliminate Gypsies: more than 200,000 European Gypsies, including many Dutch, were exterminated. Homosexuals, too, were threatened with extermination, but their persecution was less systematic: public morality acts prohibited homosexual behaviour, and gay pressure groups ceased their activities. Amsterdam has the world's first memorial to

Amsterdammers are from Mars, Utrechters are from Venus

Amsterdamse Wijsheden ('Amsterdam Sayings'), compiled by Hans Vermaak and illustrated by Bert Witte, may be the perfect gift idea if you happen to be invited for dinner by a Dutchie. It's nice, new and blue. It's also cheap – for less than €5 at your local bookshop (*see p161*). Hell, with a bit of dictionary action you can annoy your new Dutch friends by employing all the Amsterdam clichés found here. For instance: 'Hey, sorry *goser* for being such a lazy dry armpit for not coming to help you move house, but I woke up with a bad case of Heineken sickness.' But it's really too easy to be a smartass. Like it says in another one of the book's insights: 'There's no art in pissing into a canal. Try pissing across it.' This book literally drips with such wisdom.

Insight #1: Amsterdammers are snobs

Many sayings insist on the idea that outside Amsterdam there are only farmers. In fact Amsterdammers are such urbanites that they consider it worse to call someone a *boer*, a farmer, than a *boerenlul*, a farmer's dick. One example that reflects a disdain for the outsider translates literally as 'I figure that guy is from Utrecht' but in fact means that you are assuming that he is gay.

Insight #2: Amsterdammers are pragmatists

Yep, it's a cliché that Amsterdammers are down-to-earth straighttalkers who are forever ready to compromise on principles so long as the business gets done. And the book pumps the image with examples along the lines of 'a big ass needs big pants', 'roasted doves don't fly' and 'never leave a pretty lady alone because the fast fuckers will soon be waiting in the hall'.

Insight #3: Amsterdammers are romantics. Not.

As you leaf through this book, you get the impression that courtship in this city has been tainted by a certain pragmatism. 'Shall I drag your body about the room?' is used to ask a lady to dance, while 'Shall I whiten your hall?' asks her for very much more.

persecuted gays – the Homomonument – which incorporates pink triangles in its design, turning the Nazi badge of persecution into a symbol of pride.

THE POST-WAR ERA

The country was scarred by the occupation, losing ten per cent of its housing, 30 per cent of its industry and 40 per cent of its production capacity. Though Amsterdam escaped the bombing raids that devastated Rotterdam, it bore the brunt of deportations: only 5,000 Jews, out of a pre-war Jewish population of 80,000, remained. Despite intense poverty and drastic shortages of food, fuel and building materials, the Dutch tackled the task of post-war recovery with a strong sense of optimism. In 1948, people threw street parties, firstly to celebrate the inauguration of Queen Juliana and, later, the four gold medals won by Amsterdam athlete Fanny Blankers-Koen at the London Olympics. Some Dutch flirted briefly with communism after the war, but in 1948 a compromise was struck between the Catholic KVP and the newly created Labour party PvdA, and the two proceeded to govern in successive coalitions until 1958. Led by Prime Minister Willem Drees, the government resuscitated social programmes and laid the basis for a welfare state. The Dutch now reverted to the virtues of a conservative, society: decency, hard work and thrift.

'The generous hand of the welfare state was bitten.'

The country's first priority, though, was economic recovery. The city council concentrated on reviving the two motors of its economy: Schiphol Airport and the Port of Amsterdam, the latter of which was boosted by the opening of the Amsterdam-Rhine Canal in 1952. Joining Belgium and Luxembourg in the Benelux also brought the country trade benefits, and the Netherlands was the first European nation to repay its Marshall Plan loans. The authorities dusted off their pre-war development plans and embarked on a rapid phase of urban expansion. But as people moved into the new suburbs, businesses flowed in the opposite direction, into the centre, worsening congestion on the already cramped roads.

What the hell happened?

Pim Fortuyn.

Theo Van Gogh.

What happened to Amsterdam's emotional landscape on November 2, 2004 is still impossible to gauge. It's too soon and this space too small. But on that morning during rush hour and in front of countless witnesses, the *enfant terrible* film-maker/columnist Theo Van Gogh – yes, he's a grand nephew of Vincent's – was first shot eight times, then had his throat slit and was stabbed in the chest. A five-page letter was attached to him, held in place by one of the two knives sticking from his body. The murderer was allegedly a Salafist Islamic jihadi called Mohammed Bouyeri, a Moroccan who had grown up in Amsterdam. Bouyeri was arrested and was awaiting trial as of press time. Van Gogh had just completed work on a film, *06-05*, based on the life of the gay, populist, anti-immigration politician Pim Fortuyn who had been assassinated two years earlier by an animal-rights activist.

The motivation for his murder was probably related to the fact that he liked to refer to Moslems as 'goat fuckers'. He had also recently made a highly controversial short film, *Submission*, written by 'ex-Moslem' Somalia-born politician Ayaan Hirsi Ali – who now lives in hiding under permanent police protection – that railed against the abuse of women in Islamic countries. When asked shortly before his murder if he feared reprisals, Van Gogh scoffed at the idea and asked, 'Who would murder the village idiot?' And indeed, Van Gogh revelled in his own obnoxiousness. He was a notorious provocateur in a city that prides itself on its 'big mouth'. In his career as a columnist and equal-opportunity offender (Christianity was a 'fan club for that rotting fish in Nazareth'), he had been fired by almost every major newspaper and magazine in the country and often accused of abusing his freedom of speech. Meanwhile as a much loved 'actors' director', he built up an impressive *oeuvre* that covered everything from multicultural soaps to thrillers (*see p196*). He was also regularly seen as a TV interviewer: chainsmoking and scratching at his orifices, while ripping into his guest's hypocrisy. Politicians tended to squirm the most. In short, he was a complex and contradictory individual who was as good at making friends as he was at making enemies.

His death brought in its wake a succession of attacks, mainly on Islamic schools, but also on Christian churches, as anger on both sides simmered or flared into arson.

While many hope that this will all act as a wake-up call to deal more directly and honestly with the problems around immigration, integration and extremism, others regard it as the frustrated act of one delusional man. After all, Amsterdam has been welcoming immigrants for centuries and there's no reason why it can't for centuries to come. The only real conclusion that can now be drawn, however, is that Amsterdam has lost some of its colour.

After the war, the Dutch colonies of New Guinea and Indonesia were liberated from the Japanese and pushed for independence. With Indonesia accounting for 20 per cent of their pre-war economy, the Dutch launched military interventions in 1947 and 1948. But these did not prevent the transfer of sovereignty to Indonesia on 27 December 1949, while the dispute with New Guinea dragged on until 1962 and did much to damage the Netherlands' reputation abroad. Colonial immigrants to the Netherlands – including the later arrival of Surinamese (fully half the population of that country) – and Turkish and Moroccan 'guest workers' now comprise 16 per cent of the population. Though poorer jobs and housing have been their lot, racial tensions were low until the mid 1990s.

Although the economy and welfare state revived in the 1950s, there was still civil unrest. Strikes flared at the port and council workers defied a ban on industrial action. In 1951 protesters clashed with police outside the Concertgebouw, angered by the appointment of a pro-Nazi conductor and in 1956 demonstrators besieged the Dutch Communist Party, outraged by the Soviet invasion of Hungary.

In the late '40s and '50s Amsterdammers returned to pre-war pursuits: fashion and celebrity interviews filled the newspapers and cultural events mushroomed. In 1947 the city launched the prestigious Holland Festival, while the elite held the Boekenbal, an annual event where writers met royalty and other dignitaries. New avant-garde movements emerged, notable among them the CoBrA art group, whose 1949 exhibition at the Stedelijk Museum of Modern Art caused an uproar, and the *vijftigers*, a group of experimental poets led by Lucebert. Many of these artists met in brown cafés around Leidseplein.

FAREWELL TO WELFARE

The '60s proved to be one of the most colourful decades in Amsterdam's history. There were genuine official attempts to improve society. The IJ Tunnel eased communications to north Amsterdam just as the national economy took off. There were high hopes for rehousing developments such as the Bijlmermeer, and influential new architecture from the likes of Aldo van Eyck and Herman Herzberger.

Yet the generous hand of the welfare state was being bitten. Discontent began on a variety of issues, among them the nuclear threat, urban expansion and industrialisation, the consumer society and authority in general. Popular movements similar to those in other west European cities were formed, but with a zaniness all their own. Protest and dissent have

always been a vital part of the Netherlands' democratic process, yet the Dutch have a habit of keeping things in proportion; so, popular demonstrations took a playful form.

Discontent gained focus in 1964, when pranks around *'t Lieverdje* statue, highlighting political or social problems, kick-started a new radical subculture. Founded by anarchist philosophy student Roel van Duyn and 'anti-smoke magician' Robert Jasper Grootveld, the Provos – their name inspired by their game plan: to provoke – numbered only about two dozen, but were enormously influential. Their style influenced the anti-Vietnam demos in the US and the Situationist antics in 1969 Paris, and set the tone for Amsterdam's love of liberal politics and absurdist theatre. Their finest hour came in March 1966, when protests about Princess Beatrix's controversial wedding to the German Claus van Amsberg turned nasty after the Provos let off a smoke bomb on the carriage route, and a riot ensued. Some Provos, such as Van Duyn, went on to fight the system from within: five won city seats under the Kabouter (forest-dwelling dwarves) banner in 1970.

'The city isn't ready to relinquish its rebel status.'

Perhaps the most significant catalyst for discontent in the '70s – which exploded into civil conflict by the '80s – was housing. Amsterdam's small size and historic city centre had always been a nightmare for its urban planners. The city's population increased in the '60s, reaching its peak (nearly 870,000) by 1964. Swelling the numbers further were immigrants from the Netherlands' last major colony, Surinam, many of whom were dumped in the Bijlmermeer. It degenerated into a ghetto and, when a 747 crashed there in October 1992, the number of fatalities was impossible to ascertain: many victims were unregistered.

The Metro link to Bijlmermeer is itself a landmark to some of Amsterdam's most violent protests. Passionate opposition erupted against the proposed clearance in February 1975 of the Jewish quarter of Nieuwmarkt. Civil unrest culminated in 'Blue Monday', 24 March 1975, when police sparked clashes with residents and supporters. Police fired tear gas into the homes of those who refused to move out and battered down doors. Despite further violence, the first Metro line opened in 1977, with the Centraal Station link following in 1980, though only one of the four planned lines was completed.

City planners were shocked by the fervent opposition to their schemes for large, airy suburbs. It was not what people wanted: they cherished the narrow streets, the small squares and the cosy cafés. The public felt the council was selling out to big business, complaining that the centre was becoming unaffordable for ordinary people. In 1978, the council decided to improve housing through small-scale development, renovating houses street by street. But with an estimated 90,000 people still on the housing list in 1980, public concern grew.

Speculators who left property empty caused acute resentment, which soon turned into direct action: vacant buildings were occupied illegally by squatters. In March 1980 police turned against them for the first time and used tanks to evict the squatters from a former office building in Vondelstraat. Riots ensued, but the squatters were victorious. In 1982, as Amsterdam's squatting movement reached its peak, clashes with police escalated: a state of emergency was called after one eviction battle. Soon, though, the city – led by new mayor Ed van Thijn – had gained the upper hand over the movement, and one of the last of the city's big squats, Wyers, fell amid tear gas in February 1984 to make way for a Holiday Inn. Squatters were no longer a force to be reckoned with, though their ideas of small-scale regeneration have since been absorbed into official planning.

BACK TO BASICS
Born and bred in Amsterdam, Ed van Thijn embodied a new strand in Dutch politics. Though a socialist, he took tough action against 'unsavoury elements' – petty criminals, squatters, dealers in hard drugs – and upgraded facilities to attract new businesses and tourists. A new national political era also emerged, where the welfare system and government subsidies were trimmed to ease the country's large budget deficit, and aimed to revitalise the economy with more businesslike policies. The price of Amsterdam's new affluence (among most groups, except the very poorest) has been a swing towards commercialism, with the squatters largely supplanted by well-groomed yuppies. Flashy cafés, galleries and nouvelle cuisine restaurants replaced the alternative scene and a mood of calm settled on the city. Still, a classic example of Dutch free expression was provoked by the city's mid-'80s campaign to host the 1992 Olympics. Amsterdam became the first city ever to send an (ultimately successful) official anti-Olympics delegation.

Current mayor Job Cohen stills holds to a course that hopes to see Amsterdam re-invented as 'Business Gateway to Europe', where future visitors will be more prone to point their cameras towards the arising eastern docklands than towards the ever-photogenic Red Light District. But with the current economic decline, the advantages – both for business and the general atmosphere – of nurturing Amsterdam's long-held reputation as a hotbed for edgy creativity are becoming more apparent. So worry not: the city isn't ready to relinquish its rebel status just yet.

The **Vondelstraat riots**: a temporary defeat for the squatters.

Key events

EARLY HISTORY

1204 Gijsbrecht van Amstel builds a castle in the coastal settlement that eventually becomes Amsterdam.
1270 The Amstel is dammed at Dam Square.
1300 Amsterdam is granted city rights by the Bishop of Utrecht.
1306 Work begins on the Oude Kerk.
1313 The Bishop of Utrecht grants Aemstelledamme full municipal rights and leaves it to William III of Holland.
1342 The city walls (*burgwallen*) are built.
1421 The St Elizabeth's Day Flood occurs, as does Amsterdam's first great fire.
1452 Fire destroys most wooden houses.
1489 Maximilian grants Amsterdam the right to add the imperial crown to its coat of arms.

WAR AND REFORMATION

1534 Anabaptists try to seize City Hall but fail. A period of anti-Protestant repression begins.
1565 William the Silent organises a Protestant revolt against Spanish rule.
1566 The Beeldenstorm (Iconoclastic Fury) is unleashed. Protestant worship is made legal.
1568 The Eighty Years War with Spain begins.
1577 The Prince of Orange annexes the city.
1578 Catholic Burgomasters are replaced by Protestants in the Alteration.
1579 The Union of Utrecht is signed, allowing freedom of religious belief but not of worship.
1589 Antwerp falls to Spain; there is a mass exodus to the north.

THE GOLDEN AGE

1602 The Verenigde Oost Indische Compagnie (VOC) is founded.
1606 Rembrandt van Rijn is born.
1611 The Zuiderkerk is completed.
1613 Work starts on the western stretches of Herengracht, Keizersgracht and Prinsengracht.
1623 WIC colonises Manhattan Island; Peter Stuyvesant founds New Amsterdam in 1625.
1642 Rembrandt completes the *Night Watch*.
1648 The Treaty of Munster is signed, ending the Eighty Years War with Spain.
1654 England declares war on the United Provinces.
1667 England and the Netherlands sign the Peace of Breda.

DECLINE AND FALL

1672 England and the Netherlands go to war; Louis XIV of France invades.

1675 The Portuguese Synagogue is built.
1685 French Protestants take refuge after the revocation of the Edict of Nantes.
1689 William of Orange becomes King William III of England.
1696 Undertakers riot against funeral tax.
1787 Frederick William II, King of Prussia, occupies Amsterdam.
1795 French Revolutionaries are welcomed to Amsterdam by the Patriots. The Batavian Republic is set up and run from Amsterdam.
1806 Napoleon's brother is made King.
1810 King Louis is removed from the throne.
1813 Unification of the Netherlands. Amsterdam is no longer a self-governing city.
1815 Amsterdam becomes capital of Holland.

BETWEEN THE OCCUPATIONS

1848 The city's ramparts are pulled down.
1876 Noordzee Kanaal links Amsterdam with the North Sea.
1880s Oil is discovered in Sumatra. The Royal Dutch Company (Shell Oil) is founded.
1883 Amsterdam holds the World Exhibition.
1887 The Rijksmuseum is completed.
1889 Centraal Station opens.
1922 Women are granted the vote.
1928 The Olympics are held in Amsterdam.
1934 Amsterdam's population is 800,000.

WORLD WAR II

1940 German troops invade Amsterdam.
1941 The February Strike, in protest against the deportation of Jews.
1944-5 20,000 die in the Hunger Winter.
1945 Canadian soldiers free Amsterdam.
1947 Anne Frank's diary is published.

THE POST-WAR ERA

1966 The wedding of Princess Beatrix and Prince Claus ends in riots.
1968 The IJ Tunnel opens.
1976 Cannabis is decriminalised.
1977 First Metrolijn (underground) opens.
1980 Queen Beatrix's coronation (30 April).
1986 The controversial 'Stopera' civic-headquarters-cum-opera-house is built.
1997 The euro is approved as a European currency in the Treaty of Amsterdam.
1999 Prostitution is made legal after years of decriminalisation.
2002 The guilder is dead; long live the euro. Pim Fortuyn murdered.
2004 Film-maker/columnist Theo Van Gogh murdered.

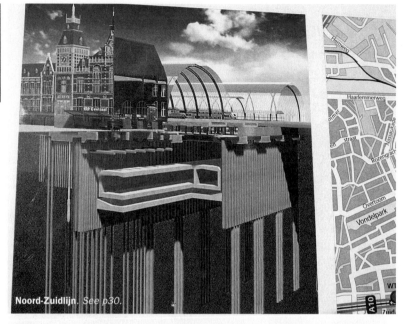

Noord-Zuidlijn. *See p30.*

Amsterdam Today

The times are a-changing fast here in fun town, but yes: it's still fun.

Amsterdammers are a strange breed. There's nothing that perks them up more than a good moan about their city: from the inordinate amounts of ordure deposited on the streets by the resident canine population to the latest baffling maze of regulations emanating from the council. But at the same time they would never think of packing up and moving. They love it here, and at least some of the reasons are obvious. It remains a relatively cheap place to live (as long as you do your own cooking) and anywhere you're likely to want to visit is within easy walking or bicycling distance. Gays and lesbians love the liberal ambience, the arts are thriving, and there are countless happening bars, clubs and theatres. Oh, and then there's the Red Light District and the coffeeshops that are synonymous with the capital. It's also a creative city, reflected in the rich party scene and other artistic initiatives. Hey, even Jamie Oliver decided to open a branch of Fifteen (*see p133*) here rather than in another European capital. True, the flower power atmosphere that used to hang in the air and the 'anything is possible' anarchic attitude in the streets are things of the past, having been replaced by a more serious and sombre manner. But the grown-up version of Amsterdam still has a lot to offer to its inhabitants and guests.

THE RIGHT TO PARTY

The city is a magnet for singletons, who make up 58 per cent of the population. Thanks to its relaxed laws, Amsterdam also attracts many people who think that they can get away with almost anything. Since in the recent past much illegal activity was condoned by the police, many complain that morals and values have drained away, with a resultant increase in the sort of petty crime and anti-social behaviour that can make the living of everyday life unpleasant. In response Mayor Job Cohen, who took office at the beginning of 2001, continues down the path laid by his predecessor to clean up the city. Apart from a zero-tolerance campaign to scare off potential offenders, this also meant goodbye to Koninginnenacht, the much-loved party night before the actual **Queen's Day** celebration (*see p188* **Orange squash**). But luckily in 2003, following a great deal of pressure, Cohen decided to give the green light to its trial return. The kinder, gentler Koninginnenacht proved to be a success and has now returned to the annual party agenda much to the pleasure of those who can't get enough of letting their (orange) hair down.

'I amsterdam.'

There's more good news for party animals, as the council plans to follow the advice of the *Nachtwacht* ('Night Watchmen', www.nacht wachtamsterdam.nl). No, nothing to do with the artist, Rembrandt, this is a collective of prominent DJs and party organisers who have lobbied to allow bar and club owners to decide for themselves when to open and close. Currently bars and most clubs shut at the same time, with the inevitable consequence that the streets are crowded with beered-up Amsterdammers and tourists, all struggling to get home, while getting into fights, making noise and generally indulging in all sorts of anti-social behaviour. It's hoped that relaxing the law on opening hours will stop this. Also, the council realises that in order to compete with other European capitals Amsterdam must make itself more attractive by repealing other bureaucratic rules and regulations – including the strict licenses on terraces. There are even councillors who want to clean up the Red Light District, or at least shine a different coloured light on this most historic of areas, thus attracting a better class of tourist.

I-AMSTERDAM, WHO ARE YOU?
All these ideas resonate with the city's new promotion slogan 'I amsterdam' (*see p28* **I amconfused**), designed to enhance the inhabitants' pride in their city and at the same time to draw foreign visitors. And Amsterdam could do with a new impetus, for in 2003 the number of tourists dropped under ten million for the first time in decades. In particular, affluent Americans are staying away and those tourists that do come are spending less because of the high Euro. As a result Stoeltie Diamonds, a top attraction, closed and lots of hotels were

forced to drop their room rates. And it's not just tourists that are staying away: international corporations are beginning to favour cities like Barcelona, Madrid and Warsaw, both as the locations for their European offices and as conference venues. So Amsterdam's promotion and marketing could do with a boost.

Money was the main objection to the €1.2 million Job Cohen wanted to fork out to celebrate Queen Beatrix's Silver Jubilee. After an outcry from the public, not to mention councillors, it was decided to plan a more low-key event and to spend the money saved on more urgent matters: such as safety, crime prevention and cracking down on youth gangs.

ART-ATTACK
The latter is a sensitive issure throughout the Netherlands, but especially in Amsterdam. Ever since the late 1990s there have been tensions between a small part of the Moroccan community, mostly youngsters, and the police. It started with a huge riot on August Allebéplein in West Amsterdam, an area populated by many immigrants. After more incidents, it got really nasty in mid-2003 when a policeman shot dead a Moroccan man who threatened him with a 20-centimetre knife. The demonstration following this incident resulted in yet another riot, which only fed the growing anti-foreigner feelings. Then in 2004 a Dutch couple in the Pijp was forced to literally flee their house as a result of months of intimidation and aggression by youngsters.

But the xenophobia really got out of hand at the beginning of November 2004, following the brutal slaughter of film director/columnist/TV presenter Theo van Gogh (*see p196* and *p22* **What the hell happened**). When his alleged killer, Mohammed Bouyeri, was caught and turned out to be a Salafist *jihadi* holding a Dutch/Moroccan passport, the simmering discontent exploded. Throughout the country mosques and Islamic schools were set on fire, and churches burned in tit-for-tat attacks, while in Amsterdam buildings of Moroccan companies were damaged and Turkish and Moroccan shops were sent fake anthrax letters. Has the Dutch experiment in multiculturalism failed? When even Paul Scheffer, the prominent Labour social critic, can write an article in *NRC Handelsblad* saying: 'Tolerance can survive only within clear limits. Without shared norms about the rule of law, we cannot productively have differences of opinion,' then it's clear that change is coming to the Netherlands. However, despite the current troubles, the 170-plus nationalities that make up the city's population of 740,000 do spend most of their time living happily side by side.

I amconfused

It was all much simpler in the 1970s. To entice people to visit Amsterdam all you had to do was what KLM did: put out some posters cajoling its long-haired American targets to come 'Sleep in Hippie Park'. Word of mouth did the rest. And before that there was the tourist board's 'Get In Touch With The Dutch' campaign during the 1960s – surely a slogan from a more innocent period. Compared to that halcyon era the boom years of the 1990s were surely the most boring of times, if you take their yawn-inducing slogans ('Capital of Inspiration' and 'Business Gateway to Europe') as typical.

But now it's the 21st century, and every city needs its own marketing campaign to establish its advantages over every other city on the planet. 'City marketing' is the rather dubious science that might never have been called into existence save for the stratospheric success of the 'I (heart shape) NY' logo. Now it seems we are all doomed to adopt our own version of the slogan, whatever we think of our place of residence. So in 2004, the city of Amsterdam paid the usually inspired advertising bureau KesselsKramer to work their glamourous magic. And they came up with 'I amsterdam'.

Unfortunately a year earlier, the designer Vanessa van Dam had already invented an 'I amsterdammer' logo with a similar accent on 'I am'. This logo even graced 120,000 postcards – it was sort of hard to miss. So it seemed only fair that Van Dam was awarded a 20,000 settlement from the city. So almost before it got off the mark, the city's 'I amsterdam' campaign made a big oopsie. (Let's hope van Dam will not get sued in turn by the estate of that other local boy René Descartes, who is known to have remarked: 'I think therefore I amsterdam'. But at least no one is accusing anyone of a crime. Like those other inspired plays on the city's name, 'Amsterdamned' and the even better 'Amsterdamaged', 'I amsterdam' is so obvious that we can assume that the slogan has occurred independently in many different minds on many different occasions. The only really annoying thing about the campaign is that it's trying to peddle the idea that the logo will not only attract outside business but also work to unify regular Amsterdammers. This is solidly contradicted whenever an actual Dutchie tries to say 'I amsterdam' out loud. Their accent makes them stutter out something that sounds more like 'I hamster', as if they were arrogant rodents rather than proud Amsterdammers.

Okay, it's easy to mock. We admit that marketing a city can't be easy. There must be more to it than producing a catchy T-shirt slogan. But what other choices were there? 'Ich bin ein Amsterdammertje' would probably generate the same confusion and controversy as JFK's grammatical gaffe, 'Ich bin ein Berliner'. And 'Handy airport, lotsa coffeeshops', while appealing to both the business and leisure-minded, lacks something in the way of elegance.

But it can be argued that 'Amsterdamned' and 'Amsterdamaged' are in fact much better ambassadors for the city. After all, today's visiting dope heads may hold the city's economic future in their rather shaky hands. It's happened before: sentimental (and rich) ex-hippies, looking for somewhere to recover their lost youth and salve their consciences, were the ones who invested in the place during the booming 1990s. They figured it would be a good excuse to come and visit a few times a year, in the hopes of re-creating those perfect relaxed coffeeshop moments from decades long past.

Thinking of which, isn't being relaxed one of the things Amsterdam has always been famous for? And neither the campaign nor the brouhaha surrounding it have contributed to this most obvious of brand benefits… Shame on them.

TICKET TO SAFETY

While Amsterdam might be growing up hard and fast, it's still a safe city. Despite some rundown areas like Ganzenpoort in Bijlmermeer – not exactly a tourist hangout anyway – there aren't any no-go areas and the 2004 crime figures from the Amsterdam Police reflect this, with a drop of 11 per cent in reported crime compared to 2003. Pickpocketing, burglary and street theft have particularly decreased, deterred by an increased police presence and the introduction of CCTVs in many areas. The increasing aggression on public transport has also been addressed, with more frequent inspectors, CCTV installed on some trams and police patrolling high-risk stations like Lelylaan. Slightly less comforting were the self-defence courses given to tram drivers. In an effort to target the habitual criminals responsible for the vast majority of crime, the police were also issued with a set of cards depicting the men most wanted by the law. Then, to make sure the police really took notice, wanted posters were put up in police canteens. Sure enough, many of the thugs and thieves were caught. However, the police were less successful in solving the ten gangland killings that have taken place in the last two years. Most were drug related and took place in residential areas in broad daylight. One of them even occurred in Dam Square on a busy Saturday afternoon. It was a miracle that none of the many bystanders got hurt…

GOING UNDERGROUND

On leaving Centraal Station the first thing you'll notice is that the city looks like a huge building site. At the start of 2005, there were more than 300 excavations in town, resulting in blocked roads, diverted traffic, clueless pedestrians and cyclists, and lost tourists. The work giving the most misery is the Noord–Zuidlijn. This new Metro line, set to open in 2011, will run from Amsterdam North via Centraal Station and the Pijp to the World Trade Centre in the south of the city – and later all the way to Schiphol. From the start, the project met with criticism. Wasn't the existing

Bike, leather, truncheon: Amster cop.

transport network adequate to the task, and thus couldn't the millions being spent on a possibly redundant metro be better spent on housing and crime prevention? But both government and council remain firm that the new line is vital for the economic future of the city. They claim it will attract international business, while the project itself will create 10,000 (much needed) jobs. Meanwhile, the office buildings in the south, near the WTC, stand empty and even Dutch companies like Ahold, who are relocating to Amsterdam in 2006, have opted for a different location. Another problem is the stations themselves. The original plans were shelved due to safety issues raised by the locals. So, it's back to the drawing board and a deeper dig into the taxpayer's pocket.

> ## 'The Dutch work to live, rather than the other way round.'

But if a city really wants to reinvent itself, what does it most need? Yes, you guessed it, yuppies. So the council plans to abandon rent controls on its own flats and apartments. After all, €300-€400 per month for a place in the centre of town is a bit of a bargain, and it does mean that the city foregoes the spending power of all those young professionals who might be renting these desirable residences at much higher prices. Critics claim this will result in the creation of ghettos, as the poor are priced out to grottier parts of town. But then, since the ghettos already exist, why not tidy things up and move all the poor people to them?

FAB FUN CITY

But it's not all doom and gloom. Far from it. Amsterdam remains a fun and fab city for both its residents and the many visitors. The Dutch work to live, rather than the other way around, and there's a big underground and squat scene that continues to organise the most inventive events, exhibitions and performances. The canals are serene and beautiful, and so are the different styles of architecture, from the old-fashioned Amsterdam School houses to the hippest office in town, the glass shoe-shaped ING House in the Zuid. Then there are the locals: while Amsterdammers can be blunt, they are always friendly and normally delighted to show off their near perfect command of English. And when the city just gets too crowded then the shortest of train rides will whisk you out into the countryside. Add all these factors together and it's not hard to see why visitors and locals can't get enough of the place.

The bridge between Borneo and Sporenburg in the eastern docklands.

Architecture

From Golden Age glory to 'Wild Living', Amsterdam is one flirtatious brick tease.

'The colours are strong and sad, the forms symmetric, the façades kept new,' wrote Eugène Fromentin, the French 19th-century art critic, of Amsterdam. 'We feel that it belongs to a people eager to take possession of the conquered mud.' The treacherous, blubbery soil on which the merchants' town of Amsterdam is built meant that most attempts at monumental display were destined soon to return to their original element. It's this unforgiving land, combined with the Protestant restraint that characterised the city's early developments and the fact that there were no royals out to project monstrous egos, that ensures Amsterdam's architectural highlights are warehouses, homes, the stock exchange and the former City Hall, rather than palaces and castles.

Amsterdam's architectural epochs have followed the pulse of the city's prosperity. The decorative façades of wealthy 17th- and 18th-century merchants' houses still line the canals. A splurge of public spending in the affluent 1880s gave the city two of its most notable landmarks – Centraal Station and the Rijksmuseum. Conversely, social housing projects in the early 20th century stimulated the innovative work of the Amsterdam School, while Amsterdam's late-'80s resurgence as a financial centre and transport hub led to an economic upturn and to thickets of ambitious modern architecture on the outskirts of town and along the eastern docklands.

Prime viewing time for Amsterdam architecture is late on a summer's afternoon, when the sun gently picks out the varying colours and patterns of the brickwork. Then, as twilight falls, the canal houses – most of them more window than wall – light up like strings of lanterns, and you get a glimpse of the beautifully preserved, frequently opulent interiors that lie behind the façades.

MUD, GLORIOUS MUD
Amsterdam is built on reclaimed marshland, with a thick, soft layer of clay and peat beneath the topsoil. About 12 metres (39 feet) down is a

Brick, glorious brick on **Brouwersgracht.**

hard band of sand, deposited 10,000 years ago during the Little Ice Age, and below that, after about five metres (16 feet) of fine sand, there is another firm layer, this one left by melting ice after the Great Ice Age. A further 25 metres (82 feet) down, through shell-filled clay and past the bones of mammoths, is a third hard layer, deposited by glaciers over 180,000 years ago.

The first Amsterdammers built their homes on muddy mounds, making the foundations from tightly packed peat. Later, they dug trenches, filled them with fascines (thin, upright alder trunks) and built on those. But still the fruits of their labours sank slowly into the swamp. By the 17th century builders were using longer underground posts and were rewarded with more stable structures, but it wasn't until around 1700 that piles were driven deep enough to hit the first hard sand layer.

The method of constructing foundations that subsequently developed has remained more or less the same ever since, though nowadays most piles reach the second sand level and some make the full 50-metre (164-foot) journey to the third hard layer. To begin, a double row of piles is sunk along the line of a proposed wall (since World War II, concrete has been used instead of wood). Then, a crossbeam is laid across each pair of posts, planks are fastened longitudinally on to the beams, and the wall is built on top.

From time to time piles break or rot, which is why Amsterdam is full of buildings that teeter precariously over the street, tilt lopsidedly or prop each other up in higgledy-piggledy rows.

STICKS AND STONES

Early constructions in Amsterdam were timber-framed, built mainly from oak with roofs of rushes or straw. Wooden houses were relatively light and less likely to sink into the mire, but after two devastating fires (in 1421 and 1452), the authorities began stipulating that outer walls be built of brick, though wooden front gables were still permitted. In a bid to blend in, the first brick gables were shaped in imitation of their spout-shaped wooden predecessors.

But regulations were hardly necessary, for Amsterdammers took to brick with relish. Granted, some grander 17th-century buildings were built of sandstone, while plastered façades were first seen a century later and reinforced concrete made its inevitable inroads in the 20th century. But Amsterdam is still essentially a city of brick: red brick from Leiden, yellow from Utrecht and grey from Gouda, all laid in curious formations and arranged in complicated patterns. Local architects' attachment to – and flair with – brick reached a zenith in the fantastical, billowing façades designed by the Amsterdam School early in the 20th century.

TOUCH WOOD

Only two wooden buildings remain in central Amsterdam: one (built in 1460) in the quiet courtyard of **Begijnhof** (No.34, known as the Houtenhuis, *see p92*), and the other on Zeedijk. The latter, **In't Aepjen** (Zeedijk 1; *see p82 and p144*), was built in the 16th century as a lodging house, getting its name from the monkeys that impecunious sailors used to leave behind as payment. Though the ground floor dates from the 19th century, the upper floors provide a clear example of how, in medieval times, each wooden storey protruded a little beyond the one below it, allowing rainwater to drip on to the street rather than run back into the body of the building. Early brick gables had to be built at an angle over the street for the same reason, though it also allowed objects to be winched to the top floors without crashing against the windows of the lower ones.

'Hendrik de Keyser gave Amsterdam's skyline its oriental appearance.'

Amsterdam's oldest building, though, is the **Oude Kerk** (Old Church, Oude Kerksplein 23; *see p88*). It was begun in 1300, though only the base of the tower dates from then: over the ensuing 300 years the church, once boasting the simplest of forms, developed a barnacle crust of additional buildings, mostly in a Renaissance style with a few Gothic additions. The Gothic building in town is the **Nieuwe Kerk** (at Dam and Nieuwezijds Voorburgwal; *see p80*), still called the 'New Church' even though work on it began at the end of the 14th century.

When gunpowder arrived in Europe in the 15th century, Amsterdammers realised that the wooden palisade that surrounded their settlement would offer scant defence, and so set about building a new stone wall. Watchtowers and gates left over from it make up a significant proportion of the city's surviving pre 17th-century architecture, though most have been altered over the years. The **Schreierstoren** (Prins Hendrikkade 94-95; *see p82*) of 1480, however, has kept its original shape, with the addition of doors, windows and a pixie-hat roof. The base of the **Munttoren** (Muntplein; *see p92*) originally formed part of the Regulierspoort, a city gate built in 1490. Another city gate from the previous decade, the St Antoniespoort (Nieuwmarkt 4), was converted into a public weighhouse (or 'Waag') in 1617, then further refashioned to become a Guild House before finally settling into its current role of a café-restaurant (**In de Waag**; *see p85 and p143*).

DUTCH RENAISSANCE

A favourite 16th-century amendment to these somewhat stolid defence towers was the addition of a sprightly steeple. Hendrick de Keyser (1565-1621) delighted in designing such spires, and it is largely his work that gives Amsterdam's present skyline a faintly oriental appearance. He added a lantern-shaped tower with an openwork orb to the Munttoren, and a spire that resembled the Oude Kerk steeple to the Montelbaanstoren (Oudeschans 2), a sea-defence tower that had been built outside the city wall. His **Zuiderkerk** (Zuiderkerkhof 72; *see p101*), built in 1603, sports a spire said to have been much admired by Christopher Wren. The appointment of De Keyser as city mason and sculptor in 1595 had given him free reign, and his buildings represent the pinnacle of the Dutch Renaissance style (also known as Dutch Mannerist) – the greatest perhaps being **Westerkerk** (Prinsengracht 279; *see p97*), completed in 1631 as the biggest Protestant church in the world.

Since the beginning of the 17th century Dutch architects had been gleaning inspiration from translations of Italian pattern books, adding lavish ornament to the classical system of proportion they found there. Brick façades were decorated with stone strapwork (scrolls and curls derived from picture frames and leather work). Walls were built with alternating layers of red brick and white sandstone, a style that came to be called 'bacon coursing'. The old spout-shaped gables were replaced with cascading step-gables, often embellished with vases, escutcheons and masks (before house numbers were introduced in Amsterdam in the 18th century, ornate gables and wall plaques were a means of identifying addresses).

The façade of the Vergulde Dolphijn (Singel 140-42), designed by De Keyser in 1600 for Captain Banning Cocq (the commander of Rembrandt's *Night Watch*), is a lively mix of red brick and sandstone, while the Gecroonde Raep (Oudezijds Voorburgwal 57) has a neat step-gable, with truly riotous decoration featuring busts, escutcheons, shells, scrolls and volutes. However, De Keyser's magnificent 1617 construction that followed the curve of a canal, the Huis Bartolotti (Herengracht 170-72, now part of the Theater Instituut; *see p95*), is the finest example of the style.

This decorative step-gabled style was to last well into the 17th century. But gradually a stricter use of classical elements came into play; the façade of the Bartolotti house features rows of Ionic pilasters, and it wasn't long before others followed where De Keyser had led. The Italian pattern books that had inspired the Dutch Renaissance were full of the less

ornamented designs of Greek and Roman antiquity. This appealed to many young architects who followed De Keyser, and who were to develop a more restrained, classical style. Many, such as Jacob van Campen (1595-1657), went on study tours of Italy, and returned fired with enthusiasm for the symmetric designs, simple proportions and austerity of Roman architecture. The buildings they constructed during the Golden Age are among the finest Amsterdam has to offer.

THE GOLDEN AGE

The 1600s were a boom time for builders as well as for businessmen. There was no way it could have been otherwise, as Amsterdam's population more than quadrupled during the first half of the century. Grand new canals were constructed, and wealthy merchants lined them with mansions and warehouses. Van Campen, along with fellow architects Philips Vingboons (1607-78) and his brother Justus (1620-98), were given the freedom to try out their ideas on a flood of new commissions.

Stately façades constructed of sandstone began to appear around Amsterdam, but brick still remained the most popular material. Philips Vingboons's Witte Huis (Herengracht 168, now part of the Theatre Instituut) has a white sandstone façade with virtually no decoration: the regular rhythm of the windows is the governing principle of the design. The house he built in 1648 at Oude Turfmarkt 145 has a brick façade adorned with three tiers of classical pilasters – Tuscan, Ionic and Doric – and festoons that were characteristic of the style. However, the crowning achievement of the period was Amsterdam's boast to the world of its mercantile supremacy and civic might: namely, the Stadhuis (City Hall) on the Dam, designed by Van Campen in 1648 and now known as the **Koninklijk Paleis** (*see p79*).

There was, however, one fundamental point of conflict between classical architecture and the requirements of northern Europe. For practical reasons, wet northern climes required steep roofs, yet low Roman pediments and flat cornices looked odd with a steep, pointed roof behind them. The architects solved the problem by adapting the Renaissance gable, with its multiple steps, into a tall, central gable with just two steps. Later, neck-gables were built with just a tall central oblong and no steps. The right angles formed at the base of neck-gables – and again at the step of elevated neck-gables – were often filled in with decorative sandstone carvings called claw-pieces.

On very wide houses, it was possible to build a roof parallel to the street rather than end-on, making a more attractive backdrop for a

classical straight cornice. The giant **Trippenhuis** (Kloveniersburgwal 29; *see p85*), built by Justus Vingboons in 1662, has such a design, with a classical pediment, a frieze of cherubs and arabesques, and eight enormous Corinthian pilasters. It wasn't until the 19th century, when zinc cladding became cheaper, that flat and really low-pitched roofs became feasible.

THE 18TH CENTURY

Working towards the end of the 17th century, Adriaan Dortsman (1625-82) had been a strong proponent of the straight cornice. His stark designs – such as for the Van Loon house at Keizersgracht 672-4 – ushered in a style that came to be known as Restrained Dutch Classicism (or the 'Tight Style' as it would translate directly from the Dutch description: *Strakke Stijl*). It was a timely entrance. Ornament was costly and, by the beginning of the 18th century, the economic boom was over.

'Good honest brick appealed to Berlage.'

The merchant families were prosperous, but little new building went on. Instead, the families gave their old mansions a facelift or revamped the interiors. A number of 17th-century houses got new sandstone façades (or plastered brick ones, which were cheaper), and French taste – said to have been introduced by Daniel Marot, a French architect living in Amsterdam – became hip. As the century wore on, ornamentation regained popularity. Gables were festooned with scrolls and acanthus leaves (Louis XIV), embellished with asymmetrical rococo fripperies (Louis XV) or strung with disciplined lines of garlands (Louis XVI). The baroque grandeur of Keizersgracht 444-6, for example, hardly seems Dutch at all. Straight cornices appeared even on narrow buildings, and became extraordinarily ornate: a distinct advantage, this, as it hid the steep roof that lay behind, with decorative balustrades adding to the deception. The lavish cornice at Oudezijds Voorburgwal 215-17 is a prime example.

ONE FOOT IN THE PAST

Fortunes slumped after 1800, and during the first part of the century more buildings were demolished than constructed. When things picked up after 1860, architects raided past eras for inspiration. Neo-classical, neo-Gothic and neo-Renaissance features were sometimes lumped together in mix-and-match style. The Krijtberg Church (Singel 446) from 1881 has a soaring neo-Gothic façade and a high, vaulted basilica, while the interior of AL van Gendt's

ARCAM.
See p39.

Hollandsche Manege (Vondelstraat 140; *see p115*), also 1881, combines the classicism of the Spanish Riding School in Vienna with a state-of-the-art iron and glass roof.

In contrast, the **Concertgebouw** (Van Baerlestraat 98; *see p223*), a Van Gendt construction from 1888, borrows from the late Renaissance, with 1892's **City Archive** (Amsteldijk 67) De Keyser revisited. But the period's most adventurous building is the Adventskerk (Keizersgracht 676), which crams in a classical rusticated base, Romanesque arches, Lombardian moulding and fake 17th-century lanterns.

The star architect of the period was **PJH Cuypers** (1827-1921), who landed the commissions for both the **Rijksmuseum** (Stadhouderskade 41; *see p113*) of 1877-85 and what would become its near mirrored twin on the other side of town, Centraal Station (Stationsplein), built from 1882 to 1889. Both are in traditional red brick, adorned with Renaissance-style decoration in sandstone and gold leaf. Responding to those who thought his tastes too catholic, Cuypers – while still slipping in some of his excesses later during construction – decided to organise each building according to a single coherent principle. This idea became the basis for modern Dutch architecture.

THIS IS THE MODERN WORLD

Brick and wood – good, honest, indigenous materials – appealed to Hendrik Petrus Berlage (1856-1934), as did the possibilities offered by industrial developments in the use of steel and glass. A rationalist, he took Cuypers' ideas a step further in his belief that a building should openly express its basic structure, with a modest amount of ornament in a supportive role. Notable also was the way he collaborated with sculptors, painters and even poets throughout construction. His **Beurs van Berlage** (Beursplein; *see p79*), built between 1898 and 1903 – all clean lines and functional shapes, with the mildest patterning in the brickwork – was startling at the time, and earned him the reputation of being the father of modern Dutch architecture.

Apart from the odd shop front and some well-designed café interiors, the art nouveau and art deco movements had little direct impact on Amsterdam, though they did draw a few wild flourishes: HL de Jong's **Tuschinski** cinema (Reguliersbreestraat 26; *see p198*) of 1918-21, for example, is a delightful and seductive piece of high-camp fantasy. Instead, Amsterdam architects developed a style of their own, an idiosyncratic mix of art nouveau and Old Dutch using their favourite materials: wood and brick.

This movement, which became known as the **Amsterdam School** (*see p38* **Back to school**), reacted against Berlage's sobriety by producing whimsical buildings with waving, almost sculptural, brickwork. Built over a reinforced concrete frame, the brick outer walls go through a complex series of pleats, bulges, folds and curls that earned the work the nickname *Schortjesarchitectuur* ('apron architecture'). Windows can be trapezoid or parabolic; doors are carved in strong, angular shapes; brickwork is decorative and often polychromatic; and sculptures are abundant.

The driving force behind the school came from two young architects, Michel de Klerk (1884-1923) and Piet Kramer (1881-1961). Commissions for social housing projects – one for the Dageraad (constructed around PL Takstraat, 1921-23), one for Eigen Haard (in the Spaarndammerbuurt, 1913-20) – allowed them to treat entire blocks as single housing units. Just as importantly, the pair's adventurous clients gave them freedom to express their ideas. The school also produced more rural variants suggestive of village life such as the BT Boeyinga-designed 'garden village' Tuindorp Nieuwendam (Purmerplein, Purmerweg).

In the early 1920s a new movement emerged that was the antithesis of the Amsterdam School – although certain crossover aspects can be observed in JF Staal's 1930-completed *Wolkenkrabber* (Victorieplein), the first residential high-rise in the country, whose name appropriately translates as 'cloudscraper'. Developing rather than reacting against Berlage's ideas, the **Functionalists** believed that new building materials such as concrete and steel should not be concealed, but that the basic structure of a building should be visible. Function was supreme, ornament anathema. Their hard-edged concrete and glass boxes have much in common with the work of Frank Lloyd Wright in the USA, Le Corbusier in

France and the Bauhaus in Germany. Unsurprisingly, such radical views were not shared by everyone, and the period was a turbulent one in Amsterdam's architectural history. Early Functionalist work, such as 1930's *Openluchtschool* (Open-air School, Cliostraat 40), 1934's Cineac Cinema (Reguliersbreestraat 31) and the **Round Blue Teahouse** (in Vondelpark; *see p115*), has a clean-cut elegance, and the Functionalist garden suburb of Betondorp (literally, 'concrete village'), built between 1921 and 1926, is much more attractive than the name might suggest. But after World War II, Functionalist ideology became an excuse for dreary, derivative, prefabricated eyesores. The urgent need for housing, coupled with town-planning theories that favoured residential satellite suburbs, led to the appearance of soulless, high-rise horrors on the edge of town, much the same as those put up elsewhere in Europe.

'My favourite colour is the rainbow' – Aldo van Eyck.

A change of heart during the 1970s refocused attention on making the city centre a pleasant jumble of residences, shops and offices. At the same time, a quirkier, more imaginative trend began to show itself in building design. The ING Bank (Bijlmerplein 888), inspired by

Living inside of the box. Container living at **NDSM**. *See p39.*

anthroposophy and built in 1987 of brick, has hardly a right angle in sight. A use of bright colour, and a return to a human-sized scale, is splendidly evident in Aldo van Eyck's Hubertushuis (Plantage Middenlaan 33-35) from 1979, which seems to personify the architect's famed quotation: 'my favourite colour is the rainbow'. New façades – daringly modern, yet

Back to school

Amsterdam's monuments are not the products of imperial imaginations, imposing their stone wills on an unwilling populace, but rather the homes of merchants, and working men and women. And it was for the workers that the **Amsterdam School** largely built its gentler versions of Gaudí, working with a socialist vision during the early part of the twentieth century.

While due credit can be given to the stonemasons who perforce had to practise non-geometrical brickwork when repairing houses slowly sinking into the mud, it was Hendrik Berlage who formed the nexus of the movement. Not only did his work strip things down, rejecting all the neo-styles that had defined most 19th-century Dutch architecture, but he also provided the opportunity to experiment with new forms by coming up with Plan Zuid, an urban development meant to provide housing for the working classes.

Although the Amsterdam School was short-lived – it was forced to simplify within a decade when money ran out, the Functionalism-obsessed De Stijl started to diss its more self-indulgent tendencies, and its greatest proponent, Michel de Klerk, died – examples of its work remain on view in Rivierenbuurt, Spaarndammerbuurt and Concertgebouwbuurt, plus the area around Mercantorplein. What follows, though, are some of the highlights.

Located along the waterfront, the eerie and epic Scheepvaarthuis (Prins Hendrikkade 108-114) is generally considered to be the school's first work. Completed in 1916, it was the work of three big names: JM van der Mey, Piet Kramer and de Klerk. Among the hallmarks on show are obsessively complex brickwork, allegorical decorations (reflecting its use as offices for shipping companies), sculptures and wrought-iron railings fused with the building.

Behind Westerpark lies the Spaarndammer neighbourhood, which sports the school's most frolicsome work. The Ship, as the locals like to call it, takes up a whole block, its boundaries Zaanstraat, Hembrugstraat and Oostzaanstraat. Completed in 1919, it was commissioned by the Eigen Haard housing association and includes 102 homes and a school. Be sure to pop your head through the archway at Oostzaan 1-21, where you can see the courtyard and its central meeting hall, before visiting **Museum Het Schip** next door. This former post office organises Amsterdam School boat and walking tours and is an exhibition space devoted to the school. You can also visit an apartment that has been returned to the state envisioned by de Klerk.

However, the school's playground is Plan Zuid, at the border of the Pijp and Rivierenbuurt. Josef Israelkade, between 2e Van der Helststraat and Van Woustraat, is a pleasant stretch along the Amstelkanaal; enter PL Takstraat and then circle Burg Tellegenstraat without forgetting to pop into the courtyard of Cooperatiehof. Socialist housing association de Dageraad (the Dawn) allowed de Klerk and Kramer to do their hallucinatory best and while employing their favourite sculptor, Hildo Krop. Kramer, incidentally, went on to design over 200 bridges; after visiting the Plan, you shouldn't have any problem recognising his work elsewhere in the city.

It's a different story elsewhere, though. Backtrack and cross the Amstelkanaal, and then walk down Waalstraat; here you'll find later examples of the school's work, where tightening purse-strings resulted in more restraint. Nearby, on Vrijheidslaan and its side-streets, are some more classic buildings, all scrubbed and renovated. Conclude your tour at Roelof Hartplein, where a window seat at Wildschut (see p152) affords a panorama of goodies. Look out for House Lydia (across the street at No.2), which served as a home to Catholic girls; finished in 1927, it stands as one of the last buildings in which wacky window shapes and odd forms were allowed.

Museum Het Schip
Spaarndammerplantsoen 140 (475 0924/ 418 2885/www.hetschip.nl). Bus 22. **Open** 1-5pm Thur-Sun. **Admission** €5; €2.75 over-65s; €2 students; free MK. **No credit cards**. **Map** p309 A1.

built to scale – began to appear between the old houses along the canals. The 1980s also saw, amid an enormous amount of controversy, the construction of what became known as the Stopera, a combined city hall (Stadhuis) and opera house on Waterlooplein. The eye-catching brick and marble coliseum of the Muziektheater is more successful than the dull oblongs that make up the City Hall.

Housing projects of the 1980s and 1990s have provided Amsterdam with some imaginative modern architecture – especially on the islands of the once derelict eastern docklands (*see p108* **Take a walk on the water side**). You can get a view of some it from the roof of Renzo Piano's already classic **NEMO** building (1997).

THE FUTURE

At the municipal information centre for planning and housing in **Zuiderkerk** (*see p101*), visitors can admire models of current and future developments set to transform the city in the near future. Those interested should pay a visit to NEMO's neighbour **ARCAM – Architectuurcentrum Amsterdam** (*see p204*) – or pick up a copy of their excellent publication *25 Buildings You Should Have Seen, Amsterdam*. Bureau Monumentenzorg Amsterdam, meanwhile, provides an overview of the city's architecture from its origins to 1940 at www.bmz.amsterdam.nl. Another excellent resource is www.amsterdamarchitecture.nl.

Architectural travesties of the past have politicised the populace and referendums are held prior to many developments. Although 130,000 votes against the construction of **IJburg** (*see p108* **Take a walk on the water side**) – a residential community currently being built on a series of man-made islands in the IJmeer, just east of Amsterdam – was not enough to stop development around this ecologically sensitive area, they did inspire the promise that ƒ15 million (now around €7 million) would be invested in 'nature-development'. Parts of the area will also be a showcase for the recently hyped Dutch concept of *wilde wonen* – 'wild living' – where residents get to design and build their own houses. (Yes: this is a radical concept in this space-constrained country…)

Similarly, the referendum result against the laying of the new **Noord-Zuidlijn** (*see p30*) on the Metro network didn't halt the project, but it did establish that the city needed to be considerably more diligent in its thinking. The powers that be apparently overlooked such significant details as financing, loss of revenue for shopkeepers and the potential for all this digging to cause the speedier sinking of historical buildings above when planning the line, none of which endeared them to voters.

Now that the facelift of **Museumplein** (*see p113*) has long been completed save for the extension being planned for the Stedelijk Museum in 2006-8, all eyes are on the eastern docklands (*see p108* **Take a walk on the water side**). It's hoped that redevelopments will turn it into a harbourfront not unlike that of Sydney. Similarly, construction around the ArenA stadium in the south-east will hopefully pump some life into the nearby architectural prison known as Bijlmermeer. This should become home to many businesses and – thanks to the recent leaps and bounds made in building vertically on bog – the largest residential tower in the country. In 2004 a building called Living Tomorrow (www.livingtomorrow.com) also opened here as a joint project of companies out to pedal their 'visionary' designs in this 'house and office of the future'…

Another hotspot currently roping in a who's who of architects is Zuidas (www.zuidas.nl) in the South. Zuidas is grouped around the World Trade Center, near the wacky ING House (Amstelveenseweg 500): no doubt it caught your eye on the ride in from Schiphol airport.

Dutch architecture – thanks in part to exponents like Rem Koolhaas (who coincidentally has his embarrassingly ugly 1991 work, *Byzantium*, viewable at the north entrance to Vondel Park on Stadhouderskade) – is currently very much in vogue. Brad Pitt's favourite architecture firm, MVRDV, who just renovated **Lloyd Hotel** (*see p70* **Cooking culture with Lloyd**), also helped put Dutch architecture back on the map at Hanover World Expo 2000 with their 'Dutch Big Mac', featuring such delicious ingredients as water- and windmills for electricity on the roof, a theatre on the fourth floor, an oak forest on the third floor, flowers on the second floor, and cafés, shops and a few dunes on the first floor. Yes dunes.

International periodicals, no longer casting LA and Hong Kong as the primary visionaries, now see the 'Dutch Model' – where boundaries between building, city and landscape planning have blurred beyond recognition – as both pragmatic and futuristic. After all, ecological degradation is now a worldwide phenomenon, and the space-constrained Netherlands has long seen nature as a construct that needs to be nurtured. Expect this principle to define some of the Dutch architecture of the future – although knowing what's gone before, it'll likely be implemented in an unexpected fashion. For instance, in 2004, hundreds of steel containers were re-invented as living spaces for students at both **NDSM** (*see p250*) in the north and Houthavens in the west (where they were joined by a cruise ship to house an additional 200 students). Now how's that for pragmatic?

④

Art

The Golden Age started a love for all things golden framed.

Ah, the Golden Age. The living was sweet during those first six decades of the 17th century, starting with the founding of the East India Company (VOC) and ending when the British changed New Amsterdam to New York. Not only did the economic benefits of being the world's leading trading power result in the building of Amsterdam's image-defining ring of canals, but it also led to a flourishing of the arts.

But the groundwork for this efflorescence was laid by a rich medieval artistic tradition under the sponsorship of the Church. Later artists, not content to labour solely *ad majorem dei gloriam,* found more 'individual' masters in the Flemings Bosch and Brueghel. Foremost among these early artists was Jacob Cornelisz. van Oostsanen (c.1470-1533). Also known as Jacob van Amsterdam, Oostsanen represents the beginning of the city's artistic tradition, and his sharpness of observation went on to become a trademark for all the Dutch art that was to follow. The only painting of his to survive the

iconoclastic fury of the sixteenth century, *Saul and the Witch of Endor,* tells the whole biblical story in one panoramic, almost comic book, sweep and depicts a time when witches obviously lacked PR.

In contrast, painters had no problems with PR once the Golden Age proper arrived and the aspirant middle classes became hungry for art. Rembrandt van Rijn is, of course, the best known of all those who made art while the money shone, and his *Night Watch* (on display at the Rijksmuseum) remains Amsterdam's most famous painting. He couldn't decorate Amsterdam on his own, however, and the likes of Jan Vermeer, Frans Hals, Ferdinand Bol, Jan Steen and Jacob van Ruisdael all thrived creatively and economically during this time.

Although it couldn't last, art continued to develop after the Golden Age began to tarnish. Jacob de Wit (1695-1754), long before the invention of sticky glow-in-the-dark stars, brightened up many a local ceiling with cloud

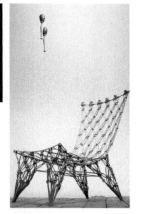

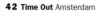

dappled skies, gods and flocks of cherubs. His work can be seen at the **Theater Instituut** (*see p95*), the attic church at the **Museum Amstelkring** (*see p87*), **Pintohuis** (*see p101*), the **Bijbels Museum** (*see p95*), and **Huis Marseille** (*see p95*).

The 18th century produced Monet's inspirer, Johan Jongkind, while the 19th century offered George Breitner and Vincent van Gogh, and the 20th led off with such varied talents as MC Escher, Piet Mondriaan and Karel Appel. With so many 'names' coming from such a tiny country, one cannot help wonder if the Netherlands' battle with the sea is really all about creating small wall-space for the pictures.

But the Dutch are as famed for their business acumen as their dykes, and this no doubt leads the less scrupulous to a somewhat free and easy attitude towards a work's provenance. An estimated 30 per cent of the world art market consists of forgeries, and even the most famous institutions can be caught out. In 1938 the Rijksmuseum, to its eventual relief, lost a bidding war for a Vermeer to Rotterdam's Boijmans Van Beuningen (*see p276*) who bought it for a then-astronomical 550,000 guilders. Proof, if it were needed, that desire blinds, for how else could Hans van Meegeren's heavy-handed *De Emmaüsgangers* be mistaken

for a Vermeer? It was only in 1945, when the forger was facing a traitor's death penalty for selling the Nazis another 'Vermeer', that van Meegeren admitted both were forgeries, painted to avenge himself on a critic's poor reviews. That self same critic had fallen for the forgeries, although whether the satisfaction of facing his nemesis with his own incompetence was sufficient compensation for van Meegeren's subsequent jail term is unlikely: van Meegeren died in 1947 while serving it.

But despite this lapse you can generally trust the provenance of the art in Amsterdam's museums. And to miss out on the heritage on show would be a sin, comparable to anything you might contemplate in the Red Light District. So open your eyes to sensual bliss.

Jan Vermeer ❶

Delft-born painter Jan Vermeer (1632-75) painted pictures, like the *Kitchen Maid*, that radiate an extraordinary serenity. In his essential essay, *Vermeer in Bosnia*, Lawrence Weschler suggests that the artist's works are not depictions of actual peace but rather hopeful invocations of a peace yet to come. For Vermeer was painting at a time when Europe was slowly emerging from the ravages of the Thirty Years War (1618-1648), and at the time peace still remained a hope rather than an expectation for the exhausted, war-weary peoples of Europe. On display: **Rijksmuseum** (*see p113*).

Jan Steen ❷

Leiden's Jan Steen (1625/6-1679) has always got a
bad rap as a rowdy. While he did run a tavern in
his own home, his patchy reputation is more likely
based on the drunken folk that inhabit his paintings
of everyday life. But in fact, the *Merry Family* (1668)
is a thoroughly moralistic painting. Through a
plethora of symbols representing the emptiness of a
life spent smoking, drinking and talking crap, this
picture offers a lesson as valid today as the day it
was painted. Steen cameos as the bagpiper.
On display: **Rijksmuseum** (*see p113*).

Vincent van Gogh ❸

The career of everyone's favourite earless genius,
Vincent van Gogh (1853-90), is on full display in
Amsterdam. Here you can marvel at the fact that
the creator of the dark shadows of the *Potato Eaters*
went on to paint, a mere four years later in 1888,
the almost kinetic *Bedroom* and this self portrait
(*pictured*). By then he had settled in France's clearer
light and abandoned the Vermeer-inspired subdued
colouring of his earlier work to embrace the
Expressionist style that would make him famous.
While the self portrait clearly reflects his restless
nature, the *Bedroom* depicts the bed he would have
perhaps been better off sleeping in. Two months later
he had the first of the breakdowns that led finally to
his suicide. *See p116* **Vincent in Amsterdam**.
On display: **Van Gogh Museum** (*see p114*).

Isaac Israëls ❹

Like Van Gogh and GH Breitner, Israëls (1865-1934)
sought to re-invent painting's relevance in a post-
photographic age. But unlike his buddy Breitner who

chose to embrace this new technology by using
photographs as the basis for his paintings,
Israëls chose a more athletic path and achieved the
'snapshot' feel of his paintings by running around
like a ninny and painting very fast. And *Two Girls by
a Canal* does successfully reflect a quintessentially
Impressionist view of dynamic Amsterdam.
On display: **Amsterdams Historisch Museum**
(*see p92*).

Marcel Wander ❺

The 1997-produced *Knotted Chair* could not be
more different from that other iconic Dutch chair
of the 20th century: the highly geometric *Red-Blue
Chair* (1918/1923) by De Stijl guy Gerrit Rietveld. But
Knotted Chair – which re-invents the frumpy hippy
art of macramé with the aid of hi-tech epoxy – came
to represent the work of a new vanguard of local
designers (*see p178* **Living for design**) who seek to
achieve a fusion of wit, hipness and function.
On display: **Stedelijk Museum** (*see p114*).

Piet Mondriaan

Piet Mondriaan (1872-1944), can be used as a
one-man weathervane of modern art. He moved
through realism, impressionism and cubism, before
embracing the purely abstract. His use of only lines
and primary colour blocks inspired accusations of
sterility, but actually represent a very personal and
subjective quest for essence and harmony. He was
also a wit, at least by artistic standards: he tilted his
late and ultra-minimal canvas, *Composition with Two
Lines* (1931) – the title essentially describes it as well
as any reproduction – by 45 degrees.
On display: **Stedelijk Museum** (*see p114*).

①

Sex & Drugs

Some call Amsterdam the 'vagina of Europe', but others call it home.

It's pragmatism at its finest: what better way to stamp out crime than by legalising it? Granted, the story of Amsterdam's liberal attitudes ain't quite so straightforward, but here's a fact known the world over: this city does sex and drugs with fewer hang-ups than anywhere else on the planet. It's little wonder that the visitors keep sliding in like iron filings to a magnet.

Some elements of the local authorities would prefer to re-invent Amsterdam as a business capital and attract a higher-minded breed of tourist (read: people with money). However, if you ask most non-residents, the first words that come to mind when they hear 'Amsterdam', their answers will be 'Red Light District' or 'coffeeshops'. And since the city has such forward-thinking policies on sex and drugs, who can really blame them?

Of course, we wouldn't want you to forget the other 95 per cent of the guide to this most multi-faceted city – but we'd be shirking our duty if we didn't tell you the history behind the hundreds of naked ladies in their neon-framed windows, and the availability of joints the size of Oklahoma. The fun starts here.

Sex

What is it about travel that makes people so frisky? Even if you've never had a one night stand with a hotel bartender, nor applied for membership of the Mile High Club, you can't deny that there's something about strange places and new faces that kindles an appetite for adventure. However, the legal consequences of, say, hiring a prostitute vary from country to country: most governments prohibit prostitution but then selectively police the more public levels of the sex industry, or hand out licences to escort agencies and dance clubs, or create 'special zones' where men can let off steam without getting busted. But the Netherlands has chosen a more open approach.

The recorded history of prostitution in Amsterdam dates from the city's 13th Century roots. Amsterdam has always resisted all efforts to banish sex as an industry, and eventually the Dutch came to accept the advantages of a more pragmatic approach. Although working as a prostitute has been completely legal here since 1911, it was not

By the 15th century, Amsterdam was a bustling port attracting money, merchants and sailors – or, more specifically, merchants and sailors with money – which in turn increased the amount of sex for sale. But it wasn't only randy men who influenced the industry's growth, but also the fact that many local women, separated from their seafaring husbands for months on end, were left with little or no means to sustain themselves or their children. Prostitution was one of the few money-making options available.

In the Middle Ages prostitutes had been permitted to work in one of the brothels located on what is now Damstraat. Keeping a whorehouse was then the exclusive privilege of the city's sheriff, and women found working elsewhere in the city were forcibly marched back to said sheriff to the 'sound of drums and flutes'. But in the 15th century prostitutes began working the area around Zeedijk; and by the 17th century some were walking through the Old Side with red lanterns to advertise their profession. Soon after, enterprising women turned to advertising themselves in the windows of their own homes, or from front-facing rooms rented from other homeowners; it's from this practice that today's rather more garish window trade is descended.

'In the game of commercial sex, the big losers are female customers.'

More 'traditional' methods of conducting business still apply, but it's the red-lit windows that have earned Amsterdam's notoriety as a major sex capital. And no matter how prepared you think you are, you'll be taken aback the first time you see street after street of huge picture windows, each decorated with red velvet-effect soft furnishings, each sparingly lit, and each dominated by a nearly-naked woman. The women are in your face, obliging you to notice them. They come in all shapes, sizes, skin tones and ages. Not all of them look terribly excited to be there, but neither would you if your job involved standing up for hours and answering a string of stupid questions. Many of the women pass the time between clients by gossiping with colleagues, dancing and cavorting or teasing passers-by. If you see someone who takes your fancy, talk to her politely and you'll be behind the curtain before you can say, 'I love Amsterdam'.

Amsterdam's best-known Red Light District spreads out around Oudezijds Voorburgwal and Oudezijds Achterburgwal canals, and the famous windows alternate with the butcher, the

until 2000 that the ban on brothels was lifted, thus formally permitting window and brothel sex-work. But with the legalisation of brothels came bureaucratisation: now all sex-workers must have an EU passport; and a 200-page rule book was introduced to govern the business of selling sexual services, covering everything from fire escapes to the appropriate length of a prostitute's fingernails.

baker and the candlestick maker. Two smaller, less heralded Red Light areas sit on the New Side (between Kattengat and Lijnbaanssteeg) and in the Pijp (Ruysdaelkade, from Albert Cuypstraat to 1e Jan Steenstraat).

What you see is not all you get; there are loads of other options to choose from. A quick scan of the internet or *Gouden Gids* (*Yellow Pages*) will lead you to escort services, professional S&M services, sex clubs, striptease clubs, swingers' clubs, brothels, live sex shows, sex services for gay men, peep shows, sex cinemas and more. The only thing that is not permitted is street prostitution. Although a *tippelzone* (tolerated 'walking zone') was set up on Theemsweg, complete with private parking stalls, police security, and prostitute support services, the city elected to close it in December 2003, since the prostitutes it was intended for were using it less. Some street prostitution does occur in the centre, most notoriously in the area behind Centraal Station.

In the game of commercial sex, the big losers are female customers. Sorry, gals: your options are limited. There are a few escort services that will supply male or female prostitutes for you, and you may find a window prostitute who is happy to get busy with a woman – though this is more likely to happen if you visit her with your male partner. Another option for the adventurous is to visit a swingers club; they generally have an overabundance of single men looking for a free frolic. You could also make a

point of visiting the most female-friendly sex shop in Amsterdam, **Female & Partners** (*see p182*), to pick up a little consolation gift for yourself (though remember, batteries are rarely included). For visitors who want to look but not touch, a visit to a live sex show, at **Casa Rosso** (*see p86*) for instance, might inspire an evening of private fun elsewhere.

The most unique quality about the Red Light District is its integration into the Old Centre neighbourhood (for more, *see p80*). Police patrol the area with just enough visibility to dissuade most troublemakers. CCTV cameras keep a close eye on street activity and every window is equipped with an emergency alarm system that the woman behind it can activate if necessary. While the majority of clients, almost half of whom are locals, have no interest at all in harming a prostitute, these safeguards give workers a feeling of reassurance. One misdemeanour that's guaranteed to cause trouble is taking a photo of a window prostitute. If you get the urge, try to imagine yourself in their place and remember that they're not zoo animals. If you really need a picture of an Amsterdam window gal, some of the tourist shops sell suitable postcards.

The subject of prostitution always raises concerns about STDs. Sex workers take their healthcare seriously and will insist on using a condom – and clients should do likewise. There are no laws requiring prostitutes to have medical check-ups but there's an STD clinic in

Ask a silly question

Founded in 1994 by ex-prostitute Mariska Majoor, the Prostitution Information Centre (PIC, *pic* also being Dutch slang for 'dick') is right by Oude Kerk and open to absolutely everyone out to expand their understanding of prostitutes and prostitution. PIC supports its efforts through the sale of print information and books related to prostitution, PIC and Red Light souvenirs, and donations. Interested groups can also arrange a lecture session or private walking tour.

PIC
Enge Kerk Steeg 3, Old Centre: Old Side (420 7328/www.pic-amsterdam.com). Tram 4, 9, 16, 24, 25, 26. **Open** noon-7pm Tue-Sat. **Map** p310 D2.

PIC quiz:
1. How do I negotiate a date with a prostitute?
2. How much will it cost?

3. Are all the prostitutes legally required to have medical checks for sexually transmitted diseases (STDs)?
4. Who controls the girls?
5. Has legalisation made working conditions better for prostitutes?

1. Be polite and make clear arrangements about your desires, the duration and fee.
2. Expect to pay €35-€50 for 20 minutes.
3. While medical checks are not required by law, prostitutes do visit local clinics and will insist on condoms.
4. Window workers are self-employed; they decide for themselves who they will see and what they will do with clients.
5. Legalisation recognizes prostitution as work and thereby allows prostitutes to demand better working conditions, health care, protection, and benefits.

the Old Side's Red Light District where sex workers can go anonymously for free check-ups. There's also a prostitute rights organisation, De Rode Draad (the Red Thread), and a sex workers' union, Vakwerk. You can find out about both at the Prostitution Information Centre (*see p47* **Ask a silly question**).

That said, the situation is by no means perfect. 2000's legal reforms were aimed in part at reducing the number of illegal immigrants working in prostitution, but in actual fact only a minority of prostitutes have no legal status. There are still exploitative situations involving coercion, parasitic and controlling 'boyfriends', and problems related to substance abuse. The most positive effect of the legal changes has been to legitimise prostitution as a profession, which means that sex workers have access to social services and can legitimately band together to improve their working conditions. However, the stigma remains. Even in the most ideal circumstances it's still difficult for prostitutes to balance their work and private lives. Further, prostitutes have problems when trying to get bank accounts, mortgages and insurance, despite being liable for taxes and generating an estimated €450 million a year.

Certainly, the locals' liberal, grown-up attitudes merit applause, and the methods they've employed to deal with the inevitability of a sex industry have arguably resulted in a better deal for both customer and sex worker. Visit with an open mind, but don't be surprised if Amsterdam's fabled Red Light District falls short of at least some of the hype.

Drugs

You strut in through the front door of the coffeeshop, engage in a simple transaction and then smoke the sweet smoke. You strut out through the front door, wiggly, wasted and – most importantly, for you have done no wrong – free of paranoia. Welcome to the Netherlands.

A large part of the country's image has been defined by its apparently lax attitude towards drugs. But this is misleading: soft drugs are still only semi-legal. Simply put, the famously pragmatic Dutch began to put drug laws into perspective back in the early 1970s. Swamped with heroin and repeatedly reminded by the ex-Provos and hippies then entering mainstream politics of the relatively benign nature of pot, the fight against wimpy drugs came to be seen as a ludicrous waste of time and money.

And so, in 1976, a vaguely worded law was passed to make a distinction between hard and soft drugs, effectively separating their markets from each other's influence and allowing the use and sale of small amounts of soft drugs – under

30 grams (one ounce). The 'front door' of the then embryonic 'coffeeshop' was now legal, although the 'back door', where produce arrived by the kilo, looked out on an illegal distribution system. While the coffeeshop owner deals on the condoned side of this economy and can redirect his profits into other legal ventures (as many do, investing in hotels and nightclubs), and while suppliers experience the profitability of being illegal, the couriers who provide the link and run the risks without high returns remain in a legal limbo where such clichés as 'Kafkaesque' or 'Catch 22' are very real.

And yet the wobbly system has worked. Time passed without the increase in soft drug use that doomsayers expected. The coffeeshop became a part of the Amsterdam streetscape. And the concerted efforts against hard-drug use – less through law enforcement and more via education, methadone programmes, needle exchanges, drop-in shoot-up centres and counselling – have resulted in one of the lowest junkie populations in the world. Junkies may have more street visibility here than in other European cities, but that's more to do with an openness that lets junkies dare to be seen.

> **'Some visitors show up on Friday, spend three days getting wasted, then go home again.'**

Moves towards complete legalisation of soft drugs have always been thwarted by a variety of factors: pressure from fellow EU members (France – which, funnily enough, is Holland's pipeline for heroin – and more recently Germany); tension between the government and coffeeshop owners (who have come to enjoy testing the boundaries of the vague laws); and the lack of a local supply. This last factor, though, was weakened by the 'green wave' of the early '90s, when the US-designed skunk blew over and was found to grow very nicely under artificial light; its descendants are the basis for the near-infinite variety of Nederweeds. Technology has even produced viable hash from the local harvest: foreign suppliers need no longer be involved.

After years of derision, many countries are now waking up to the advantages of Dutch policies. Vancouver is now cited as the 'New Amsterdam', especially since British Columbian buds like Love Potion No.1 and God Bud won as best sativa resin and indica Indian cannabis respectively at the 2004 Cannabis Cup. So you might think it would be a good time for the Netherlands to fully legalise the growth, distribution and use of soft drugs. But as it turns out, the opposite seems to be happening. A conservative stream in government began to crack down on home-growing, allowing only the cultivation of four plants at a time and banning the use of artificial light. Tighter restrictions also caused a decline in the number of coffeeshops: from 1,200 in 1997 to 782 in 2002. Amsterdam, home to about 20 per cent of these, now won't let any new coffeeshops open, and is also busy forcing coffeeshops that sell alcohol to choose between dope and booze.

In 2003 – the same year that saw the appearance of (albeit overpriced) prescription marijuana in the nation's pharmacies – coffeeshops narrowly avoided demise threatened by new anti-smoking legislation for smoke-free workplaces. Ever pragmatic, the authorities soon realised that non-smokers are unlikely to look for a job in a coffeeshop. And

Put that in your bong and smoke it.

international shock and horror greeted the much-publicised suggestion later in the same year by the Christian Democrat Justice Minister that drug tourism could be eradicated by letting only Dutch residents buy from coffeeshops. But the municipalities – the level of government that he wanted to take responsibility for the mind-boggling logistics – turned the idea down.

There's an obvious difference between the locals blasé attitude and how visitors behave. The majority of Amsterdammers treat soft drugs as just something else to do. Dope tourists, though, hit the coffeeshops with wide-eyed, giggling greed, then face a painful comedown when they belatedly realise that Dutch drugs are far stronger than those they're used to at home. (Perhaps that third spacecake might have been two too many…)

The easy availability of soft drugs has produced its own brand of tourist: those who come to the city merely to get so stoned they can't remember a thing about it. A full six per cent of visitors cite coffeeshops as the reason they come here (with 25 per cent of all visitors finding time to at least visit a coffeeshop). And it's this six per cent that has led the authorities to look upon their city's most famous law with ambivalence. On the one hand, the coffeeshops attract many visitors to the city. On the other, the kind of visitors the law attracts are, not to put too fine a point on it, hardly the kind of tourists the authorities welcome with open arms. Two thirds of ambulances called for drug problems are for tourists.

Although many of Amsterdam's weekend funseekers only blight the Red Light District the authorities' displeasure is less a matter of principle than a question of economics. Such visitors show up on Friday, spend three days getting wasted on spliffs, spacecake and Amstel, then go home on Monday having made a negligible contribution to the Dutch GNP.

Then there's the issue of organised crime. Every country has it in some form, of course, but the gangs in the Netherlands are able to go about their drug-running businesses with more ease than the government would like. Worse still, many Dutch gangs are believed to be freely trafficking drugs both hard and soft all over Europe, a fact that hasn't exactly endeared the Netherlands to its neighbours.

And yet, and yet… The policy works. And before the world has caught up, the Dutch have moved on: in fact since 1998, the pleasure-seeking public has become less hedonistic, smoking fewer joints (from 28 per cent to 19 per cent), dropping less ecstasy (from 27 per cent to eight per cent) and snorting less coke (ten per cent to three per cent). So you might want to put a bit of that in your pipe and blow.

Bicycles

I want to ride my *fietsicle*.

Bicycles may largely be taken for granted these days, but as 'iron horses that need no feeding', they are still majestic beasts whose invention transformed life as much as the car and commercial flight. The *fiets* – as the Dutch call it – democratised movement by being both functionally and financially accessible. As an efficient agent of mobility, freeing up time for more noble pursuits, bikes also participated in the emancipation of women and found one of their biggest local cheerleaders in pioneering feminist Alleta Jacobs (1854-1929), the Netherlands' first female doctor and inventor of the family-planning 'Dutch cap'. And thanks to a bicycle's mechanical nudity – the artist Saul Steinberg called it an 'X-ray of itself' – bikes are easy to maintain as well.

Don't mention it to the Dutch (more on this later), but it was a German, Karl van Drais (1785-1851), who envisioned two in-line wheels being steered by handlebars at the front. But this was only a 'walking bike', and it was not until 1861 that Ernest Michaux, a son of a Parisian wagon-maker, put pedals on the front wheel and created the *vélocipède*. Then in 1871, the Englishman James Starley made the discovery that a huge front wheel made things more efficient – only to be outdone in 1885 by his own nephew John Kemp Starley who made his 'Rover' with two equal-sized wheels being back-propelled with a chain. While later appended with inflatable rubber tyres to cure riders of their headaches, this design had

already achieved near-perfection. And it's this standard old 'bone-shaker', called an *oma fiets* ('granny bike'), that you still see most around town. This horizontal land – where only the wind offers any real challenges – has no need for those light frames that enable overachievers like Lance Armstrong to pedal at lightning speeds. Bicycles, in their simplest incarnations, are intrinsic to Dutch identity: sensible, sober and befitting of the Calvinist doctrine of 'no pain, no gain'. Politicians and royals always take to the saddle for a photo shoot.

The Dutch also show their respect by buying 1.5 million bikes annually and then, in Amsterdam alone, stealing 150,000 of them. (Professional thieves steal 40 per cent, junkies 30 per cent, and 'occasion stealers' – read: broke students – account for the other 30 per cent.) It has been calculated that if the city's 540,000 bikes were all put together, they would fill Vondelpark twice over.

The term *fiets* has entered the language in many ways. 'Bicycle bread' refers to raisin bread that is so skimpy on the raisins that a bike could ride between them. And if you see someone with gapped teeth, feel free to point, laugh and call them 'bike rack'. But the most widely used cycling phrase is 'Okay, first return the bike', which means 'first things first'. This commemorates the requisition by retreating Germans of the nation's bikes at the end of World War II, and provides part of the reason why spiteful locals will direct German tourists to the Anne Frankhuis when asked about the location of the nearest coffeeshop.

Bicycles played a particularly heady role for the Provos in the 1960s. This left-wing group combined anti-capitalist politics with a sense of the absurd and their 'happenings' – which were to become blueprints for both the Yippies in America and the Situationists in France – were actually orchestrated mind games meant to provoke the authorities into embarrassing actions like drug busts of hay stacks. Their 1965 'White Bicycle Plan' donated a white painted bicycle to the citizens of Amsterdam for their free use in the hope that the city would follow through with thousands more. But it only provoked the police to impound it. While there were many other 'White Plans' – such as the 'White Constable Plan' that envisioned white-clad cops equipped with lighters for joint-smokers, chickens for the hungry, and oranges for the thirsty – only the 'White Bicycle Plan' managed to enter the realm of the nearly-real. The idea was formulated by Luud Schimmelpenninck who, as a newly elected councillor in 1967, tried to push the plan through. A limited test run did not begin until 1998. A designer, Schimmelpenninck had clung to his bicycle vision for 30 years. He managed to deal with the logistics of finding sponsorship, weaving through the required bureaucracy, inventing an 'asshole-proof' bicycle and developing a computerised distribution system that would minimise theft. But after several trials and millions of guilders of investment, the plan proved unworkable.

But there are many other local bike visionaries. VMX Architect's temporary shed for 2,500 bicycles, currently pile-drived in a canal just west of Centraal Station to keep the bike clutter at bay while the Noord–Zuid metro line is being constructed, won first prize at the 2002 Venice International Architecture Biennial. There's also a whole posse of squatters who weld together 'tall bikes' for jousting contests (*see p242* **Get on your bike and ride**). You can even hire a *fietscafe* ('bike café', *see 144* **A barrel and a bicycle**) to pedal while drinking. Meanwhile, the obsessives at Workcycles (Veemarkt 150, 689 7879, www.workcycles.com) can build or rent you any manner of work bike.

But Amsterdam-based American artist Eric Staller (www.conferencebike.com), famed for his *Lightmobile* (1985), a Volkswagen Beetle covered with 1659 computerised lights, has truly embraced the bicycle as long-term muse. Inspired by Dutch socialism and bike culture, he invented the ConferenceBike, where seven people sit in a circle elbow to elbow. One person steers while all seven pedal to propel the bike forward. In 2003 Staller re-invented his

ConferenceBike as a PeaceTank with the hopes of getting seven world leaders to pedal towards peace. None have yet dared to take the plunge.

For those who want to get on a bike and ride, here are some tips. Firstly, ignore traffic lights (unless the police are around of course). Amsterdam cyclists hate to queue behind people waiting for a red light and in general regard traffic lights as charmingly inconsequential pop-art town-decorations. And if you do get into an accident, it's usually the car drivers who lose in court and hence are the ones who will pay for your shiny new wheelchair. Also, remember to stick to your right and to watch out for the tram tracks and deer-like tourists reading maps on the bike path. It may also help to read a few books on chaos theory before setting out. And for the love of God do not regard Amsterdam as some sort of Disney-esque pedal world (*see p90* **Disneyland Amsterdam**). Only bike if you know how. Oh, and avoid travelling in packs; yes, we're talking to you British rugby players and Italians… This is real life people!

But in general, cycling – or even merely gracefully side-saddling on the back of one – will help link you to the city and its singular vibe. Imagine if you will if everyone drove a car here; the city would be unliveable. And the fact that this city is so very liveable may help account for why Amsterdam's cyclists are rightfully proud – or psychotically smug, depending on your view – about their rights to the road. And with a third of all gasoline pumped in the developed world being used for trips of five kilometres (three miles) or less (with the majority of these rides for a single passenger), the bike can still play a much larger role in the long-term future of our sweet little planet. So happy pedalling!

ConferenceBike

Where to Stay

Where to Stay

From beds on water to water beds, there's no better place for knocking out zeds.

For most of the time the hotel trade in Amsterdam ambles along, with few major openings or closures. But someone must have slipped go-juice in the water in 2004, because the whole business underwent a shake-up. At the bottom end the city council began a clamp-down on the touts who pounce on unwary tourists around Centraal Station, leading them off to unregulated rooms in who knows where. At the top, Anoushka Hempel's boarding house for the jet set, Blakes, will disappear early in 2005 to re-emerge as the **Dylan**, while Intercontinental put the **American Hotel** on the market. Amsterdam's most talked-about hotel venture for yonks, **Lloyd Hotel** (*see p70* **Cooking culture with Lloyd**) opened in the summer of 2004, followed by a fully-operational training hotel for caterers and hoteliers – The College – in the autumn. After a year of unprecedented activity, things are bound to settle down to the old peaceful pace…

Walking through the city (or browsing through this guide) you'll notice that hotels tend to cluster: you're spoiled for choice in the Museum District or along the canals, yet the Jordaan and the Pijp, have few options for a bed, and we pretty much list the lot. Don't fret if you can't find a place to stay in your chosen 'hood: in this dinky city, nothing is far-flung.

Rather less accessible – especially if you're in a wheelchair – are the rooms. The haphazard buildings that make Amsterdam so charming are an obstacle course for anyone with mobility problems. Lots of the quirkiest hotels are in listed buildings, making lifts a no-no. If you can't afford to pay top-whack, you may have to grit your teeth and stay at a chain.

Once you've checked in, you'll also notice that you don't get much for your money. Rooms are rather, ahem, bijoux, and often, there's not much difference in price between a hotel in the centre or in the suburbs.

Breakfast, normally a help-yourself-buffet, is usually included, except at the very top and bottom of the market, where it will almost certainly be extra. You will also have to pay a city tax of five per cent, which may or may not be included in the advertised rate.

If there's just one piece of advice you should heed, it's to book as far in advance as possible. Also be aware of the weekend, three-night

RHO Hotel. *See p57.*

minimum stay policy, which is, alas, both increasingly popular and downright cheeky in a weekend-break destination. If you don't book independently, the **Nederlands Reserverings Centrum** (Dutch Reservations Centre) will do so for you by phone (0299 689144, 8.30am-5.30pm, with a message-service out of hours) or online (www.hotelres.nl).

If you turn up without accommodation, your best bet is the **Amsterdam Tourist Board** (VVV), who'll find you a hotel room for a small fee; there are branches at the airport, Centraal Station and Leidseplein (*see p295*).

The website www.weekendhotel.nl is an excellent resource for B&B and smaller luxury hotels across the Netherlands and Belgium.

Hotels

The Old Centre

Deluxe

The Grand
*Oudezijds Voorburgwal 197, 1012 EX (555 3111/
fax 555 3222/www.thegrand.nl). Tram 4, 9, 14, 16,
24, 25.* **Rates** €420-€465 single/double; €560-€1,495
suite. **Credit** AmEx, DC, MC, V. **Map** p310 D3.
Though just a short walk away, the Grand Sofitel
Demeure Hotel ('The Grand') is a million miles from
red light sleaze. An oasis of wealth and good taste,
there are six suites, three named after old
Amsterdam mayors and three after former blue-
blooded guests (reflecting the building's history as
town hall and royal staging post). Mere mortals stay
in more modest quarters, but rooms are huge by
Amsterdam standards, drenched in light, and the
marble bathrooms are filled with covetable goodies.
You won't get bargain-breaks here, but deals – like
the 'Excellence' (with use of the spa and late check-
out) – represent good value. The hotel is also host to
wine and culinary events – appropriate for a place
with an in-house Albert Roux restaurant (*see p127*).
Hotel services *Air-conditioning. Babysitting. Bar.
Business services. Concierge. Garden. Gym.
Limousine service. No-smoking rooms. Parking.
Restaurant. Swimming pool.* **Room services**
*Dataport. Minibar. Room service (24hrs). TV:
cable/pay movies/VCR (by request).*

Grand Hotel Krasnapolsky
*Dam 9, 1012 JS (554 9111/fax 622 8607/www.nh-
hotels.com). Tram 1, 2, 4, 5, 9, 13, 14, 16, 17, 24,
25.* **Rates** €290-€320 single/double; €450-€700
suites; €60 extra bed. **Credit** AmEx, DC, MC, V.
Map p310 D3.
Accommodation in this landmark ranges from the
super-deluxe Tower Suite, to rather cramped rooms
at the back – where you'll end up if you've booked
one of their frequent specials. All have plenty of
facilities, including hair trigger minibars (where you
pay for anything you touch!) and rooms without
baths have invigorating multi-headed showers.
Sunday brunch (€33, non-residents welcome) in the
listed glass confection of the Winter Garden, is truly
indulgent. Step out of the revolving door and you're
bang in the centre of town.
Hotel services *Air-conditioning. Babysitting. Bar.
Business services. Concierge. Disabled: 1 adapted
room. Garden. Gym. No-smoking floors. Parking.
Restaurants.* **Room services** *Dataport. Minibar.
Room service (24hrs). TV: satellite/pay movies.*

Hotel de l'Europe
*Nieuwe Doelenstraat 2-8, 1012 CP (531 1777/fax
531 1778/www.leurope.nl). Tram 4, 9, 14, 16, 24,
25.* **Rates** €290-€355 single; €360-€440 double;
€460-€970 suite. **Credit** AmEx, DC, MC, V.
Map p310 D3.

Commanding wonderful views over the Amstel,
l'Europe is swish through-and-through, from the
attentive service to the 100 (individually decorated)
rooms and suites. For nuptial indulgence there's a
bridal suite with a jacuzzi, while the seriously
wealthy feel on top of the world in the duplex pent-
house, with its city panorama.
Hotel services *Air-conditioning. Babysitting. Bar.
Business services. Concierge. Gym. Limousine service.
No-smoking rooms. Parking. Restaurants. Swimming
pool.* **Room services** *Dataport. Minibar. Room
service (24hrs). TV: cable/pay movies/VCR.*

Sofitel Amsterdam
*Nieuwezijds Voorburgwal 67, 1012 RE (627 5900/
fax 623 8932/www.accorhotels.com/nl). Tram 1, 2,
5, 13, 17.* **Rates** €304-€378 single/double; €351-
€424 triple; €499-€620 suite. **Credit** AmEx, DC,
MC, V. **Map** p310 C2.
An immaculately restored 17th century building
near Centraal Station, the Sofitel is well situated for
shopping, sightseeing and eating. The rooms are
tastefully furnished, with swathes of rich fabrics
(though avoid the place if you're allergic to Regency
stripe). The gentleman's club feel is continued in the
Duke of Windsor bar-brasserie, designed to evoke
the romance of the Orient Express.
Hotel services *Air-conditioning. Babysitting. Bar.
Concierge. Disabled: 1 adapted room. Gym. No-
smoking rooms. Parking (€32/24hrs). Restaurant.*
Room services *Dataport. Minibar. Room service
(24hrs). TV: cable/pay movies.*

The best Hotels

For meeting royalty and rock stars
Amstel. *See p63.*

For all-inclusive indulgence
Banks Mansion. *See p63.*

For Pijp dreams
Hotel Savoy. *See p69.*

For flower power
Hotel Agora. *See p64.*

For a bargain break
Bellington. *See p67.*

For escaping the hurly-burly
Seven Bridges. *See p64.*

For romantic getaways
Truelove Guesthouse and Antiek. *See p67.*

For on-your-doorstep entertainment
Arena. *See p65.*

Winston Hotel. *See p59.*

Expensive

Die Port van Cleve

Nieuwezijds Voorburgwal 176-80, 1012 SJ (624 4860/fax 622 0240/www.dieportvancleve.com). Tram 1, 2, 5, 9, 13, 14, 16, 17, 24, 25. **Rates** €199-€340 single; €215-€350 double; €350-€525 suites; €47.50-€50 extra bed. **Credit** AmEx, DC, MC, V. **Map** p310 C3.

Refreshing the parts other hotels cannot reach, this hotel was where Heineken first began brewing in the 1870s (*see p120*). And if you choose to partake in a little liquid history, you can follow it with a new(er) speciality: steak – nearly six million have been seared, grilled, roasted and generally burnt to various degrees of carboniferous perfection here over the years. When the time comes to walk off all that ingested indulgence, you can always repair to the nearby Magna Plaza, or the Nieuwezijds scene, for alternative forms of conspicuous consumption.

Hotel services *Bar. Business suite. Restaurant.* **Room services** *Minibar. TV: cable, pay.*

Moderate

Avenue

Nieuwezijds Voorburgwal 33, 1012 RD (530 9530/ www.avenue-hotel.nl). Tram 1, 2, 5, 13, 17. **Rates** €110 single; €155-€185 double; €210 triple; €240 quad. **Credit** AmEx, MC, V. **Map** p310 C2.

They've managed to squeeze two lifts in among the four old East India Company warehouses that now hold people rather than the fabulous spices of the Orient that marinaded Amsterdam's wealth. Useful for the less fit among us, since the 80 rooms are arranged over six floors. It's good for the canals and Nieuwezijds nightlife, with fine rooms, but, but... First rule of hotel management: never, never run out of food at breakfast time. Bears with sore heads are nothing next to cornflake-deprived clubbers.

Hotel services *Bar. Concierge. Internet.* **Room services** *TV: pay.*

Hotel Citadel

Nieuwezijds Voorburgwal 98-100, 1012 SG (627 3882/fax 627 4684/www.hotelcitadel.nl). Tram 1, 2, 4, 5, 9, 13, 14, 16, 17, 24, 25. **Rates** €85-€110 single; €120-€160 double; €160-€190 triple. **Credit** AmEx, DC, MC, V. **Map** p310 C2.

This unremarkable though thoroughly reliable little place (38 rooms) opened in 1992. Lying between the Jordaan and the Red Light District, it's also handy for a night exploring the groovy Nieuwezijds club scene. Pets are welcome, and the lift makes it a good choice for the less than fully mobile.

Hotel services *Bar.* **Room services** *TV: cable.*

Hotel Des Arts

Rokin 154-6, 1012 LE (620 1558/fax 624 9995/ www.hoteldesarts.nl). Tram 4, 9, 14, 16, 24, 25. **Rates** €79-€85 single; €95-€130 double; €135-€168 triple; €168-€183 quad; €159-€177 family room. **Credit** AmEx, DC, MC, V. **Map** p310 D3.

Family-run, family-orientated hotel with 18 big rooms and a couple of smaller ones (all en suite): they're dark, but have lovely touches like chandeliers and plasterwork ceilings. With Kalverstraat behind, it's well located for shopaholics. But we give a big thumbs down to the weekend three-night minimum stay policy and the early (10am) check-out – hoteliers, weekends are two, not three, days long.

Hotel services *Internet.* **Room services** *TV: cable.*

Hotel Sint Nicolaas

Spuistraat 1A, 1012 SP (626 1384/fax 623 0979/ www.hotelnicolaas.nl). Tram 1, 2, 5. **Rates** €65-€95 single; €90-€120 double; €120-€150 triple; €180 quad. **Credit** AmEx, DC, MC, V. **Map** p310 C2.

When they say this place has a 'large lift' they mean it: the building was once a mattress factory, hence the bumper-size elevator. Cared for by the Mesker family, and handy for Centraal Station and the Jordaan, the 24 bright, plain rooms are all en suite, and there's free use of wireless internet, too.
Hotel services *Bar. Concierge. Internet (free).* **Room services** *TV: cable.*

Residence Le Coin

Nieuwe Doelenstraat 5, 1012 CP (524 68 00/fax 524 6801/www.lecoin.nl). Tram 4, 9, 14, 16, 24, 25. **Rates** €110 single; €130-€145 double; €218 quad; €35 extra bed. **Credit** AmEx, DC, MC, V. **Map** p310 D3.

Good for families and longer stays (ask about monthly rates), the rooms are comfortable and airy, thanks to huge windows, and come equipped with kitchenettes and email connections. Because it's owned by the university, it's regularly full up with conference delegates. Breakfast is taken at Café Katoen a couple of doors down and you might like to know that Rembrandt lived on this street.
Room services *Internet. Kitchen.*

RHO Hotel

Nes 5-23, 1012 KC (620 7371/fax 620 7826/www. rhohotel.nl). Tram 1, 2, 4, 5, 9, 13, 14, 16, 17, 24, 25. **Rates** €90-95 single; €115-145 double; €135-175 triple. **Credit** AmEx, MC, V. **Map** p310 D3.

The fabulous art deco lobby in this former gold-merchants will whisk you to the '30s, but the rooms, alas, are stuck in the '80s – and the single ones are tiny.

Mind you, you can't knock the location. Nes is crammed with bars, restaurants and theatres, and is metres away from the Dam – ask for a room overlooking the square as there's no extra charge. They don't accept bookings for Saturday night only.
Hotel services *Bar. Concierge. No-smoking rooms. Internet. Parking (paid).* **Room services** *TV: satellite.*

Y Boulevard

Prins Hendrikkade 145, 1011 AT (623 0430/fax 620 0709/www.hotelyboulevard.nl). Trams 1, 2, 4, 5, 7, 9, 13, 17, 24, 25/Metro Centraal Station. **Rates** €50-€135 single/double; €110-€195 quad; €135-€225 quintuple; €155-€245 sextuple. **Credit** MC, V. **Map** p311 E2.

This small (35 rooms) hotel overlooks Oosterdok, just over the water from hip 'n' happening Oostelijke Handelskade and Post CS (*see p107* **View to the future**). Rooms, though nothing special, are well looked after, en suite and some can accommodate up to six. The downside is their cheeky bookings policy: no Sunday check out (!) and during loosely defined 'convention periods' you must book a minimum of four nights (five at Christmas).
Room services *TV: cable.*

Budget

Greenhouse Effect

Warmoesstraat 55, 1012 HW (624 4974/fax 489 0850/www.the-greenhouse-effect.com). Tram 4, 9, 17, 24, 25. **Rates** €60 (shared facilities), €75 (private facilities) single; €90-€105 double/twin; €120-€130 triple; €160 quad; €195 quintuple; €230 sextuple; €120-€180 apartments. **Credit** AmEx, MC, V. **Map** p310 D2.

Looking for a hostel?

Stayokay, your best bed in low budget!
Stayokay Amsterdam Vondelpark is situated in the heart of Amsterdam, on the edge of the beautiful Vondelpark. The exciting nightlife at the Leidseplein, the Van Gogh Museum and the Rijksmuseum, you will find them all at your doorstep.

We offer you...
- 24 Hours access.
- Shared rooms & private rooms
- Prices from € 19,50 (incl. Breakfast)
- Ensuite facilities
- WIFI internet & internet desks
- Brasserie Backpackers & terrace
- € 2,50 Discount for HI-members
- And much more…

Stayokay Amsterdam Vondelpark
tel +31 20 589 89 96

www.stayokay.com

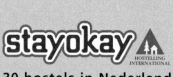

30 hostels in Nederland

Welcome to Stoner Central! This small, 17-room hotel atop the coffeeshop of the same name (*see p155*) isn't quite as scuzzy as it sounds: there's a variety of rooms, many with suitably trippy themes (FLUO, Outer Space and – hoho – Mary Jane) sleeping from one to six people. You'll fit in best if you're young and/or on the drugs trail, and there's plenty of that in this area. But with a bar (happy hours daily) and smoking room below, you may find you needn't – or simply can't – leave. Note that some rooms can only be booked for two nights or more. **Hotel services** *Bar.* **Room services** *Kitchen (apt/studio). Minibar. TV: cable.*

Hotel Vijaya

Oudezijds Voorburgwal 44, 1012 GE (638 0102/ 626 9406/fax 620 5277/www.hotelvijaya.com). Tram 4, 5, 16, 24, 25. **Rates** €45-€75 single; €70-€105 double; €90-€145 triple; €110-€175 quad; €120-€195 quintuple. **Credit** AmEx, DC, MC, V. **Map** p310 D2.

Many places round the Red Light District are decidedly dodgy, but not this one. Vijaya is basic but cheerful, and rooms (some sleep up to five) are all en suite and well looked-after – a perfectly adequate choice if you just want somewhere to dump your stuff and sleep at night. A few rooms come with canal views – it's worth asking for one, since you never know what you'll see in this lively area. Includes continental breakfast.
Hotel services *Bar.* **Room services** *TV: cable.*

Winston Hotel

Warmoesstraat 129, 1012 JA (623 1380/fax 639 2308/www.winston.nl). Tram 4, 9, 14, 16, 24, 25. **Rates** €62-€70 single; €75-€89 double; €110-€118 triple; €124-€137 quad; €149-€162 quintuple; €174-€192 sextuple. **Credit** AmEx, DC, MC, V. **Map** p310 D2.

A young, funky bunch come here to stay in the art rooms (there are artless and cheaper ones, but that kind of defeats the point), which range from Peik Suyling's uber-minimalist *Emptyness* to fetish-store Absolute Danny's study in scarlet and leopardskin. There's also a 24-hour residents' bar and ever-changing club-nights (*see p228*) next door. Deals mean you often get 20% off Mon-Wed.
Hotel services *Bar. Disabled: adapted room.*

Hostels

Flying Pig Hostels

Flying Pig Downtown *Nieuwendijk 100, 1012 MR (420 6822/group bookings 421 0583/fax 428 0802/www.flyingpig.nl). Tram 1, 2, 3, 5, 13, 17.* **Rates** €19.40-€29.60 dorm bed; €29.10-€35.10 queen-size; €71.60-€78.40 single/twin.
Flying Pig Palace *Vossiusstraat 46-7, 1071 AJ (400 4187/group reservations 421 0583/fax 421 0802/www.flyingpig.nl). Tram 2, 5, 20.* **Rates** €18.40-€27.90 dorm bed; €27.60-€34.40 queen-size; €57.50-€64.40 single; €56.50-€64 twin; €80.40-€90 triple. **Credit** *both* MC, V. **Map** *Downtown* p310 D2; *Palace* p314 C6.

Very much a part of the youthful traveller scene, this curfew-free hostel is still going strong after ten years. Perhaps it's because they work hard at creating a party atmosphere – the cheap booze (€2 a pint) on Thursday is justly popular. You can book anything from a (pricey) en suite twin to a place in a large (22-bed) or small (four-bed) dorm; in the summer there's a women-only one. There are some queen-size beds: big enough for two, though hardly suited to romantic liaisons (unless you're an exhibitionist) – they're in shared dorms. There's a branch in the Vondelpark (with free skate hire) called Flying Pig Palace and, in summer, at Noordwijk-aan-Zee. They don't accept guests under 16 or over 40.
Hotel services *Bar. Kitchen. Internet (free).*

Stayokay

Stadsdoelen *Kloveniersburgwal 97, 1011 KB (624 6832/fax 639 1035/www.stayokay.com). Tram 4, 9, 14, 16, 24, 25.*
City Hostel Vondelpark *Zandpad 5, 1054 GA (589 8996/fax 589 8955/www.stayokay.com). Tram 1, 2, 5, 6, 7, 10.* **Rates** *Stadsdoelen* €19.50-€23.50 (€2 surcharge per person per night on Fri, Sat) dorm bed. *City Hostel Vondelpark* €19.50-€24 dorm/quad bed; €67.50-€79.50 twin; €108-€116 quad (€1 surcharge per person per night on Fri, Sat). Both hostels HI members €2.50 reduction. **Credit** AmEx, MC, V. **Map** *Stadsdoelen* p310 D3; *City Hostel Vondelpark* p314 C6.

More low-key than other Amsterdam hostels, the national Stayokay organisation aims for older travellers and families as much as the backpack and bum-fluff crowd. There are special deals like New Year packages and they can even provide a packed lunch. Stadsdoelen is on a lovely canal, with dorms for 8-20 people. Tree-huggers can opt for the branch next to Vondelpark.
Hotel services *Bar (both). Disabled: adapted rooms 3 (Vondelpark only). Internet (both). Kitchen (Stadsdoelen only). Launderette (both). No-smoking rooms (both). Restaurant (Vondelpark full menu, Stadsdoelen snacks).*

Western Canal Belt

Deluxe

Amsterdam Marriott Hotel

Stadhouderskade 12, 1054 ES (607 5555/fax 607 5511/www.marriott.com). Tram 1, 2, 5, 6, 7, 10. **Rates** €140-€278 room (for 1-4 people); €478-€525 suite (for 1-4 people). **Credit** AmEx, DC, MC, V. **Map** p314 C5.

Your first thought on seeing this brick bulk on the fringe of Vondelpark is 'great location, lousy building'. But once inside the green-carpeted, rather country-clubbish rooms, you get all the little comforts standard to this class of hotel to help you forget the blandness of it all. It's a very child-friendly place – with cots for babies and an on-site Pizza Hut, and of course, acres of green play-space round the back.

't Hotel. *See p61.*

Hotel services *Air-conditioning. Babysitting. Bars. Business services. Concierge. Disabled: adapted rooms. Gym. No-smoking floors. Parking (€25/day). Restaurants.* Room services *Dataport. Minibar. Room service (24hrs). TV: satellite/pay movies. VCR.*

The Dylan

Keizersgracht 384, 1016 GB (530 2010/fax 530 2030/www.dylanamsterdam.com). Tram 1, 2, 5. Rates €255-€305 single; €405-€505 double; €695-€995 duplex; €1,095-€1,492 suite. Credit AmEx, DC, MC, V. Map p314 C4.

Switching poets in midstream, what was once Blakes became, in early 2005, the Dylan. But while tygers burning bright may have been replaced by lazy lounging under milk wood, this will remain the epitome of designer hotel elegance – and expense. There'll be renovations aplenty to Anoushka Hempel's fortress of style: a chic 20m stainless-steel swimming pool, rooms incorporating plasma-screen TVs, WiFi, and all the little luxuries that ensure you do go gentle into that good night's sleep.

Hotel services *Air-conditioning. Babysitting. Bar. Concierge. Garden. Limousine service. Parking (valet). Restaurant.* Room services *Dataport. Minibar. Room service (24hrs). TV: cable/VCR.*

Hotel Pulitzer

Prinsengracht 315-31, 1016 GZ (523 5235/fax 627 6753/www.sheraton.nl). Tram 13, 14, 17. Rates €260-€390 double deluxe; €485-€550 double exec; €650-€765 jr suite; €885-€1,015 suite; €47 extra bed. Credit AmEx, DC, MC, V. Map p310 C3.

A palace of a place, with 230 rooms spread over some 25 canal houses. Glorious for culture-seekers

with abundant funds, there's a good restaurant, a lovely garden and lots of art on the walls. Rooms, as you're entitled to expect at these sort of prices, are wonderful, with marble bathrooms just one of the highlights. In August, the Pulitzer is host to many events in the Grachtenfestival of classical music. Lots of recitals take place in the courtyard garden, and it culminates with a spectacular closing concert on pontoons right outside the hotel.

Hotel services *Air-conditioning. Babysitting. Bar. Business services. Concierge. Garden. Limousine service. No-smoking rooms. Parking (valet). Restaurant.* Room services *Dataport. Minibar. Room service (24hrs). TV: cable/pay movies/VCR.*

Expensive

Ambassade Hotel

Herengracht 341, 1016 AZ (555 0222/fax 555 0277/www.ambassade-hotel.nl). Tram 1, 2, 5. Rates €165 single; €195 double; €227 triple; €270-€340 suite; €305 apartment; €32 extra bed. Credit AmEx, DC, MC, V. Map p314 C4.

A subtly opulent, medium size (59 rooms and suites) hotel, decked out in antiques, with CoBrA paintings hung here and there. The large rooms, in calming shades, are light and continue the classy theme. Ambassade is famous for literary guests and they offer everything a scribe about town could dream of, from laptop rental to flotation tanks (at nearby Koan Float) to soothe away the RSI.

Hotel services *Babysitting. Business services. Concierge. Limousine service. No-smoking rooms.* Room services *Internet. Room service (24hrs). TV: cable/VCR.*

Hotel services *Air-conditioning (selected rooms).
Babysitting. Bar. Business services. Garden. Internet:
WiFi. Parking (paid). Restaurant.* **Room services**
Minibar. TV: cable/pay movies.

Moderate

Amsterdam Wiechmann

*Prinsengracht 328-32, 1016 HX (626 3321/fax
626 8962/www.hotelwiechmann.nl). Tram 1, 2, 5, 7,
17.* **Rates** €75-€95 single; €125-€145 double; €175-
€185 triple/quad. **Credit** MC, V. **Map** p314 C4.
Half a century old, the Wiechmann occupies a prime
canal-side spot, is ideally placed for the Jordaan, and
is within walking distance of all the sights. The 38
rooms include some family ones – though those with
a watery view come at a premium. The breakfast
room is lovely, with enormous picture-windows and
quirky old teapots and toasters.
Hotel services *Babysitting. Bar.* **Room services**
Internet. TV: cable.

Belga

*Hartenstraat 8, 1016 CB (624 9080/fax 623 6862/
www.hotelbelgahotel.nl). Tram 1, 2, 5.* **Rates** €41-
€81 single; €61.50-€125 double. **Credit** AmEx, MC,
DC, V. **Map** p310 C3.
In a listed 17th-century building, the lace-curtain
chintz of Belga couldn't be further from the stealth-
wealth of the surrounding Nine Streets. Most rooms
here are en suite, though a few share facilities in the
corridor. Some rooms are big enough for five, so it's
a great family place and very child-friendly: they
even offer a baby-sitting service.
Hotel services *Babysitting.* **Room services** *TV.*

't Hotel

*Leliegracht 18, 1015 DE (422 2741/www.thotel.nl).
Tram 1, 2, 5, 13, 14, 17.* **Rates** €135-€148 double.
Credit MC, V. **Map** p310 B3.
There's more to this bolt-hole than the prosaic name
implies. Run with tons of tender loving care by the
charmingly scatty owners, rooms are furnished in
glamorous but understated '30s style, decorated
with framed Bauhaus posters, and, in this cramped
town, you be glad to know that they are all a good
size. Room eight, up among the eaves, sleeps up to
five – two of the beds are on a lovely mezzanine. The
reception is in the antique shop downstairs that specialises in art deco, so you can browse at leisure.
Room services *TV: cable.*

Budget

Hotel Brouwer

*Singel 83, 1012 VE (624 6358/fax 520 6264/www.
hotelbrouwer.nl). Tram 1, 2, 5.* **Rates** €50 single;
€70 single use of double; €85 double; €105 triple.
No credit cards. Map p310 C2.
Run by the same family since 1917, the eight-room
Brouwer makes a snug base for lazy Jordaan or
canal wanderings, as well as town-centre
shopathons. All rooms in this (recently renovated)
1652 building are named after Dutch painters, and

Estherea

*Singel 303-9, 1012 WJ (624 5146/fax 623
9001/www.estherea.nl). Tram 1, 2, 5.* **Rates**
€160-€225 single; €170-€285 double; €240-€320
triple; €272-€348 quad. **Credit** AmEx, DC, MC, V.
Map p310 C3.
Still a family concern, the Estherea has expanded
since the war from its original modest complement
of 12 rooms, until it now lodges guests in 71 bedrooms, spread over six connecting canal houses, just
off restaurant-rich area around Spuistraat. It's luxurious – with a lovely canal-side lounge and a library
– but never stuffy, and even the smallest guests are
looked after, with high chairs, cots, and even toys
and colouring books. There's a lift, too.
Hotel services *Babysitting. Bar. Concierge. No-
smoking rooms.* **Room services** *Dataport. Minibar.
Room service (7am-11pm). TV: cable.*

Toren

*Keizersgracht 164, 1015 CZ (622 6352/fax 626
9705/www.hoteltoren.nl). Tram 13, 14, 17.* **Rates**
€125-€180 single; €140-€240 double; €205-€215
triple; €280-€350 suites. **Credit** AmEx, DC, MC, V.
Map p310 C3.
This Golden Age house oozes class. Standard doubles are cramped, though: splash out, if you can, on
the deluxe summer-house room with its own private
terrace. There are no fewer than three bridal suites,
all with jacuzzis – big enough for two, naturally –
the grandest has a four-poster bed. (Ring them for
honeymoon packages.) Be sure to ask about the
building's amazing history – it's been a prime minister's house, part of the VU and it even sheltered
Jews from the Nazis in World War II.

What Londoners take when they go out.

are individually decorated. Each one is en suite, no-smoking and enjoys canal views, making the place great all-round value. Email for reservations. **Room services** *TV.*

Singel Hotel

Singel 13-17, 1012 VC (626 3108/fax 620 3777/ www.singelhotel.nl). Tram 1, 2, 5. **Rates** €59-€104 single; €79-€149 double; €99-€199 triple. **Credit** AmEx, MC, V. **Map** p310 C2.

An excellently priced, medium-sized hotel in a 17th century house. A great location at the top of Singel makes for easy canal wandering and a short hop to Brouwersgracht and hip Haarlemmerstraat. The 32 rooms are all en suite and decoration is simple but bright. If you can, try to bag a room with a watery view. Triple rooms are a real bargain. **Hotel services** *Bar.* **Room services** *TV.*

Southern Canal Belt

Deluxe

American Hotel

Leidsekade 97, 1017 PN (556 3000/fax 556 3001/ www.amsterdam-american.crowneplaza.com). Tram 1, 2, 5, 6, 7, 10. **Rates** €150-€320, €320-€373 single/double (low/high season); €35 extra bed. **Credit** AmEx, DC, MC, V. **Map** p314 C5.

The art nouveau architecture is glorious. The café, with its vaulted ceilings and enormous windows (each weighing 1,600kg), is spectacular. Rooms are big and full of deluxe facilities (moguls can fill idle moments with the in-room golf-sets) and the sort of touches, like stained-glass windows and granite bathrooms, you'd expect for the price. Yet, somewhere along the way the hotel's character ebbed away. Now things are looking up: the place was sold in 2004 and Rob Spiekerman, the new manager, is keen to restore its fin-de-siècle glory, bringing back, for example, the original table-top lamps that were rediscovered in an attic. One to watch. **Hotel services** *Air-conditioning. Babysitting. Bars. Business services. Concierge. Disabled: adapted room. Gym. Internet: WiFi. Limousine service. No-smoking floors. Parking (paid). Restaurants.* **Room services** *Dataport. Minibar. Room service (24hrs). TV: cable/pay movies.*

Inter-Continental Amstel Amsterdam

Professor Tulpplein 1, 1018 GX (622 6060/fax 622 5808/www.interconti.com). Tram 6, 7, 10. **Rates** €550-€600 single/double; €700-€3,500 suites. **Credit** AmEx, DC, MC, V. **Map** p315 F4.

Commanding wonderful views over the Amstel, the grande dame of Amsterdam hotels has been lodging the great and the good since 1867. There are only 79 rooms and suites – astonishing for a building this size – which indicates how spacious they are, and how many in-house facilities are available. With a Michelin-starred restaurant (La Rive, *see p131*), health club (with pool), and privacy (all rooms are

soundproof) it's the obvious choice for the powerful and pretty (Bill Clinton and Brad Pitt), and there are often screaming gaggles camped out front to prove it. Its reputation was tarnished somewhat in October 2004 when legionella bacteria were found, however things are back to normal now. **Hotel services** *Air-conditioning. Bars. Business services. Concierge. Gym. Internet: WiFi. Limousine service. No-smoking rooms. Parking. Restaurants. Swimming pool.* **Room services** *Minibar. Room service (24hrs). TV: cable/pay movies/VCR.*

Hotel 717

Prinsengracht 717, 1017 JW (427 0717/fax 423 0717/www.717hotel.nl). Tram 1, 2, 5. **Rates** €398-€650 suites; extra bed €50; small dogs €25. **Credit** AmEx, DC, MC, V. **Map** p314 D4.

From marble hall to manicured garden, 717 whispers taste. There are only eight suites, which allows staff to shower attention on guests. Bouquets blossom in every corner, guests help themselves to wine beneath the chandeliers of the lounge, and antique furniture is polished to mirrored perfection. All this makes it a classy place to lay down your head (on cotton pillowcases specially imported from New York, of course). The suites, named after writers and composers, are all huge: two so big they outstrip most Amsterdam flats in size. On request your small canine accessory can stay for €25 a night, too. **Hotel services** *Air-conditioning . Business services. Garden. No-smoking rooms. Parking (paid).* **Room services** *Dataport. Minibar. Room service (7.30am-1am). TV: cable/pay movies/VCR.*

Expensive

Banks Mansion

Herengracht 519-25, 1017 BV (420 0055/fax 420 0993/www.banksmansion.nl). Tram 16, 24, 25. **Rates** €185-€205 single; €205-€230 double. **Credit** AmEx, DC, MC, V. **Map** p315 E4.

Opened April 2004, this is luxury at non-prohibitive prices. In a stately former bank, the 51 rooms have all kinds of indulgent flourishes: DVD players, help-yourself bars, breakfast in bed. The best views are over Herengracht, though even those on noisier Vijzelstraat offer something interesting. In the bar, you can snuggle down in an armchair by the open fire with a magazine and a (free) drink or snack from the serve-yourself counter. Check online for packages (such as 'Shop 'til you Drop'). **Hotel services** *Air-conditioning. Bar. Internet. No-smoking rooms.* **Room services** *Internet. Minibar (free). TV: cable/DVD.*

Eden Hotel

Amstel 144, 1017 AE (530 7878/fax 623 3267/ www.edenhotelgroup.com). Tram 4, 9, 14. **Rates** €115-€145 single; €135-€190 twin/double; €180-€215 triple; €205-€240 quad; €140-€220 apartments. **Credit** AmEx, DC, MC, V. **Map** p311 C3.

A big (340 rooms) hotel with the Amstel flowing in front, the fleshpots of Rembrandtplein behind and all of Amsterdam's attractions within walking distance. It's a good bet for families (with rooms taking up to four), business travellers (there's a dedicated floor with extra big desks and modems) or longer stays (ask about the apartments). Rooms are bland, but for individuality pay a supplement for a room decorated by students from the Rietveld Academie. **Hotel services** *Babysitting. Bar. Business services. Concierge. Disabled: adapted room. Internet: WiFi. No-smoking rooms. Parking nearby. Restaurant.* **Room services** *Dataport (selected rooms). TV: cable/pay movies.*

HEM Hotel Maas

Leidsekade 91, 1017 PN (623 3868/fax 622 2613/ www.hemhotels.nl). Tram 1, 2, 5, 6, 7, 10. **Rates** €105 single; €145-€205 double; €210 triple; €250 quad. **Credit** AmEx, DC, MC, V. **Map** p314 C5.

If your budget won't stretch to the American (*see p63*) a couple of doors down, then this hotel enjoys a similarly splendid spot, on the water between the temptations of Leidseplein and the cerebral pursuits of the museums. It's worth paying the extra €15 for a canal-side room, and, if you're feeling particularly sybaritic, splash out on one with a king-size waterbed and jacuzzi. There's a lift, too. **Hotel services** *Air-conditioning.* **Room services** *Internet. Minibar. TV.*

Jolly Hotel Carlton

Vijzelstraat 4, 1017 HK (521 6810/fax 626 6183/ www.jollyhotels.nl). Tram 16, 24, 25. **Rates** €99-€200 single; €150-€300 double. **Credit** AmEx, DC, MC, V. **Map** p314 D4.

Right in the centre, near Muntplein and the canals, this 218-room hotel is great for business travellers: there are nine meeting spaces, a business centre and specially adapted office-apartments, which come complete with kitchenette and ISDN line. The restaurant, Caruso, is good for carousing with clients. For indulgence, deluxe rooms are fitted with hydro-massage baths. Standard rates are expensive, though by checking their online deals, you'll almost certainly never have to fork out the full whack: weekend packages drop as low as €40 per person per night. Breakfast is a whopping €34. **Hotel services** *Air-conditioning. Bar. Business centre. Concierge. Parking (€30/24 hrs). Restaurant.* **Room services** *ISDN. Kitchen (office apartments). Minibar. TV: pay/satellite.*

Moderate

Bridge Hotel

Amstel 107-11, 1018 EM (623 7068/fax 624 1565/ www.thebridgehotel.nl). Tram 4, 6, 7, 9, 10. **Rates** €85-€95 single; €98-€140 double; €130-€150 triple; €195-€275 apartments. **Credit** AmEx, DC, MC, V. **Map** p311 E3.

Cosily isolated on a quiet stretch of the Amstel, yet just a couple of minutes' walk from Rembrandtplein, this pleasant hotel occupies a former marble and stone works. The 36 rooms (all en suite) are spacious and simply furnished; those with river views cost extra. There are also apartments for stays of three

nights or more, which accommodate up to four people and have their own living room and kitchen; the Gold Apartment even has two bathrooms. **Hotel services** *Bar.* **Room services** *TV: cable.*

Hotel Agora

Singel 462, 1017 AW (627 2200/fax 627 2202/ www.hotelagora.nl). Tram 1, 2, 5. **Rates** €100 single; €120-€135 double; €155 triple; €180 quad. **Credit** AmEx, DC, MC, V. **Map** p314 D4.

Unassuming from without, within the Agora is a gem, with lovely staff and well turned-out rooms (some en suite), five of which overlook Singel. It's ideally situated for the horticulturally inclined, with Bloemenmarkt (*see p170*) a few steps away, and the green theme continues with the inner-garden: the conservatory-style breakfast room overlooks it, making for a blooming marvellous start to the day. **Hotel services** *Garden. Internet: WiFi.* **Room services** *ISDN (by request). Room service (8am-10.30pm). TV: cable.*

Hotel de Munck

Achtergracht 3, 1017 WL (623 6283/fax 620 6647/ www.hoteldemunck.com). Tram 4. **Rates** €63-€68 single; €78-€110 double; €130-€160 triple; €160-€180 quad; €210-€230 apartment. **Credit** AmEx, DC, MC, V. **Map** p315 F4.

There's been a hotel in this quiet street off the Amstel since the 1940s, but the building's history stretches way back: built in 1727, it was the home of an East India Company captain. The 14 higgledy-piggledy rooms (and an apartment for five) are neat but plain. The same can't be said for the breakfast room, which is plastered with vinyl platters, samples of which play on the Wurlitzer while you eat. **Hotel services** *Bar.* **Room services** *Dataport. TV: cable.*

Nicolaas Witsen

Nicolaas Witsenstraat 4, 1017 ZH (623 6143/fax 620 5113/www.hotelnicolaaswitsen.nl). Tram 4. **Rates** €65-€90 single; €89-€110 double; €116-€142 triple; €142-€156 quad. **Credit** AmEx MC, V. **Map** p315 E5.

Rooms in this well-maintained hotel (with lift) are fine, if plain and basic for the price. But it's well located if you plan on stuffing your pipe in the Pijp, and the museum quarter is only a short stroll away. One danger we must warn you of: you may find yourself shedding Euros (and gaining pounds in the process) at the delicious deli on the corner. **Hotel services** *Bar. Internet.* **Room services** *TV: cable.*

Seven Bridges

Reguliersgracht 31, 1017 LK (623 1329). Tram 16, 24, 25. **Rates** €80-€150 single; €100-€180 double. **Credit** AmEx, MC, V. **Map** p315 E4.

A comely little place – there are only eight rooms – where relaxation is fiercely enforced: no email, no internet, nothing to shatter the calm that wafts through the hotel, kitted out in antique furniture and handmade carpets. Rooms are spacious by the

Inter-Continental Amstel. *See p63.*

cramped city standards and one even has its own terrace. Choose between a soporific garden or soothing canal view. Lack of a breakfast room means, dammit, that breakfast in bed is compulsory! **Hotel services** *Garden. No-smoking rooms.* **Room services** *TV: cable.*

Budget

Hotel Leydsche Hof

Leidsegracht 14, 1016 CK (623 2148/www. freewebs.com/leydschehof). Tram 1, 2, 5, 6, 7, 10. **Rates** €105 double. **No credit cards.** **Map** p314 C4.

On a rather genteel stretch of canal – the Finnish consulate is opposite – the Hof has seven simple but attractive rooms with low-beamed ceilings and dark wood furniture. They all have showers, but you have to share the toilets in the hall. There's no breakfast, but with so much in the vicinity – Leidseplein is two-minutes away – it's not a problem. There are no extras in this simple place, but who's arguing at this price? A good bet for night-owls on a budget.

Hotel Prinsenhof

Prinsengracht 810, 1017 JL (623 1772/fax 638 3368/www.hotelprinsenhof.com). Tram 4. **Rates** €45-€80 single; €65-€85 double; €90-€110 triple; €110-€140 quad. **Credit** AmEx, MC, V. **Map** p315 E4.

In a great location off Utrechtsestraat, this homely canal house dating from the 1700s has rooms with beams and big windows (some looking on to Prinsengracht). They're comfortably furnished with relaxing armchairs in a chintzy style. Only a couple of rooms are en suite, but those with shared facilities do have sinks, and all are reasonably priced.

Jodenbuurt, the Plantage & the Oost

Moderate

Arena

's Gravesandestraat 51, 1092 AA (850 2400/fax 850 2415/www.hotelarena.nl). Tram 3, 6, 9, 10, 14. **Rates** €100-€125 small double; €125-€175 medium double; €140-€165 large double. **Credit** AmEx, DC, MC, V. **Map** p316 G3.

Far removed from its early days as a hostel (and even further from its origin as an orphanage), this stylish hotel remains convinced that minimalism is cutting edge. Six new suites have recently been added, designed by the company IDing: most are duplex and all are fleshed out furniture-wise by big names like Piet Hein Eek. The only drawback is the location – a bit of a trek out east – but when there's a top-notch nightclub (*see p231*), and its own groovy bar and restaurant on site, you don't really need to go anywhere else. Check online for packages. **Hotel services** *Bar. Concierge. Disabled: adapted rooms. Garden. Parking (paid). Restaurant.* **Room services** *Internet. TV: cable/DVD/PlayStation.*

Ibis Stopera

Valkenburgerstraat 68, 1011 LZ (531 9135/fax 531 9145/www.ibishotel.com). Tram 9, 14/Metro Waterlooplein. **Rates** €77-€112 single; €97-€124 double. **Credit** AmEx, DC, MC, V. **Map** p311 E3.

No surprises at this international chain: it's all a bit bland and anonymous, but the air-conditioned rooms are always reliable, and pets can stay, too. The location – on a busy through road – also seems soulless, but duck off the main drag and you're in the heart of the old Jewish quarter, full of rewarding backstreet wanderings. There are also Ibis hotels at Centraal Station, Schiphol and Transformatorweg. **Hotel services** *Air-conditioning. Bar. Concierge. Parking. Restaurant.* **Room services** *Internet. TV: cable.*

Budget

Fantasia Hotel

Nieuwe Keizersgracht 16, 1018 DR (623 8259/ www.fantasia-hotel.com). Trams 4, 6, 7, 10/Metro Weesperplein. **Rates** €55-€65 single; €84-€94 double; €120 triple; €140 family room. **No credit cards.** **Map** p311 F3.

A couple of doors down from Adolesce (*see p67*), and cut from the same cloth, this is a good family bet. Of the 19 rooms, only one isn't en suite and all have tea-

and coffee-making facilities in them (a rarity in this price category). Check for off-season specials, but note that they close from Oct 31-Mar 15 (except for the first three weekends in December.)
Hotel services *TV lounge.*

Hotel Adolesce

Nieuwe Keizersgracht 26, 1018 DR (626 3959/fax 627 4249/www.adolesce.nl). Trams 4, 6, 7, 10/Metro Weesperplein. **Rates** €60-€65 single; €90-€100 double; €120 triple. **Credit** MC, V. **Map** p311 F3.
In a lovely location near Waterlooplein this little, ten-room (all en suite) hotel is great for media munchers on a budget. Rooms are clean and simple and although there's no breakfast, you can help yourself to coffee, tea and biscuits all day long.
Room services *TV: cable.*

The Jordaan

Moderate

Hotel de Looier

3e Looiersdwarsstraat 75, 1016 VD (625 1855/ fax 627 5320/www.hoteldelooier.com). Tram 1, 2, 5, 7, 10. **Rates** €79-€129 double; €99-€159 triple; €120-€140 family room. **Credit** AmEx, DC, MC, V. **Map** p314 C4.
There's nothing fancy at this spotlessly clean hotel in a former diamond factory, but all the 28 rooms are neatly furnished and en suite and there's a bar for nightcaps. It's in a great location, tucked down a side street on the lower fringes of the Jordaan. It's perfect for market hopping: De Looier bric-a-brac arcade is opposite, and the Jordaan's street markets (*see p180*) are within strolling distance.
Hotel services *Bar.* **Room services** *TV.*

Truelove Antiek and Guesthouse

Prinsenstraat 4, 1015 DC (320 2500/06 248 056 72 mobile after 6pm/fax 847 1149 50/www.truelove.be). Tram 1, 2, 5. **Rates** €90-€110 double; €120 suite; €130 apartments. **No credit cards. Map** p310 C2.
Who could resist a name like this? Nestling above an antique shop (which also serves as reception) this romantic, two-room hidy-hole has the romantic touches that let the lurve flow: fresh flowers, mineral water and wine in both rooms. Breakfast isn't included, but you're spoiled for choice in this area. They don't accept one-night stays Fri-Sun and it's completely non-smoking – so no post-coital fag.
Hotel services *Non smoking throughout.* **Room services** *TV: cable.*

Budget

Hotel Acacia

Lindengracht 251, 1015 KH (622 1460/fax 638 0748/www.hotelacacia.nl). Tram 1, 2, 5, 13, 17. **Rates** €65 single; €80 double; €99 triple; €120 quad; €90 studio; €95-€110 (double on boat); €115-125 (triple on boat); €130 (quad on boat). **Credit** MC, V. **Map** p309 B2.

It's back to basics at Acacia – the only frills here are on the bedspreads – leading some guests to liken it to a Blackpool B&B. Still, it's a friendly place, in a nice corner of the Jordaan, with en suite showers (no baths) and WCs. They also rent studios and a couple of houseboats.
Room services *Kitchen (boat/studio). TV: cable.*

Hotel van Onna

Bloemgracht 102-108, 1015 TN (626 5801/ www.hotelvanonna.nl). Tram 13, 17. **Rates** €40 single; €80 double; €120 triple. **No credit cards**. **Map** p309 B3.
Probably the most picturesquely placed hotel in town, on a heart breakingly beautiful stretch of canal in the Jordaan, Van Onna is a moment's stroll from Westerkerk and Anne Frankhuis. The hotel is arranged across three canal houses spanning the 17th to late 20th century, the 42 rooms all have shower and toilet en suite, and the entire place is no smoking. Cinephiles and Harry Mulisch fans will also be intrigued to know that some of the 1979 movie *Twee Vrouwen* was filmed here.
Hotel services *Non smoking throughout.*

The Museum Quarter, Vondelpark & the South

Moderate

Hotel V

Victorieplein 42, 1078 PH (662 3233/fax 676 6398/ www.hotelv.nl). Tram 4, 12, 25. **Rates** €75-€85 single; €110-€130 double; €155 triple. **Credit** AmEx, DC, MC, V.
Firmly in the 'great hotel in bland location' slot, only the glowing purple doors hint at the jewel of a joint hiding inside three ordinary-looking houses in residential Rivierenbuurt. The breakfast room/bar has a gorgeous pebbly fireplace, and the 24 rooms are similarly designer-orientated. Perhaps a bit pricey for the location, though the number 4 tram stops right outside to whisk you into town, and the Pijp's a short walk away. If you're in town for the RAI exhibition centre (ten minutes by foot) or the WTC, this is a splendid way of being where you need to be while avoiding impersonal, corporate chain-hotels.
Hotel services *Bar. Garden. Parking (street).* **Room services** *TV: cable.*

Budget

Bellington

PC Hooftstraat 78-80, 1071 CB (671 6478/fax 671 863/www.hotel-bellington.com). Tram 4, 12, 25. **Rates** €45-€95 double; €70-€110 triple; €90-€138 quad. **Credit** AmEx, MC, V. **Map** p314 D6.
Perched above a boutique on Amsterdam's glitziest shopping street, this basic-but-tidy hotel is a welcome break from all the consumption around you, and is a great base camp for those setting out on

Find **Truelove**. *See p67.*

some serious museum exploration. Shockingly cheap for the city and the surroundings, if you don't mind sharing facilities in the low season you could pay as little as €35 for a double, knocking hostel accommodation into a cocked hat.
Room services *Minibar. TV: cable.*

Hostels

For **Flying Pig Hostels** and **Stayokay Hostels**, *see p59.*

The Pijp

Deluxe

Hotel Okura Amsterdam

Ferdinand Bolstraat 333, 1072 LH (678 7111/ fax 671 2344/www.okura.nl). Tram 12, 25. **Rates** €260-€345 single; €295-€380 double; €425-€1,950 suites; €73 extra bed. **Credit** AmEx, DC, MC, V. **Map** p315 E6.

On the edge of the Pijp a short walk from RAI, this massive (370 rooms, 23 floors) hotel aims very much at business travellers, with its endless expense-account frills and conference facilities. Rooms are big and comfortable – as they should be for this price – with plenty of work-related facilities including wireless internet and fax. You can work off your executive stress in the full-size pool and saunas, then schmooze with clients: Okura has no fewer than six bars and restaurants (among them the top-dollar, top-floor Ciel Bleu, with its epic views and French food) and then, to help with the digestion, it can even hook you up with a golf course.
Hotel services *Air-conditioning. Babysitting. Bars. Business services. Concierge. Disabled: adapted rooms. Gym. Limousine service. No-smoking rooms. Parking (paid). Restaurants. Swimming pool (indoor).* **Room services** *Dataport. Minibar. Room service (24hrs). TV: satellite/pay movies/VCR (suites only).*

Expensive

Hotel Savoy

Ferdinand Bolstraat 194, 1072 LW (644 7445/ fax 644 8989/www.hampshirehotels.nl/savoy). Tram 3, 12, 16, 24, 25. **Rates** €150 single; €175 double; €200 triple. **Credit** AmEx, DC, MC, V. **Map** p315 F6.

Just what the Pijp needed: a hotel going some way to bridging the previously gaping price void between the opulent Okura and the basic Bicycle. In a rather forbidding Amsterdam School building, the Savoy is pitched – because of its proximity to RAI – at business travellers, but it's ideal for holidaying pleasure seekers, too: you could easily spend a weekend eating and boozing your way along Ferdinand Bolstraat alone. Cool, pale minimalism is the key throughout. It's enlivened by friendly staff: charm them, and you may find you've negotiated yourself a discount. Look for online deals, too: some

like the €90pp two-night special, knock the place down a category in price. Whatever else happens, at least you're guaranteed a safe night's sleep – the hotel adjoins a huge police station.
Hotel services *Bar.* **Room services** *Air-conditioning. Dataport. Internet. TV.*

Budget

Van Ostade Bicycle Hotel

Van Ostadestraat 123, 1072 SV (679 3452/fax 671 5213/www.bicyclehotel.com). Tram 3, 12, 16, 24, 25. **Rates** €50-€65 single; €55-€105 double; €70-€130 triple; €99-€150 quad. **Credit** AmEx, MC, V. **Map** p315 F6.

One of the strangely few places to stay in the Pijp, this hotel slots into the cheap 'n' cheery category. The rooms are basic, but the breakfast area/internet lounge is airy, with a view of the garden. No prizes for guessing that cycling is central to the hotel: you can hire a bike for (a very reasonable) €5 a day, or bring your own and park it in the hotel. Staff will be delighted to offer advice on routes and give you maps. But we're sorry to report that this is another one of those irritating hotels which insist on a three-night-minimum weekend stay.
Hotel services *Free Internet. No-smoking rooms. Parking (paid).* **Room services** *TV: satellite.*

Other options

Floating accommodation

Being surrounded by canals, it's only natural to want to stay afloat in Amsterdam, though there are surprisingly few options for a city awash with waterways. Below, we've listed the best ways for making your holiday HQ on H$_2$0. *See also p67* **Hotel Acacia.**

The Old Centre

Amstel Botel

Oosterdokskade 2-4, 1011 AE (626 4247/fax 639 1952/www.amstelbotel.nl). Tram 1, 2, 5, 9, 13, 17, 24, 25. **Rates** €87 (rear side)-€92 (water side) single/double/twin; €117-€122 triple. **Credit** AmEx, DC, MC, V. **Map** p311 E1.

Bobbing alongside Centraal Station, this floating hotel is something of an Amsterdam institution. While it may not qualify as the *QE2*, all 176 simple rooms are clean and come with en suite facilities and free in-house movies. Redevelopment of the area means the back overlooks building work, while the front looks onto the heads (or feet) of people on their way to Post CS (*see p107* **View to the future**): try and get a room on the top floor. The early-opening, late-closing bar with retro-games and pool table is ideal place for pacifying truculent teenagers.
Hotel services *Bar. Internet.* **Room services** *TV: cable.*

The Waterfront

Captain's Place

Levantkade 184, 1019 BG (419 8119/www. meesvof.nl). Tram 10, 26. **Rates** €95-€155 double; €250 for 4 people; €35 for each extra person (up to 6). **No credit cards. Map** p108.

The *Pas Meprise*, a lovely old boat moored on KNSM island, has been restored and turned into a floating hotel, with two large rooms, Orion and Cassiopeia, and a garden, protected by a sliding glass roof from the vagaries of the Dutch climate. It's an excellent option for group travel, as it sleeps up to eight. However, note that it's not escaped the tendency of hoteliers here to stipulate how long their guests must stay: the minimum is a lengthy four nights.

Ideaal II

Opposite No.51 Levantkade, 1019 MJ (419 7255/ www.houseboats.nl). Tram 10, 26. **Rates** €150-€190 per person per night. **Credit** V. **Map** p108.

A few berths down from Captain's Place, Ideaal II is indeed the ideal of indulgence adrift. Sleeping up to five, there are waterbeds, a jacuzzi, a state-of-the-art kitchen, and a deck for sunbathing and swimming. Minimum stay one week.

The Jordaan

Frederic Rentabike

Brouwersgracht 78, 1013 GZ (624 5509/www. frederic.nl). Bus 18, 22. **Rates** €50 per person per night (double occupancy). **No credit cards. Map** p310 C2.

For what is a fairly reasonable sum, you can indulge your *Wind in the Willows* fantasies and rent one of two houseboats moored on lovely Brouwersgracht; one sleeps two people, the other three. Basic but neat. After all, as Rattie says, there's nothing so much fun as simply messing around in boats.

Apartment rentals

If you like the city so much that a weekend break won't suffice, there are several options for finding longer-term accommodation. Many hotels have apartments which are specifically designed for lengthy stays, and they often have special rates. We've listed them in the hotel section wherever appropriate. You could also try the places listed below. If you're moving to Amsterdam, *see p283* **Don't come here**.

Cooking culture with Lloyd

The idea was simple: create as much space and freedom as possible. But the transformation of a youth prison into a hotel and 'cultural embassy' – complete with 120 rooms that run from one- to five-stars – took another eight years. However, **Lloyd Hotel** finally opened in the eastern docklands area to much hoopla in late 2004.

That original idea came from several prime movers of the local underground culture scene, including one of the founders of the singular **Supperclub** (*see p128*). They were inspired to seek a way to take fuller advantage of the global arts scene and the 'eternal immigration' of its participants. Hence, a hotel! But not any old hotel. No! This one would be completely flexible and open-for-all, 24-7. It would act as a showcase for visitors and the local arts scene.

Aha, I hear you say: designer hotel! Bite your tongue. Don't you dare compare Lloyd to New York's Chelsea Hotel or Rotterdam's New York, this is something completely different: a unique vision and a singular experiment in the human/space interface, as signalled by the way the idea of a 'guest' has changed in the building's history. It began as a hotel for immigrants, sheltering East Euros en route to becoming South

Americanos. During World War II the 'guests' became less willing: captured Dutch Resistance fighters. After the war the residents were no more willing, but less worthy: Nazi collaborators. And to finish Lloyd's long history of unwilling visitors, from 1964 to 1989 it was Amsterdam's prison for young offenders.

Now, what better place for a hotel? MVRDV, the architects who gave the world the strange concept of 'Pig City 2001' (a skyscraper for pig breeding) and the real life 'Dutch Big Mac' (*see p39*), transformed a claustrophobic hellhole (it was a prison, after all) into a citadel of light and space while still retaining the original elements such as stained-glass windows, tiled walls, exposed timbers, and jail doors re-invented as open concept linen storage.

Meanwhile some of the more inspired names of Dutch art and design – Atelier van Lieshout, Bureau Lakenvelder, Richard Hutten, Marcel Wanders, Hella Jongerius and many others – took responsibility for the interiors. And the result is a party pack of rooms. Most are best described via their bathrooms: some are shared, some fold-away, some have translucent walls, some only exist as an open shower in the middle

Amsterdam Apartments

Kromme Waal 32, 1011 BV (626 5930/fax 622 9544/www.amsterdamapartments.nl). Tram 4, 9, 16, 24, 25. **Open** by appointment. **Credit** AmEx, MC, V. **Map** p311 E2.

More than 20 flats, all of them fully-furnished, fitted with all mod cons and in the town centre. It's not cheap though: the bottom line is €550 a week for a studio or one-person flat. Minimum let one week.

Apartment Services AS

Waalstraat 58, 1078 BX South (672 1840/fax 676 4679/www.apartmentservices.nl). Tram 4, 12, 25. **Open** 9.30am-5pm Mon-Fri. **No credit cards.**

For longer stays, this agency has a selection of (mostly) furnished accommodation, from studios to flashier apartments to houses. Rent – normally for at least two months – starts at €1,000 per month.

Bed & breakfast

B 'n' B (*Logie en Ontbijt* or L&O in Dutch) options are limited in the Netherlands because of restrictions on the number of people (four) allowed to stay in a house at any one time. Nevertheless, there are a few possibilities around. The best way to find a B&B is through City Mundo, which deals with private accommodation and longer stays.

City Mundo

Schinkelkade 47 II, 1075 VK (676 5270/fax 676 5271/www.citymundo.com). **Open** 10am-6pm Mon-Fri, 11am-6pm Sat. **Credit** AmEx, MC, V.

A service linking up visitors with private accommodation, City Mundo will find you a room in anything from someone's home to a windmill. Ten per cent discount for stays of longer than a week. Use the online booking service to get an overview of what's available for the period you want.

Southern Canal Belt

Marcel van Woerkom

Leidsestraat 87, 1017 NX (622 9834/fax 772 7446/ www.marcelamsterdam.com). Tram 1, 2, 5. **Rates** €60-€110 per person. **Credit** V. **Map** p314 D4.

The owner, Marcel, is an artist and his home may perhaps be his greatest work. Not just the art that lines the walls, but the atmosphere of creative exchange that draws visitors here time and again. The downside of this is that you'll need to book well

of the room, and yet others are wholly customised from polyester resin...

But forming the very heart of the building and its unique philosophy is the Cultural Embassy. It is located on four open balconies hanging above what was the city's first 24-hour restaurant, *Snel*, (Fast) where you can construct one's own meals from a menu packed with single dishes and ingredients that cover the range from butter to toast to fries to caviar. (The experiment failed and Snel is no longer 24 hour but 7am-1am: still pretty impressive for this town. Room service remains 24-hour however.) The other, more posh, dinner-time restaurant, *Sloom* (Slow – reservations essential), dispenses with a menu altogether and forces the diner to test both the chef and the kitchen with their own personal requirements. Already the floating spaces above *Snel* are buckling under the weight of donations: for instance, a library from local art college, Rietveld Academie. The Cultural Embassy can also arrange event tickets 24/7, advise guests on how to take best advantage of their time and even connect them with the like-minded.

Remember though: at Lloyd's everything is for everybody – including your luggage. No, we're joking. But Lloyd Hotel is serious.

Lloyd Hotel

Oostelijke Handelskade 34, 1019 BN (561 3636/www.lloydhotel.com). Tram 10, 26. **Rates** €80-€300 doubles. **Credit** AmEx, DC, MC, V. **Map** p108.

ahead for one of the four rooms, and if you do stay, the mornings will see you stumbling blearily out to neighbouring cafés, since breakfast is not included in the price – but the previous night's conversation will probably more than compensate.

Westerpark

Mark's B&B

Van Beuningenstraat 80 A, 1051 XS (m.noordam@ chello.nl/www.alegriamedia.com/BBamsterdam/best_ B&B.html). **Rates** €95-€110 studio. **No credit cards. Map** p309 A2.

Mark has just one non-smoking, double room. Swathed in silks, it's camp and gay-friendly. Despite the B&B moniker, you'll get no food, but there are plenty of cafés nearby. There are studios, which sleep up to four, nearer to town on Westerkade; these aren't quite as nice but, yes, you can smoke in them. Enquire for B&B and apartment rates, which fluctuate according to season, length of stay and number of people. You can only book via email. **Room services** *Kitchen (apartment/studio). TV: satellite.*

The Museum Quarter, Vondelpark & the South

Xaviera Hollander Bed & Breakfast

Stadionweg 17, 1077 RV (673 3934/fax 664 3687/ www.xavierahollander.com). Tram 5, 24. **Rates** €120 double (with breakfast, but fluctuating based on required services). **No credit cards.**

Local legend, columnist, erstwhile madam, novelist, raconteur, theatrical producer (*see p246*) and now B&B landlady, eccentric Ms Hollander is probably best known as the *Happy Hooker*. She always has a tale to tell guests about her extraordinary life. Probably not the best bet for prudes or the incurably shy, you'll find yourself staying in an upstairs bedroom or a hut in the back garden of her voluptuous villa, situated quite incongruously in the heart of Amsterdam's banker-belt. There's always someone dropping by or something going on, so don't place your bets on a quiet mini-break. Only in Amsterdam.

Cake Under My Pillow

Eerste Jacob van Campenstraat 66, 1072 BH (751 0936/fax 776 4604/www.cakeundermypillow.com). Tram 16, 24, 25. **Rates** €80-€150 single/double. **Credit** AmEx, DC, MC, V. **Map** p315 E5.

From the purveyors of the campest confectionery in town, Taart van m'n Tante (*see p140*), this glorious little B&B sits atop their kitchens in a groovy corner of the Pijp, in an area bursting with nightlife, but also a few minutes' walk from the museums. There are three rooms, two of which are en suite, and all are equipped with orthopaedic beds for the best night's sleep. You definitely won't find any cake under your pillow, but there might be a slice with your breakfast (and if there isn't, you'll get a reduction). Unsurprisingly, it's very gay-friendly.

Camping

Although none of the four camp sites is particularly close to the centre, all are well served by good transport links. Zeeburg is a young people's site – not ideal if you plan on turning in early; Gaasper and Amsterdamse Bos are family campsites (with designated youth fields), while everyone is mixed in together at Vliegenbos.

Gaasper Camping Amsterdam

Loosdrechtdreef 7, 1108 AZ (696 7326/fax 696 9369/www.gaaspercamping.nl). Metro 53 Gaasperplas/night bus 75. **Open** mid Mar-June, Sept-Nov 9am-8pm daily. *July-Aug* 9am-10pm daily. Closed 2 Nov-14 Mar. **Rates** €4.50 per person per night. *Tent* from €5.25. *Vehicles* €4-€8. *Dog* €2.50. **No credit cards.**

Gaasper is a well-maintained campsite with good facilities like a shop, a café/snackbar and a launderette. It's located in a positively rural setting in Gaasperpark, near a lake teeming with watersport possibilities. A hot shower will set you back 75c.

Het Amsterdamse Bos

Kleine Noorddijk 1, 1187 NZ (641 6868/fax 640 2378/www.campingamsterdamsebos.nl). Bus 171, 172, 199. **Open** 1 Apr-15 Oct 9am-12.30pm, 1.20-9pm daily. **Rates** €5 per person per night. *Vehicles* €3. **Credit** AmEx, MC, V.

Buses stop nearby, though if you aren't loaded down it's a lovely cycle through the woods to this shady site on the edge of Amsterdam Bos (*see p117*). There are snack opportunities, a launderette and supermarket, and huts to hire. It's worth exploring nearby, scenic Aalsmeer, too (*see p117*).

Vliegenbos

Meeuwenlaan 138, 1022 AM (636 8855/fax 632 2723/www.vliegenbos.com). Bus 32, 36/nightbus 73. **Open** 1 Apr-1 Oct 9am-9pm daily. **Rates** €7.60 per person per night. *Tent* €1-€4. *Vehicles* €4-€8. **Credit** MC, V.

The most expensive campsite (although still very reasonable when compared to any other sort of accommodation) is pet-free and full of facilities (restaurant, café, shop, launderette and lockers, as well as hut-hire). Up in north Amsterdam, it's a short hop by bus to the centre, and also well placed for exploring pretty Waterland villages.

Zeeburg

Zuider IJdijk 20, 1095 KN (694 4430/fax 694 6238/ www.campingzeeburg.nl). Tram 14/bus 22, 37. **Open** all year round. **Rates** €4.50 per person per night. *Vehicles* €4.00. *15 Oct-15 Mar* 20% reduction. **Credit** AmEx, MC, V.

The nearest campsite to town (with a handy tram stop, too) is also near Blijburg and occupies a fabulous site on the edge of the water. A young crowd makes good use of the facilities which include a shop, café, laundrette and a kicking 24-hour bar. A place better suited to night owls than morning larks.

Sightseeing

Features

Introduction

Put on those walking shoes and pack an umbrella: it's time to tiptoe through tulip town.

If you're looking for sex, drugs and/or rock 'n' roll, you'll find all you need for a lost weekend in Amsterdam without much preparation. But this town is also dense with plenty of higher pursuits. And while packing the cultural punch of a metropolis, Amsterdam is a remarkably convenient size. Most things are within half an hour's walk and the trams provide back-up for those low on energy. You can also slipstream the locals and saddle up on a bike (though beware of trams and cycle thieves).

In the centre are Amsterdam's old port, its medieval buildings, the red lights that denote a hotspot of the world's oldest trade, the grand 17th-century merchants' houses, the spires of ancient religious institutions, the earliest and prettiest canals, and many of its most famous sights. Except to stroll Museumplein and its three major art museums, few visitors go

beyond the *grachtengordel*, the calming belt of Golden Age canals – likened in Albert Camus' *The Fall* to the circles of hell – that ring the fascinating and historic Old Centre. Don't make the same mistake. While primarily residential, the Jordaan and the Pijp are hugely attractive places. Further out, too, there's much to enjoy, on the Waterfront to the north and north-east, or south around the idyllic Amsterdamse Bos. For more on Amsterdam's various areas, *see p76* **Neighbourhood watch**.

TICKETS AND INFORMATION

While most Amsterdam museums charge for admission, prices are reasonable: rarely more than €7. However, if you're thinking of taking in a few, the **Museumkaart** (Museum Card) is a steal: €25 for adults and €12.50 for under-25s (plus a €4.95 administration fee for first-timers).

Sightseeing

The best Things to do in Amsterdam

For entering the past
A morning in **Amsterdams Historisch Museum** (*see p92*), an afternoon in the **Museum Amstelkring** (*see 87*), and an evening at the **Concertgebouw** (*see p223*).

For going back to the future
A morning in **Nemo** (*see p106*), an afternoon walk around the eastern docklands (*see p108* **Take a walk on the water side**), and a night in **Jimmy Woo's** (*see p228*).

For art both ancient and modern
Rijksmuseum (*see p113*) or the galleries in the Jordaan (*see p205*).

For a religious experience
The **Oude Kerk** (*see p88*), the **Joods Historisch Museum** (*see p102*) or the **Chinese Fo Guang Shan Buddhist Temple** (*see p85*).

For a trinity of Dutch clichés
A drink at the Brouwerij 't IJ, next to a **windmill** (*see p150*); shopping at **cheese** emporium Wegewijs (*see p172*); and a wander around the floating **flower market** Bloemenmarkt (*see p170*).

For the party to end all parties
The canals on **Queen's Day** (*see p188* **Orange squash**) or **New Year's Eve** on Nieuwmarkt (*see p190*).

For the desperate, the horny or the just plain curious
A walk around the **Red Light District** (*see p80*), a visit to the **Sexmuseum** (*see p80*) or an evening in the **Casa Rosso** (*see p86*).

For the longest queues in town
Anne Frank Huis (*see p97*), the **Van Gogh Museum** (*see p114*) or **boat tours** from near Centraal Station (*see p77*).

For getting away from it all
Vondelpark (*see p114*), **Artis** (*see p104*), **Hortus Botanicus** (*see p105*), **Begijnhof** (*see p92*) or the **Amsterdamse Bos** (*see p117*).

For sitting, drinking and thinking
The cafés that surround the **Nieuwmarkt** (*see p85*) and the **Spui** (*see p90*). Or for something extra you can always take a trip to a **coffeeshop** (*see p153*).

... ground zero of consumerism, ..., entertainment and history, the Old Centre is bounded by Prins Hendrikkade to the north, Oudeschans and Zwanenburgwal to the east, the Amstel to the south and Singel to the west. Within these borders, the Old Centre is split into the New Side (west of Damrak and Rokin) and the Old Side (east of Damrak and Rokin). Within the Old Side, roughly in the triangle formed by Centraal Station, the Nieuwmarkt and the Dam, is the famed Red Light District.

THE CANALS

The *grachtengordel* (girdle of canals) that guards the Old Centre is idyllic, pleasant and quintessentially Amsterdam. In the listings for shops, restaurants and the like in this guide we've split the canals in half. Western Canal Belt denotes the stretch of canals to the west and north of Leidsegracht, while Southern Canal Belt covers the area east of here, taking in Leidseplein and Rembrandtplein.

JODENBUURT, THE PLANTAGE AND THE OOST

The area around Waterlooplein was settled by Jews two centuries ago and took its name – Jodenbuurt — from them. The Plantage, which lies east and south-east of Waterlooplein, holds many delights, among them the Hortus Botanicus and Artis. Further east – or Oost – lies the Tropenmuseum, before the city opens up and stretches out.

THE WATERFRONT

Once the gateway to the city's prosperity, Amsterdam's waterfront is now the setting for one of Europe's most exciting new architectural developments and an increasing number of nightlife options.

THE JORDAAN

Bordered by Brouwersgracht, Prinsengracht, Leidsegracht and Lijnbaansgracht, the Jordaan is arguably Amsterdam's most charming neighbourhood. Working-class stalwarts rub shoulders with affluent newcomers in an area that, while lacking the grandiose architecture of the canals, wants for nothing in character.

THE MUSEUM QUARTER, VONDELPARK AND THE SOUTH

With its world-class museums and stupendously posh fashion emporia, Amsterdam's Museum Quarter is a mix of culture and couture. South of Singelgracht, with approximate borders at Overtoom (west) and Hobbemakade (east), it's also home to many pleasant hotels and, at its northernmost tip, is within a stone's throw of both Leidseplein and Vondelpark.

THE PIJP

Against all the odds, the Pijp has managed to remain a wonderful melting pot of many cultures and nationalities. Located east of the Museum Quarter and south of the canals, it's an area short on tourist sights but long on character and fun.

The card offers free or discounted admission to over 400 attractions in the Netherlands and is valid for a year from date of purchase; discounted or free entry offered to holders of the Museumkaart is denoted in our listings by the letters 'MK'. You can buy the card at most participating museums. The **Amsterdam Tourist Board** (*see p295*) also sells a savings pass, the I amsterdam Card, that gives you free entry to major museums, free public transport and a free canal trip, along with a 25 per cent discount at participating tourist attractions and restaurants. It costs €33 for 24 hours, €43 for 48 hours and €53 for 72 hours.

Three final tips. Call ahead if you plan to visit a museum on a public holiday, as many shut for the day. And don't worry about language: in Amsterdam, almost all the big museums (and many of the smaller ones) have either captions and/or guidebooks in English – or English-speaking staff on hand. The website www.amsterdammuseums.nl lists all major Amsterdam museums and their programmes.

Tours

Bicycle tours

For bicycle hire, see p284.

Yellow Bike
Nieuwezijds Kolk 29, Old Centre: New Side (620 6940/www.yellowbike.nl). Tram 1, 2, 5, 13, 17. **Open** *Mar-Nov* 8.30am-5.30pm daily. **No credit cards. Map** p310 C2.
Of the many options, there's a three-hour City Tour (€17) that departs daily at 9.30am and 1pm; the six-hour Waterland Tour (€22.50), leaving daily at 11am, includes a visit to a pancake house.

Boat tours

There's not an awful lot of difference between the various boat tours that rove Amsterdam's waterways for an hour at a time – just pick the one with the shortest queues. For longer tours, though, choose more carefully. As well as day cruises, all the firms listed run night cruises at 9pm daily in summer (less often in winter), costing from €20 to €25. Lovers and Holland International (for both, see below) do dinner cruises for €65 to €75. Booking is vital. Or there's Het Varend Restaurant (428 8996, www.varendrestaurant.nl) which, for €75, tours the canals while serving a meal prepared by a changing roster of highly regarded local chefs. They depart from the dock in front of the café 't Smalle *(see p152)*.

There's also a **water taxi** (535 6363, www.water-taxi.nl) for groups of one to 44, but their relatively small size means that you have access to the smaller, more charming canals; and a **canal bus** (626 5574, www.canalbus.nl) where a €16 day card, available at the Amsterdam Tourist Board and various kiosks around town, allows you unlimited use of 14 stops until noon the next day. For information on **St Nicolaas Boat Club**, a non-profit outfit that gives toke-friendly cruises on small open-topped boats, ask **Boom Chicago** *(see p253)* or surf to www.boatclub.nl. For boat hire, see p283.

Best of Holland
Departure point at Damrak 34, by Centraal Station, Old Centre: New Side (420 4000/www.thebestof holland.nl). Tram 4, 9, 16, 24, 25. **Cruises** every 30min, 10am-5pm daily. **Tickets** €8.50; €5.50 under-13s. **Credit** AmEx, DC, MC, V. **Map** p309 D2.

Holland International
Departure point at Prins Hendrikkade 33a, by Centraal Station, Old Centre: New Side (622 7788). Tram 4, 9, 16, 24, 25. **Cruises** *Summer* every 15min, 9am-10pm daily. *Winter* every 30min, 10am-6pm daily. **Tickets** €8.50; €5 under-13s or free for two children when accompanied by two paying adults. **Credit** AmEx, MC, V. **Map** p309 D2.

Lovers
Prins Hendrikkade, opposite 25-7, nr Centraal Station, Old Centre: New Side (530 1090/www.lovers.nl). Tram 4, 9, 16, 24, 25. **Cruises** *Summer* every 30min, 9am-6pm daily. *Winter* every 30min, 10am-5pm daily. **Tickets** €8.50; €5.75 under-13s. **Credit** AmEx, MC, V. **Map** p309 D2.

Rondvaarten Rederij Kooij
Corner of Rokin and Spui, Old Centre: New Side (623 3810/www.rederijkooij.nl). Tram 4, 9, 16, 24, 25. **Cruises** *Summer* every 30min, 10am-10pm daily. *Winter* every 30min, 10am-5pm daily. **Tickets** €6.50; €3.75 under-13s. **No credit cards. Map** p310 D3.

Walking tours

The Amsterdam Tourist Board publishes brochures in English that suggest easy routes.

Archivisie
Postbus 14603, 1001 LC (625 9123). Tailor-made architectural tours and regular theme tours. Phone for appointments and prices.

Mee in Mokum
(625 1390). **Tours** 11am Tue-Sun. **Tickets** €3; free under-12s. **No credit cards. Map** p310 C3. Locals, all over 55, give two-hour tours (in English and Dutch) of the Old Centre, the Jordaan and Jewish Amsterdam. Tours leave from the Amsterdams Historisch Museum *(see p92)*. Booking is required; when you call, tell them if you plan to bring children.

Urban Home & Garden Tours
(688 1243/www.uhgt.nl). **Tours** *Apr-Sept 30,* 10.15am Mon, Fri; 11.15am Sat. **Tickets** €25 (includes lunch). **No credit cards. Map** p315 E4. Professional garden designers and art historians give tours in English of the 17th-, 18th- and 19th-century canal houses. Tours leave from the Museum Willet-Holthuysen *(see p100)*; booking is essential.

Van Aemstel Produkties
(683 2592/www.amsterdamexcursies.nl). Various times and prices. **No credit cards.** Generally only available for groups of ten or more, these inspired folk have long branched out from offering tours of the Old Centre led by medieval guardsmen types. Now you can learn about the world of edible flowers from a homeless man, drink tea with a transvestite, get the inside scoop on Amsterdam's most special toilets, or learn to use a hand bow in an ancient monastery. With prices starting at €9/hour, they are even competitive on cost with their less visionary and exciting peers.

The Old Centre

The unholy trinity: shops, sex and history.

A horse, a carriage and a **Koninklijk Paleis**. *See p79*.

One side embraces shopping and pursuits of the mind, while the other – with the Red Light District as its red neon centrepiece – is more about sex and religion. Common feature? They both drip with history. In short: Amsterdam's compelling Old Centre (aka Oud Centrum) surfs on a wave of contradiction.

Marked off by Centraal Station, Singel and Zwanenburgwal, the area is bisected by Damrak, which turns into Rokin south of Dam Square. Within the Old Centre, the saucier area to the east is the ancient Old Side (Oude Zijde), while the gentler area to the west – whose most notable landmark is Spui Square – is the far-from-new New Side (Nieuwe Zijde).

The Old Side

Around the Dam

Map p310

Straight up from Centraal Station, just beyond the once-watery but now-paved and touristy strip named Damrak, lies Dam Square, the heart of the city since the first dam was built across the Amstel here in 1270. Today it's a convenient meeting point for many tourists, the majority of whom convene under its mildly phallic centrepiece, the **Nationaal Monument**. The 22-metre (70-foot) white obelisk is dedicated to the Dutch servicemen who died in World War II. Designed by JJP Oud, with sculptures by John Raedecker, it has 12 urns, 11 filled with earth collected from the (then) 11 Dutch provinces and the 12th containing soil from war cemeteries in long-time Dutch colony Indonesia.

Both the monument and the square recently had much-needed facelifts: the roughness of the new cobblestones now deters errant bikers (and wheelchairs), and their lighter colour disguises the Jackson Pollock splodges of pigeon droppings. If you can, see it in the quiet of dawn, when the square reflects an elusive sense of the epic; appropriate, since the Dam has seen many singular social and political activities: nude running through the square (by Anabaptists, testing the boundaries of religious freedom in 1535), chilling in the name of peace (by hippies in the 1960s) and a catalogue of protests, coronations and executions.

The west side of Dam Square is flanked by the **Koninklijk Paleis** (Royal Palace; *see below*); next to it is the 600-year-old **Nieuwe Kerk** (New Church, so named as it was built a century after the Oude Kerk, or Old Church, in the Red Light District; *see p80*). In kitsch contrast, on the south side, is **Madame Tussaud's Scenerama** (*see below*).

Beurs van Berlage

Damrak 277, entrance at Beursplein 1 (530 4141/Artiflex tours 620 8112/www.beursvanberlage.nl). Tram 4, 9, 14, 16, 24, 25. **Open** during exhibitions 11am-5pm Tue-Sun. **Admission** varies; discount with MK. **No credit cards. Map** p310 D2.

Designed in 1896 by Hendrik Berlage as the city's stock exchange, the palatial Beurs, while incorporating a broad range of traditional building styles, represents a break with 19th-century architecture and prepared the way for the Amsterdam School (*see p38* **Back to school**). Although some jaded critics thought it just 'a big block with a cigar box on top', it's now considered the country's most important piece of 20th-century architecture. By exposing the basic structures and fusing them with stunning decorations, it celebrates the workers and artisans who built it (as opposed to the stockbrokers who were to inhabit it). In fact, it's a socialist statement: much of the artwork warns against capitalism, and each of the nine million bricks was intended by Berlage to represent the individual; the resulting monolith stands for society at large.

Having long driven out the moneychangers, the Beurs is now all things to all other people: a conference centre, concert halls (*see p223*), a mosaic-ed café/restaurant, and an exhibition space for excellent shows that range from Harley Davidsons to organic architecture to beer festivals (*see p188*). In addition, 90-minute tours of the building are conducted by art historians from Artiflex, though booking is compulsory; call the number above.

Koninklijk Paleis (Royal Palace)

Dam (information 620 4060/tours 624 8698/www.koninklijkhuis.nl). Tram 1, 2, 4, 5, 9, 13, 14, 16, 17, 24, 25. **Open** July, Aug 11am-5pm daily. *Sept-June* times vary. **Admission** €4.50; €3.60 5s-16s, over-65s; free under-6s. **No credit cards. Map** p310 C3.

Seemingly following a citywide trend, the Royal Palace will be closed for renovations from October 2005 until 2008. And it's a damn shame. Designed along classical lines by Jacob van Campen in the 17th century, built on 13,659 wooden piles that were rammed deep into the sand, the Royal Palace was originally built and used as the city hall. The poet Constantijn Huygens hyped it as 'the world's Eighth Wonder', a monument to the cockiness Amsterdam felt at the dawn of its Golden Age. It was intended as a smugly epic 'screw you' gesture to visiting monarchs, a species that the people of Amsterdam had happily done without.

The exterior is only really impressive when viewed from the rear, where Atlas holds his 1,000-kilogram (2,205-pound) copper load at a great height. It's even grander inside than out: the Citizen's Hall, with its baroque decoration in grand marble and bronze that depicts a miniature universe (with Amsterdam as its obvious centre), is meant to make you feel about as worthy as the rats seen carved in stone over the Bankruptcy Chamber's door.

Though much of the art on display reflects the typically jaded humour of a people who have seen it all, the overall impression is one of deadly seriousness: one screw-up and you could end up among the grotesque carvings of the Tribunal and sentenced to die in some uniquely torturous and public way. Kinder, gentler displays of creativity, though, can be seen in the chimney pieces, painted by artists such as Ferdinand Bol and Govert Flinck, both pupils of Rembrandt (who, oddly enough, had his own sketches rejected). The city hall was transformed into a royal palace in 1808, shortly after Napoleon had made his brother, Louis, King of the Netherlands, and a fine collection of furniture from this period can be viewed on a guided tour. The Palace became state property in 1936 and is still used occasionally by the royal family. During the summer there are free guided tours (upon admission) in English on Wednesdays and Sundays at 2pm.

Madame Tussaud's Scenerama

Peek & Cloppenburg, Dam 20 (523 0623/www.madame-tussauds.nl). Tram 4, 9, 14, 16, 24, 25. **Open** 10am-5.30pm daily. **Admission** €23; €20 over-60s; €17.50 5s-16s; free under-5s. **Credit** AmEx, DC, MC, V. **Map** p310 D3.

A recent €4 million facelift has done nothing to dilute the queasy kitsch factor here. Waxy cheese-textured representations from Holland's own Golden Age of commerce are depicted alongside the Dutch royal family, local celebs and global superstars. Some of the models look like their subjects, some don't. But while there's some campy fun to be had, it comes at a price, and it's hard not to leave without a renewed respect for candles.

Sightseeing

De Waag.
See p85.

Nieuwe Kerk (New Church)

Dam (626 8168/recorded information 638 6909/
www.nieuwekerk.nl). Tram 1, 2, 4, 5, 9, 13, 14, 16,
17, 24, 25. **Open** hours vary. **Admission** varies
with exhibition. **No credit cards**. **Map** p310 C3.

While the 'old' Oude Kerk in the Red Light District
was built in the 1300s, the sprightly 'new' Nieuwe
Kerk dates from 1408. It is not known how much
damage was caused by the fires of 1421 and 1452,
or even how much rebuilding took place, but most
of the pillars and walls were erected after that time.
Iconoclasm in 1566 left the church intact, though
statues and altars were removed in the Reformation.
The sundial on its tower was used to set all of the
city's clocks until 1890.

In 1645, the Nieuwe Kerk was gutted by the Great
Fire; the ornate oak pulpit and great organ (the latter designed by Jacob van Campen) are thought to
have been constructed shortly after the blaze. Also
of interest here is the tomb of naval hero Admiral de
Ruyter (1607-76), who initiated the ending of the
Second Anglo-Dutch war – wounding British pride
in the process – when he sailed up the Medway in
1667, inspiring a witness, Sir William Batten, to
observe: 'I think the Devil shits Dutchmen'. Behind
the black marble tomb of De Ruyter is a white marble relief depicting the sea battle in which he died.
Poets and Amsterdam natives PC Hooft and Joost
van den Vondel are also buried here. These days, the
Nieuwe Kerk hosts organ recitals, state occasions
and consistently excellent exhibitions.

Sexmuseum Venus Tempel

Damrak 18 (622 8376). Tram 4, 9, 14, 16, 24, 25.
Open 10am-11.30pm daily. **Admission** €2.50. **No**
credit cards. **Map** p310 D2.

The Sexmuseum is one of two museums devoted to
doin' the dirty in Amsterdam, and a tawdry little
operation it is, too. The Damrak location, just by
Centraal Station, is designed to lure in masses of
passing tourists, and on this count it succeeds. But
with the exception of a splendid and often hilarious
collection of pornographic Victorian photographs,
the exhibition is largely botched. There's a fascinating exhibition on the history of porn movies to
be staged, but the one here ain't it. Ivory dildos,
filthy porcelain, joyless cartoons, peeling pin-ups,
'happy breastday cakes' and ugly art are all shaved
of eroticism by the context and the leering gangs of
gigglers that make up the majority of the punters.
At least admission is appropriately cheap…

The Red Light District

Maps p310 & p311

The Red Light District, situated in an
approximate triangle formed by Centraal
Station, Nieuwmarkt and the Dam, is at the
root of Amsterdam's international notoriety.
While overheated imaginations the world over
construct images of sexual abandon framed in
red neon-lit windows, the reality depicted in the
postcards on sale locally is a sort of small,

cutesy version of Las Vegas. If truth be told, the cheesy joke shop has here been supplanted by the cheesy sex shop: instead of electric palm buzzers and comedy nose glasses, you get multi-orifice inflatables and huge dildos.

Most of the historical significance of the Red Light District – of which there is plenty, this being the oldest part of Amsterdam – has been veneered by another old and greasy trade: marketing. Although sex is the hook upon which the area hangs its reputation, it's actually secondary to window-shopping. People do buy – it's estimated to be a €500-million-per-year trade – but mostly they wander around, gawping at the live exhibits.

Most of the window girls are self-employed and, even though prostitution was only defined as a legal and taxable profession in 1988 and bordellos have only been officially legitimate since October 2000 (a tactic hoped to make taxation easier), the women have had their own union, De Rode Draad, since 1984. The prostitutes are, indeed, mostly women: despite attempts to launch male and transsexual prostitution, men have so far found it difficult to get their dicks into this particular door of opportunity. With legality has come a plethora of new rules, governing anything from the temperature at which lingerie is washed to the cleansers used to clear the adjoining showers

of 'liquid-loving insects'. (For more on the sex trade and its history, *see p45*.)

As at more traditional markets like **Albert Cuypmarkt** (*see p180*), where cheese merchants line up alongside cheese merchants and fishmongers group with fishmongers, women with specialities also tend to clump together. Sultry Latinos gather on the Molensteeg and the beginning of Oudezijds Achterburgwal; ambiguously sexed Thais on Stoofstraat; amply girthed Africans around Oude Kerk, and the model-ish and skinny on Trompettersteeg, Amsterdam's smallest street. But there is much else to absorb in this most iconoclastic of neighbourhoods. Prostitutes, clerics, school kids, junkies, carpenters and cops all interact with a strange brand of social cosiness, and the tourists are mere voyeurs. It's all good fun and pretty harmless, just so long as you remember that window girls do not like having their pictures taken and that drug dealers react to eye contact like dogs to bones.

And why all the red lights? It's simple: it's most flattering to the skin.

Zeedijk

Facing away from Centraal Station to the left are two churches, **St Nicolaaskerk** (whose interior of funky darkness can be viewed from

Easter to mid October, and where one can hear Gregorian vespers every Sunday at 5pm from September to June) and the dome and skull-adorned exterior of **St Olafkerk** (known locally as the 'Cheese Church', having housed the cheese exchange for many years). Between the two, you can enter Zeedijk, a street with a rich and tattered history.

Before this dyke was built, some time near 1300, Amsterdam was a fishing village with barely enough bog to stand on. But by the 15th and 16th centuries, with the East India Company raking in the imperialist spoil, Zeedijk was where sailors came to catch up on their boozing, brawling and bonking – or 'doing the St Nicolaas', as it was fondly termed in those days (a tribute to their patron saint, a busy chap who watches over children, thieves, prostitutes and the city of Amsterdam).

Sailors who had lost all their money could trade in their pet monkey for a flea-infested bed at Zeedijk 1, which still retains its old name – **In't Aepjen**, meaning 'In the Monkeys' – and is one of the oldest wooden houses and certainly the oldest bar in the city (see p144). Just off the street down Oudezijds Kolk, you can spot the **Schreierstoren**, aka the 'Weeping Tower' (see p33). It is said that wives would cry there, perhaps with relief, when husbands set off on a voyage, then cry again if the ship returned with

Going with the flow

Farmers, beer and water. An unlikely recipe for success, but they made Amsterdam what it is today. Not that the city's rise was universally greeted with delight. In 1652, during one of those periodic downturns in Anglo-Dutch relations, the poet Owen Felltham described the Low Countries as 'the buttock of the world, full of veins and blood but no bones'. But it's that boggy basis that is the foundation of Amsterdam's historical success and go-with-the-flow reputation.

Originating as a village that subsisted on a bit of fishing and some small-town frolicking, Amsterdam fostered some of the first cheerleaders of democracy: stubborn farmers, who set themselves to build dykes to keep the sea and the mighty Amstel at bay. The teamwork needed for such a massive task formed the basis for today's famed but seemingly fading 'polder model', where all conflicts are resolved at endless meetings fuelled by coffee and the thirst for consensus. Of course, since flexibility and compromise also made good business sense, the approach turned out to be highly profitable.

Amsterdam was only properly set up as a centre of pragmatic trade and lusty sin in the 14th century, when it was granted beer tax exemption status. This opened the floodgates to a river of the stuff (flowing from Hamburg) and to lots of beer-drinking settlers. After beer profits other profits followed – from sea travels to both the East and the West – and before long Amsterdam became the richest and most powerful port on the planet. The resulting Golden Age saw the construction of the image-defining canal girdle (see p93), and these and the more ancient ones of the Old

Centre formed a full circulatory system – and er, sewage system – in which the goods and the people from all over the world could flow in and out.

Besides a knack for building canals, dykes, windmills and ships, the Dutch came up with a whole bevy of other water-worthy inventions during the Golden Age. The inventor Cornelis Drebbel (1572-1634) designed the first submarine prototype (basically a rowing boat fitted with rawhide and tubes), and local genius Jan van der Heyden (1637-1712) invented the first pump-action fire hose (see p14 **The hose master**). More curious were the 'Tobacco-Smoke-Enema-Applicators', developed to attempt the reanimation of the drowners who were regularly pulled from the canals. This ancient technique – also applied with reversed 30-centimetre (12-inch) Gouda pipes – was standard practice and all part of the canalside scenery in Amsterdam until the 1850s, when the less dramatic but more effective mouth-to-mouth technique gained prominence. Talk about progress.

The fine-tuning of technologies at the end of the 19th century allowed the building of the North Sea Channel, thus giving Amsterdam a more direct route to the open sea and triggering a second Golden Age of sorts. The 1990s can be seen in a similar light, thanks to the huge influx of corporations seeking a central location for their European headquarters. The eastern docklands (see p106) began transforming into a showcase for modern architecture that sought to blend both private and public spaces with its watery surrounds. The artificial islands of IJburg further east continue this trend, as do

news that said spouse was lost at sea. If the latter happened, then it was but a short walk to Zeedijk, where the bereaved lady would often continue life as a 'merry widow'. Prostitution was often the female equivalent of joining the navy: the last economic option.

During the 20th century Zeedijk has been sparked by cultural diversity. In the 1930s, the first openly gay establishments appeared, and at the now-closed – though a replica is on display in the **Amsterdams Historisch Museum** (*see p92*) – Het Mandje (Zeedijk 65), there's a window shrine to flamboyant owner Bet van Beeren (1902-67), who has gone down in local mythology as the original lesbian biker

chick. In the '50s, jazz greats Chet Baker and Gerry Mulligan came to jam and hang out in the many after-hours clubs here, among them the still-functioning-as-a-shadow-of-what-it-was Casablanca (Zeedijk 26).

Unfortunately, this subculture marked Zeedijk as a place where heroin could be scored with comparative ease. By the 1970s the street had become crowded with dealers, junkies and indifferent cops, with most of the restaurants and cafés renting their tables to dealers. It was one big druggie convention. The junkies' magic number was 27: *f*25 for the drugs and *f*2 for the drink that owners insisted the junkies purchase to maintain the façade of legality.

ambitious plans to build vast windmill parks in the North Sea and create a floating runway for Schiphol airport. While acceptance of this last idea is still far off, it's not as ridiculous as it sounds: Schiphol itself used to be five metres (16 feet) under water. What's more, the fuel of the future, hydrogen – the mighty H in H_2O – is being taken seriously, as proved by the 2004 debut of hydrogen-powered buses in Amsterdam.

That water is of national importance in a country where two thirds of the land is reclaimed was shown recently, when Crown Prince Willem Alexander decided to slough off his image of rather doltish young manhood and embrace water as a personal crusade. 'Water is fantastically beautiful. It's essential to life. It's about health, environment, and transport. There's the fight against water and the fight against too little water. You can actually do everything with it, and it's primordially Dutch.'

Anything you say, Crown Prince.

Still, water does play a fundamental role in the recreational lives of more regular folk. While eel-pulling (*see p15* **Eel-advised?**) is no longer practised as a canal sport, boating remains the most popular of calm pastimes. (Sadly its winter counterpart, ice-skating, has suffered greatly from climate change.) The opening of the city's first bonafide beach in IJburg was the news story of summer 2003 (and a worthy one at that: *see p109* **Take a walk on the water side**), that was only tarnished when the beach claimed its first drowning victim in 2004. And while the concept of making Prinsengracht swimmable remains a ploy by fringe political parties to

get headline space, the more realistic plan to re-dig canals – like Elandsgracht and Lindengracht – that were filled to cope with motor traffic was all set for the go ahead until it was quashed by residents who decided that since the city is already one-quarter water they didn't need any more. But regardless, Amsterdam remains aware that water remains one of its strongest tourist magnets.

As an almost mystical form of male communion with the elemental basis of the city there is, of course, the practice of urinating into a canal. However, this form of *wildplassen* ('wild pissing') now risks a €50 fine, levied to stop that other unique form of historical loss, urine erosion. To prevent this, 'Wild Pissing Symposiums' – no shit – have been convened, and consensus-building pow-wows even came up with 'A Plan of Action: Wild Pissing'. But since the canal waters are essentially flushed daily, ever since a hi-tech alternating sluice system was implemented, what's the problem?

When compared to the original Venice, also known as the 'sewer of the south', the waters of the 'Venice of the North' are essentially stench-free. And now that Amsterdam even has its own gondola service (*see p112* **Great gondola!**), there's really no competition. In fact, here you can meditate on the wiggly reflections in the canals from up close without fear of succumbing to fumes. Not merely trippy, they act as a constant reminder that Amsterdam is a happily twisted and distorted town – and also remarkably user-friendly; where you can throw your cares overboard and go with the flow. Just don't take that last part too literally.

THE WORLD'S YOUR OYSTER

Amsterdam's reputation became littered with needles and foil, never more so than when a wasted Chet Baker took his final curtain call in 1988 – on to a cement parking pole – from a window (second floor on the left) of the Prins Hendrik Hotel at the entrance of Zeedijk. A brass plaque commemorating the crooning trumpeter has been put up to the left of the hotel's entrance. Although there was a time when a German tour operator's 'criminal safari' was not even allowed on Zeedijk and street cleaners needed armed escorts, the police claim to have cleaned the street up in recent years (but only after long and sustained pressure from residents); indeed, the scene is today infinitely less intimidating and packed with newish businesses and restaurants. The famed dance and ambient label Outland Records has its store at No.22; **Demask** offers its posh line of leathers and latexes at No.64 (*see p215*); and excellent cheap Chinese food can be found at **Nam Kee** at Zeedijk 111-13 (*see p125*). Across the street from Nam Kee, the relatively new **Chinese Fo Guang Shan He Hua Buddhist Temple** (420 2357, www.ibps.nl, open noon-5pm Tue-Sat, 10am-5pm Sun), where monks and nuns provide a library, internet café and vegetarian restaurant, says a lot for this street's spiritual growth.

Nieuwmarkt

At the bottom of Zeedijk, your eyes will be drawn to the huge and menacing castle-like **De Waag**, or 'the Weigh House'. The Waag, previously called St Antoniespoort, stands in the centre of Nieuwmarkt and dates from 1488, when it was built as a gatehouse for the city defences. If you have a yen for mankind's darker traits, try to imagine the body parts that used to garnish the Waag's south-east side. The majority of Amsterdam's many public executions took place here, providing a steady supply of corpses for the medical guild to dissect in the Waag's Anatomical Theatre (and for Rembrandt to study and paint – as in his *Anatomy Lesson of Dr Nicolaes Tulp*). In the black days of the Nazi occupation the square was surrounded by barbed wire and used as one of the collection points to hold captives from the Jewish quarter who were to be shipped off to concentration camps via the **Hollandse Schouwburg** (*see p104*). More recently, in 1980, Nieuwmarkt was the site of riots when the city demolished housing to make way for the Metro. In 1991 it was saved by a citizens' committee from being irrevocably revamped by designer Phillippe Starck. Today, de Waag is home to trendy café **In de Waag** (*see p143*) and the Society for Old and New Media (557

9898, www.waag.org), which surfs the interface between technology and culture and often organises events in the Anatomical Theatre.

The streets leading north-east from Nieuwmarkt contain Amsterdam's small Chinatown, while the colourfully named side streets – among them Monnikkenstraat (Monk Street), Bloedstraat (Blood Street) and Koestraat (Cow Street) – on the south-west lead into the reddest part of the Red Light District. Heading south from Nieuwmarkt along the length of Kloveniersburgwal canal, though, makes for a more interesting stroll.

At Kloveniersburgwal 29 is **Trippenhuis**, now home to the Dutch Academy of Sciences, who formerly shared it in the 18th century with the original Rijksmuseum collection. During the Golden Age the building was owned and equally shared (witness the bisecting wall in the middle window) by the two Trip brothers and their respective families. Their fortune was made by arms dealing (witness, now, the mortar-shaped chimneys and the cannons engraved on the gable), and they could easily afford the imposing gunpowder grey exterior. They even – or so the story goes – built the **House of Mr Trip's Coachman** at No.26, in response to a one-liner the coachman reputedly made about being happy with a house as wide as the Trips' front door. He got his wish. The house, capped with golden sphinxes, is now home to a clothing store and appropriately anorexic display figures.

'De Wallen'

The canals Oudezijds Voorburgwal and Oudezijds Achterburgwal, with their interconnecting streets, are where carnal sin screams loudest. So it's ironic that, right in the middle of Sin City, you'll stumble across a pair of churches. The **Oude Kerk** (*see p88*), Amsterdam's oldest building, is literally in the centre of the sleazy action, with hookers in windows ringing the mammoth church like bullies taunting the class geek. Keep your eyes peeled for the small brass bosom inlaid by a mystery artist into the pavement by the front entrance. The **Museum Amstelkring** (*see p87*), meanwhile, is tucked away a little distance from the red-lit action, but shouldn't be overlooked on your journey around the area.

The Oudezijds Voorburgwal was known as the 'Velvet Canal' in the 16th century due to the obscene wealth of its residents. Now, though, at least along its northern stretch, the velvet has been replaced by red velour, illuminated by scarlet fluorescent lighting and complemented by bored-looking girls sat in the windows of the lovely canal houses. It's perhaps incongruous,

Sightseeing

then, that this canal should also be so densely populated with churches, chapels and orders. Representatives from the Salvation Army lurk on many a corner, although less so near the **Agnietenkapel** (*see p88*) to the quieter south end of the street, and more so around the aforementioned Oude Kerk and Museum Amstelkring to the north.

The parallel Oudezijds Achterburgwal offers some of the more 'tasteful' choices for the eroto-clubber. The **Casa Rosso** nightclub (Oudezijds Achterburgwal 106-108, 627 8954) is certainly worth a look, if only for the peculiar marble cock-and-rotary-ball water fountain at its entrance. A short walk away at No.37 is the Bananenbar (622 4670), where improbably dextrous female genitalia can be seen performing night after night – and, as the central part of their belief-buggering act, spitting out an average of 15 kilograms (33

Irvine Welsh: Amster mage

In the mid-1990s, out to escape the chaos of fame, best-selling Scottish writer Irvine Welsh set up camp in Amsterdam for a couple of years. 'I'd been coming to Amsterdam for years and had some friends there and always vibed on the city... It's very laid back, cool people, pretty girls, town's very easy on the eye... Also, with *Trainspotting* kicking off big time in the UK I wasn't getting much peace to work. It was nice to vanish for a bit... I lived in the Jordaan in an apartment looking on to the Brouwersgracht where I had a local baker, hash café and cheese shop.'

So why would he ever leave such a trinity? 'My buddies got to know where I was and there was a posse over every week looking for me to take them out and show them around. I was getting less done than I was back home.' But his sojourn did allow him to do research that helped him depict the perfect dirty weekend in his most depraved novel, *Filth*, whose main character, a cop named Bruce, makes the *Bad Lieutenant* look like *SpongeBob*. But sadly for literary tourists, the hotel Cok City where Bruce stays went out of business. When asked why he chose that particular hotel as a setting, Welsh answers honestly: 'It was irresistible.'

But it was more of a personal connection that led him to employ such middle-of-the-road settings as the Warmoesstraat bars, Stones Café, Hunters Bar and **Hill Street Blues** (actually the latter is quite charming, *see p155*). In all three of them Welsh claims to have 'passed out and split my head open on the pool table'.

But when pressed to name his truly favourite Amsterthings, Welsh betrays more taste than most of his Amstercharacters: 'De Meer for football (sadly gone), Seymour Likely 2, Mazzo, Trance Buddah and every brown bar in the Jordaan. I liked cycling around on my bike.' However, besides the bikes, the brown bars and Seymour Likely 2 (that lives on to a

degree as Getaway, *see p145*), all these other places are about as obsolete as snorting coke with a 'rolled 50-guilder note' (p180, *Filth*). But another Welsh favourite, **Barney's** (*see p157*) – advertised in *Filth* as a delight for not serving that 'continental breakfast shite' and being 'full of fuckin' students and crusty trash' – remains unchanged as a purveyor of weed and greasy breakfasts. 'Fuck me, I was never out of there at one time. In the morning go for a smoke and nosh to take the edge off the hangover. Thank fuck it remains unchanged. There just might be a god after all.'

In his most recent novel, *Porno*, that sees the *Trainspotting* gang reunite to make a porn film, Amsterdam is consistently depicted as a lovely town. But of course Welsh would not be Welsh if he did not also deal with the less romantic aspects of continental living like the way small apartments and large chunks of hash do not combine particularly well: 'our wee flat overlooking the canal has developed an atmosphere highly conducive to paranoia' (p126, *Porno*). In particular there is one other negative, recurring Amstermotif in his writing: Dutch hippie-shits. 'I was coming up on a pill in the Mazzo, off my tits saying something daft like, "These e's are the best ever..." and this smug cunt in the company goes, "But of course, this is Amsterdam." There is a type of fucker the place attracts that almost makes me think that George Bush isn't that bad.'

But in fact, the insertion of the odd git into his Amsterwritings just helps Welsh to paint a richer picture of this city and goes to prove that he lived here long enough to recognise both Amsterdam's beauty and its ambiguity and to write about both in a natural way. And as he stresses at the end of the short story 'Eurotrash' – which opens with Amsterdam being described as a port 'where all the scum gets washed up' – the city is in fact just full of 'people trying to get by'.

pounds) of fruit every evening. A former owner of the Bananenbar once attempted to stave off the taxman – and get round the fact his drinking licence had lapsed – by picking Satan as a deity and registering the Bananenbar as a church. It was a scam that worked for years – until 1988, when the 'Church of Satan' claimed a membership of 40,000 overseen by a council of nine anonymous persons. The tax police were called in to find the loopholes and bust the joint, but the bar was tipped off and the 'church' disbanded. Now under the same owner, Janot Entertainment, as Casa Rosso and the Erotic Museum, the Bananenbar has kept its name and returned to its roots as a purveyor of sleaze.

If your urges are more academic, you can conduct some, ahem, research at the **Erotic Museum** (*see below*), following it in semi-traditional fashion with a smoke at the **Hash Marihuana Hemp Museum** (which doesn't actually sell dope, but you get the picture; *see below*). Other than that, sleaze and stag parties dominate this strip, with it all becoming particularly unpleasant and busy on weekends.

It's a far cry from the **Spinhuis**, a former convent tucked away at the southern end of the canal (on Spinhuissteeg) that used to set 'wayward women' to work spinning wool. The male equivalent was over on the New Side at Heiligeweg 9 – now an entrance to the Kalvertoren shopping complex – where audiences used to watch the prisoners being branded and beaten with a bull's penis. In a curious foreshadowing of Amsterdam's contemporary S&M scene, the entrance gate sports a statue that bears a striking resemblance to a scolding dominatrix.

Erotic Museum
Oudezijds Achterburgwal 54 (624 7303). Tram 4, 9, 16, 24, 25/Metro Nieuwmarkt. **Open** 11am-1am Mon-Thur, Sun; 11am-2am Fri, Sat. **Admission** €5. **No credit cards. Map** p310 D2.
While the Sexmuseum (*see p80*) benefits from its Damrak location in terms of passing trade, the Erotic Museum is in the more appropriate location: slap bang in the Red Light District. That's not to say, though, that it's any more authentic or interesting. Its prize exhibits are a bicycle-powered dildo and a few of John Lennon's erotic drawings, while lovers of Bettie Page (and there are many) will enjoy the original photos of the S&M muse on display. In general, though, the museum's name is somewhat inaccurate: despite its best intentions, it's as unsexy as can be. All in all, you're probably best off going to one of the many nearby sex shops for your kicks.

Hash Marihuana Hemp Museum
Oudezijds Achterburgwal 130 (623 5961/ www.hashmuseum.com). Tram 4, 9, 14, 16, 24, 25/Metro Nieuwmarkt. **Open** 11am-11pm daily. **Admission** €5.70. **No credit cards. Map** p310 D3.

A city built on water.

Given the decriminalised nature of dope here, it figures that Amsterdam should have a museum devoted to hash. It's just a pity that it has to be this slightly shabby, ridiculously named operation, which tries to be all things to all people and ends up being nothing to anyone, aside from a pricey way for a backpacker to waste around half an hour in the Red Light District. There's some interesting information here, sure: the display on the medical benefits of the drug is enlightening, as are a few nuggets on the history of hemp. But the small exhibition lacks cohesion and entertainment value, and comes across alternately as hippyish and – surprisingly – po-faced. Definitely a missed opportunity.

Museum Amstelkring
Oudezijds Voorburgwal 40 (624 6604/www. museumamstelkring.nl). Tram 4, 9, 14, 16, 24, 25. **Open** 10am-5pm Mon-Sat; 1-5pm Sun. **Admission** €7; €5 students, over-65s; €1 5s-18s; free under-5s, MK. **No credit cards. Map** p310 D2.
The Amstelkring takes its name from the group of historians who succeeded in saving it from demolition in the late 1800s. Good job they did save it, too, for what remains is one of Amsterdam's most unique spots, and one of its best-kept secrets. The lower floors of the house have been wonderfully preserved since the late 17th century, and offer a look at what life might have been like back then.

The main attraction is upstairs, and goes by the name of Ons' Lieve Heer op Solder, or 'Our Sweet

Dam Square.
See p78.

Lord in the Attic'. Built in 1663, this attic church was used by Catholics during the 17th century when they were banned from worshipping after the Alteration. It's been beautifully preserved, too, the altarpiece featuring a painting by 18th-century artist Jacob de Wit. The church is often used for services and a variety of other meetings. Don't miss it.

Oude Kerk

Oudekerksplein 1 (625 8284/www.oudekerk.nl). Tram 4, 9, 16, 24, 25, 26. **Open** 11am-5pm Mon-Sat; 1-5pm Sun. **Admission** €4; €3.20 over-65s, students; free under-12s, MK; may vary during special exhibitions. **No credit cards. Map** p310 D2.
Originally built in 1306 as a wooden chapel, and constantly renovated and extended between 1330 and 1571, the Oude Kerk is the city's oldest and most interesting church. One can only imagine the Sunday Mass chaos during its heyday of the mid-1500s when it had 38 altars each with its own guild-sponsored priest. Its original furnishings were removed by iconoclasts during the Reformation, but the church has retained its wooden roof, which was painted in the 15th century with figurative images. Keep your eyes peeled for the Gothic and Renaissance façade above the northern portal, and the stained-glass windows, parts of which date from the 16th and 17th centuries. Rembrandt's wife

Saskia, who died in 1642, is buried here. The inscription over the bridal chamber, which translates as 'Marry in haste, mourn at leisure', is in keeping with the church's location in the heart of the Red Light District, though this is more by accident than design. If you want to be semi-shocked, check out the carvings in the choir benches of men evacuating their bowels – apparently they tell a moralistic tale… The church is now as much of an exhibition centre as anything else, with shows covering everything from modern art installations to the annual World Press Photo Exhibition (*see p185*).

Universiteitsmuseum de Agnietenkapel

Oudezijds Voorburgwal 231 (525 3339/information universiteitsmuseum@uva.nl). Tram 4, 9, 14, 16, 24, 25. **Open** 9am-5pm Mon-Fri (ring bell for entry). **Admission** free. **Map** p310 D3.
Of Amsterdam's 17 medieval convents, this Gothic chapel is one of a few remnants to have survived intact. Built in the 1470s and part of the university since its foundation in 1632, the chapel has an austere, Calvinistic beauty highlighted by stained-glass windows, wooden beams and benches, and a collection of portraits of humanist thinkers. The Grote Gehoorzaal (Large Auditorium), the country's oldest lecture hall, is where 17th-century scholars

Vossius and Barlaeus first taught; its wooden ceiling is painted with soberly ornamental Renaissance motifs including angels and flowers. Exhibitions are held here only occasionally. It is closed for renovations until 2007 but a temporary exhibit can be visited at Herengracht 182 by appointment only.

Warmoesstraat & Nes

It's hard to believe that Warmoesstraat, Amsterdam's oldest street, was once the most beautiful of lanes, providing a sharp contrast to its evil and rowdy twin, Zeedijk. The poet Vondel ran his hosiery business at Warmoesstraat 101; Mozart's dad would try to flog tickets at the posh bars for his young son's concerts; and Marx would later come here to write in peace (or so he claimed: he was more likely to have been in town to borrow money from his cousin-by-marriage, the extremely wealthy Gerard Philips, founder of the globe-dominating Philips corporate machine).

But with the influx of sailors, the laws of supply and demand engineered a heavy fall from grace for Warmoesstraat. Adam and Eve in their salad days can still be seen etched in stone at Warmoesstraat 25, but for the most

part, this street has fallen to accommodating only the low-end traveller. However, hip hangouts such as gay/mixed bar **Getto** (*see p213*) and the **Winston Hotel** (*see p59*), shops including the **Condomerie het Guiden Vlies** (*see p182*) and gallery **W139** (*see p203*) have ensured that the strip has retained some brighter and less commercial colours, while the council's serial clean-up operation reached the street quite recently and has at least had some of the desired cosmetic effect.

Just as Warmoesstraat stretches north from the Nationaal Monument into the Old Side, so Nes leaves the same spot to the south, parallel and to the west of Oudezijds Achterburgwal. Dating from the Middle Ages, this street was once home to the city's tobacco trade and the Jewish philosopher Benedict Spinoza (1623-77), who saw body and mind as the two aspects of a single substance. Appropriate, then, that you can now witness the alignment of body and mind on the stages of the many theatres that have long graced this street. You can also stop, recharge and realign your own essence at one of the many charming cafés hereabouts. At the end of Nes, either take a turn left to cross a bridge where the junkies are often out selling freshly stolen bicycles for next to nothing (be warned that buying one will have you risking jail and deportation) towards **Oudemanhuis Book Market** (where Van Gogh used to get prints to decorate his room; *see p116* **Vincent in Amsterdam**) on the University of Amsterdam campus; or turn right and end up near the **Allard Pierson Museum** (*see below*).

Allard Pierson Museum

Oude Turfmarkt 127 (525 2556/www.uba. uva.nl/apm). Tram 4, 9, 14, 16, 24, 25. **Open** 10am-5pm Tue-Fri; 1-5pm Sat, Sun. **Admission** €5; €2.50 4s-15s, over-65s; free under-4s, MK. **No credit cards. Map** p310 D3.
Established in Amsterdam in 1934, the Allard Pierson claims to hold one of the world's richest university collections of archaeological exhibits, gathered from ancient Egypt, Greece, Rome and the Near East. So far, so good. And, if archaeological exhibits are your thing, or your children would like their names written in hieroglyphics, then it's probably a destination that will go down well. However, if you didn't spend several years at university studying stuff like this, you'll probably be bored witless. Many of the exhibits (statues, sculptures, ceramics, etc) are unimaginatively presented, as if they are aimed solely at scholars. English captions are minimal – though for the record, the Dutch ones are scarcely more helpful – and few staff are on hand to help explain exactly what you're looking at. Some items are instantly accessible and interesting – the full-size sarcophagi, the model of a Greek chariot – but otherwise this is a frustrating experience.

Sightseeing

Map p310

Rhyming (nearly enough) with 'cow', the Spui is the square that caps the three main arteries that start down near the west end of Centraal Station: the middle-of-the-road walking and shopping street Kalverstraat (called Nieuwendijk before it crosses the Dam), Nieuwezijds Voorburgwal and the Spuistraat.

Coming up Nieuwezijds Voorburgwal – translated literally as 'the New Side's Front of the Town Wall', to distinguish it from the Oudezijds Voorburgwal ('the Old Side's Front of

Sightseeing

Disneyland Amsterdam

Ain't Amsterdam cute? It's certainly hard not to be charmed by the city's cutesy dollhouse proportions. Even the radical hippie party that arose from the ashes of Provo (see p23) and ended up winning five seats in city government in 1970, called themselves the Kabouters, after the happy-go-lucky forest-dwelling dwarves who feature in local folk tales. It also makes sense that the Dutch have a reputation for quality theme parks: **Efteling** (see p195) is a favourite among connoisseurs who like a dash of the surreal in their roller-coaster experiences, and then there's the 'world's largest miniature village', **Madurodam** (see p195).

But in many ways, Amsterdam itself can be seen as a theme park – or may at least eventually become one. This process is best seen in, of all places, the Red Light District. What were once furtive pleasures have been sanitised to the point that the district has got as close to being 'fun for the whole family' as it's possible to imagine an area that makes its living by spreading its legs becoming. Long gone are the days when you would walk around and see – as you could still in the 1960s – condoms hanging out to dry until their next go. Yep, things have certainly been cleaned up.

Disturbed by this trend, plenty of locals – call them cynics or call them soothsayers – warn of the 'Disneyfication' of Amsterdam. They fear that the residents will be pushed out of the inner-city in favour of hotels and restaurants, turning Amsterdam into a water-girdled tourist attraction. Already this scenario seems to be backed up by the fact that most visitors, whether stoner or businessperson, rarely bother to look both ways when crossing a road, tramline or bike path. Do the intimate dimensions of Amsterdam lull people into a false sense of security? Regardless, you should not make the same mistake. Amsterdam remains a city where one can be rendered into road pizza in the gap betwen milliseconds. You have been warned.

What would happen if Atlas shrugged? **Koninklijk Paleis.** *See p79.*

the Town Wall') found in near mirror image in the Red Light District, though both city walls have long since been destroyed – the effects of tragically half-arsed urban renewal are immediately noticeable. The Crowne Plaza hotel at Nieuwezijds Voorburgwal 5 was formerly the site of the large Wyers squat, which was dramatically emptied by riot police in 1985, after a widely supported campaign by squatters against the mass conversion of residential buildings into commercial spaces (or, in the case of the domed Koepelkerk at Kattengat 1, a Lutheran church painted by Van Gogh, turned into a hotel convention centre).

The multinational, perhaps predictably, proved victorious, as did the ABN-Amro Bank further up, with its in-your-face glass plaza at the corner with Nieuwezijds Kolk. But urban renewal – not to mention the digging of new subway lines – does have its benefits, in that it allows an opportunity for city archaeologists to

dig down and uncover Amsterdam's sunken history (in general, every 50 centimetres downwards represents a century backwards). For instance, while the underground car park was being dug on the ABN-Amro site, researchers uncovered 13th-century wall remains which were, for a short time, surmised to be the remains of a marsh-surrounded castle belonging to the Lords of the Amstel. While this proved to be jumping the gun, it did prove that the so-called 'New Side' is not new at all.

A quiet backwater accessible via the north side of Spui square or, when that entrance is closed, via Gedempte Begijnensloot (the alternating entrances were set up to appease residents), the **Begijnhof** is a group of houses built around a secluded courtyard and garden. Established in the 14th century, it originally provided modest homes for the Beguines, a religious and, as was the way in the Middle Ages with religious establishments for women, rather liberated, sisterhood of unmarried ladies from good families who, though not nuns and thus taking no formal vows, lived together in a close community and had to take vows of chastity. Since they did not have to take vows of poverty, the Beguines were free to dispose of their property as they saw fit, further ensuring their emancipation as a community. They could, however, renounce their vows at any moment and leave, for instance if they wanted to get married. The last sister died in 1971 and one of her predecessors never left, despite dying back in 1654. She was buried in a 'grave in the gutter' under a red granite slab that's still visible – and often still adorned with flowers – on the path. Nowadays, it's the best-known of the city's numerous hofjes (almshouses).

Most of the neat little houses in the courtyard were modernised in the 17th and 18th centuries. In the centre stands the **Engelsekerk** (English Reformed Church), built as a church in around 1400 and given over to Scottish (no, really) Presbyterians living in the city in 1607; many became pilgrims when they decided to travel further to the New World in search of religious freedom. Now one of the principal places of worship for Amsterdam's English community, the church is worth a look primarily to see the pulpit panels, designed by a young Mondriaan.

Also in the courtyard is a Catholic church, secretly converted from two houses in 1665 following the banning of open Catholic worship after the Reformation. It once held the regurgitated Eucharist host that starred in the Miracle of Amsterdam (*see p185*), a story depicted in the church's beautiful stained-glass windows. The wooden house at Begijnhof 34, known as the **Houtenhuis**, dates from 1475 and is the oldest house still standing in the city, while Begijnhof 35 is an information centre. The Begijnhof is also close to one of the several entrances to the **Amsterdams Historisch Museum** (*see below*), which in turn is the starting point for the informal **Mee In Mokum** walking tours (*see p77*).

The Spui square itself plays host to many markets – the most notable being the busy book market on Fridays – and was historically an area where the intelligentsia gathered for some serious browbeating and alcohol abuse, often after an honest day's graft at one of the many newspapers that were once located on Spuistraat. The *Lieverdje* ('Little Darling') statue in front of the **Athenaeum Nieuwscentrum** store (*see p161*), a small, spindly and guano-smeared statue of a boy in goofy knee socks, was the site for wacky Provo 'happenings' in the mid 1960s.

You can leave Spui by going up Kalverstraat, Amsterdam's main shopping street, or Singel past Leidsestraat: both routes lead to the **Munttoren** (Mint Tower) at Muntplein. Just across from the floating flower market (the **Bloemenmarkt**; *see p170*), this medieval tower was the western corner of Regulierspoort, a gate in the city wall in the 1480s; in 1620, a spire was added by Hendrick de Keyser, the foremost architect of the period. The tower takes its name from when it minted coins after Amsterdam was cut off from its money supply during a war with England, Munster and France. There's a shop on the ground floor selling fine Dutch porcelain (Holland Gallery de Munt, Muntplein 12, 623 2271), but the rest of the tower is closed to visitors. The Munttoren is prettiest when floodlit at night, though daytime visitors may hear its carillon, which often plays for 15 minutes at noon.

From here, walk down Nieuwe Doelenstraat past the Hôtel de l'Europe (a mock-up of which featured in Hitchcock's *Foreign Correspondent*; *see p200* **Lights! Camera! Clog action!**). This street connects with scenic Staalstraat – so scenic, in fact, that it's the city's most popular film location, having appeared in everything from *The Diary of Anne Frank* to *Amsterdamned*. Walk up here and you'll end up at **Waterlooplein** (*see p101* and *p180*).

Amsterdams Historisch Museum

Kalverstraat 92 (523 1822/www.ahm.nl). Tram 1, 2, 4, 5, 9, 14, 16, 24, 25. **Open** 10am-5pm Mon-Fri; 11am-5pm Sat, Sun. **Admission** €6; €3 6s-16s; free under-6s, MK. **No credit cards. Map** p310 D3.
A note to all those historical museums around the world who struggle to present their exhibits in an engaging fashion: head here to see how it's done. Amsterdam's Historical Museum is a gem: illuminating, interesting and entertaining. It starts with the buildings in which it's housed: a lovely, labyrinthine collection of 17th-century constructions built on the site of a 1414 convent. You can enter it down Sint Luciensteeg, just off Kalverstraat, or off Spui, walking past the Begijnhof (*see p92*) and then through the grand Civic Guard Gallery, a small covered street hung with huge 16th- and 17th-century group portraits of wealthy burghers.

And it continues with the museum's first exhibit, a computer-generated map of the area showing how Amsterdam has grown (and shrunk) throughout the last 800 years or so. It then takes a chronological trip through Amsterdam's past, using archaeological finds (love those 700-year-old shoes), works of art (by the likes of Ferdinand Bol and Jacob Corneliszoon) and plenty of quirkier displays: tone-deaf masochists may care to play the carillon in the galleried room 10A, while lesbian barflies will want to pay homage to Bet van Beeren, late owner of celebrated Het Mandje. It's all linked together with informative, multilingual captions and the occasional audio-visual exhibit. Amsterdam has a rich history, and this wonderful museum does it justice.

The Canals

Cruising down the (man-made) rivers…

The Dutch call them *grachten*. There are 165 in Amsterdam. They stretch for 75.5 kilometres (47 miles) around the city, are crossed by 1,400 bridges and are, on average, three metres (ten feet) deep. They keep the sea and all the surrounding bog at bay. Some 10,000 bicycles, 100 million litres (22 million gallons) of sludge and 50 corpses (usually of drunk tramps) are dredged from their murky depths every year.

The major canals and their radial streets are where the real Amsterdam exists. What they lack in sights, they make up for as a place for scenic coffee slurping, quirky shopping, aimless walks and meditative gable gazing. The *grachtengordel* – 'girdle of canals' – rings the centre of town, its waterways providing a border between the tourist-laden centre and the gentler, artier and more 'local' locales of the Museum Quarter, the Jordaan and the Pijp.

Singel was the original medieval moat of the city, and the other three canals that follow its line outward were part of a Golden Age urban renewal scheme; by the time building finished, Amsterdam had quadrupled in size. Herengracht (named after the gentlemen who

initially invested in it), Keizersgracht (named after Holy Roman Emperor Maximilian I) and Prinsengracht (named after William, Prince of Orange) are canals where the rich lived; but though parts are still residential, many properties now house offices, hotels and banks.

The connecting canals and streets, originally built for workers and artisans, have a higher density of cafés and shops, while the shopping stretches of Rozengracht, Elandsgracht, Leidsestraat and Vijzelstraat are all former canals, filled in to deal with the traffic. Smaller canals worth seeking out include Leliegracht, Bloemgracht, Egelantiersgracht, Spiegelgracht and Brouwersgracht.

In this guide, for ease of use, we've split venues on the canals into the Western Canal Belt (between Singel and Prinsengracht, south of Brouwersgracht, north and west of Leidsegracht) and the Southern Canal Belt (between Singel and Prinsengracht, from Leidsegracht south-east to the Amstel). This splitting is historically justified by the fact that the western girdle was completely finished before work on the eastern half began.

Huis Marseille. *See p95.*

Singel

One of the few clues to Singel's past as the protective moat surrounding the city's wall is the bridge that crosses it at Oude Leliestraat. It's called the Torensluis and did, indeed, once have a lookout tower; the space under the bridge, now ironically populated with drinkers on its terraces, was supposedly used as a lock-up for medieval drunks. The statue of the writer, Multatuli, on it, depicting his head forming as smoke from a bottle, is a reference to the way he let the genie out of the bottle by questioning Dutch imperialism in such novels as *Max Havelaar* (1860), and not to the fact that he was the first Dutchman to be cremated.

While you're wandering this lazy canal, you may want to join the debate on whether Singel 7 or Singel 166 is the smallest house in town. Located between them, and adored by cat lovers, is the **Poezenboot** (Cat Boat, 625 8794, www. poezenboot.nl, open 1-3pm daily) opposite Singel 40, home to stray and abandoned felines, though funding problems may see a demise of this institution. Slightly further down, and always good for a snort, is the **House with Noses** at Singel 116, though arty types may be more interested in Singel 140-42, once the home of Banning Cocq – the principal figure of Rembrandt's *Night Watch*, once referred to as 'the stupidest man in Amsterdam'. Further south, you may want to stake out the town's poshest sex club, **Yab Yum** (Singel 295, 624 9503/www.yabyum.com) to watch the country's elite enter for a good old-fashioned servicing.

Multatuli Museum

Korsjespoortsteeg 20 (638 1938/www.multatuli-museum.nl). Tram 1, 2, 5, 13, 17. **Open** 10am-5pm Tue; noon-5pm Sat, Sun; also by appointment. **Admission** free. **Map** p310 C2.
Just off Singel, this museum to the writer Eduard Douwes-Dekker (1820-87), aka Multatuli, is in the house where he was born. The various literary artefacts pay testament to his credo: 'the human calling is to be human'. There's also a small library.

Herengracht

Cross Singel at Wijde Heisteeg, and opposite you on Herengracht is the **Bijbels Museum** (Bible Museum, *see p95*). A few doors south, at the **Netherlands Institute of War Documentation** (Herengracht 380, 523 3800, www.niod.nl) – whose three kilometres (1.8 miles) of archives include Anne Frank's diary, donated by her father Otto – stonemasons knocked up a copy of a Loire mansion, complete with coy reclining figures on the gable and frolicking cherubs around its bay window.

The northern stretch of Herengracht, from here up to Brouwersgracht, is fairly sight-free; the canal also wants for cafés and decent shops. Still, it's a very pleasant walk. Try to peek into the windows of the **Van Brienenhuis** at Herengracht 284: the excesses of bygone eras will soon become apparent. Keep walking, and you'll reach a Vingboons building at No.168, dating from 1638. Along with De Keyser's Bartolotti House, this architectural gem now houses the **Theater Instituut** (*see below*).

Bijbels Museum

Herengracht 366-8 (624 2436/www.bijbels museum.nl). Tram 1, 2, 5. **Open** 10am-5pm Mon-Sat; 11am-5pm Sun, public holidays. **Admission** €6.50; €3.50 13s-17s; free under-13s, MK. **No credit cards. Map** p314 C4.

Housed in two handsome Vingboons canal houses, Amsterdam's Bible Museum aims to illustrate life and worship in biblical times with archaeological finds from Egypt and the Middle East (including the remarkable mummy of an Israeli woman), models of ancient temples and a slideshow. There's also a splendid collection of Bibles from several centuries (including a rhyming Bible from 1271). A little dry in places, this museum does attract folk merely looking to admire the restored houses, the splendid Jacob de Wit paintings, and the grand garden with biblical plants and a wild sculpture entitled *Apocalypse*.

Theater Instituut

Herengracht 168 (551 3300/www.tin.nl). Tram 1, 2, 5, 13, 17. **Open** 11am-5pm Mon-Fri; 1-5pm Sat, Sun. **Admission** €4.50; €2.25 students, 6s-16s, over-65s; free under-6s, MK. **Credit** AmEx, MC, V. **Map** p310 C3.

The ever-changing displays here are largely drawn from the institute's collection of costumes, props, posters, memorabilia and ephemera, which will soon all be digitally catalogued. Upstairs there is a massive library; call ahead for information on hours and prices. Inside is a ceiling painting by Jacob de Wit while outside there's an idyllic garden.

Keizersgracht

Walk down Keizersgracht from its northern tip (by Brouwersgracht), and you'll soon encounter the **House with the Heads** at Keizersgracht 123, a pure Dutch Renaissance classic. The official story has these finely chiselled heads representing classical gods, but according to local folklore they are the heads of burglars, chopped off by a lusty maidservant. She decapitated six and married the seventh.

Another classic is at **Keizersgracht 174**, an art nouveau masterpiece by Gerrit van Arkels which, rumour has it, will become a

hotel – you might want to admire from **Café Brandon** (Keizersgracht 157, 626 4191) whose decorations remain seemingly unchanged since the Dutch lost the 1974 World Cup Final to the Germans. Similarly hard to ignore is the **Felix Meritis Building** at Keizersgracht 324, given that it's a neo-classical monolith with the motto 'Happiness through achievement' chiselled over its door. And achieve it did: after housing a society of arts and sciences in the 1800s, it went on to house the Communist Party and is now the European Centre for Art and Science – complete with a high-minded and high-ceilinged café. Nearby is the equally lofty home of the photography foundation, **Huis Marseille**. This whole stretch was also the site of the Slipper Parade, where the posh-footed rich strolled about every Sunday to see and be seen. From here, take a right turn down Molenpad and you'll reach Prinsengracht.

Huis Marseille

Keizersgracht 401 (531 8989/www.huis marseille.nl). Tram 1, 2, 5. **Open** 11am-5pm Tue-Sun. **Admission** €3; free under-12s, MK. **No credit cards. Map** p314 C4.

Located in a monumental 17th-century house, the walls of this photography foundation might host the latest from such hotshots as Jacqueline Hassink, Axel Hütte or Naoya Hatakeyama, classic work from perhaps contemporary photography's most influential duo, Bernd and Hilla Becher, or landscapes of Amsterdam or even the moon. Don't miss the videos and mags in the 'media kitchen'.

Keep it cheap

There's a wealth of, well, wealth on display in this neighbourhood, but don't think you have to spend a fortune to enjoy yourself in Amsterdam. This list of freebies shows how easily cheapskates can have fun.
● The view from **Nemo**'s roof (*see p108*).
● Complimentary coffee at many **Albert Heijn** stores (*see p177* **Heijnie ho!**).
● The **ferry** trips from behind Centraal Station to the north (*see p106*).
● **Rijksmuseum**'s garden on its west side (*see p113*).
● Open-air concerts and the fresh open air of **Vondelpark** (s
● 'Civic Guard Gall
Historisch Museum
Begijnhof (for both;
● **Noordermarkt** fl
mornings (*see p18*
● **Concertgebouw**
Wednesday lunchti

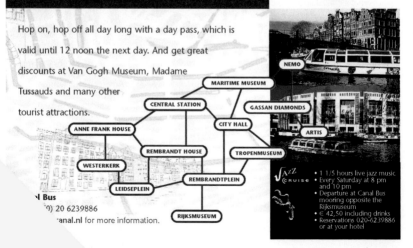

Prinsengracht

The most charming of the canals. Pompous façades have been mellowed with shady trees, cosy cafés and some of Amsterdam's funkier houseboats. The **Woonbootmuseum** (Houseboat Museum, *see p98*), one of the funkiest, is a short stroll away. Also around here are some lovely shopping thoroughfares. Working northwards, the 'Nine Streets' linking Prinsengracht, Keizersgracht and Herengracht, between Leidsestraat and Raadhuisstraat, all offer a delightfully diverse pick of smaller, artier speciality shops that perfectly flavour a leisurely walk by the water.

On your way up Prinsengracht, the tall spire of the 375-year-old **Westerkerk** (*see below*) should loom into view. Its tower is easily the tallest structure in this part of town and if you choose to climb it, you'll be able to look down upon the expanded – but still modestly dimensioned – **Anne Frank Huis** (*see below*). Mari Andriessen's statue of Frank (dated 1977) stands nearby, at the corner of Westermarkt and Prinsengracht. Meanwhile, any fans of René Descartes – and if you think, you therefore probably are – can pay tribute to the great savant by casting an eye on his former house around the corner at Westermarkt 6, which looks out on the pink granite triangular slabs of the **Homomonument** (*see p207*), the planet's first memorial to persecuted gays and lesbians.

If it's a Monday and you find yourself at the weekly **Noordermarkt** (*see p180*), make sure you stop for coffee at the **Papeneiland** (Prinsengracht 2). According to local legend, a tunnel used to run under the canal from here to a Catholic church that was located at Prinsengracht 7 at the time of the Protestant uprising. Also on this odd-numbered side of the canal, you can check to see if the doors to the courtyards of the Van Briennen hofje (No.85-133) or the De Zon hofje (No.159-71) are open.

Anne Frank Huis

Prinsengracht 267 (556 7105/www.annefrank.nl). Tram 13, 17. **Open** *Jan-Mar, Sept-Dec* 9am-7pm daily. *Apr-Aug* 9am-9pm daily. **Admission** €7.50; €3.50 10s-17s; free under-10s. **Credit** MC, V. **Map** p310 C2.

Prinsengracht 263 was the 17th-century canal-side house where young Jewish girl Anne Frank and her family hid for two years during World War II. Today it's one of the most popular attractions in Amsterdam, with almost a million visitors a year.

Having fled from persecution in Germany in 1933, Anne, her sister Margot, their parents and four other Jews went into hiding on 5 July 1942. Living in an annexe behind Prinsengracht 263 they were sustained by friends who risked everything to help them; a bookcase marks the entrance to the sober,

The swaying tower of **Westerkerk**.

unfurnished rooms. But on 4 August 1944 the occupants were arrested and transported to concentration camps, where Anne died with Margot and their mother. Her father, Otto, survived, and decided that Anne's diary should be published. The rest, as they say, is history: tens of millions of copies of the diary have been printed in a total of 55 languages.

In the new wing, there's a good exhibition about the Jews and their persecution during the war, as well as displays charting racism, neo-Fascism and anti-Semitism, and exploring the difficulties in fighting discrimination; all have English texts. To avoid the famously long queues, arrive first thing in the morning, or (in summer) after 7pm.

Interestingly, the Amsterdam South apartment the Franks previously lived in will begin in 2005 to host persecuted writers from around the world.

Westerkerk

Prinsengracht 277-9 (624 7766/tower 689 2565/ www.westerkerk.nl). Tram 13, 14, 17. **Open** *Apr-July* 11am-3pm Mon-Fri. *July-Sept* 11am-3pm Mon-Sat. **Services** 10.30am Sun. **Admission** *Tower* €5. **No credit cards. Map** p310 C3.

Before noise pollution it was said that if you could hear the bells of Westerkerk, built in 1631 by Hendrick de Keyser, you were in the Jordaan. These days, its tower is just a good place from which to view its streets and canals, provided you don't suffer from vertigo: the 85m (278ft) tower sways by 3cm (1.2in) in a good wind. Although the last tour up the

The Golden Bend. *See p99.*

186 steps is at 5pm, and tours are only scheduled in summer, groups may call to book for other times.

It's thought that Rembrandt is buried here, though no one is sure where. Rembrandt died a pauper, and is commemorated inside with a plaque. Though his burial on 8 October 1669 was recorded in the church register, the actual spot was not; there's a good chance he shares a grave with his son, Titus.

From the street you can see that the tower is emblazoned with a gaudy red, blue and gold 'XXX' crown. Not a reference to the porn industry, it's the crown granted to the city in 1489 by Maximillian, the Holy Roman Emperor, in gratitude for treatment he received during a pilgrimage to Amsterdam. The triple-X came to be used by local traders to denote quality. It also emblazons the phallic parking poles scattered throughout the city; which incidentally can be bought for around €85 at the city's Material depot (Pieter Braaijweg 10, 561 2111).

Woonbootmuseum

Prinsengracht, near No.296 (427 0750/www.house boatmuseum.nl). Tram 13, 14, 17. **Open** *Mar-Oct* 11am-5pm Tue-Sun. *Nov-Feb* 11am-5pm Fri-Sun. Closed last 2wks of Jan. **Admission** €3; €2.25 children under 152cm (5ft). **No credit cards**. **Map** p314 C4.

The Houseboat Museum is not just a museum about houseboats: it's actually on one. In fact, it more or less is one: aside from some discreet explanatory panels, a small slide show and a ticket clerk, the *Hendrika Maria* is laid out as a houseboat would be, to help visitors imagine what it's like to live on the water. It's more spacious than you might expect and does a good job of selling the lifestyle afforded by its unique comforts. Until, that is, you notice the pungent scent of urine emanating from the public 'curlie' (as they are locally called) toilet right by the boat.

The Southern Canal Belt

Map p314

Around Rembrandtplein

In better days Rembrandtplein was called Reguliersmarkt. Then it hosted Amsterdam's butter market and in 1876 the square was renamed in honour of Rembrandt; a statue – today the oldest in the city – of the Dutch master, looking decidedly less scruffy than he does in his self portraits, stands in the centre of the gardens, gazing in the direction of the Jewish quarter. Though there's no longer a market, it's still the centre of commercial activity, with a profusion of neon and a cacophony of music blaring out from the cafés, bars and restaurants on all sides.

The area is unashamedly, unconsciously, unbearably tacky. The square is home to a variety of establishments, from the faded and fake elegance of the traditional striptease parlours to seedy modern peepshow joints and nondescript cafés. There are a few exceptions to the prevailing tawdriness – places like the zoological sample-filled grand café **De Kroon** (No.17), the art deco **Schiller** (No.26) and HL de Jong's insanely colourful dream-as-reality eclectic masterpiece, the **Tuschinski** cinema on Reguliersbreestraat (*see p198*). Carry on past here and you'll end up at Muntplein, by the floating flower market at the southern tip of Singel (the **Bloemenmarkt**; *see p170*) that now also sports the largest miniature art gallery on the planet, **Reflex Minituur Museum** (*see p118* **The collectors' collectors**). Around the corner on the Amstel is a stretch of lively gay cafés and bars (*see p210*); and on the façade of Amstel 216, the city's freakiest graffiti. This 'House with the Bloodstains' was home to former mayor Coenraad van Beuningen (1622-93), whose brilliance was eclipsed by insanity. After seeing visions of fireballs and fluorescent coffins above the Reguliersgracht, he scrawled the still visible graffiti of sailing ships, stars, strange symbols and his and his wife's name with his own blood. Attempts to scrub the stains off have proved futile.

From Rembrandtplein, walk south along the prime mid-range shopping and eating street Utrechtsestraat, or explore Reguliersgracht and Amstelveld. Whichever you choose, you'll cross Herengracht as you wander.

The canals

As the first canal to be dug in the glory days, Herengracht attracted the richest of merchants, and this southern stretch is where you'll find the most stately and overblown houses on any of Amsterdam's canals. The **Museum Willet-Holthuysen** (*see p100*) is a classic example of such a 17th-century mansion.

However, it's on the stretch built between Leidsestraat and Vijzelstraat, known as the Golden Bend, that things really get out of hand. By then the rich saw the advantage of buying two adjoining lots so that they could build as wide as they built high. Excess defines the Louis XIV style of Herengracht 475, while tales of pre-rock 'n' roll excess are often told about Herengracht 527, whose interior was trashed by Peter the Great while he was here learning to be a ship's carpenter and picking up urban ideas for his dream city, St Petersburg. Around the corner on Vijzelstraat is the imposing building, Gebouw de Bazel; in 2006 this will become the new home of the city archives **Gemeentearchief Amsterdam** (*see p36*). Mischievous types, meanwhile, may relish the chance to annoy the mayor by mooring up on his personal dock in front of the official residence at Herengracht 502. If you're caught, try palming off the authorities with the excuse that you're just visiting the **Kattenkabinet** (Cat Cabinet, *see right*).

It's a similarly grand story on this southern section of Keizersgracht, too. For evidence, pop into the **Museum van Loon** (*see right*) or the photography museum **Foam** (*see right*), both on Keizersgracht just east of Vijzelstraat. But for an alternative view of this area, head half a block south to Kerkstraat, parallel to and directly between Keizersgracht and Prinsengracht. The houses here are less grand, but what they lack in swank they more than make up for in funkiness,

with their galleries and shops – including smart drugs central **Conscious Dreams** (*see p162*) – only adding to the community feel. The pleasant oasis of Amstelveld helps, too, with **Amstelkerk** – the white wooden church that once took a break from sacred duties to act as a stable for Napoleon's horses – worth a nose around.

Heading east along Kerkstraat will get you to the **Magerebrug** (Skinny Bridge), the most photographed bridge in the city and one said to have been built in the 17th century by two sisters – living on opposite sides of the Amstel – who wanted an easy way to get together for morning coffee. If you cross it and go down Nieuwe Kerkstraat, you'll get to the **Plantage** (*see p103*). Alternatively, turn right at Amstel and right again down Prinsengracht for more grand canal houses, peace and general loveliness – or if you want to smoke your way through the 2,000-plus exhibits at the **Pijpenkabinet** (Pipe Cabinet, *see p118* **The collectors' collectors**).

Foam (Photography Museum Amsterdam)

Keizersgracht 609 (551 6500/www.foam.nl). Tram 16, 24, 25. **Open** 10am-5pm Mon-Wed, Sat, Sun; 10am-9pm Thur, Fri. **Admission** €6; free MK. **No credit cards. Map** p315 E4.

This relatively new photography museum, located in a renovated canal house, holds excellent exhibitions of works by shutter-button maestros like fashion guy Paul Huff and war dude Don McCullin, and shows covering local themes such as the history of Amsterdam panoramas. They also organise discussions and events for the photographically obsessed.

Kattenkabinet (Cat Cabinet)

Herengracht 497 (626 5378/626 9040/www.katten kabinet.nl). Tram 1, 4, 9, 14, 16, 24, 25. **Open** 10am-2pm Mon-Fri; 1-5pm Sat, Sun. **Admission** €4.50; €2.25 under-12s. **No credit cards. Map** p314 D4.

Housed in a grand 17th-century canal house (and a location for *Oceans 12*; *see p200* **Lights! Camera! Clog action!**), the Cat Cabinet differs from Amsterdam's more notorious pussy palaces. It's a veritable temple to the feline form: in fact, it boasts that it's the world's only museum with a permanent exhibition devoted to cats, and so far no one's come forward to disagree. Paintings, statues, posters and cattish ephemera fill the vast rooms, guarded (after a fashion) by moggies who spend the whole time lying around, cocking a silent snook at guests.

Museum van Loon

Keizersgracht 672 (624 5255/www.museumvan loon.nl). Tram 16, 24, 25. **Open** Sept-June 11am-5pm Mon, Fri-Sun; *Jul-Aug* 11am-5pm daily. **Admission** €5; €4 students; free MK, under-12s. **No credit cards. Map** p315 E4.

Amsterdam's waterways are chock-a-block with grand houses. Few of their interiors have been preserved in anything approaching their original state, but the former Van Loon residence is one that has.

Designed by Adriaan Dortsman, the house was orig-inally the home of artist Ferdinand Bol. Hendrik van Loon, after whom the museum is named, bought the house in 1884; it was opened as a museum in 1973.

The posh mid-18th-century interior is terrifically grand, and admirers of Louis XIV and XV decor will find much that excites. So will art-lovers. The house holds a collection of family portraits from the 17th to the 20th centuries; perhaps more unexpectedly, it hosts a modern art show every two years. The 18th-century, French-style garden contains Ram Katzir's striking sculpture of a headless man, *There*.

Museum Willet-Holthuysen

Herengracht 605 (523 1870/www.museumwillet holthuysen.nl). Tram 4, 9, 14. **Open** 10am-5pm Mon-Fri; 11am-5pm Sat, Sun. **Admission** €4; €3 over-65s; €2 6s-18s; free under-6s, MK. **Credit** MC, V. **Map** p315 E4.

Built in the 1680s, this mansion was purchased in the 1850s by the Willet-Holthuysen family. When Abraham, remembered as 'the Oscar Wilde of Amsterdam', died in 1889, his wife Sandrina Louisa, an hermaphrodite (that's right: a chick with a dick) left the house and its contents to the city on the con-dition it was preserved and opened as a museum – a nice gesture, were it not for the fact that cats were the main residents for many years. The family had followed the fashion of the time and decorated it in the neo-Louis XVI style: it's densely furnished, with the over-embellishment extending to the collection of rare *objets d'art*, glassware, silver, fine china and paintings – including a portrait of a rather shocked looking Abraham (taken on his honeymoon per-haps?). English texts accompany the exhibits, and there's an English-language video explaining the history of the house and the city's canal system. The view into the recently renovated 18th-century gar-den almost takes you back in time, but the illusion is disturbed by the adjoining modern buildings.

Torture Museum

Singel 449 (320 6642/www.torturemuseum.nl). Tram 1, 2, 4, 5, 9, 16, 24, 25. **Open** 10am-11pm daily. **Admission** €5; €3.50 under-12s. **No credit cards**. **Map** p314 D4.

The Torture Museum is just another one of those Amsterdam tourist traps that should really have been more informative, engaging and – most impor-tantly – fun. OK, torture museums don't really have to be fun, but this one's a particularly frustrating experience, riddled with tattily maintained exhibits and uninvolving, even illegible, captions. Torturous.

Around Leidseplein

Leidseplein, which from Prinsengracht is reached via the chaotic pedestrian- and tram-packed Leidsestraat, is the tourist centre of Amsterdam. It's permanently packed with merrymakers drinking at pavement cafés, listening to buskers and soaking up the atmosphere (and the Amstel Light).

Leidseplein lies on the bottom of the 'U' made by the Canal Belt; and although it's called a square, it is, in fact, L-shaped, running south from the end of Leidsestraat to the Amsterdam School-style bridge over Singelgracht and east towards the 'pop temple' **Paradiso** (*see p220*) – where you can admire brass iguanas in the grass in front of an entrance made of classical columns and a chiselled Latin profundity that translates as 'Wise men don't piss into the wind' – to the Max Euweplein (a handy passage to **Vondelpark**; *see p114*) with its **Max Euwe Centrum** (*see below*) and giant chess set.

Leidseplein has always been a focal point. Artists and writers used to congregate here in the 1920s and 1930s, when it was the scene of clashes between Communists and Fascists. In the war, protests were ruthlessly broken up by the Nazis: there's a commemorative plaque on nearby Kerkstraat. But Leidseplein's latter-day persona is more jockstrap than political, especially when local football team Ajax wins anything and their fans take over the square.

The area has more cinemas, theatres, clubs and restaurants than any other part of town. It's dominated by the **Stadsschouwburg** (the municipal theatre; *see p224*) and by the cafés that take over the pavements during summer; this is when fire-eaters, jugglers, musicians and small-time con-artists and pickpockets fill the square. Unfortunately, development has meant that there are now fast food restaurants on every corner, and many locals feel that the Dutch flavour of the district has been destroyed.

The café society associated with Leidseplein began with the opening of the city's first terraced bar, the Café du Théâtre. It was demolished in 1877, 20 years before the completion of Kromhout's **American Hotel** (*see p63*) at the south-west end of the square. Opposite the American is a building, dating from 1882, that reflects Leidseplein's transformation: once grand, it's now illuminated by huge, vile adverts. Just off the square, in the Leidsebos, is the *Adamant*, a pyramid-like, hologram-effect sculpture that commemorated 400 years of the city's diamond trade in 1986. Wittier is the sculpture of a sawing man in one of the trees.

Max Euwe Centrum

Max Euweplein 30a (625 7017/www.maxeuwe.nl). Tram 1, 2, 5, 6, 7, 10. **Open** 10.30am-4pm Tue-Fri; 10.30am-4pm first Sat of mth. **Admission** free. **No credit cards**. **Map** p314 D5.

Named after the only chess world champion the Netherlands has produced and occupying the city's old House of Detention – it held Resistance leaders in World War II – the Max Euwe Centrum harbours a library of works in dozens of languages, various chess artefacts, vast archives, and chess computers that visitors can use and abuse at their leisure.

Jodenbuurt, the Plantage & the Oost

A zoo, gardens and museums – lots of them. Welcome to Amsterdam's other Museum Quarter.

Jodenbuurt

Map p311

Located south-east of the Red Light District, Amsterdam's old Jewish neighbourhood is a peculiar mix of old and new architectural styles. If you leave the Nieuwmarkt along Sint Antoniesbreestraat, you'll pass several bars, coffeeshops, chic clothes stores and the modern yet tasteful council housing designed by local architect Theo Bosch. In contrast, there's the Italian Renaissance-style **Pintohuis** at No.69, renovated by the Jewish refugee and a VOC founder, Isaac de Pinto. It now houses a public library where you can browse under Jacob de Wit's ceiling paintings. Pop through the skull-adorned entrance across the street between Sint Antoniesbreestraat 130 and 132, and enter the former graveyard and now restful square around **Zuiderkerk** (South Church). Designed by De Keyser and built between 1603 and 1614, it was the first Protestant church to appear after the Reformation, and is now the municipal information centre for planning and housing:

Waterlooplein Market.

development plans are presented as interactive scale models. But as you walk around the neighbourhood – or view it from the church's tower (552 7977, 11am-4pm Mon, 9am-4pm Tue-Fri; noon-4pm Sat) – it becomes obvious that shiny ideals can often create obtuse realities.

Crossing the bridge at the end of Sint Antoniesbreestraat, you'll arrive at the obtuse reality of a performing arts school, the Arts Academy (aka De Hogeschool voor de Kunsten), on the left and the **Rembrandthuis** (*see p103*) on the right, next door to the **Holland Experience** (*see p102*). Immediately before this, though, some steps will take you to **Waterlooplein Market** (*see p180*). Though touristy, it can be a bargain-hunter's dream if you're a patient shopper.

Nearby is the 19th-century **Mozes en Aäronkerk**, built on Spinoza's birthplace. This former clandestine Catholic church, where Liszt reportedly played his favourite concert in 1866, is on the corner where Waterlooplein meets Mr Visserplein – the square-cum-traffic roundabout where the obtuse reality of the copper-green Film and Television Academy meets the much chirpier underground children's playground **TunFun** (*see p192*). Also near at hand is the **Joods Historisch Museum** (Jewish Historical Museum; *see p102*) and the new **Hermitage aan de Amstel** (*see p102*).

Dominating Waterlooplein is the **Stadhuis-Muziektheater** (the City Hall-Music Theatre; *see p254*). The area where it stands was once a Jewish ghetto and later, in the 1970s, site of dozens of gorgeous 16th- and 17th-century squatters' residences, before it was decided to replace them with a €136-million civic headquarters cum opera house. The decision was controversial, as was the 'denture'-like design by Wilhelm Holtzbauer and Cees Dam, and locals showed their discontent by protesting: in 1982, a riot caused damage estimated at €450,000 to construction equipment. Such displays of displeasure are the reasons why the home to the Nederlands Opera and the Nationale Ballet is still universally known as the 'Stopera'.

Sightseeing

A girl's best friend

Amsterdam is famous for diamonds and the city has long been a centre of the gem trade. It's sparklers still rate as a top five tourist attraction. Just remember, though: falling in love with a piece of crushed carbon is the easy part – working out how you're going to pay for it may prove to be a little more tricky.

Amsterdam Diamond Centre

Rokin 1-5, Old Centre: New Side (624 5787/www.amsterdamdiamond centre.nl). Tram 4, 9, 14, 16, 24, 25. **Open** 10am-6pm Mon-Wed, Fri-Sat; 10am-7.30pm Thur; 11am-6pm Sun. **Credit** AmEx, DC, MC, V. **Map** p310 D2.

Coster Diamonds

Paulus Potterstraat 2-8, Museum Quarter (305 5555/www.costerdiamonds.com). Tram 2, 5. **Open** 9am-5pm daily. **Credit** AmEx, DC, MC, V. **Map** p314 D6.

Gassan Diamond BV

Nieuwe Uilenburgerstraat 173-5, Old Centre: Old Side (622 5333/www.gassandiamond. com). Tram 9, 14. **Open** 9am-5pm daily. **Credit** AmEx, DC, MC, V. **Map** p311 E2.

It's rare that science and art meet on the level, but in the passage between City Hall and the Muziektheater, the Amsterdam Ordnance Project includes a device showing the NAP (normal Amsterdam water level) and a cross-section of the Netherlands detailing its geological structure.

Hermitage aan de Amstel

Gebouw Neerlandia, Nieuwe Herengracht 14 (626 8168/www.hermitage.nl). Tram 9, 14/Metro Waterlooplein. **Open** 10am-5pm daily; free under-16s, MK. **No credit cards. Map** p311 E3.
Partly opened in 2004, this outpost of the Hermitage in St Petersburg is expected to put on two exhibitions a year, using objects and art taken from its prestigious Russian parent collection. While the projected massive exhibition space will only be completed by 2007, but meanwhile visitors can have a look around part of this 19th-century building and all of its 17th-century courtyard.

The Hermitage's riches owe much to the collecting obsession of Peter the Great (1672-1725), who came to Amsterdam to learn shipbuilding and how to build a city on a bog – the latter knowledge was applied to his pet project, St Petersburg. A giant of a man, Peter befriended local doctor Frederik Ruysch, perhaps the greatest ever anatomist and preserver of body bits and mutants. Not content with pickling Siamese foetuses in jars, Ruysch constructed moralistic 3D collages with gall and kidney stones piled up to suggest landscapes, dried veins woven into lush shrubberies and testicles crafted into pottery, and he animated his scenes with dancing skeletal foetuses. After kissing the forehead of a preserved baby, Peter paid Ruysch *f* 30,000 for the whole lot (much of which is still on display in St Petersburg's Kunstkammer collection). With luck, some of Peter's souvenirs – including Rembrandts – will return for a visit. But so far it's focused on Greek jewellery, the last Tsar and Tsarina, Nicolas and Alexandra, and Venetian painters.

Holland Experience

Waterlooplein 17 (422 2233/www.holland-experience.nl). Tram 9, 14/Metro Waterlooplein. **Open** 10am-6pm daily. **Admission** €8.50; €7.25 over-65s, under-16s. **Credit** AmEx, DC, MC, V. **Map** p311 E3.
A monumentally peculiar attraction, this, and one that's hard to recommend unless you have a fetish for Euro-kitsch. For your money you get to sit on an undulating platform wearing 3-D glasses and watch a half-hour film that acts as a roll-call of Dutch clichés. Windmills? Check. Canals? Check. Clogs? Check. Tulips? Check. Cheese? Yep, it's cheesy all right. And while children may enjoy it, and the actual technology isn't unimpressive, one can't help wondering who needs the virtual when the actual is just outside the door. The attraction has recently broadened its repertoire with two other films: *3D Mania* and *Alien Adventure…*

Joods Historisch Museum (Jewish Historical Museum)

Nieuwe Amstelstraat 1 (531 0310/www.jhm.nl). Tram 9, 14/Metro Waterlooplein. **Open** 11am-5pm daily; closed Yom Kippur. **Admission** €6.50; €4 over-65s, students; €3 13s-17s; €2 6s-12s; free MK, under-6s. **No credit cards. Map** p311 E3.
Housed since 1987 in four former synagogues in the old Jewish quarter, the Jewish Historical Museum is full of religious items, photographs and paintings detailing the rich history of Jews and Judaism in the Netherlands. A recent revamping has created more warmth and a sense of the personal in its permanent displays that concentrate on religious practice and Dutch Jewish culture; among the exhibits is the painted autobiography of artist Charlotte Salomon, killed at Auschwitz at the age of 26. An excellent new children's wing crams interactive exhibits on aspects of Jewish culture (including a nice one on music) into its space. The temporary shows explore various aspects of Jewish culture, while the Jonas Daniël Meijerplein site, with its *Dock Worker* statue

commemorating the February Strike of 1941 in protest against Jewish deportations, is across the street, beside the Portuguese Synagogue (*see below*).

Portuguese Synagogue

Mr Visserplein 3 (624 5351/guided tours 626 9945/ www.esnoga.com). Tram 4, 9, 14, 20. **Open** *Apr-Oct* 10am-4pm Mon-Fri, Sun. *Nov-Mar* 10am-4pm Mon-Thur, Sun; 10am-3pm Fri; closed Yom Kippur. **Admission** €6.50; €5 10s-15s; free under-10s. **No credit cards. Map** p311 E3.

Architect Elias Bouwman's mammoth synagogue, one of the largest in the world and reputedly inspired by the Temple of Solomon, was inaugurated in 1675. It's built on wooden piles and is surrounded by smaller annexes (offices, archives, the rabbinate, and one of the oldest libraries in the world). Renovation in the late 1950s restored the synagogue well and the low-key tours are informative and interesting.

Rembrandthuis

Jodenbreestraat 4 (520 0400/www.rembrandthuis.nl). Tram 9, 14/Metro Waterlooplein. **Open** 10am-5pm Mon-Sat; 11am-5pm Sun. **Admission** €7.50; €5 students; €1.50 6s-16s; free under-6s, MK. **Credit** AmEx, DC, MC, V. **Map** p311 E3.

Rembrandt bought this house in 1639 for ƒ13,000 (around €6,000), a massive sum at the time. Indeed, the pressure of the mortgage payments eventually got to the free-spending artist, who went bankrupt in 1656 and was forced to move to a smaller house (Rozengracht 184). When he was declared bankrupt, clerks inventoried the house room by room; it's these records that provided the renovators with clues as to what the house looked like in Rembrandt's time.

You can't help but admire the skill and effort with which craftsmen have tried to re-create the house, nor the antiquities, *objets d'art* (Rembrandt was a compulsive collector) and 17th-century furniture. However, the presentation is, on the whole, dry and unengaging. Nagging at you all the time is the knowledge that this isn't really Rembrandt's house, but rather a mock-up of it – which lends an unreal air that is only relieved when guest artists are allowed to use the studio. There's also a remarkable collection of Rembrandt's etchings which show him at his most experimental, and explain why this was the medium in which he gained European fame during his lifetime. But if it's his painting you're after, make for the Rijksmuseum (*see p113*).

The Plantage

Map p311 & p316

The largely residential area known as the Plantage lies south-east of Mr Visserplein and is reached via Muiderstraat. The attractive Plantage Middenlaan winds past the **Hortus Botanicus** (*see p105*), passes close to the **Verzetsmuseum** (Museum of the Dutch Resistance; *see p105*), runs along the edge of the zoo **Artis** (*see p104*), and heads towards the **Tropenmuseum** (*see p105*).

Jews began to settle here 200 years ago, and the area was soon redeveloped on 19th-century diamond money. The headquarters of the diamond cutters' union, designed by Berlage as a more outward expression of socialism than his Stock Exchange (aka **Beurs van Berlage**; *see p79*), still exists on Henri Polaklaan as the **Vakbondsmuseum** (Trade Unions Museum;

Portuguese Synagogue.

Sightseeing

Living history: plants ancient and modern thrive at the **Hortus Botanicus**. *See p105.*

see p105), and other extant buildings like the Gassan, the Saskiahuis and the Coster act as reminders that the town's most profitable trade was once based here (*see p102* **A girl's best friend**). However, the spectre of World War II again raises its head at the **Hollandse Schouwburg** (*see below*) and the Van Eyck's **Moedershuis** at Plantage Middenlaan 33 that was used as a mother and child refuge then.

The Plantage is still a wealthy part of town, with graceful buildings and tree-lined streets, although its charm has somewhat faded over the years. The area has seen extensive redevelopment, and work is continuing, with mixed results: while the housing association flats and houses erected where the army barracks and dockside warehouses once stood (just past Muiderpoort city gate) are unattractive, **Entrepotdok** works far better: to wander down this stretch is to admire a delicate balance between the new and the old, with docked post-hippie houseboats and views of Artis providing a charming contrast to the apartment buildings.

Artis

Plantage Kerklaan 38-40 (523 3400/www.artis.nl). Tram 6, 9, 14. **Open** *Summer* 9am-6pm daily; *Winter* 9am-5pm daily. **Admission** €14.50; €13.50 over-65s; €11.50 4s-11s; free under-4s. **No credit cards. Map** p311 F3.

The first zoo on mainland Europe (and the third oldest in the world) provides a great day out for children and adults. Along with the usual animals, Artis has an indoor 'rainforest' for nocturnal creatures and a 120-year-old aquarium that includes a simulated Amsterdam canal (the main difference is the clear water improves your chances of spotting the eels). The zoo expanded a couple of years ago after a long battle for extra land, and now features a savannah that wraps around a light-infused restaurant.

The narration in the planetarium is in Dutch, but an English translation is available. Further extras include a geological museum, a zoological museum, an aquarium and, for kids, a petting zoo and playgrounds; you could easily spent a day here. And while there's no guarantee, they often let you hang out long after closing hours…

Hollandse Schouwburg

Plantage Middenlaan 24 (626 9945/www. hollandscheschouwburg.nl). Tram 6, 9, 14. **Open** 11am-4pm daily. **Admission** free. **Map** p311 F3.

In 1942, this grand theatre became a main point of assembly for between 60,000 and 80,000 of the city's Jews before they were taken to the transit camp at Westerbork. It's now a monument with a small but very impressive exhibition and a memorial hall displaying 6,700 surnames by way of tribute to the 104,000 Dutch Jews who were exterminated. The façade has been left intact, with most of the inner structure removed to make way for a memorial.

Hortus Botanicus

Plantage Middenlaan 2a (625 9021/www.dehortus.nl).
Tram 9, 14/Metro Waterlooplein. **Open** *Feb-June,*
Sept-Nov 9am-5pm Mon-Fri; 10am-5pm Sat, Sun.
Jul, Aug 9am-9pm Mon-Fri; 10am-9pm Sat, Sun.
Jan, Dec 9am-4pm Mon-Fri; 10am-4pm Sat, Sun.
Admission €6; €3 5s-14s; free under-5s.
No credit cards. Map p316 G3.

You don't have to be green-fingered to enjoy these
beautiful gardens, although, if you are, its entertainment value will be higher still. The Hortus has
been here since 1682, although it was set up 50 years
earlier when East India Company ships brought
back tropical plants and seeds originally intended
to supply doctors with medicinal herbs. Some of
those specimens (which include the oldest potted
plant in the world, a 300-year-old cycad) are still here
in the palm greenhouse – which itself dates from
1912 – while three other greenhouses maintain
desert, tropical and subtropical climates. There are
also descendants of the first coffee plant to tour the
world: it was smuggled out of Ethiopia before finding its way via Hortus to Brazil, which would later
become the biggest producer in the world. The terrace is one of the nicest in town, with only the dis-
tant noise of the city to remind you where you are.

Vakbondsmuseum (Trade Unions Museum)

Henri Polaklaan 9 (624 1166/www.deburcht-
vakbondsmuseum.nl). Tram 6, 9, 14. **Open** 11am-
5pm Tue-Fri; 1-5pm Sun. **Admission** €2.50; €1.25
12s-18s; free under-12s, MK. **No credit cards.**
Map p311 F3.

The Vakbondsmuseum offers a permanent exhibition
showing the progress and history of unions in Dutch
history. If you think that kind of thing sounds interesting, you'll enjoy it; if not, don't make a special trip
– unless, perhaps, for the fascinating collection of
posters. That said, for those whose interest in labour
relations is even casual, the building itself is worth
a peek: it was designed by Berlage, who viewed it
as his favourite, to house the offices of the country's
first trade union – that of the diamond workers.

Verzetsmuseum (Museum of the Dutch Resistance)

Plantage Kerklaan 61 (620 2535/www.
verzetsmuseum.org). Tram 6, 9, 14. **Open** noon-5pm
Mon, Sat, Sun; 10am-5pm Tue-Fri; **Admission** €5;
€2.75 7s-16s; free under-6s, MK. **No credit cards.**
Map p311 F3.

The Verzetsmuseum is one of Amsterdam's most
illuminating museums and quite possibly its most
moving. It tells the story of the Dutch Resistance
through a wealth of artefacts: false ID papers, clandestine printing presses and illegal newspapers, spy
gadgets and an authentic secret door behind which
Jews hid. The exhibits all help to explain the ways
people in the Netherlands faced up to and dealt with
the Nazi occupation. The engaging presentation is
enhanced by the constant use of personal testimo-
ny; indeed, the museum's disparate exhibits are

linked effectively by these stories – told, by those
who lived through the war, on small panels that act
as adjuncts to the main displays. Regular temporary
shows explore wartime themes (like the much more
predominant flipside of resistance – collaboration)
and modern-day forms of oppression, and there's a
small research room, too. An excellent enterprise.

The Oost

Map p316

South of Mauritskade is Amsterdam Oost
(East), where the **Arena** hotel complex (*see*
p65 and p231) is located along the edge of
a former graveyard that was long ago
transformed into **Oosterpark**. While hardly
Amsterdam's most beautiful, it's not without its
charms, not least because the area isn't notable
for much else, the **Tropenmusem** (*see below*)
and **Dappermarkt** (*see p180*) excepted.

It's a similar story in the Indische Buurt
(Indonesian neighbourhood) north-east of here,
although the **Brouwerij 't IJ**, a brewery in a
windmill (*see p150*), is a good place to sip on a
culturally reflective beer. North of here are the
eastern docklands (*see p108* **Take a walk**
on the water side), but as you head east from
the centre of Amsterdam, you'll find little of
interest save for the pleasant green expanses
of **Flevopark** and the new beach in **IJburg**.

Tropenmuseum

Linnaeusstraat 2 (568 8215/www.tropenmuseum.nl).
Tram 9, 14/bus 22. **Open** 10am-5pm daily.
Admission €7.50; €5 students, over-65s; €3.75 6s-
17s; free under-6s, MK. *Tropenmuseum Junior* €2
extra (6s-12s only). **Credit** MC, V. **Map** p316 H3.

It's a handsome and vast building, this, sitting
grandly in a slightly out-of-the-way (by the pocket
handkerchief standards of Amsterdam, anyway)
location. Better still: the exhibitions in the Tropical
Museum are terrific. Through a series of informative and lively displays – the majority of which come
with English captions – the visitor gets a vivid, interactive glimpse of daily life in the tropical and sub-
tropical parts of the world (a strange evolution for a
museum originally erected in the 1920s to glorify
Dutch colonialism). Exhibits – from religious items
and jewellery to washing powder and vehicles – are
divided by region and broad in their catchment. A
musical display allows visitors to hear a variety of
different instruments at the push of a button (the
Tropenmuseum is also the city's leading venue for
world music); walk-through environments include
simulated African and South Asian villages and a
Manilan street; and a Latin American exhibit is highlighted by a fun room complete with videos of sporting highlights and a jukebox. Temporary art and
photography exhibitions fill a large central space on
the ground floor, the shop has a excellent selection
of books and souvenirs, and the restaurant offers
fine global eats with a view-worthy terrace.

The Waterfront

Watery past and trippy future.

Map p108 & p311

Amsterdam's historic wealth owes a lot to the city's waterfront, for it was here that all the goods were unloaded, weighed and prepared for storage in the warehouses still found in the area. During Amsterdam's trading heyday in the 17th century, most maritime activity was centred east of Centraal Station, along Prins Hendrikkade and on the artificial islands east of Kattenburgerstraat. At the time, the harbour and its arterial canals formed a whole with the city itself. A drop in commerce slowly unbalanced this unity and the construction of Centraal Station late in the 19th century served as the final psychological cleavage. This neo-Gothic monument to modernity blocked both the city's view of the harbour and its own past.

However, that's not to say that the harbour ever really slacked. While Rotterdam is the world's largest port, Amsterdam and the nearby North Sea Canal ports of Zaanstad, Beverwijk and IJmuiden rank in the top 15.

North-west of Centraal Station the **Westelijke Eilanden** (Western Islands) are artificial islands created in the 17th century for shipping-related activities. Although there are now warehouse flats and a yacht basin on Realeneiland, Prinseneiland and Bickerseiland, where once shipyards, tar distillers, fish-salters and smokers were located, the area remains the city's best setting for a scenic stroll that hearkens back to more seafaring times.

Since 1876 access to the sea has been via the North Sea Canal. Because the working docks are also to the west, there is little activity on the IJ behind Centraal Station beyond a handful of passenger ships and the free ferries that run across to Amsterdam Noord – an area of little interest except as a bicycling route towards the scenic fishing villages of **Waterland** (see p262) or the cultural breeding ground of **Kinetic Noord**, which is located in the former shipping yard NDSM (see p250).

Directly south of **Post CS** (see p107 **View to the future**), the **Schreierstoren**, or 'Weeping Tower', you'll notice on the right if you walk east from Centraal Station. It's the most interesting relic of Amsterdam's medieval city wall. Built in 1487, it was successfully restored in 1966. In 1927, though, a bronze memorial plaque was added by the Greenwich Village Historical

Society of New York: its text states that it was from this point, on 4 April 1609, that Henry Hudson departed in search of shorter trade routes to the Far East. He failed, and ended up colonising a small island in the mouth of a river in North America. The river was later named after him and the colony was called New Amsterdam, only to have its name changed by the English to New York. (Today, some of the boroughs still have a 'nederstamp' on them: in particular, Harlem, after Haarlem, and Brooklyn, after Breukelen.) The next eye-opener you'll see is **Nemo** (see below), a science museum whose green building dominates the horizon. It dwarfs the silver shell-shaped **ARCAM** architecture gallery (see p204) and the nautically inclined **Nederlands Scheepvaartmuseum** (see below), itself a very grand structure and major tourist draw.

Nederlands Scheepvaartmuseum

Kattenburgerplein 1 (523 2222/www.scheepvaart museum.nl). Bus 22, 42. **Open** *Mid Jun-mid Sept* 10am-5pm daily. *Mid Sept-mid Jun* 10am-5pm Tue-Sun. **Admission** €7.50; €6 over-65s; €4 6s-17s; free under-6s, MK. **Credit** AmEx, MC, V. **Map** p311 F2.
Dutch nautical history is rich and fascinating and it follows, that the country should boast one of the world's finest nautical museums; second only, say experts, to London's National Maritime Museum.

However, non-Dutch speakers may get a tad frustrated. There's no doubt as to the importance of the collection of models, portraits, boat parts and other naval ephemera; nor can there be any quibbling with the wonderful building in which it's housed (built 350 years ago by Daniel Stalpaert). But while the Dutch captions are excellent, the British, French and German ones are unilluminating. Many of the portraits on display are captioned in Dutch with mini-biographies, or at least details of why the subjects merit inclusion in the museum; the non-Dutch captions consist only of a name and the dates the subject was alive and it's a similar deal with the objects. Only the huge replica VOC ship at the rear, complete with costumed 'sailors', really excites. Given the full English captioning in almost all Amsterdam's other major museums, it seems fair to criticise; it's an oversight that, for the foreign visitor, turns a potentially fascinating museum into a largely dull one.

Nemo

Oosterdok 2 (531 3233/www.e-nemo.nl). Bus 22, 42. **Open** 10am-5pm Tue-Sun. *School holidays* 10am-5pm daily. **Admission** €11; €8.50 students; free under-3s. **Credit** AmEx, DC, MC, V. **Map** p311 F2.

Nemo opened in 1998 and has gone from strength to strength as a kid-friendly science museum. It eschews exhibits in favour of hands-on trickery, gadgetry and tomfoolery (in English and Dutch): you can play DNA detective games, blow mega soap bubbles or explode things in a 'wonderlab'. The museum's open-plan interior means that, aside from the film theatre, there's no escape from the young 'uns.

Renzo Piano's mammoth structure resembles a green ship rising from the water, and never fails to raise a gasp from people seeing it for the first time. Energetic types will enjoy the (free) climb to the top via the long, sloping roof, where you'll get a breathtaking view of the city and a variety of historical boats below. The outdoor café at the top is a lovely place to spend an afternoon and early evening.

View to the future

The big cultural success story of 2004 was the reinvention of **Post CS** (Oosterdokskade 5), the former post office building just east of Centraal Station (CS). This late modernist classic from 1969, designed by architect Piet Elling, is the only building on Oosterdokeiland, an artificial isle, to have temporarily escaped destruction while this whole area is being transformed into a home for 'New China Town', the city's music conservatory, the country's largest library and a whole mess of shops and hotels. While Post CS is due to be stripped of its walls and then encased in glass some time late in 2006, it is meanwhile the temporary home to the **Stedelijk Museum of Modern Art** (see p114), gallery **W139** (see p203), interior design showroom **Post Amsterdam** (see p178 **Living for design**), and hip club-restaurant **Eleven** (see p133).

People are already expressing a desire that Post CS stays exactly as it is. Besides offering spectacular views of the whole city from Eleven, Post CS has a certain vital rawness that has been missed since the demise of such cultural fulcrums as the squats Vrieshuis Amerika and the Silo. So catch the flavour while you can.

Post CS

Oosterdokskade 5, Old Centre. Tram 1, 2, 4, 5, 6, 9, 13, 16, 17, 24, 25. **Map** p311 E1.

Eleven.

Persmuseum (Press Museum)

Zeeburgerkade 10 (692 8810/www.persmuseum.nl).
Bus 22, 43. **Open** 10am-5pm Tue-Fri; noon-5pm
Sun. **Admission** €3.50; €2.50 6s-18s; free under-6s,
MK. **No credit cards**.

This newly revamped museum covers the 400-year
history of journalism, both magazine and newspaper, in Amsterdam and the Netherlands. The temporary exhibitions are usually focused on graphics,
cartoons, photography and particular magazines.

Take a walk on the water side

Once a mecca for squatters, Amsterdam's
eastern dockland is now the city's up-and-
coming eating and entertainment hot-spot.
The city hopes the transformed boardwalk
will prove as image-enhancing as the one in
Sydney, Australia. So if you want to explore
the future, put on those walking shoes or hop
on a bike and get moving. Hugging the water
eastward from behind Centraal Station,
follow Oostelijk Handelskade to pass the
new **Muziekgebouw** (*see p225*), and the
glass, wave-shaped Passenger Terminal for
cruise ships (www.pta.nl lists docking times,
should you want to admire them).

Take Jan Schaeferbrug to the left. This goes
through the de Zwijger warehouse – formerly
used for storing cocoa and now being turned
into a cultural space – to the tip of Java
Eiland. Here you'll find a showcase for the
Netherlands' experiments in residential living.
At first glance, Java Eiland may look like a
dense designer prison. But it's not hard to
be charmed by the island's bisecting walking
street, which will have you crossing canals
on funkily designed bridges and passing a
startling variety of architecture. At Azartplein,
with its funky **Ship of Fools** (*see p246*), the
island changes its name to KNSM Eiland,

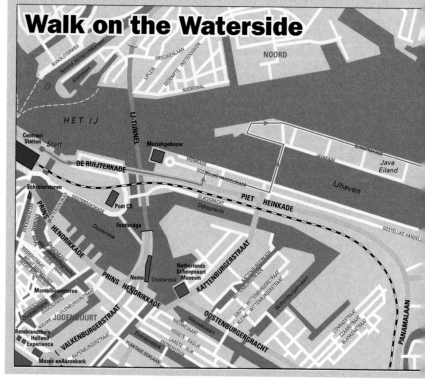

Walk on the Waterside

Werf 't Kromhout

Hoogte Kadijk 147 (627 6777/www.machine kamer.nl/museum). Bus 22. **Open** 10am-3pm Tue. **Admission** €4.50; €2.75 under-15s. **No credit cards. Map** p311 F2.

A nostalgic museum, full of old, silent ship engines and tools. The shipyard is proud of the fact that it's the oldest remaining original yard still in use, but its 18th-century heritage is no longer very apparent, nor is the yard especially active nowadays.

named for the Royal Dutch Steam Company that was once located here. Follow Surinamekade before returning on its southern parallel, Levantkade and popping through the strangely suggestive sculpted steel archway to Barcelonaplein, stopping for refreshment at one of the waterside cafés, or investing in an art coffin at the alternative burial store De Ode. Then linger and look at the imposingly dark-brown residential Piraeus building, by German architect Hans Kollhoff, with its eye-twisting inner courtyard.

The two peninsulas to the south are Borneo-Sporenburg, designed by the urban planners and landscape architects of West 8. The lots are all of different sizes, in an attempt to inspire the many participating architects to come up with creative solutions for low-rise living. Cross to Sporenburg via the Verbindingsdam to the building that has probably already caught your eye: the raised silver Whale residential complex, designed by architect Frits van Dongen, on Baron GA Tindalplein. From here, cross to Borneo via the red and swoopy bridge and turn left past a yet swoopier bridge. At the end, return via Scheepstimmermanstraat, the city's most eccentric architectural street. Each façade, whether twisting steel rods or haphazard plywood, seems odder than the next.

If you want to visit **IJburg** and its official swimming beach, **Blijburg**, complete with an official beach restaurant bar, **Blijburg aan Zee** (*see p135*), backtrack to the Whale where you can get on Oostelijk Handelskade and reach **Lloyd Hotel** (*see p70* **Cooking culture with Lloyd**) and its neighbouring café De Kantine (Rietlandpark 375, 419 4433). This is a good spot for a break before catching the tram to IJburg by the huge public art piece *Folly for the Bees*, (those unmissable huge stacked tables). By its completion in 2012, the seven fake islands that make up IJburg, will be home to 18,000 residences for 45,000 people and join the area you have just explored as a modern landscaping and architectural mecca.

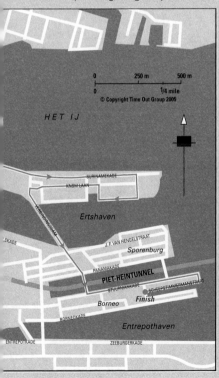

HET IJ

0   250 m   500 m

0   1/4 mile

© Copyright Time Out Group 2005

Ertshaven

SURINAMEKADE

KNSM LAAN

SKADE

J. F. VAN HENGELSTRAAT

Sporenburg

PANAMAKADE

PIET-HEINTUNNEL

STUURMANKADE

SCHEEPSTIMMERMANSTRAAT

Borneo   Finish

BORNEOKADE

ENTREPOTKADE

ZEEBURGERKADE

Entrepothaven

Scheepstimmermanstraat.

Sightseeing

The Jordaan

Wander that hangover away in the most charming 'hood in town.

The Jordaan is roughly sock-shaped, with borders at Brouwersgracht, Prinsengracht, Leidsegracht and Lijnbaansgracht. The area emerged when the city was extended in the 17th century and was designated for the working classes and smelly industries; it also provided a haven for victims of religious persecution, such as Jews and Huguenots. In keeping with the residents' modest financial circumstances, the houses are small and densely packed, at least when compared to dwellings along the swankier canals to the east.

The area is a higgledy-piggledy mixture of old buildings, bland modern social housing and the occasional eyesore. Despite its working-class associations, properties are now highly desirable, and though the residents are mainly proud, community-spirited Jordaansers, the nouveaux riches have moved in to yuppify the 'hood: once one of the most densely populated areas in Europe, with 80,000 residents at the end of the 19th century, it now houses less than a fifth of that number.

There are several theories about the origin of the name 'Jordaan'. Some say it's based on the area being on the wrong side of the River Jordan, as the Prinsengracht was once nicknamed. Others believe it to be a corruption of *joden*, Dutch for Jews, while linguistic dissenters think it's from *jardin*, the French word for garden. The latter seems more

plausible: the area was formerly a damp meadow, and many streets are named after flowers or plants. Other streets are named after animals whose pelts were used in tanning, one of the main – and stinkiest – industries here in the 17th century. Looiersgracht ('Tanner's Canal') sits near streets like Hazenstraat ('Hare Street'), Elandsgracht ('Elk Canal') and Wolvenstraat ('Wolf Street').

North of Rozengracht

Map p309

The Jordaan has no major sights; it's more of an area where you just stumble across things. It's also constantly surprising to wander through its streets and see hardly a soul. In general, the area north of the shopping-dense Rozengracht, the Jordaan's approximate mid-point, is more interesting and picturesque, with the area to the south more commercial.

Much of the area's charm comes from what's hidden from the uninformed eye. Chief among these treats are the *hofjes* or almshouses, many of which are pretty and deliciously peaceful. As long as you behave well the residents don't mind people admiring their garden courtyards. Best known are **Venetiae** (Elandsstraat 106-36; the only one on this list south of Rozengracht), **Sint Andrieshofje** (Egelantiersgracht 107-14),

Noordermarkt. See p111.

Big Brother is watching

Imagine if you will, a part of town where the hungry feed the hungrier, the poor buy beer for the poorer, and the sense of family extends to all one's neighbours. Sound like an idealised view of London's East End? Not far off, since it's easy to see the folks of the Jordaan as clog Cockneys, sharing – or rather, having shared – working-class backgrounds, cramped living spaces, a fierce sense of identity renowned throughout the nation, and a unique and rich vocabulary that betrays a special savvy at generating new words to describe drunkenness.

But a sense of community – even a mythical one – not only means that people are looking after each other, it also means that people are looking *at* each other. And whether through pragmatism or indifference, the Dutch are comfortable living with the curtains open.

So it makes sense that the Netherlands is the birthplace of reality TV. In 1999 nine people spent three months cooped up in a house in Almere (a satellite city where many of the 'real' Jordaaners moved during the 1970s) and made TV history. *Big Brother* seemed to strike a universal chord, exposing humans as craven beasts who craved their 15 minutes of fame so much that they were willing to publicise their private lives 24-7. But this trend – which spawned everything from *Survivor* to webcam exhibitionism – seemed also to feed some sort of nostalgia for authenticity that the more traditional soaps could never muster.

So what's next in the big bad world of 'reality'? Well, *Big Brother* creators Endemol have not been resting on their laurels. 2005 seems set to be the year when their *Sperm*

Race (guy with the best sperm wins a 'sexy sports car') and *Make Me a Mum* (a woman gets to pick her impregnator) will debut in Germany and/or the UK. Curiously, these shows will not get produced locally as they contravene the 'Dutch Embryo Law', which bans the commercial use of sperm or eggs.

But besides these exceptions, Amsterdam will undoubtedly remain at the vanguard of tasteless television. Recent highpoints include everything from €500 being offered to anyone willing to kiss a stranger's arse to getting up close and personal with celebrity enemas. We kid you not! So stay tuned (or not) for further developments in turn-off TV.

Karthuizerhof (Karthuizerstraat 21-31), **Suyckerhofje** (Lindengracht 149-63), **Claes Claesz Hofje** (1e Egelantiersdwarsstraat 3), **Raepenhofje** (Palmgracht 28-38), and the oldest, **Lindenhofje** (Lindengracht 94-112). Hofje-hopping is a gamble, as entrances are sometimes locked in deference to the residents. But take a chance, and you may get lucky.

The area north of Rozengracht is easy to get pleasantly lost in. Little lanes and alleys link the already quiet main streets in a mazy haze, and it's no surprise that such a chilled atmosphere incorporates some of the city's best cafés: **'t Smalle** (Egelantiersgracht 12; *see p152*), for example, set on a small canal, where Peter Hoppe (of Hoppe & Jenever, the world's

first makers of gin) founded his distillery in 1780. (The Japanese have built an exact replica of 't Smalle in Nagasaki's Holland Village.)

Between scenic coffees or decadent daytime beers, check out some of the specialist shops tucked away on these adorable side streets. Apart from these shops, many of the best of the outdoor markets are also found nearby: Monday morning's bargain-packed **Noordermarkt** and Saturday's organic foodie paradise **Boerenmarkt** (for both, *see p180*) are held around the Noorderkerk, the city's first Calvinist church, built in 1623. Adjacent to the Noordermarkt is the bargain-packed **Westermarkt**, while another general market fills **Lindengracht** on Saturdays (*see p180*).

Between Brouwersgracht and the blisteringly scenic **Westelijk Eilanden** (*see p106*), more quirky shopping opportunities can be found on Haarlemmerstraat and its westerly extension Haarlemmerdijk. Though not officially part of the Jordaan, this strip and its alleys share an ambience. Head east towards Centraal Station past **West Indische Huis** (Herenmarkt 93-7). This home to the West Indies Trading Company (WIC) stored the silver that Piet Hein took from the Spanish after a sea battle in 1628, and was the setting for such dubious decisions as selling Manhattan for 60 guilders and running the slave trade between Africa and the Caribbean. Today you can pop your head into the courtyard to say hello to the statue of Peter Stuyvesant. Heading west, Haarlemmerdijk ends at Haarlemmerplein, where you'll see the imposing Haarlemmerpoort city gate, built in 1840. Behind it is wanderful **Westerpark**, which connects to the happening arts complex **Westergasfabriek** (*see p250*).

Rozengracht & further south

Map p309, p313 & p314

As its name suggests, Rozengracht was once a canal. It's now filled in, and scythes through the heart of the Jordaan in unappealing fashion. It's unlikely it was so traffic-clogged when Rembrandt lived at No.184 from 1659 until his death a decade later; all that remains of his former home is a plaque on the first floor bearing an inscription that translates into 'Here stood Rembrandt's home 1410-1669'. While you're here, look up at the gable of Rozengracht 204 to spy an iron stickman wall anchor or visit some of the many Jordaan galleries (*see p205*).

The area south of Rozengracht is notable for two antique markets: **Rommelmarkt** and **Looier** (*see p180*). Nearby, Elandsgracht 71-7 is where the labyrinthine Sjako's Fort once stood. Sjako is often referred to as the 'Robin Hood of Amsterdam', which glosses over the fact that while he was happy stealing from the rich, he usually neglected to give to the poor. Still, he had style: not many burglars go about their business dressed in white and accompanied by henchmen clad in black. In 1718 his 24-year-old head ended up spiked on a pole where the Shell Building now stands, but local band Sjako!, anarchist bookstore Fort van Sjako (Jodenbreestraat 24, 625 8979), and a shrine in the window of the building that replaced his fort keep his name alive. More tributes can be paid where Elandsgracht hits Prinsengracht: here you'll find statues of Tante Leni, Johnny Jordaan and Johnny Meijer, who personified the spirit of the Jordaan by crooning of lost love and spilt beer in local cafés.

Great gondola!

It's got canals, it's got tourists, so where are the gondolas? Having taken its time, Amsterdam can now boast its own single oar boat service, and it's suitably unique: you will be piloted by either 'Hans, the tallest gondolier on the planet' or 'Tirza, the world's first woman gondolier'. (She now has a rival in Hamburg, but in Venice, the city we call the 'Amsterdam of the South', gondolier remains a trade that is restricted to short males.)

It all started in 1998 when Tirza decided to build a gondola as part of her shipbuilding studies. It proved an instant success and even won a city-sponsored prize for innovation. But in a typically contradictory fashion, another arm of city government refused to give her and her business partner, Hans, an operating licence. Undaunted, they incorporated a charitable foundation which will take suitable sponsors for trips on the canals.

Becoming a 'sponsor' is easy, both for romantic couples or groups of up to five or six. You can also choose to bring your own food or drink or have them arrange it at cost price. The standard route is around the Jordaan but you are always welcome to formulate your own.

And if you see them sculling by, don't bother to sing *O Sole Mio*: they've heard that one a million times before. But do keep an eye open for their cameo in *Deuce Bigelow II: European Gigolo* (*see p200* **Lights! Camera! Clog action!**). **Battello Foundation**. 686 9868/mobile 06 474 64545/www.gondel.nl.

The Museum Quarter, Vondelpark & the South

Pots of money, culture and plants.

The Museum Quarter

Map p314

Just over a century ago, the area now known as the Museum Quarter was still outside the city limits. Towards the end of the 19th century, though, the city expanded rapidly and the primarily upper-class city fathers decided to erect a swanky neighbourhood between the working-class areas to the west and south. Most of the beautiful mansions, with their art deco gateways and stained-glass windows, were built in the late 1890s and early 1900s.

The heart of the area is Museumplein, the city's largest square, bordered by the **Rijksmuseum** (*see p113*), the **Stedelijk Museum of Modern Art**, the **Van Gogh Museum** (for both, *see p114*) and the **Concertgebouw** (*see p223*). However, the heart will be beating fainter in the coming years, what with the Rijksmuseum being partially closed and the Stedelijk moving to a temporary space by Centraal Station (*see p107* **View to the future**). Museumplein itself is not really an authentic Amsterdam square, its recent revamp accenting its more park-like – or, rather, rural – aspects. Developed in 1872, it served as a location for the World Exhibition of 1883, and was then rented out to the Amsterdam ice-skating club between 1900 and 1936. During the Depression the field was put to use as a sports ground and during World War II the Germans built bunkers on it. The square was further mucked around in 1953 when the country's 'shortest motorway', Museumstraat, cut it in two. But the recent additions of grass, wading pool, skate ramp, café and wacky new addition to the Van Gogh Museum have helped.

As you'd expect in such high-falutin' cultural surroundings, property doesn't come cheap, and the affluence is apparent. Van Baerlestraat and, especially, PC Hooftstraat are as close as Amsterdam gets to Rodeo Drive, their boutiques offering solace to ladies who would otherwise be lunching. It's little wonder that this is where you'll find the majority of Amsterdam's diamond retailers (*see p102* **A girl's best friend**).

While you're in the area, it's worth visiting nearby Roemer Visscherstraat. This road, which leads to Vondelpark, is notable not for its labels but rather for its buildings. The houses from Nos.20 to 30 each represent a different country and are each built in the appropriate 'national' architectural style: Russia comes with a miniature dome, Italy has been painted pastel pink, and Spain's candy stripes have made it one of the street's favourites.

Rijksmuseum

Stadhouderskade 42 (674 7047/www.rijkmuseum.nl).
Tram 2, 5, 6, 7, 10. **Open** 10am-5pm daily.
Admission €9; free under-19s, MK. **Credit** AmEx, MC, V. **Map** p314 D5.

Designed by PJH Cuypers and opened in 1885, the Rijksmuseum holds the country's largest collection of art and artefacts, including 40 Rembrandts and four Vermeers. However, most of its million exhibits will be out of the public eye until 2008 while the Rijksmuseum gets a €200 million facelift at the hands of Spanish architect Cruz y Ortiz. The closure may turn out to be a blessing in disguise: instead of overdosing on the vastness of the place, visitors will be able to see the 400 most masterful masterpieces in the Philips Wing. Some of the collection will be used in other exhibitions organised by museums throughout the Netherlands. In addition, the Rijksmuseum Amsterdam Schiphol (Schiphol Airport, Holland Boulevard between E and F) has a few choice pieces by the likes of Rembrandt, Steen and Ruysdael. In short: there will still be plenty of Golden Age art to look at, but you'd do well to make the museum's excellent website before you visit.

The collection was started when William V began to acquire pieces just for the hell of it, and has been growing ever since: it includes Dutch paintings from the 15th century until 1900, as well as decorative and Asian art. The Old Masters that will almost certainly stay on display will include such jewels as Rembrandt's *Night Watch* and Vermeer's *Kitchen Maid* and *Woman Reading a Letter*; and a selection of the likes of Frans Hals, Jacob de Wit and Ferdinand Bol. There should also be a wealth of decorative arts on display, including 17th-century furniture and intricate silver and porcelain, 17th- and early 18th-century dolls' houses, plus furniture to give a glimpse of how the interiors of canal houses looked. Eighteenth- and 19th-century paintings, art

objects from Asia, statues, lacquer work, paintings, ceramics, jewellery, weaponry and the Textile and Costume collection will also undoubtedly be visible; the freely accessible garden, filled with Golden Age gateways and architectural fragments on the west side, will remain an oasis of rest.

Stedelijk Museum of Modern Art

Paulus Potterstraat 13 (573 2911/www.stedelijk.nl). Tram 2, 3, 5, 12. **Open** 10am-6pm Mon-Wed, Fri-Sun; 10am-9pm Thur. **Admission** €9; €4.50 7s-16s; free MK, under-7s. **Credit** *Shop* AmEx, MC, V. **Map** p314 D6.

Er, it's moved. Until 2006 the best collection of modern art in Amsterdam is on display on the second and third floors of the Post CS building near Centraal Station (*see p107* **View to the future**). But since the Stedelijk's rebuilding will take until at least 2008 there may be yet another transfer before the collection returns to Paulus Potterstraat. But wherever it finds itself, the museum remains a winner. Pre-war highlights include works by Cézanne, Picasso, Matisse and Chagall, plus a collection of paintings and drawings by Malevich. Post-1945 artists represented include De Kooning, Newman, Ryman, Judd, Stella, Lichtenstein, Warhol, Nauman, Middleton, Dibbets, Kiefer, Polke, Merz and Kounellis. Displays change regularly: some exhibitions are drawn from the collection, while others are made up from works loaned to the museum, but each tends to focus on a particular trend or the work of a specific artist.

Van Gogh Museum

Paulus Potterstraat 7 (570 5200/www.vangogh museum.nl). Tram 2, 3, 5, 12. **Open** 10am-6pm Mon-Thur, Sat, Sun; 10am-10pm Fri. **Admission** €9; €2.50 13s-17s; free under-13s, MK. *Temporary exhibitions* prices vary. **Credit** MC, V. **Map** p314 D6.

As well as the bright colours of his palette, Vincent van Gogh (*see p116* **Vincent in Amsterdam**) is known for his productivity, and that's reflected in the 200 paintings and 500 drawings that form part of the permanent exhibition here. In addition to this collection, there are also examples of his Japanese prints and works by the likes of Toulouse-Lautrec that add perspective to Van Gogh's own efforts.

After a major and impressive refurbishment, the enlarged Rietveld building remains the home base for the permanent collection, while the new wing by Japanese architect Kisho Kurokawa is usually the home to temporary exhibitions that focus on Van Gogh's contemporaries and his influence on other artists. These shows are assembled from both the museum's own extensive archives and private collections. Do yourself a favour and get there early in the morning, though: the queues in the afternoon can get frustratingly long, and the gallery unbearably busy. And it's worth noting that Friday evenings often feature lectures, concerts and films.

Vondelpark

Map p314

Amsterdam's largest green space is named after the city's most famous poet, Joost van den Vondel (1587-1679), whose controversial play *Lucifer* caused the religious powers of the time to crack down hard on those who engaged in what was termed 'notorious living'. The campaign helped bring about the downfall of Rembrandt and Vondel; the latter ended his days as a pawnshop doorman.

Vondelpark is the most central of the city's major parks, its construction inspired by the development of the Plantage, which had formerly provided the green background for the leisurely walks of the rich. It was designed in the 'English style' by Zocher, with the emphasis on natural landscaping; the original ten acres opened in 1865. The last few years has seen much renovation as the park has sunk two to three metres (seven to ten feet) since it was first built – some of the larger trees are in fact 'floating' on huge blocks of styrofoam or are re-inforced with underground poles.

There are several ponds and lakes in the park – no boating, though – plus a number of play areas and cafés; most pleasant are **Het Blauwe Theehuis** (Round Blue Teahouse; *see p152*) and Café Vertigo at the **Nederlands Filmmuseum** (*see p199*). The NFM is less a museum and more a cinema with a café attached and a library nearby. Keep your eye out for a huge Picasso sculpture in the middle of the park, and wild parakeets who were mistakenly released in 1976. Around the corner – and providing a unique place for coffee – is the epic Hollandsche Manege (Vondelstraat 140, 618 0942), a wooden version of the Spanish Riding School in Vienna.

Vondelpark gets fantastically busy on sunny days and Sundays, when bongos abound, dope is toked and football games take up any space that happens to be left over. The dicky-tickered would do well to look out for rollerbladers, who meet here weekly for the **Friday Night Skate** (*see p242*). Films, plays and concerts are also put on, with a festival of free open-air performances in summer (*see p220*).

Further south

The Museum Quarter is the northernmost tip of Amsterdam's Oud Zuid (Old South), which stretches down beyond Vondelpark. This area is defined by residential housing, with the more bohemian streets around the park contrasting nicely with their smarter equivalents by the museums and comparing favourably with the uglier modern buildings nearby.

Nieuw Zuid

Stretching out in a ring beneath Vondelpark is a fairly indeterminate region known as Nieuw Zuid (New South), bordered to the north by Vondelpark, to the east by the Amstel and to the west by the Olympisch Stadion (www.olympisch-stadion.net). It was built for the 1928 Olympics, recently renovated to its original Amsterdam School glory and now notable primarily for its club/restaurant **Vakzuid** (*see p139*). The New South was planned by Berlage and put into action by a variety of Amsterdam School architects, who designed both private and public housing for the area. It's the former that's given the New South what character it has, most notably around Apollolaan and Beethovenstraat (worth visiting simply for the **Oldenburg** bakery at No.17; *see p171*).

The few visitors are here on business, especially around the **World Trade Center**. The controversial Noord-Zuidlijn Metro is set to link this district with the centre of town and Amsterdam Noord. East of here is another

Museumplein. *See p113.*

Vincent in Amsterdam

Most people know the Van Gogh Museum is in Amsterdam. Few realise that Vincent lived for over a year in the Dutch capital. **Ken Wilkie**, 'art detective' and author of *The Van Gogh File*, reports.

Vincent was 24 when he arrived in Amsterdam in May 1877. He was beardless, with a freckled face framed in a mop of red hair. The young Van Gogh had not yet begun to paint and his passions at that time were focused on the Bible. A few years earlier he had been working as an assistant in a London art gallery. But following a rejection in love, he began to immerse himself in religion and planned to follow his father's footsteps into the pulpit.

But to study theology at a university, he first had to pass a state examination. He boarded with his Uncle Jan, in a house still standing, next to the **Dutch Maritime Museum** (*see p106*). Uncle Jan was a Vice Admiral in the Dutch navy. Another uncle, the Reverend Stricker, arranged for Vincent to study Greek and Latin with Dr Mendes da Costa. While in yet another uncle's art gallery, in Leidsestraat, he could indulge his love of paintings.

But, well-read and highly intelligent as he was, Vincent was not studious. Rather than sweating over Greek verbs, he wandered all over the city. Never a person to do anything in half measures, on a Sunday he would take in three or four church services, in different churches, starting at 7am. You can follow his footsteps today, from the Maritime Museum, through the Red Light District, to the **Oude Kerk** (*see p88*), and on along the canals to the **Agnietenkapel** (*see p88*), the **Begijnhof** (*see p92*), the **Zuiderkerk** (*see p101*), **Noorderkerk** (*see p224*), **Westerkerk** (*see p97*), **Nieuwe Kerk** (*see p80*) and **Amstelkerk** (*see p99*). Canal houses and canals like the Binnenkant have changed very little since Vincent's time.

Although his studies were not going well, Vincent endeared himself to his young teacher, Mendes da Costa, who admired his concern for the poor and society's outcasts. Vincent's guilt in not meeting the academic expectations of Mendes took on masochistic dimensions. When he felt he was underperforming, he would beat himself with a cudgel in bed at night and often slept out in the winter to punish himself. Mendes said later that Vincent had a 'pervading expression of indescribable sadness and despair'. Bringing his teacher a bunch of snowdrops, he would say: 'Don't be mad at me, Mendes, I have brought you some little flowers again because you are so good to me.'

Vincent abandoned his studies in September 1878 and before long was working as a missionary in the coalfields of the Belgian Borinage, which led to his decision to become a painter. But even in his Amsterdam days, there were many glimpses of the artist to come. On Monday 4 June 1877, he wrote to Theo: 'Today when I passed the flower market on the Singel (still there, *see p170*), I saw something very attractive and amusing. A man was selling a bunch of pots with all kinds of flowers and plants; there was a backdrop of ivy, and his little girl was sitting between it all, such a child as Maris would have painted, so simple in her little black bonnet, and with a pair of bright smiling eyes. She was knitting; the man was praising his wares – and if I could have spared the money I should have liked to buy some – and he said, pointing, unintentionally, at his little daughter: "Isn't this beautiful?"'

Vincent returned to Amsterdam in 1881, in an ill-fated declaration of love for his cousin Kee, when he held his hand over a candle until he was allowed to see her, and again in 1885 to visit the newly-built Rijksmuseum (*see p113*) when he spent a day looking at Rembrandt's *Jewish Bride*. On that visit he painted two pictures, one of a view of De Ruijterkade and another view of the Singel, both scenes that have changed little in the intervening 120 years.

staple of Amsterdam business life: the ugly **RAI Exhibition and Congress Centre**, which holds numerous trade fairs, conventions and public exhibitions throughout the year.

However, in between the RAI and the WTC lies one of Amsterdam's loveliest parks. Extended and renovated in 1994, **Beatrixpark** is a wonderfully peaceful place, handy if you want to avoid the crowds in town on a summer's day. The Victorian walled garden is worth a visit, as is the pond, complete with geese, black swans and herons. Amenities include a wading pool and play area for kids; there are concerts staged in July and August.

Still further south, **Amstelpark** was created for a garden festival in 1972, and now offers recreation and respite to locals in the suburb of Buitenveldert, near the RAI. A formal rose garden and rhododendron walk are among the seasonal spectacles, and there are also a labyrinth, pony rides and a children's farm, plus tours on a miniature train. The Rosarium Restaurant serves expensive meals, though its outdoor café is less pricey. Just north of Amstelpark, along the scenic banks of the Amstel, lies the city's most evocative cemetery, **Begraafplaat Zorgvlied** (Amsteldijk 273, 644 5236), which is filled with ancient and arty headstones – perfect for an introspective stroll.

Amstelveen

Of all Amsterdam's southern suburbs, Amstelveen is the most welcoming to the casual visitor. Though the **CoBrA Museum** (*see right*) helps, the main attraction here is the **Amsterdamse Bos**, a mammoth, artificially built wood that's treasured by locals yet neglected by visitors. The 2,000-acre site sprawls beautifully, and comes with a great many attractions in case the tranquillity isn't enough. The man-made Bosbaan is used for boating and swimming, with canoe and pedalo rental available. Other attractions include play areas, a horticultural museum, jogging routes, a buffalo and bison reserve, a bike-hire centre (open March to October), a water sports centre, stables and a picnic area. The goat farm sells

cheese, milk and ice-cream: you can even feed the goats. The wood feels a lot further away from Schiphol than it actually is: the airport is less than a mile from the wood's western edge. Kids also love the petting farm and pancake restaurant Boerderij Meerzicht (679 2744, www.boerderijmeerzicht.nl, open Mar-Oct 10am-7pm Tue-Sun, Nov-Feb 10am-6pm Fri-Sun).

Bosmuseum

Koenenkade 56, near Amstelveenseweg, Amsterdamse Bos (676 2152). Bus 170, 171, 172. **Open** 10am-5pm daily. **Admission** free.
The Bosmuseum recounts the history and use of the Amsterdamse Bos. Its mock woodland grotto, which can turn from day to night at the flick of a switch, is wonderful for kids.

CoBrA Museum of Modern Art

Sandbergplein 1 (547 5050/www.cobra-museum.nl). Tram 5/Metro 51/bus 170, 172. **Open** 11am-5pm Tue-Sun. **Admission** €7; €4 over-65s; €3 5s-16s; free under-5s, MK. **Credit** *Shop* MC, V.
The CoBrA group (an acronym of Copenhagen, Brussels and Amsterdam, *see p202*) attempted to radically reinvent the language of paint in 1948, preaching an ethos of participation and believing everyone should make art, regardless of ability or education. Artists such as Karel Appel, Eugene Brands and Corneille were once regarded as little more than eccentric troublemakers; they've now been absorbed into the canon. This museum provides a sympathetic environment in which to trace the development of one of the most influential Dutch art movements of the 20th century.

'Ere, 'ere. **Van Gogh Museum**.

Sightseeing

Hortus Botanicus (Vrije Universiteit)

Van de Boechorststraat 8, Zuid (444 9390/www.vu. nl/hortus). Tram 5/Metro 50, 51/bus 142, 170, 171, 172. **Open** *5 Sept-4 Jun* 8am-4.30pm Mon-Fri; *5 Jun-4 Sept* 8am-4.30pm Mon-Fri; 9am-5pm Sat. **Admission** free.

This small garden is, rather curiously, wedged between the high buildings of a university and a hospital. It doesn't have the charm of its city centre counterpart (*see p105*), but it's a pleasant place for a stroll. The fern collection is one of the largest in the world; the Dutch garden next door shows the great variety of flora found in this country.

The collectors' collections

For planes

Aviodome *Pelikaanweg 50, Lelystad Airport (0900 284 6376/www.aviodome.nl). Bus 147 from Lelystad NS station.* **Open** *Jan-June, Sept-Dec* 10am-5pm Tue-Sun. *July, Aug* 9am-6pm daily. **Admission** €13.50 adults; €11.50 4s-12s; free under-4s. **No credit cards.**
Aeroplane enthusiasts will loop the loop over this aviation theme park and museum. They have a 1903 Wright Flyer, a Spider (designed by Dutch pioneer Anthony Fokker), and more recent aeronautical exhibits.

For trams

Electrische Museumtramlijn Amsterdam *Haarlemmermeerstation, Amstelveenseweg 264 (673 7538 Sunday only/info 0900 423 1100/www.museumtram.nl). Tram 16.* **Open** *Apr-June, Sept, Oct* every 20mins, 11am-5pm Sun, public holidays. *July, Aug* every 20mins, noon-5pm Wed. **Tickets** €3.50 round trip; €2.80 4-11s, over-65s; free under-4s. **No credit cards.**
The pride and *raison d'être* of the Electric Tram Museum, housed in a beautiful 1915 railway station, is its rolling stock. For its one-hour round trips, colourful antique streetcars from several cities take you along a track through the nearby Amsterdamse Bos.

For pianolas

Pianola Museum *Westerstraat 106, the Jordaan (627 9624/www.pianola.nl). Tram 3, 10.* **Open** 11.30am-5.30pm Sun. **Admission** €4; €3 over-65s; €2.50 children. **No credit cards. Map** p309 B2.
Ever wanted the full scoop on piano-playing devices? Look no further. But do call ahead: budget cuts may see its demise.

For mutants

Museum Vrolik *Entrance on south side of AMC medical faculty, Meibergdreef 15 (info 566 9111). Metro Holendrecht.* **Open** 9am-5pm Mon-Fri. **Admission** free.
This museum way out in the south-east contains 18th- and 19th-century specimens of human embryos and malformations collected by Professor Gerardus Vrolik and his son: clearly not for those with weak stomachs. Funny fact: '*vrolijkis*' is Dutch for cheerful.

For mini modern art

Reflex Minituur Museum voor Hedendaagse Kunst *Singel 548, in the Fortis Bank (627 2832/www.reflex-art.nl). Tram 1, 2, 4, 5, 9, 14.* **Open** 1-5pm Mon; 9.30am-5pm Tue-Fri. **Admission** free.
Some 1,500 works no larger than ten centimetres (four inches) across: artists on show include Warhol, Appel, Scholte, Beuys, Kienholz, Lichtenstein, Leibovitz and LeWitt.

For pipes

Pijpenkabinet *Prinsengracht 488, Southern Canal Ring (421 1779/www.pijpenkabinet.nl). Tram 1, 2, 5.* **Open** noon-6pm Wed-Sat. **Admission** €5. **No credit cards. Map** p314 D5.
This national pipe museum staggers mind and lungs with a vast collection: clay pipes, opium pipes and paraphernalia. Good 'Smokiana' shop for connoisseurs and souvenir hunters.

For lifts

EnergeticA *Hoogte Kadijk 400, Amsterdam East (422 1277/www.energetica.nl/ actueel.html). Tram 9, 14/bus 22, 32.* **Open** 10am-4pm Mon-Fri. **Admission** €3; free under-12s, MK. **No credit cards. Map** p311 F2.
This museum of 'energy techniques, elevators, household appliances and city gas' is a world leader among functioning lift collections; it includes the famous 'Pater Noster'. But funding may soon be cut off, so ring first to check.

For all and sundry

For **cats** see p99; for **Bibles** see p95; for **coffee and tea** see p175; for **beer** see p120; for **torture** see p100; for **drugs** see p48 and p87; for **condoms** see p182; for **sex** see p80 and p87.

The Pijp

Draw deep on the most multicultural part of town.

Map p315

Doing the Pijp is a spunky experience, even if it has nothing to do with the Dutch slang for giving a blow job, 'piping'. While it's hardly a treasure trove of history and sights, the Pijp's time is the present, with over 150 different nationalities keeping its global village vibe alive and the recent economic upturn seeing the opening of more upmarket and trendy eateries and bars than ever before.

The Pijp is the best known of the working-class quarters built in the late 19th century. Harsh economics saw the building of long, narrow streets, which probably inspired the change in name from the official, double-yawn-inducing 'Area YY' to its appropriate nickname, 'the Pipe'. Because rents were high many tenants were forced to sublet rooms to students, who then gave the area its bohemian character.

That said, the many Dutch writers who lived here helped add to it. Among the locals were luminaries like Heijermans, De Haan and Bordewijk, who famously described World War I Amsterdam as a 'ramshackle bordello, a wooden shoe made of stone'. Many painters had studios here, too – people like Piet Mondriaan, who once lived in the attic of Ruysdaelkade 75, where he began formulating de Stijl while enjoying a view of the decidedly old-school Rijksmuseum. It's estimated that over 250 artists currently live in the area, and the current crop is gaining status in a district where most streets are named after their forebears. Jan Steen, Ferdinand Bol, Gerard Dou, and Frans Hals (whose street, Frans Halsstraat is particularly pretty, and rich with cafés and bars) are just a few of the artists honoured.

And, of course, the area was packed with brothels and drinking dens. In the basement of Quellijnstraat 64 the Dutch cabaret style – distinguished by witty songs with cutting social commentary for lyrics – was formulated by Eduard Jacobs and continues to live on through the likes of Freek de Jonge, Hans Teeuwen and Najib Amhali.

At the turn of the century the Pijp was a radical socialist area. The area has lost much of its bite since those days and many families with children have fled to suburbia. Still, the number of cheap one- and two-bedroom places, combined with the reasonably central location, makes the area very attractive to students, young single people and couples, and the area has the densest gay population in Amsterdam.

During the last 40 years, many immigrants have found their way to the Pijp, setting up shop and inspiring the general economic upswing of the area. The Pijp now houses a mix of nationalities, providing locals with halal butchers, Surinamese, Spanish, Indian and Turkish delicatessens, and restaurants offering authentic Syrian, Moroccan, Thai, Pakistani, Chinese and Indian cuisine. Thanks to these low-priced exotic eats, the Pijp is the best place in town for quality snacking treats, the ingredients for which are mostly bought fresh from the largest daily market in the Netherlands: **Albert Cuypmarkt** (*see p180*), the hub around which the Pijp turns. The market attracts thousands of customers every day, and spills merrily into the adjoining roads: the junctions of Sweelinckstraat, Ferdinand Bolstraat and 1e Van der Helststraat, north into the lively Gerard Douplein, and south towards Sarphatipark. The chaos will be heightened over the next few years by the construction of the Metro's controversial Noord–Zuidlijn, whose route will run pretty much right underneath Ferdinand Bolstraat.

Still on Albert Cuypstraat, cross Ferdinand Bolstraat and you'll find a cluster of fine, cheap Chinese-Surinamese-Indonesian restaurants. After passing the coach-party attraction of the Van Moppes & Zoon Diamond Factory, diamond turns to ruby around the corner on Ruysdaelkade, the Pijp's very own mini red light district. Enjoy the sight of steaming, hooter-happy motorists caught in their own traffic gridlock while you lounge casually around an otherwise restful canal.

Head back away from the water (and the red lights) a few blocks along 1e Jan Steenstraat, passing splendid bric-a-brac shop Nic Nic as you go, and you'll soon run across the Pijp's little green oasis: the grass-, pond- and duck-dappled **Sarphatipark**, designed and built as a mini Bois de Boulogne by the slightly mad genius Samuel Sarphati (1813-66). Aside from building the Amstel hotel and the Paleis voor Volksvlijt, Sarphati showed philanthropic tendencies as a baker of inexpensive bread for the masses, and as initiator of the city's rubbish collection. The centrepiece fountain comes complete with a statue of Sammy himself.

Edging along and beyond the south edge of Sarphatipark, Ceintuurbaan offers little of note for the visitor, with the exception of the buildings at Nos.251-5. Why? Well, there aren't many other houses in the city that incorporate giant ball-playing green gnomes with red hats in their wooden façades. The unique exterior of the **Gnome House** was inspired by the owner's name: Van Ballegooien translates (clumsily) as 'of the ball-throwing'. Around the corner stands the archive, **Gemeentearchief Amsterdam** (Amsteldijk 67, 572 0202, www.gemeentearchief.amsterdam.nl), where you can peruse the library or one of its excellent exhibitions (though they plan to move in 2006).

After a stroll in the park, wander north up 1e Van der Helststraat towards Gerard Douplein. This little square, with its cafés, coffeeshops, chip shops and authentic Italian ice-cream parlour, turns into one big terrace during the summer, and is hugely popular with the locals. Bargain second-hand knick-knacks can be bought from **Stichting Dodo** at No.21; trivia hounds should know that the Dutch – or rather their egg-eating animals – were responsible for this bird's extinction after they colonised Mauritius in 1598. A few streets away is the old **Heineken Brewery** (*see below*).

Heineken Experience

Stadhouderskade 78 (523 9666/www. heinekenexperience.com). Tram 6, 7, 10, 16, 24, 25. **Open** 10am-6pm (no entry after 5pm) Tue-Sun. **Admission** €10. **Credit** MC, V. **Map** p315 E5.
Once upon a time, this vast building was the main Heineken Brewery. Beer pilgrims can find this out by reading the blurb next to the entrance that states – cue intake of hushed breath – that the building is 'where Heineken was actually brewed'. However, in 1988, Heineken stopped brewing here, but kept the building open for endearingly unflashy tours: for a charitable donation of *f*2 (less than €1 in today's money), you got an hour-long guided walk through the site, followed by as much Heineken as you could neck. It's safe to say that more punters were there for the free beer than the brewing education.

Unfortunately, Heineken cottoned on to this, and recently renovated the huge building so tourists can enjoy the Heineken Experience. And while it's a lot flashier, it's a little less illuminating and a lot less fun. There's an interesting story to be told here, but this botched affair fails to narrate it. Plus points: the quasi-virtual reality ride through a brewery from the perspective of a Heineken bottle is easily the most ludicrous exhibit in Amsterdam, and you still get three free beers plus a surprise free gift (and not a bad one at that) at the end. But all in all, you're probably better off just going to a bar.

Albert Cuypmarkt. *See p119.*

Eat, Drink, Shop

Features

Restaurants

It's not just melted cheese and raw fish.

Smokin'. **Brasserie Harkema**. *See p123.*

While many restaurants have dropped like flies into soup, there has been an almost endless stream of new – and often daring – ventures to replace them. Gossip has focused along the eastern harbour front with the dizzyingly high views of **11** (*see p133*), the tasty do-goodery of Jamie Oliver franchise **Fifteen** (*see p133*), and Snel and Sloom (fast and slow) at **Lloyd Hotel** (*see p70* **Cooking culture with Lloyd**).

All this action makes one forget that the term 'Dutch cuisine' once tended to inspire peals of laughter. But well-travelled chefs have returned home to apply their lessons to fresh local, and often organic, ingredients (you can source your own at Noordermarkt's Saturday organic market; *see p180*). Transcending its setting on a land best suited to spuds, cabbages, carrots and cows, the nation is now employing its greenhouses to grow an array of ingredients.

But visitors should still take advantage of the traditional grub (the carrots taste all the better when you know that 17th-century Dutch royalists grew them for their orange colour). And watch for it: 2005 will see the debut of the Dutch-designed low-carb potato.

Fish, gruel and beer formed the trinity of the medieval diet. (Yes, Homer: beer! Would you want to drink the canal water?) But during the Golden Age, the rich indulged in hogs and pheasants, although apparently only after having these table-groaning meals painted for posterity – as the Rijksmuseum attests. But it was with Napoleonic rule at the dawn of the 19th century that the middle classes were seduced by innovations like herbs, spices and the radical concept that overcooking is bad. Sadly, a century later a well-meaning section of the bourgeoisie developed simplified recipes for the working classes that instead proved popular with the next generation of the bourgeoisie; the subtleties of southern cuisine were thereby eradicated from the home and passed down via a few of the town's top-end restaurants. But still, there's nothing quite like a hotchpotch of potato, crispy bacon and still-crunchy greens, all diligently dammed to hold a pool of gravy.

The spicy food of Indonesia re-eroticised the Dutch palate after World War II, when the colony was granted independence and the Netherlands took in Indonesian immigrants.

Take your pick from the various cheap Surinamese-Indonesian-Chinese snack bars or visit the purveyors of the *rijsttafel* ('rice table'), where every known fish, meat and vegetable is worked into a filling extravaganza. Along with fondue – a 'national' dish shamelessly stolen from the Swiss because its shared pot appealed to the Dutch sense of the democratic – Indo is the food of choice for any celebratory meals. Other waves of immigrants helped create today's vortex of culinary diversity.

If you prefer to stroll, here are a few tips. Rocket salad grows like weed in IJburg (*see p108*). Go to the Pijp if you crave econo-ethnic. Cruise Haarlemmerstraat, Utrechtsestraat, Nieuwmarkt, the 'Nine Streets' area and Reguliersdwarsstraat if you want something posher; and only surrender to Leidseplein – though we note some worthy exceptions – if you don't mind being overcharged for a cardboard steak and day-old sushi.

Sure, check out the posh places, but quality and economic snack opportunities (*see p136* **Give grease a chance**) can be found in the form of fish (*see p128* **Tails of herring-do**), rolled 'pizzas' from Turkish bakeries, Dutch *broodjes* (sandwiches) from bakers and butchers, and spicy Surinamese *broodjes* from 'Suri-Indo-Chin' snack bars. And you really should visit an Albert Heijn (*see p177* **Heinie ho!**) to get an insight into Dutch eating habits.

In addition to the restaurants listed below, there are many cafés and bars serving good food at fair prices; for these, *see p142*. For gay-friendly restaurants and cafés, *see p213*. For places to take the children, *see p194*.

LEISURELY DINING

Dining in Amsterdam is a laid-back affair, although those who keep nocturnal hours should note that the Dutch tend to eat early: many kitchens close by 10pm. All bills should, by law, include 19 per cent tax and a 15 per cent service charge, though it's customary to round up between five and ten per cent if the service merits it. If you have any special requirements, like high chairs or disabled access, it's always best to phone the restaurant before setting out.

Since the Euro was adopted in 2002, prices have shot up; prices listed here should only be used as a guideline. Local foodies weigh in at www.iens.nl and www.specialbite.nl – with the latter being a real winner that can reliably scoop you on such anticipated 2005 openings as Park Pacific in the Westergasfabriek (*see p250*). This is also a good place to check to see if the fantastic urban views of Inez IPSC (Amstel 2, 639 2899, www.inezipsc.com) were saved from bankruptcy thanks to it being the last work of late, lamented designer Peter Giele.

The Old Centre: Old Side

Cafés & snack stops

1e Klas

Centraal Station, Line 2B (625 0131). Tram 1, 2, 4, 5, 6, 9, 13, 16, 17, 24, 25. **Open** 8.30am-11pm daily. **Main courses** €16-€22. **Credit** AmEx, DC, MC, V. **Map** p310 D1.

This former brasserie for first-class commuters is now open to anyone who wants to kill some time in style – with a full meal or snack – while waiting for a train. The art nouveau interior will whisk you to the 1890s. But if you are running for the train, score a coffee, shake and bagel from Shakies (West Tunnel by stairs to lines 10/11, 423 4377, www.shakies.nl).

Brasserie Harkema

Nes 67 (428 2222/www.brasserieharkema.nl). Tram 4, 9, 14, 16, 24, 25. **Open** 11am-1am Mon-Sun. *Kitchen* 11am-11.30pm Mon-Thur, Sun; 11am-midnight Fri-Sat. **Main courses** *Lunch* €7-€14. *Dinner* €11-€16. **Credit** MC, V. **Map** p310 D3.

A new landmark, this former tobacco factory has titillated the local scene with its sense of designer space, excellent wines and a kitchen that stays open late pumping out reasonably priced French classics.

De Bakkerswinkel

Warmoesstraat 69 (489 8000/www.bakkerswinkel.nl). Tram 1, 2, 4, 5, 9, 13, 14, 16, 17, 24, 25. **Open** 8am-6pm Tue-Fri; 8am-5pm Sat; 10am-5pm Sun. **Main courses** €3.50-€11. **No credit cards**. **Map** p310 D3.

A bakery-tearoom where you can indulge in lovingly prepared, hearty sandwiches, soups and the most divine slabs of quiche you've ever had.
Other locations: Roelof Hartstraat 68 (662 3594).

The best Restaurants

Bazar
We want to believe. *See p141*.

Blijburg
A good place for a picnic. *See p135* **Son of a beach, that's tasty!**

Blue Pepper
Designer Indo. *See p131*.

Nam Kee
Cheap, central, divine oysters. *See p125*.

Riaz
Where Gullit scores rice and beans. *See p140*.

La Rive
A *grande bouffe* wallet weakener. *See p131*.

Eat, Drink, Shop

Café Bern. *See p127.*

De Jaren

Nieuwe Doelenstraat 20-22 (625 5771/www.cafe-de-jaren.nl). Tram 4, 9, 14, 16, 24, 25. **Open** *Café* 10am-11pm Mon-Thur, Sun; 10am-midnight Fri, Sat. *Restaurant* 5.30-10.30pm daily. **Main courses** *Café* €3-€12. *Restaurant* €10-€15. **Credit** V. **Map** p310 D3.
The grand De Jaren occupies a beautifully restored former bank complete with, depending on the Dutch weather, a potentially sunny terrace. The food in the ground-floor café is OK; upstairs in the restaurant service can be painfully slow, but worth it.

Latei

Zeedijk 143 (625 7485/www.latei.net). Tram 4, 9, 14, 16, 24, 25/Metro Nieuwmarkt. **Open** 8am-6pm Mon-Wed; 8am-10pm Thur, Fri; 9am-10pm Sat; 11am-6pm Sun. **Main courses** €3-€8. **No credit cards. Map** p310 D2.
Packed with kitsch and funky Finnish wallpaper – all of which, including wallpaper, is for sale – this little café serves up healthy juices and snacks all day long, plus vegetarian dinners based around couscous (after 6pm from Thursdays to Saturdays).

Chinese & Japanese

A Fusion

Zeedijk 130 (330 4068). Tram 4, 9, 14, 16, 24, 25/ Metro Nieuwmarkt. **Open** noon-11pm daily. **Main courses** €7-€14. **Credit** AmEx, DC, MC, V. **Map** p310 D2.
This loungey affair obviously took notes from the hip side of NYC's Chinatown. The dark and inviting interior harbours big screens playing Hong Kong music videos, bubble teas (lychee!), and some of the tastiest confusion-free pan-Asian dishes in town.

Nam Kee

Zeedijk 111-13 (624 3470/www.namkee.nl). Tram 4, 9, 14, 16, 24, 25/Metro Nieuwmarkt. **Open** noon-11pm Mon-Sat; noon-10pm Sun. **Main courses** €6-€19. **No credit cards. Map** p310 D2.
Cheap and terrific food has earned this Chinese joint a devoted following: the oysters in black bean sauce have achieved classic status. If it's busy, try massive sister operation and dim sum maestros Nam Tin nearby (Jodenbreestraat 11-13, 428 8508) or neighbour New King (Zeedijk 115-17, 625 2180). **Other locations:** Geldersekade 117 (639-2848).

Oriental City

Oudezijds Voorburgwal 177-9 (626 8352). Tram 4, 9, 14, 16, 24, 25. **Open** 11.30am-11.30pm daily. **Main courses** €8-€23. **Credit** AmEx, DC, MC, V. **Map** p310 D2.
The views overlook Damstraat, the Royal Palace and the canals. And that's not even the best bit: they serve some of city's most authentic dim sum.

Dutch & Belgian

De Brakke Grond

Nes 43 (626 0044/www.brasseriedebrakkegrond.nl). Tram 4, 9, 14, 16, 24, 25. **Open** *Café* 11am-1am Mon-Thur; 11am-2am Fri; noon-2am Sat; noon-1am Sun. *Restaurant* 6-10pm daily. **Main courses** €14-€18. **Credit** AmEx, MC, V. **Map** p310 D3.
Though Chez Georges (Herenstraat 3, 626 3332) offers a more sophisticated take on Belgian cuisine, De Brakke Grond shows more sensitivity to those who have an abiding love for Belgium's glory, its beers, by recommending the best choice of beverage to accompany each dish. Great patio, too.

Café Bern

Nieuwmarkt 9 (622 0034). Tram 4, 9, 14, 16, 24, 25/Metro Nieuwmarkt. **Open** 4pm-1am daily. *Kitchen* 6-11pm daily. **Main courses** €9-€14. **No credit cards. Map** p310 D2.

Despite its Swiss origins, the Dutch adopted the cheese fondue as a 'national dish' long ago. Sample its culinary conviviality at this suitably cosy brown bar that was established by the rather unlikely fiat of a nuclear physicist: the menu is affordable and the bar stocked with a generous variety of grease-cutting agents. It's best to book ahead.

French & Mediterranean

Blauw aan de Wal

Oudezijds Achterburgwal 99 (330 2257). Tram 9, 16, 24. **Open** 6.30-11.30pm Mon-Sat. **Main courses** €24.50-€25.50. **Set menu** 3 courses €38.50. **Credit** AmEx, MC, V. **Map** p310 D2.

Down an alley in the carnal heart of the Red Light District lies this oasis of reverence for the finer things in life. The hallmarks of this culinary landmark are tempting dishes (largely French in origin) and a inspired wine list likely to inspire long bouts of grateful contemplation in visiting oenophiles.

Café Roux

The Grand, Oudezijds Voorburgwal 197 (555 3560/www.thegrand.nl). Tram 4, 9, 14, 16, 24, 25. **Open** *Breakfast* 6.30-10.30am. *Lunch* noon-2.30pm. *Tea* 3-5pm. *Dinner* 6-10.30pm daily. **Main courses** €17-€39. **Credit** AmEx, DC, MC, V. **Map** p310 D3.

The food here is identical to that of the Grand Hotel itself, and is overseen by the great man himself. But despite Albert Roux's extraordinary status among gastronomes, meals here still represent good value for money, especially at lunch and afternoon tea. The sommelier is excellent, too. *See also p55.*

Centra

Lange Niezel 29 (622 3050). Tram 4, 9, 14, 16, 24, 25. **Open** 1.30-11pm daily. **Main courses** €7-€17. **No credit cards. Map** p310 D2.

Good, wholesome, homely Spanish cooking with a suitably unpretentious atmosphere to match. The tapas, lamb and fish dishes are all great.

Indonesian & Thai

Thaise Snackbar Bird

Zeedijk 72 (snack bar 420 6289/restaurant 620 1442). Tram 1, 2, 4, 5, 9, 13, 14, 16, 17, 24, 25. **Open** *Snack bar* 2-10pm daily. *Restaurant* 5-11pm daily. **Main courses** €10-€17. **Credit** (restaurant only) AmEx, DC, MC, V. **Map** p310 D2.

The most authentic Thai place in town. No doubt because of that fact, it's also the most crowded, but nevertheless it's worth waiting for, whether you drop by to pick up a pot of tom yam soup or go for a full-blown meal. If you plan to linger, settle down in the restaurant rather than the snack bar.

Cafés & snack stops

Al's Plaice

Nieuwendijk 10 (427 4192). Tram 1, 2, 4, 5, 9, 14, 16, 17, 24, 25. **Open** noon-10pm daily. **Main courses** €3-€8. **No credit cards. Map** p310 D2.

Brits will spot the pun from 50 paces: yep, it's an English fish 'n' chip gaff. Besides fish, there's a selection of pies, pasties, peas and downmarket tabloids.

Delores

Nieuwezijds Voorburgwal, opposite No.289 (626 5649). Tram 1, 2, 5. **Open** noon-10pm Mon-Wed; noon-1am Thur; noon-3am Fri, Sat. **Main courses** €7-€15. **No credit cards. Map** p310 C2.

Conveniently located in the hipster bar zone, this former police post is now a snack bar. Greasy fries have been replaced with healthy snacks and meals, harsh colours and neon forsaken for funky warmth.

Helder

Taksteeg 7 (320 4132/www.helderamsterdam.com). Tram 4, 9, 14, 16, 24, 25. **Open** 10am-6pm Wed-Sat; noon-6pm Sun. **Main courses** €2.50-€5.50. **No credit cards. Map** p310 D3.

The tiny 'Clear', in an alley off Kalverstraat, has inspired chefs who only use the freshest ingredients in their often perfect salads, soups, sandwiches, and pastas. Groups from ten to 27 people can arrange a private three or four-course dinner for €30-€35 a head and there's a takeaway option, too.

Chinese & Japanese

Kung Fu

Rokin 84 (528 9590/www.restaurant-kungfu.nl). Tram 4, 9, 14, 16, 24, 25. **Open** 5-11pm Mon-Thur, Sun; 5pm-midnight Fri, Sat. **Main courses** €6.50-€17. *Dim Sum* €1.75-€5. **Credit** AmEx, MC, V. **Map** p310 D3.

As in a computer game where you go on to a bigger and better arena when all the bad guys are dispatched and the boss obliterated, this is the next level Chinese restaurant. It has flat screens playing Kung Fu film classics (*Drunken Master!*), back-lit fish tanks separating the tables and providing diners with a sense of privacy and, most importantly of all, the food tastes great and is reasonably priced.

Tokyo Café

Spui 15 (489 7918/www.tokyocafe.nl). Tram 1, 2, 4, 5, 9, 14, 16, 24, 25. **Open** 11am-11pm daily. **Main courses** €10-€23. **Set menu** *Lunch* €12-€14. *Dinner* €19-€50. **Credit** AmEx, DC, MC, V. **Map** p314 D4.

Thought to be haunted, this Jugendstil monument now hosts its umpteenth eatery in the form of a Japanese café, complete with lovely terrace, teppanyaki pyrotechnics and sushi and sashimi bar. Their high quality – and the cocktail hour (from 5pm to 7pm) – will likely keep the ghosts at bay.

Eat, Drink, Shop

Dutch & Belgian

Brasserie De Roode Leeuw

*Damrak 93-4 (555 0666/www.restaurant
deroodeleeuw.com). Tram 4, 9, 14, 16, 24, 25.*
Open 7am-11.30pm daily. *Kitchen* 10am-10pm daily.
Main courses *Lunch* €4-€29.50. *Dinner* €18-€29.50.
Credit AmEx, DC, MC, V. **Map** p310 D2.
This brasserie is housed in the oldest covered terrace in Amsterdam. As you might guess, it harks
back to classier times but what's more surprising is
its embrace of the digital age as a WiFi point. It specialises in rather expensive Dutch fare – there's a
hotchpotch festival if you can't make up your mind
– and even has a selection of Dutch wine.

Keuken van 1870

*Spuistraat 4 (620 4018/ www.keukenvan1870.nl).
Tram 1, 2, 5.* **Open** 4-10pm Mon-Sat. **Main
courses** €6-€12. **Set menu** 3 courses €7.50.
No credit cards. Map p310 C2.
This former soup kitchen has been renovated and
re-invented but retains a menu of authentic Dutch
standards and, in a homage to its roots, the promise
to continue serving a set three-course menu for
€7.50. Another aspect of the restaurant that may
take you back is the fact that diners often end up
sharing tables, so we hope you'll enjoy the opportunity to rub shoulders with the Dutch.

D'Vijff Vlieghen

*Spuistraat 294-302 (530 4060 624 8369/
www.d-vijffvlieghen.com). Tram 1, 2, 5, 13, 17.*
Open 5.30-10pm daily. **Main courses** €22-€28.
Set menu 4-6 courses €39-€51. **Credit** AmEx, DC,
MC, V. **Map** p310 C3.
The Five Flies achieves a rich Golden Age vibe – it
even has a Rembrandt room, with etchings – but
also works as a purveyor of over-the-top kitsch. The
food is best described as poshed-up Dutch. Unique.

Kung Fu feasting. *See p127.*

Global

Supperclub

*Jonge Roelensteeg 21 (344 6400/www.supperclub.nl).
Tram 1, 2, 5, 13, 17.* **Open** 7.30pm-1am Mon-Thur,
Sun; 7.30pm-3am Fri, Sat. **Set menu** 5 courses €60.
Credit AmEx, DC, MC, V. **Map** p310 D3.
With its white decor, beds for seating, irreverent
food combos that change weekly and wacky acts;
this arty and utterly unique joint is casual to the
point of being narcoleptic. At the very least, we can

Tails of herring-do

You must, yes, you really *must* try raw herring.
We don't want to hear any excuses. The best
time is between May and July when the *nieuw*
(new) catch hits the stands, as this doesn't
need any extra garnish like onions and
pickles, since their flesh is at its sweetest –
thanks to the high fat content that the herring
was planning to burn off in the arduous
business of breeding. There's a quality fish
stall or store around most corners, but here
are some of the best purveyors of not only
herring but also smoked eel and other –
perhaps less controversial – fish for the
sandwich. And they're as cheap as chips
(or at least a lot cheaper than sushi).

Altena

*Stall at Stadhouderskade/Jan Luijkenstraat,
the Museum Quarter. Tram 2, 5, 6, 7, 10.*

Huijsman

*Zeedijk 129, Old Centre: New Side
(624 2070). Tram 4, 9, 14, 24, 25/
Metro Nieuwmarkt.*

Kromhout

*Stall at Singel/Raadhuisstraat, Old Centre:
New Side. Tram 13, 14, 17.*

Volendammer Viswinkel

*1e Van der Helststraat 60, the Pijp
(676 0394). Tram 6, 7, 10.*

promise that you'll remember your visit. And if you do go, remember to be nice to host Howie (*see p234* **Howie says 'Amsterdam rules!'**). They have their own cruise ship (www.supperclubcruise.nl).

Vegetarian

Green Planet
Spuistraat 122 (625 8280/www.greenplanet.nl). *Tram 1, 2, 5, 13, 17.* **Open** 5.30pm-midnight Mon-Sat; 5.30-10.30pm Sun. *Kitchen* 5.30-10.30pm daily. **Main courses** €13-€17. **No credit cards.** **Map** p310 C2.
The best veggie in town builds organic ingredients into soups, lasagne and stir fries. Finish with the house cognac and a slice of chocolate heaven.

Western Canal Belt

Cafés & snack stops

Foodism
Oude Leliestraat 8 (427 5103). *Tram 1, 2, 5, 13, 17.* **Open** 11am-10pm Mon-Sat; noon-10pm Sun. **Main courses** €8-€13. **No credit cards.** **Map** p310 C3.
English and Serbo-Croat are the languages of choice in this comfortable snack bar, perfect for post-joint munchies. Choose from sandwiches, salads, pastas and hearty shakes; it's also good for takeaway.

Greenwoods
Singel 103 (623 7071). *Tram 1, 2, 5.* **Open** 9.30am-6pm Mon-Thur; 9.30am-7pm Fri-Sun. **Light meals** €3-€12.50. **No credit cards.** **Map** p310 C3.

Service at this teashop is friendly but can tend to be on the slow side. Everything is freshly made, though, so forgive them: cakes, scones and muffins are baked daily on the premises. In summer, take your purchase and sit on the terrace by the canal.

't Kuyltje
Gasthuismolensteeg 9 (620 1045). *Tram 1, 2, 9, 24, 25.* **Open** 7am-4pm Mon-Fri. **Sandwich** €1.75-€3.30. **No credit cards.** **Map** p310 C3.
The wonderful, and deeply filling, world of Dutch *broodjes* (sandwiches) has its greatest champion in this takeaway, one of the very few that still features proper homemade meat and fish salads in your bun, rather than the almost ubiquitous factory prepared product that's taken over the sandwich market.

Loekie
Prinsengracht 705a (624 4230). *Tram 1, 2, 5, 6, 7, 10.* **Open** 9am-5pm Mon-Fri; 10am-6pm Sat; 11am-5pm Sun. **Sandwich** €1.50-€10. **No credit cards.** **Map** p314 D4.
Loekie isn't cheap, and you'll have to queue, but a French stick with Italian fillings makes for a meal. Fine quiche, cheesecake and tapenade, too.
Other locations: Utrechtsestraat 57 (624 3740).

Lust
Runstraat 13 (626 5791/www.lustamsterdam.nl). *Tram 1, 2, 5.* **Open** 10am-11pm daily. **Main courses** *Lunch* €3-€9. *Dinner* €15-€18. **Credit** MC, V. **Map** p314 C4.
Lust means 'appetite' in Dutch, and you'll soon have one at this slick, trendy but friendly, Dutch lunch venue that has a healthy array of dinners as well.

French & Mediterranean

Van Harte

Hartenstraat 24 (625 8500/www.vanharte. com). Tram 13, 14, 17. **Open** 10am-1am daily. *Kitchen* 11am-11pm. **Main courses** *Lunch* €3- €6. *Dinner* €16-€21. **Credit** AmEx, MC, V. **Map** p310 C3.

Both a snack stop (lunch-time sandwiches) and a place to settle back and masticate (dinner-time clam chowder is particularly good), Van Harte, under its new chef, has become a local favourite.

Indonesian & Thai

Blue Pepper

Nassaukade 366 (489 7039/www.diningcity.com/ ams/bluepepper). Tram 7, 10. **Open** 6-10pm daily. **Main courses** €18-€23. **Set menu** €40-€55. **Credit** AmEx, DC, MC, V. **Map** p314 C5.

An Indonesian restaurant near Leidseplein that combines tongue tantalising with designer decor. Combined with wine, it's the perfect romantic date.

Southern Canal Belt

Cafés & snack stops

Café Américain

Leidseplein 97 (556 3232). Tram 1, 2, 5, 6, 7, 10. **Open** 7am-11pm Mon-Wed, Sun; 7am-midnight Thur-Sat. **Main courses** €15.50-€21.50. **Set menu** 2-4 courses €27.50-€37.50. **Credit** AmEx, DC, MC, V. **Map** p314 C5.

Café Américain's glorious art deco interior – murals, stained glass and marbled lampshades – is a listed monument; Mata Hari is said to have held her wedding reception here. While threatening to hip up, it's still mostly tourists meeting for coffee and a pastry.

Chinese & Japanese

An

Weteringschans 76 (624 4672). Tram 6, 7, 10. **Open** 6-10pm Tue-Sat. **Main courses** €17-€22. **No credit cards. Map** p315 E5.

An serves some of the city's best Japanese cuisine – sushi as well as starters and grilled dishes. Staff are friendly and the place is comfortable.

Dim Sum Palace

Leidsestraat 95 (622 7878) Tram 1, 2, 5, 6, 7, 10. **Open** noon-1am Sun-Thur; noon-3am Fri-Sat. **Dim Sum** €3-€5. **Credit** AmEx, DC, MC, V. **Map** p314 C5.

With late hours and belly-gelling dim sum, this chaotic castle is the perfect pit stop near Leidseplein.

Japan Inn

Leidsekruisstraat 4 (620 4989/www.japaninn.nl). Tram 1, 2, 5, 6, 7, 10. **Open** 5.30pm-midnight daily. **Main courses** €10-€35. **Credit** AmEx, DC, MC, V. **Map** p314 D5.

Japan Inn offers quality and quantity. The fresh sushi and sashimi are served from the open kitchen and are hits with students (who dig the quantity) and Japanese tourists (who come for the quality).

Wagamama

Max Euweplein 10 (528 7778/www.waga mama.com). Tram 1, 2, 5, 6, 7, 10. **Open** noon-10pm Mon-Wed, Sun; noon-11pm Thur-Sat. **Main courses** €9-€15. **Credit** AmEx, MC, V. **Map** p314 D5.

Amsterdam's branch of the popular London franchise of quick 'n' cheap noodle bars. You may not fancy lingering in the minimalist canteen setting, but you certainly can't fault the speedy service or the tasty noodle dishes and soups. **Other locations**: Zuidplein 12 (620 3032).

Dutch & Belgian

Hap Hmm

1e Helmersstraat 33 (618 1884). Tram 1, 6, 7, 10. **Open** 4.30-8pm Mon-Fri. **Main courses** €5-€10. **No credit cards. Map** p314 C5.

Hungry but hard up? You need some of the Dutch grandma cooking served up in this canteen with a living-room feel. Yummy Bite, near Leidseplein, will be pleased to pack your empty insides with meat and potatoes for not much more than €5.

Fish

Le Pêcheur

Reguliersdwarsstraat 32 (624 3121/www.le pecheur.nl). Tram 1, 2, 5. **Open** *Lunch* noon-2.30pm Mon-Fri. *Dinner* 6-10.30pm Mon-Sat. **Main courses** €21-€40. **Credit** AmEx, MC, V. **Map** p314 D4.

Multilingual menus let you choose from à la carte or the menu of the day with minimal effort. The service is friendly but formal; the mussels and oysters are particularly excellent, as is the Golden Age patio.

French & Mediterranean

La Rive

Amstel Hotel, Prof Tulpplein 1 (520 3264/www. amstelhotel.nl). Tram 6, 7, 10/Metro Weesperplein. **Open** 7-10.30am, noon-2pm, 6.30-10.30pm Mon-Sat; 7am-noon Sun. **Main courses** €22.50-€45. **Set menu** €85-€97.50 **Credit** AmEx, DC, MC, V. **Map** p315 F4.

While Hôtel de l'Europe (*see p55*) has Excelsior, it's really the Amstel Hotel's (*see p63*) La Rive that overshadows all the rest of the high-end competition, and it does this by serving chef Edwin Kats's superb regional French cuisine without the excessive formality that can too often mar such a restaurant. For the perfect meal when money's no object…

Segugio

Utrechtsestraat 96a (330 1503/www.segugio.nl). Tram 4, 6, 7, 10. **Open** 6-11pm Mon-Sat. **Main courses** €23-€32. **Set menu** (5 courses) €52.50. **Credit** AmEx, MC, V. **Map** p315 E4.

Eat, Drink, Shop

All aboard the **Supperclub cruise**.
See p128.

Best. Risotto. Ever. In fact, this Italian has all the ingredients to make the perfect lingering meal for foodies and romantics alike. Bellissima!

Global

Beddington's

Utrechtsedwarsstraat 141 (620 7393). Tram 4.
Open 7-10.30pm Tue-Sat. **Set menu** 3 courses €42, 4 courses €48. **Credit** AmEx, MC, V. **Map** p315 E4.
Back from a revitalising break, proprietor and chef Jean Beddington is doing what she does best: cooking up creations, where one dish can hint at French haute cuisine, Japanese macrobiotic and English country cooking. The restaurant's peaceful interior allows you to concentrate on the inspired interplay of delicate flavours. Book far ahead!

Eat at Jo's

Marnixstraat 409 (638 3336). Tram 1, 2, 5, 6, 7, 10. **Open** noon-9pm Wed-Sun. **Main courses** €10.90-€11.90. **No credit cards**. **Map** p314 C5.
Each day brings a different fish, meat and vegetarian dish to the menu of this cheap and tasty international kitchen. Star spotters take note: whichever act is booked to play at the Melkweg (*see p219* and *p229*) may very well chow down here beforehand.

Janvier Proeflokaal

Amstelveld 12 (626 1199/www.janvier.nu). Tram 16, 24, 25. **Open** 10am-1am Mon-Thur; 11.30am-2am Fri, Sat; 11am-1am Sun. *Kitchen* 10am-10pm daily. **Main courses** €16-€18. **Credit** AmEx, DC, MC, V. **Map** p315 E4.
While this new 'tasting room' with lots of global eating and sipping options still had to prove itself as of press-time, its location conquers all: a wooden church – once the stable for Napoleon's horses – with the city's greatest terrace. Evaluate with a coffee.

Pygma-Lion

Nieuwe Spiegelstraat 5a (420 7022/www.pygma-lion. com). Tram 1, 2, 5. **Open** 11am-11pm Tue-Sun. *Kitchen* 11am-5pm, 6-10pm Tue-Sun. **Main courses** *Lunch* €5.50-€10. *Dinner* €18-€21. **Credit** AmEx, MC, V. **Map** p314 D4.
This South African restaurant is open all day for sandwiches, but it's only at dinner that the zebra, the crocodile and other oddities get thrown in the pot. History and geography have made this country's food an exotic blend of African, Asian and Dutch sensibilities. Quite pricey but nice.

Indonesian & Thai

Bojo

Lange Leidsedwarsstraat 51 (622 7434). Tram 1, 2, 5. **Open** 5pm-2am Mon-Thur, Sun; 5pm-4am Fri, Sat. **Main courses** €8-€12. **Credit** AmEx, MC, V. **Map** p314 C5.
Bojo is a fine Indo-eaterie, and one of the few places that stays open into the small hours. The price is right and the portions are large enough to glue your insides together before or after an evening of excess. Its sister operation at No.49 compensates for its earlier closing time by serving alcohol.

Puri Mas

Lange Leidsedwarsstraat 37-41 (627 7627/www. purimas.nl). Tram 1, 2, 5. **Open** 5-11pm daily. **Main courses** around €14. *Rice table* €18.50-€37.50. **Credit** AmEx, DC, MC, V. **Map** p314 C5.
Puri Mas has impeccable service and fine rice tables which, unlike most places, they offer to solo diners.

Tempo Doeloe

Utrechtsestraat 75 (625 6718/www.tempodoeloe restaurant.nl). Tram 4, 6, 7, 10. **Open** 6-11.30pm daily. **Main courses** €19.50-€25. *Rice table* €26.50-€35. **Credit** AmEx, DC, MC, V. **Map** p315 E4.

Eat, Drink, Shop

This cosy and rather classy Indonesian restaurant (heck, it even has white linen) is widely thought of as one of the city's best and spiciest purveyors of rice table, and not without good reason. Book ahead or, if you turn up on the off chance and find the place full, use neighbour Tujuh Maret (Utrechtsestraat 73, 427 9865, www.tujuh-maret.nl) as a tasty Plan B.

South American

Los Pilones
Kerkstraat 63 (320 4651/www.lospilones.nl). Tram 1, 2, 5, 11. **Open** 4pm-midnight Tue-Thur, Sun; 4pm-1am Fri, Sat. **Main courses** €10-€12.50. **Credit** AmEx, DC, MC, V. **Map** p314 D4.
A splendid Mexican cantina with an anarchic bent, Los Pilones is run by two young and friendly Mexican brothers; one of them does the cooking, so expect authentic grub rather than standard Tex-Mex fare. There are 35 – yes, 35 – tequilas on offer.

Jodenbuurt, the Plantage & the Oost

Global

De Kas
Kamerlingh Onneslaan 3 (462 4562/www.restaurant dekas.nl). Tram 9/bus 59, 69. **Open** noon-2pm, 6.30-10pm Mon-Sat. **Set menu** *at Bar* €25. *Lunch* 4 courses €32. *Dinner* 5 courses €43.50. **Credit** AmEx, DC, MC, V.
In Frankendael Park, way out east, is a renovated 1926 greenhouse. It's now a posh and peaceful restaurant that inspires much fevered talk among local foodies. Its international menu changes daily, based on what was harvested earlier in the day.

The Waterfront

French & Mediterranean

Wilhelmina-Dok
Noordwal 1 (632 3701/www.wilhelmina-dok.nl). Take the ferry from behind Centraal Station to Ijplein-Meeuwenlaan. **Open** noon-midnight Mon-Thur, Sun; noon-1am Fri, Sat. *Kitchen* 6-10pm daily. **Main courses** *Lunch* €3.75-€8.50. *Dinner* €15-€18. **Credit** AmEx, MC, V.
Through the large windows of this cubic building you get great views of the eastern docklands. Come for soup and sandwiches by day and a daily menu of Mediterranean dishes by night. DJs, terrace and an open-air cinema spice it up in summer.

Global

11
Oosterdokskade 3-5, 11th Floor (625 5999/www. ilove11.com). Walk from Centraal Station. **Open** 11am-midnight Sun-Wed, 11am-4am Thur-Sat; *kitchen* 11am-10pm. **Main courses** *Lunch* €4-€9. *Dinner* 4-courses €30. **No credit cards.** **Map** p311 E1.
This vertical wonder on the top of Post CS (*see p107* **View to the future**) is very un-Amsterdam. While acting as the Stedelijk café by day with soups, salads and sandwiches, its celeb chefs offer a fixed globe-hopping four-course dinner in the evening before the whole place evolves into a club by night (*see p229*). Book ahead and do it before 2007, when the whole place is closing down.

Fifteen
Jollemanhof 9 (0900 343 8336/www.fifteen.nl). Tram 16, 26. **Open** 4-11pm daily. **Set menu** €42.50. **No credit cards.** **Map** p311 F1.

positive eating + positive living

max euweplein 10
1017 mb amsterdam
telephone +31 (0) 20 528 7778

opening hours:
sunday – wednesday 12noon-10pm / thursday – saturday 12noon-11pm

world trade centre
zuidplein 12 1077 xv amsterdam
telephone +31 (0) 20 620 3032

opening hours:
monday – friday : 11.30am-9pm

for menu visit: www.wagamama.com
uk ı dublin ı amsterdam ı australia ı dubai

While Jamie Oliver has only found one gap in his hectic TV and cooking schedule to visit the Amsterdam outpost of his culinary empire, yet this franchise of sorts – complete with TV show that documented the transformation of challenged street kids into a well-oiled kitchen brigade – is inspired by his love for dishes honest and fresh. The beautiful and massive waterfront location is marred by the bogus graffiti and the fact that there's only one set menu. We think it's downright cheeky having a premium rate number as the only telephone contact.

Kilimanjaro

Rapenburgerplein 6 (622 3485). Bus 22, 43. **Open** *5-10pm Tue-Sun.* **Main courses** €10-€18. **Credit** AmEx, MC, DC, V. **Map** p311 F2.

This relaxed and friendly pan-African eaterie offers an assortment of traditional recipes from Senegal, the Ivory Coast, Tanzania and Ethiopia. Once you've eaten your way from the east coast through to the west coast of Africa, you'll probably need some serious refreshment, in the cooling form of the fruitiest of cocktails and the strongest of beers.

Son of a beach, that's tasty!

Being 25 kilometres (15 miles) from the sea, Amsterdam was hardly anyone's choice for a beach holiday until sand was tipped on the artificial islands of IJburg where 45,000 people will come to live. While construction continues, the vast expanses of sand and surrounding fresh water lake are being exploited for their surreal beach-like properties. The restaurant/bar Blijburg – which has a regular programme of barbecues, bands and DJs – is on hand to cater to your eating/drinking whims. (Or you can picnic...)

Equally visionary is Amsterdam Plage (www.amsterdamplage.nl), which has set up sandy shop in various locations around the Western docklands. They usually serve snacks, tapas and a three-course Mediterranean menu at weekends, when the party vibe is enhanced by groove-oriented DJs. Check out the website to discover their ever-changing locations.

From April 2005, Plage will have competition in the Houthavens. This area has been re-invented as a temporary student village, housing 1,000 in a former cruise ship and redundant containers. Set to operate year-round, Strand West (www.strandwest.nl) will begin by spreading 20,000 square metres of sand on which are to be built a café-restaurant and sports- and kid-friendly areas.

Already established as ultimately child-friendly, NEMO Summertime (531 3233, www.nemosummertime.nl) takes place every July and August on the sloping roof of the NEMO science and tech museum (*see p108*). Children go nuts building sandcastles and splashing around in the built-in waterfall. Come the night, things change: DJs, tapas, BBQ nights, salsa nights and the fruitiest of exotic cocktails... The programme varies so call first or check the website.

More shipyard than beach, one can still enjoy a similar relaxing vibe at the NDSM arts complex (*see p250*) by visiting the charming wasteland-as-wonderland café/restaurant De Houten Kop. It offers a quirky meat, fish or vegetarian menu. Figuring that it's winter more than it's summer in the Netherlands, they improved the insulation by building bales of straw over the premises. DJs and bands often add to the atmosphere at weekends. With such a middle-of-nowhere feel, it's hard to believe you are but a ten-minute ferry ride from Centraal Station.

You can also try your luck at the squatty-vibed Buitenland (www.buitenland.org), one of the few remaining 'free zones' near Amsterdam, and home to regular family affairs on summer weekends, when a changing roster of talented cooks provides the eats while DJs play the tunes. And if the weather permits, there's a lake to swim in – making this the only place besides Blijburg where swimming is feasible.

But remember: most of these places tend to be as transient as the sand they are found on, so be sure to check ahead. You can opt to visit the real thing at Bloemendaal or Wijk Aan Zee (*see p232*). And if beaches don't really float your boat, then you can always climb aboard Odessa (*see p150*) or the very posh Supperclub Cruise (*see p128*)....

Blijburg

Bert Haanstrakade 2004, IJburg (416 0330/ www.blijburg.nl). Tram 26/bus 326. **Open** *Summer 10am-10pm daily. Winter 10am-10pm Thur-Sun.* **Main courses** €5-€15. **No credit cards**.

De Houten Kop

TT Neveritaweg 15, NDSM-werf (062 749 2690/www.dehoutenkop.nl). Ferry from behind Centraal Station. **Open** *11am-11pm Tue-Thur, Sun; 11am-3am Fri; 11am-1am Sat.* **Main courses** €3-€10. **No credit cards**.

Eat, Drink, Shop

Give grease a chance

The correct local terminology for a greasy snack – *vette hap* – can be translated literally as 'fat bite', which says a lot for the honesty of the Dutch when it comes to the less healthy spectrum of belly-ballast. And honestly, why go to a multinational burger merchant when there's such a rich local grease tradition to indulge in? After all, variety is not only the spice but the lubricant of life.

The best chips

Vleminckx *Voetboogsteeg 31, Old Centre: New Side (no phone). Tram 1, 2, 5.* **Open** 11am-6pm Mon-Sat; noon-5.30pm Sun. **No credit cards. Map** p314 D4.
Chunky Belgian (*Vlaamse*) potatoey goodness served with your pick of toppings. Go for *oorlog* (war): chips with mayo, spicy peanut sauce and onions.

The best 'ball'

Het Koffiekeldertje *Frederiksplein 4, Southern Canal Belt (626 3424). Tram 4, 6, 7, 10.* **Open** 9am-5pm Mon-Fri. **No credit cards. Map** p315 F4.
A large melts-in-your-mouth ground-beef sphere served on a bun, and with a smile, in a charming basement café. Watch your head.

The best pancake

Pancake Bakery *Prinsengracht 191, the Jordaan (625 1333/www.pancake.nl). Tram 13, 17.* **Open** noon-9.30pm daily. **Main courses** €5-€10. **Credit** AmEx, MC, V. **Map** p310 C2.
Dutch recipes stress the importance of sheer density so that the pancake can hold a dense array of toppings, from sweet to hardcore savouries like bacon and cheese.

The best steak

Eetcafé Loetje *Johannes Vermeerstraat 52, Museum District (662 8173). Tram 16.* **Open** 11am-1am Mon-Fri; 5.30pm-1am Sat. *Kitchen* 11am-10pm Mon-Fri; 6-10pm Sat. **Main courses** €5-€18. **No credit cards. Map** p314 D6.
After a day's tourism there's nothing better than beef steak served with fries and mayo. A fine antidote to the rarefied air you may have inhaled while gazing at a Rembrandt.

The best *kroket*

Van Dobben *Korte Reguliersdwarsstraat 5-9, Southern Canal Belt (624 4200). Tram 4, 9, 16, 24, 25.* **Open** 9.30am-1am Mon-Thur;

9.30am-2am Fri, Sat; 11.30am-8pm Sun. **Main courses** €2-€8. **No credit cards. Map** p315 E4.
A *kroket* is a version of a croquette: a mélange of meat and potato with a crusty, deep-fried skin best served on a bun with lotsa hot mustard. And while this 1945-vintage late-nighter is the uncontested champion, you can also find a more refined shrimp *kroket* nearby at famous bakery Holtkamp (Vijzelgracht 15, 624 8757).

The best all-round grease merchant

Febo *Venues across town (www.febo.nl).*
Grease goes space age at the Febo (pronounced 'Fay-bo') automats: you put your change into a glowing hole in the wall and, in exchange, get a dollop of grease in the form of a hot(-ish) hamburger, *kroket*, *bamibal* (a deep-fried noodle-y ball of vaguely Indonesian origin) or a *kaas* soufflé (a cheese treat that's surprisingly tasty if eaten when still hot).

Odessa

Veemkade 259 (419 3010/www.de-odessa.nl).
Tram 10, 26/bus 26. **Open** *Apr-Nov* noon-1am Mon-Thur, Sun; noon-3am Fri, Sat. *Dec-Mar* 4pm-1am
Mon-Thur, Sun; 4pm-3am Fri, Sat. *Kitchen* 6-9.30pm
Mon-Thur, Sun; 6-11pm Fri, Sat. **Main courses**
€15-€21. **Set menu** 3 courses €27.50. **Credit**
AmEx, MC, V.

Hipsters make the trek to the unlikely environs of a
Ukrainian fishing boat for the fusion food and the
revamped interior. The vibe is 1970s James Bond fil-
tered through a modern lounge sensibility. On
warmer nights, dine on the funkily lit deck, while
DJs spin from 10pm at weekends. On Sundays,
between 5pm and midnight, you can walk the plank
to neighbours Lizboa (419 1338/www.lizboa.nl) who
open for cheap booze, tapas and live music.

The Jordaan

Cafés & snack stops

Small World Catering

Binnen Oranjestraat 14 (420 2774/www.smallworld
catering.nl). Bus 18, 22. **Open** 10.30am-8pm Tue-
Sat; noon-8pm Sun. **Main courses** €6-€10. **No**
credit cards. **Map** p309 B2.

The home base for this catering company is a tiny
deli, which feels like the kitchen of the lovely proprietor. Besides superlative coffee and fresh juices,
enjoy salads, lasagne and sublime sandwiches.

Dutch & Belgian

Amsterdam

Watertorenplein 6 (682 2666/www.cradam.nl). Tram
10. **Open** 11am-midnight Mon-Thur, Sun; 11am-1am
Fri, Sat. *Kitchen* 11am-10.30pm Mon-Thur, Sun;
11am-11.30pm Fri, Sat. **Main courses** €10-€16.50.
Credit AmEx, DC, MC, V.

This spacious monument to industry just west of the
Jordaan pumped water from the coast's dunes for
around a century. Now it pumps out honest Dutch
and French dishes – from *krokets* to caviar – under
a mammoth ceiling and floodlighting rescued from
the old Ajax stadium. It's a truly unique – and child-
friendly – experience.

Moeder's Pot

Vinkenstraat 119 (623 7643). Tram 3, 10. **Open** 5-
9.30pm Mon-Sat. **Main courses** €4-€11. **No credit**
cards. **Map** p309 B1.

Mother's Pot serves up – you guessed it – the sort
of simple and honest fare a Dutchman would expect
to get from his mum. The decor is woody farmer's
kitsch, and the grub's not bad at all.

French & Mediterranean

Balthazar's Keuken

Elandsgracht 108 (420 2114/www.balthazarskeuken.
nl). Tram 7, 10. **Open** 6-11pm Wed-Fri. **Set menu**
€23.50. **Credit** AmEx, DC, MC, V. **Map** p314 C4.

This tiny restaurant is always packed tight. So you
really need to book ahead to make sure of enjoying
its excellent set menu of meat or fish.

Bordewijk

Noordermarkt 7 (624 3899). Tram 3. **Open** 6.30-
10.30pm Tue-Sun. **Set menu** €37-€49. **Credit**
AmEx, DC, MC, V. **Map** p309 B2.

Ideal for sampling some of the city's finest original
food and palate-tingling wines in a designery interior. The service and atmosphere are both relaxed,
and Bordewijk has a very reliable kitchen. A perfectly balanced restaurant.

Cinema Paradiso

Westerstraat 186 (623 7344). Tram 10. **Open**
6-11pm Tue-Sun. **Main courses** €14-€20. **Credit**
AmEx, DC, V. **Map** p309 B2.

This Italian purveyor of fine pizza and even finer
antipasti is agreeably situated in a former cinema
and loved by the fashionista crowd. There's a bit of
an echo, and their no-reservation policy sometimes
makes for a long wait by the bar.

Duende

Lindengracht 62 (420 6692/www.cafeduende.nl).
Tram 3, 10. **Open** 4pm-1am Mon-Thur, Sun; 4pm-
3am Fri, Sat. **Tapas** €2.50-€10. **Credit** AmEx, MC.
Map p309 B2.

Get a taste of Andalusia with the good tapas at
Duende. Place your order at the bar and prepare to
share your table with an amorous couple or a fla-
menco dancer who might offer you free lessons
before getting up to stamp and strut. There are performances every Saturday night (11pm).

Toscanini

Lindengracht 75 (623 2813/www.toscanini.nu).
Tram 3, 10. **Open** 6-10.30pm Mon-Sat. **Main**
courses €17.50-€19. **Credit** AmEx, DC, MC, V.
Map p309 B2.

The authentic and invariably excellent Italian food
at this bustling spot is prepared in an open kitchen.
Don't go expecting pizza, but do make sure that you
book early (from 3pm) if you want to get a table.

Yam-Yam

Frederik Hendrikstraat 90 (681 5097/www.yam
yam.nl). Tram 3. **Open** 6-10pm Tue-Sun. **Main**
courses €7-€15. **No credit cards.** **Map** p309 A3.

Unparalleled and inexpensive pastas and pizzas in
a hip and casual atmosphere: no wonder Yam-Yam
is a favourite of clubbers and locals alike. Well worth
the trip west of the Jordaan after booking.

Global

Nomads

Rozengracht 133 (344 6401/www.restaurantnomads.
nl). Tram 13, 14, 17. **Open** 7pm-1am Tue-Thur,
Sun; 7pm-3am Fri, Sat. **Mezzes** €3-€8. **Set menu**
€42.50. **Credit** AmEx, DC, MC, V. **Map** p309 B3.

With a wonderfully evocative decor of curtains,
mosaics and marbles, Nomads (from the people who

Eat, Drink, Shop

Killer Comedy and Fantastic Food!

Welcome to...

BOOM CHI-CA-GOOOOOO!

Boom Chicago is hard-hitting, in-your-face, intensely energetic improv and sketches that never lose a beat. But don't believe us... here's the word on the street

★ ★ ★ ★ ★ Kill to get a ticket!" The Scotsman

"They are smart, fast, loud, irreverent...and serve suprisingly good food" The Wall Street Journal

" It's fun, fast and very, very clever. Miss them at your peril." The Independent

"Big Talents turn in a very funny show!" Chicago Tribune

"Innovative, multimedia-driven, improv wizardry... dynamic, and intensely funny." Backstage

For dinner reservations, tickets and info: www.boomchicago.nl or call +31 (0) 20 . 423 01 01

brought you Supperclub; *see p128*) has taken lounging back to its oriental roots. After 11pm, it's time for drinking, dancing or some more lounging.

Semhar

Marnixstraat 259-261 (638 1634/www.semhar.nl).
Tram 10. **Open** 4-10pm daily. **Main courses**
€10.50-€14. **Credit** MC, V. **Map** p309 B3.
A great spot to sample the *injera*-based (a type of pancake) and veggie-friendly food of Ethiopia (best washed down with a calabash of beer) after an afternoon spent wandering the Jordaan.

Indian

Balraj

Haarlemmerdijk 28 (625 1428/www.balraj.nl). Tram
3. **Open** 4.30-11pm daily. **Main courses** €9-€13.
No credit cards. Map p309 B2.
A small, cosy eating house with several decades of experience. The food is reasonably priced and well done, with vegetarians generously catered for.

Vegetarian

De Vliegende Schotel

Nieuwe Leliestraat 162 (625 2041/www.vliegende
schotel.com). Tram 13, 14, 17. **Open** 4-11.30pm
daily. *Kitchen* 4-10.45pm daily. **Main courses**
€8.50-€10.50. **Credit** AmEx, MC, V. **Map** p309 B3.
The venerable Flying Saucer serves up a splendid array of dishes, buffet style. If it's booked up, the nearby De Bolhoed (Prinsengracht 60-62, 626 1803) offers hearty vegan dishes as a consolation prize.

The Museum Quarter, Vondelpark & the South

Café & snack stops

Bagels & Beans

Van Baerlestraat 40 (675 7050/www.bagelsbeans.nl).
Tram 3, 5, 12. **Open** 8.30am-6pm Mon-Fri; 9am-
6pm Sat; 10am-6pm Sun. **Main courses** €3-€5.
Credit AmEx, DC, MC, V. **Map** p315 E6.
An Amsterdam success story, this branch of B&B has a wonderfully peaceful back patio. Perfect for an economical breakfast, lunch or snack; sun-dried tomatoes are employed with particular skill.
Other locations: Ferdinand Bolstraat 70 (672 1610);
Keizersgracht 504 (330 5508).

Fish

Vis aan de Schelde

Scheldeplein 4 (675 1583/www.visaandeschelde.nl).
Tram 5, 25. **Open** *Lunch* noon-2.30pm Mon-Fri.
Dinner 5.30-11pm daily. **Main courses** €23.50-€38.
Credit AmEx, DC, MC, V.
This eaterie out near the RAI convention centre has become a fish temple for the connoisseur. French favourites collide with Thai fish fondue.

French & Mediterranean

Eetcafé I Kriti

Balthasar Floriszstraat 3 (664 1445/ www.ikriti.nl).
Tram 3, 5, 12, 16. **Open** 5pm-1am Mon-Thur, Sun;
5pm-3am Fri, Sat. **Main courses** €12-€16. **Credit**
DC, V.
Eat, and party, Greek style in this evocation of Crete, where a standard choice of dishes is lovingly prepared. Bouzouki-picking legends drop in on occasion and pump up the frenzied atmosphere, further boosted by plate-lobbing antics. Nearby, De Greikse Taverna (Hobbemakade 64-5, 671 7923, 6pm-midnight daily) may lack plates but competes on taste.

Le Garage

Ruysdaelstraat 54-6 (679 7176/www.restaurant
legarage.nl). Tram 3, 5, 6, 12, 16. **Open** *Lunch*
noon-2pm Mon-Fri. *Dinner* 6-11pm daily. **Set menu**
2 courses €39.50; 3 courses €49.50. **Credit** AmEx,
DC, MC, V. **Map** p315 E6.
Don your glad rags to blend in at this fashionable brasserie, which is great for emptying your wallet while watching a selection of Dutch glitterati do exactly the same. The authentic French regional cuisine – and 'worldly' versions thereof – is pretty good. They also have a more loungey sister establishment, En Pluche (Ruysdaelstraat 48, 471 4695), next door.

Pulpo

Willemsparkweg 87 (676 0700/www.restaurant-
pulpo.nl). Tram 2. **Open** noon-midnight Mon-Sat.
Kitchen noon-3pm; 5.30-10pm Mon-Sat. **Main**
courses €12-€18. **Set menu** €26. **Credit** AmEx,
DC, MC, V. **Map** p314 C6.
Pulpo serves original, well-priced Mediterranean food – including a killer polenta and a mighty fine selection of wines to wash it down with – to diners who are looking for trendy surrounds, complete with a hipster lounge soundtrack and shaggy walls.

Global

De Peperwortel

Overtoom 140 (685 1053/www.peperwortel.nl).
Tram 1, 6, 7, 10. **Open** 4-9pm daily. **Main courses**
€5-€10.50. **No credit cards. Map** 310 C6.
One could survive for weeks on take-aways from Riaz (*see p140*) and the Pepper Root. After all, a range of dishes that embraces Dutch, Mexican, Indian and Spanish cuisines is not hard graft.

Vakzuid

Olympisch Stadion 35 (570 8400/www.vakzuid.nl).
Tram 16, 24/bus 15, 23. **Open** 10am-1am Mon-
Thur; 10am-3am Fri; 4pm-3am Sat; 3-10pm Sun.
Kitchen noon-3pm, 6-10.30pm daily. **Main courses**
Lunch €6-€13. *Dinner* €12-€27. **Credit** AmEx, DC,
MC, V.
Vakzuid, with its view over the Olympic Stadium and modish cons, is popular with working trendies. Thursday to Saturday nights it transforms into a club, with Sundays child-friendly.

Sushi for the masses at **Albert Cuypmarkt**. *See p180.*

Indonesian & Thai

Djago

Scheldeplein 18 (664 2013). Tram 4. **Open** 5-9.30pm Mon-Fri, Sun. **Main courses** €7.40-€23. **Credit** AmEx, DC, MC, V.

Djago's West Javanese eats are praised to the hilt by Indo-obsessives. Set near the RAI convention centre, it's a bit out of the way, but worth the trip south.

Middle Eastern

Paloma Blanca

JP Heyestraat 145 (612 6485). Tram 7. **Open** 6-10pm Mon-Wed; 5pm-midnight Fri-Sun. **Main courses** €7-15. **No credit cards**.

This is the place for consumers of couscous. The surroundings are simple and there's no alcohol.

South American

Riaz

Bilderdijkstraat 193 (683 6453). Tram 3, 7, 12, 17. **Open** noon-9pm Mon-Fri; 2-9pm Sun. **Main courses** €5-€14. **No credit cards**. **Map** p313 B5.

Amsterdam's finest Surinamese restaurant is where Ruud Gullit scores his rotis when he's in town.

Vegetarian

De Peper

Overtoom 301 (779 4913/http://squat.net/overtoom 301). Tram 1, 6. **Open** 8pm-1am Thur; 9pm-1am Fri; 6pm-1am Sun. **No credit cards**. **Map** p313 B6.

The purveyor of the cheapest and best vegetarian food in town has found a new home in this 'breeding ground' located in 0T301 (*see p199*). De Peper is a collectively organised, non-profit project combining culture with kitchen. Thursdays has a lounge bar night with vegan snacks, Fridays has DJs and sushi, and Sundays combine dinner and cabaret (for which book from 2pm on 412 2954).

The Pijp

Cafés & snack stops

De Taart van m'n Tante

Ferdinand Bolstraat 10 (776 4600/www.detaart.nl). Tram 16, 24, 25. **Open** 10am-6pm daily. **Average** €2.20-€5. **No credit cards**. **Map** p315 E6.

My Aunt's Cake started life as a purveyor of over-the-top cakes (which they still make) before becoming the campest tea-room in town. In a glowing pink space filled with mismatched furniture, it's particularly gay-friendly (note the Tom of Finland cake).

Chinese & Japanese

Albine

Albert Cuypstraat 69 (675 5135). Tram 16, 24, 25. **Open** 10.30am-10pm Tue-Sun. **Main courses** €4-€12. **No credit cards**. **Map** p315 E6.

One in a whole row of cheap Suri-Chin-Indo spots, Albine – where a Chinese influence predominates – gets top marks for its lightning service and solid vegetarian or meat meals of roti, rice or noodles.

Balkan food comes in huge heaps, as does the hospitality. Surrender to the grilled selections and the *slivovic*, a plummy and poetic hard liquor that will have you hymning the frog's legs and snails.

Bazar

Albert Cuypstraat 182 (675 0544/www.hotel bazar.nl). Tram 16, 24, 25. **Open** 8am-1am Sun-Thur, 9am-2am Fri-Sat. **Main courses** *Breakfast/lunch* €3-€8. *Dinner* €8-€13.90. **Credit** AmEx, DC, MC, V. **Map** p315 F5.

If you can't find Bazar, look up at the sky and search there for the angel. This former church, now downgraded to an Arabic-kitsch café, is one of the glories of Albert Cuypmarkt (*see p180*). While yet to open at the time of going to press, we want to believe that, if they stick to the winning formula set by its Rotterdam mothership, it will become a proper temple to gastronomy. Expect to find a menu that travels the world but lingers long and lovingly in the environs of North Africa.

Mamouche

Quellijnstraat 104 (673 6361) Tram 3, 12, 24, 25. **Open** 6.30-10.30pm Tue-Sun. **Main courses** €15-€20. **Credit** AmEx, DC, MC, V. **Map** p315 E5.

In the heart of the multicultural Pijp is a new Moroccan restaurant with a difference: it's posh, stylish (in a sexy minimalist sort of way) and provides groovy background music that can only be described as 'North African lounge'.

Indian

Balti House

Albert Cuypstraat 41 (470 8917). Tram 6, 7, 10, 16, 24, 25. **Open** 5-11pm daily. **Main courses** €10.50-€13.50. **Credit** AmEx, MC, V. **Map** p315 E6.

Balti and tandoori dishes at Amsterdam's only balti house come in big portions, which are mildly seasoned to suit the average Dutch palate. But ask for hotter and you shall receive.

Indonesian & Thai

Siriphon

1e Jacob van Campenstraat 47 (676 8072). Tram 6, 7, 10. **Open** 3-10.30pm daily. **Main courses** €8-€14. **Credit** MC, V. **Map** p315 E5.

A small comfy Thai with a green kaeng khiaw curry that's positively to die for and many other dishes that are worthy of at least a culinary coma.

Warung Spang-Makandra

Gerard Doustraat 39 (670 5081). Tram 6, 7, 10, 16. **Open** 11am-10pm Tue-Sat; 1-10pm Sun. **Main courses** €2-€5. **No credit cards**. **Map** p315 E6.

An Indonesian-Surinamese restaurant where the Indo influence always comes up trumps with their addictive Javanese rames. The decor is kept properly simple, but the relaxed vibe and beautifully presented dishes will make you want to sit down and linger over a meal rather than taking it away.

Yamazato

Okura Hotel, Ferdinand Bolstraat 333 (678 8351/ www.okura.nl). Tram 12, 25. **Open** 7.30-9.30am, noon-2pm, 6-9.30pm daily. **Main courses** €25-€37. **Set menu** €25-€70. **Credit** AmEx, DC, MC, V.

If you want class, head out here and surrender to the charming kimono-clad staff, the too-neat-to-eat presentation and the restful views over a fishpond.

Zen

Frans Halsstraat 38 (627 0607). Tram 16, 24, 25. **Open** noon-8pm Tue-Sat. *Kitchen* noon-7.30pm Tue-Sat. **Main courses** €7-€19. **No credit cards**. **Map** p315 E6.

This Japanese delicatessen with limited seating lives up to its name: calm, friendly and delicious.

French & Mediterranean

District V

Van der Helstplein 17 (770 0884). Tram 12, 25. **Open** 6pm-1am daily. **Set menu** 3 courses €28.50. **No credit cards**. **Map** p315 F6.

District V not only offers a good and economical French-inspired, daily menu, but sells the locally designed plates, cutlery and tables it is served on. The patio is a lovely spot to sit in summer.

Global

Aleksandar

Ceintuurbaan 196 (676 6384). Tram 3. **Open** 5-10pm daily. **Main courses** €16-€31. **No credit cards**. **Map** p315 E6.

Bars

The beer necessities.

De Bekeerde Suster. *See p143*.

While crawling around Amsterdam's bars a visitor may find time to question that other type of Dutch cap, frothing at the top of his glass. But rest assured: there's a rationale behind serving beer with two fingers of foam on top (*see p151* **AmsterBarflying for Rummies**). Also never failing to take visitors by surprise is the inherent slow service. Whilst Haarlem might be just up the road, this ain't New York.

However, muster patience and you'll discover that Amsterdam's canals run with gold, and that's even before the nocturnal stagger home when so often the waters internal and external are joined. After all, the Dutch built this city on beer and its bars reflect that in their variety. Most common is the *bruin café* or brown bar, so called because over the years, nicotine has stained their walls. Wood, warmth and well-worn *gezelligheid* (a uniquely Dutch brand of social cosiness) typify the best. They usually have a good range of local and national brews, but uncompromising enthusiasts should head to specialist purveyors such as **'t Arendsnest** or **In de Wildeman** (for both, *see p147*). For fine, locally-produced beer, take a trip to **De Bekeerde Suster** (*see p143*) or **Brouwerij 't**

IJ (*see p150*). However, there's much more to Amsterdam's bars than boozing. Some simply ooze history, like **In 't Aepjen** (*see p144*) or **In de Waag** (*see p143*). Others preserve an important Dutch tradition. For instance, a *proeflokaal* (a tasting house) specialises in *jenever* (a gin-like spirit made from juniper berries), *brandewijn* (literally, burnt – or distilled – wine) and other old Dutch liquors. The best place to get a taste for tasting houses is undoubtedly **Wynand Fockink** (*see p144*).

Recent years have seen a trend towards lounge bar louche and the emergence of DJ bars such as **Café Tetra** (*see p145*), **Twstd** (*see p149*), **Café Vaaghuyzen** (*see p145*), and **Vibing** (*see p149*). But thankfully, other types of bar – geared towards the political, literary, musical, trad or mad – are still out there.

Outdoor terraces – which enhance the drinking experience – abound for the larger part of the year (many are heated in an effort to stave off winter's approach) – but leave the city looking a little desolate in the colder months. But don't despair: it's the ideal time to hole up in a bar with a hot chocolate and whisky and discover the true meaning of *gezilligheid*.

The Old Centre

The Old Side

De Bekeerde Suster
*Kloveniersburgwal 6-8 (423 0112/www.beiaard
groep.nl). Tram 4, 9, 14, 16, 24, 25.* **Open**
4pm-1am Mon; noon-1am Tue-Thur; 11am-2am Fri,
Sat; noon-midnight Sun. **Credit** AmEx, DC, MC, V.
Map p310 D3.
In 1544 nuns, determined not to let their monkish
brethren have all the fun, began producing beer at
the cloisters on this site. But in this case it really was
medicinal, the drinking water was that bad. And –
praise the Lord – 'The Converted Sister' still produces beer: taps on the bar connect to huge copper
vats of the stuff. They serve decent 'pub grub' too.

De Buurvrouw
*St Pieterspoortsteeg 29 (625 9654/www.
debuurvrouw.nl). Tram 4, 9, 14, 16, 24, 25.*
Open 9pm-3am Mon-Thur; 9pm-4am Fri-Sun.
No credit cards. Map p310 D3.
A lively and popular, late-night alternative haunt
notable for its sawdust-strewn floor and quirky art.
DJs spin regularly and there's occasional live music,
offbeat performances and pool competitions.

Café Cuba
*Nieuwmarkt 3 (627 4919). Tram 4, 9, 14, 16,
24, 25/Metro Nieuwmarkt.* **Open** 1pm-1am Mon-
Thur, Sun; 1pm-3am Fri, Sat. **No credit cards.**
Map p310 D2.
One of the Nieuwmarkt square's most beautiful
cafés, Café Cuba is spacious and lively with plenty
of snug seating. Black and white photos of the communist country and posters of Che Guevara adorn
the walls. But most importantly, they never skimp
on the mint in their wicked Mojito cocktails. Ernest
Hemingway would have loved it.

Café Fonteyn
*Nieuwmarkt 13-15 (422 3599). Tram 4, 9, 14, 16,
24, 25/Metro Nieuwmarkt.* **Open** 10am-1am Mon-
Thur, Sun; 10am-3am Fri, Sat. **No credit cards.**
Map p310 D2.
The 'Fountain' sprinkles a warm, home-from-home
feel through its drawing room interior. Local customers devour the dailies and the decent cooked
breakfasts. The only dampener is the busker traffic
on their doorstep – and in your face – during the
summer. Still, the heated terrace allows for late-night
conversations on nippy evenings when the noise-
mongers are elsewhere, drinking the day's takings.

Captein & Co
*Binnen Bantammerstraat 27 (627 8804). Tram 4, 9,
14, 16, 24, 25/Metro Nieuwmarkt.* **Open** 4pm-1am
Mon-Thur; 4pm-2am Fri; noon-midnight Sat, Sun.
No credit cards. Map p311 E2.
Had enough of Nieuwmarkt? Take a trip off the
tourist tram lines to a peaceful locals' haven, order
a beer and settle down on the terrace. *Proost!*

De Diepte
*St Pieterspoortsteeg 3-5 (06 29 00 59 26 mobile).
Tram 4, 9, 14, 16, 24, 25.* **Open** 10pm-3am Mon-
Thur, Sun; 10pm-4am Fri, Sat. **No credit cards.**
Map p310 D3.
Its name – the Depth – refers to the bowels of damna-
tion. In this unholy hole, with its walls seemingly on
fire, you can toss back beers to DJs mixing a soundtrack of randy rockabilly, snotty punk and filthy
rock 'n' roll. We don't know what Dante would have
thought, but hell has never seemed so *gezellig*.

Engelbewaarder
*Kloveniersburgwal 59 (625 3772). Tram 4, 9, 14,
16, 24, 25/Metro Nieuwmarkt.* **Open** noon-1am
Mon-Thur; noon-3am Fri, Sat; 2pm-1am Sun.
Credit MC, V. **Map** p310 D3.
Popular with quasi-academics and beer lovers enjoying the fine brews or those simply admiring the
views from the huge picture windows. Live jazz
brightens Sundays from 4.30-7pm.

't Hoekje
*Krom Boomssloot 47 (622 8131). Metro
Nieuwmarkt.* **Open** 4-11pm Mon-Thur, Sun; 4pm-
1am Fri, Sat. **No credit cards. Map** p311 E2.
Five women run this charming little bar, which still
retains its 1929 art deco fittings and beautifully tiled
mosaic floor. There's delicious bar food (with lots of
choice for vegetarians) and a varied wine list.

In de Waag
*Nieuwmarkt 4 (422 7772/www.indewaag.nl). Tram
4, 9, 14, 16, 24, 25/Metro Nieuwmarkt.* **Open**
10am-midnight daily. **Credit** AmEx, DC, MC, V.
Map p310 D2.
The building is imposing and the terrace uninspir-
ing, but walk through the doors of this former weigh
house (*see p85*) and you'll be wafted back in time:
there's no music here – piped or otherwise – and candles are the only lighting. However, the price of the
beer remains all too contemporary.

The best ## Bars

Blauwe Theehuis
Vondelpark's best-kept secret. *See p152.*

Café Cuba
Commie heaven. *See above.*

Suite
Sweet lounging. *See p147.*

Wynand Fockink
Charming, evocative and romantic.
See p144.

Wolvenstraat
A haven for hedonists. *See p148.*

Eat, Drink, Shop

In 't Aepjen

Zeedijk 1 (626 8401). Tram 4, 9, 14, 16, 24, 25.
Open 3pm-1am Mon-Thur, Sun; 3pm-3am Fri, Sat.
No credit cards. Map p310 D2.
Located in one of the oldest wooden houses in town
(it dates from 1550, although the ground floor is 19th
Century), this is a terrific bar. The name – 'In the
Monkeys' – comes from when Zeedijk was fre-
quented by sailors: those who couldn't pay their bills
in what was then a lodging house would settle up
by handing over a monkey from the Dutch East
Indies, sailors being inveterate animal collectors.
(Note: apes are no longer legal tender.) *See p33.*

Kapitein Zeppos

*Gebed Zonder End 5 (624 2057/www.zeppos.nl).
Tram 4, 9, 14, 16, 24, 25.* **Open** 11am-1am Mon-
Thur; 11am-2am Fri, Sat; noon-1am Sun. **Credit**
AmEx, MC, V. **Map** p310 D3.
Once used for storing horse-carriages and as a cigar
factory, Kapitein Zeppos has retained a seductive
olde worlde feel. Hidden away down a narrow alley-
way, with a terrace glittering with fairy lights and
a conservatory-style restaurant, it's quite a find.
There's live music every Wednesday from 10pm.

Lime

*Zeedijk 104 (639 3020). Tram 4, 9, 14, 16, 24, 25/
Metro Nieuwmarkt.* **Open** 5pm-1am Mon-Thur,
Sun; 5pm-3am Fri, Sat. **Credit** AmEx, MC, V.
Map p310 D2.
Snuggling up to the Buddhist temple next door, the
minimalist Lime is the trendiest bar in this area.
However, it's also surprisingly unpretentious. The
music is upbeat, the cocktails are fab, service is
attentive and it's particularly popular with locals in
the evening as a pre-club destination.

The Tara

*Rokin 85-89 (421 2654/www.thetara.com). Tram 4,
9, 14, 16, 24, 25.* **Open** 10am-1am Mon-Thur, Sun;
11am-3am Fri, Sat. *Kitchen* 10am-10pm daily. **Credit**
AmEx, MC, V. **Map** p310 D3.

Huge, yet surprisingly intimate, this cosmopolitan
Irish venue has three bars, two pool tables and a couple of log fires. DJs play at weekends, there's regular live music, the food is superb, and TVs – mainly
screening football – remain unobtrusive to the non-
fan. The best Irish pub in town and also, incidentally, where the German Expressionist artist, Max
Beckman, lived (at No.85) between 1937-1947.

't Tuinfeest

*Geldersekade 109 (620 8864). Tram 4, 9, 14, 16,
24, 25/Metro Nieuwmarkt.* **Open** 4pm-1am Mon-
Thur, Sun; 4pm-3am Fri, Sat. **Credit** AmEx, MC, V.
Map p310 D2.
This 'Garden Party' is almost as popular as the ones
at Buckingham Palace, but you don't need an invi-
tation to try the delicious, well-presented food at
decent prices. The music is turned up loud to appeal
to its young crowd, but somehow manages the trick
of not being too obtrusive.

VOC Café

*Schreierstoren, Prins Hendrikkade 94-5 (428
8291/www.schreierstoren.nl). Tram 4, 9, 14, 16,
24, 25.* **Open** 10am-6pm Mon; 10am-1am Tue-
Thur; 10am-3am Fri, Sat; noon-8pm Sun. **Credit**
V. **Map** p310 D2.
Housed in the city's oldest defence tower, the
Schreierstoren (*see p33*), the VOC Café has two ter-
races overlooking Geldersekade, a faux-historic inte-
rior plus a good range of *jenevers* and liqueurs: try
De Zeedijker Schoot An, which is brewed to an old
East India Company recipe.

Wynand Fockink

*Pijlsteeg 31 (639 2695/www.wynand-fockink.nl).
Tram 4, 9, 14, 16, 24, 25.* **Open** 3-9pm daily.
No credit cards. Map p310 D3.
Dating from 1679, this is without doubt the city's
best tasting house. Around 50 old Dutch liquors
(produced on the premises and described in delightfully charming detail on the menu – in English), plus
20 *jenevers* are served. Don't miss it!

A barrel and a bicycle

A beer on the hop? A moving terrace with
ever-changing views and a guarantee to turn
heads wherever you go? Start pedalling the
Fietscafé® (literally 'bicycle café').

The ever ingenious Dutch have come up
with the marvellous idea of combining beer,
bicycling and sightseeing. This mobile bar
for hire carries up to 17 people – but only
ten have pedal-power – and dispenses fresh
pils as you drunkenly navigate the streets of
the city (one caveat: the sole pilot should
probably be sober). The VIP version offers
bottom-friendlier saddles and a CD player.

However, while the latest addition to the
burgeoning fleet of bicycles, the *Trouwfiets*
('Wedding Bike'), will get the bride to the
church on time, at least she'll arrive sober.
This particular bike is dry. But regardless
of whether you wed sober or just wet your
whistle, it's all a barrel of laughs.

Fietscafé

*Oude Essenerweg 10, 3774 JK
Kootwijkerbroek (mobile 06 53 86 40 90/
fax 0342 442 681/www.fietscafe.nl).*
Open *Telephone* 8am-8pm Mon-Sat.
No credit cards.

In 't Aepjen. *See p144.*

The New Side

Absinthe

Nieuwezijds Voorburgwal 171 (623 4413/www. absinthe.nl). Tram 1, 2, 5. **Open** 8pm-3am Mon-Thur, Sun; 8pm-4am Fri, Sat. **No credit cards.** **Map** p310 D3.

An upbeat late-opener in the heart of cool clubland, this grotto-like lounge has absinthe on tap.

Bep

Nieuwezijds Voorburgwal 260 (626 5649). Tram 1, 2, 4, 5, 9, 13, 14, 16, 17, 24, 25. **Open** 5pm-1am Mon-Thur; 5pm-3am Fri, Sat; 4pm-1am Sun. **No credit cards. Map** p310 D3.

An avant-garde hangout that sits among similarly cool neighbours Diep and the Getaway (for both, *see below*). Go there to be seen, by all means, but don't pass up the terrific bar food and cocktails.

Café Luxembourg

Spui 24 (620 6264/www.luxembourg.nl). Tram 1, 2, 5, 16, 24, 25. **Open** 9am-1am Mon-Thur, Sun; 9am-2am Fri, Sat. **Credit** AmEx, DC, MC, V. **Map** p314 D4.

Ignore the aloof service and make the most of a fine vantage-point. This elegant bar – with its white-aproned waiting staff and high-ceilinged, art deco interior – has a well-placed conservatory and terrace for people who need to see and be seen.

Café Tetra

Nieuwezijds Voorburgwal 89 (no phone/www.cafe-tetra.nl). Tram 1, 2, 4, 5, 9, 13, 14, 16, 17, 24, 25. **Open** 4pm-1am Mon-Thur, Sun; 4pm-3am Fri, Sat. **No credit cards. Map** p310 C2.

DJs spin nightly at this spliff-friendly bar (next to Homegrown Fantasy, *see p157*) which also serves absinthe – complete with accompanying pyro-theatrics. Wednesday's hard trance nights are popular.

Café Vaaghuyzen

Nieuwe Nieuwstraat 17 (420 1751/www. vaaghuyzen.net). Tram 1, 2, 4, 5, 9, 13, 14, 16, 17, 24, 25. **Open** 3pm-3am daily. **No credit cards.** **Map** p310 C2.

An endearingly scruffy and chaotic DJ-bar that affords the chance to meet – and mix – with some of Amsterdam's coolest. Has some inspired nights.

De Drie Fleschjes

Gravenstraat 18 (624 8443/www.driefleschjes.nl). Tram 1, 2, 4, 5, 9, 13, 14, 16, 17, 24, 25. **Open** 2-8.30pm Mon-Sat; 3-7pm Sun. **No credit cards.** **Map** p310 C3.

While the saints are in De Nieuwe Kerk, the sinners can be found next door in one of the oldest tasting houses in Amsterdam. Its street is calm and picturesque and, since opening in 1650, the place has specialised in *jenever*, wine and traditional Dutch liquors – one wall is lined with barrels of the stuff.

Diep

Nieuwezijds Voorburgwal 256 (420 2020). Tram 1, 2, 5, 13, 14, 17. **Open** 5pm-1am Mon-Thur, Sun; 5pm-3am Fri, Sat. **No credit cards. Map** p310 D3.

Dieply cool, this brown café-meets-opulent disco palace interior should ring bells with anyone who likes their bars camp and crushed. DJs spin often.

The Getaway

Nieuwezijds Voorburgwal 250 (627 1427). Tram 1, 2, 5, 13, 14, 17. **Open** 5pm-1am Mon-Thur, Sun; 5pm-3am Fri, Sat. **No credit cards. Map** p310 D3.

Formerly the infamous Seymour Likely Lounge, this place remains a very handy escape, especially if you've just got Dieply Bepped at its neighbours, Diep and Bep (for both, *see above*). DJs play upbeat music and, despite The Getaway's perpetually hip reputation, the crowd here is chilled and approachable. There's a lunch and dinner menu, too.

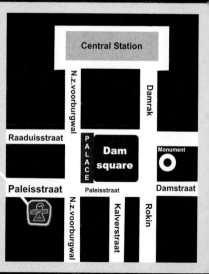

'You missed a bit.' **Getaway.** *See p145.*

Hoppe

Spui 18-20 (420 4420). Tram 1, 2, 4, 5, 9, 14, 16, 24, 25. **Open** 8am-1am Mon-Thur, Sun; 8am-2am Fri, Sat. **Credit** AmEx, DC, MC, V. **Map** p314 D4.
This brown café is always popular, with the left-hand entrance leading to the more relaxed of its two bars. A haunt of radicals in the '60s, its old pews and beer barrels make a refreshing change from the chrome fittings in most New Side haunts.

In de Wildeman

Kolksteeg 3, by Nieuwezijds Kolk (638 2348/www.indewildeman.nl). Tram 1, 2, 5, 13, 17. **Open** noon-1am Mon-Thur, Sun; noon-2am Fri, Sat. **No credit cards. Map** p310 D2.
A beer-tasting tavern offering a selection of 200 bottled brews from around the world, as well as 17 – plus one cider – on tap. The only drawback can be the noise from some of the customers – portly male pissheads who tend to dribble froth on to their beards. Happily, the small no-smoking room provides a degree of refuge from the din.

Schuim

Spuistraat 189 (638 9357). Tram 1, 2, 5, 13, 14, 17. **Open** 11am-1am Mon-Thur; 11am-3am Fri, Sat; 1pm-1am Sun. **No credit cards. Map** p310 C2.
A large rustic, arty bar particularly popular with students and the coolest of the creatives. Chilled music makes it a dreamy hangout on a rainy day; beats go-up tempo as night falls and DJs spin.

De Schutter

Voetboogstraat 13-15 (622 4608). Tram 1, 2, 4, 5, 9, 14, 16, 24, 25. **Open** 4pm-1am Mon-Wed; noon-1am Thurs, Sun; noon-3am Fri, Sat. **No credit cards. Map** p314 D4.
A spacious and restful wooden-floored, first-floor bar with fine, wallet-friendly fare on offer, too. It's popular with students and worn-out shoppers dragging their bags from nearby Kalversstraat.

De Still

Spuistraat 326a (427 6809/www.destill.nl). Tram 1, 2, 4, 5, 9, 13, 14, 16, 24, 25. **Open** 5pm-1am Mon-Thur; 5pm-3am Fri; 3pm-3am Sat; 3pm-1am Sun. **No credit cards. Map** p310 D3.
De Still's defining feature is its giant range of whiskies (from bottle and vat): around 400 in total. Arrange your own tastings at the bar, priced at €27.50 for a selection of six (minimum two people). And watch out for their regular special tastings when the latest whiskies are introduced.

Suite

Sint Nicolaasstraat 43 (489 6531/www.suite.nu). Tram 1, 2, 4, 5, 9, 13, 14, 16, 17, 24, 25. **Open** 6pm-midnight Mon-Thur, Sun; 6pm-3am Fri, Sat. **Credit** AmEx, MC, V. **Map** p310 C2.
Advertising darlings, celebrities and Amsterdam's beautiful people – in short, the usual mediacrities – head here after a hard day's work to chill on both floors of the city's lushest lounge bar. You, too, can sip on cocktails and dine on Japanese-Mediterranean fusion tapas as DJs dish up a diverse soundscape.

The Canals

Western Canal Belt

't Arendsnest

Herengracht 90 (421 2057/www.arendsnest.nl). Tram 1, 2, 5, 13, 14, 17. **Open** 4pm-midnight Mon-Thur; 4pm-2am Fri, Sat. **Credit** MC, V. **Map** p310 C2.
A haven of Dutch beer, 'The Eagle's Nest' serves around 150 (plus seasonal brews, such as *Bokbier*), produced by some 60 breweries from all over the Netherlands – with 12 on tap. Try their home-brewed *Nestvlieder* (Fledgling). If you want to drink your way around the country – geography can be fun! – €6 will get you a taste of four different beers.

Het Molenpad

Prinsengracht 653 (625 9680/www.good foodgroup.nl). Tram 1, 2, 5, 7, 10. **Open** noon-1am Mon-Thur, Sun; noon-2am Fri, Sat. *Kitchen* noon-4pm, 6-10.30pm daily. **No credit cards. Map** p314 C4.
The 'Mill Path' is particularly popular with studious literary types, who pop in on their way back from the nearby library. Delicious lunches and dinners are served, artists' exhibits rotate on a monthly basis and there's a decent canal-side terrace. Pull up in your boat and they'll serve you on board!

Eat, Drink, Shop

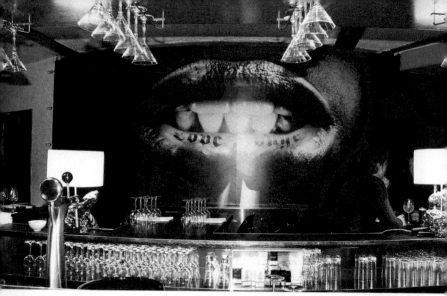

Van Puffelen

Prinsengracht 375-7 (624 6270 www.good foodgroup.nl). Tram 1, 2, 5, 7, 10, 13, 14, 17.
Open 3pm-1am Mon-Thur; 3pm-2am Fri; noon-2am Sat; noon-1am Sun. *Kitchen* 6-11pm Mon-Sat; 6-10pm Sun. **Credit** AmEx, DC, MC, V. **Map** p310 C3.
Amsterdam's biggest brown café and hedonistic hotspot is a favourite haunt of the beautiful people, especially on balmy summer evenings. Arrive by boat to really make an impression.

Wolvenstraat

Wolvenstraat 23 (320 0843). Tram 1, 2, 5. **Open** 8am-1am Mon-Thur; 8am-3am Fri; 9am-3am Sat; 10am-1am Sun. **No credit cards. Map** p314 C4.
Sublimely retro, this beleathered lounge bar attracts affluent beings who sink into its sofas, attracted by the gentle grooves and quirky art exhibitions. It's terrific for breakfast, lunch or champagne; at night, take a culinary trek from Shanghai to Beijing.

Southern Canal Belt

Het Land van Walem

Keizersgracht 449 (625 3544/www.cafewalem.nl). Tram 1, 2, 5. **Open** 10am-1am Mon-Thur, Sun; 10am-2am Fri, Sat. **Credit** AmEx, DC, MC, V. **Map** p314 D4.
One of the first designer bars in Amsterdam, this long, narrow and bright filling station was the work of the renowned Dutch architect Gerrit Rietveld. There are two terraces, one out front by the canal, the other in the small garden at the back.

Morlang

Keizersgracht 451 (625 2681/www.morlang.nl). Tram 1, 2, 5. **Open** 11am-1am Tue-Thur, Sun; 11am-2am Fri, Sat. *Kitchen* 11am-11pm daily. **Credit** AmEx, MC, V. **Map** p314 D4.

Although it has a large canalside terrace, the two-floor Morlang lacks the bright designer looks of Het Land van Walem next door, but it's still a stylish hangout. The food is good, and the selection of spirits stunning, both in apprehension and consumption.

Around Leidseplein

De Balie

Kleine Gartmanplantsoen 10 (553 5130/www.balie.nl). Tram 1, 2, 5, 6, 7, 10. **Open** 10am-1am Mon-Thur, Sun; 10am-2am Fri, Sat. **No credit cards. Map** p314 D5.
The café within this cultural and political centre is always crowded with the arty and political: eavesdropping can serve as a complete education. Meet here before attending a lecture or movie, or enjoy the elevated view across the hectic Leidseplein.

BoomBar

Leidseplein 12 (530 7307/www.boomchicago.nl). Tram 1, 2, 5, 6, 7, 10. **Open** 11am-1am Mon-Thur, Sun; 11am-3am Fri, Sat. **Credit** AmEx, MC, V. **Map** p314 C5.
Expats converge and comedy fans grab a drink before adjourning to Boom Chicago's theatre out back for some American-style humour (*see p253*). It's small but functional, and DJs play Wed-Sat.

Café de Koe

Marnixstraat 381 (625 4482/www.cafedekoe.nl). Tram 1, 2, 5, 6, 7, 10. **Open** 4pm-1am Mon-Thur; 4pm-3am Fri, Sat; 3pm-1am Sun. *Kitchen* 6-10.30pm daily. **Credit** AmEx, DC, MC, V. **Map** p309 B2.
The decor at this lively, two-level bar-restaurant takes its thematic lead from the venue's name: 'Cow'. Drinkers find their good-mooed pasture upstairs, while diners descend to a restaurant serving appetising fodder at reasonable prices.

Blender. *See p150.*

De Zotte

Raamstraat 29 (626 8694). Tram 1, 2, 5, 6, 7, 10.
Open 4pm-1am Mon-Thur, Sun; 4pm-3am Fri, Sat.
Credit AmEx, MC, V. **Map** p314 C4.

De Zotte, appropriately enough, is Belgian for 'drunken fool': nothing like a bar that makes no pretence of advertising double talk. It's likely to be a state of being that you will come to know rather well after sampling their selection of the neighbouring country's 130 beers. However, you can stave off sottishness by soaking up some of the excess with the hearty, beer absorbing food from the kitchen.

Hard Rock Café

Max Euweplein 59 (523 7625/www.hardrock.com). Tram 1, 2, 5, 6, 7, 10. **Open** 11am-midnight Mon-Thur, Sun; 11am-1am Fri, Sat. **Credit** AmEx, MC, V. **Map** p314 D5.

The Hard Rock formula with an Amsterdam twist – complete with a waterside terrace. Child-friendly during the day, it's food-friendly at night: the kitchen is open till 12.30am at weekends.

Lux

Marnixstraat 403 (422 1412). Tram 1, 2, 5, 6, 7, 10. **Open** 8pm-3am Mon-Thur, Sun; 8pm-4am Fri, Sat. **No credit cards. Map** p314 C5.

One of the best late-opening hangouts in the city, this split-level designer bar has DJs every night and draws a trendy, alternative crowd. Lux's owners also run Weber, nearby at No.397.

Twstd

Weteringschans 157 (320 7030/www.twstd.nl). Tram 6, 7, 10, 16, 24, 25. **Open** 6pm-1am Mon-Thur; 6pm-3am Fri, Sat; 4pm-1am Sun. **No credit cards. Map** p315 E5.

Amsterdam's definitive DJ bar boasts a great sound system and varied nights that welcome both established spinners and raw-but-eager beginners.

Vibing

Raamstraat 27 (624 4410/www.vibing.nl). Tram 1, 2, 5, 6, 7, 10. **Open** 7pm-1am Wed-Thur, Sun; 7pm-3am Fri, Sat. **Credit** MC, V. **Map** p314 C4.

A chic American-owned cocktail lounge hidden away down a small street off the neon wastes of Leidseplein. DJs mix contemporary tunes and you can rent the place out on Mondays and Tuesdays.

Around Rembrandtplein

For Irish live music bar **Mulligans**, *see p219.*

De Duivel

Reguliersdwarsstraat 87 (626 6184/www. deduivel.nl). Tram 4, 9, 14. **Open** 8pm-3am Mon-Thur, Sun; 8pm-4am Fri, Sat. **No credit cards. Map** p315 E4.

Cypress Hill, The Roots and Gang Starr have all popped by this small but lively hip hop bar since it opened a decade ago. Nowadays DJs at 'The Devil' mix it up with funk, rare groove and breakbeats.

L'Opera

Rembrandtplein 27-29 (620 4754/www.l-opera.nl). Tram 4, 9, 14. **Open** 10am-1am Mon-Thur, Sun; 10am-2am Fri, Sat. **Credit** AmEx, MC, V. **Map** p315 E4.

Exceptional service and a grand interior – not too unlike the wondrous Tuschinski cinema nearby (*see p198*) – makes this a great place for a drink and directorial dissection before or after that auteur's latest film. However, it's perhaps a place you'd more expect to find in Paris than in Amsterdam.

Schiller

Rembrandtplein 26 (624 9846). Tram 4, 9, 14. **Open** 4pm-1am Mon-Thur, Sun; 4pm-3am Fri, Sat. *Kitchen* 5.30-10pm daily. **Credit** AmEx, DC, MC, V. **Map** p315 E4.

Eat, Drink, Shop

Got a light? **Twstd**. *See p149*.

An absolute godsend for anyone feeling lost amid Rembrandtplein's crass, packed terraces, this renowned art deco café dating – and virtually unchanged – from 1913 maintains a highbrow sensibility with the literati and mediacrities it attracts.

Jodenbuurt, the Plantage & the Oost

Brouwerij 't IJ
Funenkade 7 (622 8325/www.brouwerijhetij.nl). *Tram 6, 10.* **Open** 3-8pm Wed-Sun. **No credit cards.**
In the shadow of the 1814 De Gooyer windmill, this former bathhouse is home to a micro-brewery that turns out some of the finest beer in the country. Unfortunately its bar often resembles a smoky working men's club, but after a couple of jars you'll be one of the lads. Divine on summer nights.

Café de Sluyswacht
Jodenbreestraat 1 (625 7611/www.welcome. to/sluyswacht). *Tram 9, 14/Metro Waterlooplein.* **Open** 11.30am-1am Mon-Thur; 11.30am-3am Fri, Sat; 11.30am-7pm Sun. **Credit** MC, V. **Map** p311 E3.

Built in 1695, this former lock-keeper's house has retained much of its charm, as well as its dodgy foundations: the building leans heavily. It's across from the Rembrandthuis (*see p103*), and the terrace at the rear is one of the most peaceful in town.

Eik & Linde
Plantage Middenlaan 22 (622 5716/www. eikenlinde.nl). *Tram 7, 9, 14.* **Open** 11am-1am Mon-Thur; 11pm-2am Fri; 2pm-2am Sat. **No credit cards. Map** p311 F3.
'The Oak & Lime' is an old-fashioned, family-run neighbourhood bar. Local memorabilia on the walls, including posters from radio shows held on the premises, give it historical appeal; low prices and a laid-back air make it a fine hostelry.

Entredok
Entrepôtdok 64 (623 2356). *Tram 7, 9, 14.* **Open** 4-11pm daily. **No credit cards. Map** p311 F2.
A characterful, two-floor bar on an oft overlooked picturesque canal behind Artis Zoo, with a quiet waterside terrace that catches the sun's last rays.

De Ponteneur
1e van Swindenstraat 581 (668 0680/www. ponteneur.nl). *Tram 9, 14.* **Open** 9am-1am Mon-Thurs; 9am-2am Fri, Sat; 11am-1am Sun. **No credit cards. Map** p316 H3.
Spacious and perpetually popular. Come here for some hearty sustenance after a browse at the local Dappermarkt (*see p180*), or to kick back with a newspaper or magazine from their reading table.

The Waterfront

Kani's & Meiland
Levantkade 127 (418 2439). *Bus 28, 32, 59, 61.* **Open** 10am-1am Mon-Thur, Sun; 10am-3am Fri, Sat. **No credit cards.**
K&M is in the middle of Amsterdam's redeveloped eastern docklands. The waterfront terrace is perfect in the summer – and the food's terrific.

Odessa
Veemkade 259 (419 3010/www.de-odessa.nl). *Bus 28, 39.* **Open** 4pm-1am Mon-Thur, Sun; 4pm-3am Fri, Sat. **Credit** AmEx, DC, MC, V.
A hip Ukrainian fishing boat with a bar on deck, regular DJs and a lounge bar in its hold. *See also p137*.

The Jordaan

Blender
Van der Palmkade 16 (486 9860/www.blender.to). *Tram 10.* **Open** 6pm-1am Tue-Sun. **Kitchen** 6-11pm Tue-Sun. **Credit** AmEx, MC, V.
Bizarrely juxtaposed with the dull suburban building in which it is located, this designer restaurant and bar has a sleek interior and a *looong* curving bar (30m). Like its cocktail menu, it's an inspired concoction of bright colours – from the lounge chairs right through to the toilets. Worth the trek.

Café Nol

Westerstraat 109 (624 5380). Tram 10. **Open**
9pm-3am Mon-Thur, Sun; 9pm-4am Fri, Sat.
No credit cards. Map p309 B2.
Kitsch doesn't come more hardcore than Café Nol,
and this over-the-top Jordaan bar/institution, with
red leatherette interiors and crowds of lusty-voiced
locals, is supposed to sum up the true 'spirit' of this
famously cohesive neighbourhood. But as with the
East End in London, times and populations have
changed. Be warned: its brand of social cosiness
comes with much jolly spittle flying through the air.

Café Soundgarden

*Marnixstraat 164-6 (620 2853). Tram 10, 13,
14, 17.* **Open** 1pm-1am Mon-Thur; 1pm-3am Fri;
3pm-3am Sat; 3pm-1am Sun. **No credit cards.**
Map p309 B3.
Popular with a grungy crowd, which flocks to its
garden terrace on warm, summer days, the bar also
has plenty to while away those frequent rainy afternoons in the form of pool, darts, pinball and table
football. Regular DJs spin it all: from reggae to country to snotty punk. Many regulars round off the
night at the nearby Korsakoff (*see p231*).

AmsterBarflying for rummies

There are certain rituals that will enrich your
Amsterdam barflying experience – whether
it takes place in a lounge, a DJ bar, or an
endemic 'brown café' where the wood is
stained and the ceiling nicotine-soaked.

Most importantly, feel no guilt since it
was beer that built this city (*see p11*).

Other basic rules: ask before lighting your
spliff, buy rounds when in a group, do not use
German when ordering and expect a long,
honest and drawn-out answer if you do ask
a bartender 'How are you?'

But perhaps the most fundamental rule
is not to whine about the 'two-fingers' of
head that comes with a glass of draught pils
('lager'). You are not being ripped off. It's the
'crown' and the reasoning behind it is sound:
by letting a head form during tapping, some of
the beer's carbon dioxide is released, which
both liberates the beer's hoppy aroma and
minimises the client's gas intake (room for
more beer!). And if the head remains semi-
stable for three minutes you will know two
things: the glass is clean and the beer is
not watered down. And since the head is
30 per cent beer anyway, the 'wastage'
only comes to about a thumb's worth.
So who's complaining? Not you, surely?

A barfly can also score points by giving the
Dutch their rightful credit for inventing gin.
Once upon a time – let's call it 1650 – a
doctor in Leiden came up with the alchemy
that allowed juniper berries to be infused
into distilled spirits and lo! Gin was born – or
rather *jenever*, as the Dutch version is called.
A few decades later, the Dutch were exporting
ten million gallons of what was supposed to
be an innocent cure for stomach and kidney
ailments. While the basic recipe was later
swiped by Gordon's and the like, the Dutch
continued to innovate, grading it by age –
jong, *oud* and *zeer oud* ('young', 'old' and

'truly ancient') – and adding various herbs,
spices and flavours and giving different
varieties evocative names such as 'Parrot
Soup', 'Prunes Prick In' and 'Assurance for
Bitter Suffering'. Should your sufferings
indeed be bitter you can assuage them at
proeflokalen ('tasting houses') such as
Wynand Fockink (*see p144*). And like all
good inventions, *jenever* can multi-task
as a *kopstoot* or 'blow to the head' when
served with a glass of beer.

Another tip is not to get so drunk that
you start calling everyone cheeseheads. As
the local barfly/journalist Simon Carmiggelt
once observed: 'Going for one drink is like
jumping off a roof with the plan of falling only
one floor.' So a basic knowledge of *borrel
hapjes* ('bar snacks') is essential. These are
– trust us – scientifically formulated to gel
belly and mind back together. Inevitably, such
menus begins with the strongest of Dutch
stereotypes: *kaas* (cheese), ingested either
via *tostis* (grilled cheese sandwiches) or pure
with dipping mustard. But the most universal
and tastiest of *hapjes* are *bitterballen* ('bitter
balls'), which are essentially just poshed-up
cocktail versions of the *kroket* (*see p136*
Give grease a chance).

And please, be experimental. While the
late Freddie Heineken deserves our undying
respect for saying, 'Death is about becoming
a worm cookie,' there are many beers tastier
than Heineken. For instance, the sweet yet
tangy *witbier* may very well be the ultimate
summer drink. And when the bartender asks
if you want a lemon wedge with it you will, of
course, answer, 'Naturally'.

Which brings us to our last point: don't take
the citrus habit to Belgium when you go there
for a *true* beer vacation. They will think you a
savage. Cultural diversity, doncha just love it.
But anyway: *Proost!*

Dulac

Haarlemmerstraat 118 (624 4265). Bus 18, 22.
Open noon-1am Mon-Thur, Sun; noon-3am Fri, Sat.
Credit AmEx, DC, MC, V. **Map** p310 C2.
A wildly OTT grand café fitted out in surreal art deco style (stuffed alligators, mutant trees and more besides). The cosy corners, raised gallery, secret garden and glass-walled conservatory pack in trendies by the hundred. DJs spin Thur-Sat.

Finch

Noordermarkt 5 (626 2461). Tram 1, 2, 5, 13, 17, 20. **Open** 7am-1am Mon; 10am-1am Tue-Thur; 10am-3am Fri, Sat; 11am-1am Sun.
No credit cards. Map p309 B2.
Located in one of the city's more scenic squares, Finch attracts the expected hip and artistic crowd to its *Wallpaper**-like interior, whose trendiness is happily muted by the carefully cultivated, carefree vibe. The excellent eats, grooving tunes and charming staff make it a top place to hangout.

De Kat in 't Wijngaert

Lindengracht 160 (622 4554). Tram 1, 2, 5, 13, 17. **Open** 10am-1am Mon-Thur, Sun; 10am-2am Fri, Sat.
No credit cards. Map p309 B2.
From 'The Cat in the Vineyard', you can spy the site of the infamous 1886 Eel Riot. It's a neighbourhood café that evokes a truer image of the spirit of the Jordaan than even Café Nol (*see p151*), with locals drawn from every walk of life. Purrrfect.

P96

Prinsengracht 96 (622 1864). Tram 10, 13, 14, 17. **Open** 8pm-3am Mon-Thur, Sun; 8pm-4am Fri, Sat.
No credit cards. Map p310 C2.
A friendly and spacious, split-level 'night bar' on the city's premier canal, offering a more civilised end to a night out than most of its competitors.

't Smalle

Egelantiersgracht 12 (623 9617). Tram 13, 14, 17, 20. **Open** 10am-1am Mon-Thur, Sun; 10am-2am Fri, Sat. **No credit cards. Map** p309 B3.
In 1786 Pieter Hoppe (of Hoppe & Jenever) opened a liquor distillery here. Though a few artefacts remain – including an original *jenever* pump on the bar – this charming establishment now earns its reputation as a wine bar. You can even park your boat at their quayside terrace in the summer time.

The Museum Quarter, Vondelpark & the South

Het Blauwe Theehuis

Vondelpark 5 (662 0254/www.blauwetheehuis.nl). Tram 1, 2, 6. **Open** 9am-11pm Mon-Thur, Sun; 9am-1am Fri, Sat. **No credit cards. Map** p314 C6.
Looking like a flying saucer, the 'Blue Teahouse' – a functionalist masterpiece from 1936 – is a charming and romantic spot. There are two bars: one upstairs where DJs spin on Sundays and one downstairs for those with dogs and small children in tow.

Decent snacks are available all day. It's an excellent place to come in summer (when an outdoor cocktail bar is set up), though it can get very crowded, particularly when there are events on in the park.

Café Ebeling

Overtoom 50-52 (689 4858/www.cafeebeling.com). Tram 1, 3, 6, 12. **Open** 11am-1am Mon-Thur; 11am-3am Fri, Sat; noon-1am Sun. *Kitchen* noon-10pm daily. **Credit** AmEx, MC, V. **Map** p314 C5.
Located in an old bank – the toilets are in the safe – Café Ebeling is a split-level bar-restaurant that aims itself at the young without being snobby or needing to have the music on so loud you can't think. Another plus: it's one of the few non-Irish bars in town that serves a decent Guinness.

Toussaint

Bosboom Toussaintstraat 26 (685 0737). Tram 1, 3, 6, 7, 12, 17. **Open** 10am-midnight Mon-Thur, Sun; 10am-1am Fri, Sat. **No credit cards. Map** p314 C5.
Rustic charm abounds at this café-cum-bar. You'll find it on a quiet street a ten-minute walk from Leidseplein, and it's well worth the detour. The small, open kitchen serves up super grub all day and night, and there's even a decent selection for vegetarians. For hipper fare, carry on down the road to Wanka (Bosboom Toussaintstraat 70, 412 6169) – pronounced, you'll be glad to hear, 'vanker'.

The Pijp

Chocolate

1e van der Helststraat 62a (675 7672). Tram 16, 24, 25. **Open** 10am-1am Mon-Thur, Sun; 10am-3am Fri, Sat. **Credit** V. **Map** p315 E6.
Despite the name, its notoriously slow service won't leave your mouth watering – so only come if you have the time and inclination to lounge around for a while. The Chocolate experience does improves with the cool clientele and regular DJs, however. On Mondays they screen cult, rare and classic films with dinner served in the style of the movie.

Kingfisher

Ferdinand Bolstraat 24 (671 2395). Tram 16, 24, 25. **Open** 11pm-1am Mon-Thur; 11pm-3am Fri, Sat. **No credit cards. Map** p315 E6.
Of the many local-ish brown cafés that actually let in some fresh light and a little international style, the Kingfisher does the best job, balancing impeccable service with inventive snacks and a daily dinner special that'll take your taste buds on a global roller coaster ride. The archetypical locals' local.

Wildschut

Roelof Hartplein 1-3 (676 8220/www.good foodgroup.nl). Tram 3, 5, 12, 24. **Open** 9am-1am Mon-Thur; 9am-3am Fri; 10.30am-2am Sat; 9.30am-1am Sun. **Credit** (over €15) AmEx, DC, MC, V.
The faded glory of Amsterdam School architecture can be found at this popular semicircular bar. In the summer, snag a seat on the large terrace, which overlooks the Roelof Hartplein, for all-day sun.

Coffeeshops

The lowdown on blow town.

Watch the grass grow at **Abraxas**.
See p155.

What's Amsterdam's biggest draw (pun intended)? The many places where you can sip a coffee and smoke a spliff are one answer. In 1976 the Dutch, taking their normal pragmatic approach to humanity's weaknesses, realised that the use of marijuana was widespread and (re)classified it as a soft drug. As a result, locals and visitors can now walk into a coffeeshop and purchase up to five grams of the stuff for personal use – as long as they're over 18.

Technically, however, although it has been decriminalised, cannabis remains illegal. Albeit of little concern to the visitor, this does make for some rather potty laws. For example, coffeeshops (all licensed and taxed) can sell you the stuff but they are not allowed to buy it. So it comes through the back door illegally but lawfully goes out the front.

The city also has a strangely symbiotic relationship with its coffeeshops. On one hand, it values – and can't deny – their contribution to tourism but, on the other, relentlessly puts pressure on them. Thus a few years ago the council weeded out the more disreputable establishments and stopped granting new licenses. They also clamped down on the selling

The best Toking paradises

Abraxas
A goblin's cave of cannabis and chess.
See p155.

Barney's
Bangers and hash: one for high fryers.
See p157.

De Rokerij
Say, 'Open sesame' and wish. *See p158.*

Hill Street Blues
Cop your cannabis here. *See p155.*

La Tertulia
Greenly serene pastures. *See p158.*

Dampkring.

of spacecake and banned coffeeshops from any form of advertising. Owners were even advised to remove any mention of cannabis (in word or image) from their websites.

Obviously, in a community of paranoid stoners, a mild panic ensued. Some coffeeshops removed their websites completely and many still just list their address and little else besides. However, the more canny simply found creative ways around the restrictions (keep an eye out).

And – for those who like to spend their time in Amsterdam hallucinating in the middle of a street while lying in a pool of their own vomit – several coffeeshops have started to bake spacecake once more.

It does seem perverse, however, that while coffeeshops aren't even allowed to put an image of a cannabis leaf on their shop windows, junkies publicly shoot up. Many feel the council should spend more time chasing the real criminals and leave peace-loving potheads to their pipe dreams. Still, perhaps not a huge price to pay for a unique liberty. For a broader survey of Dutch drugs culture, *see p48*.

SCORING SAVVY

Walk into a coffeeshop and ask to see the menu. Listed before you will be the different types of hash and weed available.

The hash side of things is fairly clear, as varieties are usually named after their country of origin. Weed, though, is more complicated. It divides roughly into two categories: 'brown' weed grown naturally, such as Thai; and Nederwiet or the stronger variety, Skunk, an indigenous Dutch product grown under UV lights for maximum THC (the active

ingredient). As with Guinness in Ireland – well, kinda – the Skunk here is worlds away from anything available elsewhere, and caution is advised if you want to remember anything.

Most of the stuff is sold by the gram – either in ready-prepared bags or weighed and bagged in front of you. Quality can vary and, of course, as quality goes up, the price follows. The average amount you can expect to pay for a gram of run-of-the-mill weed or hash is around €5 or €6. Staff will usually let you see, smell and touch your wares before you part with your euros – and even let you choose your own buds.

Go for the organically grown stuff for a purer hit. And, as you get more experienced, you'll find yourself slipping into the role of connoisseur, taking time to pick your poison, on a par with selecting a fine wine.

Most shops sell pre-rolled joints and supply free rolling papers and tips; some have bongs and vaporisers (but go easy on the hits if you're not used to it). The same caution should be exercised when it comes to spacecake: effects can take an hour to kick in, and the return to planet Earth can be protracted.

If you're not used to it, don't drink and draw. If you do overdo it, eat or drink something sweet. Tourists passed out on the street are an all too common sight. Sure, it'll make for a funny story when you get home, but at the time you'll never have felt so ill in your life.

Finally a couple of 'don'ts' that really need to be stressed: never ever buy anything from junkies. And, although it should go without saying, make sure you empty your pockets before you get on that plane. But, in the meantime, happy smoking!

Coffeeshops

One of the few decent lesbian bars in town, **Saarein II** (*see p216*), organises a homegrown contest every November.

The Old Centre: Old Side

Greenhouse

Oudezijds Voorburgwal 191 (627 1739/www.green house.org). Tram 4, 9, 14, 16, 24, 25. **Open** 9am-1am Mon-Thur, Sun; 9am-3am Fri, Sat. **No credit cards. Map** p310 D3.

The Greenhouse has a worldwide reputation for its menu, which will bring a long slow smile of delight to the face of the cannabis connoisseur (although, of course, all this comes at a price). It also serves alcohol and, since it is handily located next door to the Grand Hotel, there is always a chance you could spot a furtive celeb spliffing up in here.

Other locations: Waterlooplein 345 (no phone); Tolstraat 91 (673 7430, a members-only establishment).

Greenhouse Effect

Warmoesstraat 53 (623 746/www.greenhouse-effect.com). Tram 4, 9, 16, 24, 25. **Open** 9am-1am Mon-Thur, Sun; 9am-3am Fri, Sat. **No credit cards. Map** p310 D2.

Not to be confused with the Greenhouse (*see above*), this is a small but hip joint that also sells alcohol. However, if you fancy a modest line-up of DJs, a bit more chill-out space while falling into the gap between the beats and a chance to sample the dubiously named Cream In Your Pants cocktail, take a trip next door to the bar-hotel of the same name (*see p57*). While just on the other side is Getto, arguably the best gay/mixed bar in town, where the green smoke is also allowed (*see p214*).

Hill Street Blues

Nieuwmarkt 14 (no phone/www.hill-street-blues.nl). Tram 4, 9, 14, 16, 24, 25/Metro Nieuwmarkt. **Open** 9am-1am daily. **No credit cards. Map** p310 D2.

It's long, loungey and chilled, has an international vibe, a more-hash-for-your-cash menu and a small terrace overlooking busy and bustling Nieuwmarkt square. Hill Street Blues also makes some wicked fruit smoothies and shakes (ideal for munchies), and sells a discerning array of space cookies, space truffles and marijuana tea. Its other, more established, branch at Warmoesstraat 52, serves alcohol (with a daily happy beer and cider hour – well, hours – from 6-9pm), has a pool table and table football – but is invariably more hectic. It does ooze street cred, however: as proof of that, it's a favourite of Irvine Welsh (*see p82* **Irvine Welsh: Amster mage**).

Rusland

Rusland 16 (627 9468). Tram 4, 9, 14, 16, 24, 25/ Metro Nieuwmarkt/Waterlooplein. **Open** 10am-midnight Mon-Thur, Sun; 10am-1am Fri, Sat. **No credit cards. Map** p310 D3.

'Russia' claims to be the first (legal) coffeeshop in Amsterdam and has been welcoming comrades for over 30 years on the street of the same name. Unsurprisingly perhaps, they have a Russian theme throughout, a variety of levels, plus cosy nooks and crannies. They sell a whopping 39 different types of tea, spacecake and fresh juices (including their renowned Vitamin Cocktail).

The Old Centre: New Side

Abraxas

Jonge Roelensteeg 12-14 (625 5763/www.abraxas.tv). Tram 4, 9, 16, 24, 25. **Open** 10am-1am daily. **No credit cards. Map** p310 D3.

Comfortable and colourful, this veritable goblin's dwelling is located down a small alley in the heart of the city's cool clubland. As well as alcohol, they sell cannabis-infused spacecakes, shakes, bonbons and tea. It seems about the only thing missing in the way of drug delivery systems is a cannabis drip. And to complement the experience there's occasional DJs, internet (free to customers) and chess, or watching the grass grow (literally).

Dampkring

Handboogstraat 29 (638 0705). Tram 1, 2, 5. **Open** 10am-1am Mon-Thur; 10am-2am Fri, Sat; 11am-1am Sun. **No credit cards. Map** p314 D4.

Hidden away down a small alley behind the bustle of one of Amsterdam's main shopping streets, Kalverstraat, is this haven of haze. It's renowned, not just for its exquisite (mostly) organically grown weed, but for the fact that scenes for *Ocean's Twelve* (*see p200* **Lights! Camera! Clog action!**), starring Brad Pitt and George Clooney, were filmed here. (And, unashamedly cashing in on that, they even have Ocean's Twelve Haze on the menu.) Don't miss their cat Bowie – he's quite the local legend.

Eat, Drink, Shop

A duality becomes one, maannn...

Bruce Brewster – aka Bastard to friends and family alike – began life as just a regular Scottish lad. He claims to have been a 'perfectly normal student brewer' as well as a 'perfectly normal hash dealer'. He moved to Amsterdam after some messiness involving a Poll Tax riot. And here, in the 'magical centre of the universe', his two passions became, like, one, man. He began brewing THC-infused ciders, meads and wines. Alcohol and marijuana no longer have to bicker about who was humankind's earliest intoxicant. May the healing begin!

He sold his first batch of crisp and dry Cycocyder – best served chilled – on Queen's Day 1995. It was finally deemed too strong by both Bastard himself and a member of the Hell's Angels. (Wimps!) 'I always try to do the decent thing and experiment on myself first.' His hobby grew quickly and soon the grassroots demand surpassed supply, reaching a peak in 2004 when his Strawberry Scorpion – a fresh and fruity strawberry rosé that 'tastes of summer' – won the coveted Food & Beverage award at the prestigious 2004 International Cannagraphic Independent Growers Cup.

Bastard keeps his techniques close to the chest. But he will say that the weed is processed into a state high in THC and low in cannabinoids. 'This makes one nice and high and not red-eyed and fried.' It is also the reason why he has no time for beer brewing,

since those nasty cannabinoids only get neutered by alcohol levels above 11 per cent. He also claims that his products have aphrodisiac properties: 'You really do get quite touchy-feely on them.'

Bastard generally makes batches of 25-30 bottles at a time. Each bottle, retailing at about €17.50, is formulated to get 3-4 people righteously wasted. And like any farmer, his selection flows with the seasons. Besides Cycocyder and Strawberry Scorpion, Bastard has also achieved ample respect for his Chambrain, a sparkling semi-dry white wine; Bastard Brew, a thick and spicy mead that follows a medieval recipe; and Bloody Brew, a light, fruity, semi-sweet red wine with lots of complementing Purple Haze bud. Oenophiles note that his products combine well with chocolate. Lots of it.

But Bastard is the first to admit that both the brewing and the legality still remain decidedly 'seat-of-the-pants', although he's hoping the famous local pragmatism will keep him safe: 'As long as you pay taxes no one busts you here.' But remember kids: this is not an export product. And don't try any DIY brewing at home. However, do feel free to drop Bastard an email (bastardbrewer @yahoo.co.uk) for his latest list of offerings. He also remains very welcoming to any interested investors and 'any good will trimmings for the next batch...'
www.bastardbrewer.com.

Homegrown Fantasy

Nieuwezijds Voorburgwal 87a (627 5683/www. homegrownfantasy.com). Tram 1, 2, 5, 13, 17. **Open** 10am-midnight Mon-Thur, Sun; 10am-1am Fri, Sat. **No credit cards**. **Map** p310 D2.
Just a few minutes' walk from Centraal Station this pleasant coffeeshop cum art gallery is a popular destination for the jet-lagged inbound. It also has one of the widest selections of Dutch-grown weed in Weedsville (most of it organically grown), including their infamous Cheese. For those keen to get themselves wasted on arrival, spacecake is also for sale.

Tweede Kamer

Heisteeg 6 (422 2236). Tram 1, 2, 5. **Open** 10am-1am Mon-Sat; 11am-1am Sun. **No credit cards**. **Map** p310 D3.
Smoky, poky and usually packed, Tweede Kamer is frequented by locals for its deserved reputation of having a wide range of imported grass. It might be best to purchase your indulgence here but, to smoke it, head to greener, less crowded, pastures.

Western Canal Belt

Amnesia

Herengracht 133 (no phone). Tram 13, 14, 17. **Open** 9.30am-1am daily. **No credit cards**. **Map** p310 C2.
The Amnesia has a certain home-from-home, boudoir charm. Its refined menu is unlike most other coffeeshops in Amsterdam – offering more non-commercial varieties. There's also a chess table to challenge your powers of concentration.

Barney's

Haarlemmerstraat 102 (625 9761/www.barneys-amsterdam.com). Tram 13, 14, 17. **Open** 7am-8pm daily. **No credit cards**. **Map** p310 C2.
The best thing about Barney's is its early opening hours and range of international breakfasts (complete with vegetarian and vegan options). Come here if you arrive in Amsterdam in the morning (it's just a five-minute walk from Centraal Station) or for a

civilised end to a night on the tiles. Additionally, the weed is 100% organic. A few doors away, at No.98, is Barney's Brasserie, which serves hearty meals, plus alcohol. They don't trade in marijuana but you're welcome to smoke the weed there.

Siberië
Brouwersgracht 11 (623 5909/www.siberie.nl). Tram 1, 2, 4, 5, 13, 17. **Open** 11am-11pm Mon-Thur, Sun; 11am-midnight Fri, Sat. **No credit cards.** **Map** p310 C2.
Friendly and mellow, Siberië has regular free horoscope readings, open mic nights and exhibitions, and DJs spin at weekends. For those wishing to see how THC effects concentration, there's internet access and plenty of board games. All in all, Siberia is a cool place to while away any rainy day while drinking some of the best coffee in town (it's also cheap at €1.35; tea is €1.15). The same owners run the small but modern De Supermarkt (Frederik Hendrikstraat 69, 486 2479, www.desupermarkt.net) and well-established neighbourhood coffeeshop De Republiek (2e Nassaustraat 1a, 682 8431, www.republiek.nl), both west of the Jordaan.

La Tertulia
Prinsengracht 312 (no phone). Tram 7, 10, 13, 14, 17. **Open** 11am-7pm Tue-Sat. **No credit cards.** **Map** p314 C4.
A stoned-looking Van Gogh is painted on the outer wall of this charming split-level corner coffeeshop where Michelle from *East Enders* took her first toke years ago. Inside the place is bright and airy; weed brownies are served at the sunken counter and there's a miniature garden, complete with fountain. In summer, the canal-side terrace is a peaceful spot to spliff up while settling back for a relaxing afternoon watching the world drift by.

Southern Canal Belt

De Rokerij
Lange Leidsedwarsstraat 41 (622 9442/ www.rokerij.net). Tram 1, 2, 5, 6, 7, 10. **Open** 10am-1am Mon-Thur, Sun; 10am-3am Fri, Sat. **No credit cards.** **Map** p314 D5.
A marvellous discovery on an otherwise hideous tourist street by Leidseplein, De Rokerij is an Aladdin's cave: lit by wall-mounted candles and beautiful metal lanterns, it's decorated with colourful Indian art and a variety of seating (ranging from mats on the floor to decorative 'thrones'). In line with its central location, it gets very busy in the evening and at the weekend.
Other locations: Amstel 8 (620 0484); Singel 8 (422 6643); Elandsgracht 53 (623 0938).

The Jordaan

Brandend Zand
Marnixstraat 92 (528 7292/www.brandendzand.nl). Tram 3, 10. **Open** 9.30am-1am Mon-Fri; 10am-1am Sat, Sun. **No credit cards.** **Map** p309 B2.

This spacious, designer split-level coffeeshop is a real find on this ugly street. Downstairs is cushion heaven (even if you're capable of movement you won't want to leave), while upstairs you'll find four computers with internet access, a pool table and big-screen MTV. The crowning glory is the upright aquarium – although we're not sure if the fish are really that keen on swimming vertically.

Grey Area
Oude Leliestraat 2 (420 4301/www.greyarea.nl). Tram 1, 2, 5, 13, 14, 17. **Open** noon-8pm Tue-Sun. **No credit cards.** **Map** p310 C3.
The joint venture of two wacky Americans, Grey Area is small but has a big reputation. It also has a reputation for not opening exactly at noon, so if it's not long past twelve you might want to phone first to make sure they've surfaced. But they do sell top-quality weed and are particularly proud of their Bubblegum and Grey strains. They're also the only place in town to offer free refills of organic coffee. On the same street is Foodism (*see p129*), ideal for when you get the munchies.

Paradox
1e Bloemdwarsstraat 2 (623 5639/www.paradox amsterdam.demon.nl). Tram 10, 13, 14, 17. **Open** 10am-8pm daily. **No credit cards.** **Map** p309 B3.
When compared to the dingy coffeeshops that dominate much of Amsterdam, Paradox lives up to its name. A bright, cheerful contradiction, it serves healthy food, fruit shakes and fresh fruit/vegetable juices on top of all the usual dope (though if you're feeling peckish, it's worth remembering that the kitchen shuts at 3pm). Comfortable and cosy, it's ideal for a deep-and-meaningful – and you could probably bring your mum here, too.

Samenentereng
2e Lauriedwarsstraat 44 (624 1907). Tram 10, 13, 14, 17. **Open** 11am-midnight daily. **No credit cards.** **Map** p313 B4.
If you're after an experience on a par with one of *Mr Benn*'s visits to the fancy-dress shop, then pop into Samenentereng, ostensibly a bric-a-brac store crammed to the nines with both brac and bric. But tucked at the back is an unusual African hut-style coffeeshop-cum-conservatory, complete with reggae, rastas and table football. Definitely worth a ganja.

The Museum Quarter, Vondelpark & the South

Kashmir Lounge
Jan Pieter Heijestraat 85-87 (683 2268). Tram 1, 6, 7, 11, 17. **Open** 10am-1am Mon-Thur; 10am-3am Fri, Sat; 11am-1am Sun. **No credit cards.** **Map** p313 B6.
Kashmir Lounge's non-central location means cheaper drinks (including alcohol) and more flexible deals on weed. Spacey and spacious, the cushioned area is a great place for a horizontal smoke and to kick back to the DJs – who play daily.

The Pijp

Yo-Yo
2e Jan van der Heijdenstraat 79/entrance on Hemonystraat (664 7173). Tram 3, 4. **Open** noon-7pm Mon-Sat. **No credit cards**. **Map** p315 F5.
A popular neighbourhood coffeeshop situated out in the Pijp, Yo-Yo is spacious and calm. The atmosphere is mellow and the weed organic. Don't leave without trying Helga's home-made apple pie.

Events

For the *High Times* Cannabis Cup, *see p187.*

Highlife Hemp Fair
Highlife, Discover Publisher BV, Postbus 362, 5460 AJ, Veghel (073 549 8112/www.highlife.nl).
Organised by *Highlife* magazine, this huge international event celebrates the cannabis plant, with an emphasis on the industrial uses of hemp. The exhibition holds displays detailing the many uses for the plant, and there are around 100 stands selling smart drugs, weed tea and coffee, and all sorts of soft drugs paraphernalia. Highlight is the presentation of the *Highlife* Cup for the best Dutch weed and hash. The event takes place in the Jaarbeurs (Utrecht) every January and usually attracts around 13,000 people.

Legalize! Street Rave
Stichting Legalize!, Postbus 59723, 1040 LE, Amsterdam (www.legalize.net).
In an attempt to raise awareness on drugs issues this voluntary group organises a street rave through the city every first Saturday in June – attracting both party and political animals to the festivities. They also stage a rally in May and organise a number of international actions and benefit parties. Check their website for more details.

Information

For the Hash Marijuana Hemp Museum, *see p87.*

Cannabis College
Oudezijds Achterburgwal 124, Old Centre: Old Side (423 4420/www.cannabiscollege.com). Tram 4, 9, 14, 16, 24, 25/Metro Nieuwmarkt. **Open** 11am-7pm daily. **Admission** free. **Map** p310 D3.
The College, occupying two floors in a 17th-century registered monument in the Red Light District, provides the public with an impressive array of information about the cannabis plant (including its medicinal uses). The place is run by volunteers and admission is free; however, staff request a €2.50 donation if you take a look at their indoor garden.

Drugs Information Line
0900 1995. **Open** 1-9pm Mon-Fri; Dutch recorded message at other times.
A national advice and information line for the Trimbos Institute (Netherlands Institute of Mental Health and Addiction). To the relief of drug-addled tourists, the operators speak excellent English.

Grey Area. *See p158.*

Shops & Services

Craving some of that only-in-Amsterdam individuality?

Bricks and fauna at **Architectura & Natura**. *See p161.*

Feeling so out of touch with new trends and fashions that you're convinced your family and friends are in cahoots to expose your flaws to a mocking television audience as the next victim for a total makeover for misfits programme? Not the slightest clue as to what's the new black; whether to go virgin or rustic, or if a tennis bracelet is the thing, or if that's just too much bling? Relax. The answer is simple. All you need to do is walk down one of the streets or tree-lined canals in Amsterdam and the chances are that every other person is going to look sharp; Amsterdammers have *STIJL*. In a tiny town like this, hemmed in by sea, river and marsh, every millimetre counts. Hence wherever you look, everything and everyone is saturated with culture; be it good eats, classical or more progressive architecture, a vibrant and varied arts scene and naturally some very tasty shopping. So if you just set off to do a little exploring of your own, some of the magic is bound to rub off on you on the way. Here is our cheat's guide to Amsterdam's global village chic; all the best places where Amsterdammers shop, and now you can too.

Antiques & auctions

Visit Spiegelgracht, Nieuwe Spiegelstraat or the markets (*see p180*). For a more rarefied air, try **Sotheby's** (De Boelenlaan 30, 550 2200, www.sothebys.com) and **Christie's** (Cornelis Schuytstraat 57, 575 5255, www.christies.com).

Art & art supplies

Check museum shops for prints and postcards.

Art Multiples

Keizersgracht 510, Southern Canal Belt (624 8419/www.artmultiples.nl). Tram 1, 2, 5. **Open** 1-6pm Mon; 10am-6pm Tue, Wed, Fri, Sat; 10am-9pm Thur; noon-5pm Sun. **Credit** AmEx, DC, MC, V. **Map** p314 C4.
The most comprehensive collection of international photographs and posters in the Netherlands, and the largest collection of postcards in Western Europe.

J Vlieger

Amstel 34, Southern Canal Belt (623 5834). Tram 4, 9, 14, 16, 24, 25. **Open** noon-6pm Mon; 9am-6pm Tue-Fri; 11am-5.30pm Sat. **Credit** AmEx, DC, MC, V. **Map** p311 E3.

Papers and cards of every description monopolise the ground floor; upstairs are paints, pens and inks, as well as small easels and hobby materials.

Peter van Ginkel

Bilderdijkstraat 99, Oud West (618 9827). Tram 3, 7, 12, 17. **Open** 10am-5.30pm Mon-Fri; 10am-4pm Sat. **Credit** MC, V. **Map** p313 B5.

Heaven for creative types. Shelves groan with paints and pigments, canvas and many types of paper.

Bookshops

The best of Dutch literature is celebrated in the third week of March; while the second week of October sees the focus turn to children's books. Note: English-language books are pricey. For book markets, *see p180*.

General

American Book Center

Kalverstraat 185, Old Centre: New Side (625 5537/ www.abc.nl). Tram 1, 2, 4, 5, 9, 14, 16, 24, 25. **Open** 10am-8pm Mon-Wed, Fri, Sat; 10am-9pm Thur; 11am-6.30pm Sun. **Credit** AmEx, DC, MC, V. **Map** p310 D3.

Since 1972, this shop has brought a vast stock of English-language books and magazines from the UK and US to the (mostly) bilingual Dutch.

Athenaeum Nieuwscentrum

Spui 14-16, Old Centre: New Side (bookshop 622 6248/news centre 624 2972/www.athenaeum.nl). Tram 1, 2, 5. **Open** 9.30am-6pm Tue, Wed, Fri, Sat; 9.30am-9pm Thur; noon-5.30pm Sun. *News centre* 8am-8pm Mon-Wed, Fri, Sat; 8am-9pm Thur; 10am-6pm Sun. **Credit** AmEx, MC, V. **Map** p314 D4.

This is where Amsterdam's most highbrow literary browsers like to hang out. The Athenaeum Nieuwscentrum, as its name might suggest, also stocks newspapers from all over the world, as well as a wide choice of magazines, periodicals and, the bibliophile's staple, books in many languages.

Book Exchange

Kloveniersburgwal 58, Old Centre: Old Side (626 6266). Tram 4, 9, 14/Metro Nieuwmarkt. **Open** 10am-6pm Mon-Fri; 10am-5.30pm Sat; 11.30am-4pm Sun. **No credit cards**. **Map** p310 D3.

The owner of this bibliophiles' treasure trove is a shrewd buyer who's willing to do trade deals. Choose from a plethora of second-hand English and American titles (mainly paperbacks).

Waterstone's

Kalverstraat 152, Old Centre: New Side (638 3821/ www.waterstones.co.uk). Tram 1, 2, 4, 5, 9, 14, 16, 24, 25. **Open** 10am-6pm Mon; 9am-7pm Tue, Wed, Fri; 9am-9pm Thur; 10am-7pm Sat; 11am-6pm Sun. **Credit** AmEx, MC, V. **Map** p310 D3.

Thousands of books, magazines and videos, all in English. The children's section is delightful.

Specialist

Architectura & Natura

Leliegracht 22, Western Canal Belt (623 6186/ www.architectura.nl). Tram 13, 14, 17. **Open** noon-6pm Mon; 9am-6pm Tue, Sat; 9am-6.30pm Wed-Fri. **Credit** MC, V. **Map** p310 C3.

The stock at Architecture and Nature, which includes many works in English for monoglots, is exactly what you'd expect from its name: books on architectural history, plant life, gardens and animal studies. Leliegracht 22 is also home to Antiquariaat Opbouw, which deals in antiquarian books on architecture and associated topics.

Au Bout du Monde

Singel 313, Western Canal Belt (625 1397/www. auboutdumonde.nl). Tram 1, 2, 5. **Open** 1-6pm Mon; 10am-6pm Tue-Sat. **Credit** AmEx, DC, MC, V. **Map** p310 C3.

Au Bout du Monde specialises in Eastern philosophy and religion, and stocks a daunting selection of titles on subjects ranging from psychology to sexuality. There are also magazines, plus related paraphernalia such as incense, cards and videos.

The best Shops

For cheese infusion
De Kaaskamer. *See p172.*

For vintage glitter and glamour
Laura Dols. *See p170.*

For four eyes
Donald E Jongejans. *See p165.*

For wooden shoes
't Klompenhuisje. *See p164.*

For glad rags
Bits and Pieces. *See p164.*

For molto chocolata
Pâtisserie Pompadour. *See p172.*

For suds galore
De Bierkoning. *See p175.*

For a beauty spot
Skins Cosmetics Lounge. *See p179.*

For hot wax
Get Records. *See p182.*

For naughty girls
Stout. *See p182.*

For a stinker
PGC Hajenius. *See p182.*

Eat, Drink, Shop

Intertaal

Van Baerlestraat 76, Museum Quarter (575 6756/
www.intertaal.nl). Tram 3, 5, 12, 16. **Open** *1-6pm*
Mon; 10am-6pm Tue-Fri; 10am-5pm Sat. **Credit**
AmEx, MC, V. **Map** p314 D6.
Dealing in language books, CDs and teaching aids,
Intertaal will be of use to all learners, whether grap-
pling with basic Dutch or improving their English.

Lambiek

Kerkstraat 132, Southern Canal Belt (626 7543/
www.lambiek.nl). Tram 1, 2, 5. **Open** 11am-6pm
Mon-Fri; 11am-5pm Sat; 1-5pm Sun. **Credit** AmEx,
MC, V. **Map** p314 D4.
Lambiek, founded in 1968, claims to be the world's
oldest comic shop and has thousands of books from
around the world; its on-site cartoonists' gallery
hosts exhibitions every two months.

Pied-à-Terre

Singel 393, Old Centre: New Side (627 4455/
www.piedaterre.nl). Tram 1, 2, 5. **Open** 10am-6pm
Mon-Fri; 10am-5pm Sat. *Apr-Aug* 10am-9pm Thur.
No credit cards. Map p314 D4.
Travel books, international guides and maps for
active holidays. Adventurous walkers should talk
to the helpful staff before a trip out of town.

Department stores

De Bijenkorf

Dam 1, Old Centre: New Side (552 1700/
www.bijenkorf.nl). Tram 1, 2, 4, 5, 9, 13, 14,
16, 17, 24, 25. **Open** 11am-7pm Mon; 9.30am-
7pm Tue, Wed; 9.30am-9pm Thur, Fri; 9.30am-
6pm Sat; noon-6pm Sun. **Credit** AmEx, DC, MC, V.
Map p310 D3.
Amsterdam's most notable department store has a
great household goods department and a decent mix
of clothing (designer and own-label), kidswear, jewellery, cosmetics, shoes and accessories. The Chill
Out department caters to funky youngsters in need
of streetwear, clubwear, wacky foodstuffs and
kitsch accessories, while the store's restaurant, La
Ruche, is a good lunch spot. The Christmas displays
are extravagant and hugely popular.

Maison de Bonneterie

Rokin 140-2, Old Centre: New Side (531 3400).
Tram 1, 2, 4, 5, 9, 14, 24, 25. **Open** 1-5.30pm
Mon; 10am-5.30pm Tue, Wed, Fri, Sat; 10am-9pm
Thur; noon-5pm Sun. **Credit** AmEx, DC, MC, V.
Map p310 D3.
This venerable institution stocks quality men's and
women's clothing 'By Appointment to Her Majesty,
Queen Beatrix'. As you'd expect, it's a conservative
affair: the in-store Ralph Lauren boutique is as out-
landish as it gets. There's an excellent café.

Metz & Co

Leidsestraat 34-6, Southern Canal Belt (520 7020).
Tram 1, 2, 5. **Open** 11am-6pm Mon; 9.30am-6pm
Tue-Sat; noon-5pm Sun. **Credit** AmEx, DC, MC, V.
Map p314 D4.

Metz is wonderful for upmarket gifts: designer furniture, glass and Liberty-style fabrics and scarves
are all available. For lunch with a view, make for the
top-floor restaurant designed by Gerrit Rietveld. At
Yuletide their Christmas shop will put the holiday
spirit back into the Scroogiest customer.

Vroom & Dreesmann

Kalverstraat 203, Old Centre: New Side (0900 235
8363/www.vroomendreesmann.nl). Tram 4, 9, 14,
16, 24, 25. **Open** 11am-6.30pm Mon; 10am-6.30pm
Tue, Wed, Fri; 10am-9pm Thur; 10am-6.30pm Sat;
noon-6pm Sun. **Credit** AmEx, MC, V. **Map** p310 D3.
V&D means good quality at prices just a step up
from HEMA (*see p164* **From cut-price to cutting
edge**). There's a staggering array of toiletries, cosmetics, leather goods and watches, clothing and
underwear for the whole family, kitchen items, suit-
cases, CDs and videos. The bakery, Le Marché, sells
delicious bread, quiches and sandwiches.

Drugs

Conscious Dreams Dreamlounge

Kerkstraat 93, Southern Canal Belt (626 6907/
www.consciousdreams.nl). Tram 1, 2, 5. **Open**
11am-7pm Mon-Wed; 11am-8pm Thur-Sat; noon-5pm
Sun. Closed Oct-Apr. **Credit** AmEx, DC, MC, V.
Map p314 D4.
Conscious Dreams was the original proponent of the
smart drugs wave in Amsterdam. The staff here
really know their stuff – the owner worked as a
drugs adviser for five years – and you're more or
less guaranteed to find whatever you're after.
Other locations: Kokopelli Warmoesstraat 12
(421 7000).

Head Shop

Kloveniersburgwal 39, Old Centre: Old Side (624
9061/www.headshop.nl). Tram 4, 9, 14, 16, 24,
25/Metro Nieuwmarkt. **Open** 11am-6pm Mon-Sat.
Credit AmEx, MC, V. **Map** p310 D3.
Land at the Head Shop and you'll think Jimi, Janis
and Jim are all still alive. There are wide selections
of pipes, bongs, jewellery, incense and books, and
mushrooms and spores (so green-fingered types can
cultivate their own). Like far out, man.

Hemp Works

Nieuwendijk 13, Old Centre: New Side (421 1762/
www.hempworks.nl). Tram 1, 2, 5, 13, 17. **Open**
11am-7pm Mon-Wed, Sun; 11am-9pm Thur-Sat.
Credit AmEx, DC, MC, V. **Map** p310 C2.
One of the first shops in Amsterdam to sell hemp
clothes and products, and now one of the last, Hemp
Works has had to diversify into seed sales and fresh
mushrooms: it won the Cannabis Cup in 2002 with
its strain of the stinky weed.

Interpolm

Prins Hendrikkade 11, Old Centre: Old Side (402
0232/www.interpolm.nl). Tram 1, 2, 4, 5, 9, 16, 17,
24, 25/Metro Centraal Station. **Open** 9am-6pm Mon-
Fri; 9am-5pm Sat. **Credit** MC, V. **Map** p310 D2.

Spectacular. **Brilmuseum/Brillenwinkel**. *See p165.*

Everything needed to set up a grow centre at home: Interpolm carries hydroponics and organic equipment, bio-growth books and videos.

Electronics

Expert Mons

Utrechtsestraat 80-2, Southern Canal Belt (624 5082). Tram 4/Metro Waterlooplein. **Open** noon-6pm Mon; 9.30am-6pm Tue-Sat. **Credit** AmEx, MC, V. **Map** p315 E4.

Amsterdam: white goods. See, they're as inseparable as yin and yang, or Cheech and Chong. Come here for washing machines, TVs, stereos, fridges and other appliances, most at competitive prices.

Fabrics & trimmings

Capsicum

Oude Hoogstraat 1, Old Centre: Old Side (623 1016/www.capsicumtextiles.com). Tram 4, 9, 14, 16, 24, 25. **Open** 11am-6pm Mon; 10am-6pm Tue, Wed, Fri, Sat; 10am-9pm Thur. **Credit** AmEx, DC, MC, V. **Map** p310 D3.

All the fabrics here are made from natural fibres, such as cotton woven in India. Staff spin the provenance of each fabric into the sale. A gem.

H J van de Kerkhof

Wolvenstraat 9, Western Canal Belt (623 4666). Tram 1, 2, 5. **Open** 11am-6pm Mon; 9am-6pm Tue-Fri; 11am-5pm Sat. **Credit** MC, V. **Map** p314 C4.

Tassel maniacs go wild. A sea of shakeable frilly things, lace and rhinestone banding.

Stoffen & Fourituren Winkel a Boeken

Nieuwe Hoogstraat 31, Old Centre: Old Side (626 7205). Tram 4, 9, 16, 24, 25. **Open** noon-6pm Mon; 10am-6pm Tue, Wed, Fri; 10am-8pm Thur; 10am-5pm Sat. **Credit** MC, V. **Map** p311 E3.

The Boeken family has been in the rag trade, hawking fabrics since 1920. Just try to find somewhere else with the kind of variety on offer here: latex, Lycra, fake fur and sequins abound.

Fashion

Children

Funky vintage clothes can be found at **Noordermarkt**; for budget garments, try **Albert Cuypmarkt** (for both, *see p180*).

Broer & Zus

Rozengracht 104, the Jordaan (422 9002/ www.broerenzus.nl). Tram 13, 14, 17. **Open** noon-6pm Mon; 10.30am-6pm Tue-Fri; 10am-6pm Sat. **Credit** AmEx, MC, V. **Map** p309 B3.

For the baby or toddler who has it all, Broer & Zus makes gift-giving a snap with its handmade toys, adorable T-shirts with goofy slogans, and a selection of some seriously stylish kit.

Geboortewinkel Amsterdam

Bosboom Toussaintstraat 22-4, Museum Quarter (683 1806). Tram 3, 7, 10, 12. **Open** 1-6pm Mon; 10am-6pm Tue-Fri; 10am-5pm Sat. **Credit** MC, V. **Map** p314 C5.

A beautiful range of maternity and baby clothes (including premature sizes) in cotton, wool and linen. You'll also find cotton nappies and childbirth videos.

't Klompenhuisje

Nieuwe Hoogstraat 9a, Old Centre: Old Side (622 8100/www.klompenhuisje.nl). Tram 4, 9, 14/Metro Nieuwmarkt. **Open** 10am-6pm Mon-Sat. **Credit** AmEx, DC, MC, V. **Map** p311 E3.

Delightfully crafted and reasonably priced shoes, traditional clogs and handmade leather and woollen slippers from baby sizes up to size 35.

't Schooltje

Overtoom 87, Museum Quarter (683 0444/ www.schooltje.nl). Tram 1, 2, 5, 6. **Open** 1-6pm Mon; 9am-6pm Tue, Wed, Fri; 9am-9pm Thur; 9.30am-5.30pm Sat; 9.30am-5.30pm 1st Sun of mth. **Credit** AmEx, DC, MC, V. **Map** p313 B6.

Well-heeled and well-dressed kids (babies and kids aged up to 16) are clothed and shod here. The ranges are good but costly. Party costumes a speciality.

Clubwear

Cyberdog/Clubwear House

Spuistraat 250, Old Centre: New Side (330 6385/ 622 8766/www.clubwearhouse.nl/www.cyberdog.net). Tram 1, 2, 5. **Open** 10am-6pm Mon-Wed, Fri, Sat; 10am-9pm Thur; 1-5pm Sun. *Winter* closing hours may vary. **Credit** MC, V. **Map** p310 C3.

Once two shops battled to be top of Amsterdam's glitzy club scene. But then they realised that there is strength in unity. Now you can join the love fest by scanning the rubber, furry and Day-Glo bits from designers Weber, Modevictim, Cicci, Cyberdog and in-house label CHW, or score tickets and DJ tapes.

Designer

Azurro Due

Pieter Cornelisz Hooftstraat 138, Museum Quarter (671 9708). Tram 2, 3, 5, 12. **Open** 1-6pm Mon; 10am-6pm Tue, Wed, Fri; 10am-9pm Thur; 10am-5.30pm Sat; noon-5pm Sun. **Credit** AmEx, DC, MC, V. **Map** p314 C6.

If you've got to splurge, this is as good a spot as any. Saucy picks from Anna Sui, Blue Blood, Chloé and Stella McCartney attract the usual mediacrities.

Bits and Pieces

Cornelis Schuytstraat 22, Museum Quarter (618 1939). Tram 16. **Open** noon-6pm Mon; 10am-6pm Tue-Fri; 10am-5pm Sat. **Credit** AmEx, DC, MC, V.

Innovative purchasing mixes new designers with more established names such as Martine Sitbon, Clements Ribeiro and Earl Jean. Bits and Pieces is often featured in the Dutch rags next to an A-lister's 'what is she wearing/where did she get it' tagline.

Khymo

Leidsestraat 9, Southern Canal Belt (622 2137). Tram 1, 2, 5. **Open** noon-6pm Mon; 10am-6pm Tue, Wed, Fri, Sat; 10am-9pm Thur; 1-6pm Sun. **Credit** AmEx, DC, MC, V. **Map** p314 D4.

Many 20- to 40-somethings, both male and female, come here for trendy garb. Among the labels on offer are Plein Sud, Evisu and Amaya Arzuaga.

Razzmatazz

Wolvenstraat 19, Western Canal Belt (420 0483/ www.razzmatazz.nl). Tram 13, 14, 17. **Open** noon-6pm Mon; 11.30am-6pm Tue, Wed, Fri, Sat; noon-7pm Thur; 1-5pm Sun. **Credit** AmEx, DC, MC, V. **Map** p314 C4.

From cut-price to cutting edge

A quarter of the Dutch population wakes to the ring of a HEMA alarm clock, one in three men wears HEMA underwear, and one in four women wears HEMA bras. HEMA sells 506,000 kilograms of *drop* (liquorice) every year, and the cashiers of their 250 national outlets process 14 million units of *tompouce* (a pink-glazed custard cake) annually, and one smoked sausage per second. Yes, the department store chain has come a long way since 1926, when it started as a 'one price business' selling products for ten, 25 and 50 cents. It was 1969 before they stocked a product that cost more than 100 guilders – an electric drill – wreaking havoc on the two-digit cash registers. While HEMA remains the economic place to shop for basics, it's also made a name for itself as a source of affordable, no-nonsense design objects –

even their sale flyers are graphics' classics. They've had products designed by bigwigs like Piet Hein Eek, Gijs Bakke and Hella Jongerius, and had a big hit with the Le Lapia whistle kettle, selling over 250,000. Of course, they've had some flops – the hairless toilet brush, for example – but that's life. If you like to shop, you'll love HEMA.

HEMA

Kalvertoren, Kalverstraat 212, Southern Canal Belt (422 8988/www.hema.nl). Tram 1, 2, 4, 5, 9, 14, 16, 24, 25. **Open** 11am-6.30pm Mon; 9.30am-6.30pm Tue, Wed, Fri; 9.30am-9pm Thur; 9.30am-6pm Sat; noon-6pm Sun. **Credit** MC, V. **Map** p310 D3.

Other locations: Ferdinand Bolstraat 93A (676 3222); Kinkerstraat 313 (683 4511); Nieuwendijk 174-6 (623 4176).

Although the staff can be a bit of a pain, Razz is a must-see for designers like Walter van Beirendonck, Frankie Morello and Masaki Matsushima.

Spoiled
Leidsestraat 27, Southern Canal Belt (626 3818/ www.spoiled.nl). Tram 1, 2, 5. **Open** noon-6pm Mon; 10am-6pm Tue-Sat; 10am-9pm Thur; noon-6pm Sun. **Credit** AmEx, MC, V. **Map** p314 D4.
A lifestyle shop along London or NY lines, with edgy designs by Duffer of St George, Evisu and Juicy Couture, plus LA coaster bikes, a hairdresser and music and mags to complete your transformation.

2πR
Oude Hoogstraat 10-12, Old Centre: Old Side (421 6329). Tram 4, 9, 14, 16, 24, 25. **Open** noon-7pm Mon; 10am-7pm Tue, Wed, Fri, Sat; 10am-9pm Thur; noon-6pm Sun. **Credit** AmEx, DC, MC, V. **Map** p310 D3.
This funky number's just for the boys. Two shops side by side on Oude Hoogstraat offer urban street wear and killer threads from the likes of Helmut Lang, Psycho Cowboy, D-Squared and Anglomania. **Other locations**: (womenswear): Gasthuismolensteeg 12 (528 5682).

Van Ravenstein
Keizersgracht 359, Western Canal Belt (639 0067). Tram 13, 14, 17. **Open** 1-6pm Mon; 11am-6pm Tue-Fri; 11am-7pm Thur; 10.30am-5.30pm Sat. **Credit** AmEx, MC, V. **Map** p314 C4.
Superb boutique with the best from Belgian designers: Martin Margiela, Dirk Bikkembergs, AF Vandervorst and Bernhard Willhelm, among others. Victor & Rolf form the Dutch contingent. Don't miss the itsy-bitsy bargain basement.

Glasses & contact lenses

Brilmuseum/Brillenwinkel
Gasthuismolensteeg 7, Western Canal Belt (421 2414/www.brilmuseumamsterdam.nl). Tram 1, 2, 5. **Open** noon-5.30pm Wed-Fri; noon-5pm Sat. **No credit cards**. **Map** p310 C3.
Officially this 'shop' is an opticians' museum, but don't let that put you off. The fascinating exhibits are of glasses through the ages, and most of the pairs you see are also up for sale.

Donald E Jongejans
Noorderkerkstraat 18, the Jordaan (624 6888). Tram 3, 10. **Open** 11am-6pm Mon-Sat. **No credit cards**. **Map** p309 B2.
This vintage frame specialist sells unused frames dating from the mid 1800s to the present day. Most frames are at fabulously low prices and built to last – and the staff are friendly, too. A complete treat but the hours are notoriously erratic.

Villa Ruimzicht
Utrechtsestraat 131, Southern Canal Belt (428 2665). Tram 4. **Open** 1-6pm Mon; 9am-6pm Tue, Wed, Fri; 9am-6pm, 7-9pm Thur; 9am-5pm Sat. **Credit** AmEx, MC, V. **Map** p315 E4.

Biba. *See p167.*

If you're bored with your ordinary coloured contact lenses, come here to amaze and surprise your friends with $ signs and more. Designer specs, too.

Hats & handbags

Many markets have huge selections of hats and bags, try **Albert Cuypmarkt** (*see p180*).

Accessorize

Leidsestraat 68, Southern Canal Belt (head office 010 453 1075/www.accessorize.nl). Tram 1, 2, 5. **Open** 10am-6pm Mon-Wed, Fri, Sat; 10am-9pm Thur; noon-6pm Sun. **Credit** MC, V. **Map** p314 D4.
'Ac·ces·sor·ize' means to use items such as gloves, hats, and handbags to complete an outfit. Now, about that handbag...

Cellarrich Connexion

Haarlemmerdijk 98, the Jordaan (626 5526/ www.cellarrich.nl). Tram 1, 2, 4, 5, 13, 14, 16, 17, 24, 25. **Open** 1-6pm Mon; 11am-6pm Tue-Fri; 11am-5pm Sat. **Credit** AmEx, MC, V. **Map** p309 B2.
Nab a sophisticated Dutch handbag in materials from leather to plastic. Many (but not all) of the creations are produced locally by four Dutch designers.

De Hoed van Tijn

Nieuwe Hoogstraat 15, Old Centre: Old Side (623 2759). Tram 4, 9, 14, 16, 24, 25. **Open** 11am-6pm Mon-Sat; *Oct-Dec* noon-5pm Sun. **Credit** AmEx, DC, MC, V. **Map** p311 E3.
Mad hatters will delight in this vast array of bonnets, Homburgs, bowlers, sombreros and caps, plus second-hand and handmade items.

High street

Be sure to cruise the Kalverstraat as it's high street heaven. But here are the usual suspects.

Diesel

Heiligeweg 11-17, Old Centre: New Side (638 4082/ www.diesel.com). Tram 1, 2, 4, 5, 9, 14, 16, 24, 25. **Open** noon-6pm Mon, Sun; 10am-6pm Tue, Wed, Fri, Sat; 10am-9pm Thur. **Credit** AmEx, MC, V. **Map** p314 D4.
Three storeys, filled with Diesel and Diesel only.

Hennes & Mauritz

Kalverstraat 125-9, Old Centre: New Side (524 0440). Tram 1, 2, 4, 5, 9, 14, 16, 24, 25. **Open** noon-6pm Mon, Sun; 10am-6pm Tue, Wed, Fri, Sat; 10am-9pm Thur. **Credit** AmEx, DC, MC, V. **Map** p310 D3.
Prices range from reasonable to ultra low; quality, too, varies. Clothes for men, women, teens and kids. **Other locations:** throughout the city.

Sissy Boy Homeland

Magna Plaza, Nieuwezijds Voorburgwal 182 (basement level), Old Centre: New Side (389 2589/ www.sissy-boy.nl). Tram 1, 2, 4, 5, 9, 14, 16, 24, 25. **Open** 11am-7pm Mon; 10am-7pm Tue, Wed, Fri, Sat; 10am-9pm Thur; noon-7pm Sun. **Credit** AmEx, DC, MC, V. **Map** p310 C3.

A mixture of clothing and interior items, Sissy Boy's new lifestyle shop has a decidedly upmarket rustic-urban vibe. Expect a quirky jumble of labels and wares; candles from Diptyque, Sissy Boy khakis, satin quilts, deer antler chairs and much more.

Zara

Kalverstraat 72, Old Centre: New Side (530 4050/ www.zara.com). Tram 1, 2, 4, 5, 9, 14, 16, 24, 25. **Open** noon-6pm Mon, Sun; 10am-6pm Tue, Wed, Fri, Sat; 10am-9pm Thur. **Credit** AmEx, MC, V. **Map** p310 D3.
Imagine you have a lean, mean fashion machine that can almost instantaneously churn out decent approximations of the latest catwalk creations at a fraction of the price you'd pay at the outlet shops of the designers. Now imagine how much money you'd make doing it. Oops! Too late, Zara beat you to it. The styles are hot – the quality perhaps not.

Jewellery

For crushed carbon, *see p102* **A girl's best friend**.

Biba

Nieuwe Hoogstraat 26, Old Centre: Old Side (330 5721). Tram 4, 9, 14, 16, 24, 25. **Open** 1-6pm Mon; 11am-6pm Tue-Sat; 1-5pm Sun. **Credit** AmEx, V. **Map** p311 E3.
Come here for funky designer jewellery by Gaultier, Gem Kingdom and E Beamon. There's a selection of less exclusive but still attractive brands available for those on less flamboyant budgets.

Grimm Sieraden

Grimburgwal 9, Old Centre: Old Side (622 0501/ www.grimmsieraden.nl). Tram 16, 24, 25. **Open** 11am-6pm Tue-Fri; 11am-5pm Sat. **Credit** AmEx, DC, MC, V. **Map** p310 D3.
While Elize Lutz's shop features the most avant garde of jewellery designers, she has the decency, and sound commercial sense, to concentrate her stock on the most wearable pieces from their ranges.

Jorge Cohen Edelsmid

Singel 414, Southern Canal Belt (623 8646). Tram 1, 2, 5. **Open** 10am-6pm Mon-Fri; 11am-6pm Sat. **Credit** AmEx, DC, MC, V. **Map** p314 D4.
The kind of art deco-inspired jewellery you'd be proud to pass off as the real thing. The shop creates its pieces using a combination of salvaged jewellery, silver and antique and new stones.

MK Jewelry

Reestraat 9, Southern Canal Belt (427 0727/ www.mk-jewelry.com). Tram 13, 14, 17. **Open** 11am-6pm Tue-Sat. **Credit** AmEx, DC, MC, V. **Map** p310 C3.
Pressing our noses to the immaculate windows we were hesitant about intruding. But we're glad we did. Once inside all is calm and relaxed, allowing the glitter of a million reflected, refracted rays of light to work their mesmeric magic. Prices start low.

Eat, Drink, Shop

Shiny, shiny, shiny boots of leather.
Betsy Palmer.

Large sizes

High and Mighty

Singel 465, Southern Old Centre (622 1436/ www.highandmighty.co.uk). Tram 1, 2, 5. **Open** 1-6pm Mon; 9am-6pm Tue, Wed, Fri; 9am-9pm Thur; 9am-5pm Sat; noon-5pm every 1st Sun of mth. **Credit** AmEx, DC, MC, V. **Map** p314 D4.
Big and tall men are going to love the selection: now you can have the same brands as your buddies! From Ben Sherman through to Yves Saint Laurent, if you wear a 58 or larger, you are in luck.

Mateloos

Kwakersplein 1-7, Oud West (683 2384/ www.mateloos.nl). Tram 3, 12, 13, 14, 17. **Open** 10am-6pm Mon-Fri; 10am-5pm Sat. **Credit** AmEx, DC, MC, V. **Map** p313 B5.
Mateloos cares for curves. Clothes from sizes 44 to 60: eveningwear, sportswear, lingerie, the works.

Lingerie

Hunkemöller

Kalverstraat 162, Old Centre: New Side (623 6032/ www.hunkemoller.com). Tram 1, 2, 5, 9, 14, 16, 24, 25. **Open** 11am-6pm Mon; 9.30am-6pm Tue, Wed, Fri, Sat; 9.30am-9pm Thur; noon-6pm Sun. **Credit** AmEx, MC, V. **Map** p310 D3.
Female fancy pants should check out this chain (you can call 035 646 5413 for details of other branches). The undies manage to be feminine and attractive, while simply designed and reasonably priced.

Salon de Lingerie

Utrechtsestraat 38, Southern Canal Belt (623 9857/ www.salondelingerie.nl). Tram 4. **Open** 1-6pm Mon; 10am-6pm Wed, Fri, Sat; 10am-8pm Thur. **Credit** AmEx, DC, MC, V. **Map** p315 E4.
Upscale (often uppity) lingerie shop with a wide collection of stock which, while it might tend towards the conservative, still manages to squeeze in quite a few extravagantly lacy pieces.

Tothem Underwear

Nieuwezijds Voorburgwal 149, Old Centre: New Side (623 0641). Tram 1, 2, 4, 5, 9, 13, 14, 16, 17, 24, 25. **Open** 1-5.30pm Mon; 9.45am-5.30pm Tue, Wed, Fri; 9.45am-9pm Thur; 9.45am-5pm Sat; 1-5pm Sun. **Credit** AmEx, DC, MC, V. **Map** p310 D3.
This men's underwear shop mainly sells designer items: Hom, Calvin Klein, Body Art and the like.

Repairs & cleaning

Luk's Schoenservice

Prinsengracht 500, Southern Canal Belt (623 1937). Tram 1, 2, 5, 6, 7, 10. **Open** 9am-5.30pm Tue-Fri; 9am-5pm Sat. **No credit cards. Map** p314 D5.
Reliable and speedy shoe repairs.

Powders

Kerkstraat 56, Southern Canal Belt (625 0772). Tram 16, 24, 25. **Open** 1-6.30pm Mon; 9.30am-6.30pm Tue-Fri; 9am-12.30pm Sat. **No credit cards. Map** p315 E4.
Washing and dry-cleaning in a relatively central location. Prices are reasonable.

Shoes

For new shoes go to **Leidsestraat** or **Kalverstraat**; for second-hand wares there's **Waterlooplein** or **Noordermarkt** (*see p180*).

Big Shoe

Leliegracht 12, Western Canal Belt (622 6645). Tram 13, 14, 17. **Open** 10am-6pm Wed, Fri; 10am-9pm Thur; 10am-5pm Sat. **Credit** AmEx, DC, MC, V. **Map** p310 C3.
Fashionable footwear for men and women in large sizes only. Every women's shoe on display is available in sizes 42 to 46, men's from 47 to 50.

Betsy Palmer

Rokin 9-15, Old Centre: Old Side (422 1040/ www.betsypalmer.com). Tram 4, 9, 14, 16, 24, 25. **Open** 10.30am-6.30pm Mon-Fri; 10am-6pm Sat; 1-6pm Sun. **Credit** MC, V. **Map** p310 D3.
Tired of seeing the same shoes in every shop, Dutch fashion buyer Gertie Gerards put her money where her mouth was, and set up shop. Betsy Palmer is her in-house label, and sits alongside a huge variety of other labels that change as they sell out.
Other locations: Van Woustraat 46 (470 9795).

Paul Warmer

Leidsestraat 41, Southern Canal Belt (427 8011). Tram 1, 2, 5. **Open** 1-6pm Mon, Sun; 10am-6pm Tue, Wed, Fri, Sat; 10am-9pm Thur. **Credit** AmEx, DC, MC, V. **Map** p314 D4.
Fashionista heaven: ultra-refined footwear for men and women. Gucci, Roberto Cavalli, Emillio Pucci.

Seventy Five

Nieuwe Hoogstraat 24, Old Centre: Old Side (626 4611/www.seventyfive.com). Tram 4, 9, 14/Metro Nieuwmarkt. **Open** noon-6pm Mon; 10am-6pm Tue-Sat; noon-5pm Sun. **Credit** MC, V. **Map** p311 E3.
Trainers for folk who have no intention of ever having to insert a pair of Odor-eaters: high fashion styles from Nike, Puma, Converse, Diesel.

Shoe Baloo

Koningsplein 7, Museum Quarter (626 7993). Tram 2, 3, 5, 12. **Open** noon-6pm Mon; 10am-6pm Tue, Wed, Fri, Sat; 10am-9pm Thur; 1-6pm Sun. **Credit** AmEx, MC, V. **Map** p314 C6.
A space age men's and women's shoe shop with a glowing Barbarella-pod interior. Über cool, but, despite that, worth taking the time to cruise for Miu Miu, Costume Nationale and Patrick Cox.
Other locations: Leidsestraat 10 (330 9147); PC Hooftstraat 80 (671 2210).

Street

To look good but pay less, hunt down relaxed streetwear styles in **Waterlooplein Market** (*see p180*).

America Today

Magna Plaza, Nieuwezijds Voorburgwal 182 (ground floor), Old Centre: New Side (638 8447/www.americatoday.nl). Tram 1, 2, 5, 13, 14, 17. **Open** 11am-7pm Mon; 10am-7pm Tue, Wed, Fri, Sat; 10am-9pm Thur; noon-7pm Sun. **Credit** AmEx, DC, MC, V. **Map** p310 C2.

This giant started as the tiniest of ventures; today it sells American street classics from Converse, Ben Sherman, Timberland and the like.

Other locations: Sarphatistraat 48 (638 9847).

Independent Outlet

Vijzelstraat 77, Southern Canal Belt (421 2096/ www.outlet.nl). Tram 16, 24, 25. **Open** 1-6pm Mon; 11am-6pm Tue, Wed, Fri, Sat; 11am-9pm Thur. **Credit** AmEx, MC, V. **Map** p314 D4.

Customised boards, Vans shoes and labels like Fred Perry: just some of the things in store at this temple to street cool. Great selection of punk imports.

Men at Work

Kalverstraat 172, Old Centre: New Side (624 1000/ www.menatwork.nl). Tram 1, 2, 4, 5, 9, 14, 16, 24, 25. **Open** noon-6pm Mon, Sun; 10am-6pm Tue, Wed, Fri, Sat; 10am-9pm Thur. **Credit** AmEx, MC, V. **Map** p314 D4.

The naff name doesn't stop it being the best address for denim labels like G-Star, Evisu, Kuyichi and Pepe.

Reprezent

Haarlemmerstraat 80, the Jordaan (528 5540/ www.reprezent.nl). Tram 3/bus 18, 22. **Open** 10.30am-6.30pm Tue, Wed, Fri; 10.30am-9pm Thur; 10.30am-6pm Sat; noon-6pm Sun. **Credit** V, MC. **Map** p310 C2.

Custom skateboards, snowboarding threads from Volcom Grenade and Special Blend, ass kicking accessories and in-house surf and snowboard tours arranged. If that ain't the wildest: the staff don't pose!

Tom's Skate Shop

Oude Hoogstraat 35-37, Old Centre: Old Side (625 4922/www.skateboardwinkel.tk). Tram 4, 9, 14/ Metro Nieuwmarkt. **Open** noon-6pm Mon; 10am-6pm Tue-Sat; 12am-6pm Sun **Credit** AmEx, MC, V. **Map** p310 D3.

Dual gender gear from the likes of Nike SB, Zoo York, local label Rockwell and London label Addict. Also stocks limited edition trainers, shades by Electric, and, of course, custom skateboards.

Vintage & second-hand

Loads of vintage clothes and accessories can be found (and often cheaply) at **Noordermarkt** and **Waterlooplein** (*see p180*).

Lady Day

Hartenstraat 9, Western Canal Belt (623 5820/ www.ladydayvintage.com). Tram 1, 2, 5. **Open** 11am-6pm Mon-Wed, Fri, Sat; 11am-9pm Thur; 1-6pm Sun. **Credit** AmEx, MC, V. **Map** p310 C3.

Beautifully tailored second-hand and period suits, and sportswear classics. Period wedge shoes, pumps and accessories complete the stylish ensemble.

Laura Dols

Wolvenstraat 6-7, Western Canal Belt (624 9066/ www.lauradols.nl). Tram 1, 2, 5. **Open** 11am-6pm Mon-Wed, Fri, Sat; 11am-9pm Thur; 2-6pm Sun. **Credit** MC, V. **Map** p314 C4.

A treasure trove of period clothing, mainly from the '40s and '50s, Laura Dols has many of the sumptuous dresses of the time, as well as some menswear.

Ree-member

Reestraat 26, Western Canal Belt (622 1329). Tram 1, 2, 5. **Open** 1-6pm Mon; 11am-6pm Tue-Sat. **Credit** AmEx, MC, V. **Map** p310 C3.

Ree-member stocks a terrific collection of vintage clothes and '60s standards. The shoes are the best in town and priced to match. If you're strapped for cash you'll be pleased to learn that they sell their less-than-perfect pieces on Noordermarkt – by the kilo! Ain't life sweet?

Zipper

Huidenstraat 7, Western Canal Belt (623 7302). Tram 1, 2, 5. **Open** 11am-6pm Mon-Sat; 1-5pm Sun. **Credit** AmEx, MC, V. **Map** p314 C4.

It's not cheap, but the jeans, cowboy shirts, '80s gear and '70s hipsters are worth a gander; there's treasure to be found on them there rails.

Other locations: Nieuwe Hoogstraat 8 (627 0353).

Flowers

It's tempting to bring home a selection of bulbs from Amsterdam. However, although travellers to the UK and Ireland will be fine, some other countries' import regulations either prohibit the entry of bulbs or, in the case of the US, require them to have a phytosanitary certificate. You'll find that some of the packaging is marked with flags indicating the countries into which the bulbs can be safely carried, but most Dutch wholesalers know the regulations and can ship bulbs to your home. In terms of cut flowers, travellers to the UK and Ireland can take an unlimited quantity, as long as they're not chrysanthemums or gladioli, while US regulations vary from state to state.

Bloemenmarkt (Flower market)

Singel, between Muntplein and Koningsplein, Southern Canal Belt. Tram 1, 2, 4, 5, 9, 14, 16, 24, 25. **Open** 9am-6pm Mon-Sat. **No credit cards**. **Map** p314 D4.

This fascinating collage of colour is the world's only floating flower market, with 15 florists and garden shops (although many hawk cheesy souvenirs these days) permanently ensconced on barges along the southern side of Singel. The plants and flowers usually last well and are good value.

Plantenmarkt (Plant market)

Amstelveld, Southern Canal Belt. Tram 4, 6, 7, 10. **Open** 9.30am-6pm Mon. **No credit cards**. **Map** p315 E4.

Despite the market's general emphasis on plants, pots and vases, the Plantenmarkt also has cut flowers for sale. Each spring sees the house plants go on sale, while the later months burst into colour with the transient glory of garden annuals.

Eat, Drink, Shop

Florists Gerda's
Runstraat 16, Western Canal Belt (624 2912). Tram 1, 2, 5. **Open** 9am-6pm Mon-Fri; 9am-5pm Sat. **Credit** DC, MC, V. **Map** p314 C4.

Amsterdam's most inspired florist, Gerda's diminutive shop is full of fantastic blooms and sports legendary window displays. If you're lucky, you'll spy sculptural bouquets on their way out the door. Gerda's takes orders for local deliveries from anywhere in the world – pay by phone with plastic.

Jemi
Warmoesstraat 83a, Old Centre: Old Side (625 6034). Tram 4, 9, 16, 24, 25. **Open** 9am-6pm Mon-Fri. **No credit cards. Map** p310 D2.

Amsterdam's first stone-built house is now occupied by a delightfully colourful florist. Jemi arranges splendid bouquets, provides tuition in the fragrant art of flower-arranging, throws floral brunches and stocks loads of pots and plants.

Food & drink

Bakeries

For bread, rolls and packaged biscuits, go to a *warmebakker*; for pastries and delicious cream cakes, you need a *banketbakker*.

Crust and Crumbs
Haarlemmerstraat 108, the Jordaan (528 6430/ www.crustandcrumbs.nl). Tram 3/bus 18, 22. **Open** 11am-6.30pm Mon; 8.30am-6.30pm Tue-Fri; 9am-5pm Sat. **No credit cards. Map** p310 C2.

'Inspiring bread and delicacies' is their motto: tasty sourdough breads, fine French pastries and fresh mescal salad greens from restaurant/greenhouse De Kas are just a few of their treats.

Oldenburg
Beethovenstraat 17, Zuid (662 5520). Tram 5. **Open** 9am-5.30pm Mon-Fri; 9am-5pm Sat. **No credit cards.**

Dessert cakes, *bavarois* and chocolate mousse tarts, plus great choccies, marvellous marzipan confections in winter and chocolate eggs at Easter. **Other locations**: Maasstraat 84 (662 2840); Singel 184 (427 8341).

Runneboom
1e Van der Helststraat 49, the Pijp (673 5941). Tram 16, 24, 25. **Open** 7am-5pm Mon, Wed, Fri; 7am-4pm Tue, Thur, Sat. **No credit cards. Map** p315 E5.

This Pijp bakery is a staunch favourite with locals. A huge selection of French, Russian, Greek and Turkish loaves is offered, with rye bread the house speciality. Delicious cakes and pastries are also sold.

Cheese

The younger (*jong*) the cheese, the creamier and milder it will be; riper (*belegen*) examples will be drier and sharper, especially the old (*oud*) cheese. Most popular are Goudse (from Gouda), Leidse (flavoured with cumin seeds) and Edammer (aka Edam, with its red crust). Don't miss Leerdammer, Maaslander (both mild with holes) or Kernhem (a dessert cheese).

Skate punks unite at **Reprezent**. *See p170.*

Geels & Co. See p175.

De Kaaskamer

Runstraat 7, Western Canal Belt (623 3483). Tram 1, 2, 5. **Open** noon-6pm Mon; 9am-6pm Tue-Fri; 9am-5pm Sat, noon-5pm Sun. **No credit cards.** **Map** p314 C4.

De Kaaskamer offers over 200 varieties of domestic and imported cheeses, plus pâtés, olives, pastas and wines. Have fun quizzing the staff on the different cheese types and caseus trivia: they know their stuff.

Wegewijs

Rozengracht 32, the Jordaan (624 4093/www. wegewijs.nl). Tram 13, 14, 17. **Open** 8.30am-5.30pm Mon-Fri; 9am-4.30pm Sat. **No credit cards.** **Map** p309 B3.

The Wegewijs family started running this shop more than 100 years ago. On offer are around 50 foreign cheeses and over 100 different domestic varieties of caseus, including *gras kaas*, a grassy-tasting cheese that is available in summer. For those nervous about buying a strange cheese, Wegewijs allows you to try Dutch varieties beforehand.

Chocolate

Australian

Leidsestraat 101, Southern Canal Belt (622 0897/ www.australianhomemade.com). Tram 1, 2, 5. **Open** 11am-11pm Mon-Fri, Sun; 11am-noon Sat. **No credit cards.** **Map** p314 D4.

Check out the delicious selection of bonbons, icecream and coffees with all natural ingredients as you ponder how the Amsterdam branch of a Belgian chain ended up with this name.

Other locations: throughout the city.

Huize van Wely

Beethovenstraat 72, Zuid (662 2009/www. huizevanwely.nl). Tram 5. **Open** 9.30am-6pm Mon-Fri; 8.30am-5pm Sat. **Credit** AmEx, MC, V.

Since 1922, Huize van Wely has been handmaking confectionery at its factory in Noordwijk, on the west coast of Holland. So sublime are its creations that the company has been rewarded with the honour of being the sole Dutch member of the prestigious Relais Desserts and Académie Culinaire de France.

Pâtisserie Pompadour

Huidenstraat 12, Western Canal Belt (623 9554). Tram 1, 2, 5, 7. **Open** 9am-6pm Mon-Sat. **Credit** MC, V. **Map** p314 C4.

This fabulous *bonbonnerie* and tearoom – with an 18th-century interior imported from Antwerp – is likely to bring out the little old lady in anyone. A relatively new branch (Kerkstraat 148, Southern Canal Belt; 9am-6pm daily) also sports a nice tea room serving sublime designer sandwiches.

Puccini Bomboni

Staalstraat 17, Old Centre: Old Side (626 5474/ www.puccinibomboni.com). Tram 9, 14/Metro Waterlooplein. **Open** noon-6pm Mon; 9am-6pm Tue-Sat; noon-6pm Sun. **Credit** MC, V. **Map** p311 E3.

Handmade tamarind, thyme, lemongrass, and anise chocolates made without artificial ingredients. **Other locations**: Singel 184 (427 8341).

Unlimited Delicious

Haarlemmerstraat 122, the Jordaan (622 4829/ www.unlimiteddelicious.nl). Tram 3/bus 18, 22. **Open** 9am-6pm Mon-Sat. **Credit** AmEx, V. **Map** p310 C2.

Known for such twisted treats as balsamic-vinegar-and-tomato bonbons and a caramel-balsamic-choco-late-pie-with-a-brownie-bottom, Unlimited Delicious also offers individual or group courses in bonbon-making so you can devise your own mad combos.

Delicatessens

Ron's

Huidenstraat 26, Western Canal Belt (626 1668). Tram 1, 2, 5, 7. **Open** 8.30am-6pm Tue-Fri; 8.30am-5pm Sat. **No credit cards. Map** p314 C4.
This jewel of a greengrocer-cum-deli is frequented by the most demanding food critic in Holland, Johannes Van Damme – and hence almost everyone with cash and taste buds follows suit. Great pastas, tarts, salads and fruits.

Uliveto

Weteringschans 118, Southern Canal Belt (423 0099). Tram 6, 7, 10. **Open** 11am-8pm Mon-Fri; noon-6pm Sat. **No credit cards. Map** p315 E5.
Uliveto is a superb Italian deli that – along with the usual wines, pastas and fruity olive oils for dipping bread – has an irresistible takeaway selection of tender roasted seasonal vegetables, grilled fish, rack of lamb and polenta, and ricotta cheesecake.

Ethnic & speciality

Arkwrights

Rozengracht 13, the Jordaan (320 0710/www. arkwrights.nl). Tram 13, 14, 17. **Open** 1-8pm Mon; 11am-8pm Tue-Sun. **No credit cards. Map** p310 C3.

Britons! Stop homesickness by stocking up on fresh sausages, bacon and puddings, Walkers crisps and more. Then wash it all down with the British or Irish beers and ciders also on sale.

Casa Molero

Gerard Doustraat 66, the Pijp (676 1707). Tram 16, 24, 25. **Open** 10am-6pm Tue-Fri; 9am-5pm Sat. **No credit cards. Map** p315 E6.
Aside from stocking cheeses, spices, sausages and hams from Spain, Casa Molero is also an exclusive distributor for some Spanish and Portuguese wines.

Eichholtz

Leidsestraat 48, Southern Canal Belt (622 0305). Tram 1, 2, 5. **Open** 10am-6.30pm Mon; 9am-6.30pm Tue, Wed, Fri; 9am-9pm Thur; 9am-6.30pm Sat; noon-6pm Sun. **Credit** (over €23 only) AmEx, MC, V. **Map** p314 D4.
Beloved by expats, this is the place where Yanks can get their hands on chocolate chips and Brits can source Christmas puddings. They stock a range of Dutch souvenirs, too.

Olivaria

Hazenstraat 2a, the Jordaan (638 3552). Tram 7, 10. **Open** 2-6pm Mon; 11am-6pm Tue-Sat. **No credit cards. Map** p314 C4.
What's in a name? Quite a lot, judging by Olivaria's devotion to olive oils. There's a vast array of them from around the world, both on show and for sale.

Oriental Commodities

Nieuwmarkt 27, Old Centre: Old Side (626 2797). Tram 4, 9, 14, 16, 24, 25/Metro Nieuwmarkt. **Open** 9am-6pm Mon-Sat; 9.30am-5pm Sun. **No credit cards. Map** p310 D2.
Visit Amsterdam's largest Chinese food emporium for the full spectrum of Asian foods and ingredients, from shrimp- and scallop-flavoured egg noodles to fried tofu balls and fresh veg. There's also a fine range of Chinese cooking appliances and utensils.

Waterwinkel

Roelof Hartstraat 10, Museum Quarter (675 5932/ www.springwater.nl). Tram 3, 24. **Open** 1-6pm Mon; 10am-6pm Tue-Fri; 10am-5pm Sat. **Credit** AmEx, DC, V.
Mineral water galore, both native and imported. The sheer variety may induce an emergency in the more weak-bladdered among us.

Health food

See also p180 Markets.

Delicious Food

Westerstraat 24, the Jordaan (320 3070). Tram 3. **Open** 10am-7pm Mon, Wed-Fri; 9am-6pm Sat; 11am-3pm Sun. **No credit cards. Map** p309 B2.
Organic produce has reached the self-contradictory pinnacle of urban rustic chic at what can only be described as a bulk food boutique. Come here for the enticing dispensers of pastas, nuts, exotic spices, plus oils and vinegars.

Eat, Drink, Shop

De Natuurwinkel
Weteringschans 133, Southern Canal Belt (638 4083/www.denatuurwinkel.nl). Tram 6, 7, 10. **Open** 8am-8pm Mon-Sat; 11am-7pm Sun. **Credit** MC, V. **Map** p315 E5.
The largest healthfood supermarket that there is to be found in Amsterdam. You'll find everything here, from organic meat, fruit and vegetables (delivered fresh daily) to quite surprisingly tasty sugar-free chocolates and organic wine and more.
Other locations: throughout the city.

Organic© Food For You
Cornelis Schuytstraat 26-28, Zuid (379 5195/ www.organicfoodforyou.nl). Tram 16. **Open** 9am-7pm Mon-Fri; 8.30am-6pm Sat. **No credit cards.**
Fancypants organic supermarket with daily staples like sugar and flour and more exotic fare like 30-year-old balsamic vinegar, caviar and wild salmon.

Night shops

It's 11pm, and you're in dire need of ice-cream/ condoms/cigarettes/toilet roll/beer/chocolate (delete as applicable). This is where the city's night shops come in. But since the customers are desperate and the staff costs higher, the prices are generally steeper than in their more diurnal competitors.

Avondmarkt
De Wittenkade 94-6, West (686 4919). Tram 10. **Open** 4pm-midnight Mon-Fri; 3pm-midnight Sat; 2pm-midnight Sun. **No credit cards. Map** p309 A2.
The biggest and best of all night shops, this is basically a supermarket, albeit a late-opening one. Worth the trek out just west of the Jordaan.

Big Bananas
Leidsestraat 73, Southern Canal Belt (627 7040). Tram 1, 2, 5. **Open** 9am-1am Mon-Fri, Sun; 9am-2am Sat. **No credit cards. Map** p314 D4.
A passable selection of wine, some odd-looking canned cocktails and a variety of sandwiches are stocked here. Expensive, even for a night shop.

Dolf's Avondverkoop
Willemstraat 79, the Jordaan (625 9503). Tram 3. **Open** 4pm-1am daily. **No credit cards. Map** p310 B2.
One of the best night shops in the Jordaan, Dolf's stocks all the urgent products you might suddenly need late at night. As pricey as most night shops.

Sterk
Waterlooplein 241, Old Centre: Old Side (626 5097). Tram 9, 14/Metro Waterlooplein. **Open** 8am-2am daily. **Credit** MC, V. **Map** p311 E3.
Less of a night shop and more of a deli: quiches, pastries and salads are made on site, and there's also fruit and veg. Be prepared to ask for what you want here – there's no self-service. Its branch is known as 'Champagne Corner', which hints at what's on offer.
Other locations: De Clercqstraat 1-7 (618 1727).

Off-licences (Slijterijen)

De Bierkoning
Paleisstraat 125, Old Centre: New Side (625 2336/ www.bierkoning.nl). Tram 1, 2, 5, 13, 14, 16, 17, 24, 25. **Open** 1-7pm Mon; 11am-7pm Tue, Wed, Fri; 11am-9pm Thur; 11am-6pm Sat; 1-5pm Sun. **Credit** AmEx, DC, MC, V. **Map** p310 C3.
Named for its location behind the Royal Palace, the Beer King stocks a trifling 850 brands of beer from around the world, and a range of fine glasses.

Cadenhead's Whisky
Huidenstraat 19, Western Canal Belt (330 6287/ www.cadenhead.nl). Tram 1, 2, 5, 7. **Open** 11am-6pm Tue-Sat; 11am-9pm Thur; 1-5pm Sun. **Credit** AmEx, MC, V. **Map** p314 C4.
This Shangri-la for whisky (and whiskey) lovers has a great selection of elixirs from Scotland, Ireland and America, and a range of Scottish mineral waters should you wish to pollute the true water of life.

Supermarkets

A few tips for shopping in Dutch supermarkets. Unless a per piece (*per stuk*) price is given, fruit and veg usually has to be weighed by the customers. Put your produce on the scale, press the picture of the item, and press the 'BON' button to get the receipt. You must pack your groceries yourself, too – and if you want a plastic bag, you'll have to ask (and pay) for it. *See also p177* **Heijnie ho**!

Albert Heijn
Nieuwezijds Voorburgwal 226, Old Centre: New Side (421 8344/www.ah.nl). Tram 1, 2, 4, 5, 9, 13, 14, 16, 17, 24, 25. **Open** 8am-10pm Mon-Sat; 11am-7pm Sun. **No credit cards. Map** p310 D3.
This massive Food Plaza, just behind Dam Square, is one of over 40 branches of Albert Heijn in Amsterdam. It contains virtually all the household goods you could ever need, though some of the ranges are more costly than at its competitors. Note: most branches do not have extended opening hours.
Other locations: throughout the city.

Dirk van den Broek
Marie Heinekenplein 25, the Pijp (673 9393). Tram 16, 24, 25. **Open** 9am-9pm Mon-Fri; 9am-8pm Sat. **No credit cards. Map** p315 E5.
Suddenly fashionable – its red bags are now must-haves for the town's designer lemmings and fashion rats – Dirk remains cheaper than Albert Heijn, while its choice has improved.
Other locations: throughout the city.

Tea & coffee

Geels & Co
Warmoesstraat 67, Old Centre: Old Side (624 0683/ www.geels.nl). Tram 4, 9, 14, 16, 24, 25. **Open** *Shop* 9.30am-6pm Mon-Sat. **Credit** MC. **Map** p310 D2.

Eat, Drink, Shop

Coffee beans and loose teas, plus a large range of brewing contraptions and serving utensils. Upstairs is a small museum of brewing equipment, which is open only on Saturday afternoons.

Simon Levelt

Prinsengracht 180, Western Canal Belt (624 0823/ www.simonlevelt.com). Tram 13, 14, 17. **Open** 10am-6pm Mon-Fri; 10am-5pm Sat. **Credit** AmEx, DC, MC, V. **Map** p309 B3.

Anything and everything to do with brewing and drinking, stocked in a remarkable old shop. The premises date from 1839 and the place still has much of the original tiled decor.

Other locations: throughout the city.

Furniture

For intensive browsing, don't miss **Overtoom** (*map p314 C5-C6*), re-invented as a furniture boulevard, or **Post Amsterdam** (*see p178* **Living for design**).

Bebob Design Interior

Prinsengracht 764, Southern Canal Belt (624 5763/www.bebob.nl). Tram 4. **Open** noon-6pm Tue-Fri; 11am-5pm Sat. **Credit** AmEx, MC, V. **Map** p315 E4.

Bebob stocks sought-after vintage furnishing from the likes of Eames on up. The quality of pieces is fantastic, the selection superb, the prices high.

De Kasstoor

Rozengracht 202-10, the Jordaan (521 8112). Tram 13, 14, 17. **Open** 10am-6pm Mon-Wed, Fri; 10am-9pm Thur; 10am-5pm Sat. **Credit** AmEx, MC, V. **Map** p309 B3.

De Kasstoor is not your average modern Dutch interior design shop; it also has handpicked collectors' pieces from the likes of Le Corbusier, Eames and Citterio, and a very extensive upholstery and fabrics library. Plan to pay for oversized luggage.

Pols Potten

KNSM-laan 39, The Waterfront (419 3541/ www.polspotten.nl). Tram 10, 26. **Open** 10am-6pm Tue-Fri; 10am-5pm Sat; 1-5pm Sun. **Credit** MC, V. **Map** p108.

'Pol's Pots'. Quite why a shop stocking innovative furnishings and home accessories should wish to associate itself with a genocidal mass-murderer remains a mystery. But it does have lots of pots, and a design team to help you pull off the latest trends.

Games, models & toys

Joe's Vliegerwinkel

Nieuwe Hoogstraat 19, Old Centre: Old Side (625 0139). Tram 4, 9, 16, 24, 25/Metro Nieuwmarkt. **Open** 1-6pm Mon; 11am-6pm Tue-Fri; 11am-5pm Sat. **Credit** DC, MC, V. **Map** p311 E3.

Kites, kites and yet more kites, plus a quirky array of boomerangs, yo-yos and kaleidoscopes can be found at this wonderfully colourful shop.

Kramer/Pontifex

Reestraat 18-20, Western Canal Belt (626 5274). Tram 13, 14, 17. **Open** 10am-6pm Mon-Fri; 10am-5pm Sat. **No credit cards**. **Map** p310 C3.

Broken Barbies and battered bears are restored to health by Mr Kramer, a doctor for old-fashioned dolls and teddies who has practised here for 25 years. In the same shop, Pontifex is a candle seller.

Schaak en Go het Paard

Haarlemmerdijk 173, the Jordaan (624 1171/www. schaakengo.nl). Tram 3/bus 18, 22. **Open** 1-5.30pm Mon; 10am-5.30pm Tue, Wed, Fri, Sat; 10am-8pm Thur. **Credit** AmEx MC, V. **Map** p309 B1.

This is the place to come to for a glorious selection of chess sets, from African to ultra-modern.

Schaal Treinen Huis

Bilderdijkstraat 94, Oud West (612 2670/www. schaaltreinenhuis.nl). Tram 3, 7, 12, 13, 14, 17. **Open** 1-5pm Mon; 9.30am-5.30pm Tue-Fri; 9.30am-5pm Sat. **Credit** AmEx, DC, MC, V. **Map** p313 B5.

DIY kits and a ready-made parade that includes electric trains, modern and vintage vehicles and some truly adorable dolls' houses.

Gifts & souvenirs

Delftshop

Spiegelgracht 13, Southern Canal Belt (421 8360). Tram 4, 9, 16, 24, 25. **Open** 9.30am-6pm Mon-Sat; 11am-6pm Sun. **Credit** AmEx, DC, MC, V. **Map** p314 D5.

Souvenirs with provenance. Delftshop are the official dealers of Royal Delft and Makkum pottery, the bread and butter of the Dutch antique trade. The stock here includes antiques too, with some pieces dating from the 17th century – for a price, of course.

Other locations: Prinsengracht 440 (627 8299); Rokin 44 (620 0000).

Tesselschade: Arbeid Adelt

Leidseplein 33, Southern Canal Belt (623 6665). Tram 1, 2, 5, 6, 7, 10. **Open** 11am-6pm Tue-Fri; 10am-5pm Sat. **Credit** AmEx, MC, V. **Map** p314 D5.

Everything here is sold on a non-profit basis by Arbeid Adelt ('work ennobles'), an association of Dutch women. There are plenty of toys and decorations, as well as more utilitarian household items such as tea cosies and decorated clothes hangers.

Health & beauty

Douglas

Kalverstraat 71, Southern Canal Belt (627 6663/ www.douglas.nl). Tram 1, 2, 4, 5, 9, 14, 16, 24, 25. **Open** 1-6pm Mon; 10am-6pm Tue, Wed, Fri, Sat; 10am-9pm Thur; noon-6pm Sun. **Credit** AmEx, MC, V. **Map** p310 D3.

The scents and labels you'd expect, plus rarer brands like La Prairie, Urban Decay and Versace. This new two-storey superstore also features hair products not normally found outside salons.

Other locations: throughout the city.

Heijnie ho!

There are more reasons to visit a supermarket than the upsurge of prices since the Euro came in. Note how cheap the Grolsch is when compared to that trendy bar back home. But you can also glean many insights into a people through what they eat, how they package it, and what muzak they listen to while buying it. However, while many stereotypes are true – the range of cleaning products is epic – don't expect a ballet of clogged-out *Stepford Wives*.

The Dutch have a particularly close relationship with their superest of supermarkets: **Albert Heijn** (*see p175*). Similar to how a photocopy is a 'Xerox', the Dutch often call any supermarket 'Albert Heijn'. And it's no coincidence that AH's colour scheme is blue: a shade that the Dutch, unlike Swedes, see as highly feminine and comforting. Albert Heijn was founded in 1887 in Oostzaan as a cornershop; a replica of which can be visited at the open-air museum **Zaanse Schans** (*see p263*). And today, you are always within rock-throwing range of an *Albie*: be it a regular AH, an 'AH XL' or a small 'AH to go'. Out of deference to Dutch sensibilities, we will skim over the fact that AH's holding company, Ahold, had their own Enron-like billion Euro accounting problems in 2003 when its accounts were reissued. But you may want to know that **Dirk van den Broek** (*see p175*) has increased its selection while keeping prices low; and its red shopping bags are a bona fide hype with the fashion- and design-conscious crowd. (Another tip: if you want it *really* cheap – 39 cent beer anyone? – keep your eyes peeled for chains like Aldi, Lidl and Coop.)

But enough of this pretentious drivel... The true reason to visit the supermarket is to stuff one's gob. Addictions have been fought, but rarely won, against such tantalising treats as *stroopwafels* (thin wafers united with syrup), *drop* (liquorice drops that cover the range from sweet to salty), and *hagelslag* (the nation's greatest gift to the world of bread toppings: flaked chocolate). And don't get us started on the kaleidoscopic assortment of glorious milk products... We're not just talking cheese. For instance, the lightly sour *karnemelk* (buttermilk) goes down a treat when served with those *hagelslag* sandwiches. And *vla* (custard) rates as a wonderful dessert – but, be warned, don't drink it in public as it's also *the* food group for the toothless junkie crowd.

In short: explore and ye shall be rewarded. Happy picnicking!

Jacob Hooy & Co

Kloveniersburgwal 12, Old Centre: Old Side (624 3041/www.jacobhooy.nl). Tram 4, 9, 14, 16, 24, 25/Metro Nieuwmarkt. **Open** 1-6pm Mon; 10am-6pm Tue-Fri; 10am-5pm Sat. **Credit** V. **Map** p310 C3.
Established in 1743, this chemist sells medicinal herbs, health foods and homeopathic remedies.

Lavendula

Westerstraat 45, the Jordaan (420 9140/www. lavendula.nl). Tram 1, 2, 5, 13, 17. **Open** 10am-5.30pm Mon; 10am-6pm Wed-Fri; 9.30am-5.30pm Sat. Closed Tue, Sun. **Credit** AmEx. **Map** p309 B2.
Simone will make sense of the supplements on sale in this tiny shop, or just melt into one of her facials!

Living for design

The history of Dutch design has always fluttered between intrinsic orderliness (reinforced by Calvinism and De Stijl) and a strong desire for personal expression (perhaps an echo of the stubbornness required to battle the sea). And the fact that this design is often both ingeniously functional and downright witty has resulted in worldwide acclaim – so much so that even the tourist board has jumped on the bandwagon at www.coolcapitals.com. In fact, design has infiltrated every level of Dutch life *and* death: as witnessed by designer coffin outfit **De Ode** (Levantkade 51, 419 0882, www.uitvaart.nl/ode) in the eastern docklands (*see p108* **Take a walk on the water side**).

Droog Design

Staalstraat 7a/7b, Old Centre: Old Side (523 5050/www.droogdesign.nl). Tram 4, 9, 14, 16, 24, 25. **Open** noon-6pm Tue-Sat. **Credit** MC, V. **Map** p311 E3.
This internationally acclaimed Dutch design collective has its own shop with the wittiest designers around: Marcel Wanders, Hella Jongerius, Richard Hutten and Jurgen Bey.

Frozen Fountain

Prinsengracht 629, Western Canal Belt (622 9375/www.frozenfountain.nl). Tram 1, 2, 5. **Open** 1-6pm Mon; 10am-6pm Tue-Fri; 10am-5pm Sat. **Credit** AmEx, V. **Map** p313 C4.
The 'Froz' is a haven for lovers of contemporary furniture and design items. While showing innovative young Dutch designers such as furniture god Piet Hein Eek, it also exhibits the international brigade, like Marc Newsom.

Galerie Binnen

Keizersgracht 82, Western Canal Belt (625 9603). Tram 1, 2, 5, 13, 17. **Open** noon-6pm Wed-Sat; or by appointment. **No credit cards**. **Map** p310 C2.
These industrial and interior design specialists show work by unusual names (Sottsass, Kukkapuro, Studio Atika) and host

unusual exhibits of things like toilet brushes, Benno Primsela vases, or designers subverting Dutch clichés (www.dutch-souvenirs.org).

Post Amsterdam

Oosterdokkade 3-5, Post CS, 9th and 10th floors, the Waterfront (421 1033/www. postamsterdam.nl). Tram 1, 2, 4, 5, 6, 9, 13, 16, 17, 24, 25, 26. **Open** 11am-5pm Mon-Sat; noon-5pm Sun. **No credit cards**. **Map** p311 E1.
A showroom for 30 of the top European interior design companies, next to Centraal Station. *See p107* **View to the future**.

SML.X

Donker Curtiusstraat 11, Westerpark (681 2837/www.sml-x.com)). Tram 10, Bus 18. **Open** noon-6pm Fri; noon-5pm Sat. **No credit cards**. **Map** p309 A3.
A T-shirt shop with a difference, offering an open forum for Dutch graphic/contemporary designers and graffiti artists to make their own shirts, which are then sold exclusively at this shop/gallery (and its webstore...).

WonderWood

Rusland 3, Old Center: Old Side (625 3738/ www.wonderwood.nl). Tram 6, 7, 10. **Open** noon-6pm Wed-Sat. **Credit** AmEx, MC, V. **Map** p314 D5.
The name says it all: wonderfully sculpted wood in the form of shop-made originals, re-editions of global classics and original plywood from the '40s and '50s. Wonderful.

Also...

Rozengracht, Haarlemmerstraat and the 'Nine Streets' (*see p181* **Where to spend**) are good for general design. Department store **HEMA** (*see p164* **From cut-price to cutting edge**) often has cheap but savvy knock-offs. **Athenaeum Nieuwscentrum** (*see p161*) is the place for Amsterdam-centric design books and mags. And, of course, there's **Condomerie het Gulden Vlies** (*see p182*) for functional and whimsical designer peniswear.

Lush

*Kalverstraat 98, Old Centre: New Side (330 6376/
www.lush.nl). Tram 4, 9, 14, 16, 24, 25.* **Open** noon-
6pm Mon, Sun; 10am-6pm Tue, Wed, Fri, Sat; 10am-
9pm Thur. **Credit** MC, V. **Map** p310 C3.
Lush looks lovely and smells divine. Friendly staff.

Rituals

*Kalverstraat 73, Old Centre: New Side (344 9222/
www.rituals.com). Tram 4, 9, 14, 16, 24, 25.* **Open**
noon-6pm Mon, Sun; 10am-6pm Tue, Wed, Fri, Sat;
10am-9pm Thur. **Credit** MC, V, AmEx. **Map** p310 D3.
A shop integrating products for body and home. We
all have to brush our teeth and do the dishes, so the
shop is full of products to ritualise such daily grinds.

Skins Cosmetics Lounge

*Runstraat 9, Western Canal Belt (528 6922/www.
skins.nl). Tram 1, 2, 5, 13, 14, 17.* **Open** 1-7pm
Mon; 11am-7pm Tue, Wed, Fri; 11am-9pm Thur;
10am-7pm Sat; noon-5pm Sun. **Credit** AmEx, DC,
MC, V. **Map** p314 C4.
Sleek, sexy and full of products you'll have trouble
finding anywhere else in town: REN, Benefit, Creed.

De Witte Tandenwinkel

*Runstraat 5, Western Canal Belt (623 3443). Tram
1, 2, 5, 13, 14, 17.* **Open** 1-6pm Mon; 10am-6pm
Tue-Fri; 10am-5pm Sat. **Credit** AmEx, MC, V.
Map p314 C4.
The store that's armed to the teeth with brushes and
pastes to ensure your gnashers are white.

Home accessories

Kitsch Kitchen

*Rozengracht 8, the Jordaan (622 8261). Tram 13,
14, 17.* **Open** 10am-6pm Mon-Sat. **Credit** AmEx,
DC, MC, V. **Map** p309 B3.
Mexican Mercado with a twist. Even the hardiest tat
queen will love the colourful culinary and household
objects here (including wacky wallpapers).

Outras Coisas

*Herenstraat 31, Western Canal Belt (625 7281).
Tram 1, 2, 5.* **Open** noon-5pm Mon, Sun; 10am-
6.30pm Tue-Fri; 10am-5.30pm Sat. **Credit** AmEx,
DC, MC, V. **Map** p310 C2.
All the pieces to round off your dream house:
Missoni tea towels and throws, bone spoons for sam-
pling caviar – you know, the necessities.

Santa Jet

*Prinsenstraat 7, Western Canal Belt (427 2070/
www.santajet.com). Tram 1, 2, 5.* **Open** 11am-6pm
Mon-Fri; 10am-5pm Sat; noon-5pm Sun. **Credit**
AmEx, DC, MC, V. **Map** p310 C2.
Live *la vida loca* with Mexican housewares. Olé!

What's Cooking

*Reestraat 16, Western Canal Belt (427 0630). Tram
13, 14, 17.* **Open** 11am-6pm Tue-Sat. **Credit** AmEx,
MC, V. **Map** p310 C4.
Pink salad bowls, green sauces, orange peppermills:
culinary gifts don't come any more retina-searing.

Get into the **Groovy Living**.

Vintage

Groovy Living

*Westerstraat 158, the Jordaan (06 1345 1664/
www.groovy-living.nl). Tram 13, 14, 17.* **Open** 10am-
6pm Mon-Sat, and by appointment. **No credit
cards. Map** p309 B2.
For the true collector, some supremely desirable vintage pieces and furnishings, including such bizarre
items as the painted chinoiserie-style bar that was
used to style Harrods in the '60s.

Nic Nic

*Gasthuismolensteeg 5, Western Canal Belt (622
8523). Tram 1, 2, 5, 13, 17.* **Open** noon-6pm
Mon-Fri; 10am-5pm Sat. **Credit** AmEx, MC, V.
Map p310 C3.
We consider this the best shop of its ilk in
Amsterdam, selling '50s and '60s furniture, lamps,
ashtrays and kitchenware, mostly in mint condition.

SPRMRKT

*Rozengracht 191-193, the Jordaan (330 5601/
www.sprmrkt.nl). Tram 13, 14, 17.* **Open** By
appt Mon; 10am-6pm Tue-Sat. **Credit** MC, V.
Map p309 B3.
A whopping 450m square (hey, that's exceptional
for Amsterdam) is focused on vintage '60s and '70s
furniture and home accessories. Clothing is an additional but important commodity here, as seen in
their current collection of quirky customised Levis.

Blue Note from Ear & Eye. *See p181.*

Markets

Albert Cuypmarkt

Albert Cuypstraat, the Pijp. Tram 4, 16, 24, 25. **Open** 9.30am-5pm Mon-Sat. **No credit cards.** **Map** p315 E5.

Amsterdam's largest general market sells everything from pillows to prawns at great prices. The clothes on sale tend to be run-of-the-mill cheapies.

Boerenmarkt

Westerstraat/Noorderkerkstraat, the Jordaan. Tram 3, 10. **Open** 9am-3pm Sat. **No credit cards.** **Map** p310 B2.

Every Saturday, the Noordermarkt turns into an organic farmers' market. Groups of singers or medieval musicians sometimes make a visit feel more like a day trip than a shopping binge.

Dappermarkt

Dapperstraat, Oost. Tram 3, 6, 10, 14. **Open** 9am-5pm Mon-Sat. **No credit cards.** **Map** p316 H3.

Dappermarkt is a locals' market: prices don't rise to match the number of visitors. It sells all the usual market fodder, and plenty of cheap clothes.

Looier Art & Antique Centre

Elandsgracht 109, the Jordaan (624 9038/ www.looier.nl). Tram 7, 10, 17. **Open** 11am-5pm Mon-Thur, Sat, Sun. **Credit** AmEx, DC, MC, V. **Map** p314 C4.

Mainly antiques, with plenty of collectors' items. It's easy to get lost in the quiet premises and find yourself standing alone by a stall crammed with antiquated clocks ticking eerily.

Noordermarkt

Noordermarkt, the Jordaan. Tram 3, 10. **Open** 7.30am-1pm Mon. **No credit cards.** **Map** p310 B2.

North (d'oh!) of Westermarkt, Noordermarkt is frequented by the serious shopper. The stacks of (mainly second-hand) clothes, shoes, jewellery and hats need to be sorted with a grim determination, but there are real bargains to be had. Arrive early or the best stuff will probably have been nabbed. They also have an organic farmers market on Saturdays.

Oudemanhuis Book Market

Oudemanhuispoort, Old Centre: Old Side. Tram 4, 9, 14, 16, 24, 25. **Open** 11am-4pm Mon-Fri. **No credit cards.** **Map** p310 D3.

People have been buying and selling books, prints and sheet music here since the 19th century.

Postzegelmarkt

Nieuwezijds Voorburgwal, by No.276, Old Centre: New Side. Tram 1, 2, 5, 13, 17, 20. **Open** 11am-4pm Wed, Sun. **No credit cards.** **Map** p310 D3.

A specialist market for collectors of stamps, coins, postcards and medals.

Rommelmarkt

Looiersgracht 38, the Jordaan. Tram 7, 10, 17. **Open** 11am-5pm daily. **No credit cards.** **Map** p314 C4.

A flea market where, nestled among the junk, you're likely to stumble across such bargains as a boxed set of Demis Roussos records. Tempting, no?

Waterlooplein

Waterlooplein, Jodenbuurt. Tram 9, 14, 20/Metro Waterlooplein. **Open** 9am-5pm Mon-Sat. **No credit cards.** **Map** p311 E3.

Amsterdam's top tourist market is basically a huge flea market with the added attraction of loads of clothes stalls (though gear can be a bit pricey and, at many stalls, a bit naff). Bargains can be found, but they may be hidden under cheap 'n' nasty toasters and down-at-heel (literally) shoes.

Westermarkt

Westerstraat, the Jordaan. Tram 3, 10. **Open** 9am-1pm Mon. **No credit cards.** **Map** p310 B2.

A market selling all sorts of stuff. The people packing the pavement are proof of the reasonable prices and range of goods, including new watches, pretty (and not so pretty) fabrics and cheap clothes.

Music

Vintage vinyl collectors should also head to the **Noordermarkt** and **Waterlooplein** (for both *see above*). The contemporary dance music vinyl junkie/dj will find a plethora of small independent shops on Nieuwe Nieuwstraat and its narrower parallel, Sint Nicolaasstraat.

Blue Note from Ear & Eye
Gravenstraat 12, Old Centre: New Side (428 1029). Tram 1, 2, 4, 5, 9, 13, 16, 24, 25. **Open** 11am-7pm Tue-Sat; noon-5pm Sun. **Credit** AmEx, DC, MC, V. **Map** p310 C3.
This conveniently central shop stocks a full spectrum of jazz, from '30s stompers to mainstream, avant-garde and Afro jazz. Cool.

Charles Klassiek en Folklore
Weteringschans 193, Southern Canal Belt (626 5538). Tram 6, 7, 10, 16, 24, 25. **Open** 1-6.30pm Mon; 10am-6.30pm Tue, Wed, Fri; 10am-9pm Thur; 10am-5.30pm Sat. **Credit** AmEx, DC, MC, V. **Map** p315 E5.
Literally, 'classical and folk'. A good place for some of the smaller German and French labels and, bucking trends, for good, old-fashioned vinyl.

Concerto
Utrechtsestraat 52-60, Southern Canal Belt (623 5228/www.concerto.nu). Tram 4. **Open** 10am-6pm Mon-Wed, Fri, Sat; 10am-9pm Thur; noon-6pm Sun. **Credit** AmEx, DC, MC, V. **Map** p315 E4.

Head here for classic Bach recordings, obscure Beatles items, or that fave Diana Ross album that got nicked from your party. There are also second-hand 45s and new releases at decent prices. Massive.

Distortion Records
Westerstraat 72, the Jordaan (627 0004/www. distortion.nl). Tram 10. **Open** 11am-6pm Tue, Wed, Fri; 11am-9pm Thur; 10am-6pm Sat. **No credit cards. Map** p309 B2.
Vinyl from '70s punk rock, jazz, funk, soul, Latin, and soundtracks, through lo-fi, indie, noise, garage and industrial, to '80s and '90s indie, electro, hip hop and reggae, ending up in break beats and house. Er, what else is there?

Fame
Kalverstraat 2-4, Old Centre: New Side (638 2525/ www.fame.nl). Tram 1, 2, 5, 13, 14, 17. **Open** 10am-7pm Mon-Wed, Fri-Sun; 10am-9pm Thur. **Credit** AmEx, MC, V. **Map** p310 D3.
The biggest record store in Amsterdam sits bang on its busiest shopping thoroughfare. Fame offers a vast array of stock in a variety of genres.

Where to spend

Although reckless abandon and aimless drifting can make for memorable shopping trips, sometimes having a plan doesn't hurt. So, here's a cheat sheet. Go mad.

Damstraat
A street at war with its past, Damstraat is fighting to jettison the sleaze and turn into a boutique-lined retail oasis. Alas, its proximity to the Red Light District means that laddish types can too often impinge on this otherwise lovely neighbourhood.

The Jordaan
Tiny back streets laced with twisting canals, cosy boutiques, lush markets, bakeries, galleries, restful and old-fashioned cafés and bars; the Jordaan captures the spirit of Amsterdam like nowhere else.

Kalverstraat and Nieuwendijk
Kalverstraat and its more scruffy extension Nieuwendijk are where the locals come for their consumer kicks. The shops are largely unexciting, yet they still get insanely busy on Sundays. However, it's pedestrian-only, so at least you can forget the dreaded bike menace and focus your attention on the tills.

Leidsestraat
Connecting Koningsplein and Leidseplein, Leidsestraat is peppered with fine shoe shops and boutiques but you'll have to dodge the trams. Cyclists: note that bikes aren't allowed in this part of town. And yes, the police do notice.

Magna Plaza
Right behind Dam Square, this architectural treat was once a post office. Its reincarnation as a five-floor mall is beloved by tourists, though locals are less keen.

Nine Streets
The small streets connecting Prinsengracht, Keizersgracht and Herengracht between Raadhuisstraat and Leidsegracht offer a mix of boutiques, antiques and speciality stores.

PC Hooftstraat
Amsterdam's elite shopping strip has had a rocky ride in the last few years, but with an infusion of designer establishments embracing both established and up-and-coming names, things are looking better.

The Pijp
This bustling district is notable mainly for Albert Cuypmarkt and its ethnic food shops.

Spiegelkwartier
Across from the Rijksmuseum and centred on Spiegelgracht, this area is packed with antiques shops selling authentic treasures at high prices. Dress for success and keep your nose in the air.

Fat Beats

*Singel 10, Western Canal Belt (423 0886/www.
fatbeats.com). Tram 1, 2, 5.* **Open** 1-7pm Mon; noon-
7pm Tue, Wed, Fri, Sat; noon-9pm Thur; 1-6pm Sun.
Credit AmEx, MC, V. **Map** p310 C2.

Amsterdam's one-stop hip hop shop and distributor. With its roots in NYC, Fat Beats has all the vinyl
and CDs that any DJ (or aspiring upstart) could
dream up. Staff are seriously informed and have all
the dirt on the local party and music scene.

Get Records

*Utrechtsestraat 105, Southern Canal Belt (622
3441). Tram 4.* **Open** 10am-6pm Mon-Wed, Fri, Sat;
10am-9pm Thur; noon-6pm Sun. **Credit** AmEx, DC,
MC, V. **Map** p315 E4.

Much of the vinyl has been cleared away to make
room for a savvy pick of alternative and independent CDs; it's also good for roots, Americana and
dance. Don't miss the 'cheapies' corner at the front.

Midtown

*Nieuwendijk 104, Old Centre: New Side (638 4252/
www.mid-town.nl). Tram 1, 2, 5, 13, 17, 24, 25.*
Open noon-6pm Mon; 10am-6pm Tue, Wed, Fri, Sat;
10am-9pm Thur; noon-5pm Sun. **Credit** AmEx, DC,
MC, V. **Map** p310 D2.

Dance music galore: hardcore, gabber, trance, club,
mellow house and garage are among the styles on
the shelves. Midtown is also a good source of information and tickets for hardcore parties.

Palm Guitars

*'s Gravelandseveer 5, Old Center: Old Side (422
0445/www.palmguitars.nl). Tram 4, 9, 16, 24, 25.*
Open noon-6pm Wed-Sat. **Credit** AmEx, DC, MC, V.
Map p311 E3.

Palm Guitars stocks new, antique, used and rare
musical instruments (and their parts). The excellent
website features a calendar of upcoming local gigs,
all of a worldly and rootsy nature.

Sound of the Fifties

*Prinsengracht 669, Southern Canal Belt (623 9745).
Tram 6, 7, 10.* **Open** 1-5pm Mon; noon-6pm Tue-
Sat. **Credit** AmEx, MC, V. **Map** p314 C4.

This specialist store sells vinyl from the '50s, with
artists from Liberace to Yma Sumac. Records and
sleeves are in good nick, so prices are high.

Pharmacies

Dam Apotheek

*Damstraat 2, Old Centre: Old Side (624 4331). Tram
4, 9, 14, 16, 24, 25.* **Open** 8.30am-5.30pm Mon-Fri;
10am-5pm Sat. **No credit cards**. **Map** p310 D3.
This central pharmacy has extended opening hours.
Should you need a late pharmacy, *see p288*.

Lairesse Apotheek

*Lairessestraat 40, Museum Quarter (662 1022/
www.delairesseapotheek.nl). Tram 3, 5, 12, 16.*
Open 8.30am-6pm Mon-Fri; 10am-4pm Sat. **Credit**
MC, V. **Map** p314 D6.

One of the largest suppliers of alternative medicines
in the country, chemist Marjan Terpstra wanted her
shop to reflect her speciality. Designed by Concrete,
the shop is out of the way if you're just popping in
for haemorrhoid cream, but the interior is so inspiring it should be on any design junkie's must-see list.

Sex shops

Absolute Danny

*Oudezijds Achterburgwal 78, Old Centre: Old Side
(421 0915/www.absolutedanny.com). Tram 4, 9, 16,
24.* **Open** 11am-9pm Mon-Thur, Sun; 11am-10pm
Fri, Sat. **Credit** AmEx, DC, MC, V. **Map** p310 D2.
Rubber clothes to erotic toothbrushes.

Christine le Duc

*Spui 6, Old Centre: New Side (624 8265/www.
christineleduc.com). Tram 1, 2, 4, 5, 9, 14, 16, 24,
25.* **Open** 10am-9pm Mon, Tue, Wed, Fri; 10am-
10pm Thur; 10am-6pm Sat; 1-6pm Sun. **Credit**
AmEx, MC, V. **Map** p310 D3.

A rather plebeian erotic shop: crotchless red panties,
porn and novelties like an elephant's head G-string.

Condomerie het Gulden Vlies

*Warmoesstraat 141, Old Centre: Old Side (627
4174/www.condomerie.com). Tram 4, 9, 14, 16, 24,
25.* **Open** 11am-6pm Mon-Sat. **Credit** AmEx, DC,
MC, V. **Map** p310 D2.

An astounding variety of rubbers will wrap up
trouser snakes of all shapes and sizes.

Female & Partners

*Spuistraat 100, Old Centre: New Side (620 9152/
www.femaleandpartners.nl). Tram 1, 2, 5, 13, 17.*
Open 1-6pm Mon, Sun; 11am-6pm Tue, Wed, Fri,
Sat; 11am-9pm Thur. **Credit** AmEx, MC, V.
Map p310 C2.

The opposite of most enterprises here, Female &
Partners welcomes women (and, yes, their partners)
with an array of clothes, videos and toys.

Stout

*Berenstraat 9, Western Canal Belt (620 1676/
www.stoutinternational.com). Tram 13, 14, 17.*
Open noon-7pm Mon-Fri; 11am-6pm Sat; 1-5pm Sun.
Credit AmEx, DC, MC, V. **Map** p314 C4.

Naughty and nice lingerie and sex toys for the thinking gal: La Fille D'O, Marvel & Malizia, Dolce &
Gabbana, John Galliano, Eres, and more.

Tobacconists

PGC Hajenius

*Rokin 92-6, Old Centre: New Side (625 9985/
www.hajenius.com). Tram 4, 9, 14, 16, 24, 25.*
Open noon-6pm Mon; 9.30am-6pm Tue, Wed, Fri,
Sat; 9.30am-9pm Thur; noon-5pm Sun. **Credit**
AmEx, DC, MC, V. **Map** p310 D3.

A smoker's paradise (tobacco, not dope) for over 250
years, Hajenius offers cigarabilia, from traditional
Dutch pipes to own-brand cigars. With its art deco
interior, even anti-smokers should pop in for a whiff.

Eat, Drink, Shop

Arts & Entertainment

Festivals & Events

It's raining fun, hallelujah.

'Act normal, and then you're crazy enough.' Sure, it's a local cliché, but it speaks volumes about the Dutch, and Amsterdammers have long known that fully living out the Protestant work ethic requires equal attention to work and play. So come **Oudejaarsavond** (New Year's Eve; *see p190*), **Koninginnedag** (Queen's Day; *see p188* **Orange squash**), or Ajax winning an important football match, and you'll see the city dissolve into an orange-tinted psychosis of song, drink and dance. Nor are Amsterdam's festivals solely fuelled by alcohol: there's soul food too, ranging from **Stille Omgang** (Silent Procession, *see p185*) to **Museum Night** (*see p189*). And can New York claim Cannabis Championships (*see p187*) or boatloads of men waving knitted willies (*see p186*)? We think not.

The **AUB** (0900 0191; *see p293* **Tickets please**) and the **Amsterdam Tourist Board** (0900 400 4040; *see p295*) list upcoming events in *Uitkrant* and *Day by Day* respectively, and www.timeout.com/amsterdam previews the best. For a list of public holidays, *see p295*. Unless stated, all events are free.

Frequent events

Arts & crafts markets

Spui *Old Centre: New Side (www.artplein-spui.nl).* *Tram 1, 2, 4, 5, 9, 14, 16, 24, 25.* **Map** p314 D4. **Date** year-round 10am-6pm Sun. **Thorbeckeplein** *Southern Canal Belt (www.modern-art-market.nl).* *Tram 4, 9, 14.* **Map** p315 E4. **Date** Mar-Oct 10am-5pm Sun.

These two weather-dependent open-air Sunday arts and crafts markets are decent places to browse, but don't expect the latest video art or a condom-strewn unmade bed: most of the jewellery, paintings, vases and prints are less radical. Buskers touting CDs enhance the laid-back vibe.

Antiques market

Nieuwmarkt, Old Centre: Old Side. Tram 9, 14/ Metro Nieuwmarkt. **Map** p310 D2. **Date** Apr-Aug 9am-5pm Sun.
Antiques and bric-a-brac lovers should head for this small market. There are gems nestled in amongst the tat, especially books, furniture and objet's d'art.

Rowing contests

Amsterdamse Bos, Bosbaan 6 (646 2740/ www.knrb.nl). Bus 170, 171, 172. **Date** Apr-Dec.
Visit this lovely green expanse to watch participants get wet. Check local press or phone the Amsterdam Tourist Board for details of the rowing contests.

Book markets

Various locations (627 5794). **Date** May-Aug.
Besides the year-round Friday (9am-6pm) book stalls on Spui and Oudemanhuispoort (Mon-Sat, noon-6pm, *see p180*), there are four temporary markets in summer: two along the Amstel (art book market, mid-June; religion, mid-Aug) and two on Dam (children's, mid-May; mysteries, mid-July).

Spring

Spring is when the tulips and crocuses push through the earth, and a winter's worth of dog dung defrosts: those who know about this sort

De Parade. See p186.

of thing estimate 20 million kilograms of the stuff (44 million pounds). It's also when the city shrugs off the existential gloom that defines the northern European mindset in winter. Energised by the sun, city dwellers take on the shiny *joie de vivre* that's more often associated with southern European café cultures. Lounging in a park or on a terrace is a respectable thing to do after a hard winter's cold rain and mental drain.

Stille Omgang (Silent Procession)

Starts at Spui, Begijnhof (no phone/www.stille-omgang.nl). **Date** weekend after 10 Mar.
This singular annual event commemorates the 1345 'Miracle of Amsterdam': a dying man, being administered the last rites, vomited. Since he had been given the viaticum what was thrown up was put into the fire, where the Blessed Sacrament was discovered next day, undamaged by fire or digestion, and the man later recovered. Every year since then, local Catholics make a silent nocturnal procession that begins and ends at Spui. The sight of the candle-lit procession moving through the Red Light District at night is both surreal and moving.

World Press Photo

Oude Kerk, Oudekerksplein 23, Old Centre: Old Side (625 8284/www.worldpressphoto.nl). Tram 4, 9, 16, 24, 25. **Admission** €5. **Map** p310 D2. **Date** Apr-May 11am-5pm Mon-Sat; 1-5pm Sun.
This is the world's largest photography competition, and it lines up exhibits from thousands of photojournalists. The exhibition is held in the Oude Kerk (*see p88*) and, after kicking off in Amsterdam, it goes on tour to another 70 locations around the world. In 2005, WPP celebrates its 50th anniversary with a special overview exhibition (7 Oct-15 Dec).

National Museum Weekend

Around the Netherlands (www.museumweekend.nl). **Admission** mostly free. **Dates** 8-9 April 2006; 15-16 April 2007.
Many of the more than 500 state-funded museums offer discounted or free admission and special activities during National Museum Weekend. Pick up the Museum Weekend newspaper at, yes, a museum.

Koninginnedag (Queen's Day)

Around the city. **Date** 30 Apr.
See p188 **Orange squash**.

Herdenkingsdag & Bevrijdingsdag (Remembrance Day & Liberation Day)

Remembrance Day *National Monument, Dam, Old Centre: Old Side. Tram 1, 2, 4, 5, 9, 13, 14, 16, 17, 24, 25.* **Map** p310 D3. **Date** 4 May.
Liberation Day *Vondelpark, Museum Quarter. Tram 1, 2, 3, 5, 6, 12.* **Map** p314 C6. **Date** 5 May.
Those who lost their lives during World War II are remembered at the National Monument on Dam Square on 4 May at 7.30pm. Homosexuals who died

in the war are also remembered at a gay remembrance service at the Homomonument (*see p207*).
Liberation Day is celebrated on 5 May. Rokin, Vondelpark, Museumplein and Leidseplein are the best places to make for: expect live music, speeches and information stands for political groups, and a market where you can sell everything you bought in a drunken stupor on Queen's Day a week earlier.

Oosterpark Festival

Oosterpark, Oost (www.oosterparkfestival.nl). Tram 3, 6, 9, 14. **Map** p316 H3. **Date** first wk in May.
The culturally varied east of Amsterdam makes a perfect setting for this one- or two-day free festival emphasising community between nationalities. But it's really just a great opportunity to experience different music, customs, sports and food(!).

National Windmill Day

Around the Netherlands (0900 400 4040/ www.visitamsterdam.nl). **Date** 2nd Sat in May.
The day for any budding Don Quixotes to win their spurs: over half the 1,035 state-subsidised windmills spin their sails and open to the public. Tell Sancho Panza to watch out for the blue banners on Amsterdam's six working mills.

National Cycling Day

Around the Netherlands (0900 400 4040/ www.visitamsterdam.nl). **Date** late May.
Roads are packed with cyclists as 200 special bicycling routes of varying lengths are marked out.

KunstRAI (RAI Arts Fair)

RAI Congresgebouw, Europaplein, Zuid (549 1212/ www.kunstrai.nl). Tram 4, 25/NS rail RAI station. **Admission** €10-€15. **No credit cards**. **Date** mid May-early June.
Everything from ceramics and jewellery to paintings and sculpture are featured at this huge four-day annual exhibition of contemporary art. About 100 Dutch and international galleries take part.

Kunstvlaai

Westergasfabriek, Haarlemmerweg 8-10, Westerpark (588 2400/www.sandberg.nl/www.kunstvlaai.nl). Tram 10. **Map** p309 A1. **Date** bi-annual: May 2006.
2004 saw the return of Kunstvlaai, organised by the Sandberg Institute, after a few years' absence while Westergasfabriek was renovated. This edgy art market was formulated as the twisted twin of the commercial Kunstrai (*see above*) and as such is dedicated to giving space to dozens of decidedly less middle-of-the-road artists, groups and galleries.

Open Ateliers (Open Studios): Kunstroute de Westelijke Eilanden

Prinseneiland, Bickerseiland & Realeneiland (627 1238/www.oawe.nl). **Date** mid-May.
Many neighbourhoods with populations of artists and artists' studio complexes hold open days in spring and autumn when, over a weekend or more, dozens of artists – starving and successful alike – open their doors to the public. The annual Westelijke

Arts & Entertainment

Eilanden is the most popular, situated on the picturesque and peaceful islands around Prinseneiland, all connected by traditional 'skinny bridges'. Be sure to check out the Jordaan event, which, in a triumph of programming, is held on the same weekend.

Europerve

Information: Demask, Zeedijk 64, Old Centre: Old Side (620 5603/www.demask.com). Admission prices vary. Date May.
Organised by Demask (*see p215*), Europerve brings together thousands of Europe's self-proclaimed most sexually adventurous people – with the Germans and English most in need of a buttock blushing – for a long evening of fashion, performance, dancing, naughty games and friction fun. Leather, latex, PVC and/or adult-sized nappies are required dress.

Summer

Amsterdammers move outdoors with the sunshine. Bodies pack the nearby beaches at Bloemendaal, Zandfoort, Wijk aan Zee and Amsterdam's new strand at IJburg (*see p108*); while Vondelpark gets jammed with skaters, joggers, sun-worshippers and bongo players. Many locals depart for holiday heaven, while the city's tourist load can reach critical density.

Stripdagen Haarlem (Comics Festival)

Around Haarlem (0900-616 1600/www.stripdagen haarlem.nl). Date early June 2006, 2008.
Haarlem (*see p268*) – a 15 minute train ride from Amsterdam and home to the world's first cartoonist designed theatre, Joost Swarte's Toneelschuur – falls under the spell of comics during this bi-annual festival. There are exhibitions, fairs, films, parties, concerts, workshops and special guests such as Art Spiegelman, Joe Sacco and Robert Crumb.

Holland Festival

Stadsschouwburg, Leidseplein, Southern Canal Belt (530 7110/www.holndfstvl.nl). Tram 1, 2, 5, 6, 7, 10. Admission €10-€40. Credit AmEx, MC, V. Map p314 C5. Date early-mid June.
A fixture in the diaries of the Netherlands' cultured populace, the Holland Festival features art, dance, opera, theatre and a whole lot more. The programme includes both mainstream and oddball works, and is held in the Stadsschouwburg (*see p224*) and other venues with some events in the Hague. Tickets are sold from May from the AUB Ticketshop, Amsterdam Tourist Board offices and theatres.

Canal Gardens in Bloom

Around Amsterdam. (www.amsterdamse grachtentuin.nl). Date mid June.
This event sees owners of beautiful, hidden gardens open their doors to the public, giving the chance to appreciate an art that's unappreciated but democratic, being open to anyone with some seed. Contact Museum van Loon (*see p99*) for details.

Kwakoe

Bijlmerpark, Bijlmer (416 0894/www.kwakoe.nl). Metro Bijlmer. Date Jun-mid Aug.
See p190 **A good ribbing**.

De Parade

Martin Luther Kingpark, Zuid (033 465 4555/www. deparade.nl). Tram 25/Metro Amstel. Admission free-€10. No credit cards. Date 1st 2wks in Aug (3pm-1am Mon-Thur, Sun; 3pm-2am Fri, Sat).
One of the highlights of the cultural year, this outdoor theatre festival (*see p251*) comes pretty close to re-enacting the vibes of ancient carnivals. Enter into another, alcohol-fuelled world, where a beer garden is surrounded by kitschly decorated tents that each feature a different cabaret, music or theatre act. Afternoons are child-friendly.

Landjuweel

Ruigoord (497 5702/www.ruigoord.nl). Date the full moon during July. Admission €20-€25
About 10km out of town, Ruigoord was a squatted village and arts community for decades before the powers-that-be decided it should be submerged in the name of building the harbour. Protest led to compromise and the village's ancient church survives as an island of alternative culture. This week-long festival of art, music and theatre captures the hippie-trippie-bongo-playing-spliff-smoking-we-are-all-one-big-happy-family vibe of this singular spot.

Amsterdam Gay Pride Boat Parade

Prinsengracht, Canal Belt (620 8807/www. amsterdampride.nl). Tram 13, 14, 17. Map p310 C1. Date 1st Sat in Aug 2-5pm.
If the weather's fine, there might be as many as 250,000 spectators lining Prinsengracht to watch the spectacular Gay Pride Boat Parade. Eighty boats with garish decorations and loud sound systems crewed by extravagant, and sometimes bare, sailors

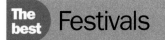

The best Festivals

Koninginnedag
A right royal knees-up. *See p188* **Orange squash**.

Museum Night
Culture in the dark. *See p189*.

Amsterdam Gay Pride Boat Parade
Madness, sheer madness. *See above and p209* **Tiaras and tantrums**.

Crossing Border
The only time to visit The Hague. *See p188*.

Kunstvlaai
Art in the coolest of parks. *See p185*.

Arts & Entertainment

set sail at this Rabelaisian climax to a whole week-end of special activities (check the website for the full array). *See also p216* **The queer year.**

Hartjesdag

Zeedijk, Old Centre: Old Side (625 8467/www. hartjesdagen.nl). Tram 4, 9, 14, 16, 24, 25. **Map** p310 D2. **Date** mid Aug.
An ancient Amsterdam celebration, 'Heart Day' was held on the last Monday of August and involved much drinking, cross-dressing and firecrackers. It was in abeyance for decades, but was resurrected in 1999, primarily to focus on the booze and drag side of things. Marvel at the parade of boys dressed as girls and girls dressed as boys: it's predictably popular with the city's transvestite population, as are its associated theatrical and music events.

SAIL2005

Around Amsterdam (681 1804/www.sail-amsterdam.nl). **Date** 17-21 Aug 2005.
Held every five years, it's scarcely possible to imagine the scale of this, the largest nautical gathering to take place in Europe. An extraordinary 2.5 million visitors are expected to stroll along Oostelijke Handelskade, admiring dozens of tall ships and thousands of more modern boats. There's a flotilla of related events to choose from, so plan ahead.

Open Haven Podium

On and around Java eiland (423 5615/www. openhavenpodium.nl). **Date** mid-Aug.
The western tip of Java eiland, along with the bars, theatres and galleries in the immediate neighbourhood, unite for a hip weekend of harbour-themed art, music, theatre and children's activities. They will return in 2006 after taking a year off for SAIL2005.

Uitmarkt

Museumplein and Leidseplein (www.uitmarkt.nl). **Date** last weekend in Aug.
The chaotic Uitmarkt previews the coming cultural season with foretastes of theatre, opera, dance and music. From Friday to Sunday outdoor stages are set up in squares around the centre of Amsterdam, presenting free music, dance, theatre and cabaret shows. Not surprisingly, it gets very crowded.

Autumn

Amsterdam has the occasional Indian summer, but otherwise this season's stormy disposition and increasing gloom is a warning of the winter despair that's sure to follow; it's a time when Amsterdammers start storing razor blades out of sight. As a visitor, though, this might be the perfect time to visit. With the tourist tide ebbing and touring bands arriving in their droves to play the Melkweg or Paradiso, the true spirit of Amsterdam comes bubbling back to the surface. Just be sure to bring a brolly and be prepared to duck into a pub to avoid the elements, which is hardly a hardship.

Bloemencorso (Flower Parade)

Around Amsterdam: route usually via Overtoom, Leidseplein, Leidsestraat, Spui, Spuistraat, Dam, Rembrandtplein, Vijzelstraat, Weteringschans (029 732 5100/www.bloemencorsoaalsmeer.nl). **Date** 1st Sat in Sept.
Since the 1950s a spectacular parade of floats bearing all kinds of flowers – except tulips as they're out of season – makes its way from Aalsmeer (the home of Holland's flower industry, *see p261*) through to Amsterdam and Hoofddorp before heading back to Aalsmeer. Crowds line the pavements for a glimpse of the beautiful, fragrant and often over-the-top displays. After the sun sets, the artificial lighting makes the sight that much more surreal.

Open Monument Days

Around Amsterdam (552 4888/www.open monumentendag.nl). **Date** 2nd weekend of Sept.
The declining light of autumn offers the chance to travel back to Holland's Golden Age and see how people lived, and continue living, in some of the country's most historic buildings. Watch for the Monumenten flag and walk through doors only open to the public for one weekend in the year.

Jordaan Festival

The Jordaan (626 5587/www.jordaanfestival.nl). **Map** p314 C4. **Date** 3rd weekend in Sept.
The Jordaan is different. Charming but, to the average *Guardian*-reading middle class white liberal, positively odd. In fact, the area is proof that multiculturalism existed in Amsterdam long before large-scale immigration. So here's your chance to mix with people for whom Raymond van Barneveld is a hero, orange the only colour, and gold jewellery best worn large, chunky and jewel encrusted.

Dam tot Damloop

Prins Hendrikkade in Amsterdam, to Peperstraat in Zaandam (72 533 8136/www.damloop.nl). **Participation fee** €3-€13.50. **Date** 3rd Sun in Sept.
The annual 'Dam to Dam Run' stretches 16.1km (ten miles) from Amsterdam to Zaandam and then back again. Up to 200,000 people gather to watch the 30,000 participants. It's easy to spot the many world-class athletes: they're the ones at the front. Bands line the route and there's also a circus and various mini-marathons in Zaandam for children.

High Times Cannabis Cup

Melkweg, Lijnbaansgracht 234a (531 8181/ www.cannabiscup.com). Tram 1, 2, 5, 6, 7, 10. **Admission** prices vary. **No credit cards.** **Map** p314 C5. **Date** Nov.
Harvest means *High Times*' annual, heavily commercialised Cannabis Cup, where all things related to wastedness are celebrated over five days. There are banquets, bands, cultivation seminars and a competition where hundreds of judges (you too, if you wish) ascertain which of the hundreds of weeds are the wickedest, dude. The event is scattered – as are the minds – all over town, but is invariably focused around the Melkweg at night.

Arts & Entertainment

Orange squash

First-time visitors to Amsterdam arriving on 30 April often get confused and exclaim, 'I heard Amsterdam was a happening town but I didn't know it was like this.' And it is indeed lucky for everyone that this chaotic day only occurs once a year. Party lovers, crap collectors and students of the surreal should, however, make sure that their visit coincides with this date when up to a million extra people pour into the city, making every single street and canal dense with excess.

Queen's Day, or *Koninginnedag* in the local lingo, is (in theory) a celebration of Beatrix's birthday. As it happens, her birthday falls in winter, but the ever-pragmatic Dutch choose to celebrate it on her mother's birthday, when the climatic conditions are more clement.

However, Her Highness is soon forgotten amid all the revelry. You might discover a leather-boy disco party on one side street, boogie through and get to an old-school Jordaan crooner on another, when suddenly a boat bellows by with a heavy metal band on deck, whose amps get short-circuited at the next bridge when a gang of boys dressed in head-to-toe orange urinate on them. If nothing else, you'll come away with a few stories of debauched derring-do to tell your grandchildren. (If you have your own offspring in tow, head straight to Vondelpark, which is dedicated to children.)

Meanwhile, the gay and lesbian festivities spread like ripples from the Homomonument (*see p207*) and the Reguliersdwaarsstraat.

Crossing Border

Various locations in The Hague (70 346 2355/www. crossingborder.nl). Den Haag CS. **Admission** day programmes €5, evening programmes €25-€28. **Date** Oct/Nov.

Sadly this 'literary festival that rocks' returned to its original home in 2003. Still, it's only a 45-minute train trip away. Even though there will be strictly defined 'authors' present, the vast majority of the more than 120 acts come from the world of music who will perform concerts and/or spoken word. Past participants include: the Harlem Gospel Choir, David Byrne, David Sedaris, Henry Rollins, Robert Crumb, Norman Mailer, Dave Eggers, Jill Scott, and Irvine Welsh (*see p82* **Amster mage**).

Amsterdam Dance Event

Around Amsterdam (035 621 8748/www. amsterdam-dance-event.nl). **Admission** varies. **Date** mid Oct.

Schmooze by day and party by night during this annual dance music conference. Felix Meritis is the location for daytime workshops where over 1,000 delegates discuss the business of boogie. During the evenings, 30,000 visitors visit 30 clubs hosting 300 DJs/acts from around the world.

ING Amsterdam Marathon

Olympic Stadium, Stadionplein 20, Zuid (663 0781/www.amsterdammarathon.nl). Tram 24. **Date** mid Oct.

This world-class marathon starts and finishes at the Amsterdam School-styled 1928 Olympic Stadium and winds through Vondelpark and some of the more scenic streets of Amsterdam. See the website if you want to be one of 15,000 runners. But prospective athletes should remember the apocryphal story of the herald of Greek victory at Marathon: he died.

Bock Beer Festival

Beurs van Berlage, Damrak, Old Centre 277 (530 4141/www.beursvanberlage.nl/www.pint.nl). Tram 4, 9, 14, 16, 24, 25. **Date** late-Oct.

The annual three-day Bock Beer Festival takes place in the former stock exchange, Beurs van Berlage (*see p79*). Here's your chance to taste up to 50 different varieties of this full-bodied, slightly sweet and usually dark beer of German origin. Boozehounds should also check the PINT website above for other local beer festivals. Meanwhile, whisky lovers will want to attend the International Whisky Festival (0297 524 834/www.whiskyfestival.nl), which is held in Leiden every November.

Dam Square becomes a fairground, the mind gets clogged with an overdose of sensations, and pockets slowly empty as punters get tricked into buying just what they always (read: never) wanted. So, how are you going to explain that pair of orange clogs when you get back home? But regardless: what with all the performances, the markets, the crowds and, of course, the alcohol, the streets of Amsterdam have all you ever dreamed of, and much that you didn't, for one day only. Just don't make too many plans for 1 May.

Museum Night

Around Amsterdam (621 1311/www.n8.nl).
Date Nov.
Almost every museum and gallery in town opens late for Museum Night. Besides regular exhibits, many organise a special event appropriate to the institution – for instance you might be able to watch Bollywood films all evening at the Filmmuseum or dance the night away under the *Night Watch*. Check out the website and plan for a unique evening. Now there's also a related event, Night Salon (www.nacht-salon.nl), that features a different museum hosting a singular event every two months.

Sinterklaas Intocht

Route via Barbizon Palace on Prins Hendrikkade, Damrak, Dam, Raadhuisstraat, Rozengracht, Marnixstraat, Leidseplein. **Date** mid Nov.
In mid November, Sinterklaas (St Nicholas) marks the beginning of the Christmas season by stepping ashore from a steamboat at Centraal Station. St Nick – with his white beard, robes and staff – is every Dutch kid's favourite patron saint, and the old boy distributes sweets during this annual parade of the city. Meanwhile, his Zwarte Piet (Black Peter) helpers represent a threat to any naughty kids.

Depending on which story you believe, Black Peter was originally the devil – the colour and appetite for mischief are the only leftovers of an evil vanquished by Sinterklaas – or he got his dark skin from climbing down chimneys to deliver sweets.

Winter

In the typical Amsterdam winter, with luck, the canals turn solid enough for skating. Otherwise, only the two family festivals – St Nicholas's Day, as important to the Dutch as Christmas, and New Year's Eve – break up the monotony.

Sinterklaas

Around Amsterdam. **Date** 5, 6 Dec.
While St Nicholas, aka Sinterklaas, is directing his Black Peter helpers down chimneys on the eve of his feast day, 6 December, families celebrate by exchanging small gifts and poems. This tradition started when the Church decided to tame the riot and disorder that had always accompanied the end of the slaughter season. It began by ruling that the traditional celebration should be based around the birthday of St Nicholas, the patron saint of children (and, curiously enough, of prostitutes, thieves and Amsterdam itself); a once violent tradition was

A good ribbing

There are not a lot of reasons to go to the south-east of Amsterdam. Sure, there's the ArenA football stadium (*see p238*), the Heineken Music Hall (*see p218*) and even an 'Office of the Future' (www.livtom.nl) for those interested in exploring the no doubt fascinating, and even more certainly lucrative, future of corporate sponsorship. But this is also where a Boeing 747 crashed in 1992, killing countless people – countless because many were unregistered illegal residents living in this most low-rent of neighbourhoods. While much economic life has been pumped into the area in the last decade, Bijlmermeer remains desperate for more positive marketing. And there are few things more positive than a good ribbing. In fact, any

barbecued Surinam snack makes a visit to Bijlmermeer worthwhile. But if you need some reason other than your stomach, **Kwakoe** is a family-orientated festival that takes place every weekend during the height of summer, where one can drop in and usually find some action in the form of excellent ass-shaking music, theatre, film, literature, sport and – yes, folks: we want to mention the excellent ribs again – a large range of exotic food stalls. In other words: if it's a sunny weekend, this is the ultimate multicultural location in this most multiculti of towns. And if you squint a bit and settle into one of the 'beach tents' in the woods beyond the football field, it's even possible to imagine yourself in a tropical paradise. Wicked.

reborn as a Christian family feast. Sinterklaas eventually emigrated to the States, changed his name to Santa Claus and gave out presents on 25 December.

Oudejaarsavond (New Year's Eve)

Around Amsterdam. **Date** 31 Dec.
After Queen's Day (*see p188* **Orange squash**), this is Amsterdam at its wildest. There's happy chaos throughout the city, but the best spots are Nieuwmarkt and Dam, both of which get crowded and noisy: the ample use of firecrackers gives a fair impression of the fall of Saigon. The Dutch often begin with an evening of coffee, spirits and *oliebollen*

with the family; many bars don't open until the witching hour. In case you're wondering, 'oil balls' are deep-fried blobs of dough, apple and raisins, with a sprinkle of icing sugar. Mmmm, yummy.

Chinese New Year

Nieuwmarkt, Old Centre: Old Side (mobile 06 2476 0060/www.zeedijk.nl). **Map** p310 D2. **Date** late Jan/early Feb.
Lion dances, firecrackers and Chinese drums and gongs may scare away evil spirits, but your children will have a roaring good time chasing the dragon through Amsterdam's scenic Chinatown.

Children

Amsterdam loves little ones – and the feeling is mutual.

Kinderkookkafe. *See p194.*

Amsterdam may be famous for more adult pursuits, but its quirky characteristics and small scale makes it appealing to children of all ages. Although there are a great many child-specific activities on offer, sightseeing by foot or bike can be an entertainment in itself. Children love the novelty of steep bridges, crooked old buildings and canals at every turn.

Amsterdammers enjoy hanging out with their kids, so there's plenty on offer to please the generations, especially on Wednesday afternoons as all Amsterdam schools finish at midday. Also look out for street performances around the main squares (Rembrandtplein, Dam Square and Leidseplein). And if you're here when a truly icy winter sets in, skating on the frozen canals will provide an unforgettable experience (but make sure *you* are under the supervision of a local).

When trundling around town you'll find that baby-changing facilities are rare – big department stores are the best bet – but no one will mind if you improvise.

The **AUB Ticketshop** (0900 0191; *see p293* **Tickets please**) is a great place to collect information about children's events. If you can grapple with Dutch, get hold of one of the city's free listings magazines: *NL20* (look under 'Kind') or *Uitkrant* (look under 'Jeugd').

For families staying longer in Amsterdam, the excellent *Kids Gids* (www.kidsgids.nl, 'the children's guide for the Netherlands') has an English edition packed with ideas. You'll be able to pick one up at **Atheneum Nieuwscentrum** (*see p161*).

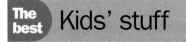

The best Kids' stuff

Linnaeushof
A playground paradise. *See p195.*

Nemo
Big fun for small techies. *See p106.*

Park life
Come rain or shine, it's fresh, fun and free! *See p193.*

De Taart van m'n Tante
Camp cake as an art form. *See p140.*

Tropenmuseum
Nurturing cultural understanding. *See p105.*

Tunfun
Let the children run riot. *See p192.*

Arts & Entertainment

GETTING AROUND

Bicycle. Not only do you get to view the city at a perfect pace, but you can also be spontaneous and reach the places that the other forms of transport can't. Young children (from about ten months) can be carried in a variety of child-seats, while older siblings can ride their own bikes (for rental, *see p284*). If you don't fancy cycling, trams provide a cheap and scenic alternative. Children love the novelty of Amsterdam's waterways, so rent some canal bikes, take a tourist cruise or splash out on a trip by water taxi. For a free ride, catch the River IJ ferry linking Amsterdam Noord to the rest of the city; boats leave from behind Centraal Station about every ten minutes. For more information about transport, *see p280*.

In Amsterdam

Tunfun

Mr Visserplein 7, entrance by Portuguese Synagogue, Plantage (689 4300/www.tunfun.nl). Tram 9, 14/ Metro Waterlooplein. **Open** 10am-7pm daily (last admission 5.30pm). **Admission** €7.50 1s-12s; free under-1s, adults accompanying children. **No credit cards**. **Map** p311 E3.

Time for an alternative

If you're a family looking further than a MacDonald's Happy Meal you'll want to check out the 'alternative' kids scene in Amsterdam's numerous squats and ex-squats (*see p206* **Good breeding**). Food in these places tends to be cheaper and you probably won't find Coca-Cola on offer. The **Binnenpret** (Amstelveenseweg 134, 671 7778/www.occii.org) is a complex of several buildings at the end of Vondelpark that was squatted for more than 20 years and houses a venue, info café, sauna (Fenomeen, *see p215*), and *voku* (people's kitchen). At *kinderpret* every Wednesday afternoon from 2.45pm, children can watch a puppet or theatre show, join a performance workshop or strut their stuff at the *kinderdisko* with DJ Barbapapa. In the same area is **Cafe de Peper** (Overtoom301, 779 4913, http:// squat.net/overtoom301). Housed in the former film academy known as **OT301** *(see p199)*, now a legalised squat, the café is one of several cultural projects based in the building. On Wednesdays from 2-5pm the café is open for children and parents to drop by. Snacks and drinks are all organic and vegan and there are toys and games to play with. See the website for occasional circus workshops or children's films. If you want the feeling that you've left the city, a 15-minute bike ride from the centre will get you to **Buurtboerderij** (Spaarndammerdijk 319, 486 5500, www.buurtboerderij.com), a little cottage set on a dyke at the edge of Westerpark run by a group of eco-activists. Inside the atmosphere has a relaxed and friendly old-time squat feel to it. The surrounding area is part of a unique 12th-century polder landscape and activities involve caring for the fauna and flora in this environment. A couple of evenings a week a meal is served (call to reserve a place) and on Sundays there are pancakes for €1. For more outside fun it's worth investigating the artists' colony **Ruigoord** (www. ruigoord.nl), with its hippie feel, and **Buitenland** (06 1130 8521/www.buiten land.org), which also attracts an 'arty' crowd. Offbeat theatre, traditional fairground rides, and cooking-your-own *poffertjes* (mini pancakes) are all among the kids' events on offer at the **De Parade** festival *(see p186)*.

Arts & Entertainment

Tunfun is quite simply *the* place to be if it rains and you've got young children to keep busy. A perfect example of Dutch resourcefulness, this big indoor playpark used to be an underpass that has been reinvented with three distinct areas for different ages to climb, slide, build and trampoline. There's football, go-karting and a little disco, too.

Applied Arts

Keramiekstudio Color Me Mine

Roelof Hartstraat 22, Museum Quarter (675 2987/ www.colormemine.nl). Trams 3, 5, 12, 24. **Open** 11am-7pm Tue, Wed; 11am-10pm Thur-Sat; noon-6pm Sun. **Cost** painting time €12.50 over-12s; €10 under-12s; plus cost of ceramic item. **Credit** MC, V. Children choose a ceramic from a selection of 400 – ranging from tiny buttons to giant vases – and then decorate them, or they can design and make their own mosaic. All the materials are non-toxic. Tots under six need to be accompanied by an adult. Reservations recommended. Check website for deals.

Klankspeeltuin

Piet Heinkade 1, Eastern Docklands (788 2010/ www.klankspeeltuin.nl). Tram 16, 26. **Age** 7-11 years. **Map** p311 F1.
Re-opening autumn 2005 at the Muziekgebouw (*see p225*), the 'noise playground' is a playground with a difference. Ingenious constructions produce diverse sounds as they are pushed, prodded, pressed and jumped on – and *voilà* everyone becomes a musician.

't Landje

Rembrandtpark, off Postjesweg, West (618 3604). Tram 13, 17/bus 15, 18 (and a short walk). **Open** noon-5pm Mon-Fri; 10am-5pm Sat. *Holidays* 10am-5pm Mon-Sat. **Admission** free. **Age** 6-14 years.
Situated on a little island in the midst of one of the city's great parks, 'The Little Land' has something for everyone who wants to get down and dirty (so don't dress up!). Outside the focus is on building wooden constructions and taking care of animals. Indoors, there's cooking, sport and climbing.

Films

Most films are dubbed, but you can often catch the same movies being shown in their original language at off-peak times. A number of independent cinemas have regular international children's programmes, usually on Wednesday and Sunday afternoons. Check the **Kriterion** (*see p198*), the **Rialto** (*see p198*) and the **Nederlands Filmmuseum** (*see p199*). Also, the children's bookshop **Helden en Boeven** *(*De Waag, Nieuwmarkt, 427 4407, www. heldenboeven.nl*)* has regular film screenings in the impressive old Waag (*see p85*) opposite their shop. The *filmladder* (hung in most cafés) has times and other information on all but the smallest of cinemas. During the autumn

holidays, the excellent **Cinekid** film festival (*531 7890/www.cinekid.nl*) takes place across the nation, offering quality films from around the globe (including many in English).

Museums

Dry and dull they ain't. From small and quirky to big and high-tech, the Dutch pride themselves on their innovative approach. Museums are highly interactive, and either extraordinarily life-like or they simply eschew simulacrums and bring in the real thing, like the **Woonbootmuseum** (*see p98*), where you can experience life on a houseboat. The **CoBrA Museum** (*see p117*) in Amstelveen features the brightly coloured style of the Cobra artists and on Sundays from 11am to 2pm it hosts the *kinder atelier* where children can paint, draw and discuss art under the guidance of a teacher. Other child-friendly museums are: **Anne Frank Huis** (*see p97*), **Nemo** (*see p106*) and **Tropenmuseum** (*see p105*).

Parks

Parents seeking outdoor entertainment need look no further than the city's parks. Of course **Vondelpark** (*see p114*) remains the most popular – in particular its playgrounds, paddling pools and free Wednesday afternoon summer performances on the outdoor stage – but you'll find at least one park in each district, as well as smaller play areas and city farms. The re-vamped **Westerpark** (*see p112*) has been transformed into an innovative terrain that has nature reserves, a children's farm, a 'roughground' play park, a paddling pool and a café. At **Amstelpark** (*see p117*) kids can catch the miniature train that runs around the park, get lost in the maze or take a pony ride. For a wilder experience take the whole day to explore the **Amsterdamse Bos** (*see p117*). A bit out of town but well worth the trip is **Waterspeelplaats De Blauwe Poort** (075 684 4338), an enormous, toddler-friendly water park fed by fresh lake water continually pumped in from the Sloterplas. There's an artificial beach with a fort and pirate ship in the middle of a lake for bigger kids. It's only open in the warmer half of the year, but it is free.

Restaurants

The city is dotted with eateries and brown cafés where children are welcome. We recommend Amsterdams Historisch Museum's **David & Goliath** (*see p92*); **De Taart van m'n Tante** (*see p140*); **De Jaren** (*see p125*); **Latei** (*see p125*); and **Vakzuid** (*see p139*).

Arts & Entertainment

Kinderkookkafe

Kattenlaan, Vondelpark (625 3257/www.kinder kookkafe.nl). Tram 1,6. **Open** 10am-8.30pm daily. **Admission** kids cooking €10; guests: €2.50 under-5s; €5 6-12s; €10 over-13s. **Age** 4-12 years. **No credit cards. Map** p314 C6.

Children take on the whole culinary caboodle at this specially designed space: cooking, serving, washing-up and presenting the bill – with a little help from the grown-up staff. Two set meals are on offer for the children to prepare according to age: lunch on Wed, Sat and Sun (12.30-3.30pm) for over-sixes; and dinner, including veggie options, from Wed-Sun (3.30-8pm) for over-eights. The café is also open every day from 10am for pre-schoolers and their minders to drop by and munch out. Children must be accompanied by an adult. Reservations recommended.

Swimming pools & saunas

Good for children are **De Mirandabad** (a subtropical pool with a wave machine, whirlpool, toddler pool and slide), the **Zuiderbad** indoor pool, and the **Brediusbad** and **Flevoparkbad** outdoor pools. For local pools, check the phone book under 'Zwembad'. Most saunas tolerate quiet children, especially off-peak, and some offer family-only sessions. The most child-friendly sauna is **Fenomeen** (*see p215*). For saunas, *see p242*; for pools, *see p243*.

Theatre & circus

The Dutch love of all things cultural readily extends to children with a wide selection of shows for all ages: the Concertgebouw's (*see p223*) *Kijk met je Oren*, for example, combines classical music and puppetry. Check with **Uitlijn** (0900 0191) for details or look under 'Jeugd' in *Uitkrant*.

Circustheater Elleboog

Passeerdersgracht 32, Western Canal Belt (626 9370/www.elleboog.nl). Tram 1, 2, 5, 7, 10. **Open** 9am-5pm Mon-Fri. *Bookings* 10am-2pm Mon-Fri. *Activities* times vary Sat, Sun. *Shows* times vary. **Admission** €7.50 adults; €5 under-15s. **No credit cards. Map** p314 C4.

Children between four and 17 can learn circus and clowning tricks, juggling, and stilt and tightrope walking. Days end with a performance for parents and friends. Non-member sessions are always busy, mostly with Dutch children, but the troupe does not see language as a barrier.

Other locations: Circustheater Elleboog ZO, Hoogoord 1A, 365 8313.

De Krakeling

Nieuwe Passeerdersstraat 1, Western Canal Belt (625 3284/reservations 624 5123/www.krakeling.nl). Tram 7, 10. **Shows** 2.30pm Wed, Sun; 8pm Thur-Sat. **Admission** €9; €7 adults with child; €8 over-65s; €6 under-18s. **No credit cards. Map** p314 C4.

De Krakeling is the only Dutch theatre that programmes only for children. There are separate productions for over-12s and under-12s: phone to check what's going on. For non-Dutch speakers, there are puppet and mime shows, and sometimes musicals.

Toy libraries

If it's raining and your toddler is running riot, a visit to the local *speel-o-theek* (toy library) could be the move that saves the day. There's space for the little ones to run around and toys galore to play with, and it's all free! To find the nearest, look up 'Speel-o-theek' in the *Telefoongids*. The **Centraal Bibliotheek** (*see p290*) has English-language books, a play area, changing room and story-telling in English on Friday mornings.

Urban farms

Free entertainment for small animal lovers is to be found at any of the 17 or so children's farms. Horses, pigs, goats, rabbits, ducks, chickens, and sheep – if it's not too exotic and clucks, baas or quacks, they've got it. Kids can just visit or muck in, helping to feed and groom the animals. Some have 'petting' hours where you can, er, pet the furry ones and there are often special activities organised. Admission is usually free, check the *Gouden Gids* (*Yellow Pages*) under 'Kinderboerderijen'. And there's also **Artis** (*see p104*), the zoo.

Outside Amsterdam

These attractions are easy to reach by train or car. Check with the local **Amsterdam Tourist Board**, ANWB shops or the Netherlands Railways (**NS**) for ideas on day trips. The NS also has walking and cycling routes available; tickets for **NS Rail Idee** (*see p258*), which runs to all of the following attractions, cover the cost of transport and maps to and from the walking or cycling location. For details of other out-of-town attractions, *see pp259-278*.

Archeon

Archeonlaan 1, Alphen aan den Rijn (0172 447744/ www.archeon.nl). 50km (31 miles) from Amsterdam; A4 to Leiden, then N11 to Alphen aan den Rijn. **Open** *Easter weekend-Oct* 10am-5pm Tue-Sun. *Aug* 10am-5pm daily. Some winter events from Nov to opening. **Admission** €14.90; €13.90 over-65s; €12.90 under-10s. **Credit** MC, V.

The Archeon plunges visitors into life as it was in the Netherlands during three different periods: the pre-historic, the Roman Empire and the Middle Ages. You can walk through authentically constructed streets and buildings and talk to the 'residents' about how everyday life was then. The price of admission includes a meal from the buffet.

Arts & Entertainment

Circustheater Elleboog. *See p194.*

Efteling

Europalaan 1, Kaatsheuvel, Noord Brabant (0900 0161/UK agent 01242 528877/www.efteling.nl). 110km (68 miles) from Amsterdam; take A27 to Kaatsheuvel exit, then N261. **Open** *2005 Mar 25-Oct 31* 10am-6pm daily. *11 July-28 Aug* 10am-9pm Mon-Fri, Sun; 10am-midnight Sat. *For Nov-Mar* check website. **Admission** €24-€26 general; €22-€24 over-60s, disabled (2 caregivers permitted at same price); free under-4s. **Credit** DC, MC, V.

If your children insist on the big Disney experience (with prices to match) this is the next best thing. An enormous fairy-tale forest peopled with dwarves and witches, characters from Grimm stories and the *Arabian Nights*, enchanted and haunted castles, and even talking rubbish bins. This massive (and massively popular) amusement park is packed with state-of-the-art thrills, as well as more traditional fairground rides for the real tiny. Busy in summer.

Linnaeushof

Rijksstraatweg 4, Bennebroek (023 584 7624/ www.linnaeushof.nl). 20km (13 miles) from Amsterdam; take A5 to Haarlem, then head south on N208. **Open** *Apr-Sept* 10am-6pm daily. Closed Oct-Mar. **Admission** €8 over-2s; €6.25 over-65s, disabled; free under-2s. **No credit cards.**

Billed as Europe's biggest playground, this leisure park is host to 350 attractions including a Wild West train, cable cars, mini-golf, trampolines, water play area and go-carts. For the under-five's there's a separate play area. Very good value for money.

Madurodam

George Maduroplein 1, the Hague (070 355 3900/ 070 416 2400/www.madurodam.nl). 57km (35 miles) from Amsterdam; take A4 to the Hague. **Open** *Apr-June* 9am-8pm daily. *July, Aug* 9am-10pm daily. *Sept-Mar* 9am-6pm daily. **Admission** €12; €11 over-65s; €8.75 3-11s; free under-2s. **Credit** AmEx, DC, MC, V.

Apparently the largest miniature village in the world, with scale models of the Netherlands' most famous sights, built on a 1:25 ratio. Go on a summer evening, when the models are lit from the inside by over 50,000 tiny lamps.

Museum van Speelklok tot Pierement

Steenweg 6, Utrecht (030 231 2789/www.museum speelklok.nl). 38km (24 miles) from Amsterdam; take A2 to Utrecht. **Open** 10am-5pm Tue-Sat; noon-5pm Sun. **Admission** €6; €4 4-12s; under-4s free. **Credit** MC, V.

This Utrecht attraction houses a unique collection of antique mechanical instruments. Music boxes, circus, fairground and street organs and wondrous tin toys dating from as far back as the 15th century.

Childminders

Check the *Gouden Gids* under 'Oppascentrales'.

Oppascentrale Kriterion

624 5848/www.kriterionoppas.org. **Bookings** 9-11am, 4.30-8pm daily. **Rates** from €5-€6/hr; additional charge Fri, Sat. *Administration charge* €3.50. *Compulsory annual membership fee* €12.50. **No credit cards.**

This service uses male and female students aged over 18, all of whom are vetted. Book in advance. English-speakers can register and book online.

Tante Josine

420 5165/www.tantejosine.nl. **Bookings** 9am-5.30pm Mon-Thur; or leave a message. **Rates** €7.50/hr occasional use (€2.50 administration fee). **No credit cards.**

This friendly new service tries to match sitter to family. Employees are all well vetted and are either students or older 'auntie' types. Book by email at info@tantejosine.nl.

Film

It was the best of times, it was the worst of times.

Half the Dutch film industry is thriving. Of course film-makers struggle to find money but never have there been more Dutch films making it to the big screen – from commercial crowd-pleasers to desperate art house. And in 2004 an unprecedented four Dutch films were selected for the Toronto Film Festival. But Dutch audiences don't seem impressed: the number of people visiting cinemas continues to fall.

'Fast Eddy' Terstall is probably the most interesting Dutch director. Following comedies such as *Hufters en Hofdames* and *Rent-a-Friend*, his latest release, *Simon,* boasted typical Dutch themes: homosexuality, hash and homicide (or euthanasia as polite society has it). *Simon* is the first part of a trilogy about Dutch society with the upcoming films, *Sextet* and *Vox Populi*, following which Terstall threatens to turn to politics. Seeing what happened to that other politically inclined film-maker, Theo van Gogh, it remains to be seen if Terstall will make good his promise. After all, it's all very well being controversial but who wants to be shot, stabbed and nearly decapitated because of a few insults? At the time of his death Van Gogh (*see p22* **What the hell happened**) had just finished

The inimitable **Pathé Tuschinski.**
See p198.

editing *06-05*, a film based on the assassination of Dutch politician Pim Fortuyn, another man whose views, in this supposedly most tolerant of societies, led to his murder.

On safer ground, Paul Verhoeven, who became the most successful Dutch director in the US with films such as *Total Recall* and *Basic Instinct*, is working on *Zwartboek*, his first Dutch film since he left for Hollywood in 1983. The film, about a Jewish girl going undercover and infiltrating German circles during World War II, was set for release in 2005, but following Verhoeven's heart problems has been postponed until 2006.

Another Hollywood success is Pieter Jan Brugge, who directed and co-wrote *The Clearing*, loosely based on the kidnapping and killing of executive Gerrit-Jan Heijn of Ahold (owner of Albert Heijn supermarkets, *see p177* **Heijnie ho!**) in the '80s. The film, starring Dustin Hoffman and Helen Mirren, is more of a character study than a fast-paced action-thriller. As usual Hollywood wanted a happy ending, but Brugge somehow managed to slip in an appropriately gloomy Dutch denouement.

But in 2004 Hollywood came to Amsterdam to film a part of *Ocean's 12* (*see p200* **Lights! Camera! Clog action!**).

THE CINEMAS

Amsterdam has a large number of cinemas and, as in many cities, they can be divided into two categories: first-run and art houses (*filmhuizen*). Amsterdammers have a good appetite for foreign fare, and these venues offer a cosmopolitan mix of art films, documentaries and retrospectives (as well as an informed selection of more intelligent Hollywood flicks).

With the exception of the Uitkijk, all cinemas have cafés, while the Movies (*see p198*) has a good restaurant, too. The Pathé Tuschinski (*see p198*), with its grand art deco architecture, is a gem and a must-see in its own right.

TICKETS & INFORMATION

Films run from Wednesdays to Wednesdays. To find what's on and where, consult the Filmladder listings in the Wednesday editions of all major newspapers or online at www.filmfocus.nl. It's also on display in many bars, cafés and cinemas. English listings and reviews, both independent and mainstream, can be found in the free *Amsterdam Weekly* (*see p286* **'Bloids of Amsterdam**). For indie and art house films, there's the website www.underwateramsterdam.com and for those who read Dutch, the free monthly *Filmkrant*, available at cinemas, has lots of articles on (inter)national films and directors, reviews, gossip and soundtrack reviews.

It's best to reserve tickets between Thursday and Sundays. You can go to the booking office during the day or phone to make a reservation. But beware, Pathé cinemas run a computerised phone line in Dutch only, some cinemas charge a small booking fee and none accept credit cards. Pick up your ticket(s) at least 30 minutes before the film, otherwise they will be sold.

Multiplexes always show about 15 minutes of commercials and previews before the film and art house theatres do the same, albeit to a lesser extent. Films are shown in their original language, with Dutch subtitles. Films in Dutch are indicated by the words *Nederlands Gesproken* after the title. Some cinemas offer discounts for students or on weekday mornings and most cinemas, including art houses, stick a 15-minutes interval in the middle of every film and only a few have midnight screenings.

Cinemas

First run

City
Kleine-Gartmanplantsoen 15-19, Southern Canal Belt (0900 1458 premium rate/www.pathe.nl). Tram 1, 2, 5, 6, 7, 10. **Tickets** €4-€8. **Screens** 7. **No credit cards. Map** p314 D5.
You can't miss this functionalist classic of a building, nor the big crowds going in and out. Inside, TVs whet your appetite for films to come. Its central location and strictly Hollywood action and feel-good film diet make it hugely popular with loud youngsters.

Pathé ArenA
ArenA Boulevard 600, Bijlmermeer (0900 1458 premium rate/www.pathe.nl). Metro Bijlmer. **Tickets** €4.50-€9. **Screens** 14. **No credit cards.**

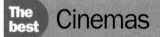
The best Cinemas

Cinecenter
Lounge, drink, watch an art flick. *See p198.*

Kriterion
Run by volunteers, enjoyed by all. *See p198.*

The Movies
For fine food and a fab film. *See p198.*

Pathé Tuschinski
Grand, gracious and over-the-top. Unmissable. *See p198.*

De Uitkijk
No thrills or frills, just quality. *See p198.*

Ever been to a multiplex near where you live? This is the same: 14 screens, 3,250 seats, digital sound and air-conditioning. You could be anywhere: just another consumer of the global entertainment industry. But at least the seats will be comfortable.

Pathé de Munt
Vijzelstraat 15, Southern Canal Belt (0900 1458 premium rate/www.pathe.nl). Tram 4, 9, 14, 16, 24, 25. **Tickets** €4.50-€9. **Screens** 7. **No credit cards. Map** p314 D4.
Locals despise the horrible brick building, but take to the Hollywood flicks and odd art house movie.

Pathé Tuschinski
Reguliersbreestraat 26-34, Southern Canal Belt (0900 1458 premium rate/www.pathe.nl). Tram 4, 9, 14, 16, 24, 25. **Tickets** €4.50-€10. **Screens** 4. **No credit cards. Map** p315 E4.
Built in 1921 as a variety theatre, the Tuschinski is Amsterdam's most prestigious venue and the city's only proper grand cinema. Have a drink in the lounge before you see a film and admire the glorious art deco interior. And for a real treat, reserve the eight-person box, complete with champagne. But if, during the film you find yourself wondering more about the cinema than Colin (*Alexander*) Farrell's hair dye, it offers guided tours.

Pathé Tuschinski Arthouse
Reguliersbreestraat 34, Southern Canal Belt (0900 1458 premium rate/www.pathe.nl). Tram 4, 9, 14, 16, 24, 25. **Tickets** €4.50-€10. **Screens** 3. **No credit cards. Map** p314 D4.
Located right next door to the Tuschinski, this Pathé shows somewhat artier films, sprinkled with a leavening of intelligent Hollywood movies.

Art houses

Cinecenter
Lijnbaansgracht 236, the Jordaan (623 6615/www.cinecenter.nl). Tram 1, 2, 5, 6, 7, 10. **Tickets** €5-€8. **Screens** 4. **No credit cards. Map** p314 C4.
The highly popular Cinecenter, complete with a hip 'lounge' décor café, always has an interesting programme, with films from all over the world. The screens, all with their own name, are small. It's very popular on Sunday afternoons and on the irregular gay-preview Monday evenings.

Filmhuis Cavia
Van Hallstraat 52-1, West (681 1419/www.filmhuiscavia.nl). Tram 3, 10. **Tickets** €5. **Screens** 1. **No credit cards. Map** p309 A3.
Housed in a former squatted school, as you might expect Cavia specialises in obscure and/or political pictures. You can also rent it for film parties.

Filmmuseum Cinerama
Marnixstraat 400-2, Southern Canal Belt (623 7814/www.filmmuseum.nl/cinerama). Tram 1, 2, 5, 6, 7, 10. **Tickets** €5.50-€8. **Screens** 3. **No credit cards. Map** p314 C5.

At some point this building will be turned into a new theatre complex. In the meantime it shows art house and non-mainstream Hollywood flicks.

Het Ketelhuis
Haarlemmerweg 8-10, the Jordaan (684 0090/www.ketelhuis.nl). Tram 10/bus 18, 22. **Tickets** €7.50. **Screens** 1. **No credit cards. Map** p309 A1.
Ketelhuis struggles to keep going on its diet of Dutch non-commercial features and documentaries. The new filmmakers who show their labours don't do much to bring in the bacon, either. And the forums and discussions are not exactly money-spinners.

Kriterion
Roetersstraat 170, Oost (623 1708/www.kriterion.nl). Tram 6, 7, 10/Metro Weesperplein. **Tickets** €5.50-€8; €5.50 children's matinées, previews. **Screens** 2. **No credit cards. Map** p316 G3.
Run by volunteer students since 1945, and overlorded by resident cats Jules and Jim, this cinema's intriguing programme includes children's matinées (Wed, Sat, Sun) and preview screenings (Thur). Then there are student flicks, late shows covering cult US movies or erotic French films and the last Sunday-of-the-month film and discussion afternoons.

The Movies
Haarlemmerdijk 161, the Jordaan (624 5790/www.themovies.nl). Tram 3. **Tickets** €8; €6.50 children; €7 students, over-65s; €65 10-visit card. **Screens** 4. **Credit** *Restaurant* MC, V. **Map** p309 B1.
The Movies might be a stupid name for a cinema, but this is one of the oldest in town, in the middle of hip Haarlemmerdijk, and with its own restaurant, too. The set menus cost €29, including film ticket, and your seat for the independent/art house movie will be reserved while you finish your meal.

Rialto
Ceintuurbaan 338, the Pijp (662 3488/www.rialtofilm.nl). Tram 3, 12, 24, 25. **Tickets** €5.50-€8; €28 5-visit card; €50 10-visit card. **Screens** 2. **No credit cards. Map** p315 F6.
Stylish and alternative, this is one of the few remaining neighbourhood cinemas in town and one of the few with disabled access. On offer are new and old international films, documentaries, the occasional European première and kids' flicks on Sat, Sun, Wed. It also organises film discussions and lectures.

De Uitkijk
Prinsengracht 452, Southern Canal Belt (623 7460/www.uitkijk.nl). Tram 1, 2, 5, 6, 7, 10. **Tickets** €5.50-€7. **Screens** 1. **No credit cards. Map** p315 D5.
De Uitkijk is Amsterdam's oldest cinema, having opened its doors to the public just before the start of the 20th century's carnage in 1913. It's a charming 158-seat converted canal house that was set up by anti-commercial filmmakers. It still shows interesting flicks and as the cinema doesn't serve snacks, you won't be disturbed by crunching or slurping.

Multimedia centres

OT301
*Overtoom 301, Oud West (779 4913/http://squat.
net/overtoom301). Tram 1, 6.* **Tickets** €2.50 and
up. **Screens** 1. **No credit cards. Map** p313 B6.
This former Dutch film academy was squatted some
years ago and transformed into an organic vegan
restaurant, a club and a cinema offering 'alternative'
films. As with most squats, check before setting out.

De Balie
*Kleine-Gartmanplantsoen 10, Southern Canal Belt
(553 5100/www.debalie.nl). Tram 1, 2, 5, 6, 7, 10,
20.* **Tickets** €5-€7. **Screens** 1. **No credit cards.
Map** p314 D5.
This cultural centre, cinema and bar/restaurant (*see
p148*) shows documentaries, art films and is the central location for the annual IDFA (International
Documentary Filmfestival Amsterdam).

Melkweg
*Lijnbaansgracht 234A, Southern Canal Belt (531
8181/www.melkweg.nl). Tram 1, 2, 5, 6, 7, 10, 20.*
Tickets €6; €5 students (incl membership).
Screens 1. **No credit cards. Map** p314 C5.
There's always something interesting to see at the
Melkweg (*see p219*), from trash to cult to art house.

Tropeninstituut
*Kleine Zaal Linnaeusstraat 2, Oost; Grote Zaal
Mauritskade 63, Oost (568 8500/www.kit.nl/
tropentheater). Tram 9, 10, 14.* **Tickets** €6-€7.
Screens 2. **Credit** MC, V. **Map** p316 H3.
Next to the Tropenmuseum (*see p105*), this venue
shows documentaries from developing countries.

Film museum

Nederlands Filmmuseum (NFM)
*Vondelpark 3, (Library: Vondelstraat 69-71)
Museum Quarter (589 1400/library 589
1435/www.filmmuseum.nl). Tram 1, 2, 3, 5,
6, 12.* **Open** *Library* 1-5pm Tue-Fri (closed for a
month every summer). **Tickets** €7.20-€7.80;
€6-€6.50 students, over-65s; €5.50 members.
Membership €20/yr. **Screens** 3. **No credit
cards. Map** p314 C6.

This government-subsidised enterprise, a combination of cinema and museum, is facing hard times following budget cuts. It was established in the 1940s
and has over 35,000 films in its vaults, culled from
every period, cinematic style and corner of the world.
Children's matinées screen Sunday and Wednesday,
and there are regular showings of silent movies with
live musical accompaniment. On Thursday at 10pm
in summer, there   are outdoor screenings on the
terrace. Students of cinema can be found poring over
the archives. Its Café Vertigo – also a restaurant –
has one of Amsterdam's most charming terraces.

Film festivals

Amnesty International
Film Festival
626 4436/www.amnesty.nl/filmfestival. **Date**
Mar-Apr.
This five-day biennial event on human rights is held
in various locations and features films, documentaries, lectures, discussions and a workshop.

De Balie/IDFA.

Lights! Camera! Clog action!

With large parts of the *Ocean's 11* sequel – *Ocean's 12*, which reunited Clooney, Pitt and Co – set and filmed in the city, the interest in Amsterdam as an international film location will undoubtedly rise. In fact, whatever the movie's merits, it does cast a refreshingly non-stereotypical glow over this filmic town. And while local response to Hollywood filming soured, the coffeeshop Dampkring (*see p155*) did extend their thanks for being chosen as a setting by introducing a special 'Ocean's 12 Haze' to its menu.

But in fact there is a rich history of Amsterdam being cast as a film extra – even when it doesn't appear in person. Alfred Hitchcock wanted the city as a location in *Foreign Correspondent* (1940) but there was a little matter of a world war on. Undaunted, Hollywood set builders made 'a piece of Amsterdam... a few hotels, a Dutch windmill and a bit of the Dutch countryside'. America being tardy in joining the struggle, Hitchcock sent a cameraman to get location footage in Amsterdam, but the war intervened when his ship was torpedoed. Undaunted, the heroic cameraman still managed to get some footage of the Jordaan for a chase scene, but a jarring left turn lands you back in a Hollywood lot complete with Spanish-style windmill. (What is it with Hollywood filmmakers and windmills? They did the same in the *South Park* movie in the 'Kyle's Mom is a Bitch' segment. Don't they realise Dutch windmills are different?)

Another thriller that used Dutch stereotypes was *Puppet on a Chain* (1971), a tale of illicit drugs and apathetic cops, which climaxed – we kid you not – with traditionally dressed women doing a murderous clog dance (for more absurd wooden shoe action check out Jackie Chan's *Who Am I?*). The same year brought Sean Connery to town for *Diamonds are Forever*, with Bond falling for the charms of a typically tough and sexy Dutch chick. In fact, finding love in Amsterdam seems to be a recurring theme in international productions: a feature-length *Love Boat* episode had the long-neglected Captain Stubing finally getting some *amore* action here. Similarly, the Italian production *La Ragazza in Vetrina* (1961) – 'The Girl in the Window' – written by Pier Paolo Pasolini is a heart-warming tale of, you guessed it, Red Light love.

Staying in an art house vein: no less a person than Monsieur Hulot slapsticked his way through town in *Trafic* (1971). This was a homecoming of sorts for director/star Jacques Tati who had a Dutch grandfather, a picture framer famed in the family for refusing Van Gogh his services in exchange for some of the artist's paintings. Also, almost the complete oeuvre of that personification of art house, Peter Greenaway, offers an orgy of local location spotting.

Sadly the film that may be the most rewarding for Amsterdam-spotters is very difficult to find. Cheech and Chong's *Still Smokin'* (1983) has the dopehead duo being consistently confused for Burt Reynolds and Dolly Parton in such landmarks as the Tuschinski Cinema, Hotel Okura and a gay sauna. In the meantime there's always *Deuce Bigalow: European Gigolo* (2005) for Amsterdam-based stereotypes and slapstick.

Let's also hope that Dutch superbaddie, Goldmember, returns to the screen in the next instalment of Austin Powers so we can learn why Austin's father hates only 'two kinds of people: people that have no respect for other cultures and the Dutch'.

Fantastic Film Festival
679 4875/www.afff.nl. **Date** Apr.
FFF will appeal to lovers of horror, fantasy and SF. The Night of Terror, which spotlights some of the goriest movies imaginable in front of an up-for-it crowd, is not to be missed.

International Documentary Filmfestival Amsterdam
627 3329/www.idfa.nl. **Date** last wk in Nov.
This fascinating annual festival has opportunities to watch and discuss the form. There's friendly competition with the Shadow Festival's (www.shadowfestival.nl) more edgy kinds of filmmaking.

International Film Festival Rotterdam
Information 010 890 9090/reservations 010 890 9000/www.filmfestivalrotterdam.nl). **Date** late Jan/early Feb.
Holland's biggest festival, with around 350,000 visitors and 100 films in both the main programme and retrospectives, has an emphasis on 'art' movies. There are also lectures, seminars and workshops.

Nederlands Film Festival
030 230 3800/www.filmfestival.nl. **Date** Sept.
This all-Dutch affair spotlights 100 new features in a variety of venues around Utrecht.

Galleries

There's more to Dutch art than applied stereoblindness.

At first, it seemed as if the theories behind why the Dutch have such a mighty reputation for rendering life in two dimensions had to be discarded when it was revealed in 2004 that Rembrandt was a big fat cheater. Analysis of his self-portraits discovered that he suffered from stereoblindness: misaligned eyes that cause one to see three-dimensional reality in two-dimensional terms. While some were quick to recast Dutch artistic achievements as freakish products of stereoblind savants, calmer minds remembered that closing one eye is an old trick to do artificially what stereoblindness does naturally: flatten things. So there's room for other theories on why Amsterdam is so arty.

Certainly, 'there's money' remains one of the more compelling explanations. Ever since the Golden Age, artists like Rembrandt and Vermeer have been able to make a living from a middle-class rabid to invest in their quest for status. And in Amsterdam, little has changed: the locals remain enthusiastic for original artworks and there are plenty of galleries to meet demand. But despite this, both Rembrandt and Vermeer went bankrupt.

Another theory is based on how the Dutch have evolved innate organisational skills, from the order required to keep the sea at bay, to the almost constant spring-cleaning required to maintain a sense of space in this modestly proportioned land. A dedication to arrangement is certainly on display as one descends on Schiphol and sees the Mondrian-like grid pattern of the landscape. Some even see it in the ballet-like elegance of Dutch football players, who open space to score and close space to defend. And, of course, you see it in much of the art, the product of what happens when these ingrained compulsions are applied to paper, canvas and the computer.

But where there's order, there's chaos. And there's been a strong Dionysian strand that has sought to rebel against the rules, both overt and hidden, required in both keeping the sea at bay and living with such a density of people. It should not come as a surprise that the major developments of Dutch art in the 20th century can be seen as a battle between order and chaos.

Representing that part of the Dutch psyche that joneses for order, the abstractionists of **De Stijl** (the Style), founded in 1917 and involving the likes of Theo van Doesburg, Piet Mondrian and Gerrit Rietveld, sought rules of equilibrium that are as useful in everyday design as in art. You just have to surf the web, leaf through *Wallpaper**, visit IKEA or buy a White Stripes

The best Galleries

Chiellerie HPVK
The ultimate hang-out; s*ee p206* **Good breeding**.

Smart Project Space
Everything you need; *see p206*.

Oude Kerk
New in old; *see p203*.

Arcam
Follow the sparkly trail to the silver snail; *see p204*.

W139
Squatty art bunker; *see p203*.

Droog Design
Art applied; *see p178* **Living for design**.

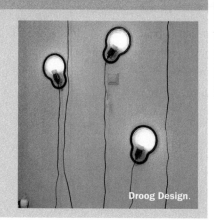

Droog Design.

The new in the **Oude Kerk**. See p203.

album to see their influence. However, some later painters chose to become disciples of chaos, embracing an antidotal muse. Under the moniker of **CoBrA**, such artists as Karel Appel and Eugene Brands interpreted the Liberation that ended World War II as a signal for spontaneity and the expression of immediate urges. Where their Surrealist forebears had embraced Freud, they preferred Jung, and sought to wire themselves into the unconscious of primitives, children and the mentally ill (for the **CoBrA Museum of Modern Art**, *see p117*). CoBrA can take a lot of credit for bringing 'outsider art' into the world's galleries.

Rebellion also defined the 1980s, when Amsterdam's 'After Nature' group, including Peter Klashorst and Jurriaan van Hall, decided to counter the reign of conceptual art with a renaissance of figurative work – but one marked by a spontaneous approach showing respect for CoBrA's abstract expressionism. This decade was also marked by the punk attitude of 'do-it-yourself', and squats became more cultural than political as artists sought settings for making and exhibiting new work.

THE 21ST CENTURY

The reaction against the anti-functionalism of conceptual art continues unabated – a trend that would have pleased adherents of De Stijl, who hoped the future would bring a frenzy of cross-disciplinary action. Not only can photographers (Anton Corbijn, Rineke Dijkstra), VJs (Ottograph, Micha Klein), cartoonists (Joost Swarte), and architects (Rem Koolhaas) easily pass themselves off as 'artists', but the inspired work of John Körmeling and Atelier van Lieshout, equal parts artistry and oddball carpentry, embodies a perfect fusion of function, whimsy and good old-fashioned aesthetics. On the other hand, many people who would have called themselves artists in the past now proudly proclaim themselves designers (*see p178* **Living for design**).

Besides straddling a fine line between order and chaos, Dutch graphic/multimedia designers are now also surfing between the pure and purely commercial. Having achieved global acclaim for formulating a universal visual language where stylistic simplicity (De Stijl) doesn't rule out personal expression (CoBrA), many are now being employed by 'guerrilla' or 'viral' ad agencies, who have been set up to take advantage of this talent pool for international campaigns. The nation's art, design and architecture colleges have helped this process by making artists and designers study together and by welcoming a large number of foreign students. However, creative Amsterdammers are not as spoiled as they once were. Generous subsidies still exist (another reason for foreign artists to visit), but things are no longer as they were in the swinging '80s.

But compared with the art factories of Paris, New York and London, Amsterdam's galleries remain adventurous and welcome up-and-comers. Even auction house Christie's (*see p160*) is trying to fight a staid image by sponsoring some hip art shows. But you will also note a backlash against all this cutting-edge stuff, with many artists returning to good ol' fashioned painting, drawing and sculpting.

With **Westergasfabriek** (*see p250*) coming of age, there's a brand new slew of exhibition spaces. And between this 'culture park' and the Jordaan, lies Stadsliedenbuurt, hosts of Art Walk (www.artwalkamsterdam.nl), that seeks to fill unused spaces and display windows with art. Just download a map from the website for an edgy and arty wander.

ON SHOW

Besides the **Stedelijk Museum of Modern Art** (*see p114*), now in **Post CS** (*see p107* **View to the future**), there are several other world-famous museums of modern art in the Netherlands: the **Haags Gemeentemuseum** in The Hague (Stadhouderslaan 41, 070 338 1111/www.gemeentemuseum.nl); the terrific outdoor Rijksmuseum Kröller-Müller (near Otterloo entrance to Hoge Veluwe, 0318 591 241/www.kmm.nl), the **Groninger Museum** in Groningen (*see p272* **Groninger rock city**), and the newly expanded Stedelijk van Abbemuseum (Bilderdijklaan 10, 040 238 1000/www.vanabbemuseum.nl) in Eindhoven.

Photography buffs would do well to visit **Huis Marseille** (*see p95*) and **Foam** (*see p99*). For the more antique/collectible side of art try gallery street Spiegelgracht/Nieuw Spiegelstraat (*see Map p314 D5/4*).

Art spaces in Amsterdam appear and vanish all the time. For the most up-to-date list, buy the monthly *Alert* (available at **Athenaeum Nieuwscentrum**; *see p161*); although it's in Dutch, galleries are sorted into areas and clearly marked on maps. Also, scan the flyers at art and design book store Artbook (Van Baerlestraat 126, Museum District, 664 0925, 10am-6pm Tue-Sat, 1-6pm Mon); check gallery shows in *Amsterdam Weekly* (*see p286* **'Bloids of Amsterdam**), *Uitkrant* (www.uitkrant.nl), or the art listings pamphlet published every two months by AKKA, whose website (www.akka.nl) links to the city's galleries.

Many galleries close during July or August and have a relaxed attitude to opening hours the rest of the time, so it's best to call ahead. For **KunstRAI** art fair, **Kunstvlaai**, its edgier equivalent, and artists' open studios, *see p185*.

Galleries

The Old Centre: Old Side

Amsterdams Centrum voor Fotographie

Bethaniënstraat 9-13 (622 4899/www.acf-web.nl). *Tram 16, 24, 25.* **Open** 2-5pm Wed-Fri; 11am-5pm Sat. Closed July, Aug. **No credit cards**. **Map** p310 D3.

Photo hounds love this sprawling space within flashing distance of the Red Light District. Besides exhibitions (also at No.39), it has workshops and a black-and-white darkroom for hire.

Oude Kerk

Oudekerksplein 23 (625 8284/www.oudekerk.nl). *Tram 4, 9, 14, 16, 24, 25.* **Open** 11am-5pm Mon-Sat; 1-5pm Sun. *During World Press Photo* 10am-6pm Mon-Sat; 1-6pm Sun. **No credit cards**. **Map** p310 D2.

The 'Old Church', home of World Press Photo (*see p185*), exhibits everything from contemporary aboriginal art to photographs documenting the life of albinos in Africa. Admission to the various exhibitions shouldn't be more than €6. *See also p88*.

W139

Warmoesstraat 139 (622 9434/www.w139.nl). *Tram 4, 9, 14, 16, 24, 25.* **Open** 1-7pm Tue-Sun, but varies with exhibitions. **No credit cards**. **Map** p310 D2.

In its two decades of existence, W139 has never lost its squat, nor occasionally overly conceptual edge. And they have found the perfect location, complete with stellar bar, in the basement of Post CS (*see p107* **View to the future**) until the renovations of their Warmoesstraat location are finished in late 2006.

The Old Centre: New Side

Arti et Amicitiae

Rokin 112 (623 3508/www.arti.nl). Tram 4, 9, 14, 16, 24, 25. **Open** 1-6pm Tue-Sun. **No credit cards**. **Map** p310 D3.

This marvellous building houses a private artists' society, whose members gather in the first-floor bar. But members of the public can climb a Berlage-designed staircase to its large exhibition space, home to some excellent temporary shows.

Western Canal Belt

Galerie Paul Andriesse

Prinsengracht 116 (623 6237/www.galeries.nl /andriesse). Tram 13, 14, 17. **Open** 11am-6pm Tue-Fri; 2-6pm Sat; 2-5pm Sun of mth. **No credit cards**. **Map** p310 C2.

While perhaps no longer all that innovative, there's still a selective savvy at work that embraces both older and wiser artists (Marlene Dumas often shows new works here) and up-and-coming names such as horse portraitist Charlotte Dumas.

Montevideo/TBA

Keizersgracht 264 (623 7101/www.montevideo.nl).
Tram 13, 14, 17. **Open** 1-6pm Tue-Sat. **No credit**
cards. **Map** p310 C3.
Montevideo is dedicated to applying new techniques
to visual arts, alongside photography and installations. Admire tech in an olde worlde space, or read
up on an assortment of topics in the reference room.
There's usually a token entry fee for exhibitions.

Southern Canal Belt

De Appel

Nieuwe Spiegelstraat 10 (625 5651/www.deappel.nl).
Tram 16, 24, 25. **Open** 11am-6pm Tue-Thur, Sat,
Sun; 11am-10pm Fri. **Admission** €4; free 1st Sun
of mth. **No credit cards**. **Map** p314 D4.
An Amsterdam institution that showed its mettle by
being one of the first galleries in the country to
embrace video art. It still has a nose for things modern, and gives international and rookie guest cura-
tors freedom to follow their muse.

Galerie Akinci

Lijnbaansgracht 317 (638 0480/www.akinci.nl).
Tram 6, 7, 10, 16, 24, 25. **Open** 1-6pm Tue-Sat.
No credit cards. **Map** p315 E5.
Part of a nine-gallery complex that includes Lumen
Traven, Art Affair, Oele, Meti and the office of the
Gate Foundation (an 'intercultural contemporary art
multicultural society' with a massive website at
www.gatefoundation.nl), Akinci thrives on surprise,
with shows that employ every imaginable contem-
porary medium: from the body-hair art of Yael
Davids, to the mutant puppets of Gerben Mulder.

Gallery Lemaire

Reguliersgracht 80 (623 7027/www.gallery-lemaire.
com). Tram 4, 16, 24, 25. **Open** 11am-5pm Tue-Fri;
11am-4pm Sat. **Credit** AmEx, MC, V. **Map** p315 E4.
In the same family for three generations, this maze-
like gallery fills a huge canal house with tribal art
from around the world – in short: a heaven for collectors. Phone ahead to confirm opening times.

Melkweg

Marnixstraat 409 (531 8181/www.melkweg.nl).
Tram 1, 2, 5, 6, 7, 10. **Open** 1-8pm Wed-Sun.
No credit cards. **Map** p314 D5.
The Melkweg reflects the broad interests of director
Suzanne Dechart, with quality shows of contempo-
rary photography. Expect anything from meditative
studies of trees to portraits of Hong Kong ravers. *See*
also p219 and p229.

Reflex Modern Art Gallery

Weteringschans 79a (627 2832/www.reflex-art.nl).
Tram 6, 7, 10. **Open** 11am-6pm Tue-Sat. **Credit**
AmEx, MC, V. **Map** p314 D5.
You can almost smell the Big Apple in Reflex. The
New York flavour extends to its international
names, like Araki and Christo, as well as celebrity
locals such as Dadara and Erin Olaf. And here's
where to come to for that blow-up *Scream* doll.

Walls

Prinsengracht 737 (616 9597/www.walls.nl). *Tram*
1, 2, 5. **Open** 10am-6pm Tue-Fri; noon-5pm Sat, 1st
Sun of mth. **Credit** AmEx, MC, V. **Map** p314 D5.
The walls are filled with everything and anything
of the painterly persuasion: most of which is well
priced, local and unpretentious – in contrast to
neighbour Hang (Prinsengracht 715, www.hang.nl).

Jodenbuurt, the Plantage & the Oost

Arcam

Prins Hendrikkade 600 (620 4878/www.arcam.nl).
Tram 9, 14/Metro Waterlooplein/bus 42, 43. **Open**
1-5pm Tue-Sat. **No credit cards**. **Map** p311 E3.
Architecture Centrum Amsterdam is obsessed with
the promotion of Dutch contemporary architecture,
and organises tours, forums, lectures and exhibits
in their fresh new 'silver snail' location.

East Area

Jodenbreestraat 24sous (624 5747/www.eastarea.nl).
Tram 9, 14/Metro Waterlooplein. **Open** 1-7pm Thur-
Sun. **No credit cards**. **Map** p311 E3.
Located in the basement of radical leftist bookstore
Fort van Sjako (625 8979/www.fortvansjakoo.nl),
this new initiative from party-throwers Salon USSR
(*see p235*) presents the work of artists from Eastern
Europe in a tiny squatty setting. Poetry readings
and concerts round out the programme.

East 66

Sumatrastraat 66h (no phone/www.66east.org).
Tram 7, 14/Metro Muiderpoort. **Open** 2-8pm Fri,
noon-6pm Sat during exhibitions. **No credit cards**.
This rather small 'Centre for Urban Culture' surfs a
singular wave between art, architecture and urban-
ism with exhibitions, installations and lectures that
reflect the 'living city'. Located a long way from the
normal tourist trail in Amsterdam's far oost, East
66 can be combined with a visit to Pakt (*see p205*)
and Dappermarkt (*see p180*). They may move to a
nearby location in 2006, so check the website.

The Waterfront

Many more galleries are likely to follow the Stedelijk – now temporarily housed in Post CS (*see p107* **View to the future**) – to the eastern docklands. Besides **Consortium** (*see below*) and **Lloyd Hotel** (*see p70* **Cooking culture with Lloyd**), the former warehouse Loods6 (KNSM-Laan 143, www.loods6.nl) puts on occasional exhibitions of an art/design nature, as does hip street accessory shop, 90 Square Meters (Levantplein 52, KNSM-Eiland, 419 2525/www.90sqm.com).

Consortium

Pakhuis Wilhelmina, Veemkade 570 (06 2611 8950 mobile/www.xs4all.nl/~conso). Bus 32. **Open** 2-6pm Fri-Sun during exhibitions. **No credit cards**.
Consortium puts on exhibitions dedicated to international underground up-and-comers. Its warehouse home has recently been renovated as a studio space and 'breeding ground' (*see p206* **Good breeding**) for local artists and has an excellent bar/café.

Mediamatic

Post CS building 5th floor, Oosterdokskade 5 (638 9901/www.mediamatic.net). A 10 min walk from Centraal Station. **Open** varies. **No credit cards**. **Map** p311 E1.
This organisation dedicated to the outer reaches of technology and multimedia lost its exhibition space in 2004 but is now housed in the happening Post CS. They hope to get an exhibition space on the 1st floor in 2005, so check their excellent website.

Pakt

Zeeburgerpad 53 (06 5427 0879 mobile/www. pakt.nu). Tram 7, 10. **Open** 2-8pm Thur-Sun. **No credit cards**.
This new, slightly out-of-the-way address is worth a visit for sheer inspired quirkiness. Expect the 'pure image and sound' of Park 4DTV (www.park.nl), the mobile art/hotdog kiosks of aptly named Ki-osk, or the rolling printing logs of Alex Fischer.

The Jordaan

Annet Gelink Gallery

Laurierstraat 187-9 (330 2066/www.annetgelink. com). Tram 13, 14, 17. **Open** 11am-6pm Tue-Fri; 1-6pm Sat. **No credit cards**. **Map** p313 B4.
Annet Gelink has plenty of space and light to lavish on notable names in Dutch and international art: Ed van der Elsken (the photographer of 1960s Amsterdam), Alicia Frames, Barbara Visser and Virgil Marti, who achieved fame with a wallpaper patterned by the web of a marijuana-wasted spider.

Donkersloot

Leidsegracht 76 (572 2722/www.gallery donkersloot.nl). Tram 1, 2, 5. **Open** noon-midnight daily; *July, Aug* noon-6pm Tue-Sun. **Credit** AmEx, DC, MC, V. **Map** p314 C4.
Hyping itself as a 'night gallery', Donkersloot hosts 'live painting events' (such as getting 80 women together to paint each other) and works by rock 'n' roll types like the late Herman Brood. Its openings are a who's who of the city's more decadent artists.

Galerie Diana Stigter

Hazenstraat 17 (624 2361/www.dianastigter.nl). Tram 7, 10, 13, 14, 17. **Open** 1-6pm Tue-Sat; 2-5pm 1st Sun of mth. **No credit cards**. **Map** p314 C4.
The extreme and the extremely committed have found a home with curator Diana Stigter: the scary animation of Martha Colburn, the magical videos of Baloise art prize winner Saskia Olde Wolbers, while Maaike Schoorel had most of her exhibition bought up by Saatchi. Stigter may move in 2005 so call ahead.

Galerie Fons Welters

Bloemstraat 140 (423 3046/www.fonswelters.nl). Tram 13, 14, 17. **Open** 1-6pm Tue-Sat; 2-5pm 1st Sun of mth. **No credit cards**. **Map** p309 B3.
Venerable doyen of the scene, Fons Welters likes to 'discover' the latest new (and often local) talent and has shown remarkable taste in both sculpture and installation, having provided a home to Merijn Bolink, Rob Birza, Jennifer Tee and Roy Villevoye. Worth it for the Atelier van Lieshout entrance alone.

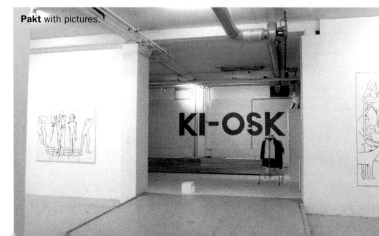

Pakt with pictures.

GO Gallery

Prinsengracht 64 (422 9580/www.gogallery.nl).
Tram 13, 14, 17. **Open** noon-6pm Wed-Sat; 1-5pm
Sun. **Credit** AmEx, DC, MC, V. **Map** p309 B2.
Owner Oscar van den Voorn is an energetic sup-
porter of art that manages to display a sense of
humour. Visitors can expect stained-glass, graffiti,
LSD-inspired art and sporadic themed dinners
(check the website for details).

Motive Gallery

Elandsgracht 10 (330 3668/www.motivegallery.nl).
Tram 7, 10. **Open** 1-6pm Wed-Sat; 2-5pm 1st Sun
of mth. **No credit cards. Map** p314 C4.
Focusing on photography and drawings by younger
artists, this Haarlem-expat was a welcome addition
to the scene in 2004. Don't miss neighbour, the art
book publisher/store Artimo (Elandsgracht 8, 625
3344/www.artimo.net).

Serieuze Zaken

Elandsstraat 90 (427 5770). Tram 7, 10, 17. **Open**
noon-6pm Tue-Sat; 1-5pm 1st Sun of mth. **No credit
cards. Map** p314 C4.
Rob Malasch was already known as a quirky theatre type and journalist before opening this gallery
in the Jordaan. Shows here might feature Brit Art,
works by contemporary Chinese painters or the
'Punk Pictures' of Max Natkiel.

Stedelijk Museum Bureau Amsterdam

*Rozenstraat 59 (422 0471/www.smba.nl). Tram 13,
14, 17.* **Open** 11am-5pm Tue-Sun. **Map** p313 B4.
The Stedelijk's Rozenstraat outpost is often hipper
than its mothership, with shows including the scary
styrofoam sculptures of Folkert de Jong and the, er,
sperm paintings of Arnoud Holleman.

Torch

Lauriergracht 94 (626 0284/www.torchgallery.com).
Tram 7, 10. **Open** 2-6pm Thur-Sat. **Credit** AmEx,
DC, MC, V. **Map** p313 D4.
If you like your art edgy you'll love Torch, which
brings Richard Kern, Jake & Dino Chapman, Micha
Klein and Anton Corbijn to Amsterdam.

The Museum Quarter, Vondelpark & the South

Smart Project Space

*Arie Biemondstraat 101-111 (427 5951/www.smart
projectspace.net). Tram 1, 3, 6, 12.* **Open** noon-
10pm Tue-Sun. **No credit cards. Map** p313 B6.
Relocated and reopening in May 2005, Smart will no
doubt remain loyal to 'hardcore art' in its huge new
exhibition space, which also has two cinemas, a
media lab, lecture hall and a café-restaurant.

Good breeding

This town has a lot of nostalgists weeping for
those '80s and '90s salad days when cultural
squats like Silo and Vrieshuis Amerika were
the coolest, edgiest and most frolicsome
things around. But while no one likes a
whiner, when the powers-that-be closed
these cultural beehives in order to make
Amsterdam the 'business gateway to Europe'
it was soon seen to be a monumental blunder
in a city defined by its artistic traditions. So
the city bureaucrats, in an effort to claw back
lost prestige and emigrating artists, did what
all such functionaries do and threw money at
the problem, creating non-squat squats called
'broedplaatsen' (breeding grounds).

Don't worry if it all gets confusing, the
world of amstersquats is nothing if not
divided into umpteen different categories.
In addition to *broedplaatsen* there are proper
squats (reappropriated buildings that had
been left empty for more than a year), 'anti-
squats' (buildings with temporary residents
paying no rent so that squatters can't squat
in them); and 'bought squats' (old squats that
were then sold cheaply by the city to their
inhabitants – like Vrankrijk (Spuistraat 216,

www.vrankrijk.org), which remains a hotbed
of cheap beer and radical politics.

It seems those places that began as
bona fide squats are the ones making
the crossover most efficiently. The former
film academy **OT301** (*see p199*) is totally
happening; as is former shipping yard
art complex **NDSM** (*see p250* and *p252*).
And while not actually itself a *broedplaats*,
Westergasfabriek (*see p250*) retains street
smarts due its reclaimed industrial cred.

But the sexiest breeding ground is
Chiellerie HPVK (Raamgracht 58, 320 9448,
www.hpvk.nl, open 5pm-fashionably late Fri,
2-6pm Sat, Sun). Organised by artist and old
skool squatter Chiel van Zelst, his gallery is a
Hang Plek Voor Kunstenaars ('Hanging Spot
for Artists' – Dutch has the same double
meaning for 'hanging'). There's a weekly
opening: the first Friday of the month is
dedicated to a 'Curator of the Month', while
every other Friday is under the spell of an
'Artist of the Week'. The website has already
become a rather impressive collection of the
local art scene, so check it all out before
dropping by for a quality hang.

Gay & Lesbian

Explore the dykes and cruise the canals.

For gays and lesbians worldwide, Amsterdam is the number-one destination. The city's liberal reputation is legendary and has, over the centuries, attracted flocks of differently feathered birds from all over the planet.

Holland decriminalised homosexuality in 1811 and lowered the age of consent for gay men to 16 in 1971. But it made headlines in 2002, as the first nation to legalise same-sex marriage for nationals and residents. In the first year 1,339 male and 1,075 female couples tied the knot. But in 2003 the number of gays and lesbians saying 'I do' dropped 25 per cent.

Although there's been stiff competition from hip cities like Barcelona and Berlin, the old queen is not giving in. True, locals sometimes curse the lack of new initiatives, but at the same time they are a lazy bunch and tend to stick to their favourite hang-outs, giving new places a hard time. That said, for a small city it still has much to offer, whatever your flavour or fetish.

But not everything is pink-tinted. The lesbian scene is small with only half a dozen or so bars and club nights, and there's not a lot of mixing between gays and lesbians. And the council and gay organisations seem forever on opposite sides, while homophobia is on the rise.

Essential information

Although Amsterdam deserves its reputation, the warmth with which gay people are received in the Netherlands is cooling. In autumn 2004, there was a kerfuffle in the papers over some schools' refusal of a special educational edition of young people's gay mag *Expreszo*, and with the CDA (Christian Democrats) in power there's a palpable change in the moral climate. This has translated into a clampdown on cruising: the layout of Nieuwe Meer, near Amsterdamse Bos, has been changed to make it more family-friendly, and Highland cattle have been introduced; they not only trim the grass but keep sylvan sexual activity under control, too – would you want a cow stepping on your delicate bits? The most central cruising area is the rose garden in Vondelpark (though only after dark). Since there aren't many public toilets, cottaging is pretty much impossible, and *ijzerkrullen* (the curly metal urinals dotted all over the city) are designed to let you see if they are occupied – and by how many people.

Most of these changes are directed toward gay men. The city councillor most vocal in the current campaign to close down darkrooms outside the red light district and clean up nudity on the Pride parade is, ironically, a lesbian (*see p209* **Tiara and tantrums**).

The relaxed laws about prostitutes include gay ones (prostitutes for lesbians are unheard of) and the *Gouden Gids* (*Yellow Pages*) and gay press list dozens of escort agencies aimed at gay men. But the rent-boy bars on Paardenstraat are exploitative, miserable and dangerous: you have been warned.

Attitudes to HIV/AIDS have been proactive right from the start. Safe-sex information is compulsory in darkrooms – which are regulated – and plenty of the leather places organise safe-sex parties (*see p214*). Free condoms aren't universal on the scene, however, and it's a depressing fact that STDs – including HIV – are on the up and barebacking is as popular and controversial here as elsewhere.

For information about HIV and other gay/lesbian matters, *see p288*.

Homomonument

Westermarkt, Western Canal Belt. Tram 13, 14, 17. **Map** p310 C3.
Unveiled in 1987, Karin Daan's three-sectioned pink triangle – symbolising past, present and future – was a world first. The monument is treated with respect – flowers are left on it for *Herdenkingsdag*

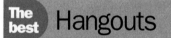

The best Hangouts

Venus Freaks
Girls. Music. Action! *See p216.*

De Trut
Dykes, queers and bargain beers. *See p212.*

Coffeeshop Downtown
A happy bunch for a tasty lunch. *See p213.*

Eagle
The staff might be rude, but the men are hot, willing and cute. *See p210.*

Exit
Dancing queens. *See p211.*

(Remembrance Day, *see p185*) and World AIDS day – but not reverence: you're likely to see people dancing around and on the monument when it becomes homo HQ for Queen's Day and Pride.

Pink Point

Westermarkt, Western Canal Belt (428 1070/www. pinkpoint.org). Tram 13, 14, 17. **Open** noon-6pm daily. *Jan, Feb* noon-6pm Fri-Sun. **Map** p310 C3.
From party flyers to political pamphlets, from books to magazines, this year-round information kiosk near to the Homomonument has got it all. Do you have a queer question? The friendly staff will try their best to answer it. Pink Point also publishes the *Bent Guide To Amsterdam* (€5.99).

Publications

Gay News Amsterdam (www.gaynews.nl) and *Gay & Night*, both in Dutch and English, are published monthly. Top-notch journalism they ain't, but they are at least free in many gay establishments and handy for party information and the latest gossip. Pocket-sized *BUTT*, a sexy/trashy/arty anti-glossy English quarterly (on pink paper!) manages to interview both established artists, such as Michael Stipe, as well as up-and-coming ones. For extensive queer listings see the website www.underwater amsterdam.com. Gay and lesbian health organisation **Stichting AIDS Fonds** (*see p289*) produces the free *Safeguard* safe sex booklet and gay tourist map (with the usual male bias) in English every year.

For those who read Dutch, *PS*, the Saturday supplement of newspaper *Het Parool*, has extensive pink listings. Dutch glossy *sQueeze* is a must-read for fashion-queens and for those who like to keep their finger on the hip pulse. while *De Gay Krant* (www.gaykrant.nl) is the longest-running Dutch-language gay publication. It focuses on national and international political news, including lesbian issues, plus interviews with (Dutch) artists and those in the public eye. Sadly, but not unexpectedly, lesbian bookworms are less well-served. There are just two dedicated dyke mags. Monthly, middle-of-the-road *Zij aan Zij* has an all-things-to-all-lesbians editorial policy, and a useful national listings section (Dutch only); go to their website at www.zijaanzij.nl. The similar, North-Holland specific *La Vita*, meanwhile, is online at www.la-vita.nl.

Radio & TV

MVS Radio

106.8 FM or 88.1 on cable (620 0247/www.mvs.nl). **Times** 6-8pm Mon-Sat; 7-8pm Sun.
Daily news supplemented with features and interviews. At the weekend they up the ante to include all the latest scene information. In Dutch.

MVS TV

A1 (Salto): channel s39+/616MHz (620 0247 /www.mvs.nl). **Times** 8-9pm Mon; repeated 2am 1st Fri of the mth.
Gay life in all forms: news, culture, lifestyle and politics. Usually in Dutch but with occasional English-language items. You can also go to pages 137, 138 and 139 on SBS6's teletext service, to read *De Gay Krant*'s pages of news, dating and national listings.

Pucker up at the **Queen's Head**. *See p210.*

Tiaras and tantrums

Amsterdam, not the gay capital of Europe, you say? Some would argue the toss as tourists offload their pink Euro elsewhere, because the same things happen here time and again. Locals think the city is becoming less liberal and there's one helluva catfight between GBA (Gay Businesses Amsterdam) and the council. But never fearing to tread in queenly puddles, we dish the dirt.

In 2004 the council wanted to stop gay businesses flying rainbow flags because they spoiled the city's beauty, yet giant (revenue-spinning) ads were going up on scaffolds. A guerrilla group hijacked one and raised a 100-square-metre rainbow flag; then everyone realised that the flags were actually good for Amsterdam's image so they stayed.

And then there are darkrooms. The council wanted to close them as they weren't within the Red Light District and, legally, didn't exist (since local laws dictate that you can be licensed as a bar or a sex club but not both).

However, the argument that darkrooms are great ways of spreading safe-sex information eventually won, and it all turned out to be a storm in a pink teacup. And now it's back to playtime as usual.

Then the council wanted a less-naked Pride parade. GBA spokesperson Siep De Haan, threatened to relocate Amsterdam's second-most popular event to Rotterdam, which caused a rift within the GBA and accusations of drama-queen tactics. And, since the final thing we saw last Pride was a barge full of dancers waving knitted willies floating down Prinsengracht, things looked to be heading towards confrontation. So it came as a big surprise that, at the end of 2004, the retiring head of police said that gays should be given designated cruising areas where they could play without the general public taking offence. Also, the council finally gave the go-ahead for a gay museum, which will materialise over the next few years. Watch this space.

Where to stay

The hotels listed below are specifically gay-run. The Gay & Lesbian Switchboard (*see p288*) has more details of gay and lesbian friendly hotels. For more hotels, *see p54*.

Aero Hotel
Kerkstraat 45-49, Southern Canal Belt, 1017 GB (622 7728/www.aerohotel.nl). Tram 1, 2, 5. **Rates** €85 double. **Credit** AmEx, MC, V. **Map** p314 D4.
Settle down here in gay central. You're next to the Bronx sex shop, opposite the Thermos Night sauna and only a stone's throw from Spijker. The rooms have modern furnishings but an old Amsterdam feel and the bar gets very busy at night.

The Amistad
Kerkstraat 42, Southern Canal Belt, 1017 GM (624 8074/www.amistad.nl). Tram 1, 2, 5. **Rates** €67-€104 single; €81-€135 double; €100-€158 triple. **Credit** AmEx, DC, MC, V. **Map** p314 D4.
'Sleep with us.' Owners Johan and Joost know how to make their guests feel at home. Even if you decline their offer, the colourful IKEA-meets-Phillipe Starck rooms are inviting. The breakfast area on the ground floor doubles as a gay internet lounge (it's also open to non-residents) after 1pm.

Black Tulip Hotel
Geldersekade 16, Old Centre: Old Side, 1012 BH (427 0933/www.blacktulip.nl). Tram 1, 2, 4, 5, 9, 13, 16, 17, 24, 25. **Rates** €110 single; €140-€200 double. **Credit** AmEx, DC, MC, V. **Map** p310 D2.

Leather, luxury, lust. The key words at men-only Black Tulip, housed in a 16th-century building. All rooms come with TV, VCR, sling, cage and bondage hooks. More expensive rooms have additional S&M facilities. But will you be allowed to leave?

Golden Bear
Kerkstraat 37, Southern Canal Belt, 1017 GB (624 4785/www.goldenbear.nl). Tram 1, 2, 5. **Rates** €58-€104 single; €72-€118 double. **Credit** AmEx, MC, V. **Map** p314 D4.
Housed in two 17th-century buildings, the Golden Bear's rooms are spacious and comfortable, though not all have private bathrooms. Single rooms have double beds. Champagne breakfasts on Sunday.

Bars & nightclubs

The gay scene is concentrated around four areas in the centre. Going back and forth is easy and quick, though each has its own identity. Clubs and bars are listed by area below, with specialist establishments – restaurants, cafés, coffeeshops and lesbian bars – and the pick of one-off club nights and sex parties listed separately. Entry to bars and clubs listed here is free unless stated otherwise.

Warmoesstraat/Zeedijk

Warmoesstraat, the oldest street in town, is just around the corner from the red-lit HQ of the oldest profession. It's full of cheap hostels and eateries, coffeeshops, bars and sex shops aimed at the visitor with only **Getto** (*see p213*) providing a decent place to rest and eat. The rest of Warmoesstraat is dominated by leather/sex bars, which often don't have hygiene as a high priority. The area attracts junkies and drug sellers, so act streetwise.

Argos

Warmoesstraat 95 (622 6595/www.argosbar.com). Tram 4, 9, 16, 24, 25. **Open** 10pm-3am Mon-Thur, Sun; 10pm-4am Fri, Sat. **No credit cards.** **Map** p310 D2.

The oldest and most famous leather bar in town is still alive and kicking. Its basement darkroom with cabins and a sling attracts all ages and can get crowded. Every second and last Sunday of the month it hosts SOS (aka Sex on Sunday; *see p214*).

Cockring

Warmoesstraat 96 (623 9604/www.clubcockring. com). Tram 4, 9, 16, 24, 25. **Open** 11pm-4am Mon-Thur, Sun; 11pm-5am Fri, Sat. **Admission** free Mon-Fri, Sun; €5 on Sat & special events. **No credit cards.** **Map** p310 D2.

This men-only club is one of a few gay venues where you need to queue at weekends, particularly after 1am. It's cruisey, touristy, throbs with hard house from a female (!) DJ, and there are strip shows, cruise nights and a darkroom. Not enough? Twice a month, on Sundays, it hosts daytime sex parties (*see p214*).

Eagle

Warmoesstraat 90 (627 8634). Tram 4, 9, 16, 24, 25. **Open** 10pm-4am Mon-Thur, Sun; 10pm-5am Fri, Sat. **No credit cards.** **Map** p310 D2.

It's an enigma why people come to this cruisey, leatherish men-only bar, with expensive drinks (order one the second you set foot here, or the unfriendly staff will get sniffy) and less than pristine toilets. Maybe it's the downstairs action-filled darkroom and the upstairs pool table – complete with adjustable sling above it. Eagle is also home to FF parties (*see p214*) and also co-hosts regular Rubber Only parties with shop Black Body (*see p214*).

The Web

Sint Jacobsstraat 6 (623 6758). Tram 1, 2, 3, 5. **Open** 2pm-1am Mon-Thur, Sun; 2pm-2am Fri, Sat. **No credit cards.** **Map** p310 D2.

Another popular men-only leather/cruise bar, but with friendly staff, cheap beer and a DJ playing cheesy/classic dance tunes to the (younger) crowd. The ubiquitous darkroom, sling (and bath tub for WS) are upstairs. Sundays from 5pm is snack afternoon, and on Wednesdays after 10pm there's a lottery with sex shop vouchers for prizes.

Zeedijk

This evocative street has been cleaned up (but hold on to your handbags – there are still dodgy sorts about). Pop down to Café 't Mandje (Zeedijk 63) for a glimpse of the olden days.

De Barderij

Zeedijk 14 (420 5132). Tram 4, 9, 16, 24, 25/Metro Centraal Station. **Open** 3pm-1am Mon-Thur, Sun; 3pm-3am Fri; noon-3am Sat; noon-1am Sun. **No credit cards.** **Map** p310 D2

It's only been open a couple of years, but this no-frills brown bar feels like it's been around for ever, supplying unpretentious guys with booze until the early hours in the canal-side premises.

Queen's Head

Zeedijk 20 (420 2475/www.queenshead.nl). Tram 4, 9, 16, 24, 25/Metro Centraal Station. **Open** 4pm-1am Mon-Thur; 4pm-3am Fri, Sat; noon-1am Sun. **No credit cards.** **Map** p310 D2

Drag-legend Dusty has slung her slingbacks and headed for the country, but the bar's still fab under new management: rows of camp Kens, a gorgeous view and diverse, attitude-free guys. Sunday afternoon is Queen's High Tea, Tuesday's Show Night.

Rembrandtplein

Rembrandtplein is one of Amsterdam's oldest bar areas. The centre's a grass square where a statue of the famous painter eyes up the party people, including a diverse gay crowd. Half of Amsterdam's lesbian venues – Vive La Vie and You II – are here, while Paardenstraat is the city's rent boy hangout. In bright and breezy contrast are the bars along Halvemaansteeg: loud, entirely attitude-free, and ready for a knees-up. This continues along the Amstel, where a strip of bars attract punters and their fag hags to cheesy music and river views.

Amstel Taveerne

Amstel 54 (623 4254). Tram 4, 9, 14, 24, 25. **Open** 5pm-1am Mon-Thur, Sun; 5pm-3am Fri-Sat. **No credit cards.** **Map** p315 E4.

This bar, on the corner of Halvemaansteeg, has been dedicated to boozing since 1574 and was the area's first gay bar. The older, unpretentious crowd hums to cheesy/chart pop tunes and is chatty.

Entre Nous

Halvemaansteeg 14 (623 1700). Tram 1, 2, 4, 5, 9, 14, 16, 24, 25. **Open** 8pm-3am Mon-Thur; 8pm-4am Fri-Sun. **No credit cards.** **Map** p315 E4.

Don't come too early as the young, local crowd gathers late at this tiny bar. Enjoyed most when you like Britney and Maddy and know the lyrics of every *Eurovision Song Contest* entry.

Lellebel

Utrechtsestraat 4 (427 5139/www.lellebel.nl). Tram 4, 9, 14, 20. **Open** *June-Sept* 8pm-3am Mon-Thur; 8pm-4am Fri, Sat; 3pm-3am Sun. *Oct-May* 9pm-3am Mon-Thur, Sun; 8pm-4am Fri, Sat. **No credit cards.** **Map** p315 E4.

The city's only bar for drag queens, transvestites and cross dressers, but you don't need to don a wig and stilettos to enjoy the loud madness in this tiny bar. Karaoke night's Tuesday.

ARC.

Rouge

Amstel 60 (420 9881). Tram 4, 9, 16, 24, 25. **Open**
4pm-1am Mon, Thur, Sun; 4pm-3am Fri, Sat. Closed
Tue, Wed. **No credit cards. Map** p315 E4.
Friendly bar staff pull a happy diverse crowd. When
the French windows are opened on warm evenings
and drinkers spill outside, it all gets very convivial.

Reguliersdwarsstraat

The strip that runs between Koningsplein
and Vijzelstraat is Amsterdam's gay village
(though wags refer to it as the 'gay cul-de-sac'),
and you can get everything for your trendy
queer lifestyle here: a haircut at Hot Heads
(Reguliersdwarsstraat 4, 626 8075); lunch at
Downtown (*see p213*); underwear at Mantalk
(No.39, 627 2525) and outerwear at The Shirt
Shop (No.64, 423 288). It's a bit of a catwalk but
seldom intimidating, with guys (and it mainly
is guys) of all ages, shapes and sizes.

ARC

*Reguliersdwarsstraat 44 (689 7070/www.bararc.
com). Tram 1, 2, 4, 5, 9, 16, 24, 25.* **Open** 4pm-
1am Mon-Thur, Sun; 9pm-3am Fri, Sat. **Credit**
AmEx, MC, V. **Map** p313 D4.
The screams of delight that greeted ARC's slickly
designed, multi-tasking (café/restaurant/dance-bar)
space have quietened, but the posiest point on the
street is still packed every weekend with a polysex-
ual crowd who come to suck cocktails and show that
they damn well can afford the prices.

Café April

*Reguliersdwarsstraat 37 (625 9572/www.april-
exit.com). Tram 1, 2, 4, 5, 9, 16, 24, 25.* **Open**
4pm-1am Mon-Thur; 4pm-3am Fri; 2pm-3am Sat;
2pm-1am Sun. **No credit cards. Map** p313 D4.
Well-known for its trippy, rotating bar, this dark
place is always packed for Sunday's happy hour.
When the sun shines punters spill on to the street.

Exit

*Reguliersdwarsstraat 42 (625 8788/www.april-
exit.com). Tram 1, 2, 4, 5, 9, 16, 24, 25.* **Open**
11pm-4am Thur-Sun; 11pm-5am Fri, Sat.
Admission €5 Fri; €7 Sat. **No credit cards.**
Map p313 E4
A tall, narrow club with a different theme on every
level: a pop basement, a main room of thumpin'
house, a quieter bar, an excellent R&B floor. The
cherry on top is the top floor darkroom. Women who
go here tend to be of the straight-best-friend variety,
though lesbians aren't made to feel unwelcome.

Reality

*Reguliersdwarsstraat 129 (639 3012). Tram 1, 2, 4,
5, 9, 16, 24, 25.* **Open** 8pm-3am Mon-Thur, Sun;
8pm-4am Fri, Sat. **No credit cards. Map** p313 E4.
Popular, multi-culti dance-bar attracting men from
every corner of the earth. Monday is Surinamese,
Sabor de Salsa is Wednesday, and R&B Thursday.

Soho

*Reguliersdwarsstraat 36 (no phone/www.april-
exit.com) Tram 1, 2, 4, 5, 9, 16, 24, 25.* **Open**
9pm-3am Mon-Thur, Sun; 9pm-4am Fri, Sat.
No credit cards. Map p313 E4.
An English boozer – with Churchillian portraits to
prove it – and a bad case of gigantism. Barn-like proportions mean there's room for everyone to cruise,
chat or hunker-down in an armchair by the fire.

Kerkstraat

Only minutes away from the super self-
conscious confines of Reguliersdwarsstraat –
we saw you preening in the mirror – is
Kerkstraat; less obviously gay and thankfully
more attitude-free. Nearby you'll find Holland's
only Arabian gay bar, **Habibi Ana** (Lange
Leidsedwarsstraat 4-6, no phone), with a strict
Arabian-music-only policy, but a mixed,
young and handsome, international crowd.

De Spijker

Kerkstraat 4 (620 5919). Tram 1, 2, 5. **Open**
1pm-1am Mon-Thur, Sun; 1pm-3am Fri, Sat.
No credit cards. Map p314 C4.

Young and cute muscle boys, leather fans, women,
bears and limp-wristed queens, all drink together at
this friendly and delightfully seedy bar. In a rather
disorientating juxtaposition, porn and cartoons are
shown side-by-side and upstairs is a small darkroom. The pool table is always occupied.

Other areas

Mankind

*Weteringstraat 60, Southern Canal Belt (638 4755/
www.mankind.nl). Tram 6, 7, 10, 16, 24, 25.* **Open**
noon-midnight Mon-Sat. **No credit cards.**
Map p314 D5.

Tucked down a side-street near the Rijksmuseum,
so an excellent stop for culture cruisers, this bar is
often overlooked and is thus very much a locals'
place. This is a pity, because the drinks are cheap
and it has a pleasant canal-side patio as well. A good
place to unwind and watch the world go by.

One-off club nights

For one-off lesbian club nights, *see p215*.

Blue Monday

A long-running night for alternatively inclined
queers, but particularly for those who don't have to
go to work in the morning, held at Vrankrijk
(Spuistraat 216, www.vrankrijk.org), a (now-legal)
squat. Cheap booze and changing DJs.

Kid Ory

Held at Jimmy Woo's (*see p229*), the Fash Mag Slags
kick off the weekend early at what is probably the
plushest venue in Amsterdam, to a slinky soundtrack of hip-hop, R&B and soul.

Queer Planet

www.spellbound-amsterdam.nl.

Held at OCCII (*see p220*), this is a cheap and alternative club night which is popular with a non-scene
crowd. It's success is easily explained by the underground beats, performances and the cosy bar.

MAF

www.artlaunch.nl.

The Multiple Arts Festival works its magic with
like-minded gay organisations from all around the
world. Recent collaborations sound like a roll call of
the hip and happening, bringing Berlin, Barcelona
and Istanbul to Amsterdam. Every party includes
DJs, fashion shows, visuals, dance and performance.

Salvation

www.salvation-amsterdam.nl.

Fills the Escape club (*see p229*) on the month's first
Friday with an international crowd of scenesters
who rip off their designer shirts and wave their
hands in the air. For those who can't get enough, it's
always followed by a sexy after-party at Thermos
Night sauna (*see p215*) – hip, hip, hooray!

De Trut

*Bilderdijkstraat 165, Oud West (612 3524). Tram 3,
7, 12, 17.* **Open** 11pm-4am Sun. **Admission** €1.50.
No credit cards. Map p313 B5.

It's Sunday night, and of course you don't want the
weekend to end just yet, but Saturday burnt a hole
in your wallet. So spend the Sabbath at this dirt-
cheap institution. Although there's usually more
DKNY than dyke action, there's always a reasonable
garnish of lesbians. Dykes and queers only.

Unk

New-ish, alternative-ish gay night every fourth
Saturday of the month at Club 8 (www.club-8.nl). A
bit of a trek west, the venue, atop a snooker hall with
groovy graffiti art, makes the journey worthwhile.

Cafés

Backstage

Utrechtsedwarsstraat 67, Southern Canal Belt (622 3638). Tram 4, 6, 7, 10. **Open** 10am-5.30pm Mon-Sat. **No credit cards. Map** p315 E4.

The mad, multicoloured exterior is a must-see. Inside, you'll be glad to hear, it is all equally bonkers. The whole place is presided over by local character Gary Christmas, who's as happy to tell you his life story as he is to sell you knitwear.

Coffeeshop Downtown

Reguliersdwarsstraat 31, Southern Canal Belt (622 9958/www.coffeeshopdowntown.nl). Tram 4, 9, 16, 24, 25. **Open** 11am-8pm daily. **No credit cards. Map** p314 D4.

This coffeeshop of the non-smoking kind is an attractive place to stop and relax, with an inventive list of breakfasts, sandwiches and drinks. However, the service starts to crumble if there are more than a couple of queens in attendance.

Le Monde

Rembrandtplein 6, Southern Canal Belt (626 9922) Tram 4, 9, 14. **Open** 8.30am-1am Mon-Thur, Sun; 8.30am-2am Fri, Sat. *Kitchen* 8.30am-10.30pm daily. **Credit** V. **Map** p315 E4.

The long opening hours make this the ideal spot to kick-start or wind down a night out.

Film & theatre

Amsterdam art-house cinemas like **Rialto**, and **Filmhuis Cavia** frequently screen gay and lesbian flicks and **CineCenter** (for all three, *see p198*) often has gay-previews on Monday nights. **De Balie** (*see p199*) and Filmhuis Cavia are home in December to *De Roze Filmdagen* (Pink Film Days, the Gay &

Lesbian Film Festival (www.rozefilmdagen.nl), a three-day event showing underground gay and lesbian shorts and documentaries with an accent on Dutch-made flicks, while De Balie plays host to the biennial Nederlands Transgender Film Festival (www.transgender filmfestival.com) in May. The Gay & Lesbian Switchboard (*see p288*) lists cinemas and theatres with gay and lesbian programmes. The Queen's English Theatre Company (www.qetc.nl) performs popular English plays a few times a year.

Restaurants

Plenty of restaurants in Amsterdam, though not specifically gay, have more than their fair share of gay diners. A good rule of thumb: if a place is brand spanking new or has spectacular decor it's sure to attract the homo herds.

Garlic Queen

Reguliersdwarsstraat 27, Southern Canal Belt (422 6426/www.garlicqueen.nl). Tram 1, 2, 4, 5, 9, 16, 24, 25. **Open** 6pm-1am Wed-Sun. *Kitchen* 6-11pm Wed-Sun. **Main courses** €17-€22. **Credit** AmEx DC, MC, V. **Map** p314 D4.

Its prime position on the main gay drag and delightful name mean this place attracts lovers of the pungent bulb, and, (well, what did you expect?), queens aplenty. The name is well earned: one dish uses 60 cloves, so make sure you bring a packet of mints with you if you intend getting lucky elsewhere.

Getto

Warmoesstraat 51, Old Centre: Old Side (421 5151/ www.getto.nl). Tram 4, 9, 16, 24, 25. **Open** 4pm-1am Tue-Thur; 4pm-2am Fri, Sat; 4pm-midnight Sun. *Kitchen* 6-11pm Tue-Sun. **Main courses** €10-€15. **Credit** AmEx, DC, MC, V. **Map** p310 D2.

Gatto **Getto**.

Food at this sparkly spot ain't gonna win Michelin stars but it won't break the bank either. Tasty and generous portions include plenty for veggies. In the bar you can sup happy hour 2-for-1 cocktails (5-7pm daily), then drink until late with a mixed bunch of regulars, locals and visitors. On Sundays, cocktails are €4 all night and, for those wanting to know whether their future includes someone tall, dark and handsome, tarot readings are available.

Hemelse Modder

Oude Waal 9-11, Old Centre: Old Side (624 3203/ www.hemelsemodder.nl). Tram 1, 2, 4, 5, 9, 13, 16, 17, 24, 25/Metro Nieuwmarkt. **Open** 6pm-midnight daily. *Kitchen* 6-10pm daily. **Set menu** €26 (3 courses); €32 (5 courses). **Credit** AmEx, MC, V. **Map** p311 E2.

This restaurant on a handsome canal has been a favourite with the pink community for years, who come for its up-to-date menu and friendly service.

Kitsch

Utrechtsestraat 42, Southern Canal Belt (625 9251/ www.restaurant-kitsch.nl). Tram 4, 9, 14. **Open** 6pm-2am Mon-Sun. *Kitchen* 6-11pm. **Main courses** €15-€30. **Credit** AmEx, DC, MC, V. **Map** p315 E4.

The Blessed Virgin Mary in the window, the cheeky to downright naughty dishes ('Pussy and Potatoes' is oysters and chips), and quirky touches (tables are fitted with water-taps, so you can help yourself): Kitsch lives up to its name. Food is serious, though, from the casual (salads or burgers) to the indulgent (Sevruga caviar or those bivalves again).

Sex parties

Apart from the lesbian leather and S&M group Wild Side (www.wildside.dds.nl) who organise events, parties and workshops in different venues, there are no women-only sex parties in Amsterdam; just occasional, mixed fetish parties. But gay visitors will have no difficulty finding relief. Just remember to play it safe.

Stable Master (Warmoesstraat 23, 625 0148, www.stablemaster.nl) hosts jack-off parties at 9pm Thursdays through Mondays. **SOS** (Sex on Sunday) is held every second and last Sunday of the month between 3-7pm (doors close 4pm) at Argos (*see p210*). The **COC** (*see p215* or www.stop.demon.nl) holds immensely popular safe sex leather parties. Call or check their website as the party's future is uncertain. The **Cockring** (*see p210*) – you get in for free if you peak at 18cm (7.2in) or more – hosts a 'shoes-only' Nude Club every first Sunday of the month and its 'nude or underwear-only' Horsemen & Knights is on every third Sunday of the month. Meanwhile 'erotic café' **Same Place** (Nassaukade 12, 475 1981, www.same place.nl), goes gay every Monday night between 9pm and 1am and attracts a less hedonistic body-fascist crowd.

Shops and Services

Bookshops

The stores below all have dedicated gay stock, though you'll find gay books and magazines on sale in most of Amsterdam's bookshops. The **American Book Center** has a well-stocked lesbian and gay section. **Waterstone's** (for both, *see p161*) doesn't have a dedicated gay section, but it does at least carry the major British gay magazines if you can't bear to miss an issue while you're away.

Intermale

Spuistraat 251, Old Centre: New Side (625 0009/ www.intermale.nl). Tram 1, 2, 5, 13, 14, 17. **Open** 11am-6pm Mon; 10am-6pm Tue, Wed, Fri, Sat; 10am-9pm Thur; noon-5pm Sun. **Credit** AmEx, MC, V. **Map** p310 C3.

Well-stocked shop full of gay men's books from across the spectrum, bulked out with gifts to carry back for those you love (or fancy).

Vrolijk

Paleisstraat 135, Old Centre: New Side (623 5142/ www.vrolijk.nu). Tram 1, 2, 5, 13, 14, 17. **Open** 11am-6pm Mon; 10am-6pm Tue, Wed, Fri; 10am-9pm Thur; 10am-5pm Sat; 1-5pm Sun. **Credit** AmEx, DC, MC, V. **Map** p310 C3.

The best selection of rose-tinted reading you'll find in town: fiction, fact, sex and academic, with an excellent English-language selection.

Hairdressers

Cuts 'n' Curls

Korte Leidsedwarsstraat 74, Southern Canal Belt (624 6881/www.cutsandcurls.nl). Tram 1, 2, 5, 6, 7, 10. **Open** 10am-8pm Tue-Thur; 10am-7pm Fri; 10am-4.30pm Sat. **Credit** AmEx, DC, MC, V. **Map** p314 D5.

Come to this no-appointments barbers for a manly haircut, whatever your gender.

Leather/rubber/sex

Amsterdam's Leather Lane, is home to a couple of very kinky boutiques: spacious **Mr B** (Warmoesstraat 89, 420 8548, www.mrb.nl), the place to come for a tattoo, piercing (there's a female piercer too) and tickets for all the big gay events, and compact **RoB of Amsterdam** where you can pick up a Muir cap before hitting the bars (Warmoesstraat 89, 422 003, www. mrb.nl); the Weteringschans branch (No.253, 428 3000) has the full complement of leather/ rubber gear. Rich pervy pickings can also be found at **Black Body** (Lijnbaansgracht 292, 626 2553). Two sex shops with in-house porn cinemas are **Bronx** (Kerkstraat 53-5, 623 1548) and **Drakes** (Damrak 61, 627 9544). Women with one-track minds should head to **Female & Partners** or **Stout** (for both, *see p182*). **Demask** (Zeedijk 64, 620 5603) is fun for all. For erotic and fetish shops, *see p182*.

Saunas

Fenomeen
1e Schinkelstraat 14, Zuid (671 6780). Tram 1, 2. **Open** 1-11pm daily. *Women only* Mon. **Admission** €6 before 6pm, €8 after. **No credit cards.**
A relaxed, legalised squat sauna, housed in old horses' stalls, that's popular with lesbians on women-only Mondays. It's open-plan and split-level, with a sauna, steam bath, cold bath, chill-out room with mattresses, showers in the courtyard, and café.

Thermos Day
Raamstraat 33, Southern Canal Belt (623 9158/ www.thermos.nl). Tram 1, 2, 5, 7, 10. **Open** noon-11pm Mon-Fri; noon-10pm Sat; 11am-10pm Sun. **Admission** €18; €13.50 under-24s with ID. **Credit** AmEx, DC, MC, V. **Map** p314 C4.
Quite busy during the week and absolutely packed at weekends, this four-level sauna offers it all: a tiny steam room, large dry-heat room, darkroom, porn cinema, private cubicles, bar, hairdresser, masseur, gym and small roof terrace. For those who want to heat, meet and eat, there's a restaurant, too.

Thermos Night
Kerkstraat 58-60, Southern Canal Belt (623 4936/www.thermos.nl). Tram 1, 2, 5. **Open** 11pm-8am Mon-Sun. **Admission** €18; €13.50 under-24s &over-65s with ID. **Credit** AmEx, DC, MC, V. **Map** p314 D4.
Even more popular than the day operation, especially when it hosts 'Salvation' after-parties.

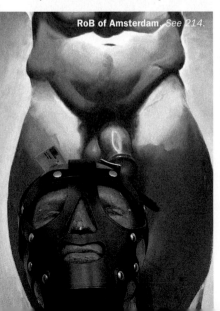

RoB of Amsterdam. *See 214.*

Lesbian

In contrast to the vibrant men's scene, dyke Amsterdam trundles along as unchanging as the tides. Most places have been around for a while, though new stuff pops up and disappears now and then. Although the lesbian and gay men's scenes are quite divided, remember everywhere below (except Flirtation) welcomes male friends. Similarly, if you've experienced all that lesbian Amsterdam has to offer, you might want to try dropping into the places aimed at gay men; you could be the only dyke in the place, but at least you'll be welcome.

COC
The Amsterdam branch of COC (*see p288*) hosts a number of women-only events: Just Girls (Sat, 8-10pm) a social evening for women under 26; Venus Freaks (1st Saturday in the month, 10pm-4am, *see p216*); Wild Side SM Workshop (3rd Saturday, 8-11pm, *see p288*) and 30+ Women's Night (2nd Saturday, 10pm-4am); Lady Liberty (4th Saturday in the month, after Just Girls) – bring ID if you're particularly fresh-faced. However, do watch out for the extremely irritating drinks policy: you have to buy tokens at the door to pay for drinks at the bar.

Flirtation
www.letsbeopen.nl.
Glamming-up the women's scene with a quarterly club-night that outstrips all the competition, Flirtation regularly attracts 1,000 clubbers to its women-only (though not solely lesbian) events at cool venues. Vocal house is the dish of the day, with side orders of live percussion and erotic dancing.

InRealLife Swingmiddag
Café Crea, Grimburgwal, Old Centre: Old Side (525 1423/www.inreallife.nl). Tram 4, 9, 16, 24, 25. **Open** 4-9pm every 3rd Sun of mth (except July, Aug). **Admission** €6. **No credit cards. Map** p310 D3.
A women-only 'swing afternoon'. If you're wondering what that might mean, it translates as part-social club, part-disco for a slightly older crowd with a '60s-'90s and chart music policy.

Miss Riss
Van der Hoopstraat 60, Bos En Lammer (686 8686/ www.missriss.nl). Tram 3, 10. **Open** noon-11pm Tue-Sun. *Kitchen* noon-9pm Tue-Sun. **No credit cards. Map** p309 A2.
The lesbians who own and run this place in Westerpark like to describe it as a 'cantina'. So that means it lies somewhere in the margins between a bar and a restaurant. Best enjoyed on a summer evening with a house cocktail in your hand.

Saarein II
Elandstraat 119, the Jordaan (623 4901). Tram 7, 10. **Open** 5pm-1am Tue-Thur, Sun; 5pm-2am Fri, Sat. **No credit cards. Map** p314 C4.

Arts & Entertainment

The scene's *grande dame* occupies a three-storey spot in a quiet Jordaan corner. Less frenetic than the competition, it tends to attract a slightly older crowd, though youngsters crowd the basement pool table.

Sappho

Vijzelstraat 103, Southern Canal Belt (423 1509/ www.sappho.nl). Tram 16, 24, 25. **Open** 3pm-1am Tue-Thur, Sun; 3pm-3am Fri, Sat. **No credit cards.**
Sappho is the best-looking of all Amsterdam's dyke bars – which indeed it should be given that it's named after the classical queen of lesbian poetry herself. Although the place is deserted for most of the week, it's rammed on Friday's dance night.

Venus Freaks

www.venusfreaks.nl.
Going strong since 2002, and attracting male punters too (welcome with women/fliers). Freaks has strong visuals, live-performance and DJs including Funki G and Sandrien. Currently at COC (*see p288*).

Vive La Vie

Amstelstraat 7, Southern Canal Belt (624 0114/ www.vivelavie.net). Tram 4, 9, 14. **Open** 4pm-1am Mon-Thur, Sun; 4pm-3am Fri, Sat. **No credit cards.** **Map** p314 E4.
This cubby-hole is usually a visitor's first stop when she arrives in Amsterdam. Expect no frills or niceties, just honest-to-badness good-time girls from the Netherlands – and the rest of the world – eager to sing-a-long-a Dutch ballad and knock back beer.

You II

Amstel 178, Southern Canal Belt (421 0900/www. youii.nl). Tram 4, 9, 14. **Open** 10pm-4am Thur, Sun; 10pm-5am Fri, Sat. **No credit cards.** **Map** p311 E3.
You II has pokey surroundings, iffy clientele, godawful music and an unpredictable door-policy. Yet despite this, if you spend any amount of time in Amsterdam, it's certain you'll find yourself in here at some point. (And, sometimes, you'll even enjoy it.)

Queer year

Spring

Pink tourists flood into Amsterdam all the year round, but things really hit a fever pitch come **Koninginnedag** (30 April). Ostensibly a celebration of the late Queen Juliana's birthday, queens of many other descriptions turn the town centre into one big party. More sombrely, on 4 May (**Remembrance Day**) the Homomonument is where the gays and lesbians who perished during World War II are commemorated in a quiet ceremony starting at 8pm, followed the next day (**Liberation Day**) with a big freedom party.

Later in May the Dominicus church hosts **AIDS Memorial Day**; candles are lit, names are read out and white balloons are released in remembrance. Also taking place in May is the biennial **Transgender Film Festival** (www.transgenderfilmfestival.com).

Summer

At the end of June (25 June 2005) there's **Amsterdam Diner**, an HIV/AIDS fundraiser at the Heineken Music Hall, where Dutch celebs and businessmen all get stuffed for a good cause. But the absolute highlight of the calendar is, of course, **Amsterdam Pride**, a long weekend of sport, film and street-parties, culminating in a waterborne parade on the first Saturday in August (*see p186* and *p209* **Tiaras and tantrums**).

Autumn

In late October the city turns black for **Leather Pride**, two days of non-stop, men-only

Homomonument. *See p207.*

hardcore parties. Secret locations and the strictest of dress codes all add to the seriously naughty fun.

Winter

On 1 December the **World Aids Day** congress is held at RAI, attracting healthcare professionals and journalists from around the world. Also in December, the Balie turns pink for **Roze Filmdagen**, a short film festival with an international agenda (*see p213*).

Music

Think you've heard it all?

Rock, Roots & Jazz

Amsterdam is a city of musical surprises. Stepping off a train at Centraal Station for the first time, you'll soon be touched by the city's soulful, laid-back melody. From the sounds pumped out of bars, to skilled musicians busking by canals, to your first venture into one of the many concert halls, when the tune gets in your head you won't be able to shake it.

Starting from those unassuming beacons of quality, Paradiso and Melkweg, in the centre, a few minutes' walk in any direction and the choice keeps on growing. Seeking a diet of exotic sounds or pulsing samba? Get to Badcuyp or Akhnaton. Want to see the best jazz stars in the world? Camp out at Bimhuis or Alto. Our main advice: exclude nothing. Music embraces the summer joy of a warm festival evening and the cosy comfort of a snug club in the bitter heart of winter. And check listings for other cities, since a performance by your favourite band/DJ may be but a train ride away.

TICKETS AND INFORMATION

For full listings head to the AUB Ticketshop (0900 0191; *see p293* **Tickets please**) or check out Ticketmaster (www.ticketmaster.nl), the free Dutch-language monthly *Uitkrant*, or the national music magazine *Oor* (www.oor.nl). Details of notable gigs are posted weekly on the *Time Out* website (www.timeout.com/amsterdam). For alternative listings check the English-language *Amsterdam Weekly* (*see p286* **'Bloids of Amsterdam**). Book in advance.

Rock & roots

Apart from the clubs and venues below, keep an eye out for squat happenings and concerts, where new talent is nurtured. Details can be found at www.squat.net and www.underwater amsterdam.com. In particular, check out OT301 (*see p199*), Zaal 100 and Fraropa for underground occasions. For **Bitterzoet**, a multi-purpose venue that has frequent gigs, *see p228*. Cultural complex **Westergasfabriek** (*see p250*) is set to become a major vortex for

The best	Venues

Paradiso
Worship at the Pop Temple. *See p220*.

OCCII
Show a sense of adventure. *See p220*.

Concertgebouw
The world's finest concert hall? *See p223*.

Engelse Kerk
Holy shit, that's some great acoustics. *See p224*.

Bimhuis
Jazz it up babies. *See p221*.

Cristofori
A canal house for your jazz and classical needs. *See p221*.

Carré
Its circus past makes for a unique present. *See p218*.

Melkweg. See p219.

Arts & Entertainment

underground bands, DJs and musical events since it managed to lure Haarlem's famed and inspired Fietsznfabriek to bring their quirky booking savvy to Amsterdam in 2005.

Akhnaton

Nieuwezijds Kolk 25, Old Centre: New Side (624 3396/www.akhnaton.nl). Tram 1, 2, 5, 13, 17. **Open** 11pm-5am Fri, Sat. **Admission** €5-€7. **No credit cards. Map** p310 D2.

Even mighty Pharoah might find himself dancing like an Egyptian to the world music rhythms that rattle and rumble through this intimate club.

AMP

KNSM-Laan 13, the Waterfront (418 1111/www. ampstudios.nl). Bus 28, 32, 59. **Open** Mon-Thur, Sun; 4pm-3am Fri, Sat. *Café open from noon.* **Admission** €5-€12 **No credit cards.**

AMP started life as a rehearsal space for local bands and now offers regular concerts and parties, as well as full recording facilities and a licensed café.

ArenA

ArenA Boulevard 1, Bijlmermeer (311 1333/www. amsterdamarena.nl). Metro Bijlmer. **Open** hours vary. **Admission** €18-€27. **No credit cards.**

When the football season closes Ajax's grand stadium is reborn as a musical amphitheatre hosting tours by the likes of the Rolling Stones, outdoor raves, and even a few Dutch stars. You know the score: like all stadiums, bring your lighter and don't forget binoculars if trapped in those cheap seats.

Badcuyp

1e Sweelinckstraat 10, the Pijp (675 9669/www. badcuyp.nl). Tram 4, 16, 24, 25. **Open** 11am-1am Tue-Thur, Sun; 11am-3am Fri, Sat. **Admission** free-€8. **Credit** MC, V. **Map** p315 F5.

Small and friendly, the focus is on world and jazz. Besides the intriguing range of international talents in the main hall, the cute café plays host to regular salsa, African, jazz and open jam evenings.

Buurvrouw

St Pieterpoortsteeg 9, Old Centre: Old Side (625 9654/www.debuurvrouw.nl). Tram 4, 9, 14, 16, 24, 25. **Open** 9pm-3am Mon-Thur, 9pm-4am Fri-Sun. **Admission** free. **No credit cards. Map** p310 D2.

This café presents DJs on weekends and the occasional singer/songwriter or acoustic performance during the week. Check out the extraordinarily varied CD collection behind the bar.

Café Pakhuis Wilhelmina

Veemkade 576, Docklands (419 3368/www. cafepakhuiswilhelmina.nl). Tram 26/bus 42. **Open** hours vary Wed-Sun. **Admission** €5-€8. **Credit** MC, V.

Part of the Pakhuis Wilhelmina 'breeding ground' for underground young artists in the docklands (*see p108* **Take a walk on the water side** *and p205*), this café aims to host challenging dance nights, interesting live acts, and some spicy world music evenings, all while keeping the cost low.

Carré

Amstel 115-25, Southern Canal Belt (0900 252 5255/www.theatercarre.nl). Tram 4, 6, 7, 10. **Open** *Box office* in person 4-7pm daily. *Telephone reservations* 9am-9pm daily. **Admission** €15-€80. **Credit** AmEx, DC, MC, V. **Map** p315 F4.

This beautiful circus theatre was originally opened in the late 19th century and boasts a rich history. Recently refurbished, it reopened in the autumn of 2004 with a series of Tom Waits shows that sold out in minutes. Thankfully not everything sells as fast, but pop concerts, musicals and operas in such beautiful surroundings always prove popular. For two weeks in winter it hosts the World Christmas Circus.

Club 3VOOR12

Studio Desmet, Plantage Middenlaan 4A, the Plantage (035 671 2222/studio Desmet 521 7100/ www.3voor12.nl). Tram 9, 14. **Open** 10pm Wed. **Admission** free. **Map** p311 F3.

This old film theatre bursts into life on Wednesday nights to coincide with a live national radio show. Each broadcast throws up a diverse line-up – one week it's three little-known local acts, the next it's international stars in town for their sold-out gig. Entry is free, but there's limited capacity, so you must reserve by emailing club3VOOR12@vpro.nl.

Cruise Inn

Zuiderzeeweg 29, Zeeburg (692 7188/www.cruise-inn.com). Tram 14/bus 22, 37. **Open** 9pm-1am Sat (until 3am on concert nights). **Admission** free-€7. **No credit cards.**

Amsterdam's home to rockabilly and swing has had a rough time since the city confiscated its land and moved the club into temporary accommodation. Still a lively and popular haunt, keep an eye out for another – hopefully final – move late in 2005.

Heineken Music Hall

ArenA Boulevard 590, Bijlmermeer (0900 300 1250/www.heineken-music-hall.nl). Metro Bijlmer. **Open** *Box office* from 6.30pm, concert days only. **Admission** €20-€60. **Credit** AmEx, MC, V.

With a capacity of 5,500 HMH is a cosy side arena to the ArenA complex, showcasing popular mainstays and new acts reaching large audiences. Its modern design lacks character but it does allow you to get up close and personal to your musical heroes.

Last Waterhole

Korte Leidsedwarsstraat 49, Leidseplein (620 8904/www.waterhole.nl). Tram 1, 2, 5, 6, 7, 10. **Open** 8pm-3am Mon-Thur, Sun; 8pm-4am Fri-Sat. **Admission** free. **No credit cards. Map** p314 C5.

A favourite with tourists, it moved here in late 2004. However it's not likely that they will move towards booking more exciting rock acts.

Maloe Melo

Lijnbaansgracht 163, Western Canal Belt (420 4592/www.maloemelo.com). Tram 7, 10, 13, 14, 17. **Open** 9pm-3am Mon-Thur, Sun; 9pm-4am Fri, Sat. **Admission** free-€5. **No credit cards. Map** p315 E5.

Dré departed

The death of the popular singer, **André Hazes** (1951-2004), transformed restrained Amsterdam into a weepy, almost Latin, capital. *Every* bar in town began playing his songs. 50,000 people attended his memorial at the ArenA stadium, singing their tribute as his body lay in state on the centreline.

You could forgive foreigners their confusion. It's all too easy to lump dear Dré in with the kind of kitsch singing superstar that natural law dictates every country has: France's Johnny Halliday, Canada's Céline Dion, and England's, well, too many to list in a guide of this modest size. But while he did walk the line at times, André was different. He was a 130-kilo blob of heart-on-your-sleeveness, a sweaty icon who sang while dripping (literally) with the residue of tragedies and marital breakdowns that were first lived, then obsessively covered by the nation's tabloids, and then written into song with the aid of a rhyming dictionary. He had a hardcore honesty that won over even the most jaded or irony-crippled soul.

In many ways, he came to represent the inferiority complex that dwells within us all – the one that only gets relieved by tossing back a few drinks. He spun tales of broken hearts and spilt beers born from his own incapacity to keep his heart intact and his beer in its glass. André was a giant whose life tells a heart-warming tale of transcending limitations. He even transcended his obvious weight problem and – let's face it – hoggish features by using both to full humorous advantage in a series of canned wiener commercials that resulted in an immediate 35 per cent sales increase.

While he was often called 'the Netherlands' only true soul singer', André considered himself more of a bluesman like his hero Muddy Waters. But in fact, he was actually a 'life singer'. *Levenslied*, born in the Jordaan, is a genre of sing-a-long drinking songs built on lyrics that (besides dwelling suspiciously on the 'long stiff tower' of Westerkerk) tend to glorify poverty, the sense of community and the simple pleasures of 'calling down curses, making babies, drinking coffee, and hanging out on the front step'. So it's fitting that Hazes was born in the Pijp, a neighbourhood as solidly working class as the Jordaan, where he began his career standing on pool tables around Albert Cuypmarkt as an eight-year old (singing songs of broken toys and spilt milk perhaps?) before breaking through. André quickly swelled both literally and figuratively to such an extent that he could fill stadiums for week-long stretches and record countless gold records.

Although his vibrato gave Caruso imitators a run for their money, André could not really be described as a 'great' singer, but he was certainly a 'big' singer. And you can't help but like a guy who was willing to cry in the name of communication.

Well I woke up this morning, feeling Maloe Melowed. Yes, you guessed it, Mamma, this small, fun juke joint is Amsterdam's home of the blues. Quality rockabilly and roots acts play here, too.

Meervaart

Meer en Vaart 300, West (410 7777/www. meervaart.nl). Tram 1, 17/bus 23, 192. **Open** *Box office* 10am-4pm Mon-Fri; 11am-4pm Sat. **Admission** €15-€30. **Credit** MC, V.
Its modern architecture and peripheral location do nothing for the ambience, but Meervaart does offer an interesting mix of cabaret and theatre shows, along with a mish mash of musical styles.

Melkweg

Lijnbaansgracht 234a, Southern Canal Belt (531 8181/www.melkweg.nl). Tram 1, 2, 5, 6, 7, 10, 20. **Open** *Box office* 1-5pm Mon-Fri; 4-6pm Sat, Sun; also from 7.30pm to start of performance. *Club* hours vary; usually 8.30pm-4am daily. **Admission** €5-€25. *Membership* (compulsory) €2.50/mth; €14/yr. **No credit cards. Map** p314 D5.

A former dairy (the name translates as Milky Way), this, like Paradiso, is famous as a home to music of all styles. The two medium-sized concert halls (holding 750-1,000 people each) offer a full programme the whole year round. The complex is also home to a theatre, a cinema, an art gallery, a café, and holds weekend club nights to boot, so it's no surprise it's become a cultural beacon in the centre of the city. It's also much cosier than you'd expect. *See p229.*

Mulligans

Amstel 100, Southern Canal Belt (622 1330/ www.mulligans.nl). Tram 4, 9, 14, 16, 24, 25. **Open** *Bar* 4pm-1am Mon-Thur; 4pm-2am Fri; 2pm-3am Sat; 2pm-1am Sun; music starts at 10pm, sessions at 7pm. **Admission** free. **No credit cards. Map** p311 E3.
You'll find Irish pubs in every major European town, but only a handful are as much fun as Mulligans. The music on offer ranges from traditional Celtic acts to modern-day rock and pop singer/songwriters. They even have an open session on Sundays, which is great fun for onlookers and musicians alike.

Nationaal Pop Instituut

Prins Hendrikkade 142, Old Centre: New Side (428 4288/www.popinstituut.nl). Bus 22, 23. **Open** *Media Centre* 10am-5pm Mon-Fri. **Map** p310 D2.

The NPI exists to support Dutch music across the country and throughout the world – be it good, bad, or excruciatingly painful. Its lack of bias is heroic, and anyone can ask for help or access their impressive media libraries stored inside. Most jawdropping of all, however, is its online history of Dutch music (available even in English). Bone up!

OCCII

Amstelveenseweg 134, Museum Quarter (671 7778/ www.occii.org). Tram 1, 2. **Open** 9pm-2am Mon-Thur, Sun; 10pm-3am Fri, Sat. **Admission** free-€5. **No credit cards.**

Formerly a squat, this friendly bar and concert hall is tucked away at one end of Vondelpark. Mainly home to touring underground rock, experimental and reggae acts, or adventurous locals, if you turn up with an open mind there's a good chance of witnessing something special.

Panama

Oostelijke Handelskade 4, the Waterfront (311 8686/ www.panama.nl). Bus 28, 43, 39. **Open** *Box office* 2pm-closing time. *Telephone* 11am-5pm Mon, Tue; 11am-8pm Wed, Thur, Sun; 11am-11pm Fri, Sat. *Theatre/club* hours vary. **Admission** €8-€17. **Credit** AmEx, MC, V.

Panama is a music venue, restaurant and nightclub in one, offering live music, dance nights and occasional theatre events. *See also p231.*

Paradiso

Weteringschans 6-8, Southern Canal Belt (626 4521/ www.paradiso.nl). Tram 1, 2, 5, 7, 10. **Open** hours vary. **Admission** €5-€20. *Membership* (compulsory) €2.50/mth; €18/yr. **No credit cards. Map** p314 D5.

This former church is the cornerstone of the Amsterdam scene, and is in such demand that it often hosts several events in one day. The main hall has a rare sense of grandeur, with multiple balconies and stained-glass windows peering down upon per-

formers. The smaller hall upstairs is a great place to catch new talent before the big time. Both are wonderfully intimate, and bands feed off the surroundings, making for special concerts. *See also p231.*

Vondelpark Openluchttheater

Vondelpark, Museum Quarter (673 1499/www. openluchttheater.nl). Tram 1, 2, 3, 5, 7, 10, 12. **Open** *June-Sept* dawn-dusk daily. **Admission** free. **No credit cards. Map** p314 C6.

On pleasant summer days this famous Amsterdam park is packed, so from June to September organisers put on music, dance, cabaret and children's activities throughout the week.

Winston International

Warmoesstraat 125-129, Old Centre: Old Side (623 1380/www.winston.nl). Tram 4, 9, 16, 24, 25. **Open** 9pm-3am Mon-Thur, Sun; 9pm-4am Fri, Sat. **Admission** €5-€10. **No credit cards. Map** p310 D3.

Part of a weird and wonderful hotel complex (*see p59*), the Winston is where artistic decadence collides with rock 'n' roll grime. Evenings see new talent, both local and international, followed by a club. Its toilets contain the smallest art gallery in the city but never mind the bollocks, there's Punk Rock Karaoke, too. You hear that thumping noise? That's Sid Vicious, pogoing in his grave.

Jazz & blues

The best international acts tour Amsterdam regularly, but don't neglect local talent. For **Maloe Melo**, *see p218*, while **OT301** (*see p199*) is home to happening jazz improv nights, *Kraakgeluiden* ('Squat/Crack Sounds', www.kraakgeluiden.dds.nl), every Monday.

Alto

Korte Leidsedwarsstraat 115, Southern Canal Belt (626 3249/www.jazz-cafe-alto.nl). Tram 1, 2, 5, 6, 7, 10. **Open** 9pm-3am Mon-Thur, Sun; 9pm-4am Fri, Sat. **Admission** free. **No credit cards. Map** p314 D5.

It's heaven. **Paradiso**. See p220.

Small and often quite smoky, Alto is one of the city's better jazz venues. Dutch saxophonist Hans Dulfer (Candy's dad) has a weekly Wednesday night slot.

Bimhuis

Piet Heinkade 3, Docklands (623 1361/www.bimhuis. nl). **Open** *Telephone reservations* 1-5pm Mon-Fri. *Box office* 8-11pm show nights, most shows 9pm. **Admission** €12-€18. **No credit cards. Map** p311 F1.
The name is known to jazz fans the world over and musicians queue up for a chance to grace its stage. Even the transplant to the new Muziekgebouw complex (*see p225*) hasn't tarnished its reputation. Instead, the eye-catching building and familiar interior layout has provided the Bimhuis with an upgrade that will carry it towards a healthy future – great news for jazz fans everywhere.

Bourbon Street

Leidsekruisstraat 6-8, Southern Canal Belt (623 3440/www.bourbonstreet.nl). Tram 1, 2, 5, 6, 7, 10. **Open** 10pm-4am Mon-Thur, Sun; 10pm-5am Fri, Sat. **Admission** €3-€5. **Credit** AmEx, MC, V, DC. **Map** p314 D5.
Sitting in the heart of the tourist area, this blues club has a spacious bar and a very late liquor licence. Musicians are welcome at its regular jam sessions.

Brix Food 'n' Drinx

Wolvenstraat 16, Southern Canal Belt (639 0351/ www.cafebrix.nl). Tram 1, 2, 5, 13, 14, 17. **Open** 5pm-1am Mon-Thur, Sun; 5pm-3am Fri, Sat. *Kitchen* 6-10pm daily. **Admission** free. **Credit** MC, V. **Map** p314 C4.
This comfortable café is a new player in the Amsterdam jazz scene. Cool jazzy sounds are spun by enthusiastic DJs, but check out their weekly jazz and piano sessions for a taste of the real thing.

Cristofori

Prinsengracht 581-583, Western Canal Belt (626 8485/www.cristofori.nl). Tram 1, 2, 5. **Open** *Store* 1-6pm Mon; 10am-6pm Tue-Fri; 10am-5pm Sat. *Concerts* 2pm; 8pm. **Admission** €12.50-€15. **No credit cards. Map** p314 C4.

Worth a visit for the building alone: a beautiful canal house that doubles as a piano retailer. Weekends see it host sporadic live entertainment ranging from jazz singers to chamber music. Check website for details.

Festivals

As summer rolls around, the Dutch shake off the gloom of a northern winter and head off to sunnier climes. Inevitably, this slows the local club scene to a crawl, but in turn it sparks the festival circuit into life. Events are scattered all over the country from April to September – many of them completely free. Check www. festivalinfo.nl for all locations and line-ups. Tickets for the larger festivals are available from the AUB Ticketshop (0900 0191) or Ticketmaster (www.ticketmaster.nl); *see p293* **Tickets please.**

Amsterdam Roots Festival

www.amsterdamroots.nl. **Date** June.
This festival, organised by the Tropeninstituut, Melkweg and Concertgebouw, brings some of the best world music acts to Amsterdam. Free concerts by less-known names in Oosterpark add to the fun.

A Camping Flight to Lowlands

www.lowlands.nl. **Date** penultimate weekend of Aug.
The best place to bid farewell to summer is in the Lowlands. Holland's largest alternative music festival takes place over three days, attracting up to 60,000 young hipsters. The music, theatre acts and street performers all create a lively atmosphere, even when the weather turns sour in anticipation of the long cold wet nights that lie ahead.

Crossing Border

www.crossingborder.nl. **Date** Nov.
Crossing Border's move back to its original home in The Hague has revitalised it. Offering a stimulating mix of literature and music, many well-known international authors and artists arrive for both spoken-word and musical performances. *See also p188.*

London Calling

www.paradiso.nl. **Date** late-March/mid-Nov.
The twice yearly London Calling concerts are often the first opportunity for Dutch audiences to catch the hottest new rock and pop talents from the UK.

Motel Mozaique

www.motelmozaique.nl. **Date** mid-April.
Rotterdam hosts this new three-day festival combining music, theatre and art. Expect the happily edgy: Scissor Sisters, Lambchop, Youngblood Brass Band.

Music Meeting

www.musicmeeting.nl. **Date** July.
For the future of cutting-edge global grooves, head to Nijmegen for a wild weekend.

North Sea Jazz

Tickets 0900 300 1250/www.northseajazz.nl. **Date** 2nd weekend in July.
This three-day mega-event bids farewell to The Hague in the summer of 2005 and heads to the Ahoy complex in Rotterdam the following year. Regular fans aren't delirious at the prospect of its soulless caverns, but the improved facilities should cope with the expected 1,200 musicians and 25,000 daily visitors, enabling the festival to continue to grow.

Parkpop

www.parkpop.nl. **Date** late June.
Every country in Europe claims to hold the largest free festival and Parkpop is the Dutch contender – organisers usually expect 300,000 to 500,000 visitors

for this family-type affair. Three stages offer bands from around the world, as well as locals, and a huge market fills any lull in the entertainment. A great day out, particularly when the weather's onside.

Pinkpop

www.pinkpop.nl. **Date** May/June.
Attracting a slightly younger crowd than its 'indie sister' Lowlands, Pinkpop, down in the southern tip of the country, is somewhat less adventurous. Still, there are plenty of big names in the worlds of pop, rock, dance and metal at this three-day event. Just remember to wear something pink… Seriously.

Sonic Acts

www.sonicacts.com. **Date** varies.
Arguably Holland's most challenging festival, Sonic Acts fills the Paradiso with the sounds of new electronic and experimental music. Various workshops, lectures, seminars and opportunities to get your hands dirty attract fans from all over the world.

Classical & Opera

One of the most heart-warming facets of the classical scene in Amsterdam is that the city promotes a classless adoration of beautiful music, so that attending a concert is not a statement of one's arrival in society but simply a result of the love of fine music. The greatest orchestras in the world perform here and there is access for all – typically for little more than the price of the biggest rock and pop concerts, and frequently considerably less.

And while orchestras elsewhere are slipping and sliding towards financial doom, the arts in Amsterdam only seem to be improving. Funding is in the right hands and many organisations are planning for a bright future. As such, you can not only hear the classics in the grand halls, but alongside canals, in parks, and sometimes even on the streets.

Of course, the city is also home to some of the most renowned orchestras and soloists around. Led by chief conductor Mariss Jansons, who took over the reigns from Riccardo Chailly at the start of the 2004/2005 season, the **Royal Concertgebouw Orchestra** is one of the most prestigious in the world. Over the years it has hosted a thrilling series of conductors and soloists, such as Carlos Kleiber, Kurt Sanderling and Christian Thielemann. And the years seem simply to have improved the Royal Concertgebouw: if you get the chance to hear them play, don't pass it up.

Alternatively, the **Netherlands Philharmonic**, based in Beurs van Berlage, and newcomers like the **Holland Symfonia** in the Muziektheater frequently produce wonderful opera and ballet productions. And then there's the **Rotterdam Philharmonic**.

Concertgebouw. See p223.

ENSEMBLES

A healthy music scene requires diversity and on that score Amsterdam certainly delivers. On one side of the fence, the quest for authenticity to the composer's intentions has led to the foundation of many traditionalist ensembles, performing the classics with authentic period instruments. Orchestras such as the **Amsterdam Baroque Orchestra & Choir**, the **Amsterdam Bach Soloists**, and the **Orchestra of the 18th Century** have restored popular cantatas to their original state of crystalline clarity with results that are quite simply sublime.

However, classical music cannot survive simply on its back catalouge, and there is also a thriving modern-classical movement, challenging musical boundaries. Not always a comfortable ride, these performances can nevertheless be an exciting experience. Stand out collectives are the **Schönberg Ensemble**, **Asko Ensemble**, and the **Combattimento Consort**. Similarly, look out for the experimental projects of the **Maarten Altena Ensemble**, which are always unpredictable.

Fans of modern works will also appreciate the annual Proms series, which runs at Paradiso from September through January. See www.promsinparadiso.nl for programme.

TICKETS AND INFORMATION

Ticket prices in Amsterdam are reasonable compared with other European cities. However, tickets for many of the larger venues are sold on a subscription system, and it can be difficult to get tickets on an ad hoc basis. For big concerts and operas, try to book as far in advance as you can, but if you're just passing through, it's always worth checking for returns.

For full listings information, pick up a copy of the free Dutch listings magazine *Uitkrant*, published by the AUB (0900 0191; *see p293* **Tickets please**), or call in at the Amsterdam Tourist Board (0900 400 4040, *see p295*), which has information on upcoming shows. Discounts on tickets are often available for students and the over-65s on production of ID.

Concert halls

Bethaniënklooster

Barndesteeg 6b, Old Centre: Old Side (625 0078/ www.bethanienklooster.nl). Tram 4, 9, 14, 16, 24, 25. Tram 4, 9, 16, 24, 25/Metro Nieuwmarkt. **Open** hours vary. **Tickets** free-€10. **No credit cards. Map** p310 D2.

Hidden in a small alley between Damstraat and the Nieuwmarkt, this former monastery is a wonderful stage for promising new talent to cut their musical teeth. And in between the music students you may find more reputable musicians too.

Beurs van Berlage

Damrak 213, Old Centre: Old Side (521 7575/ www.berlage.com). Tram 4, 9, 14, 16, 24, 25. **Open** *Box office* 2-5pm Tue-Fri; also from 2 hours before performance. *Closed* end June-mid Aug. **Tickets** €10-€20. **No credit cards. Map** p310 D2.

This former stock exchange, designed by Hendrik Berlage, is worth a visit in its own right as perhaps the most important piece of twentieth century architecture in Amsterdam (*see p79*). But the Beurs has now forgone its role as a temple to Mammon and become instead a cathedral of culture, comprising a large exhibition room, two concert halls and the offices of the building's three resident orchestras: the Netherlands Philharmonic, the Netherlands Chamber Orchestra, and the newer Amsterdam Symphony Orchestra. The medium-sized Yakult Zaal offers comfortable seating, a massive stage and controllable but not immaculate acoustics, while the 200-seat Amvest Zaal is an odd-looking, free-standing glass box within the walls of a side room.

Concertgebouw

Concertgebouwplein 2-6, Museum Quarter, (reservations 671 8345/24hr information in Dutch and English 573 0511/www.concertgebouw.nl). Tram 2, 3, 5, 12, 16, 20. **Open** *Box office* 10am-7pm daily; until 8.15pm for that night's concert. *By phone* 10am-5pm daily. **Tickets** €13-€60. **Credit** AmEx, DC, MC, V. **Map** p314 D6.

With its beautiful architecture and clear acoustics, the Concertgebouw is a favourite venue of many of the world's top musicians, and is home to its own world famous Royal Concertgebouw Orchestra. As you'd expect, the sound in the Grote Zaal (Great Hall) is excellent. The Kleine Zaal (Recital Hall) is perhaps less comfortable, but has the virtue of being the perfect size for chamber groups and soloists. Visiting stars push prices up, but avoid the big names and concerts are very affordable, with the Robeco Summer Concerts (July, Aug) a particular bargain. For a taster, pop in to the free Wednesday lunchtime concerts, which often offer a trimmed-down recital of one of the week's key performances. For a full night of culture precede your concert with a meal at the posh and somewhat overpriced – but wonderful – Bodega de Keyzer (Van Baerlestraat 96, 675 1866/www.bodegakeyzer.nl), and round things off at the unpretentious and convivial brown bar Café Welling (JW Brouwerstraat 32, 662 0155).

IJsbreker

Piet Heinkade 1, Docklands (788 2000/www. ysbreker.nl). Tram 16, 26. **Open** *Telephone reservations* 1-5pm Mon-Fri. **Admission** €7-€20. **Credit** MC, V. **Map** p311 E1.

At the start of 2005, the Ice Breaker moved with its jazz sister, Bimhuis (*see p221*), into the new Muziekgebouw (*see p225*) complex in docklands. Existing as an innovative home to contemporary classical music and experimental jazz, its organisers are looking to compile challenging and entertaining programmes well into the future.

Arts & Entertainment

Churches

Much of the world's most exquisite music was written not for performance in a concert hall but to serve within the liturgical confines of the mass. So where better to listen to it than its natural home: Amsterdam's beautiful churches. Combine that with acoustics sound technicians can only dream of, the lingering scent of incense and a palpable sense of the holy, and you can see why classical music fans go to church.

Few churches provide a box office, and some do not publish full schedules online. Details and tickets are available from the AUB (0900 0191) and online at www.amsterdamsuitburo.nl, where you can search for 'kerk' (church).

Engelse Kerk

Begijnhof 48, Old Centre: New Side (624 9665/ www.ercadam.nl). Tram 1, 2, 4, 5, 9, 14, 16, 24, 25. **Open** hours vary. **Admission** free-€20. **No credit cards. Map** p314 D4.

Nestled in an idyllic courtyard, the English Reformed Church has hosted weekly concerts of baroque and classical music since the 1970s. Combined with a particular emphasis on the use of authentic period instruments, the church's acoustics are haunting. Free lunchtime concerts by young musicians are a platform for prospective stars, and its healthy evening schedule also raises funds to help secure the future of the church.

Noorderkerk

Noordermarkt 48, the Jordaan (427 6163/www. noorderkerkconcerten.nl). Tram 3, 10. **Open** 11am-1pm Sat; concerts 2-3pm Sat. **Tickets** €8-€25. **No credit cards. Map** p309 B2.

Sure, the wooden benches in this early 17th-century church are on the hard side, but all is soon forgotten thanks to their programmes, which attract accomplished musicians to perform classical favourites. Reservations are recommended.

Oude Kerk

Oudekerksplein 23, Old Centre: Old Side (625 8284/ www.oudekerk.nl). Tram 4, 9, 14, 16, 24, 25. **Open** 11am-5pm Mon-Sat; 1-5pm Sun. **Tickets** €7.50-€15. **No credit cards. Map** p310 D2.

Jan Sweelinck, the Netherlands' most famous 17th-century composer, was once the organist here. Concerts running from June to August include organ and carillon recitals, plus choral and chamber music.

Westerkerk

Prinsengracht 281, Western Canal Belt (624 7766/ www.westerkerk.nl). Tram 13, 14, 17. **Open** Office 10am-2pm Mon-Fri. *Box office* 45 mins before concert. **Tickets** free-€35; €6-€8 concessions. **No credit cards. Map** p310 C3.

This landmark church features a wide range of lunch and evening concerts, many of them free of charge. And to hear the music in its proper setting, remember cantatas are performed during services.

Opera

Here's a refuelling idea for hungry opera fans. Staff at Pasta E Basta (Nieuwe Spiegelstraat 8, Southern Canal Belt, 422 2229/www.pasta ebasta.nl) serve out fine Italian grub the pasta variety while singing arias.

Muziektheater

Amstel 3, Old Centre: Old Side (625 5455/www. muziektheater.nl). Tram 9, 14/Metro Waterlooplein. **Open** Box office 10am-6pm Mon-Sat; 11.30am-6pm Sun; or until start of performance. **Tickets** €17-€63. **Credit** AmEx, DC, MC, V. **Map** p311 E3.

Home of the Dutch National Ballet, the Netherlands Opera, and the newly established Holland Symfonia (the combined forces of the Netherlands Ballet Orchestra and the North Holland Philharmonic Orchestra), as well as host to countless visiting guest productions, the Muziektheater has a reputation for high-quality performances at reasonable prices. Tickets go on sale three months in advance and often sell out, so it's advisable to book early if there's a performance you really want to see.

Stadsschouwburg

Leidseplein 26, Southern Canal Belt (624 2311/ www.ssba.nl). Tram 1, 2, 5, 6, 7, 10. **Open** Box office 10am-6pm or until start of performance Mon-Sat; from 1½hrs before start of performance Sun. **Tickets** €11-€35. **Credit** AmEx, MC, V. **Map** p314 C5.

This resplendent venue on Leidseplein is known primarily for its theatre and opera productions, although occasional contemporary music performances break into the schedule. The surroundings lend a touch of splendour to proceedings.

Out of town

Doelen

Kruisstraat 2, Rotterdam (010 217 1717/ www.dedoelen.nl). NS rail Rotterdam Centraal Station. **Open** Box office noon-6pm daily. *By phone* 10am-noon, 4-6pm daily and one hour before concert. **Tickets** €12-€35. **Credit** AmEx, MC, V.

The Doelen may appear cold, dreary and grey on Rotterdam's concrete skyline, but thankfully once you get inside, its interior is a scene of grandeur, promoting an electric atmosphere and offering beautiful acoustics. And to provide something for all, a smaller concert hall accompanies the main room, enabling the complex to host over 600 events each year from opera, to classical recitals, to pop concerts. It's also home to another of the Netherlands' great orchestras, the Rotterdam Philharmonic.

Vredenburg

Vredenburgpassage 77, Utrecht (box office 030 231 4544/www.vredenburg.nl). NS rail Utrecht. **Open** Box office noon-7pm Mon; 10am-7pm Tue-Sat; also from 45min before performance. **Tickets** €17-€35. **Credit** AmEx, MC, V.

Muziekgebouw

It's going to take some getting used to...
The legendary jazz joint Bimhuis (see p221),
that has welcomed everyone from smooth
jazz legends to squawking avant-garde up-and-
comers for the last three decades, is leaving
its old and wonderfully grubby digs for the
new and hi-tech Muziekgebouw. It will be
joining the equally venerable Het IJsbreker
(see p223), a proponent of modern classical
and non-Western sounds, along with a whole
slew of the nation's top contemporary music
ensembles: Asko Ensemble, Schönberg
Ensemble, Nieuw Ensemble, Ives Ensemble,
Orkest De Volharding and Amsterdam
Sinfonietta. The 'Music Building' will also
host the KlankSpeelTuin (see p193), the
'Sound Playground', where kids learn how
music making is like baking a cake.

No effort – and little money – has been
spared in building €52 million worth of jutting,
transparent cubes, complete with all the
latest technical and acoustical mod cons.
It's hoped that the Muziekgebouw will finally
jumpstart the cultural flowering of this long
up-and-coming area along the eastern
docklands, that is envisioned by city
planners as a cultural/nightlife boulevard
linking the old city – Centraal Station is a
mere ten-minute walk away – and the new.

While its official opening is not until
September 2005, it's been in action since
February, hosting every non-commercial
combination of sound and rhythm
imaginable, and some that really aren't.
To clear your head afterwards there's a
grand café/restaurant, complete with
terrace, overlooking the scenic wateriness
of the IJ, as well as studios, rehearsal
space, congress/convention facilities
and an exhibition space.

In short: music lovers should take the
plunge and walk the plank – in this case
a narrow swoopy 65-meter (215 feet) foot
bridge – towards the new home of the
other side of music...

Muziekgebouw

Piet Heinkade 1, Docklands (788 2010/
www.muziekgebouw.nl). Tram 16, 26.
Open *Telephone reservations* 1-5pm
Mon-Fri. **Admission** varies. **Credit** varies.
Map p311 F1.

Pop quiz!

Say 'Dutch music' to anyone, including a Dutchman, and you'll likely be faced with a blanker than blank stare. But you'd be surprised at how much local music does get exported – as this quiz will attest...

1. Which crooning trumpet player accented his extended residency in Amsterdam with one last moody decrescendo from local hotel window to parking lot?

2. Which local accordionist gave up a lucrative career as a sideman to the likes of Maurice Chevalier and Josephine Baker to play the drinking holes of the Jordaan in exchange for free beer.)

3. Who is generally regarded as the nation's greatest living composer? (Hint: his name is often mentioned in the same breath as those other masters of modern music, Terry Riley, Steve Reich and Philip Glass, his music has been performed by everyone from the BBC Symphony Orchestra to the Kronos Quartet, and his operas have included several collaborations with avant garde film-maker extraordinaire Peter Greenaway.)

4. Which 'eel singer' from Urk achieved the dual honour of appearing in the first season of *Big Brother* (*see p111* **Big Brother** is

watching), and having one of his songs, 'Little Green Bag', feature in *Reservoir Dogs*?

5. Who began scoring the music for *Miami Vice* after scoring a global hit with hard rock's only yodel-driven track?

6. Which 1960s band originally recorded 'Venus', Banarama's global 1980s hit?

7. Who was the 'nation's cuddle junkie' and ex-husband of Nina Hagen, who ended his life with an appropriately rock 'n' roll thump by stepping off the Hilton Hotel?

8. Which Dutch musician/producer helped a dead Elvis to posthumously break his tie with the Beatles for the most number one hits?

9. Which Dutch DJ has been voted the world's best by *DJ Magazine* for several years running?

Answers: 1) Chet Baker (*see p83*, 2) Johnny Meijer (pay respect at his statue, *see* **p112**). 3) Louis Andriessen. 4) George Baker. 5) Jan Akkerman (the hit was 'Hocus Pocus' by Focus). 6) Shocking Blue. 7) Herman Brood (for his paintings, visit Brood Galerie, Spuistraat 320, 2th floor, 623 3766, www.brood.nl). 8) Junkie XL ('A Little Less Conversation' was Elvis' 18th number one hit). 9) DJ Tiësto.

Located in the labyrinthine Utrecht train station and shopping complex from which, it's said, some visitors have never emerged, Vredenburg offers an interesting mix of classical music, jazz, pop, rock and singer/songwriters. The setting is ugly, but the acoustics are one in a million. The free lunchtime concerts on Fridays are particularly worthwhile.

Festivals & events

Further details on all the events listed below can be obtained from the AUB (0900 0191; *see p293* **Tickets please**) and the Amsterdam Tourist Board (0900 400 4040). Another festival that features a whole range of arts, including classical music, is the Uitmarkt (*see p187*).

Grachtenfestival
Various venues (421 4542/www.grachtenfestival.nl). **Date** mid Aug. **Tickets** free-€25. **Credit** varies.
What started out as a single free concert from an orchestra floating on a pontoon in front of the Hotel Pulitzer has become the 'Canal Festival'. Handel would be delighted to hear that this modern water music has expanded to over 90 concerts, each set somewhere near or on the water. The line-up balances international names with national talent.

Holland Festival Oude Muziek Utrecht
Various venues in Utrecht. Box office at VVV Utrecht, Vinkenburgstraat 19 (030 230 3838/ www.oudemuziek.nl). **Date** late Aug-early Sept. **Tickets** €7-€31. **No credit cards.**
Top baroque and classical artists converge on Utrecht each year. The festival is a staple of the season in the Netherlands because the use of period instruments allows aficionados to hear the music of Bach, Mozart or Handel as the composer intended.

International Gaudeamus Music Week
Various venues (694 7349/www.gaudeamus.nl). **Date** early Sept. **Tickets** free-€17. **Credit** varies.
An international competition for young composers organised by the Centre for Contemporary Music, the week includes intense discussion of the state of the art and performances of selected works. Contemporary music devotees shouldn't miss it – classicists may want to plug their ears and run away.

International Jewish Music Festival
www.joodsmuziekfestival.nl. **Date** end Nov.
The festival, which features readings and concerts that embrace klezmer, Yiddish, chazzanoet and classical, is in Cristofori's evocative canalside setting.

Nightclubs

The beautiful and the Amsterdamned.

Woo hoo, it's **Jimmy Woo's**. *See p229.*

The very idea of a 'nightclub' is so, well, 1970s, don't you think? Doesn't it just call to mind visions of John Travolta parading down the street in his tight white suit while the Bee Gees warble in the background? Here in the 'Dam we have bars masquerading as clubs, pretending to be live music venues, doubling as discotheques. Ladies and gentlemen it's a crazy, mixed-up world. Let's simply assume that by 'nightclub' you mean some kind of venue which is open at night, and let the party begin.

But first, please note that the smiley-faced raver days are long gone. Rather the quest in modern-day Amsterdam is to find a nice joint to hang out in. (Or alternatively, given the relaxed Dutch attitudes towards the pointy leaved weed, a nice joint to hang out with; *see p48.*) Bigger clubs are likely to be programmed by outside organisers, so the fare on offer will vary from night to night. Check websites or flyers for the latest information.

Some words of warning. First, you must pay to pee – usually at least 50c. Legally, you can't be forced to pay, but if the loos are nice and clean and you get free candy, then why make enemies with the often surly WC lady? You don't want to be in her bad books when the urge to surge grabs you.

Our second warning is to groups of men: if you must have your bachelor party here, don't expect to be heartily welcomed by the hipper establishments – why not persuade some cute ladies to accompany you in groups of twos or threes? Or alternatively, celebrate your pal's loss of freedom in a busy bar. Most clubs won't mind you lighting up a 'jasmine cigarette', but don't be misled by this seeming show of tolerance: class A drugs are not permitted. But you weren't even considering it, were you?

Do you want to lounge? Do you want to be seen? Do you want to be out late? Do you want to be brought home in an ambulance? All of the above is still possible in this global village if you know where to go on which night. It's all about timing, since Amsterdam is a city that sleeps, but when it's awake, it's alive.

Arts & Entertainment

Marge Simpson goes green with envy at Club Vegas. **Winston International**. *See p228.*

Club venues

Particular attention has been given to the most popular club nights held at each venue. For clubs and venues where the majority of nights are aimed at the gay community (such as hetero-friendly Exit, where straights are allowed in on most evenings, *see p250*. For the **Westergasfabriek**, *see p250*. For rock, pop and jazz venues, whose concerts often run into club nights of some form or other, *see p217*. And don't forget the city's clutch of smaller, DJ-friendly bars like **Twstd** (*see p149*) and DJ **Café Vaaghuyzen** (*see p145*).

The Old Centre: Old Side

Winston International
Warmoesstraat 125-129 (623 1380/www.winston.nl). Tram 9, 14, 25. **Open** 9pm-3am Mon-Thur, Sun; 11pm-4am Fri, Sat. **Admission** €5-€10. **No credit cards. Map** p310 D2.
An intimate venue that attracts a mixed crowd with its mixed, mainly rock/alt, programming. Tuesday brings the popular hip hop/R&B night Live on the Low. Sunday's Club Vegas (www.clubvegas.nl) has been keeping the arty, cheesy-listening crowd smiling for over seven years, while the excellent Monday line-up veers from punk rock karaoke to open-mic night, Spoken Beats. When you go for a whizz, watch out for the toilet art gallery. *See also p59.*

The Old Centre: New Side

Bitterzoet
Spuistraat 2 (521 3001/www.bitterzoet.com). Tram 1, 2, 5. **Open** 8pm-3am Mon-Thur, Sun; 8pm-4am Fri, Sat. **Admission** €5. **No credit cards. Map** p310 C2.
This busy, comfy and casual bar triples as a venue for theatre and music. Both the bands and the DJs tend to embrace the jazzy, world and 'urban' side of sound, while Creme de la Gutter, monthly on Saturdays, won a 2004 'Golden Gnome' for the best new underground clubnight.

Dansen bij Jansen
Handboogstraat 11-13 (620 1779/www.dansen bijjansen.nl). Tram 1, 2, 4, 5, 9, 14, 16, 24, 25. **Open** 11pm-4am Mon-Thur, Sun; 11pm-5am Fri, Sat. **Admission** €2 Mon-Wed, Sun; €4 Thur-Sat. **No credit cards. Map** p314 D4.
It's a club Jim, but not as we know it: you'll need valid student ID to get in. DJs spin sing-along Top 40 tunes and the drink prices are cheerfully affordable. But if you're over 25, you'll feel like Barbara Cartland at a booze-infused kindergarten.

Southern Canal Belt

Cineac
Reguliersbreestraat 31-33 (530 6888/www.cineac.nl). Tram 4, 9, 14. **Open** 6pm-1am Tue-Thur, Sun; 6pm-3am Fri, Sat. **Admission** €5. **Credit** AmEx, MC, V. **Map** p315 E4.

A decadent Moulin Rouge-esque restaurant that transforms itself into a nightclub after dinner (and sometimes even during the meal, much to the chagrin of dilatory diners). It's owned by ID&T (who organise giant dance festivals Sensation and Mysteryland; *see p235*), with the power to pull in some impressive DJ names. Pricey and exclusive, under-25s might be reluctant to apply for membership.

11
Oosterdokskade 3-5 (625 5999/www.ilove11.nl).
Tram 16. **Open** 11am-1am Mon-Wed, Sun; 11am-4am Thur-Sat. **Admission** €7-€15. **Credit** AmEx, MC, V. **Map** p311 E1.
A temporary hip restaurant/club which has an unbeatable eagle's eye view over the water and a celebrity chef all the way from New Zealand. 11 attracts an arty crowd of *ID* magazine readers and fashion types. Rauw ('raw', www.meubelstukken.nl) nights with techno pioneer DJ Joost van Bellen mix rock/electro/disco all together into one almighty stompin' funky brew. Check the website for other cool one-off offers. *See also p133.*

Escape
Rembrandtplein 11 (622 1111/www.escape.nl).
Tram 4, 9, 14. **Open** 11pm-4am Thur, Sun; 11pm-5am Fri, Sat. **Admission** €6-€20. **No credit cards.**
Map p315 E4.
With a capacity of 2,000 this is about as big as clubbing gets in central Amsterdam. After a drugs bust shut the place down in 2003, the shady underworld characters have gone and the arms-in-the-air Eurohouse fun can now continue. The bouncers are slightly wary of groups of tourists, so squeeze into a slinky T-shirt, slap on some hair product and get in line early with the young, pretty, excited and excitable, oh-so-mainstream crowd waiting outside.

Jimmy Woo's
Korte Leidsedwarsstraat 18 (626 3150/www.jimmy woo.com). Tram 1, 2, 5, 6, 7, 10. **Open** 10pm-3am Wed, Thur, Sun; 10pm-4am Fri, Sat. **Admission** €7.50. **Credit** AmEx, MC, DC, V. **Map** p314 C5.
Amsterdam has never seen anything quite so luxuriously cosmopolitan as Jimmy Woo's. You too can marvel at the lounge area filled with a mixture of modern and antique furniture and then confirm for yourself the merits of its 'Golden Gnome' award in 2003 for a sound system that takes an urban soundtrack ranging from hip hop to garage and kicks it screaming into the Amsterdam ether. Fellow Gnome-winners, lady-DJs Wannabe a Star & Miss B-Have (www.wannabeastar.net) keep the crowd pleased on Saturday nights. Even Pharell Williams hosted a private party here, so wear your diamanté thong. If you have problems getting in, cool off across the street at sister cocktail bar, Suzy Wong (Korte Leidsedwarsstraat 45, 626 6769).

The Kingdom
Jan Van Galenstraat 6-10 (488 9888/www.kingdom venue.com). Bus 21. **Open** hours vary. **Admission** free-€25. **No credit cards.** **Map** p313 A4.

A capacious venue that can seem a bit shabby but then, some venues pay designers potloads of oodles to try and buy their way to the seediness that the Kingdom manages without even trying. And a little seediness is hardly likely to put off the people who organise Europe's number one, kinky, fetish fest Wastelands, which comes here (sorry) twice a year (www.wasteland.nl). Sometimes referred to as the 'Marcanti Kingdom', it's also the new home to both the popular Rush (Raw Urban Sexy House) and Chemistry nights (www.chemistry.nl).

Melkweg
Lijnbaansgracht 234a (531 8181/www.melkweg.nl).
Tram 1, 2, 5, 6, 7, 10. **Open** hours vary.
Admission €5-€25. **Membership** €2.50/mth (compulsory) or €14/year. **No credit cards.**
Map p314 C5.
Amsterdam's essential multimedia centre, the 'Milky Way' offers a galaxy of stellar programming: fancy it ain't, but great value and down to earth – with a little bit of everything thrown into the mix – it certainly is. Watch out for Friday's Latin-flavoured Que Pasa, which has built up quite a following; and the weekends also have consistently good club nights. *See also p219.*

Ministry
Reguliersdwarsstraat 12 (623 3981/www.
ministry.nl). Tram 16, 24, 25. **Open** 11pm-4am Mon, Sun; 11pm-5am Fri, Sat. **Admission** €5-€12. **No credit cards.** **Map** p314 D4.
Ministry is a small and stylish club with a music policy that tends towards the funky and soulful urban sounds. Groove to the latest hip hop, R&B and dancehall tracks on Freaky Fridays. The door staff can be a little picky, so dress up and be pretty.

Nachttheater Sugar Factory
Lijnbaansgracht 238 (626 5006/www.
sugarfactory.nl). Tram 1, 2, 5, 7, 10. **Open** 9pm-4am Thur, Sun; 9pm-5am Fri, Sat. **Admission** €5-€15. **No credit cards.** **Map** p314 C5.

The best Clubs

11
The view, the view! *See above.*

Melkweg
Straightforward fun. *See p229.*

Nachttheater Sugar Factory
New kid on the block. *See above.*

Panama
Rejuvenated. *See p231.*

Sinners
Bling appeal. *See p231.*

Arts & Entertainment

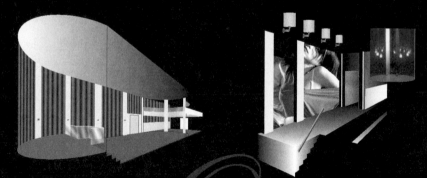

Due to open in April 2005, the 'night theatre' could well become something that really does redefine clubbing. The theatre licence means the promoters have to infuse some kind of performance element into the programming (nightly at 10pm, 1am and 3am). Art & world beats will feature on SugarH*RT on Thursdays; variety shows and live music will define Fridays; progressive theatre will fuse with a club night on Saturdays, while Sundays will see poetry jams followed by Wicked Jazz Sounds.

Odeon

Singel 460 (850 2426/www.odeonamsterdam.nl). Tram 1, 2, 5. **Open** *Club* 10pm-3am daily. *Cocktail lounge* from 5.30pm daily. *Terrace* from 11.30am daily. **Admission** free-€20. **Credit** AmEx, MC, V. **Map** p314 D4.

Due to reopen in March 2005, this three-storey multifunctional 1662-built venue comes complete with restaurant, cocktail bar, café (with great canal-side terrace), disco and cultural activities. During the day and early evening the club will host various events, presentations, concerts and performances. The café and cocktail bar will open during the day (but they are unsure of hours at the moment). Over-25s only.

Paradiso

Weteringschans 6-8 (626 4521/www.paradiso.nl). Tram 1, 2, 5, 6, 7, 10. **Open** 7pm-4am Wed-Thur, Sun; 7pm-5am Fri, Sat. **Admission** €5-€20 (incl €2.50/ mth membership). **No credit cards**. **Map** p314 D5.

As an Amsterdam institution, this large ex-church is a safe clubbing bet with a trusty formula of following on live shows with a DJ or club night. Saturday's Paradisco pulls in a youngish, up-for-it crowd, while Noodlanding (emergency landing) on a Wednesday or Thursday is particularly good for an alternative, indie feel. *See also p220.*

Sinners

Wagenstraat 3-7 (620 1375/www.sinners.nl). Tram 4, 9, 14. **Open** 11pm-4am Thur; 11pm-5am Fri, Sat. **Admission** free-€12. **No credit cards**. Map p311 E3.

The Sinners people are youthful, boo-tiful, well groomed, and well funded – some of them are even famous, albeit in a 'big in Hollandwood' sort of way. Think *Sex in the City* meets the *Fresh Prince*. Think urban and groovy house classix. Creme Fresh on Saturdays is reliably festive and dirrrty.

Zebra Lounge

Korte Leidsedwarsstraat 14 (06 223 68 039 info and reservations/www.the-zebra.nl). Tram 1, 2, 5, 7, 10. **Open** 10pm-3am Wed, Thur, Sun; 10pm-4am Fri, Sat. **Admission** €5-€10. **Credit** Amex, MC, V. **Map** p314 C5.

Refused a 'sex permit' to operate as a pole-dancing club (as if Amsterdam needs another venue for men with gyroscope obsessions), the faux-sleazy Zebra Lounge took the path of lesser profit and is now a hip, respectable and pole-less venue. Buy your booze by the bottle in order to assure yourself a place in one of their glamorous booths.

Jodenbuurt, the Plantage & the Oost

Club Arena

's Gravesandestraat 51 (850 2420/www.hotel arena.nl). Tram 3, 6, 7, 10. **Open** 10pm-4am Fri-Sun. **Admission** €6-€20. **No credit cards**. **Map** p316 G3.

Another multipurpose venue, these beautiful buildings were once an orphanage before changing into a youth hostel. From there it was only a short step to becoming a trendy hotel, bar and restaurant. Big city folk, used to long treks, will laugh at its accessibility, but Amsterdammers tend to forego the small detour eastwards, making it hard for the Arena to truly kick clubbing butt. But monthlies like Appelsap (Apple juice, www.appelsap.net) with its hip-hop/funk bias and '80s Verantwoord (duh, '80s, dude) are the exceptions. Look out for special events with top DJs or fashion shows. *See also p65.*

The Waterfront

Panama

Oostelijke Handelskade 4 (311 8686/www. panama.nl). Tram 26. **Open** 9pm-3am Thur, Sun; 9pm-4am Fri, Sat. **Admission** €8-€20. **Credit** MC, V. **Map** p108.

Recently taken over by the advertising people who used to run the now defunct Mazzo, the plush and roomy Panama is undergoing something of an identity crisis. Gone is the Latin American programming whence its name came and in its place there's a mainstream housey club agenda.

The Jordaan

Korsakoff

Lijnbaansgracht 161 (625 7854/www.korsakoff.nl). Tram 10, 13, 14, 17. **Open** 11pm-3am Mon-Thur, Sun; 11pm-4am Fri, Sat. **Admission** usually free. **No credit cards**. **Map** p314 C4.

Korsakoff strives to make the 'alternative' feel normal: the venue's hard rock/indie/metal/goth sounds reach the parts that Kylie and Justin have never even heard about. And while the decor might be rough 'n' ready, the crowd is relaxed and the drink cheap.

More

Rozengracht 133 (344 6402/www.expectmore.nl). Tram 13, 14, 17. **Open** 11pm-4am Thur; 11pm-5am Fri, Sat; 5pm-midnight Sun. **Admission** €8-€15. **No credit cards**. **Map** p313 B4.

This five-year-old club no longer tries to be the next cool hotspot. As a result the interior is less stark and more warm, the door guys have chilled out and it's a better place all round. Now it's all about uncomplicated fun of the boy-meets-girl type – and why else do most people go out clubbing? Wednesday's LAM (a Dutch acronym meaning 'up-for-it drunk chicks'), with free drinks for females between 9pm and 11pm, is an obvious winner.

Arts & Entertainment

Melkweg it. *See p229.*

Museum Quarter, Vondelpark & the South

The Mansion

*Hobbemastraat 2 (616 6664/www.the-mansion.nl).
Tram 2, 5.* **Open** 6pm-1am Wed, Thur, Sun; 6pm-
3am Fri, Sat. **Admission** free-€15. **Credit** AmEx,
DC, MC, V. **Map** p314 D5.

With the same owner as the Zebra Lounge, and
design by Concrete (also responsible for Nomads
and the Supperclub), this new restaurant/bar/club
has strong credentials. Think less Hugh Hefner and
more elegant gentleman's club (but with chicks). The
staff are bedecked in outfits designed by Europe's
answer to Donna Karan, René Lezard and the decor
is plush Chinese. Expect live music, top local and
UK DJs, loads of people keen to show off and afterwards a space in your wallet where your money was.

Powerzone

*Daniel Goedkoopstraat 1-3/corner Spaklerweg (0900
769 379 663/www.thepowerzone.nl). Metro
Spaklerweg.* **Open** 11pm-5am Fri, Sat. **Admission**
€12-€35. **Credit** AmEx, MC, V.

Packing in as many as 5,000 mainstream clubbers,
the cavernous Powerzone is more like an outdoor
dance party that has found its way indoors. The
staff, however, are not particularly welcoming to
gangs of tourists, so look pretty and feign a Swedish
accent or you risk wasting the taxi fare out to this non-
central venue. The VIP lounge includes waterbeds.

Outside Amsterdam

'What other place in the world could you find,
where all of life's comforts, and all novelties
that man could want, are so easy to obtain
as here – and where you can enjoy such a
feeling of freedom?' So wrote René Descartes
of Amsterdam in 1628. The same is still true
today, but that doesn't stop a goodly number
of Amsterdam clubbers heading out of town,
particularly for extra-late events or harder
musical styles. But if you're going out of town,
check the website or flyer and make sure to
dress the part. For venues yet further away
from Amsterdam, *see pp266-278.*

Bloemendaal beach cafés

*Beach pavilions, Bloemendaal aan Zee (023 573
2152). NS rail to Haarlem or Zandvoort, then taxi
(€12.50) or Bus 81 Bloemendaal aan Zee.* **Open**
May-Oct times vary. **Admission** free-€5.
No credit cards.

Once a wonderful secret, these beach cafés now lure
the clubbing thousands on weekends. The seven different cafés offer music, fashion and decor. There's
a venue to suit everyone – from kooky Woodstock
to chic Bloomingdale to Ibiza-esque Republiek. The
excellently programmed Beachbop (www.beach
bop.info) sees all the cafés join forces in August and
September to create the biggest beach festival in the
world: there were 20,000 visitors in 2004.

Blijburg

Berthaanstrakade 2004 (416 0330/www.blijburg.nl).
Tram 26. **Open** *Summer* 10am-1am Mon-Thur, Sun;
10am-3am Fri, Sat. *Winter* noon-1am Fri-Sat; 10am-
midnight Sun. **Admission** usually free.

Finally, Amsterdam's very own beach café. This
place is great even when the weather sucks (thanks
to the open fire perhaps?). It's not really a club, more
a restaurant/bar, but it does pull some top names
(like DJ 100% Isis) and throws a couple of super
modern-Woodstock festivals each year. A gem. *See
also p135* **Son of a beach, that's tasty!**

De Hemkade

Hemkade 48, Zaandam (075 614 8154/www.
hemkade.nl). NS rail Zaandam. **Open** 10pm-6am Fri,
Sat. **Admission** €15-€30. **No credit cards**.
De Hemkade, north of Amsterdam, is a huge hall
with adjoining rooms hosting music of the hard and
heavy house/techno variety.

Lexion

Overtoom 65, Westzaan (075 612 3999/0900 235
539 466/www.lexion.nl). NS rail Zaandam. **Open**
10pm-6am Sat. **Admission** €10-€20. **Credit**
AmEx, MC, V.
Freshly refurbished, Lexion expects you to be over
21, sans jeans or sports gear and, if you're male,
accompanied by a lot of laides, please. If you hate
the hoi polloi, take advantage of Lexion's VIP room
for four-150 people. Worth checking out for the
extra-late night events or for hard house and trance.

De Waakzaamheid

Hoogstraat 4, Koog aan de Zaan (075 628 5829/
www.waakzaamheid.com). NS rail Koogzanddijk.
Open varies. **Admission** €10-€20. **No credit**
cards.
Don't believe the doom mongers out there: techno
and hard house are not dead, and here's the proof: a
cosy, little club whose DJ line-up often includes the
top names. The club opens most Saturdays and
some Fridays. There's a separate bar area, and in
warm weather you can sit outside and catch your
breath before returning to the dance frenzy within.

Underground scene

The powers that be have tried to rid the city
of its alternative lifestylers, but underground
culture is still blossoming. However, the best
thing about Amsterdam's underground scene
is that it doesn't exclude ordinary folk: if you're
up for it, they're up for you. Should you visit
around a full moon, or a solstice or equinox
(although the summer equinox is a better
bet for outdoor shindigs than its winter
complement), there'll be some sort of mad
party going on. However, information on these
events can be hard to come by: look for flyers in
coffeeshops, eavesdrop on the conversations of
dreadlocked people, or see www.underwater
amsterdam.com. For more on squats, or erm,
'breeding grounds' *see p206* **Good breeding**.

Arts & Entertainment

Ruigoord

Ruigoord church, Ruigoord 15, Ruigoord (497 5702/ www.ruigoord.nl). Bus 82.

'Empower the Imagination', commands their website. If there's a crusty/shaman/fire-breather hidden deep down inside of you, this long-established artists' colony will bring him out. Their full-moon parties are hard to beat for all-out fun of the appropriately lunatic variety. Ruigoord is about 15km from the centre of Amsterdam and it's home to the wacky Balloon Company crew (who also throw a not-to-be missed bash at the Paradiso once a year in December). *See also p186* for their Landjuweel festival.

Club night organisers

Look out for one-off events organised by the following companies. Flyers can be picked up and tickets bought in the stores listed under **Tickets & information** (*see p235*). The most extensive party listing is to be found in www.partyscene.nl: it's in Dutch, but not impossible to decipher. Free weekly mag *NL20* is also an excellent guide – again, there's no need to be frightened off by the foreign language since most of the club listings (*Nacht* = night) are in English.

Howie says, 'Amsterdam rules!'

You may hear locals complain of how Amsterdam is no longer the magical hub of the clubbing universe that it once was. But a kinetic fiftysomething, known variously as 'Howie Krishna' and the 'The Safe Sex Pope', begs to differ. 'The city hasn't changed. People have. Don't blame this sweet and innocent city for your own troubles! There are just as many parties as before if you actually look for them.' And if there's anyone who should know, it's Howie.

After a career as a child development specialist in the States, he first came to Amsterdam in 1992 to deliver a paper on HIV and child development at the first International AIDs Conference, and then, like many others, ended up staying. 'Moving to Amsterdam at age 42 saved my life. Back home there were only bad memories from that holocaust called AIDS. And after all, travel is the ultimate way to avoid a midlife crisis. Too bad travel's wasted on the young. If I wasn't in a happy relationship, I'd be desperate to get out. Find some more tension to feed off and be forced to wake up...'

Soon after his arrival, he 'got one of the jobs I'm proudest of in my life'. He became a toilet lady at the legendary Roxy club. 'Who knew you could make money from piss? I had already done that whole define-yourself-through-your-job-thing anyway and now I just wanted to *be.*' And 'being' for Howie meant introducing such industry innovations as the Pissenkaart – '10 for the price of 7' – and evolving into a local legend thanks to a rapier wit and an even sassier dress sense.

Even the police hoped to take advantage of his talents. 'Years ago they tried to recruit toilet ladies for their war against hard drugs. During one of their workshops, I told them that I wasn't a drug enforcement agent. If you want me to find drugs then I need a drug poodle!' Sadly, the police failed to embrace Howie and his drug-busting poodle, but what was the cops' loss was the **Supperclub**'s (*see p128*) gain as they were able to recruit Howie to become one of their favoured faces behind the door.

'I am the host and make sure everyone is relaxed. People should just show enthusiasm. Otherwise there are no rules except don't be rude. So if you want be nude, be nude. Or wear a tux. Whatever. Just come and express yourself. The Supperclub is about the relationships between the guests and the staff. And while we provide a lot of the ingredients, it's really all up to you.'

'I'm also sometimes forced to return to my medical roots as a nurse fighting on the front line of that other drug war: the one against too much spacecake. It amazes me how hard soft drugs can be for some people. But I'm still learning. A while back I got into big trouble with a German lady who asked where the ladies room was and I answered "Unisex, unisex" – you know because we have unisex bathrooms at the Supperclub. But she misheard me and started to scream "How dare you? How dare you say U-Need-Sex? What do you mean I need sex?"'

'Amsterdam is one of those gifts that just keeps on opening. OK, there's a lot fewer squats and money these days, but it's still sweeter than almost anywhere else on this planet. Everybody else just keeps on debating about abortion, gay marriage and mixed babies and all that. But here it's a done deal.

'People should simply complain less. Partying, like ageing, is a learned behaviour. You just need to practise to get good at it.' So please people, remember to practise, practise, practise...

Amsterdamaged

www.amsterdamaged.org.
Often hosted by word maestro MC Quest One, their nights are dedicated to next level drum 'n' bass.

B2S

www.b2s.nl.
Hardcore and loud, loud, loud, B2S organises something like four parties a year, including Hard Bass and Decibel Outdoor near Rotterdam.

Beat Club

www.underthehat.net/beatclub.
This more intimate operation, specialising in Northern Soul and '60s Hammond jazz, regularly provides the best place to get-on-down and go-go. The nights are held about once a month in various Amsterdam locations, check the website for details.

Club Risk

www.clubrisk.nl.
Busy in the real house music scene for over a decade, Risk's resident DJs are Eric de Man and Dimitri, with international guests on hand to complete the bill.

Dance Valley

Spaarnwoude Recreation Area (www.dancevalley.nl).
NS rail to Sloterdijk, then free buses to Spaarnwoude.
Dance Valley is the biggest dance festival in the Netherlands today. On a (hopefully fine) Saturday in August 30,000 people gather in a field outside Amsterdam to listen to every imaginable genre supplied by over 100 DJs and bands. *See below* UDC.

Electronation

www.electronation.nl.
Lovers of all things electro, these organisers have become quite a force in recent years pulling names such as Chicks on Speed and even Iggy Pop-dueter Peaches to all the major clubs in town. Quality stuff.

Ex Porn Star

www.expornstar.com.
These ironic sleazefests are held about four times a year and have featured 'acts' such as Ron Jeremy, La Cicciolina and Samantha Fox. The brothers behind it are also minor stars of Dutch TV and masters of hype and controversy. Dress code enforced.

Extrema

www.extrema.nl.
Also active in Ibiza, they throw a few big techno and deep house events each year, including cruises on glamour-boat *Ocean Diva* (www.oceandiva.nl).

Gonzo

www.gonzone.com.
Fantastic costume parties with loads of innovative live acts attracting a wild and creative crowd. More like a weird acid experience than a party.

ID&T

www.id-t.com.
Also behind chic restaurant/bar Cineac and the Bloomingdale beach café, the ID&T crew throw humongous commercial hard house parties like Sensation and Innercity, and the outdoor festival Mysteryland. They pull the cream of DJ royalty like Sven Vath, Paul van Dyk and Ferry Corsten.

Loveboat

www.loveboat2.nl.
Every first Saturday of the month, the Loveboaters go sailing from an Amsterdam dock on the good ship *Ocean Diva,* with top DJs like Dimitri and Pete Heller (UK) spinning the sea-going discs.

Monumental

www.awakenings.nl.
Monumental hosts the popular Awakenings outdoor party on the first Saturday of July, where the DJs play techno until the early hours. There's also usually an indoor (for obvious reasons) winter version.

Opium

www.opium.nl.
This gang throws big, pricey indoor parties a couple of times a year for the in-crowd. Check their site or visit sister-bar the Getaway for hip tips.

Q-dance

www.q-dance.nl.
Any dance event with a 'Q' in it is probably organised by Q-dance – take the huge Houseqlassics and Qontact at the Heineken Music Hall, or Qlub-tempo in De Hemkade (*see p233*). They're also behind Q-beach on Bloemendaal beach.

Salon USSR

www.salonussr.com.
Purportedly an anagram for United Systems of Sentimental Realities, Amsterdam's very own Russian lads about town, Dima and Goldfinger, put on regular undergroundish yet charming events.

UDC

www.udc.nl,www.impulz.nl, www.hqparty.nl.
As you can see from all the websites listed above, the UDC people have their fingers and toes burning in many a clubbing pie: there's the Dance Valley festival, the monthly HQ parties at Melkweg and the Impulz festival for starters. With their glossy flyers/booklets and tickets on sale from Germany to the UK, today it's Europe, tomorrow the world.

Tickets & information

Flyers and club tickets can be acquired at a variety of city venues. Chief among them are **Cyberdog/Clubwear House** (*see p164*), **Conscious Dreams** (*see p162*), Episode (Waterlooplein 1, 320 3000), Zipper (Huidenstraat 7, 623 7302), hardcore and gabber specialist **Midtown** (*see p182*) and underground record store Groove Connection (Sint Nicolaasstraat 41, 624 7234). As well as flyers, a good many of the above shops sell tickets for a variety of events.

Sport & Fitness

Sweat out the night before.

Smaller nations often seem to carry the biggest sporting ambitions and the Netherlands is no exception to that rule. Be it the Olympics, football tournaments, tennis grand slams, or even darkened darts halls with the beer flowing freely and the air thick with cigarette smoke, the country always looks on through its fingers, holding its collective breath and hoping for something special to happen.

Sometimes success is spectacular. Inge de Bruijn and Pieter van den Hoogenband returned from the Athens Olympics as sprint swimming

champions after causing a huge splash against the Americans and Australians. Other contests don't end so happily, as emphasised by the national football team's inability to crack a major tournament since 1988 – perhaps the heaviest Dutch burden of all. Home or away, though, the orange carnival is a scene to behold, and nothing will ever quench the Dutch thirst to be the best. This means that Amsterdam has a world of sporting opportunity at its feet – both for the professional and the casual hobbyist – because every sport has a local home.

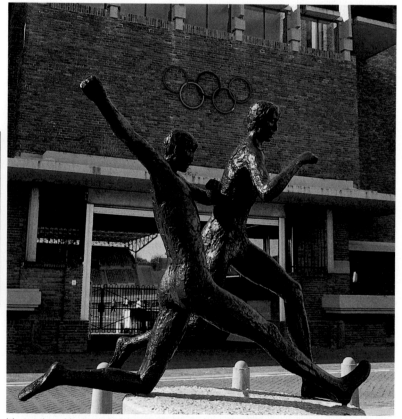

It's not the taking part, it's the winning that counts. The **Olympisch Stadion**. *See p115.*

For information on sport in the city, contact the Municipal Sport and Recreation Department at 552 2490, or see www.sport.amsterdam.nl (mostly in Dutch) for maps, schedules and links for almost every sport imaginable. The *Gouden Gids* ('Yellow Pages', again mostly in Dutch) can also help you find out what's on where.

Museums

Ajax Museum

ArenA Boulevard 29, Bijlmermeer (311 1444/ www.ajax.nl). Metro Bijlmer. **Open** 10am-5pm daily. Opening hours on match days vary. **Admission** *museum* €3.50; *with stadium tour* from €8.50. **Credit** MC, V.

A great outing for football fans of all allegiances, the Ajax Museum covers the rich history of the club, with photographs, memorabilia, trophies and videos documenting their greatest triumphs. The museum is included in the stadium tour (reserve by calling 311 1336, 9am-5.30pm Mon-Fri).

Orange Football Museum

Kalverstraat 236 at Muntplein, Old Centre: New Side (0900-1437/www.supportersclub-oranje.nl). Tram 4, 9, 16, 24, 25. **Open** 11am-5pm Sat, Sun. **Admission** €7; €5 children. **No credit cards. Map** p314 D4.

This fresh and enthusiastic museum has four floors packed with photos, paintings, songs, videos and relics relating to the 'Orange Experience' (ie, the national football team). Obsession at its purest.

Spectator sports

American football

American football continues to gain in popularity thanks to its passion, razzmatazz and cheerleading team. The Admirals are the pro team, while the Amsterdam Crusaders represent the city in the Dutch amateur league, and can be reached on 617 7450 (www.amsterdam-crusaders.nl). Full details of American football are available from governing body AFBN (www.afbn.nl).

Amsterdam Admirals

Amsterdam ArenA, Arena Boulevard 1, Bijlmermeer (465 0550/tickets 465 4545/www.admirals.nl). Metro Strandvliet or Metro/NS rail Bijlmer. **Admission** €10-€40. **Season** Apr-June. **Credit** AmEx, DC, MC, V.

The Amsterdam representatives in NFL Europe celebrated their tenth anniversary in 2004. Despite mediocre results they still draw 20,000 spectators.

Baseball

The Netherlands is currently one of the strongest baseball nations in Europe. Known locally as 'honkbal', international summer competitions such as the Haarlemse

Honkbalweek (023 525 4545/www.honkbal week.nl) have driven up the sport's popularity. Summer 2005 sees the World Championships head to Dutch venues and in 2007 the World Port Tournament returns to Rotterdam.

A surplus of local baseball and softball clubs operate at a variety of levels during the season, which runs from April to October. New players are heartily welcomed. For information contact the KNBSB (030 607 6070/www.knbsb.nl).

Cricket

Prevalent countrywide at an amateur level, Dutch cricket is played with fervour and dedication. There are over 100 men's and women's teams affiliated to the KNCB (0343 492 090/www.kncb.nl), including several clubs in Amsterdam – the biggest of which is the VRA (Volharding RAP Amstels, 641 8525/www. vra.nl). Most clubs have junior, veteran and women's teams, and welcome new players.

Cycling

In a country that seemingly depends on two rusty wheels held together by a pre-War metal frame, you would be forgiven for assuming the Dutch treat bikes merely as a crude method of transportation. But cycling is a serious business and fans of the sport turn out in huge numbers for stage, criterium (road circuit) and one-day road races, plus the track, field, cyclo-cross and mountain biking varieties.

The biggest races are the Amstel Gold around Limburg in mid-April; the popular Acht van Chaam, a 100-kilometre (62-mile) criterium held in Noord Brabant on the first Wednesday after the Tour de France (late July/early

The best Sports

Baseball
Go to bat in a party atmosphere. *See above.*

Football
A sport that unites and divides. *See p238.*

Ice skating
A must when global warming allows. *See p243.*

Road skating
It's that Friday Night Skate feeling. *See p242.*

Saunas
For a more relaxing sweat. *See p242.*

Arts & Entertainment

Klimhal Amsterdam. *See p240.*

August); and the Ronde van Nederland, a six-day race that passes through Amsterdam during late August. For more details, contact the KNWU at Postbus 136, 3440 AC Woerden (0348 484 084, www.knwu.nl).

If you have a racing bike head for Sportpark Sloten. Two cycle clubs are based here: ASC Olympia (617 7510, secretary 617 3057, www.ascolympia.nl), the oldest cycling club in Europe, and WV Amsterdam (secretary 619 3314). There's a 22-kilometre (12-mile) circuit round the park, and the 200-metre (183-yard) track is now a modern velodrome.

For those merely hoping to leave the urban behind and slip quietly into the countryside, head south to Amsterdamse Bos's 50-kilometres (30-miles) of scenic cycle paths. Alternatively, contact the NTFU (Postbus 326, 3900 AH Veenendaal, 0318 581 300, www.ntfu.nl), which offers advice on cycling routes.

Darts

Moves to have darts recognised as an Olympic sport would be supported en masse by the Dutch. Their king of kings, Raymond 'Barney' van Barneveld, has won the Embassy world title four times now, most recently in 2005, and loyal Dutch fans create a sea of orange wherever he plays, as well as flooding to Schiphol to celebrate his successes after international tournaments.

Locally, Amsterdam has around 325 teams affiliated to DORA (408 4184, www.dora.nl), which organises leagues from September to May plus smaller summer competitions in and around the city. It's usually easy to find a venue but if you're serious about darts, try De Vluchtheuvel (Van Woustraat 174, 662 5665, www.cafedevluchtheuvel.nl) or Matchroom Sloten (Slimmeweg 8, 617 7062).

Football

The Dutch turn out in huge numbers when it comes to football. From international matches played out at ArenA to amateur games on wet and cold winter afternoons, there is a devotion that never diminishes through the ups and the downs. And when it comes to Dutch football, it is always a roller-coaster ride, as shown by the agonising semi-final defeat at Euro 2004. The international squad has lacked the killer edge needed to be the very best, and many blame that on the over paid nature of the professional game. However, the fans never stop expecting greatness from the Dutch.

Unfortunately the home leagues don't demand the same level of attention, as there is a huge gap between the big clubs and the smaller ones. After Ajax, PSV and Feyenoord, it can be a long way down, but this doesn't mean the games lack excitement. The Dutch season runs from late August until late May, with a break from Christmas until early February.

To prevent hooliganism 'personal club cards' are necessary for entrance to stadiums, so you cannot turn up without pre-planning. However, most clubs offer allowances for international visitors and temporary memberships can be purchased in advance. Ruling body the KNVB (0900 8075, www.knvb.nl) provides full fixture information. Many games are available via paid-television and following them at a local café can be an exciting alternative.

Ajax

Amsterdam ArenA, Arena Boulevard 29, Bijlmermeer (311 1444/www.ajax.nl). Metro Strandvliet or Metro/NS rail Bijlmer. **Tickets** €15-€40. **Credit** AmEx, DC, MC, V.
The most famous club in the Netherlands, Ajax is renowned worldwide for flair on the field and its excellent youth training programme. Although success is not guaranteed to Ajax, it's never been far away from them either, and the battles between the club and main rivals Feyenoord and PSV are fought out fiercely each season in the gladiatorial ArenA.

Feyenoord

De Kuip, Van Zandvlietplein 3, Rotterdam (010 292 6888/tickets 010 292 3888/www.feyenoord.nl). NS rail Rotterdam Centraal Station, then bus 46. **Tickets** €13.75-€31. **Credit** AmEx, DC, MC, V.

It's impossible to predict how well Rotterdam's favourite sons will perform each year. One season they're invincible, the next they roll over and die by Sinterklaas. However, Rotterdammers are infinitely loyal to everything Feyenoord, so best not to venture south with your shiny new Ajax souvenir shirt.

PSV

Philips Stadium, Frederiklaan 10A, Eindhoven (040 250 5501/tickets 040 250 5505/www.psv.nl). NS rail Eindhoven, then bus 4, 13. **Tickets €17-€42. No credit cards.**
Originally founded in 1913 for employees of industrial giant Philips in Eindhoven, PSV remain one of the key challengers in Dutch football, and in recent years have once again tasted league success.

OTHER TEAMS

When Premier League games are sold out or too costly, try the First Division. Failing that, some of the top amateur clubs in the city – Blauw Wit, DGC and Elinkwijk among them – play decent football. Always keen to promote the future, the Netherlands play host to the FIFA World Youth Championship in summer 2005, which should provide the chance to spot the Arlen Robens and Ruud Gullits of the future.

Hockey

The rest of the world rarely has an opportunity to see just how passionate the Dutch are about (field) hockey, but the 2004 Olympic finals gave at least an inkling of the national passion. There were proud performances on the field and amazing fan backing but, cruelly, both the men's and women's teams lost their finals. However, the results only halted the party briefly. Whereas in football doubt and the memory of past failures disturb the national mentality, the Dutch know when they have great hockey talents and aren't afraid to celebrate the fact. The country boasts the largest number of affiliated teams of any equivalent association in the world, with the 7,000-capacity Wagener Stadium in Amstelveen being used for club games and internationals. The season runs from September until May and details of local teams are available from the KNHB (030 656 6444, www.knhb.nl).

Ever heard of hockey variations like salibandy, innebandy or stockey? These are all legitimate hockey-style games, with some Dutch men's teams competing internationally. For further information, contact the Netherlands Floorball and Unihockey Federation (050 521 21 96, www.nefub.nl).

For hockey of the frozen variety, the Amstel Tijgers and the Amsterdam Bulldogs are the two main local teams. Seasons run from October to February. Contact the NIJB (079 330 5050, www.nijb.nl) for schedule information.

Kaatsen

Although the history of this classical Dutch sport is rooted firmly in the province of Friesland, its branches reach out to include the KC Amsterdam Kaatsclub (0251 205 203, www.kaatsclubamsterdam.nl). Cited as a forerunner to tennis and linked loosely to modern-day handball, two teams of three players battle on a field 60 metres by 32 metres (197 feet by 105 feet) to accumulate *kaatsen*. Contact governing body KNKB (0517 397 300, www.knkb.nl) for details.

Korfball

Developed by an Amsterdam teacher in 1902, korfball is best described as a quirky form of basketball. Its appeal has always been strong in the Netherlands and has grown considerably abroad too. The season has three stages: from September to mid-November and from April to June, games are played outdoors, while from mid-November to March, it heads indoors. Contact the Amsterdam KNKV (030 656 6342, www.noordwest.knkv.nl) for more details.

Motor sport

TT Races

TT Circuit Assen (0592 321 321/www.tt-assen.com/ advance tickets from TT Assen, Postbus 150, 9400 AD Assen, fax 0592 356 911). Exit Assen south off A28, then follow signs. **Date** *Grand Prix late June.* **Tickets €40-€60. No credit cards.**
Book Grand Prix tickets and accommodation early, as this race attracts over 100,000 spectators.

Zandvoort

Circuit Park Zandvoort, Burgermeester Van Alphenstraat 108, Zandvoort (023 574 0750/www. circuit-zandvoort.nl/for tickets www.ticketbox.nl). NS rail Zandvoort. **Tickets €9-€25. No credit cards.**
Only 24 kilometres (15 miles) outside Amsterdam, this former Formula One track has a diverse programme of international races from March to October. Tickets can be bought in advance or on race day.

Rugby

There are over 100 rugby clubs currently competing throughout the the country. Rather unusually, women's rugby is almost as popular as the male game, and there is also a wealth of youth teams. AAC (www.aacrugby.com) in Amsterdam caters for all of the above and welcomes visitors and new players alike. Seasons run from September to May and are interspersed with a selection of tournaments ranging from 15-a-side to beach rugby 7s. Contact the National Rugby Board (480 8100, www.rugby.nl) for schedules.

Arts & Entertainment

Volleyball

Thanks to the growing success of both men's and women's national teams, volleyball's popularity continues to rise in Holland. For details of events and local clubs, contact the national office of NeVoBo (0348 411 994, www.volleybal.nl) or its Amsterdam office (693 6458, www.holland.nevobo.nl). In the summer, players also take to the beaches in pairs. Contact the governing body SIDBC (0900 373 3846, www.beachvolley.nl) for details.

Fitness & leisure

Athletics

The *Trimloopboekje*, published every August, lists all running events in the Netherlands. Major road events in Amsterdam are the Vondelparkloop in January – part of the Rondje Mokum series, which includes nine ten-kilometre races in the city, spread throughout the year; September's Dam tot Damloop from Amsterdam to Zaandam; and the Amsterdam Marathon in October. Further details on athletics and venues in Holland are available from the KNAU (030 608 7300, www.knau.nl).

Badminton

Perhaps in recompense for its recent dip in popularity, Dutch badminton players and sporting facilities are becoming all the more professional. Contact the NBB (030 604 7496, www.badminton.nl) for further information on local clubs and where to play.

Basketball

Although public basketball courts are a rarity, there are several clubs in Amsterdam that welcome players: contact the NBB Amsterdam office (0251 272 417, www.dunk.nl) for details.

Climbing

Yes, the Netherlands is flat. The highest point, Vaalserberg, is only 321 metres (1,053 feet) high. Fortunate, then, that climbing walls are never too far away. See 'Klimmen' in the *Gouden Gids*.

Klimhal Amsterdam

Naritaweg 48 (681 0121/www.klimhalamsterdam.nl). NS Station Sloterdijk. **Open** 5-10.30pm Mon, Tue, Thur; 2-10.30pm Wed; 4-10.30pm Fri; 11am-10.30pm Sat; 9.30am-10.30pm Sun. **Rates** €10.75 adults, €7.25 under-17s. *Rental* set €5.50. **No credit cards.**
The biggest climbing wall in the Netherlands, and easily recognisable by its exterior. It offers great facilities that cater for beginners as well as advanced climbers, with courses running throughout the year.

Golf

While golf isn't a sport that the Dutch have made much of a mark in professionally, it continues to develop as a relaxing game for men, women and children of all backgrounds and levels. You can play at a private club if introduced by a member, or if you belong to a British golf club. The public courses are open to all, with many offering driving ranges and practice holes if you wish to tune up your game. For details, see the *Gouden Gids* or contact the Amsterdam Golf Club (497 7866).

Golfbaan Sloten

Sloterweg 1045, Sloten (614 2402). Bus 145. **Open** *Mid June-mid Aug* 8.30am-dusk daily. *Mid Aug-mid June* 8.30am-6pm Mon-Fri. **Rates** €13-€18. **No credit cards.**
A nine-hole public course, with a driving range and practice green. Booking is advisable on weekends.

De Hoge Dijk

Abcouderstraatweg 46, Zuid-Oost (0294 281 241/www.dehogedijk.nl). Metro Nieuw Gein; from Holendrecht stop, take bus 120, 126 to Abcoude. **Open** dawn-dusk daily. **Rates** *18-hole* €38; €43 weekend. *9-hole* €22; €26 weekend. *Short course* €17; €20 weekend. **Credit** AmEx, DC, MC, V.
A public 18-hole polder course, with a par score of 71 and four par five holes and five par threes to complete the usual glut of par fours. The course is on the edge of Amsterdam and reservations are required.

Health & fitness

Amsterdam has an interesting collection of health clubs thanks to proprietors' willingness to set up shop in the Dutch capital's quirky old houses. Look under 'Fitnesscentra' in the *Gouden Gids* for a full listing. If you are coming for longer, check out Amsterdam's hippest health club, Shape All-In (2e Hugo de Grootstraat 2-6, 684 5857, www.shape-all-in.nl) which, alas, only offers one month minimum memberships. Or there's the University of Amsterdam's Sports Centre (De Boelelaan 46, 301 3535, www.usc.uva.nl), which is open to the public as well as students. It boasts an excellent range of great-value facilities, but long-term membership is necessary.

Barry's Fitness Centre

Lijnbaansgracht 350, Southern Canal Belt (626 1036/www.barrysfitness.nl). Tram 16, 24, 25. **Open** 7am-11pm Mon-Fri; 8am-8pm Sat, Sun. **Admission** €10/day; €25/wk; €60/mth. **No credit cards. Map** p315 E5.
This popular health club earned a very high ranking from *Men's Health* magazine. You'll find free weights and machines, cardiovascular equipment, aerobics, massage and a sauna. There are also individual trainers available by appointment.

The Garden

Jodenbreestraat 158, Jodenbuurt (626 8772/www. thegarden.nl). Tram 9, 14/Metro Waterlooplein. **Open** 9am-11pm Mon, Wed, Fri; noon-11pm Tue; noon-10pm Thur; 9am-4pm Sat, 9am-5pm Sun. **Admission** €9-€12.50/day; €47-€61/mth; €79/10 visits. **No credit cards. Map** p311 E3.

The cheapest all-in-one price in town gives you the choice of high- and low-impact and step aerobics, bodyshape, callisthenics and stretching. Despite the low price, the facilities include a sauna and Turkish bath, with hot whirlpool or cold tubs for afterwards, and free physiotherapy sessions. There's also a sun studio, hairdresser, juice bar and masseur.

Ajax!!!!!!!!!!!!

Amsterdam can be proud of its football team. In the '60s and '70s it was at the vanguard of the total football revolution, and leading the charge was Ajax's greatest son and most famous living Dutchman, Johan Cruijff. But not content with turning the Dutch into European Brazilians, the great man has found new fame for his aphorisms, the product of

base, Ajax is not a particularly Jewish club. Like the club president once said: 'These fans are about as Jewish as I am Chinese.' But there's no denying the influence Jews have had here since the 17th century when Amsterdam was the only city in Europe where Jews were free to settle. Yiddish-related words still pepper Amsterdam slang; even

either Wittgensteinian profundity or a tongue located somewhat further from his brain than his feet. Some examples: 'coincidence is logical', 'every disadvantage has an advantage' and, our favourite, 'you should never cheer before the bear is shot'.

A curious footnote to the Ajax story is how their 'F-side' football hooligans often wear a Cross of David around their neck, call themselves 'Super Jews', wave Israeli flags in the stadium and chant, 'We are the Jews, we are the Jews' (to which their counterparts from the opposing team return with a Hamas-related chant). While originating in 1900 as a middle-class club in Amsterdam East where the many resident Jews provided the fan

the city's nickname, Mokum, which means 'the place'. Sadly, WWII showed another side to how Amsterdam felt about their Jewish neighbours (*see p20*). And when the Nazis asked, Ajax axed all their Jewish members.

So why the Hebraic pride among Ajax hooligans? Well it did all begin as a response to the anti-Semitic chants of hooligans from competing teams (ie, they started it). And it has to be said that many hooligans have little idea that their 'Star of Ajax' is in fact better known as the Star of David. But rest assured: this is all simply a curious footnote to the full Ajax story of football glory. If you do go to see them play, however, it might be best to leave your Palestinian shawl at home.

Horse riding

Horse riding, while obviously difficult in town, is nevertheless fairly accessible. Two large riding centres – De Amsterdamse Manege (643 1342, www.amsterdamse-manege.com) and Nieuw Amstelland Manege (643 2468, www.nieuwamstelland.nl) – both offer rides daily in the sylvan expanses of Amsterdamse Bos for under €20 per hour; lessons are also available for children. For additional options see 'Maneges' in the *Gouden Gids*.

Saunas

Leave your modesty in the changing room: covering up is frowned upon in most places. Unless stated otherwise, saunas are mixed, but most do offer women-only sessions. For squat sauna **Fenomeen**, *see p215*. See also the *Gouden Gids* under 'Saunas'.

Deco Sauna

Herengracht 115, Western Canal Belt (623 8215/ www.saunadeco.nl). Tram 1, 2, 5, 13, 17. **Open** noon-11pm Mon-Sat; 1-6pm Sun. **Admission** from €13.50. **No credit cards. Map** p310 C2.
The most beautiful sauna in town has art deco glass panels and murals. Facilities include a Turkish bath, a Finnish sauna, a cold plunge bath and a solarium. Massages, shiatsu, and skin and beauty care are all available by appointment. Mixed bathing only.

Skateboarding, rollerblading & rollerskating

Amsterdam can be an exciting place if you like to spend your days dashing around on various types of little round wheels. There are plenty of opportunities to wow the onlookers with your skateboard skills on the half-pipe at Museumplein and the parks elsewhere in the city. Rollerblading is also hugely popular as both a sport and a method of transport, with bicycle paths doubling as skating routes. Vondelpark is typically the rollerblader's paradise but if it's dry, also check out the informal and popular tour around Amsterdam that is the **Friday Night Skate** (www.friday nightskate.nl). Protective gear is, of course, strongly encouraged. Consult the *Gouden Gids* under 'Sport en Spelartikelen' for specialist shops and rental locations.

Vondeltuin/Rent A Skate

Vondelpark 7; entrance at Amstelveenseweg, Museum Quarter (664 5091/www.vondeltuin.nl). Tram 1, 2, 3, 5, 6, 12. **Open** *Apr* 11am-9pm daily. *May* 11am-11pm daily. *Jun-Aug* 10am-11pm daily. *Sept* 11am-10pm daily. Closed Oct-Mar. **Rates** from €5 (€20 security deposit + ID). **No credit cards. Map** p314 C6.
There are two branches in Vondelpark: one at the café by Amstelveenseweg, the other at Melkgroothuis.

Get on your bike and ride

In a nation filled with the bicycle obsessed (*see p50*), it's unsurprising that some want to rise above the pack. First stop for a two-wheeler with attitude is the **Chopperdome** (Admiraal de Ruiterweg 343, 421 4864, www.fickser.nl), a feast of dune cruisers and pavement-skimming low-riders in every shade from matt black to baby pink. Prices start from 289 for an 8 Ball low-rider (if you do buy, they can ship abroad) and once you start down the road of custom bikes, you'll be hooked. With your new addiction comes the jargon: ape-hangers, double down forks and sissy bars. The shop also serves as a nerve centre for cruise-ins, races and meets: Cruiser of the Year is a winter contest for the best custom bike – pedalling a thin line between sport and art – but the annual highlight is Choppernation, a big show-off spectacle of drag-racing held each summer in Westerpark. If you fancy just a day of fat-tyred fun, **Mike's Bikes Tours** (*see p284*) rents out funky cruisers from 5 for half a day.

But to look down your nose properly at fellow cyclists, the thing to do is to climb up on a tall bike. These teetering towers of pedal power (at least twice the height of a normal bicycle) emanate from the Tall Bikes Faculty and Art Gallery (Sarphatistraat 143, no phone, www.tallbikes.net), a squat-based hothouse of research and cycle-centred jiggery-pokery. For some tips on how to make your own – and for the schedule of summer bicycle jousting contests held in Vondelpark – check out their website.

If this makes you want to get *really* close to your bike then the logical extension is participation in the Amsterdam leg – as it were – of the World Naked Bike Ride, an international event promoting body-positivity, world peace and, presumably, ultra-soft saddles. If this blows your horn, you can sign up for the next thigh-chafer on the website (www.worldnakedbikeride.org). And if you have a boring bike it hardly matters – it won't be the centre of attention, after all.

Skating

In a land where so much of the earth was once under water, it's no surprise that when the winter freeze occurs the Dutch are fearless on the ice. It's quite common to see a lone skater whooshing back and forth along the narrow canals beside city dykes. Even park ponds become popular skating areas when the conditions are right. Care must always be taken though, as the ice may be weaker than it appears. Before you head out on to a frozen canal check weather reports or ask a local: ice skates are not ideal for swimming.

Recent winters have been warmer, drastically reducing the amount of available skating time. This is highlighted by the absence of the Elfstedentocht – a 200-kilometre (124-mile) race around the towns of Friesland. It's a marathon-style event and hugely popular, with up to 16,000 skaters taking part. Unfortunately it depends on precise ice conditions and the race hasn't been held since 1997 – before that it was 1986. Despite its rarity, many skaters have permanent bookings for local accommodation just in case. If you're feeling tempted to compete, you will require membership of the Elfstedenvereniging Association, great fitness, excellent skates and a lot of patience.

When seeking something more casual, and if the weather isn't doing you any favours, head to the Jaap Edenhal 400-metre (437-yard) ice track at Radioweg 64 (694 9652, www.jaapeden.nl). Contact the KNSB in Amersfoort (0334 892 000, www.knsb.nl) for details on conditions and organised events.

Skiing & snowboarding

There may be no hills in Amsterdam but it is quite easy to spend your time on the slopes. A quick train journey out of the city and the Snow Dome (Jaap Edenweg 10, 0900 3384 8463, www.deuithof.nl) in The Hague offers one of the biggest artificial skiing and snowboarding centres in the country. Equipment hire and lessons are available.

Snooker & carambole

There are several halls in Amsterdam where you can play snooker or pool fairly cheaply. Carambole, played on a table without pockets, is a popular variation of the game. Traditionally, billiards (*biljart*) has been associated with cafés: outside the centre there are many cafés with billiards and pool tables. In town, many bars have pool tables, though they're often scruffy. Check the *Gouden Gids* under 'Biljartzalen' or contact the KNBB (www.knbb.nl).

De Keizer

Keizersgracht 256, Western Canal Belt (623 1586). Tram 13, 14, 17. **Open** 6pm-1am Mon-Fri; 1pm-1am, Sat, Sun. **Rates** €8 pool or snooker table. **No credit cards. Map** p310 C3.

The most civilised club in town has two pro-sized pool tables and seven snooker tables, all in separate rooms. Players can phone orders down to the bar and have drinks or sandwiches sent up.

Snookercentre Bavaria

Van Ostadestraat 97, the Pijp (pool 676 7903/ snooker 676 4059/www.poolensnooker.com). Tram 3, 12, 24, 25. **Open** *Pool* 1pm-1am Mon-Thur, Sun; 1pm-2am Fri, Sat. *Snooker* 2pm-1am Mon-Thur, Sun; 2pm-2am Fri, Sat. **Rates** €7.50/hr pool; €8/hr snooker. **No credit cards. Map** p315 F6.

The Bavaria boasts one carambole table, 26 billiards tables and seven snooker tables, with the first floor a pool hall. Some nights are members only.

Squash

For information on local clubs, phone the Amsterdam Squash Rackets Club on 662 8767 or look in the *Gouden Gids* under 'Squashbanen'.

Squash City

Ketelmakerstraat 6, Westerpark (626 7883/www. squashcity.nl). Bus 18, 22. **Open** 8.45am-midnight Mon; 7am-midnight Tue-Thur; 8.45am-11pm Fri; 8.45am-9pm Sat-Sun. **Rates** €7 before 5pm; €9.50 after 5pm. **Credit** MC, V.

Squash City is an all-round fitness centre, with a focus on squash. There are 12 courts, a sauna, a weights room and two aerobics rooms.

Swimming

Love swimming? It's unfortunate, then, that most Amsterdam hotels barely have space for bedrooms let alone a pool. However, the city is well-equipped with public swimming baths, although they tend to operate programmes that set aside sessions for babies, toddlers, women, families, nude swimmers and length swimmers. Look in the *Gouden Gids* under 'Zwembaden'.

Sloterparkbad (indoor & outdoor)

President Allendelaan 3, West (506 3506/ www.sloterparkbad.nl). Tram 14. **Open** 7am-10pm Mon-Fri; 9am-4pm Sat, Sun. **Admission** from €2.75. **No credit cards.**

The largest swimming complex in the country offers something for everyone. Alongside the 50-metre indoor pool that plays host to international meets, there is an outdoor water park, outdoor pool, and indoor recreational areas simply for fun.

Mirandabad (indoor & outdoor)

De Mirandalaan 9, Zuid (546 4444/www. mirandabad.nl). Tram 25/bus 15, 169. **Open** 7am-10pm Mon-Fri; 10am-5pm Sat, Sun. **Admission** from €3.25. **No credit cards.**

Arts & Entertainment

Where's Steve Redgrave when you need him? Rowing on the **Bosbaan**.

A sub-tropical pool, De Mirandabad is very clean, with a stone beach and a wave machine. It's not ideal for swimming lengths, but there's fun on the water-slide, the whirlpool and outdoor pool (opens 1 May). There are also squash courts and a restaurant.

Zuiderbad (indoor)

Hobbemastraat 26, Museum Quarter (678 1390). Tram 2, 16, 24, 25. **Open** *7am-9pm Mon; 7am-10pm Tue-Fri; 8am-3.30pm Sat; 10am-3.30pm Sun.* **Admission** from €3. **No credit cards.** **Map** p314 D6.
The mosaic-rich Zuiderbad pool was built in 1912. There's nude swimming on Sundays, 4.30-5.30pm.

Table tennis

For details of clubs, contact the Nederlandse Tafeltennis Bond (079 341 4811, www.nttb.nl).

Amsterdam 78

Schoolstraat 2, Museum Quarter (683 7829/www. amsterdam78.nl). Tram 1, 6. **Rates** €7.50/table hire per hour. **No credit cards.**
One of the few places where you can play table tennis. Advance booking is recommended as slots are arranged by age group, with priority to members.

Tennis

For details on competitions – including July's Dutch Open – and clubs, contact the KNLTB (033 454 2600, www.knltb.nl/). For a full listing of tennis courts see the *Gouden Gids* under 'Tennisparken en hallen'.

Amstelpark

Koenenkade 8, Amsterdamse Bos (301 0700/ www.amstelpark.nl). Bus 170, 171, 172 from Amsterdam Centraal Station; 169 from Amstel Station. **Open** *Apr 1-Oct 1 8am-11pm Mon-Fri; 8am-9pm Sat, Sun. Oct 1-Apr 1 8am-midnight Mon-Fri; 8am-11pm Sat, Sun.* **Rates** *Outdoor court €20/hr; indoor €25/hr.* **Credit** AmEx, DC, MC, V.
42 tennis courts: 16 indoor and 26 outdoor playable all year round, and 12 squash courts, a Turkish bath, sauna, swimming pool, a shop and racket hire.

Watersports

The Dutch are good at making do with what they've got, which is one of the reasons why watersports are popular. If you want to go sailing, visit Loosdrecht (25 kilometres/15 miles south-east of Amsterdam) or go to IJsselmeer. Catamarans can be rented in Muiden (20 kilometres/12 miles east of Amsterdam). For details on canoeing, phone the NKB (030 656 6527, www.nkb.nl). Most watersports schools ask for a deposit and ID when you rent a boat.

There are rowing clubs on the Amstel and at the Bosbaan (the former Olympic rowing course) in Amsterdamse Bos. For information call the KNRB on 646 2740, www.knrb.nl.

Gaasperplas Park

Gaasperplas Park, South-East. Metro Gaasperplas/ bus 59, 60, 174. **Open** *24hrs daily.*
This park's large lake is a centre for watersports and windsurfing. There's also a campsite (*see p72*).

Theatre, Comedy & Dance

Diversity rules and nothing is impossible.

Boom Chicago. *See p252*.

Arts & Entertainment

Theatre

Theatre goers rejoice: anything that's any good, and plenty that isn't, finds a place on Amsterdam's liberal stages. And if a traditional theatre can't be found, then performers will adopt and adapt the most outlandish of spaces, all in the effort to provide the audience with an experience that will linger in the memory.

Diversity is the name of the game as dance and theatre groups offer everything from political satire and slapstick about a post-Pim-Fortuyn-society to serious classical drama and ballet. The narrow Nes is the street to explore if you are after more daring works. And rest assured, while there is a lot of Dutch-language theatre, many of the Netherlands' theatre-makers have made their name by being intensely visual. The now venerable

Dogtroep can be considered the spiritual forebears of this particular school of theatre. Seeing themselves more as laboratory than theatre troupe, they have a huge output of sculpted dreamscape happenings rich in colour, technical wizardry, alien costumes and random exploding bits, all of which have evolved organically in response to the performance's site and context – be it Moscow's Red Square or Belgium's highest-security prison. Also keep an eye out for performances by such like-minded artists as Warner&Consorten and Vis a Vis.

Many summer festivals feature happily eccentric artists in a befittingly unique environment. Don't miss the **Over het IJ** festival or **De Parade** (for both, *see p251*). These are best combined with friends, food and booze. Also keep your eye on the **Sugar Factory** (*see p229*), a nightclub that is due to

open mid-2005, offering an international program of 'night theatre'. English-language theatre also has a very happy booker in Xaviera Hollander (673 3934, www.xavierahollander.com/booker; *see p72*), who regularly brings Edinburgh Festival talent to town.

The more commercial productions are often produced by the country's very own theatre tycoon, Joop van den Ende. While most of his touring shows now hit the Carré or De Meervaart, he will have his own huge Vandenende Theater from 2007.

TICKETS AND INFORMATION

For further information about what's on in Amsterdam, call or visit the **Uitburo** on Leidseplein (*see p293* **Tickets please**) or the **Amsterdam Tourist Board** (*see p295*). Browsing through *Uitkrant* will give a sound idea of programming in and around the city.

The three Nes theatres – **De Brakke Grond**, **De Engelenbak** and **Frascati** (*see p247*) – all have a central box office (Nes 45, 626 6866, www.indeNes.nl, 1pm to 7.30pm Mon-Sat). Their own box offices only open after 7.30pm on the night of performances.

Theatres

Amsterdam Marionetten Theater

Nieuwe Jonkerstraat 8, Old Centre: Old Side (620 8027/www.marionettentheater.nl). **Box office** 2hrs before performances; *telephone* 10am-5pm Mon-Fri. **Tickets** €12-€15. **No credit cards. Map** p311 E2.

Ever wanted to see a velvet-clad wooden puppet sing Mozart? Here's your chance. One of the last outposts of an old European tradition, the Amsterdam Marionetten Theater can also provide dinner or high tea for you and your children while you listen to Papageno and company sing *The Magic Flute*. *Thunderbirds* will never seem the same again.

Amsterdam RAI Theater

Europaplein, Zuid (549 1212/www.rai.nl). **Box office** 2hrs before performances. **Tickets** €20-€50. **Credit** AmEx, MC, V.

New for the RAI convention centre (*see p285*): a huge convention hall by day turns into a huge theatre by night and at weekends. There's all the mod-cons you'd expect so that up to 1,750 spectators can enjoy musicals, ballets, concerts, etc…

Azart Ship of Fools

Azartplein, Eastern Docklands (06 1790 0252 mobile/www.azart.org). Tram 10/bus 42/nightbus 79. **Tickets** free-€7. **No credit cards.**

Based upon medieval comic theatre, the Ship of Fools is a theatre company 'living' in a large and happily apocalyptic boat docked amid some decidedly unchaotic architecture. In the summer they put on performances that combine cabaret, over-the-top costumes, music and slapstick. They also host a free nightclub every Friday night from 11pm.

De Balie

Kleine-Gartmanplantsoen 10, Southern Canal Belt (553 5100/www.balie.nl). Tram 1, 2, 5, 6, 7, 10. **Box office** 1-6pm or until start of performance Mon-Fri; 90min before performance Sat, Sun. **Tickets** €5-€8.75. **No credit cards. Map** p314 D5.

Stadsschouwburg. *See p249.*

Theatre, new media, cinema (*see p199*) and literary events sit alongside lectures, debates, discussions and political projects at this cultural centre, which all acts together to influence the local intelligentsia. That, and the café, too. What's culture without cake?

De Brakke Grond
Nes 45, Old Centre: Old Side (622 9014/www.brakke grond.nl). Tram 4, 9, 14, 16, 24, 25. **Box office** see p246. **Tickets** €8-€10. **No credit cards.** **Map** p310 D3.
Belgian culture does stretch beyond beer, and De Brakke Grond is here to prove it. Mind you, some good Belgian beer will go down a treat after your fix of progressive Flemish theatre, and if you're really lucky you might find a Belgian actor joining you in propping up the bar at the adjoining café/restaurant.

De Engelenbak
Nes 71, Old Centre: Old Side (information 626 3644/ www.engelenbak.nl). Tram 4, 9, 14, 16, 24, 25. **Box office** see p246. **Tickets** €8-€10. **No credit cards.** **Map** p310 D3.
The draw here is Open Bak, an open-stage event (Tuesdays at 10.30pm) where anything goes. It's the longest-running theatre programme in the country, where everybody gets their 15 minutes; arrive half an hour early to get a ticket (€6.50). The best amateur groups perform Thursday to Saturday.

Felix Meritis
Keizersgracht 324, Western Canal Belt (623 1311/ www.felixmeritis.nl). Tram 1, 2, 5, 13, 17. **Box office** 9am-7pm Mon-Fri, or until performance; 90min before performance Sat, Sun. **Tickets** prices vary. **No credit cards.** **Map** p314 C4.

The Felix Meritis stages a variety of international dance and theatre performances alongside its programme of discussions, lectures and courses about Europe and other subjects. Worth visiting, if only for the handsome 1787-built surrounds, complete with an excellent café that overlooks the canal.

Frascati
Nes 63, Old Centre: Old Side (751 6400/tickets 626 6866/www.indenes.nl). Tram 4, 9, 14, 16, 24, 25. **Box office** see p246. **Tickets** €8-€10. **No credit cards.** **Map** p310 D3.
A cornerstone of progressive Dutch theatre since the 1960s, Frascati gives promising writers the chance to stage their productions on one of its three stages. Check out the 250 Kuub, a freestyle production that lets actors make up their acts as they go along, albeit within certain constraints. Members of the audience are free to come and go as they please, which is probably just as well, and there's no cover charge. If you want to meet a thespian rather than just see one on stage, the adjoining café, Blincker, has actors in permanent, loquacious residence at its bar.

Gasthuis Werkplaats & Theater
Marius van Bouwdijk Bastiaansestraat 54, entrance opposite 1e Helmerstraat 115, Museum Quarter (616 8942/www.theatergasthuis.nl). Tram 1, 3, 6, 12. **Box office** *Phone* 10am-5pm Mon-Fri. *In person* 1hr before performance. **Tickets** from €8. **No credit cards.** **Map** p309 B6.
Gasthuis emerged from a group of squatters who became critical darlings in just a few years. Even when their home, a former hospital, was threatened with demolition, their activities contributed a great deal towards the building's final salvation. The programme is, as you might expect, mainly youthful and experimental. Some productions are in English; check the website beforehand to make sure .

The best Theatre

Boom Chicago
Good for a laugh; *see p252.*

Muziektheater
Programming and acoustic perfection; *see p254.*

Over het IJ
Spectacle theatre in a post-apocalyptic setting; *see p251.*

Parade
Wacky and wonderful with an old carny vibe; *see p251.*

Stadsschouwburg
All the world has been staged here in gilded and plush surrounds; *see p249.*

Arts & Entertainment

De Kleine Komedie

Amstel 56-58, Southern Canal Belt (624 0534/ www.dekleinekomedie.nl). Tram 4, 9, 14, 16, 24, 25. **Box office** noon-6pm Mon-Sat; noon-performance on performance days. **Tickets** €10-€18. **No credit cards. Map** p311 E3.

Amsterdam's oldest (built in 1786) and one of its most important theatres, De Kleine Komedie is the country's premier cabaret stage, though it also offers a wide range of musical acts. Popular with locals, it's one of the more characterful Amsterdam venues.

Koninklijk Theater Carré

Amstel 115-25, Southern Canal Belt (0900 252 5255 premium rate/www.theatercarre.nl). Tram 4, 6, 7, 10/Metro Weesperplein. **Box office** 4-9pm daily. *Telephone* 9am-9pm daily. **Tickets** €15-€80. **Credit** AmEx, MC, V. **Map** p315 F4.

It's the dream of many to perform in this glamorous space. Formerly home to a circus, and recently refurbished in the grand style, Theater Carré hosts some of the best Dutch cabaret artists and touring shows. However, if mainstream theatre is more your thing, this is the place to come to see and hear Dutch versions of popular, blockbuster musicals like *Mamma Mia!*, *Cats* and *Oliver! See p218.*

Het Compagnietheater

Kloveniersburgwal 50, Old Centre: Old Side (520 5320/www.theatercompagnie.nl). Tram 4, 9, 14, 16, 24, 25. **Box office** 1-5pm Mon-Sat, until 8pm on performance nights. **Performances** 8pm. **Tickets** €12-€16. **No credit cards. Map** p310 D3.

This is the home to De Theatercompagnie, a huge performance ensemble that emerged from the fusion of De Trust and Art & Pro. With Theu Boermans as director, culturally- and politically-aware pieces are being produced that are usually in Dutch. The company also performs in the Rozentheater and in the Stadsschouwburg (*see below and p249*).

Het Rozentheater

Rozengracht 117, the Jordaan (620 7953/ www.rozentheater.nl). Tram 13, 17. **Box office** *Telephone* 1-5pm Mon-Sat, until 8pm on performance nights. *In person* 5pm to start of performance. **Performances** 8.30pm. **Tickets** €7.50-€12.50 **No credit cards. Map** p309 B3.

Ah, politics, don't you just love it? Give with one hand, tax with the other. The Rozentheater paid the penalty last year of dropping its collecting cap in front of the city fathers. In a moment of generosity they agreed to pay for renovating the theatre into a

Dance festivals

In July every year, the Stadsschouwburg (*see p249*) hosts **Julidans** (www.julidans.nl), a month-long showcase of international dance in all the theatres around Leidseplein. The International Concours for Choreographers in Groningen, meanwhile, is a competition event at which prizes are awarded for ensemble choreographies. Details about the various festivals, competitions, performances, courses and workshops are available from the Theater Instituut Nederland (*see p95*).

For details of the **Holland Festival** and **Uitmarkt**, both of which include a number of dance performances worthy of the attention of any dance aficionado in their calendars, *see p186* and *p187* respectively.

Dansweek & Nederlandse Dansdagen

Nederlandse Dansdagen *diverse locations in Maastricht (www.nederlandsedansdagen.nl).* **Date** the first weekend of October.
Dansweek *diverse theatres in the Netherlands (626 2062/www. dansweek.nl).* **Date** 1st wk of Oct.

In October, the Nederlandse Dansdagen in Maastricht forms the official start of the national Dansweek, held in theatres all over the country to promote Dutch dance to a larger audience. During the opening

Nederlandse Dansdagen, the best dance performances from the last theatre season are repeated and the main Dutch dance prizes are presented.

Holland Dance Festival

Nobelstraat 21, The Hague (070 361 6142/information 070 356 1176/ www.hollanddancefestival.com). **Date** biennial; Oct-Nov 2005.

The Holland Dance Festival takes place at three different venues, including The Hague's Lucent Danstheater (*see p254*), and is one of the biggest and most important festivals in the Dutch dance calendar. Many of the world's larger companies are attracted to it and the quality of the work is consistently of the highest standard. Though a variety of Dutch acts usually perform, the Nederlands Dans Theater (*see p255*) is invariably the country's main representative.

Springdance

Postbus 111, 3500 AC Utrecht (030 230 2032/www.springdance.nl). **Date** 14 Apr-24 April 2005; April 2006.

Spring Dance, held annually in Utrecht in late April, attempts to give an overview of recent developments in contemporary dance, film and music from around the world.

Muziektheater. *See p254.*

space suitable for 15- to 30-year-olds. Then, they cut off all funding since, of course, a special youth theatre is not necessary in Amsterdam, thus proving the dictum: he who lives by subsidy shall die by it.

Stadsschouwburg
Leidseplein 26, Southern Canal Belt (624 2311/ www.ssba.nl). Tram 1, 2, 5, 6, 7, 10. **Box office** 10am-6pm or until start of performance Mon-Sat; 90min before start of performance Sun. **Tickets** €11-€21.50. **Credit** AmEx, MC, V. **Map** p314 C5.
The Stadsschouwburg (or Municipal Theatre) is a beautiful and impressive baroque building, built in the traditional horseshoe shape and seating 950. In common with what seems like most of the rest of Amsterdam, it's currently being renovated, which will lead to it linking up with the Melkweg, but productions by Ivo van Hove's Toneelgroep continue in the meantime. It also stages contemporary national and international music, dance and theatre shows.

Theater Bellevue/Nieuwe de la Mar Theater
Theater Bellevue *Leidsekade 90, Southern Canal Belt (530 5301/www.theaterbellevue.nl). Tram 1, 2, 5, 6, 7, 10.* **Box office** 11am-start of performance daily. **Tickets** prices vary. **Credit** AmEx, DC, MC, V. **Map** p314 C5.
Nieuwe de la Mar Theater *Marnixstraat 404, Western Canal Belt (530 5302/www.nieuwe delamartheater.nl). Tram 1, 2, 5, 6, 7, 10.* **Box office** 6pm-start of performance daily. **Tickets** prices vary. **Credit** AmEx, DC, MC, V. **Map** p314 C5.
They may have fused in 1987, but these two theatres close to Leidseplein have distinct histories and specialities. The Theater Bellevue dates from 1840 and presents popular theatre on its three stages: one for modern theatre, dance and music, one devoted to cabaret and a third for literary events. Meanwhile, the Nieuwe de la Mar Theater offers both home-grown and international dance, theatre, cabaret and an increasing number of musical productions. However, as early as late 2005, the theatre entrepreneur Joop van den Ende – the Netherlands' answer to Cameron Mackintosh – may take over these and the adjoining film houses to build a more commercial theatre complex with three stages.

Theater de Cameleon
3e Kostverlorenkade 35, West (489 4656/www. decameleon.nl). Tram 1. **Box office** noon-6pm daily. **Tickets** €5-€15. **No credit cards. Map** p309 A3.
A relatively new theatre in the old western part of town, De Cameleon offers a wide variety of theatre performances (often in English) along with theatre and voice workshops for all ages.

Theater Het Amsterdamse Bos
Amsterdamse Bos, Amstelveen (643 3286/ www.bostheater.nl). Bus 66, 170, 172 , 176, 199. **Performances** *July-Aug* dusk. **Tickets** €7 donation appreciated. **No credit cards.**
What better place to spend a summer evening than picnicking beneath the stars, in the midst of the night-whispering of trees, while a great classical drama is performed before you? No wonder the trees are talking. Get to the Bos early with your hamper, bag a place, settle back, open the wine, and enjoy.

Theater Fabriek Amsterdam
Czaar Peterstraat 213 (522 5260/www.theater fabriekamsterdam.nl). **Box office** open 2hrs before performance. **Performances** times vary. **Tickets** €25-€40. **No credit cards.**

In an old factory that built ship engines, Theater Fabriek organises big musical shows, popular operas and post-Cirque Soleil performances for people who like mixtures of avant-garde and spectacle.

Cultural complexes

Kinetic Noord at the NDSM Shipyard

TT Neveritaweg 15, Noord (330 5480/www. ndsm.nl). Ferry from Centraal Station/bus 35, 94.
NDSM was a shipbuilding yard at the beginning of the last century. Today, in a rather unlikely turn of events, it's become a cultural complex that has yet to be completed, a fact that is actually in step with the changing needs of Amsterdam's vibrant artistic community. Despite not being finished it stages some of the most provocative dance, mime and theatre productions in Amsterdam and its future looks bright. Apart from two stages (one of which is to be made completely of recycled materials), it serves as a 'breeding ground' for artists (*see p206* **Good breeding**). Small-scale workshops and performances are held here almost daily in its labyrinth of studios and performance areas. The large outdoor area, meanwhile, affords spectacular views out over the IJ River and of Amsterdam beyond.

Westergasfabriek

Haarlemmerweg 8-10, West (586 0710/www.wester gasfabriek.com). Tram 10/bus 18, 22.
On the sprawling terrain of the city's century-old former gas works, Westergasfabriek re-opened in 2003 with much fanfare. There were years of renovation, asbestos removal and soil detoxification before this culture and arts complex, complete with acres of water and cypress-accented landscaping, could be finally completed. With a plethora of industrial monuments being re-invented as performance, event and exhibition spaces, Westergasfabriek is quickly evolving into one of the city's premier cultural hubs (as it was through the 1990s when it was an ultra-happening underground squat village). The grounds are a lovely place for wandering around, complete with a range of cafés including the one belonging to cinema Ketelhuis (*see p198*). In short, it's a place well worth keeping your eye on, not only for theatre performances but also sporadic club nights, concerts, art exhibition and festivals. From September 2005, the complex is also likely to be the new home for Cosmic (623 7234, www.cosmictheater.nl), a theatre troupe that has long been addressing the multicultural realities of the modern world.

Theatre festivals

For Robodock, *see p252*.

Boulevard

's Hertogenbosch (073 613 7671/www.bossenova.nl).
Date mid-Aug.
In an effort to promote the arts in the province of Brabant, the Boulevard Festival is an initiative that fills the medieval town of Den Bosch (short for 's Hertogenbosch) with a summer of theatre, dance and children's activities. The main festival venues are tents erected in the square next to St Jan Cathedral, though performances are also staged in theatres and other, more unlikely, locations. Among the companies, both national and international, who've taken part in recent years are Warner & Consorten, Hans Hof Ensemble and Australia's Snuff Puppets.

Kinetic Noord at the NDSM Shipyard.

ITs Festival

Around Amsterdam (530 5566/www.itsfestival.nl).
Date June.
Something of a theatrical talent-spotter's dream, the International Theaterschool Festival is where students from all over the world show what they can do. A mix of cabaret, dance, mime and drama takes place in the Theaterschool (*see p253*) and other venues in town. If you want to meet an actor, head for the ITs lounge in the Theaterschool building.

Noorderzon

Noorderplantsoen Groningen (050 314 02 78/ www.noorderzon.nl). **Date** Aug.
In a lovely park in faraway Groningen (*see p272* **Groningen rock city**), you'll find a crossover festival with theatre, music, radio shows and cabaret. Under the sterling leadership of the appropriately named Briton, Mark Yeoman, a village fete has evolved into a true international meeting place.

Oerol

The whole island of Terschelling (0562 448448/ www.oerol.nl/). **Date** June.
Terschelling, one of five Frisian islands that sit off the north coast of Holland, has a unique landscape of dunes, dykes and woodlands, shaped and shifted by the interaction of wind and man. A popular holiday destination among teenagers and bird lovers (more than half the island is a bird sanctuary), it becomes a bohemian haven during the Oerol festival. Around 200 acts perform: there might be international theatre groups creating their own environments, world music events on the beaches, theatre expeditions through the woods or bicycle tours. There's a regular ferry service to the island.

Over het IJ

NDSM-werf Amsterdam Noord (624 6380/ www.overhetij.nl). **Date** July.
A summer feast of large theatrical projects and avant-garde mayhem, Over het IJ is usually interesting and frequently compelling. The festival of performance, set in the appropriately apocalyptic setting of former shipping yard NDSM (*see p250*), brings together international troupes united by a love of absurdity, spectacle and the latest in multimedia technology. Highly recommended.

Parade

Martin Luther Kingpark, Zuid (033 465 4555/ www.deparade.nl). Tram 25. **Date** Aug.
This unique event has captured the essence of the old circus/sideshow atmosphere that's usually so conspicuously absent at today's commercial fairgrounds. Parade offers a plentiful selection of bizarre shows, many in beautiful circus tents; spread between them are cafés, bars and restaurants, as well as the odd roving performer. The event has now become very popular, and many shows sell out quickly, so it's best to go early, have dinner or a picnic, and book your tickets at the Parade Kiosk for the night (some smaller shows, however, sell their own tickets separately). For more, *see p186*.

Vondelpark Openluchttheater

Vondelpark (673 1499/www.openluchttheater.nl).
Tram 1, 2, 3. **Date** late May-Aug.
Theatrical events have been held in Vondelpark since 1865, and the tradition continues each summer with a variety of free shows. Wednesdays offer a lunchtime concert and a mid-afternoon children's show; Thursday nights find a concert on the band-

stand; there's a theatre show every Friday evening; various events (including another theatre show) take place on Saturdays; and yet more theatrical events and pop concerts are held on Sunday afternoons.

Bookshop

International Theatre & Film Books

Leidseplein 26, in the Stadsschouwburg building, Southern Canal Belt (622 6489/www.theatreand filmbooks.com). Tram 1, 2, 5, 7, 10. **Open** noon-6pm Mon; 10am-6pm Tue, Wed, Fri, Sat; 10am-7pm Thur. **Credit** (min €35) AmEx, DC, MC, V. **Map** p314 C5.
This shop caters to the theatre and film enthusiast, and how. It's the largest store of its kind in Europe, offering everything from books on circuses and musicals to production and technical manuals. There's plenty of stock in English.

Museum

For the **Theater Instituut**, *see p95.*

Comedy

While the Dutch have their own history in hilarity, thanks in large part to their own, very singular, take on the art and practice of cabaret, stand-up comedy is a fairly recent import to the Netherlands in general and Amsterdam in particular. However, it's grown more popular in recent years and the shows usually feature a mix of international and local acts, often performing in English, although it's best to call ahead to check).

Boom Chicago

Leidseplein Theater, Leidseplein 12, Southern Canal Belt (423 0101/www.boomchicago.nl). Tram 1, 2, 5, 6, 7, 10. **Box office** 11am-8.30pm Mon-Thur, Sun; 11am-11.30pm Fri; 11.30am-11pm Sat. **Shows** 8.15pm Mon-Fri, Sun; 7.30pm, 10.45pm Sat. *Heineken Late Nite* 11.30pm Fri. **Tickets** €18-€20. *Heineken Late Nite* €13. **Credit** AmEx, MC, V. **Map** p314 C5.

Robodock

One could describe Robodock as a three-day squatter-organised festival dedicated to 'spectacle theatre'. The organisers themselves have variously called it a 'manifestival', a 'free zone alternation' and an 'unsubsidised international multisubcultural event'. But basically it's a temporary post-apocalyptic village of open spaces, warehouses and haphazard structures that are all bursting with battling robots, orchestral pyrotechnics, brain-melting video projections, frolicking mutants and musical performances. In fact, Robodock can simply be seen as radical recycling taken to the outer limits of guerrilla street theatre.

In any given year, one may encounter the Large Hot Pipe Organ (www.lhpo.nl), a massive MIDI-controlled propane-powered explosion organ with a reputation for breaking all the windows within a one-mile radius. Or one might find hundreds of people with headsets silently grooving to the sounds broadcast by the inspired folks of Silent Disco (www.433fm.com). A particular joy is the reaction of these quiet contemplatives to the sudden appearance of Big Dog Monkey, a five- by ten-metre robotic ape created by the famed American robot-builder Chico MacMurtrie (www.amorphicrobotworks.org). Your timing will really be spot on if you manage to catch the German theatre group Antagon (www.antagon.de) as two girls burst forth from a balloon filled with 70 litres of red

liquid. And if anything becomes too much, you can always opt to sway to more traditional DJs, drink oneself silly, or take a nice relaxing bath in a ten-meter tall 'bathing flat'.

And as wacky as this all sounds, it can be rationalised as a natural progression from a long legacy in Dutch theatre where all things absurd, over-the-top and technologically cutting-edge are embraced. Indeed, the Dutch seem to be enamoured with a unique brand of what can only be called circus-opera, apparently all directed by a hallucinating cartoonist. You will witness only slightly tamer versions of this particular school of performance at more mainstream (although only barely) festivals such as **Parade** and **Over het IJ** (for both, *see p251*). But really the main aim of Robodock is to free theatre from the constraints of a lot of pretentious baggage. The results are a more pure – and purely fun – form of entertainment.

For years, Robodock had its home at the ADM squat (Hornweg 6, 411 0081, www.contrast.org/adm), only to move it once in 2003 to a similarly post-industrial setting in Rotterdam to make a statement against Amsterdam's perceived 'frumpification' of recent years. For its eighth incarnation in 2005, Robodock will hopefully settle in a more permanent home at **NDSM** (*see p250*), where they hope to soon expand to fill ten days. Just keep an eye on that website. *(www.robodock.org).* **Date** late September.

American improv troupe Boom Chicago is one of Amsterdam's biggest success stories. With several different shows running seven nights a week (except Sundays in winter), all in English, the group offers a mix of audience-prompted improvisation and rehearsed sketches. The bar offers cocktails and DJs (*see p148*) and is something of an unofficial meeting point for wayward Americans; a restaurant serves lunch from noon-4pm daily; and they even publish a free magazine for visitors to the city.

Comedy Café Amsterdam
Max Euweplein 43-5, Southern Canal Belt (638 3971/www.comedycafe.nl). Tram 1, 2, 5, 6, 7, 10. **Shows** 9pm Wed-Sun; 9pm, 11.30pm Sat. **Tickets** €5 Wed; €14 Thur-Sat; €11 Sun. **Credit** AmEx, MC, V. **Map** p314 C5.
The Comedy Café has been doing a decent job of bringing the art of stand-up to a wider audience. From Thursday to Saturday, there's a stand-up show in a heady blend of Dutch and English. On Wednesdays, comics try out new material at the venue's open-mic night, while Sunday nights offer improvisation show Off Your Head.

Toomler
Breitnerstraat 2, Zuid (670 7400/www.toomler.nl). Tram 2, 5, 16, 24. **Box office** from 7pm (phone reservations 5-10pm) Tue-Sat. **Shows** 8.30pm. **Tickets** €4-€12.50. **No credit cards.**
Located next to the Hilton, this café has acts four nights a week. Most programming is stand-up in Dutch, but it's the English-language Comedy Train International, in January, July and August, that has come to be most closely associated with the venue.

Dance

Anyone who associates dance with classical ballet, skinny dancers and pink tutus, should visit one of the many other forms being performed in Amsterdam and beyond. The Dutch scene is one of the richest in the world, and dance – together with general 'movement theatre' – is continuing to blossom.

For instance, you can join Italian-Dutch Emio Greco in his unending quest for new movements, or engage in Hungarian-Dutch Krisztina de Châtel's breath-taking dialectical polemic. The two big Dutch companies, **Het Nationale Ballet** in Amsterdam and the **Nederlands Dans Theater** in The Hague, are legendary, with dancers and choreographers the world over seeking some sort of collaboration or employment. A more recent development is skate-, break- and hip hop dance by groups such as Danstheater Aya, Jongerentheater 020, and ISH. And then we certainly can't forget Leine & Roebana, whose dancer Tim Persent won the 2004 Golden Swan, the national prize for best dancer.

Dance lovers will find themselves particularly well catered for in July, when all the theatres around Leidseplein stage the Julidans festival whose sheer diversity is a good reflection of the local scene. Other Amsterdam-based choreographers worth checking out, besides those of the companies listed below, are Hans Hof, Beppie Blankert, Shusaku Takeuchi, Andrea Leine and Harijono Roebana, and Marcello Evelin.

TICKETS AND INFORMATION
Tickets for the majority of performances can be bought at the venues themselves, or from any of the various phone, online or drop-in AUB operations (*see p293* **Tickets please**); their *Uitkrant* offers information on dance in the city.

Venues

Dance is performed at a variety of venues in Amsterdam, the biggest of which are detailed below. Other venues, such as the **Theater Bellevue**, **Stadsschouwburg** (for both, *see p249*), and **Kinetic Noord** (*see p250*) also stage some dance.

DVA-Studio Theatre
Arie Biemondstraat 107b, Museum Quarter (689 1789/www.danswerkplaats.nl). Tram 1, 11. **Open** *By phone* 10am-5pm Mon-Fri. *In person* 7.45pm to performance. **Tickets** €5.50-€7. **No credit cards.**
Danswerkplaats' dance studio has been staging performances once a month, both here and elsewhere in the city or country, since 1993. 'Contemporary Dance in Evolution' is its motto. See website for full details.

Het Veem Theater
Van Diemenstraat 410, Western Docklands (626 9291/www.hetveemtheater.nl). Bus 35. **Box office** *telephone* 10am-4pm on performance days. In person 1hr before performance. **Tickets** €9; €8 try-out; €3.50 theatre students. **No credit cards.**
A homophone for 'fame', Veem occupies the third floor of a renovated warehouse and hosts modern dance and multimedia productions from home and around the world. Performances usually take place at 8.30pm; between October and March, to keep the winter gloom at bay, there's a Sunday slot at 4pm.

Theaterschool
Jodenbreestraat 3, Old Centre: Old Side (527 7700/www.theatreschool.nl/). Tram 4, 9, 14, 16, 24, 25/Metro Waterlooplein. **Box office** times vary. **Tickets** free-€10. **No credit cards. Map** p311 E3.
The International Theaterschool brings together students and teachers from all over the world to learn and create in the fields of dance and theatre. Performances – some of which are announced in *Uitkrant* – vary from studio shots to evening-long events in the Philip Morris Dans Zaal. An annual showcase of talent takes place in June (*see p251*).

KIT Tropentheater

Kleine Zaal Linnaeusstraat 2, Oost; Grote Zaal Mauritskade 63, Oost (568 8500/www.kit.nl/theater). Tram 9, 10, 14. **Box office** noon-6pm, & 1hr before start of performance Mon-Sat. *Phone reservations* 10am-6pm Mon-Fri; noon-6pm Sat. **Tickets** €12-€20. **Credit** MC, V. **Map** p316 H3.

The Tropeninstituut, just by the Tropenmuseum (*see p105*), organises performances in music, dance and, occasionally, theatre that are related to or drawn from various non-Western cultures. The dance programme varies from classical Indian to South African, and from Indonesian to Argentinean.

Melkweg

Lijnbaansgracht 234a, Western Canal Belt (531 8181/www.melkweg.nl). Tram 1, 2, 5, 6, 7, 10. **Box office** 1-5pm Mon-Fri; 4-6pm Sat, Sun; also 7.30pm-start of performance. **Tickets** €5-€10. *Membership* (compulsory) €2.50/mth. **No credit cards.** **Map** p314 C5.

This multidisciplinary venue (*see also p219 and p229*) opened its doors to national and international dance and theatre groups in 1973. For many years the small stage hosted mainly dancers and choreographers at the start of their careers. Its renovated theatre lives up to tradition, as many of the country's hottest new companies perform here – scheduled between the higher-profile mainstays. As befits its reputation for one-stop eclecticism, special focus is placed on multimedia performances.

Muiderpoorttheater

2e Van Swindenstraat 26, Oost (668 1313/www. muiderpoorttheater.nl). Tram 3, 9, 10, 14. **Box office** 1hr before performance. **Performances** usually at 8.30pm. **Tickets** €8. **No credit cards.** **Map** p316 H2.

Muiderpoorttheater is known primarily for its performances by international acts. After a brief renovation during 2003, its fortnightly Mad Sunday programme has resumed, combining music, dance and improvisation. There are plenty of other activities in between those lunatic Sabbaths; check the theatre's website or call for details.

Muziektheater

Amstel 3, Old Centre: Old Side (625 5455/ www.muziektheater.nl). Tram 9, 14/Metro Waterlooplein. **Box office** 10am-6pm or until start of performance Mon-Sat; 11.30am-6pm or until start of performance Sun. **Tickets** €17-€63. **Credit** AmEx, DC, MC, V. **Map** p311 E3.

The Muziektheater is Amsterdam at its most ambitious. This plush, crescent-shaped building, which opened in 1986, has room for 1,596 people and is home to both Het Nationale Ballet (*see p255*) and De Nederlandse Opera (*see p224*), though the stage is also used by visiting companies such as Nederlands Dans Theater (*see p255*), the Royal Ballet and the Martha Graham Company. On top of that, the lobby's panoramic glass walls offer impressive views out over the River Amstel.

Out-of-town venues

Lucent Danstheater

Spuiplein 152, the Hague (070 880 0333/www. ldt.nl). NS rail Den Haag Centraal Station. **Box office** noon-6pm Mon-Sat; 1hr before performance. *Phone reservations* 10am-6pm Mon-Fri; noon-6pm Sat. **Tickets** €14-€30. **Credit** AmEx, DC, MC, V.

The Lucent Danstheater, located in the centre of the Hague, is the wonderful home of the world-famous Nederlands Dans Theater (*see p255*). As well as staging high-quality Dutch productions in both dance and opera, it's also become one of the country's most important venues in which to see touring international dance companies.

Rotterdamse Schouwburg

Schouwburgplein 25, Rotterdam (010 411 8110/ www.schouwburg.rotterdam.nl). NS rail Rotterdam Centraal Station. **Box office** 11am-7pm Mon-Sat. Closed July-mid Aug. **Tickets** €10-€18. **Credit** AmEx, DC, MC, V.

This large, square-shaped theatre opened in 1988 and quickly became known by the waggish moniker Kist van Quist (Quist's Coffin; Mr Quist was its architect). The building hosts a generous variety of classical ballet and modern dance, from both Dutch and international troupes, in its two auditoriums – one has 900 seats, the other 150 seats.

Toneelschuur

Lange Begijnestraat 9, Haarlem (023 517 3910/ www.toneelschuur.nl). NS rail Haarlem Centraal Station. **Box office** 2-9.45pm Mon-Sat; 1.30-9.45pm Sun. **Tickets** €10-€18. **No credit cards.**

With two stages and two cinemas in its hypermodern home, designed by cartoonist Joost Swarte, Haarlem's Toneelschuur has every reason to be proud. Their nationally renowned programme of theatre and modern dance has many Amsterdam culture vultures swooping in specially.

Companies

The following dance companies are all based in Amsterdam. Their performances can be rather sporadic and no one company is necessarily tied to a particular venue. For details on shows, call the numbers listed, check online or pick up a copy of *Uitkrant*.

Dance Company Leine & Roebana

489 3820/www.leineroebana.com.

Harijono Roebana and Andrea Leine's company performs its exciting, inventive modern dance works at various venues across Amsterdam.

Dansgroep Krisztina de Châtel

669 5755/www.dechatel.nl.

Over 25 years, Hungarian Krisztina de Châtel's company has grown into an internationally recognised dance group. Most productions last a whole evening, and combine dance, music and visual art.

Het Internationaal Danstheater
Box office 623 5359/company 623 9112/
www.intdanstheater.nl.
This Amsterdam-based company has been performing since 1961. Their aim is to give traditional
dance a theatrical form without compromising its
music, costumes or choreography. The corps of 24
dancers works with guest choreographers on a regular basis and prides itself on being the only professional dance company that is not bound by a
particular culture or tradition.

Magpie Music Dance Company
616 4794/www.magpiemusicdance.com.
Founded by the marvellously named dancer, Katie
Duck, and her partner in music, Michael Vatcher, in
1994, Magpie uses improvisatory techniques to mix
up a remarkable blend of dance, music and text into
surprising all-night events. While touring extensively, they still manage to maintain a season of performances at the Melkweg (*see p254*).

Het Nationale Ballet
Muziektheater box office 551 8225/
www.het-nationale-ballet.nl.
Amsterdam's premier dance company calls the
Muziektheater its home. Seventy seems to be their
magic number: there are that many productions
each year, performed by a selection of as many
dancers (the largest ensemble to be found anywhere
outside that capital of modern dance, New York).
Toer van Schayk and Rudi van Dantzig have been
instrumental in developing the company's distinc-
tive style. The current repertoire consists of
works written exclusively for Het Nationale Ballet.

Stichting Colors Amsterdam Dance Theatre
662 7310/www.cadt.nl.
This dance troupe aims to make dance as accessible
to the general public as possible without actually
selling out. The productions largely target the young
and address universal human themes: 2003's show,
House of Fear, was particularly well received.

Out of town

The Amsterdam performances by the
companies below are usually held in the
Stadsschouwburg (*see p249*).

Danceworks Rotterdam
010 436 4511/www.danceworksrotterdam.nl.
This ambitious troupe, under the guidance of Ton
Simons and visiting choreographers, combines live-
liness, purity and creative technique to make it a vig-
orous exponent of New York modern dance.

Nederlands Dans Theater
Lucent Danstheater box office 070 880 0333/
070 880 0100/www.ndt.nl.
The Nederlands Dans Theater was founded in 1959
and is the country's most high-profile company.
With two world-famous choreographers leading it –

Jiri Kylian and Hans van Manen – the company has
a firm artistic foundation and has toured the world
extensively. Apart from the main company, it's also
worth looking out for NDt2 for sightings of future
dance stars, since the troupe is made up of novices
and up-and-coming dancers, and NDt3, which offers
an opportunity to see dancers you may have missed
in the past, as it comprises veterans. They usually
perform at the Muziektheater (*see p254*).

RAZ/Hans Tuerlings
013 583 5929/www.raz.nl.
Hans Tuerlings conceives his performances as a nar-
rative without a set story, the meaning conveyed
with nonchalant, yet pure and particularly well-
timed movements. The RAZ company, meanwhile,
consists of a group of international dancers and performs regularly at the Bellevue (*see p249*).

Scapino Ballet
010 414 2414/www.scapinoballet.nl.
Scapino is the oldest dance company in the country
and used to be a little on the stuffy side. But in the
1990s attention shifted from convention to innovation (without losing sight of profits).

Movement theatre groups

Griftheater
419 3088/www.grif.nl.
Griftheater is a giant on the colossus that is the international mime scene. The company produces movement theatre productions for existing theatre spaces
and special locations, and it does this while combining the plastic arts with modern mime.

Courses & workshops

Dansstudio Cascade
Koestraat 5, Old Centre: Old Side (689 0565/
www.createrre.nl/cascade.html). Tram 4, 9, 14,
16, 24/Metro Nieuwmarkt. **Classes** 6-10.30pm
Mon-Fri. **Cost** varies. **Map** p310 D3.
No credit cards.
Modern dance technique, Brazilian capoeira, contact
improvisation and Indonesian Pentjak Silat are all
taught at this studio. Most of the teachers work within the new dance paradigm.

Henny Jurriens Foundation
1e Rozendwarsstraat 10, the Jordaan (412 1510/
http://hjs.nl). Tram 1. **Classes** 9.30am, 11am,
12.30pm Mon-Fri; 11am Sat. **Cost** €7 per class;
€55 for 10 classes. **No credit cards. Map** p309 B3.
The Henny Jurriens Foundation provides open training for professional dancers in both classical and
modern dance techniques throughout the year, with
classes in modern dance taking place at the
Danswerkplaats Amsterdam (*see p253*). The teachers are a mixture of locals and visiting teachers from
abroad, and the foundation also offers workshops.
for which pre-registration is necessary. Telephone
for more information about their programme.

Hotel BELGA

Hartenstraat 8
1016 CB Amsterdam
The Netherlands

Tel: +31 20 624 9080
Fax: +31 20 623 6862
EMail: hotelbelga@zonnet.nl
Website: www.hotelbelga.nl

Hotel Belga is a monumental mansion designed by Rembrandt's frame makers in the 17th century, centrally located in the Jordaan, just **10 minutes'** walk fom **Centraal Railway station** and **2 minutes** from **Dam Square**. With its peaceful atmosphere, our small street is a real oasis in the heart of Amsterdam, surrounded by picturesque canals and close to **historic sights**, **cafes**, **restaurants**, **bars** and **business and conference facilities**, **shopping areas**, one-of-a-kind **boutiques** and all main **public transport links**.

All our rooms come fully equipped with colour TV, direct-dial telephone with wake up service, a personally coded safe and washstand. The majority of our rooms have an en-suite bathroom. Our hearty buffet breakfast will provide you with the energy you need to explore this vibrant city.

With our hospitality and assistance we'll make sure your stay in Amsterdam is a memerable one!

Rates range from

EUR 41 - EUR 81.50
for single rooms

EUR 61.50 - EUR 125
for double/twin rooms

All rates are per night and include VAT and city tax
Larger rooms also available

Trips Out of Town

Features

Introduction

Who says Don Quixote was Spanish? This is the place to tilt at windmills.

Amsterdam is special. But before you can say you've truly visited the Netherlands, you must escape that city's suction and get to 'the real country'. Not that hard: it's a small place where most of the towns and cities worth visiting are under an hour away. Even the country's remotest corners are accessible within a half-day drive or train ride. And be careful not to fall asleep: you might wake up in Belgium or Germany.

TRAVEL INFORMATION

The **Netherlands Board of Tourism** or VVV (Vlietweg 15, 2266 KA Leidschendam, 070 370 5705, www.visitholland.com) can help with general information and accommodation, as can the **Netherlands Reserverings Centrum** (*see p54*). For national transport information and timetables (trains, buses and the Metro), call the **OV Reisinformatie** information line (0900 9292, premium rate); use the website www.ov9292.nl, *see p280*, or you can get train information at www.ns.nl, in Dutch but decipherable.

Getting around

Driving

The Netherlands' road system is extensive, well maintained and clearly signposted. For driving advice and details of the motoring organisation **ANWB**, *see p282*.

Buses & coaches

The national bus service is reasonably priced, but not as easy to negotiate as the railway. For information and timetables, phone **OV Reisinformatie** (*see above*).

Cycling

The Netherlands is flat (though windy); little wonder the bike is the country's favourite mode of transport, *see p50*. Cycle paths are abundant and the ANWB and VVV offices sell cycle maps. Most major railway stations have bike hire depots and offer discounts to rail ticket holders. Road bikes cost around €7 per day and €25 per week; mountain bikes about twice that. Both are in short supply in summer; book at least a day ahead. You'll need proof of identity and a cash deposit (ranging from €50 to €200). For bike hire in Amsterdam, *see p284*.

Rail

Nederlandse Spoorwegen (aka NS, translatable as Netherlands Railway) offers an excellent service in terms of cost, punctuality and cleanliness. Aside from singles and returns, you can also buy family and group passes, tickets that entitle you to unlimited travel on any given day (Dagkaarten), one that also entitles you to use buses, trams and the Metro (OV Dagkaarten) and, for selected places, NS Rail Idee tickets, all-in-one tickets that'll get you to a destination and also include the admission fee to one or more of the local sights. Services are frequent, and reservations are unnecessary.

As a rule, tickets are valid for one day only: if you make a return journey spanning more than one day you need two singles. A weekend return ticket is the exception to the rule: it's valid from Friday night until Sunday night. Credit cards are rarely accepted at ticket offices.

With a rail ticket, you can avail yourself of **Treintaxi**, a special cab that takes you to any destination within a fixed distance of 110 stations for under €5.

DISABLED TRAVELLERS

NS produces a booklet in English called *Rail Travel for the Disabled*, available from all main stations or from the above number. There is disabled access to refreshment rooms and toilets at all stations. For special assistance, call 030 235 7822 at least a day in advance.

Centraal Station Information Desk

Stationsplein 15, Old Centre: New Side (0900 9292/ www.ns.nl). Tram 1, 2, 4, 5, 9, 13, 16, 17, 24, 25. **Open** *Information desk* 6.30am-10pm daily. *Bookings* 24hrs daily. **Credit** MC, V. **Map** p310 D1.

The best Trips

For the future now
Rotterdam. *See p275.*

For inducing dreams
Gouda. *See p259.*

For irritating Sancho Panza
Kinderdijk Windmills. *See p261.*

Excursions in Holland

Worship the Dutch trinity: cheese, tulips and windmills.

Stereotypes: you know you love 'em – especially when they are as charmingly presented as in the Netherlands. And happily, the majority of the most enduring sights are concentrated close to Amsterdam in Noord and Zuid Holland, and are readily accessible by public transport. Besides the tourist boards listed below, there's an excellent new website, www.goudencirkel.nl, that covers the 'golden circle' of towns that surround the lake (and former sea) Ijsselmeer to the north. Note that none of the establishments listed in this chapter takes credit cards.

Charming Clichés

Cheese

Ah, yes. Cheese. It gives you strange dreams, apparently. Not that the 'cheeseheads' – a nickname that dates from medieval times, when the Dutch sported wooden cheese moulds on their heads in battle – seem to mind. When they're not munching it or exporting more than 400,000 tonnes of it every year, they're making a tourist industry of it.

One ritual for both tourists and members of the cheese porters' guild is the **Alkmaar Cheese Market** – the oldest and biggest cheese market in the world – which runs from 10am to noon every Friday between April and mid September. Pristine porters, wearing straw hats with coloured ribbons denoting their competing guilds, weigh the cheeses and carry them on wooden trays hung from their shoulders. Then buyers test a core of cheese from each lot before the ceremony, which takes place at the Waag (weighhouse); here you can also find a variety of craft stalls and a **Cheese Museum**. But Alkmaar has more than cheese on offer and the VVV provides a walking tour of the medieval centre. Among the attractions at the **Biermuseum** is a cellar in which to taste various beers and the **Stedelijk Museum** has impressive art and toy collections.

The Netherlands' famous red-skinned cheese is sold at **Edam**'s cheese market, held every Wednesday in July and August from 10am until noon. Though the town, a prosperous port during the Golden Age, tells many stories through its exquisite façades and bridges, they can't compete with the cheese. In 1840, Edams

De Zaanse Schans. *See p262.*

were used as cannon balls in Uruguay to repel seaborne attackers (imagine the humiliation of dying from a cheese injury). And in 1956 a canned Edam, a relic from a 1912 expedition, was found at the South Pole – and when opened proved to be merely a trifle 'sharp'. The town itself added to this lore in 2003 by building a colossal cheese cathedral from 10,000 of the unholey orbs to raise repair funds for their ancient Grote Kerk (Big Church).

Meanwhile, over in **Gouda**, golden wheels of cheese go on sale at the market every Thursday from 10am in July and August. There are also many thatched-roof *kaasboerderijen* (cheese farms) near Gouda, several of which are on the picturesque River Vlist. See '*kaas te koop*' (cheese for sale) and you may be able to peer behind the scenes as well as buy fresh Gouda.

Still, Gouda does have other things going for it besides the yellow stuff. There are clay pipes and pottery, which can be seen in the **De Moriaan Museum** and an annual pottery festival in the second week of May. Gouda's candles are another classic: 20,000 of them light the square during the Christmas tree ceremony.

Alkmaar Biermuseum

Houttil 1, Alkmaar (072 511 3801/www. biermuseum.nl). **Open** *Apr-Nov* 10am-4pm Tue-Fri; 1-4pm Sat; 1.30-4pm Sun. *Dec-Mar* 1-4pm Tue-Fri; 1-4pm Sat; 1.30-4pm Sun. **Admission** €3; €1.50 concessions.

Alkmaar Cheese Museum

De Waag, Waagplein 2, Alkmaar (072 511 4284/ www.kaasmuseum.nl). **Open** *Apr-Oct* 10am-4pm Mon-Thur, Sat; 9am-4pm Fri. **Admission** €2.50; €1.50 under-11s.

De Moriaan Museum

Westhaven 29, Gouda (0182 588444). **Open** 10am-5pm Mon-Sat; noon-5pm Sun. **Admission** €4; €3 over-65s; free under-18s, MK.

Stedelijk Museum

Canadaplein 1, Alkmaar (072 548 9789/www. stedelijkmuseumalkmaar.nl). **Open** 10am-5pm Tue-Fri; 1pm-5pm Sat, Sun. **Admission** €4; €2 over-65s; free under-18s, MK.

Getting there

Alkmaar

By car 37km (22 miles) north-west. By train direct.

Edam

By car 10km (5 miles) north. By bus 110, 112, 114 from Amsterdam Centraal Station.

Gouda

By car 29km (18 miles) south-west. By train direct.

Tourist information

Alkmaar VVV

Waagplein 2, Alkmaar (072 511 4284/www. vvvweb.nl). **Open** *Apr-Sept* 10am-5.30pm Mon-Wed; 10am-9pm Thur; 9am-6pm Fri; 9.30am-5pm Sat. *Oct-Mar* 10am-5.30pm Mon-Fri; 9.30am-5pm Sat.

Edam VVV

Stadhuis, Damplein 1, Edam (0299 315125/ www.vvv-edam.nl). **Open** *Mid Mar-June, Sept-mid Oct* 10am-5pm Mon-Sat. *July, Aug* 10am-5pm Mon-Sat; 1.30-4.30pm Sun. *Mid Oct-mid Mar* 10am-3pm Mon-Sat.

Floral calendar

For a complete list of all the many flower-related parades and events in the country there's the Dutch-language website www.bloemencorso.pagina.nl.

Spring

The year kicks off in mid to late February with the indoor **Holland Flowers Festival** (0228 511644, www.hollandflowersfestival.nl) in the town of Zwaagdijk-Oost. From late March to late May, the bulb district from Den Helder to Den Haag is carpeted with blooms of the principal crops: daffodils, crocuses, gladioli, hyacinths, narcissi and – of course – tulips. The **Noordwijk-Haarlem Flower Parade** (0252 428237, www.bloemencorso-bollenstreek.nl) takes place on the first Saturday after 19 April, departing from Noordwijk at 9.30am and arriving in Haarlem at 7pm. The floats are on show in Lisse and Hobahohallen for two days prior to the parade.

Summer

In the Hague, the **Japanese garden** at Clingendael is in full flower from early May to mid June, while the **rose garden** in Westbroek Park, containing 350 varieties, bursts into colour during July and August. In late June, there's the **Floralia** exhibition at the Zuider Zee Museum in Enkhuizen. And on the third

weekend in August, it's the **Rijnsburg Parade** (0900 2222 333, www.rijnsburgcorso.nl). The floats leave Rijnsburg at 11am on Saturday, reach Leiden at 1pm and journey to Nordwijk by 4pm, where they show at the Boulevard that evening and the next day.

Autumn

Heather purples the landscape – especially in Veluwe, in the province of Gelderland – during August and September, when greenhouse flowers also emerge. The **Bloemencorso** (0297 325 100, www.bloemencorso aalsmeer.nl, *see p187*), Europe's biggest flower parade, winds from Aalsmeer to Amsterdam and back on the first Saturday in September, with float viewing the day before and after the parade in Aalsmeer. On the fourth Sunday in September, a wackier flower parade takes place in the small West Frisian town of Winkel, the **Bloemencorso Winkel** (no phone, www.bloemencorso.com/winkel), complete with street theatre.

Winter

In November, the public and florists from all over the world view new varieties at the **Professional Flower Exhibition** at Aalsmeer Flower Auction. At Christmas, there's the **Kerstflora** show at Hillegom near Lisse.

Gouda VVV

Markt 27, Gouda (0900 4683 2888 premium rate/www.vvvgouda.nl). **Open** *Apr, May, Sept, Oct* 9am-5pm Mon-Sat. *June-Aug* 9am-5pm Mon-Sat; noon-3pm Sun. *Nov-Mar* 9am-5pm Mon-Fri; 10am-4pm Sat.

Flowers

Want a statistic that boggles the mind? Try this: the Netherlands produces a staggering 70 per cent of the world's commercial flower output, and still has enough left to fill its own markets, botanical gardens, auctions and parades all year round.

The world's biggest flower auction is in the world's biggest trading building (120 football fields' worth, to be precise) in Aalsmeer. The **Verenigde Bloemenveilingen** handles more than 18 million cut flowers and two million pot plants each day, mostly for export. Its unusual sales method gave rise to the phrase 'Dutch auction'. Dealers bid by pushing a button to stop a 'clock' that counts from 100 down to one; thus, the price is lowered – rather than raised – until a buyer is found. Bidders risk either overpaying for the goods or not getting them if time runs out. The best action here is usually before 9am, except on Thursdays.

The 'countdown' bidding style was invented at **Broeker Veiling**, the oldest flower and vegetable auction in the world. It's a bit of a tourist trap, but nonetheless includes a museum of old farming artefacts, and a boat trip.

There have been flowers everywhere at the **Keukenhof Bulb Gardens** since 1949. This former royal 'kitchen garden' dates from the 14th century, and contains 500 types of tulip and over six million bulbs in 1.25 square miles (over three square kilometres). The glass flower pavilion, all 6,500 square metres (70,480 square feet) – is just as interesting. Arrive early, as the gardens get packed. For more on the district's history, visit the **Museum de Zwarte Tulp**.

Broeker Veiling

Museumweg 2, Broek-op-Langerdijk (0226 313807/ www.broekerveiling.nl). **Open** *1 Apr-1 Nov* 10am-5pm Mon-Fri; 11am-5pm Sat, Sun. **Admission** *Auction & museum* €6; €3.50 under-15s. *Auction, museum & boat trip* €9.55; €5.55 under-15s.

Keukenhof Bulb Gardens

Keukenhof, near Lisse (0252 465555/www.keukenhof.nl). **Open** *Mid Mar-mid May* 8am-7.30pm daily (ticket box closes 6pm). **Admission** €12.50; €11.50 over-65s; €5.50 4-11s; free under-4s.

Museum de Zwarte Tulp

Grachtweg 2a, Lisse (0252 417900/www.museumdezwartetulp.nl). **Open** 1-5pm Tue-Sun. **Admission** €3; €2 under-12s.

Verenigde Bloemenveilingen

Legmeerdijk 313, Aalsmeer (0297 392185/ www.bloemenveiling-aalsmeer.nl). **Open** *Apr-Sept* 7am-11am Mon-Fri. **Admission** €4.50; €2.50 under-12s.

Getting there

Aalsmeer

By car 15km (9 miles) south-west. By bus 172 from Amsterdam Centraal Station.

Broek-op-Langerdijk

By car 36km (22 miles) north. By train, Amsterdam Centraal Station to Alkmaar, then bus 155.

Keukenhof/Lisse

By car 27km (17 miles) south-west. By train, Amsterdam Centraal Station to Leiden, then bus 54.

Dutch Traditions

Small historic towns in the Netherlands – the ones that depend on tourism – are expert at capitalising on their traditions, right down to the lace caps, wooden shoes and windmills. Authentic they ain't, but connoisseurs of kitsch should set course for them immediately.

Zuid-Holland & Utrecht

It's hardly catwalk glamour, but a sizeable minority of **Bunschoten-Spakenburg** residents still strut – or, rather, klog – their stuff in traditional dress on midsummer market Wednesdays between mid July and mid August; some older people wear it every day. Costumes are also worn at the summer markets in Hoorn, Medemblik (for both, *see p263*) and Schagen, and on folkloric festival days in Middelburg.

In **Alblasserdam** a posse of 19 **Kinderdijk Windmills**, called a gang, can be seen. Although they were clustered to drain water from reclaimed land, they are now under sail for the benefit of tourists (from 2 to 5pm on Saturdays in July and August, and the first Saturday in May and June). During the second week in September they're illuminated, and a spectacular sight it is; from April to September, you can take a €3 boat trip to see them.

Schoonhoven has been famous since the 17th century for its silversmiths. You can see antique pieces in the **Nederlands Goud-, Zilver- en Klokkenmuseum** and the former synagogue **Edelambachtshuis** (Museum of Antique Silverware). Olivier van Noort, the first Dutchman to sail around the world, and Claes Louwerenz Blom, who, locals believe, introduced the windmill to Spain in 1549, are buried in the 14th-century Bartholomeuskerk, whose tower leans 1.6 metres (five feet). Not buried here is Marrigje Ariens, the last woman to be burned as a witch in the country – but a circle of coloured stones by the city hall marks the spot where she died in 1591.

Dating from the 11th century, **Oudewater** (north of Schoonhoven), once famed for its rope-making, also has a rich witch-hunting past. Reaching its peak in the 1480s, the fashion didn't die out until the beginning of the 17th century, and Oudewater achieved fame for its weighing of suspected witches and warlocks in the **Heksenwaag** (Witches' Weigh House); today, swarms of tourists step on the scales.

Edelambachtshuis

Haven 13, Schoonhoven (0182 382614). **Open** 10am-5pm Tue-Sat. **Admission** €1.

Heksenwaag

Leeuweringerstraat 2, Oudewater (0348 563400/ www.heksenwaag.nl). **Open** Apr-Oct 10am-5pm Tue-Sat; noon-5pm Sun. **Admission** €1.50; €0.75 4-12s; €0.25 over-65s, MK; free under-4s.

Kinderdijk Windmills

Molenkade, Alblasserdam (078 692 1355/www. kinderdijk.nl). **Open** Apr-Sept 9.30am-5.30pm daily. **Admission** €3; €1.80 under-16s, over-65s.

Nederlands Goud-, Zilver- en Klokkenmuseum

Kazerneplein 4, Schoonhoven (0182 385612/ www.ngzkm.nl). **Open** noon-5pm Tue-Sun. **Admission** €4; €2 under-12s.

Getting there

Alblasserdam

By car 55km (34 miles) south-west. By train, Centraal Station to Utrecht, then bus 154.

Bunschoten-Spakenburg

By car 35km (22 miles) south-east. By train, Centraal Station to Amersfoort, then bus 116.

Oudewater

By car 40km (25 miles) south. By train, Centraal Station to Utrecht, then bus 180.

Schoonhoven

By car 50km (31 miles) south. By train, Centraal Station to Utrecht, then bus 195.

Tourist information

Alblasserdam VVV

Cortgene 2, inside City Hall, Alblasserdam (0786 921355). **Open** 9am-4pm Mon-Fri.

Bunschoten-Spakenburg VVV

Oude Schans 90, Spakenburg (0332 982156/ www.vvvspakenburg.nl). **Open** Apr-Sept 1-5pm Mon; 10am-5pm Tue-Fri; 10am-4pm Sat. Oct-Mar 1-5pm Mon-Fri; 10am-3pm Sat.

Oudewater VVV

Kapellestraat 2, Oudewater (0348 564636/www.vvv oudewater.nl). **Open** Apr-end-Sept 10am-4pm Tue-Sat; 11am-3pm Sun. Oct-Mar 10am-1pm Tue-Sat.

Schoonhoven VVV

Stadhuisstraat 1, Schoonhoven (0182 385009/ www.vvvschoonhoven.nl). **Open** May-Sept 1.30-4.30pm Mon; 9am-4.30pm Tue-Fri; 10am-3pm Sat. Oct-Apr 9.30am-4pm Tue-Fri; 10.30am-3pm Sat.

Waterland

Until the IJ Tunnel opened in 1956, the canal-laced peat meadows of Waterland north of Amsterdam were accessible mainly by ferry and steam railway. This isolation preserved much of the area's heritage; for a prime example, look around the old wooden buildings at **Broek in Waterland**. This area is best explored by bike before switching over to a canoe or electric motor boat, both of which can be rented from Zeilkamp Waterland (403 3209, www.kano-electroboot.nl).

Marken, reached via a causeway, was once full of fishermen (some of whom give excellent boat tours), but is now awash with tourists. Visit off-season, however, and you'll likely find it quieter and more authentic than Volendam (*see below*). To protect against flooding, many houses are built on mounds or poles. **Marker Museum** offers a tour of the island's history.

The number of preserved ancient buildings, from Golden Age merchants' houses to the famous herring smokehouses, is what makes **Monnickendam** special. There's also a kitschy collection of music boxes at the Stuttenburgh fish restaurant (Haringburgwal 2-4, 0299 651869), and a fine antique carillon on the bell-tower of the old town hall.

Such was **Volendam**'s success as a fishing village that it's said the town flag was flown at half-mast when the Zuider Zee was enclosed in 1932, cutting off access to the sea. The village's enterprise was soon applied to devising a theme park from its fascinating historic features but, sadly, the cheerily garbed locals can barely be seen for the coachloads of tourists dumped there every day – and invariably pointed to the world's biggest collection of cigar bands (11 million in all) on view at the **Volendams Museum** (Zeestraat 37, 0299 369 258, www.volendams-museum.com).

De Zaanse Schans is not your typical museum village: people still live here. One of the world's first industrial zones, Zaan was once crowded with 800 windmills that powered the production of paint, flour and lumber. Today, amid the gabled green and white houses, attractions include an old-fashioned Albert Heijn store. Nearby in Zaandam, you can visit

Czaar Peterhuisje, the tiny wooden house where Peter the Great stayed in 1697 while he was honing his new ship-building skills.

Czaar Peterhuisje
Het Krimp 23, Zaandam (075 616 0390). **Open** *Apr-Oct* 1-5pm Tue-Sun. *Nov-Apr* 1-5pm Sat, Sun. **Admission** €2; €1 under-12s; free MK.

Marker Museum
Kerkbuurt 44-7, Marken (0299 601514/www.omvis ion.nl/marken). **Open** *Apr-Nov* 10am-5pm Mon-Sat; noon-4pm Sun. **Admission** €1.82; €0.91 under-12s.

De Zaanse Schans
Schansend 1, Information Center Pakhuis Vrede (0756 168218/ www.zaanseschans.nl). **Open** *Apr-Sept* 9am-5pm daily. *Museums* 10am-5pm Tue-Sun. *Shops & windmills* 9am-5pm Tue-Sun. **Admission** free-€10; free-€4 under-13s.

Getting there

Broek in Waterland
By car 10km (6 miles) north-east. By bus 110, 111, 114 or 116 from Amsterdam Centraal Station.

Marken
By car 20km (12 miles) north-east. By bus 111 from Amsterdam Centraal Station to Marken, or 110, 114 or 116 to Monnickendam, then boat to Marken.

Monnickendam
By car 15km (9 miles) north-east. By bus 110, 114 or 116 from Amsterdam Centraal Station.

Volendam
By car 20km (12 miles) north-east. By bus 110 from Amsterdam Centraal Station.

De Zaanse Schans
By car 15km (9 miles) north-west. By train to Koog-Zaandijk. By bus 89 from Marnixstraat.

Tourist information

Volendam VVV
Zeestraat 37, Volendam (0299 363747/www.vvv-volendam.nl). **Open** *Mid Mar-Oct* 10am-5pm daily. *Nov-mid Mar* 10am-3pm Mon-Sat.

Waterland VVV
Nieuwpoortslaan 15, Monnickendam (0299 651998/ www.waterlandinfo.nl). **Open** 9am-5pm Mon-Fri.

Zaandam VVV
Gedempte Gracht 76, Zaandam (0900 400 4040). **Open** noon-5pm Mon; 9am-5pm Tue-Fri; 9am-4pm Sat. It's due to relocate sometime in 2005, so best to call ahead first.

West Friesland

West Friesland faces Friesland across the northern IJsselmeer. Despite being a part of Noord Holland for centuries, it has its own

Flying the flag in **Volendam**. *See p262.*

customs, and fewer visitors than its near-neighbour. One way to get there is to take a train to Enkhuizen, then a boat to Medemblik. From here, take the **Museumstoomtram** (Museum Steam Train) to Hoorn.

The once-powerful fishing and whaling port of **Enkhuizen** has many relics of its past, but most people come here for the **Zuider Zee Museum**. Wander either the indoor Binnenmuseum, which has exhibits on seven centuries of seafaring life around the IJsselmeer, or the open-air Buitenmuseum, a reconstructed village (complete with 'villagers') of 130 authentic late 19th- and early 20th-century buildings transplanted from nearby towns.

The Gothic Bonifaciuskerk and Kasteel Radboud dominate **Medemblik**, a port which dates from the early Middle Ages. The 13th-century castle is smaller than it was when it defended Floris V's realm, but retains its knights' hall and towers. Glassblowers and leatherworkers show off their skills at the Saturday market in July and August. Nearby is the 'long village' of **Twisk**, with its pyramid-roofed farm buildings, and the circular village of **Opperdoes**, built on a mound.

The pretty port of **Hoorn**, which dates from around 1310, grew rich on the Dutch East Indies trade; its success is reflected in its grand and

Trips Out of Town

Make your mark in **Marken**: arrive by boat. *See p262.*

ancient architecture. Local costumes and crafts can be seen at the weekly historic market, Hartje Hoorn (9am-5pm Wednesdays in July and August only). The **Museum van de Twintigste Eeuw** (Museum of the 20th Century), while hardly living up to its name, does have plenty of interest in its exhibits. The **Westfries Museum**, which focuses on art, decor and the region's past, was recently robbed of its major paintings, although, on the plus side, 'disaster tourism' has led to a sharp increase in the number of visitors.

Museum van de Twintigste Eeuw

Bierkade 4, Hoorn (0229 214001/www.museum hoorn.nl). **Open** 10am-5pm Tue-Fri; noon-5pm Sat, Sun. **Admission** €4; €2 4s-16s, concessions.

Museumstoomtram Hoorn-Medemblik

Hoorn-Medemblik; tickets behind the station at Van Dedemstraat 8, Hoorn (0229 214862/www.museum stoomtram.nl), or Hoorn VVV. **Admission** (with boat trip) *Single* €9.80; €7.45 4s-11s. *Return* €16.15; €12.25 4s-11s.

Westfries Museum

Rode Steen 1, Hoorn (0229 280028/www.wfm.nl). **Open** 11am-5pm Mon-Fri; 2-5pm Sat, Sun. **Admission** €2.50; €1.25 4s-16s; free MK.

Zuider Zee Museum

Wierdijk 12-22, Enkhuizen (0228 351111/www. zuiderzeemuseum.nl). **Open** *Nov-Apr* 10am-5pm daily (indoor museum only); *Apr-July, Sept-Nov*
10am-5pm Tue-Sun; *July-Aug* 10am-5pm daily. **Admission** *May-Oct* €10; €7.50 4s-12s. *Nov-Apr* €5.50; €5 4s-12s.

Getting there

Enkhuizen

By car 55km (34 miles) north-east. By train direct from Amsterdam Centraal Station.

Hoorn

By car 35km (22 miles) north-east. By train direct from Amsterdam Centraal Station.

Medemblik

By car 50km (31 miles) north. By train direct from Amsterdam Centraal Station.

Tourist information

Enkhuizen VVV

Tussen Twee Havens 1, Enkhuizen (0228 313 164/ www.vvvweb.nl). **Open** *Apr-Nov* 9am-5pm daily. *Nov-Apr* 1-5pm Mon; 10am-1pm Tue-Fri; 10am-3pm Sat.

Hoorn VVV

Veemarkt 4, Hoorn (072 511 4284/www. vvvweb.nl). **Open** *May-Aug* 1-6pm Mon; 9.30am-6pm Tue, Wed, Fri; 9.30am-9pm Thur; 10.30am-5pm Sat, 1-5pm Sun. *Sept-Apr* 1-5pm Mon; 9.30am-5pm Tue-Sat.

Medemblik VVV

Kaasmarkt 1, Medemblik (072 511 4284). **Open** *Apr-Oct* 9.30am-5pm Mon-Sat.

Ancient Castles

What Amsterdam lacks in palaces and castles, the rest of Holland more than makes up for. The country is studded with 400 castles, and many towns retain large parts of their medieval defences. Some of the best are in the province of **Utrecht**, within half an hour of Amsterdam. Almost 100 of the castles are open for tourists or business conferences: the 15th-century Stayokay Heemskerk, between Haarlem and Alkmaar, has been turned into a hostel (025 123 2288, www.stayokay.com), while the ultimate in power lunches can be had at Château Neercanne in Maastricht (043 325 1359, www.neercanne.nl) or Kasteel Erenstein in Kerkrade (045 546 1333, www.erenstein.com).

The fairy-tale splendour of **De Haar** is appealing but misleading. Though it looks the quintessential medieval castle, it's actually relatively recent. In 1892, the baron who inherited the ruins of De Haar (dating from 1391) re-created the original on a majestic scale, moving the entire village of Haarzuilens 850 metres (259 feet) to make room for Versailles-styled gardens. The lavish interior is visible only on one of the informative guided tours.

Many important events in Dutch history took place in the legendary stronghold **Muiderslot**. This moated castle, situated strategically at the mouth of the River Vecht, was originally built in 1280 for Count Floris V, who was murdered nearby in Muiderberg in 1296. Rebuilt in the 14th century, the fortress has been through many sieges and frequent renovations. The 17th-century furnishings originate from the period of another illustrious occupant, PC Hooft, who entertained in the castle's splendid halls. Between April and October you can take a boat from the dock here to the medieval fort island of Pampus.

The star-shaped stronghold of **Naarden** is not only moated, but has arrowhead-shaped bastions and a very well-preserved fortified town; it was in active service as recently as 1926. All is explained in the **Vestingmuseum**. The fortifications date from 1675, after the inhabitants were massacred by the Duke of Alva's son in 1572; the slaughter is depicted above the door of the Spaanse Huis (Spanish House). Today, however, Naarden is the perfect setting for a leisurely Sunday stroll.

Meandering up the River Vecht into Utrecht, boat passengers can glimpse some of the homes built in the 17th and 18th centuries by rich Amsterdam merchants. Two of the trips afford close-up views of castles, the first stopping on the way back downriver for a one-hour tour of **Slot Zuylen**, a 16th-century castle that was renovated in 1752. The collections of furniture, tapestries and *objets d'art* displayed here gives insight into the lives of the residents. The local tour boat company, **Rondvaartbedrijf Rederij Schuttevaer**, can arrange English guides with advance notice. Another boat drops passengers in the charming town of **Loenen**, which has the restored castle of Loenersloot; sadly, it's not open to the public.

De Haar
Kasteellaan 1, Haarzuilens, Utrecht (030 677 8515/ www.kasteeldehaar.nl). **Open** *End June-Sept* 11am-4pm Mon-Fri; noon-4pm Sat, Sun. *Mid Mar-end June, Oct* noon-3pm Tue-Fri; 1-4pm Sat, Sun. *Jan-mid Mar, Nov* 1-4pm Sat, Sun. *Dec* groups only. *Grounds* 10am-5pm daily. Closed in September and for special events so best to call ahead. **Admission** *Castle & grounds* €7.50; €5 5s-12s (no under-5s); free MK. *Grounds only* €3; €2 5s-12s; free under-5s, MK.

Muiderslot
Herengracht 1, Muiden (0294 261325/www. muiderslot.nl). **Open** *Apr-Oct* 10am-5pm Mon-Fri; 1-5pm Sat, Sun. *Nov-Mar* 1-4pm Sat, Sun (tours on the hour, more frequent Jul-Sep). **Admission** €7; €5 4s-12s, over-65s; free MK.

Rondvaartbedrijf Rederij Schuttevaer
Oudegracht, opposite No.85, Utrecht (030 272 0111/ www.schuttevaer.com). **Times** *June-Sept* half-daytrip to Slot Zuylen 10.30am Tue, 11.30am Thur, returning 4pm. *June-Sept* daytrip to Loenen 10.30am Wed (July, Aug also Fri), returning 6pm. **Tickets** €16.50-€25.25; €15-€21 under-13s; reservations essential.

Vestingmuseum Turfpoortbastion
Westvalstraat 6, Naarden (035 694 5459/ www.vestingmuseum.nl). **Open** *Mar-Oct* 10.30am-5pm Tue-Fri; noon-5pm Sat, Sun. *Nov-Feb* noon-5pm Sun. **Admission** €5; €3-€4 concessions; free under-4s, MK.

Getting there

De Haar
By car 30km (19 miles) south. By train Amsterdam Centraal Station to Utrecht, then bus 127.

Muiderslot
By car 12km (7.5 miles) south-east. By bus 136 from Amstel Station.

Naarden
By car 20km (12 miles) south-east. By train direct from Amsterdam Centraal Station. By bus 136 from Amstel Station.

Tourist information

Naarden VVV
Adriaan Dortsmanplein 1b, Naarden (035 694 2836). **Open** *May-Oct* 10am-5pm Mon-Fri; 10am-3pm Sat. *Nov-Apr* 10am-2pm Mon-Sat.

City Breaks

Check out 'Edge City' and discover that Amsterdam is just another 'burb among many.

Looking to the future in **The Hague**. *See p269.*

The Randstad – or 'Edge City', named for its coastal location on the Netherlands' western edge – is a loop bounded by Amsterdam, Delft, Haarlem, the Hague, Leiden, Rotterdam and Utrecht. In recent years, Gouda (*see p259*) and Dordrecht have come to be considered part of it. Though separately administered and fiercely independent, the individual towns work together for their common good. It's also one of the most densely populated areas in the world: no fewer than 40 per cent of the Dutch population inhabit this urban sprawl.

The road, rail and waterway networks are impressive, and the area's economy is strong. The Randstad's importance is based on several factors: Rotterdam's port; Schiphol Airport; Amsterdam's role as a financial and banking centre; the seats of government and royalty at the Hague; and a huge agricultural belt.

Regarded with a mix of awe, indifference and resentment by the outlying provinces, the Randstad is often accused of monopolising government attention and funds. However, it has no formally defined status and is prone to bitter rivalry between cities and municipalities – Amsterdam and Rotterdam in particular.

There's plenty beyond the Randstad – from the bogs of Drenthe to the frolicsome carnival celebrations of Limburg to the islands of Friesland: Texel and Terschelling can offer the perfect beach-and-dune escape weekend. You will find www.holland.com a handy resource. Hell, even the scenic Belgian towns of Ghent, Bruges and Antwerp are within a two- to three-hour train trip away. Mmmm, beer.

Delft

Imagine a miniaturised Amsterdam – canals reduced to dinky proportions, bridges narrowed down, merchants' houses shrunken – and you have the essence of Delft. However, though it's small and scoffed at for its sleepiness, Delft is a student town with plenty going on.

Everything you're likely to want to see is in the old centre. As soon as you cross the road from the station towards the city centre, you encounter an introduction to Delft's past: a representation of Vermeer's *Milkmaid* in stone.

Delft, though, is of course most famous for its blue and white tiles and pottery, known as Delft Blue (or internationally as Royal Blue). There are still a few factories open to visitors – among them **De Delftse Pauw** and **De Porceleyne Fles** – but for a historical overview of the industry, make for the **Museum Lambert van Meerten**. The huge range of tiles, depicting everything from battling warships to randy rabbits, contrasts dramatically with today's mass-produced trinkets.

Delft was traditionally a centre for trade, producing and exporting butter, cloth, Delft beer – at one point in the past, almost 200 breweries could be found beside its canals – and, later, pottery. Its subsequent loss in trade has been Rotterdam's gain, but the aesthetic benefits can be seen in the city's centuries-old gables, hump-backed bridges and shady canals. To appreciate how little has changed, walk to the end of Oude Delft, the oldest canal in Delft (it narrowly escaped being drained in the 1920s to become a sunken tram-line), cross the busy road to the harbour, and compare the view to Vermeer's *View of Delft*, now on display in the **Mauritshuis** in the Hague (*see p272*).

Delft also has two spectacular churches. The first, the **Nieuwe Kerk** (New Church) contains the mausoleums of lawyer-philosopher Hugo de Groot and William of Orange (alongside his dog, who faithfully followed him to death by refusing food and water). It took almost 15 years to construct and was finished in 1396. Across the Markt is Hendrick de Keyser's 1620 **Stadhuis** (or City Hall); De Keyser also designed Prince William's black and white marble mausoleum. Not to be outdone, the town's other splendid house of worship, the Gothic **Oude Kerk** (c1200), is known as 'Leaning Jan' because its tower stands two metres (over six feet) off-kilter. Art-lovers note that it's the final resting place of Vermeer.

Delft's museums have the air of quiet private residences. **Het Prinsenhof Municipal Museum**, located in the former convent of St Agatha, holds ancient and modern art exhibitions along with displays about Prince William of Orange, who was assassinated here in 1584 by one of many keen to earn the price put on his head by Philip II of Spain during Holland's 80-year fight for independence. The bullet holes are still clearly visible on the stairs.

But though the museums are grand, it's fun to simply stroll around town. The historic centre has more than 600 national monuments

in and around the preserved merchants' houses. Pick up a guide from the VVV and see what the town has to offer: the country's largest military collection at the **Legermuseum** (Army Museum), for example, or western Europe's largest collection of poisonous snakes at **Reptielenzoo Serpo**. One of the many places that may draw you in is the Oostpoort (East Gate), dating from 1394. And while at the VVV, ask if you can visit the Windmill de Roos and the torture chamber in Het Steen, the 13th-century tower of the historic city hall in the market square – they're both fascinating.

De Delftse Pauw

Delftweg 133 (015 212 4920/www.delftsepauw.com). **Open** *Apr-Oct* 9am-4.30pm daily. *Nov-Mar* 9am-4.30pm Mon-Fri; 11am-1pm Sat, Sun. **Admission** free. **Credit** AmEx, DC, MC, V.

Legermuseum

Korte Geer 1 (015 215 0500/www.legermuseum.nl). **Open** 10am-5pm Mon-Fri; noon-5pm Sat, Sun. **Admission** €5; €3 4s-12s; free under-4s, MK. **Credit** MC, V.

Museum Lambert van Meerten

Oude Delft 199 (015 260 2199). **Open** 10am-5pm Tue-Sat; 1-5pm Sun. **Admission** €3.50; €3 12s-16s; free under-12s. **Credit** AmEx, MC, V.

De Porceleyne Fles

Rotterdamseweg 196 (015 251 2030/www.royaldelft.com). **Open** *Apr-Oct* 9am-5pm Mon-Sat; 9.30am-5pm Sun. *Nov-Mar* 9am-5pm Mon-Sat. **Admission** €4. **Credit** AmEx, DC, MC, V.

Het Prinsenhof Municipal Museum

Sint Agathaplein 1 (015 260 2358). **Open** 10am-5pm Tue-Sat; 1-5pm Sun. **Admission** €3.50; €3 12s-16s; free under-12s. **Credit** AmEx, MC, V.

Reptielenzoo Serpo

Stationsplein 8 (015 212 2184/www.serpo.nl). **Open** 10am-6pm Mon-Sat; 1-6pm Sun. **Admission** €6.60; €4.40 4s-12s; free under-4s. **Credit** MC, V.

Where to eat & drink

Though many bars and cafés may appear to outsiders as survivors of a bygone era – white-aproned waiters and high-ceilinged interiors and all – it's the norm in Delft. Other cities offer hot chocolate finished with whipped cream; cafés here use real cream and accompany it with a fancier brand of biscuit.

Don't miss **Kleyweg's Stads Koffyhuis** (Oude Delft 133, 015 212 4625), which has a terrace barge in the summer and serves Knollaert beer, a local brew made to a medieval recipe. **De Wijnhaven** (Wijnhaven 22, 015 214 1460) and **Vlaanderen** (Beestenmarkt 16, 015 213 3311, www.vlaanderen.nl) provide delicious meals and excellent views at good prices.

Where to stay

De Ark (Koornmarkt 65, 015 215 7999, www.deark.nl) is upmarket, with rooms priced from €103.50 for a single and €132 for a double. **De Plataan** (Doelenplein 10, 015 212 6046, www.hoteldeplataan.nl) is more reasonable, costing €85 for a single, €97.50 for a double. Budget travellers should try the campsite at **Delftse Hout** (Korftlaan 5, 015 213 0040, www.delftsehout.nl), where a site for two costs €24. During colder weather, try **De Kok** (Houttuinen 14, 015 212 2125, www. hoteldekok.nl). Singles cost from €66 to €110 and doubles go for €80 to €125.

Getting there

By car

60km (37 miles) south-west on A4, then A13.

By train

1hr from Amsterdam Centraal Station, changing at the Hague if necessary.

Tourist information

Toeristische Informatie Punt (Tourist Information Point)

Hippolytusbuurt 4 (0900 515 1555/www.delft.nl). **Open** *Apr-Oct* 11am-4pm Mon; 9am-6pm Tue-Fri; 10am-5pm Sat; 10am-3pm Sun. *Nov-Mar* 11am-4pm Mon; 10am-4pm Tue-Sat; 10am-3pm Sun.

Haarlem

Lying between Amsterdam and the beaches of Zandvoort and Bloemendaal, Haarlem – a kinder, gentler and older Amsterdam – is a stone's throw from the dunes and the sea, and attracts flocks of beach-going Amsterdammers and Germans every summer. All trace of Haarlem's origins as a tenth-century settlement on a choppy inland sea disappeared with the draining of the Haarlemmermeer in the mid 19th century. But the town hasn't lost its appeal: the historic centre, with its lively main square, canals and some of the country's most charming almshouse courtyards, is beautiful.

To catch up with Haarlem's history, head to **St Bavo's Church**, which dominates the main square. It was built around 1313 but suffered fire damage in 1328; rebuilding and expansion lasted another 150 years. It's surprisingly bright inside: cavernous white transepts stand as high as the nave and are a stunning sight. The floor is made up of 1,350 graves, including one featuring only the word 'Me' and another long enough to hold a famed local giant, plus a dedication to a local midget who died of injuries from a game he himself invented: dwarf-tossing.

Then there's the famed Müller organ (1738): boasting an amazing 5,068 pipes, it's been played by Handel and the young Mozart.

Haarlem's cosy but spacious Grote Markt is one of the loveliest squares in the Netherlands. A few blocks away is the former old men's almshouse and orphanage that currently houses the **Frans Halsmuseum**. Though it holds a magnificent collection of 16th- and 17th-century portraits, still lifes, genre paintings and landscapes, the highlights are eight group portraits of militia companies and regents by Frans Hals (who's buried in St Bavo's). The museum also has collections of period furniture, Haarlem silver and ceramics and an 18th-century apothecary with Delftware pottery. Nearby is **De Hallen**, whose two buildings, the Verweyhal and the Vleeshal, house modern art.

Though it's rather in the shadow of the Frans Halsmuseum, the **Teylers Museum** is also excellent. Founded in 1784, it's the country's oldest museum; fossils and minerals sit beside antique scientific instruments, and there's a superb 16th- to 19th-century collection of 10,000 drawings by masters including Rembrandt, Michelangelo and Raphael. However, Haarlem is more than just a city of nostalgia: it's one of vision. Local illustrator/cartoonist Joost Swarte designed the Toneelschuur theatre in the town.

Frans Halsmuseum

Groot Heiligland 62 (023 511 5775/www.frans halsmuseum.nl). **Open** 11am-5pm Mon-Sat; noon-5pm Sun. **Admission** €7; free under-18s, MK. **No credit cards.**

De Hallen

Grote Markt 16 (023 5115775/www.dehallen.com). **Open** 11am-5pm Mon-Sat; noon-5pm Sun. **Admission** €5; free under-18s, MK. **No credit cards.**

Teylers Museum

Spaarne 16 (023 531 9010/www.teylersmuseum.nl). **Open** 10am-5pm Tue-Sat; noon-5pm Sun. **Admission** €5.50; €1 5s-18s; free under-5s, MK. **No credit cards.**

Where to eat & drink

There's plenty to choose from on Grote Markt but cosier is the nearby **Jacobus Pieck Drink & Eetlokaal** (Warmoesstraat 18, 023 532 6144), while the riverside **Eclectic Bar Restaurant Willendorf** (Bakenessergracht 109, 023 531 1970, www.willendorf.nl) is a hip space with regular DJs. At **Hotspot Lambermons** (Spaarne 96, 023 542 7804, www.lambermons.nl) you get a different French-inspired €8.75 course put in front of you every half hour from 6.30pm to 11pm; stay until you're full. For steak that you will remember for the rest of your life, go to **Wilma & Alberts** (Oude Groenmarkt 6, 532 1256, www.wilma-alberts.nl). For some of the best Indonesian in the country, head to **De Rijsttafel** (Kruisweg 70-d, 023 534 3456) and order the *rendang*.

If you're into wooden panelling, leather wallpaper, chaotic conviviality and infinite beer choices, there's **In Den Uiver** (Riviervismarkt 13, 023 532 5399, www.indenuiver.nl). For bands and/or DJs, check out **Patronaat** (Oostvest 54, 023 532 6010, www.patronaat.nl), Haarlem's equivalent to the Melkweg, which is moving to Zijlsingel 2 in autumn 2005. **Nightclub Stalker** (Kromme Elleeboogsteeg 20, 023 531 4652, www.clubstalker.nl) specialises in upfront dance music.

Where to stay

Carlton Square Hotel (Baan 7, 023 531 9091, www.carlton.nl) is posh, with rooms for €165 to €205. For a real splurge, book the €535 suite at **Park Tower Suite** (Florapark 13, 023 534 7773, www.parktowersuite.nl). The **Carillon** (Grote Markt 27, 023 531 0591, www.hotel carillon.com) has doubles for €58-€76, while outside the centre, **Stayokay Haarlem** (Jan Gijzenpad 3, 023 537 3793, www.stayokay.com) offers B&B for €21 to €25.25.

Getting there

By car

10km (6 miles) west on A5.

By train

15min, direct from Amsterdam Centraal Station.

Tourist information

VVV

Stationsplein 1 (0900 616 1600 premium rate/ www.vvvzk.nl). **Open** *Oct-Mar* 9.30am-5pm Mon-Fri; 10am-3pm Sat. *Apr-Sept* 9.30am-5pm Mon-Fri; 9.30am-3pm Sat.

The Hague

While never officially a city – in days of yore, the powers that be did not want to offend its more ancient neighbours, Leiden and Utrecht – the Hague (aka Den Haag) is the nation's power hub and centre for international justice. It began life as the hunting ground of the Counts of Holland before being officially founded in 1248, when William II built a castle on the site of the present parliament buildings, the **Binnenhof**. It was here that the De Witt brothers were lynched after being accused of conspiring to kill William of Orange; they were brutalised nearby in what is now the most

evocatively grim torture museum in the country: **Gevangenpoort**.

Queen Beatrix arrives at the Binnenhof in a golden coach every Prinsjesdag (third Tuesday in September) for the annual state opening of parliament. Guided tours are organised daily to the Knights' Hall, where the ceremony takes place. The **Mauritshuis**, a former regal home, is open to the public with one of the most famous collections in the world: works by the likes of Rubens, Rembrandt and Vermeer.

The Hague's city centre is lively, with a good selection of shops lining the streets and squares around the palaces and along Denneweg. The city is also one of the greenest in Europe, and has a number of lovely parks. Clingendael has a Japanese garden; Meijendael, further out, is part of an ancient forest; and the Scheveningse Bosje is big enough to occupy an entire day. Between the Bosje and the city is Vredes Paleis (the Peace Palace), a gift from Andrew Carnegie that is now the UN's Court of International Justice. (Meanwhile, on Churchillplein, the International Criminal Tribunal is the setting for Slobodan Milosevic's ongoing sulky theatrics.)

Beyond Scheveningse Bosje is Scheveningen, a former fishing village and now a resort. The highlight is the Steigenberger Kurhaus Hotel: built in 1887, it's a legacy of Scheveningen's halcyon days as a bathing place for European high society. The town's history as a spa has been resurrected with the opening of Kuur Thermen Vitalizee (Strandweg 13F, 070 416 6500, www.vitalizee.nl), a spa bath that offers a range of treatments. Also here is the 'Sculptures by the Sea' exhibition, a multi-dimensional collection of statues at the **Museum Beelden aan Zee**. The renovated **Panorama Mesdag** houses not only the largest painting in the country (120 metres, 400 feet, in circumference), from which it takes its name, but also works from the Hague (mainly seascapes) and Barbizon (peasant life and landscape) schools.

None, though, is worth as much as *Victory Boogie Woogie*, Piet Mondriaan's last work, which sold for a cool ƒ80 million (€36 million) in 1998. It's now on display at the **Haags Gemeentemuseum**, which holds the world's largest collections of works by Mondriaan as well as many works of paradoxical art by MC Escher in newly restored buildings. The Haags Gemeentemuseum is next door to the excellent Museum of Photography (Stadhouderslaan 43, 070 338 1144, www.fotomuseumdenhaag.nl) and linked to the Museon, an excellent science museum that induces wonder in both kids and adults, and the Omniversum IMAX Theatre, a state-of-the-art planetarium. The Gemeente's brand new sister museum, **Escher in het Paleis** on Lange Voorhout, is filled with further

Groningen rock city

The northern capital of Groningen is the furthest one can get from Amsterdam without actually leaving the country. Often called the 'Amsterdam of the North', it packs a similarly contemporary punch while still retaining plenty of old world charm.

With half of its population of 178,000 under 35, and with over 36,000 students, Groningen is a city that rocks – especially at night. But it's not just another student town. It's been around since BC became AD, when it was quick to evolve into a bustling walled city with a major grain market and high stakes in sugar and shipbuilding. And its history as a natural gas reserve is reflected in the Aardgas Headquarters (Concourslaan 17), a classic of organic architecture. In fact, one is greeted by several architectural classics as soon as you arrive. Not only is Centraal Station the most beautiful in the country, it is also across the street from **Groninger Museum**, the funkiest art gallery on the planet – even Bilbao's Guggenheim looks prefabricated in comparison. Also nearby is an early work by architect superstar, Rem Koolhaas: the *Urinoir* featuring stainless steel toilets and the homoerotic photography of Erwin Olaf. It's located on Kleine Der A in the very scenic Westhaven district which is also home to the brand new **Stripmuseum** (Comics Museum), that covers everything from Asterix to Zorro.

If you proceed up Folkingestraat you'll soon find yourself at Vismarkt and Grote Markt. The latter's image-defining church and tower is the Martinikerk and Martinitoren. Historians claim that they are named after St Martin rather than the cocktail. But suspicions rise, given that the surrounding square kilometre has the highest density of alcohol licences in the country. And if that isn't enough, another nearby church, Jozefkerk, has a tower nicknamed the 'Drunken Man's Tower' since each of its six faces has a clock and therefore at least two are always visible, creating a sense of double vision. Yep: it's a student town alright.

Groningen also provides the perfect base to explore nature. There's much within cycling distance – for instance the moated manors of Menkemaborg or Fraeylemaborg – but you may also choose to take a bus to the nearby port towns, whence ferries go to the Wadden islands of Schiermonnikoog and Ameland. (Incidentally, while both islands are part of

Friesland, Schiermonnikoog is due to enter Groningen province within the next ten-to twenty years as the dunes that make up its surface are blown eastward.) The VVV will bring you up to speed on any of these ideas and many other possibilities too.

Groninger Museum

Museumeiland 1 (050 366 6555/www. groninger-museum.nl). **Open** 10am-5pm Tue-Sun. **Admission** 7; 6 over-65s; 3.50 12-16s; 1.50 6-11s; free under-6s, MK. **Credit** AmEx, DC, MC, V.

Nederlands Stripmuseum

Westerhaven 71 (050 317 8470/www. stripmuseumgroningen.nl). **Open** 10am-5pm Tue-Sun. **Admission** 7; 5.75 4-11s; free under-4s. **No credit cards**.

Where to eat & drink

Welcome to the city that rocks! The always hip and happening **Vera** (Oosterstraat 44, 050 313 4681, www.vera-groningen.nl) acts as ground zero during the Eurosonic/ Noorderslag festival (www.noorderslag.nl) every January when 150 of the more happening bands and DJs come together in an almighty sound clash. Even the posh and 'high cultural' **De Oosterpoort** (Trompsingel 27, 050 368 0368, www.de-oosterpoort.nl) gets in on the decks action. Groningen also hosts an excellent theatre festival: **Noorderzonfestival** (*see p251*).

For drinking all year round, there are two main strips. Peperstraat is middle-of-the-road but has a couple of stand-outs for live music: **Jazzcafe de Spieghel** (Peperstraat 11, 050 528 0588, www.jazzcafedespieghel.nl) features jazz of both the trad and acid varieties, while **De Kar** (Peperstraat 15, 050 312 6215, www.dekar.nl) offers everything from lounge to hardcore punk. But if you have to choose between the two strips, Poelestraat is the trendier alternative. There's the happening **Club 29** (Poelstraat 29, 050 360 0024, www.club29.nl), whose DJs attract the city's hipper students and creatives, and the arthouse **Filmtheater & Café Images** (Poelstraat 30, 312 0433, www.images.nu).

For unpretentious swilling, check out **Mulder** (Grote Kromme Elleboog 22, 050 314 1469), the classic brown bar **De Drie Uiltjes** (Oude Ebbingestraat 47, 050 318 9147), or

the equally cosy **'t Proeflokaal** (Zuiderdiep 62, 050 313 6183) whose booze menu also embraces locally brewed *jenevers*. For some all night drinking in the city's own Red Light District, check out the sleazy area around **Benzinebar** (Hoekstraat 44, no phone), which is only open midnight Saturday until 10am Sunday (handy if you want to save on a hotel bill). A mellower proposition is coffeeshop **Metamorfose** (Oude Boteringestraat 53, 050 314 4460).

For eats, **'t Feithhuis** (Marinikerkhof 10, 050 313 5335, www.feithhuis.nl) is open for all the meals of the day, while **De Drie Gezusters** (Grote Markt 36, 050 313 4101) also offers reasonable food. Many consider the Italian-inspired **Groninger Museum Restaurant** (*see above*, book via 050 360 3665) to be the best place to eat in town. But for a real treat, book a table far in advance for the French-inspired **Onder de Linden** (Burgemeester van Barneveldweg 3, Aduard, 050 403 1406, www.slenema.nl), which is located in a 1733-built organic farm 10 kilometres outside town.

Check www.specialbite.com for the latest on the local culinary scene. And don't forget to order something with mustard, since Groningen is famous for it. *Bon appetit.*

Where to stay

For a bit of class, you can't go wrong with the revamped **Hotel de Ville** (Oude Boteringestraat 43-5, 050 318 1777, www.deville.nl), where doubles range from 115 to 275. Meanwhile the equally central **Martini Budget Hotel** (Gedempte Zuiderdiep 8, 050 312 9199, www.martinihotel.nl) offers doubles from 72.50/night and even better deals if you book. For the cheapest, check out **Simplon Youthhotel** (Boterdiep 73-2, 050 313 5221, www.simplonjongerenhotel.nl).

Getting there

By car
190 km (120 miles) on A7.

By train
2hr from Amsterdam Centraal Station, direct.

Tourist Information

VVV
Grote Markt 25 (0900 202 3050 premium/ www.vvvgroningen.nl). Open July-Aug 9am-6pm Mon-Fri; 10am-5pm Sat; 11am-3pm Sun. Sept-June 9am-6pm Mon-Fri; 10am-5pm Sat.

Trips Out of Town

examples of the mind-melting art of MC Escher and supplemented with much interactive multimedia. Should your stay in the country consist of only one afternoon one way of seeing everything is by visiting **Madurodam**, an insanely detailed miniature city that dishes up every Dutch cliché in the book. Windmills turn, ships sail and trains speed around on the world's largest model railway. But if you visit on a summer's evening, when the models are lit from within by 50,000 miniature lamps, then Madurodam leaves behind ironic appreciation and becomes a place of child-like wonder.

Binnenhof

Binnenhof 8a (070 364 6144/www.binnenhof bezoek.nl). **Open** 10am-4pm Mon-Sat. **Admission** €4-€6; €3-€5 under-13s. **No credit cards.**

Escher in Het Paleis

Lange Voorhout 74 (070 42 77730/www.escherinhet paleis.nl). **Open** 11am-5pm Tue-Sun. **Admission** €7.50; €5 7s-15s; free under-7s, MK. **No credit cards.**

Gemeentemuseum

Stadhouderslaan 41 (070 338 1111/www.gemeente museum.nl). **Open** 11am-5pm Tue-Sun. **Admission** €7.50; free under-18s, MK. **No credit cards.**

Gevangenpoort Museum

Buitenhof 33 (070 346 0861/www.gevangenpoort.nl). **Open** *Tours* hourly from 11am-4pm Tue-Fri; noon-4pm Sat, Sun. **Admission** €3.60; €2.70 under-13s. **No credit cards.**

Madurodam

George Maduroplein 1 (070 355 3900/www. madurodam.nl). **Open** *Mid Mar-June* 9am-8pm daily. *July, Aug* 9am-10pm daily. *Sept-mid Mar* 9am-6pm daily. **Admission** €12; €11 over-60s; €8.75 3s-11s; free under-3s. **No credit cards.**

Mauritshuis

Korte Vijverberg 8 (070 302 3456/www.maurits huis.nl). **Open** *1 Apr-1 Sept* 10am-5pm Mon-Sat; 11am-5pm Sun; *2 Sept-31 Mar* 10am-5pm Tue-Sat; 11am-5pm Sun. **Admission** €7.50; free under-18s, MK. **No credit cards.**

Museum Beelden aan Zee

Harteveltstraat 1 (070 358 5857/www.beelden aanzee.nl). **Open** 11am-5pm Tue-Sun. **Admission** €6; €3 5s-12s; free under-5s. **No credit cards.**

Panorama Mesdag

Zeestraat 65 (070 364 4544/www.mesdag.nl). **Open** 10am-5pm Mon-Sat; noon-5pm Sun. **Admission** €4; €3 over-65s; €2 3s-13s; free under-3s. **No credit cards.**

Where to eat & drink

Juliana's (Plaats 11, 070 365 0235, www. julianas.nl) is where the beautiful people dine, whereas **De Klap** (Koningin Emmakade 118A,

070 345 4060, www.klap.nl) is more down-to-earth. For inspired Indonesian cuisine try **Brasserie Surakarta** (Prinsestraat 13, 070 346 6999, www.surakarta.nl); while for Indian food there's **Bogor** (Van Swietenstraat 2, 070 346 1628). In the catacombs underneath the old City Hall, **Catacomben** (Grote Halstraat 3, 070 302 3060, www.catacomben.nl) offers reasonably priced Caribbean, French, Asian and Middle Eastern eats, while **WOX** (Buitenhof 36, 070 365 3754) is the latest chic dining address.

Alternative and dance music fans should check out the roster at **Paard van Troje** (Prinsegracht 12, 070 360 1838, www.paard.nl). Meanwhile, beer fans should try **De Paas** (Dunne Bierkade 16a, 070 360 0019, www. depaas.nl). The living-room feel at **Murphy's Law** (Dr Kuyperstraat 7, 070 427 2507, www.murphysjazz.nl) attracts a friendly if unlikely mix of alternative folk and drunk diplomats. Meanwhile **Fab** (Spui 185, 363 0880, www.fab.nl) is, well, fab. **Silly Symphonies** (Grote Markt 25, 070 312 3610, www.silly symphonies.nl) appeals to the clubber/drinker/eater, while for coffee connoisseurs there's **Cremers** (Prinsestraat 84, 070 346 2346, www.cafecremers.nl).

Where to stay

Le Meridien Hotel Des Indes (Lange Voorhout 54-6, 070 361 2345, www.hague. lemeridien.com) is arguably the most luxurious hotel in town, with prices to match: superior single/doubles start at €375. However the new **Grand Winston Hotel** (Generaal Eisenhowerplein 1, Rijswijk, 070 414 1500, www.grandwinston.nl) may soon eclipse all competition; doubles start at €135 before escalating sharply. The hostel **Stayokay Den Haag** (Scheepmakersstraat 27, 070 315 7888, www.stayokay.com) charges around €25.25 for a dorm bed and €67 to €74.50 for doubles.

Getting there

By car

50km (31 miles) south-west on A4, then A44.

By train

50min from Amsterdam Centraal Station to Den Haag Centraal Station; change at Leiden if necessary.

Tourist information

VVV

Koningin Julianaplein 30, outside Centraal Station (0900 340 3505 premium rate/www.denhaag.com). **Open** *Apr-Sept* 10am-6pm Mon; 9am-6pm Tue-Fri; 10am-5pm Sat; 11am-3pm Sun. *Oct-Mar* 10am-6pm Mon; 9am-6pm Tue-Fri; 10am-5pm Sat.

Trips Out of Town

Leiden

Canal-laced Leiden derives a good deal of its charm from the Netherlands' oldest university, which was founded here in 1575 and which boasts such notable alumni as René Descartes, US president John Quincy Adams and many a Dutch royal. The old town teems with bikes and bars, boasts the most historic monuments per square metre in the country, and is thus a most rewarding place to visit, ideal for a weekend away from comaparatively frenetic Amsterdam.

In the Dutch Golden Age of the late 16th and 17th centuries, Leiden grew fat on textiles. It also spawned three great painters of that era: Rembrandt van Rijn, Jan van Goyen and Jan Steen. Although few works by these three masters remain in the Leiden of today, the **Stedelijk Museum de Lakenhal** (Lakenhal Municipal Museum), where the Golden Age clothmakers met, does have a painting by Rembrandt, as well as works by other Old Masters and collections of pewter, tiles, silver and glass. Perhaps Leiden's most notable museum, though, is the **Rijksmuseum van Oudheden** (National Museum of Antiquities), which houses the largest archaeological collection in the Netherlands: in particular the display of Egyptian mummies should not be missed. The **Rijksmuseum voor Volkenkunde** (National Museum of Ethnology) showcases the cultures of Africa, Oceania, Asia, the Americas and the Arctic.

The ten million fossils, minerals and stuffed animals exhibited at **Naturalis** (Natural History Museum) make it the country's largest museum collection, while the 6,000 species of flora at the **Hortus Botanicus**, one of the world's oldest botanical gardens, include descendants of the country's first tulips. If Dutch clichés are the things that you came here to see, head straigth to the **Molenmuseum de Valk** (the Falcon Windmill Museum), a windmill-turned-museum where you can see living quarters, machinery and a picturesque view out over Leiden. But an even better panorama can be had from the top of the Burcht, a 12th-century fort on an ancient artificial mound in the city centre.

Hortus Botanicus Leiden

Rapenburg 73 (071 527 7249/www.hortusleiden.nl). **Open** *Apr-Oct* 10am-6pm daily. *Nov-Mar* 10am-4pm Mon-Fri, Sun. **Admission** €4; €2 4-12s; free MK. **Credit** AmEx, MC, V.

Molenmuseum de Valk

2e Binnenvestgracht 1 (071 516 5353/http://home. wanadoo.nl/molenmuseum/). **Open** 10am-5pm Tue-Sat; 1-5pm Sun. **Admission** €2.50; €1.50 concessions; free under-6s, MK. **No credit cards.**

Naturalis

Darwinweg (071 568 7600/www.naturalis.nl). **Open** 10am-6pm Tue-Sun. **Admission** €9; €5 4s-17s; free under-3s. **Credit** MC, V.

Rijksmuseum van Oudheden

Rapenburg 28 (0900 6 600600/www.rmo.nl). **Open** 10am-5pm Tue-Fri; noon-5pm Sat, Sun. **Admission** €7.50; €5.50 4s-17s; €6.50 over-65s; free under-4s, MK. **Credit** AmEx, DC, MC, V.

Rijksmuseum voor Volkenkunde

Steenstraat 1 (071 516 8800/www.rmv.nl). **Open** 10am-5pm Tue-Sun. **Admission** €6.50; €3.50 concessions; free MK. **No credit cards.**

Stedelijk Museum de Lakenhal

Oude Singel 28-32 (071 516 5360/www.lakenhal.nl). **Open** 10am-5pm Tue-Fri; noon-5pm Sat, Sun. **Admission** €4; €2.50 over-65s; free under-18s, MK. **No credit cards.**

Where to eat & drink

A trad cosy atmosphere is to be had at **De Hooykist** (Hooigracht 49, 071 512 5809, www.dehooykist.nl) and **In Den Bierbengel** (Langebrug 71, 071 514 8056), which specialise in meat, fish and wines. Bar-restaurant **Annie's Verjaardag** (Hoogstraat 1a, 071 512 5737) occupies eight candle-lit cellars underneath a bridge in the centre of town: its main selling point is the canal barge terrace.

Another unique location is **Restaurant City Hall** (Stadhuisplein 3, 071 514 4055, www.restaurantcityhall.nl), a budget hotspot in the city's ancient – yes, you guessed it – City Hall. For something ultra-cheap and cheerful, there's **La Bota** (Herensteeg 9, 071 514 6340) near the Pieterskerk, while excellent tapas can be had from early to late at **Oloroso** (Breestraat 49, 071 514 6633).

For a walk on the grungy side, try **WW** (Wolsteeg 4-6, 071 512 5900, www.deww.nl), which has bands, dartboards and graffiti. **The Duke** (Oude Singel 2, 071 512 1972, www.jazzcafetheduke.nl) offers live jazz, and **LVC** (Breestraat 66, 071 514 6449, www.lvc.nl) hosts smaller touring acts. Traditional bars are dotted along Nieuwstraat, Breestraat and Nieuwe Beestenmarkt.

Where to stay

The **Golden Tulip** (Schipholweg 3, 071 522 1121, www.goldentulipleidencentre.nl) is the town's poshest hotel, with rooms between €144 and €184. Rather cheaper is the **Mayflower** (Beestenmarkt 2, 071 514 2641, www.hotel mayflower.nl), where rooms cost €75 to €125, while the **Pension De Witte Singel** (Witte Singel 80, 071 512 4592, www.pension-ws.demon.nl) is cheaper still, at €36 to €66.

Erasmusbrug and Kijk-Kubus.

Trips Out of Town

Getting there

By car
40km (24 miles) south-west on A4.

By train
35min from Amsterdam Centraal Station, direct.

Tourist information

VVV
Stationsweg 2d (0900 222 2333 premium rate/ www.leidenpromotie.nl). **Open** 11am-5.30pm Mon; 9.30am-5.30pm Tue-Fri; 10am-4.30pm Sat.

Rotterdam

A skate city, a harbour city; an artists' haven, a multicultural fusion; the hometown to humanism, an architectural inspiration; a Cultural Capital of Europe, a historical museum centre, a jazz-lover's dream. There's no pinning Rotterdam down.

This 'Manhattan on the Maas' had a clean slate to play with after its almost complete destruction in World War II, and has recently managed to fill in the massive and long-standing gaps in both its urban and cultural landscape. Rotterdam is a city to watch.

The futuristic skyline along the banks of the River Maas is a success, with the Oude Haven (Old Harbour) now a work of imaginative modernism, the pinnacle of which is Piet Blom's witty **Kijk-Kubus**. These bright yellow cubic houses stand, a little goofily, on stilts. Of the houses, No.70 is open to visitors. Across the bridge, called Erasmusbrug for the local boy, the humanist Desiderius Erasmus, the renovation of the old harbour districts of Kop van Zuid and Entrepot is pretty much complete. Don't miss the cultural activities in the Las Palmas (Willeminakade 66, www.laspalmas rotterdam.nl) warehouse complex.

Across town, architectural wizard Rem Koolhaas designed Rotterdam's cultural heart, the Museum Park, where you'll find outdoor sculptures and five museums. The three best are the **Netherlands Architecture Institute**, which gives an overview of the history and development of architecture, especially in Rotterdam; the **Museum Boijmans Van Beuningen**, with a beautiful collection of traditional and contemporary art (including works by Van Eyck and Rembrandt) and a sizeable design collection; and the **Kunsthal**, which deals with art, design and photography of a more modern persuasion. The adjoining street Witte de Withstraat has many smaller galleries along with some excellent restaurants and bars. A bird's eye view of all

the modern development can be had from the nearby **Euromast**, if you can handle the height (185 metres, or 607 feet).

The sprawling **Historical Museum Rotterdam** includes the Dubbelde Palmboom (Double Palm Tree), housed in an old granary in Delfshaven and featuring life and work in the Meuse delta from 8000 BC to the present, and Het Schielandshuis, a 17th-century palatial mansion and another of the few buildings spared in the bombing. Now placed in bizarre juxtaposition to Quist's 1992 Robeco Tower and the giant Hollandse Bank Unie, it displays rooms and clothing from the 18th century to the present. Old world charm also abounds at the neighbouring village of Schiedam (VVV, Buitenhavenweg 9, 010 473 3000), which sports the world's tallest windmill and the planet's largest collection of Dutch gins and liqueurs in the tasting house of its museum. It's also where 14 million litres of Ketel One vodka are produced before being exported to the cocktail bars of the USA. An amazing cocktail fact!

Of the shopping areas the Koopgoot – 'buying gutter', as it was dubbed in the local dialect – was the country's first underground shopping mall. Nieuwe Binnenweg is shopping for clubbers, Van Oldenbarneveltstraat offers more upmarket fare, and Jan Evertsenplaats is a green square where you can rest from spending.

Rotterdam is the only city in the Netherlands with a growing youth population. Come face to wheel with the future by renting inline or roller-skates and falling over at the largest outdoor skate park in the country on West-Blank.

If you're a backpacker, take advantage of **Use-it** (Schaatsbaan 41-45, 010 240 9158, www.use-it.nl); you can find it by taking the west exit of the station, and following the fence to the right until you see a red building. Rather like a young person's VVV, it offers a feast of ideas for stuff to do in the city, as well as free lockers if you want to ditch your backpack and roam unburdened for a while.

Euromast
Parkhaven 20 (010 436 4811/www.euromast.nl). **Open** *Apr-Sept* 9.30am-11pm daily. *Oct-Mar* 10am-11pm daily. **Admission** €8; €5.20 4s-11s; free under-4s. **Credit** AmEx, DC, MC, V.

Historical Museum Rotterdam
Korte Hoogstraat 31 (010 217 6767/www.hmr. rotterdam.nl). **Open** 10am-5pm Tue-Fri; 11am-5pm Sat, Sun. **Admission** €3; €1.50 4s-16s; free under-4s, MK. **No credit cards**.

Kijk-Kubus
Overblaak 70 (010 414 2285/www.cubehouse.nl). **Open** *Jan, Feb* 11am-5pm Fri-Sun. *Mar-Dec* 11am-5pm daily. **Admission** €1.80; €1.30 concessions; free under-4s. **No credit cards**.

Trips Out of Town

Kunsthal

Westzeedijk 341 (010 440 0301/www.kunsthal.nl).
Open 10am-5pm Tue-Sat; 11am-5pm Sun.
Admission €7.50; €2.50 13s-18s; free under-12s.
No credit cards.

Museum Boijmans Van Beuningen

*Museumpark 18-20 (010 441 9400/www.boijmans.
rotterdam.nl).* **Open** 10am-5pm Tue-Sat; 11am-5pm
Sun. **Admission** €7; €3.50 over-65s; free under-18s,
MK. **Credit** AmEx, MC, V.

Netherlands Architecture Institute

Museumpark 25 (010 440 1200/www.nai.nl).
Open 10am-5pm Tue-Sat; 11am-5pm Sun.
Admission €6.50; €4 4s-16s; free under-4s,
MK. **Credit** AmEx, MC, V.

Where to eat & drink

Oude Haven, the Entrepot district and
Delfshaven all offer a wide choice of (grand)
cafés and restaurants. For traditional thick pea
soup while crossing town on a tram, check out
the schedule of the **Snerttram** (010 414 6183,
www.snerttram.nl). But for a full-blown French-
inspired culinary adventure head to **De Engel**
(Eendrachtsweg 19, 010 413 8256, www.engel
groep.com). For veggies, **Bla Bla** (Piet
Heynsplein 35, 010 477 4448) is expensive
but busy, so book ahead. **Foody's** (Nieuwe
Binnenweg 151, 010 436 5163, www.engel
groep.com) is the latest in international eateries;
Colosseo (Rodezand 36, 010 414 7030) is a fine
and cheap purveyor of Indonesian cuisine; **El
Faro Andaluz** (Leuvehaven 73-4, 010 414
6213) serves Spanish tapas; **La Pizza**
(Scheepstimmermanslaan 21, 010 241 7797) is
not distracted by their sexclub neighbours in
producing the best wood oven rendered pizzas;
while the best Chinese in town can be found by
cruising the Katendrecht. Check www.special
bite.com for special offers.

Bars-wise, **De Schouw** (Witte de Withstraat
80, 010 412 4253) is a stylish brown café that
now attracts artists and students. Lofty ceilings
give **Café Dudok** (Meent 88, 010 433 3102)
an arty feel. Jazz fiends should try **Dizzy** ('s
Gravendijkwal 129, 010 477 3014), one of the
best jazz venues in the country; for bands and
club nights, venture to **Nighttown** (West-
Kruiskade 26-8, 010 436 1210, www.night
town.nl). **Rotown** (Nieuwe Binnenweg 19, 010
436 2669, www2.rotown.nl) focuses on indie and
has a fine bar/restaurant (open 11am-9.30pm).
Mining a similar vein, with lots of hip hop and
dancehall thrown in for good measure, is
Waterfront (Boompjeskade 10, 010 201
0980, www.waterfront.nl).

Of the vast number of clubbing options,
Now&Wow (Maashaven ZZ 1,477 1074,
www.now-wow.com) has long been considered

one of the best dance clubs in Benelux; the
excellent **Off Corso** (Kruiskade 22, 010 411
3897, www.off-corso.nl) has won the prestigious
'Golden Gnome' award; and **Club Las Palmas**
(Wilhelminakade 66, 010 890 1075, www.club-
laspalmas.nl) finds big-name DJs for its hip,
up-for-it crowd.

Where to stay

Hotel New York is one of the most
luxurious places in town (Koninginnenhoofd
1, 010 439 0500, www.hotelnewyork.nl), but
not unreasonably priced: doubles start at €93.
Even if you don't stay here, pop in for a coffee
or a plate of *fruits de mer*. One unusual place
to stay is **De Clipper** (Scheepmakershaven,
06 5331 4244, www.hostelboat.nl), a boat
moored in the centre of the city. It'll set you
back €22.50 a night with breakfast. **Hotel
Bazar** (Witte de Withstraat 16, 010 206 5151,
www.hotelbazar.nl) is a little out of the
ordinary, too: it sports an *Arabian Nights*
decor and an excellent Middle Eastern
restaurant. Doubles range from €75 to
€125. For budget travellers there's **Stayokay
Rotterdam** (Rochussenstraat 107-9, 010 436
5763, www.stayokay.com); for about €19.75 to
€24.25, you also get the use of a kitchen.

Getting there

By car
73km (45 miles) south on A4, then A13.

By train
1hr from Amsterdam Centraal Station, direct.

Tourist information

VVV
*Coolsingel 67 (0900 403 4065 premium rate/
www.vvv.rotterdam.nl).* **Open** *Apr-Sept* 9.30am-6pm
Mon-Thur; 9.30am-9pm Fri; 9.30am-5pm Sat; noon-
5pm Sun. *Oct-Mar* 9.30am-6pm Mon-Thur;
9.30am-9pm Fri; 9.30am-5pm Sat.

Utrecht

One of the oldest cities in the Netherlands,
Utrecht was also, in the Middle Ages, the
biggest, and was a religious and political
centre for centuries. At one point there were
around 40 houses of worship in the city, all
with towers and spires. From a distance Utrecht
must have looked like a giant pincushion.

However, there's more to Utrecht than
history and scenery. Utrecht University is one
of the largest in the Netherlands – continuing
to expand and provide work for architects like
Rem Koolhaas (who designed the Educatorium)

– and the city centre is bustling with trendy shops and relaxed cafés. Happily, too, the Hoog Catharijne, the country's biggest shopping mall but also one of the biggest eyesores, is soon to be destroyed. But for some time yet, you'll have to wander its labyrinthine layout following signs to 'Centrum' in order to leave Central Station. Lovers of luxury should instead head for the boutiques and galleries tucked down the streets along the canals. Linger on Oudkerkhof, where there's a concentration of designer shops; La Vie, the shopping centre on Lange Viestraat; and the flower and plant markets along Janskerkhof and Oudegracht on Saturdays.

Though bikes can be hired from Rijwiel Shop (Sijpesteijnkade 40, 030 296 7287), the city is so compact that practically everything is within walking distance. A good place to start is the **Domtoren** (the French Gothic-style cathedral tower). At over 112 metres (367 feet), not only is it the highest tower in the country, but with over 50 bells, it's also the largest musical instrument in the Netherlands. Visitors are allowed to climb the tower. The panoramic view is worth the effort to climb its 465 steps: vistas stretch 40 kilometres (25 miles) to Amsterdam on a clear day. Buy tickets across the square at the Information Center for the Cultural History of Utrecht (Domplein 9, 030 233 3036, open 10am-5pm Mon-Sat, noon-5pm Sun) where you can also get details on the rest of the city and the castles located on its outskirts.

The space between the tower and the Domkerk was originally occupied by the nave of the huge church, which was destroyed by a freak tornado in 1674. Many other buildings were damaged and the exhibition inside the Domkerk shows interesting 'before' and 'after' sketches. Outside is the Pandhof, a cloister garden planted with many medicinal herbs. The garden, with its beautiful statuette of a canon hunched over his writing, is a tranquil spot.

Another fascinating place to explore is the Oudegracht, the canal that runs through the centre of the city, and its cafés and shops, excellent places for snacks and watching boats navigate their way under the narrow bridges.

Of Utrecht's several museums, the **Museum Catharijnecovent** (St Catharine Convent Museum), at least partially closed during renovations that will last until spring 2006, is located in a beautiful late medieval building and gives an account of the country's religious history. The excellent and sprawling **Centraal Museum**, meanwhile, harbours not only paintings by 17th-century masters but also the largest Rietveld collection in the world. The **Nationaal Museum van Speelklok tot Pierement** has the world's biggest collection of automated musical instruments, and the

Universiteitsmuseum (University Museum) focuses on the interaction between science and education. Meanwhile the country's biggest rock garden is a striking part of Fort Hoofddijk; on a cold day, the tropical greenhouse is a perfect place for thawing out and absorbing themes like 'plants as clocks' or 'magic and religion'.

Utrecht is in an area rich with castles, forests and arboretums. Slot Zuylen (Zuylen Castle, Tournooiveld 1, Oud Zuilen, 030 244 0255, www.slotzuylen.com) presides over exquisite ornamental waterfalls and gardens. Check the concerts and shows in Kasteel Groeneveld's gorgeous gardens (Groeneveld Castle, Groeneveld 2, Baarn, 035 542 0446, www.kasteelgroeneveld.nl), just north-east of Utrecht. Stroll in the lovely Arboretum von Gimborn (Vossensteinsesteeg 8, 030 253 1826) in Doorne, then pop across the town to Kasteel Huis Doorn (Doorn Castle, Langbroekerweg 10, 0343 421020, www.huisdoorn.nl). This will answer a question that has no doubt been bothering you these many years: what happened to the Kaiser after World War I? Wihelm II lived here in exile for 20 years before his death in 1941.

Centraal Museum

Nicolaaskerkhof 10 (030 236 2362/ www.centraal museum.nl). **Open** 11am-5pm Tue-Sun. **Admission** €8; €5 13-17s, free under 12s, MK. **Credit** MC, V.

Fort Hoofddijk

Budapestlaan 17, De Uithof (030 253 5455/ www.bio.uu.nl/botgard). **Open** *Mar-Dec* 10am-4pm daily. *May-Sept* 10am-5pm daily. **Admission** €4.50; €1.50 4s-12s; €3.50 over-65s; free under-4s, MK. **No credit cards.**

Museum Catharijneconvent

Lange Nieuwstraat 38 (030 231 7296/www. catharijneconvent.nl). **Open** 10am-5pm Tue-Fri; 11am-5pm Sat, Sun. **Admission** €7; €6 over-65s; €3.50 6-17s; free under-5s, MK. **No credit cards.**

Nationaal Museum van Speelklok tot Pierement

Steenweg 6 (030 231 2789/www.museum speelklok.nl). **Open** 10am-5pm Tue-Sat; noon-5pm Sun. **Admission** €6; €4 4-12s; €5 over-65s; free MK, under-4s. **Credit** MC, V.

Universiteitsmuseum

Lange Nieuwstraat 106 (030 253 8008/www. museum.uu.nl). **Open** 11am-5pm Tue-Sun. **Admission** €4; €2 4-18s; free under-4s, MK. **No credit cards.**

Where to eat & drink

De Winkel van Sinkel (Oudegracht 158, 030 230 3030, www.dewinkelvansinkel.nl) is a grand setting for coffee or a meal – especially at night, when its catacombs open for club nights

and to act as a late-night restaurant. Stadskasteel Oudaen (Oudegracht 99, 030 231 1864, www.oudaen.nl), the only urban medieval castle left in the country, is even posher – with only Goesting (Veeartsenijpad. 030 273 3346, www.restaurantgoesting.nl), a reinvented dog kennel, coming close. Casa Sanchez (Springweg 64, 030 231 9566, www.casasanchez.nl) serves tapas, while sushi can be munched at Konnichi Wa (Mariaplaats 9, 030 241 6388, www.konnichiwa.nl). If you want a local speciality, try the Pancake Bakery de Oude Munt Kelder (Oudegracht aan de Wer, 030 231 6773).

Most bars in the city centre are busy with students. ACU (Voorstraat 71, 030 231 4590, www.acu.nl) has cheap eats and some of the city's edgier musical events; Belgie (Oudegracht 196, 030 231 2666) serves over 300 types of beer; and 't Hart van Utrecht (Voorstraat 10, no phone) has the coolest crowd of all. The Tivoli (Oudegracht 245, 0900 235 8486, www.tivoli.nl) – REM's rehearsal space for their 2003 tour – is the best place to check for club nights and touring bands; while student favourite Ekko (Bemuurde Weerd Westzijde 3, 030 231 7457, www.ekko.nl) focuses on indie rock and pop. Meanwhile film fans congregate at Louis Hartlooper Complex (Tolsteegbrug 1, 030 232 0450, www.louishartloopercomplex.nl) run by famed local film-maker Jos Stelling and located in a remarkable 1928-built police station.

Where to stay

The four-star Malie Hotel (Maliestraat 2, 030 231 6424, www.maliehotel.nl) is a beautiful old merchant's house: a single costs from €105-€125; a double costs €125 to €145, including breakfast. Those on a tighter budget should take a ten-minute bus ride out from the city centre to Bunnik, where the Stayokay Bunnik (Rhijnauwenselaan 14, 030 656 1277, www.stayokay.com) offers a night in a shared room for €19 to €24.50.

Getting there

By car

40km (25 miles) south-east.

By rail

30min from Amsterdam Centraal Station, direct.

Tourist information

VVV

Vinkenburgstraat 19 (0900 128 8732 premium rate/ www.utrechtstad.com). **Open** noon-6pm Mon; 10am-6pm Tue-Sat; 10am-2pm Sun.

Directory

Features

Directory

Getting Around

Getting around Amsterdam is easy. The city has efficient and cheap trams and buses, though if you're staying in the centre most places are reachable on foot. Locals tend to get around by bike: the streets are busy with cycles all day and most of the evening. There are also boats, barges and water taxis.

If you were thinking of bringing a car, don't. The roads aren't designed for them, and parking places are elusive. Alas, public transport provision for those with disabilities is dire. Though there are lifts at all Metro stations, staff can't always help people in wheelchairs.

Handy new service 9292ov (0900 9292/www.9292ov.nl) groups national bus, train, taxi, tram and ferry boat information; besides phoning, you can use their Dutch-language website for 'door to door' advice. Under *van* (from), type in the *straat* (street), *huisnummer* (house number) and *plaats* (town) you want to start from; then, under *naar* (to), the details for your destination; select the date and time, then select *aankomst* if that's your ideal arrival time or *vertrek* if that's your ideal departure time; then press *geef reisadvies* (get travel advice).

Arriving & leaving

By air

For general airport enquiries, ring Schiphol Airport on 0900 0141 (costs €0.10/min) or go to www.schiphol.nl.
British Airways
346 95   ww.britishairways.nl.
        idland
        www.flybmi.com.

EasyJet
023 568 4880/www.easyjet.co.uk.
KLM
474 7747/www.klm.com.

Connexxion Airport Hotel Shuttle

Connexxion counter, Section A7, Arrivals, Schiphol Airport (653 4975/www.airporthotelshuttle.nl). **Times** every 30min 7am-1pm, every 60min 1-9pm. **Tickets** *Single* €11.00. *Open return* €18. **No credit cards**. This bus service from Schiphol Airport to Amsterdam is available to anyone prepared to pay, not just hotel guests. However, to get door-to-door service and the return pick-up, you'll have to be staying at one of the over 50 allied hotels (but with buses stopping at each of these, it's easy to get off very near your destination). Schedules and the expanding list of allied hotels are on their website (which also has a booking service).

Schiphol Airport Rail Service

Schiphol Airport/Centraal Station (information 0900 9292/www.9292 ov.nl). **Times** Every 10min 4am-midnight, then every hr. **Tickets** *Single* €3.20; €2 4-11s; free under-3s. *Return* €5.70; €2 4-11s; free under-3s. **Credit** MC, V.
The journey to Centraal Station takes about 20 minutes. Single, return and Railrunner tickets can also be bought on the train but you will be charged more. Note that a return ticket is valid only for that day.

Taxis

There are always plenty of taxis at the main exit. They're pricey: a fixed fare from the airport to the south and west of the city is about €25, and to the city centre is about €35.

Public transport

For information, tickets, maps and an English-language guide to the types of public transport tickets, visit the **GVB**, Amsterdam's municipal transport authority, in person (an office is conveniently located opposite Centraal Station) or at their useful website. A basic map of the tram network is on p320.

See p258 for details of NS, the Netherlands' rail network.

GVB

Stationsplein CS, Old Centre: New Side (0900 8011/www.gvb.nl). Tram 1, 2, 4, 5, 9, 13, 16, 17, 24, 25. **Open** *Telephone enquiries* 8am-10pm daily. *In person* 7am-9pm Mon-Fri; 8am-9pm Sat, Sun. **Map** p310 D1. The GVB runs Amsterdam's Metro, bus and tram services, and can provide information on all. **Other locations**: *Head Office*: Prins Hendrikkade 108-14 (lost articles); Bijlmer Station; Metro Stations; Rembrandtplein; Leidseplein (night buses only, midnight-6am Fri, Sat).

Fares & tickets

Don't travel on a bus or tram without a ticket. Uniformed inspectors make regular checks and passengers without a valid ticket will be fined €29.40 on the spot. Playing the ignorant foreigner won't work.

Strippenkaarten

A 'strip ticket' system operates on trams, buses and the Metro. It's initially confusing, but ultimately good value for money. Prices begin at €1.60 for a strip of two units or €6.40 for 8 units; these you can buy from any bus or tram driver. But you only really start saving if you spend €6.50 for a 15-unit card or €19.20 for 45 units; these can only be bought at GVB offices, post offices, train stations, major supermarkets and many tobacconists and souvenir shops. Children under 3 travel free, and older children (4s-18s) and seniors (+65) pay reduced fares (€4.30 for a 15-strip card). Prices increase annually.

Tickets must be stamped on boarding a tram or bus and on entering a Metro station. The city is divided into five zones: Noord (north), West, Centrum, Oost (east) and Zuid (south); most of central Amsterdam falls within Centrum. Strip tickets are also valid on trains that stop at Amsterdam stations, with the exception of Schiphol.

For travel in a single zone, two units must be stamped, while three are stamped for two zones, four for three zones and so on. On trams, if a conductor is not there, you can stamp your own tickets in the yellow box-like contraption near the doors: fold the ticket so that the unit you need to stamp is at the end. On buses, drivers stamp the tickets, and on the Metro there are stamping machines located at the entrance to stations.

More than one person can travel on one 'strip ticket', but the correct number of units must be stamped for each person. Stamps are valid for one hour; during this time you can transfer to other buses and trams again. If your journey takes more than an hour, you have to stamp more units, but no single tram journey in central Amsterdam should take that long. Strippenkaarten remain valid for one year from the date of the first stamp.

Dagkaarten

A cheap option for unlimited travel in Amsterdam, a 'day ticket' costs €6.30. All pensioners over 65 (with Dutch ID or valid passport), students with ID and children (4s-11s) pay €4.30. Child day tickets are valid on night buses. A day ticket is valid on trams, buses and the Metro on the day it is stamped until the last bus or tram runs. You need to buy a new ticket for night buses (€3). Only the one-day ticket can be bought from drivers on trams and buses. After you've stamped the day ticket on your first journey, you don't need to stamp it again. You can buy tickets for two days (€10), and three days (€13). The Amsterdam Pass is an extended day ticket (see p75) valid for one, two or three days (€31-€51), from GVB or the Amsterdam Tourist Board (see p295). And if you only want to make one journey, you can get a single (€3) valid for an hour and a half, or a return (€4.50), valid for an hour and a half each way.

Sterabonnement

'Season tickets' can be bought at GVB offices, tobacconists and post offices, and are valid for a week, a month or a year. A weekly pass for the central zone (Centrum) costs €10.30, monthly €34.10 and yearly €341.60. Children (4s-18s) and seniors get cheaper season tickets: €6.80/day, €22.50/month and €225/year. You'll need a passport photo to get a season ticket.

OV-Chipcard

Train, bus, tram and bus travellers will also be able to pay using an 'OV-chipkaart', a credit card of sorts, from 1 January 2006.

Trams & buses

Buses and trams are a good way to get around. Tram services run from 6am Monday to Friday, 6.30am on Saturday and 7.30am on Sunday, with a special night bus service taking over late in the evening. Night buses are numbered from 351 to 363; all go to Centraal Station. Night bus stops are indicated by a black square at the stop with the bus number printed on it. Night buses run from 1am to 5.30am from Monday to Friday, and until 6.30am on weekends.

During off-peak hours and at quieter stops, stick out your arm to let the driver know that you want to get on.

Yellow signs at tram and bus stops indicate the name of the stop and further stops. There are usually maps of the entire network in the shelters and route maps on the trams and buses. The city's bus and tram drivers are courteous and will give directions if asked; most can do so in English.

The yellow and decorated trams are synonymous with Amsterdam, but newer, bluer and higher-windowed ones are becoming more common. Other road users should be warned that they will only stop if absolutely necessary. Cyclists should listen for tram warning bells and be careful to cross tramlines at an angle that avoids the front wheel getting stuck; motorists should avoid blocking tramlines: cars are allowed to venture on to them only if they're turning right.

To get on or off a tram, wait until it has halted at a stop and press the yellow button by the doors, which will then open. On some trams you can buy a ticket from the driver at the front; on others from either a machine in the middle, or a conductor at the back.

Note that Metro 51, 53 and 54 are, confusingly, fast trams that run on Metro lines. This is not the same as the number 5 tram, actually called a *sneltram* (fast tram).

While continually threatened with termination, Opstapper, an eight-seater white van, will at least continue through 2005 going up and down Prinsengracht between Centraal Station and Waterlooplein (30min trip) picking up mostly the elderly. But anyone can use it as long as they pay with strippenkaart or €1.60 cash. Just wave it down when you see it.

Metro

The Metro uses the same ticket system as trams and buses (see p280), and serves suburbs to the south and east. There are three lines 51, 52 and 53, which terminate at Centraal Station (which is sometimes abbreviated to CS). Trains run from 6am Monday to Friday (6.30am Sat, 7.30am Sun) to around 12.15am daily.

Taxis

You can order a cab by calling 677 7777. The line is often busy Friday and Saturday nights: expect a phone queue.

Check that the meter starts at the minimum charge (€2.90). Always ask the driver to tell you the rough cost of the journey before setting out. Even short journeys are expensive: on top of €2.90, you will be expected to pay €1.80 per kilometre for the first 25 kilometres, then €1.40 per kilometre thereafter.

If you feel you've been ripped off, ask for a receipt, which you are entitled to see before handing over cash. If the charge is extortionate, phone the TCA, the central taxi office 650 6506; 9am-5pm Mon-Fri) or contact the police. Rip-offs are relatively rare but it's always a good idea to check that the cab you are getting into has the 'TCA' sign.

Directory

Sometimes it's very hard to hail a taxi in the street, but ranks are dotted around the city. The best central ones are found outside Centraal Station, by the bus station at the junction of Kinkerstraat and Marnixstraat, Rembrandtplein and Leidseplein.

Wheelchairs will only fit in taxis if they're folded. If you're in a wheelchair, phone the car transport service for wheelchair users (633 3943 7am-5pm daily). You'll need to book your journey one or two days in advance and it costs around €2 per kilometre.

Happily, there are now taxi companies out to break the monopoly of TCA. Tulip Taxi (636 3000), begins with a minimum charge of €2.55 before adding 85 eurocents/minute for the first 15 kilometres. After that they charge €1.50/kilometre. This can save you up to 50% on inner-city rides. Unfortunately, they do not have a large fleet and you are often left waiting.

Driving

If you absolutely must bring a car to the Netherlands, join a national motoring organisation beforehand. This should issue you with booklets that explain what to do in the event of a breakdown in Europe. To drive in the Netherlands you'll need a valid national driving licence, although ANWB (*see below*) and many car hire firms favour photocard licences (Brits need the paper version as well for this to be legal; the photocard takes a couple of weeks to come through if you're applying from scratch). You'll need proof that the vehicle has passed a road safety test in its country of origin, an international identification disk, a registration certificate, and insurance documents.

Major roads are usually well maintained and clearly signposted. Motorways are labelled 'A'; major roads 'N'; and European routes 'E'. Brits in particular should note that the Dutch drive on the right. Drivers and front-seat passengers must always wear seatbelts. Speed limits are 50kmph (31mph) within cities, 70kmph (43mph) outside, and 100kmph (62mph) on motorways. If you're driving in Amsterdam, look out for cyclists. Many streets in Amsterdam are now one-way.

Royal Dutch Automobile Club (ANWB)

Museumplein 5, Museum Quarter (673 0844/customer services 0800 0503/24hr emergency line 0800 0888/www.anwb.nl). Tram 2, 3, 5, 12, 16. **Open** *Customer services* 9.30am-6pm Mon-Fri; 9.30am-5pm Sat. **Credit** MC, V. **Map** p314 D6.
If you haven't joined a motoring organisation, enrol here for an annual €35-€65, which covers the cost of assistance if your vehicle breaks down. Members of a foreign motoring organisation may be entitled to free help. Remember that crews may not accept credit cards or cheques at the scene.

Car hire

Dutch car hire (*autoverhuur*) firms generally expect at least one year's driving experience and will want to see a valid national driving licence (with photo) and passport. All will require you to pay a deposit by credit card, and you generally need to be over 21. Prices given below are for one day's hire of the cheapest car available excluding insurance and VAT.

Adam's Rent-a-Car

Nassaukade 344-6, Oud West (685 0111/www.adamsrentacar.nl). Tram 7, 10, 17. **Open** 8am-6pm Mon-Fri; 8am-8pm Sat. **Credit** AmEx, MC, V. **Map** p314 C5.
One-day hire costs from €32; the first 100km (62 miles) are free, and after that the charge is €0.14/km. Branch at Middenweg 51.

Dik's Autoverhuur

Van Ostadestraat 278-80, the Pijp (662 3366/www.diks.net). Tram 3, 4. **Open** 8am-7.30pm Mon-Sat; 9am-12.30pm, 8-10.30pm Sun. **Credit** AmEx, DC, MC, V. **Map** p315 F6.
Prices start at €33 per day. The first 100km are free, then it's €0.14/km.

Hertz

Overtoom 333, Oud West (612 2441/www.hertz.nl). Tram 1, 6. **Open** 8am-6pm Mon-Fri; 8am-2pm Sat; 9am-2pm Sun, public holidays. **Credit** AmEx, DC, MC, V. **Map** p313 B6.
Prices start at €40 per day (no insurance and mileage) and €125 per day (with insurance and mileage).

Clamping & fines

Wheel-clamp (*wielklem*) teams are swift and merciless. A sticker on your windscreen tells you to call 553-0700. Someone will come to whom you can pay the fine by credit card (just over €90.20) and have the clamp removed. To pay in cash after business hours you must go to Daniel Goedkoopstraat 7-9. During business hours go to any of the branches listed below and hand over your money. Once you've paid, return to the car and wait for the clamp to be removed. Thankfully, the declampers normally turn up fairly promptly.

If you fail to pay the fine within 24 hours, your car will be towed away. It will cost around €153.90, plus parking fine, plus a tariff per kilometre to reclaim it from the pound if you do so within 24 hours, and around €45 for every 12 hours thereafter. The pound is at Daniel Goedkoopstraat 7-9. Take your passport, licence number and cash, or a major credit card. If your car has been clamped or towed away, go to any of the following *Stadstoezicht* (parking service) offices to pay.

Head office

Weesperstraat 105A, Old Centre: Old Side (553 0300/www. stadstoezicht.amsterdam.nl). Tram 6, 7, 10. **Open** 8am-6pm Mon-Fri; 8am-3.30pm Sat. **Map** p311 F3.
Other locations: *Beukenplein 50, Oost (553 0333). Tram 3, 9, 10, 14.* **Open** 8am-6pm Mon-Fri; 8am-3.30pm Sat. **Map** p316 H4.

Jan Pieter Heijestraat 94, Oud West (553 0333). Tram 1, 6, 7, 17. **Open** 8am-6pm Mon-Fri; 8am-3.30pm Sat. *Daniel Goedkoopstraat 7-9, Oost (553 0333). Metro 51, 53, 54.* **Open** 24hrs daily.

Parking

Parking in central Amsterdam is a nightmare: the whole area is metered from 9am until at least 7pm – and in many places up to midnight – and meters are difficult to find. Meters will set you back up to €3.20 an hour. You can buy day passes for the city centre (9am to 7pm: €16.80) evening passes (7pm to 12am: €11.20), or a week pass (€151.20) – from *Stadstoezicht* offices (*see above*). Car parks (*parkeren*) are indicated by a white 'P' on a blue square. After controlled

hours, parking at meters is free. Below is a list of central car parks where you're more likely to find a space at peak times. When leaving your car, be sure to empty it of valuables: cars with foreign number plates are vulnerable to break-ins.

ANWB Parking Amsterdam Centraal

Prins Hendrikkade 20a, Old Centre: New Side (638 5330). **Open** 24hrs daily. **Rates** €3.20/hr first 4 hours; €3.40 after that with a maximum day rate of €40. **Credit** AmEx, DC, MC, V. **Map** p310 D2.
Many nearby hotels offer a 10% discount on parking here.

Europarking

Marnixstraat 250, Oud West (623 6694). **Open** 6.30am-1am Mon-Thur; 6.30am-2am Fri, Sat; 7am-1am Sun. **Rates** €2.60/53min; €27.50/24hrs. **Credit** AmEx, MC, V. **Map** p313 B4.

De Kolk Parking

Nieuwezijds Kolk, Old Centre: New Side (427 1409). **Open** 24hrs daily. **Rates** €3/hr; €32/24hrs. **Credit** MC, V. **Map** p310 C2.

Petrol

There are 24-hour petrol stations (*tankstations*) at Gooiseweg 10, Sarphatistraat 225, Marnixstraat 250 and Spaarndammerdijk 218.

Water transport

Boats to rent

Amsterdam is best seen – and even better understood – from the water. Sure there are canal cruises (*see p284*) but they do not offer the freedom to do your own exploring. You can try to bond with a local boat

Don't come here

A cross that Amsterdammers sometimes have to bear is the rabid – and often stoned – ravings of visitors who are so bowled over by Amsterdam's mellow vibe that they want to move here. One word. Don't. If you feel this urge overcoming you, think of Irvine Welsh (*see p82* **Amster mage**) or Theo van Gogh (*see p22* **What the hell happened?**).

The housing situation in Amsterdam is so dire that students are actually living in revamped containers (*see p39*). That's right, people are living in boxes. So if you do manage to get your hands on one of those rare apartments, the only result will be to piss off long-suffering Amsterdammers. In short: we don't want you here.

However, stubborn expat-wannabes do have access to **Access** (Herengracht 472, 421 8445/www.access-nl.org), a new, volunteer-driven organisation founded to answer questions about life in the Netherlands. The website www.amsterdampartners.nl can also be very helpful when it comes to setting up a business. But to find a flat, you will also need friends, money and loads of luck.

There are two main price bands: below €450 per month, and above €450 per month. Anything above €450 is considered free sector housing and can be found through agencies or in newspapers (in particular, the

Wednesday, Thursday and Saturday editions of *De Telegraaf* and *De Volkskrant*) and every Tuesday and Thursday in the ads paper *Via Via*. Unfortunately, flatsharing is not common, and agency commissions are high.

If you're looking for properties under the €450 mark, you have two main choices. Both require a residents' permit (*see p295*). If you're studying here, register with Woning Net (0900 202 30 72/www.woningnet.nl) which charge a €57 one-time fee that allows you to react to any vacancies available via all the big housing co-ops. However, this method can take for ever given the shortage of properties and surfeit of clients. The other alternative is to register with one of the many non-profit agencies that hold property lotteries among would-be tenants. This may seem bizarre, but they do at least give you a chance of eventually getting a room. Call ASW Kamerbureau on Nieuwezijds Voorburgwal 32. (523 0130/www. steunpuntwonen.nl). Holders of residents' permits can also apply for council (public) housing. Alternatively, register with the Stedelijke Woning Dienst (City Housing Service; Jodenbreestraat 25; info 680 6806/www.wonen.amsterdam.nl). Bank on a very long wait before moving into that canal-side apartment you'd set your heart on.

Directory

Travel advice

For up-to-date information on travelling to a specific country – including the latest news on safety and security, health issues, local laws and customs – contact your home country government's department of foreign affairs. Most countries have websites packed with useful advice for would-be travellers and we list below a selection of useful internet addresses.

Australia
www.smartraveller.gov.au

Canada
www.voyage.gc.ca

New Zealand
www.mft.govt.nz/travel

Republic of Ireland
http://foreignaffairs.gov.ie

UK
www.fco.gov.uk/travel

USA
www.state.gov/travel

---

owner; but otherwise your options are limited to the pedal-powered canal bike or pedalo. Upon rental, don't ignore the introductory run-down of the rules of the water (put at its most basic: stick to the right and be very paranoid of the canal cruisers, who assume size makes right).

Canal Bike

Weteringschans 24, Southern Canal Belt (626 5574/www.canal.nl). **Open** *Summer* 10am-6pm; with nice weather till 9.30pm daily. *Winter* 10am-5.30pm daily at Rijksmuseum; weekends also at Westerkerk & Leidseplein. **Moorings** Leidsekade at Leidseplein; Stadhouderskade, opposite Rijksmuseum; Prinsengracht, by Westerkerk; Keizersgracht, on corner of Leidsestraat. **Hire rates** 4-person pedalo if 1 or 2 people, €8/person/hr; if 3 or 4 people, €7/person/hr. **Deposit** €50/canal bike. **Credit** AmEx, MC, DC, V. **Map** p314 D5.

Canal buses

Canal Bus

Weteringschans 27, Southern Canal Belt (623 9886/www.canal.nl). **Tram** 6, 10. **Open** 10am-7pm daily. **Tickets** 1 day €16; €11 under-12s. 1 day incl entrance to Rijksmuseum €23.50 (not available during special exhibitions). All Amsterdam Transport Pass €21. **Credit** AmEx, MC, V. **Map** p314 D5.
The All Amsterdam Transport Pass is valid for one day plus the morning of the following day.

Water taxis

Water Taxi Centrale

Stationsplein 8, Old Centre: New Side (535 6363/www.water-taxi.nl). **Tram** 1, 2, 4, 5, 9, 13, 16, 17, 24, 25. **Open** 8am-midnight daily. **Rates** 1-8 person boat €80 for first 30min, then €65/30min. 9-12 person boat €115 for first 30min, then €75/30min. 13-25 person boat €150 for first 30min, then €100/30min. 26-44 person boat €165 for first 30min, then €105/30min. **Credit** AmEx, DC, MC, V (accepted only prior to boarding). **Map** p309 D1.
They can pick you up and drop you anywhere in the city as long as they can get to the edge of the waterway. Try to book in advance.

Cycling

Cycling is the most convenient means of getting from A to B; there are bike lanes on most roads, marked by white lines and bike symbols. Cycling two abreast is illegal, as is going without reflectors on the wheels. At night you should use bike lights. The police set up periodic check points. Your option if you are stopped is to pay a fine or buy lights from the police on the spot. Watch out for pedestrians stepping into your path.

Never leave a bike unlocked: it will get stolen. Attach the bike to something immovable, preferably using two locks:

around the frame and through a wheel. If someone in the street offers you a bike for sale (*fiets te koop*), don't be tempted: it's almost certainly stolen, and there are plenty of good and cheap bike hire companies around, of which we list a selection below. Apart from these, check the *Gouden Gids* (*Yellow Pages*) under 'Fietsen en Bromfietsen Verhuur'.

You can also hail a 'bicycle cab' or order one with at least a day's notice (06 282 47550/ www.wielertaxi.nl). If you're wondering, it's basically a high-tech rickshaw. Rates €1/3 minutes per person; pets and children under 2 free; children aged 2-12 half-price. A €2.50 fee is applied for phone orders plus normal rates. For more on the national obsession with bicycles, *see p50*.

Bike City

Bloemgracht 68-70, the Jordaan (626 3721/www.bikecity.nl). **Tram** 10, 13, 14, 17. **Open** 9am-6pm daily. **Rates** from €7.50/day. **Deposit** €25. **Credit** AmEx, DC, MC, V. **Map** p309 B3.

Mac Bike

Centraal Station, Stationsplein 12, Old Centre: New Side (620 0985/www.macbike.nl). **Tram** 1, 2, 4, 5, 9, 13, 16, 17, 24, 25. **Open** 9am-5.45pm daily. **Rates** €4 for 2hrs; €9.75/day. **Deposit** €50 with a passport or credit card imprint. **Credit** AmEx, MC, V. **Map** p310 D1. **Other locations**: Weteringschans 2; M. Visserplein.

Mike's Bike Tours

Kerkstraat 134, Southern Canal Belt (622 7970/www.mikesbiketours.com). **Tram** 1, 2, 5. **Open** 9am-6pm daily; *Dec-Feb* 10am-6pm daily. **Rates** from €7/day. **No credit cards.** **Map** p314 D4.
Guided tours available.

Rent-A-Bike

Damstraat 20-22, Old Centre: Old Side (625 5029/www.bikes.nl). **Tram** 4, 9, 14, 16, 24, 25. **Open** 9am-6pm daily. **Rates** €7 til 6pm; €11.50 24 hrs; €25 deposit and passport/ID card or credit card imprint. **Credit** AmEx, DC, MC, V. **Map** p310 D3.
A 10% discount (excluding deposit) if you mention *Time Out* when you hire your bicycle.

Resources A-Z

Addresses

Amsterdam addresses take the form of street then house number, such as Damrak 1.

Age restrictions

In the Netherlands, only those over the age of 16 can purchase alcohol (over 18 for spirits), while you have to be 16 to buy cigarettes (18 to smoke dope). Driving is limited to over-18s.

Attitude & etiquette

Amsterdam is a relaxed city. However, not everything goes. Smoking dope is not accepted everywhere: spliffing up in restaurants is usually frowned upon. And while most restaurants don't have dress codes, many nightclubs ban sportswear and trainers.

Business

The construction of a new Metro line linking north and south Amsterdam is indicative of the city's status as a business centre. The south of Amsterdam is where most of the action is, with corporate hotels rubbing shoulders with the World Trade Center and the RAI convention centre. www.amsterdampartners.nl is a mine of useful information.

Banking

The branches listed below are head offices. Most do not have general banking facilities, but staff will be able to provide a list of branches that do. For information about currency exchange, *see p291*.

ABN-Amro

Vijzelstraat 68-78, Southern Canal Belt (628 9393/0900 0024/ www.abnamro.nl). Tram 6, 7, 10, 16, 24, 25. **Open** 11am-5pm Mon; 9am-5pm Tue-Fri. **Map** p314 D4. Locations all over Amsterdam.

Fortis Bank

Singel 548, Old Centre: New Side (624 9340/0900 8172/www. fortisbank.nl). Tram 4, 9, 14, 16, 24, 25. **Open** 1-5pm Mon; 9.30am-5pm Tue-Fri. **Map** p314 D4. Full facilities in 50 banks.

ING Group

Bijlmerplein 888, de Amsterdamse Poort (563 9111/0800 7011/www. ing.com). Metro Bijlmer/bus 59, 60, 62, 137. **Open** 9am-4pm Mon-Fri. ING incorporates Postbank (*see below*).

Postbank

Postbus 94780, 1090 GT (591 8200/ www.postbank.nl). **Open** *Enquiries* 8.30am-5pm Mon-Fri. One in every Amsterdam post office.

Rabobank

Dam 16, Old Centre: New Side (777 8899/www.rabobank.nl). Tram 1, 2, 5, 9, 13, 14, 16, 17, 24, 25. **Open** 9.30am-5pm Mon-Wed, Fri; 9.30am-6pm Thur. **Map** p310 D2. Some 30 locations in Amsterdam.

Conventions & conferences

Congrex Convention Services

AJ Ernststraat 595k, Southern Canal Belt (504 0200/www.congrex.nl). Tram 5/Metro 51. **Open** 9am-5.30pm Mon-Thur; 9am-5pm Fri. **Credit** AmEx, DC, MC, V. **Map** p315 E4. Specialists in teleconferencing.

RAI Congresgebouw

Europaplein 8-22, Zuid (549 1212/ www.rai.nl). Tram 4, 25/NS rail RAI Station. **Open** *Office* 9am-5.30pm Mon-Fri.
A congress and trade fair centre in the south. The building contains 11 halls and 22 conference rooms that can seat up to 1,750 people.

Stichting de Beurs van Berlage

Damrak 277, Old Centre: Old Side (530 4141/www.beursvanberlage.nl). Tram 4, 9, 14, 16, 24, 25. **Open** 9am-5pm Mon-Fri. **Map** p310 D2.
Used for cultural events and smaller trade fairs. Berlage Hall is a meeting and conference venue for between ten and 2,000 people.

Couriers & shippers

FedEx

0800 022 2333 freephone/500 5699/www.fedex.com/nl_english. **Open** *Customer services* 8am-6.30pm Mon-Fri. **Credit** AmEx, DC, MC, V.

TNT

0800 1234/www.tnt.com. **Open** 24hrs daily. **Credit** AmEx, DC, MC, V.

Office hire & business services

Many tobacconists and copy shops also have fax facilities.

Avisco

Stadhouderskade 156, the Pijp (671 9909/www.acsavcompany.com). Tram 3, 4, 16, 24, 25. **Open** 8am-

Weather report

	Temp	Rainfall	Sun (hrs/dy)
Jan	4°C/39°F	68mm/2.7in	1.8
Feb	6°C/43°F	48mm/1.9in	2.8
Mar	9°C/48°F	66mm/2.6in	3.7
Apr	13°C/55°F	53mm/2.1in	5.5
May	17°C/63°F	61mm/2.4in	7.2
June	20°C/68°F	71mm/2.8in	6.6
July	22°C/72°F	76mm/3.0in	6.9
Aug	22°C/72°F	71mm/2.8in	6.7
Sept	19°C/66°F	66mm/2.6in	4.4
Oct	14°C/57°F	73mm/2.9in	3.3
Nov	9°C/48°F	81mm/3.2in	1.9
Dec	6°C/43°F	84mm/3.3in	1.5

Directory

5pm Mon-Fri. **Map** p315 F5.
Credit AmEx, MC, V.
Slide projectors, video equipment,
screens, cameras, overhead
projectors, microphones and tape
decks hired out or sold.

Euro Business Center
*Keizersgracht 62, Western Canal Belt
(520 7500/www.eurobusiness
center.nl). Tram 1, 2, 5, 13, 14, 17.*
Open 8.30am-5pm Mon-Fri. **Credit**
AmEx, DC, MC, V. **Map** p310 C2.
Office space leases from one day to
two years, virtual offices, meeting
rooms and secretarial services.

World Trade Center
*Strawinskylaan 1, Zuid (575 9111/
www.wtcamsterdam.com). Tram
5/NS rail Amsterdam Zuid-WTC
Station.* **Open** *Office & enquiries*
9am-5pm Mon-Fri.
Offices let for long or short term and
assorted business services.

Translators &
interpreters

Amstelveens
Vertaalburo
*Ouderkerkerlaan 50, Amstelveen
(645 6610/www.avb.nl). Bus 65,
170, 172.* **Open** 9am-5pm Mon-Fri.
No credit cards.
Translation and interpreter service
for most languages.

Mac Bay Consultants
*PC Hooftstraat 15, Museum Quarter
(24hr phoneline 662 0501/fax 662
6299/www.macbay.nl). Tram 2, 3, 5,
12.* **Open** 9am-7pm Mon-Fri.
No credit cards. Map p314 C6.
Specialists in financial documents.

Useful organisations

For embassies and consulates,
see p287.

American Chamber
of Commerce
*Scheveningseweg 58, 2517 KW The
Hague (070 365 9808/www.am
cham.nl).* **Open** 9am-5pm Mon-Fri.

British Embassy
*Commercial Department, Lange
Voorhout 10, 2514 ED The Hague
(070 427 0427/fax 070 427 0348/
www.britain.nl).* **Open** 9am-5.30pm
Mon-Fri. *Enquiries* 11am-12.30pm,
2-4pm.
For the Amsterdam consulate; *see
p287.*

Commissariaat
voor Buitenlandse
Investeringen
Nederland
*Bezuidenhoutseweg 2, 2500 EC,
The Hague (070 379 8818/fax 070
379 6322/www.nfia.nl).* **Open** 8am-
6pm Mon-Fri.

The Netherlands Foreign Investment
Agency is probably the most useful
first port of call for business people
relocating to Holland.

Euronext
(Stock Exchange)
*Beursplein 5, Old Centre: New Side
(550 5555/www.euronext.com). Tram
4, 9, 14, 16, 24, 25.* **Open** free tours;
email to book. **Map** p310 D2.
Stock for listed Dutch companies is
traded here, and for Nederlandse
Termijnhandel, the commodity
exchange for trading futures, and
Optiebeurs, the largest options
exchange in Europe.

EVD: Economische
Voorlichtingsdienst
*Bezuidenhoutseweg 181, 2594 AH
The Hague (070 778 8888/www.
hollandtrade.com).* **Open** 8am-5pm
Mon-Fri.
The Netherlands Foreign Trade
Agency incorporates the Netherlands
Council for Trade Promotion (NCH),
both handy sources of information.
You need to make an appointment in
advance; don't turn up on spec.

Home Abroad
*Weteringschans 28, Southern Canal
Belt (625 5195/fax 624 7902/www.
homeabroad.nl). Tram 6, 7, 10.* **Open**
10am-5.30pm Mon-Fri. **Map** p315 E5.
Assistance in all aspects of life and
business in the Netherlands.

'Bloids of Amsterdam

2004 will go down in Amsterhistory as a
renaissance for free English-language print
publications. For years, the pickings were
slim: alternative listings 'zine *Shark* (now
solely at www.underwateramsterdam.com)
and the rather self-serving but nonetheless
worthwhile Boom Chicago magazine *Boom!*
(*see p253*) being the only two potential
sources for the linguistically challenged.

Now the city has two papers battling
for market share. But, despite a similar
format and names, they could hardly be more
different. *Amsterdam Times* was started by
Dutch journalism students using seed money
from a prominent local millionaire. While on
the rather dull side of the reading spectrum
and generally weak when it comes to covering
events and culture, the *Times* does offer a
handy overview of major local news stories.

A whole different kettle of inspired fish is
Amsterdam Weekly, which has taken on the
North American alternative weekly approach

as formulated by the likes of the *Village Voice*
and the *Chicago Reader*. As well as providing
a complete overview, along with a usually
savvy selection of critical picks, of each
week's arts, entertainment and culture
listings, the *Weekly* specialises in publishing
more personal tales of the city. What makes
it particularly special is that it is not out to
cater solely to expats or tourists. It is matter-
of-fact about being in English and often even
drops in Dutch words and phrases without
translating them if it happens to work better
in cutting to the chase. In short: it's a
publication for, by and about Amsterdammers
– even temporary ones like yourself. It's free,
and freely available, every Wednesday in
most bars and restaurants listed in this
guide. If you can't find it, the AUB Ticketshop
(*see p293* **Tickets please**) and Atheneum
Nieuwscentrum (*see p161*) are always safe
bets. We recommend it highly if you want to
put your finger on the pulse.

Kamer van Koophandel (Chamber of Commerce)
De Ruyterkade 5, the Waterfront (531 4000/fax 531 4799/www. kvk.nl). Tram 1, 2, 4, 5, 9, 13, 16, 17, 24, 25. **Open** 8.30am-5pm Mon, Tue, Thur, Fri; 8.30am-8pm Wed. **Map** p310 C1.
Amsterdam's Chamber of Commerce has lists of import/export agencies, government trade representatives and companies by sector.

Ministerie van Buitenlandse Zaken
Bezuidenhoutseweg 67, Postbus 20061, 2500 EB The Hague (070 348 6486/fax 070 348 4848/www.minbuza.nl). **Open** 10am-4.30pm Mon; 9am-4.30pm Tue-Fri.
The Ministry of Foreign Affairs. Detailed enquiries may be referred to the EVD (*see p286*).

Ministerie van Economische Zaken
Bezuidenhoutseweg 30, 2594 AV The Hague (070 379 8911/0800 646 3951/fax 070 379 4081/www.minez.nl). **Open** 9am-5.30pm Mon-Fri.
The Ministry of Economic Affairs can provide answers to general queries concerning the Dutch economy. Detailed enquiries tend to be referred to the EVD (*see p286*).

Netherlands–British Chamber of Commerce
Oxford House, Nieuwezijds Voorburgwal 328L, Old Centre: New Side (421 7040/fax 421 7003/www.nbcc.co.uk). Tram 1, 2, 5, 13, 14, 17. **Open** 9am-5pm Mon-Fri. **Map** p310 D3.

Consumer

If you have any complaints about the service you received from Dutch businesses that you were unable to resolve with them, call the National Consumentenbond on 070 445-4000/www.consumentenbond. nl (9am-9pm Mon-Thur; 9am-6pm Fri, Dutch only).

Customs

EU nationals over the age of 17 may import limitless goods into the Netherlands for their personal use. Other EU countries may still have limits on the quantity of goods they permit on entry. For citizens of

non-EU countries, the old limits still apply. These are:
● 200 cigarettes or 50 cigars or 250g (8.82oz) tobacco;
● 2 litres of non-sparkling wine or 1 litre of spirits (over 22 per cent alcohol) or 2 litres of fortified wine (under 22 per cent alcohol);
● 60cc/ml of perfume;
● 500 grams coffee or 200 grams coffee extracts or coffee essence.
● 100 grams tea or 40 grams tea extracts or tea essence.
● other goods to the value of €175.
The import of meat or meat products, fruit, plants, flowers and protected animals to the Netherlands is illegal. Check www.holland.com (under practical info).

Disabled

The most obvious difficulty people with mobility problems face here is negotiating the winding cobbled streets of the older areas. Poorly maintained pavements are widespread, and steep canal house steps can present problems. But the pragmatic Dutch can generally solve any problems quickly.
Most large museums have facilities for disabled users but little for the partially sighted and hard of hearing. Most cinemas and theatres have an enlightened attitude and are accessible. However, it's advisable to check in advance.
The Metro is accessible to wheelchair users who 'have normal arm function'. There is a taxi service for wheelchair users (*see p282*). Most trams are inaccessible to wheelchair users due to their high steps. The AUB (*see p293* **Tickets please**) and the Amsterdam Tourist Board (*see p295*) produce brochures on accommodation, restaurants, museums, tourist attractions and boat excursions with facilities for the disabled.

Drugs

The locals have a relaxed attitude to soft drugs, but smoking isn't acceptable everywhere, so use discretion. Outside Amsterdam, public consumption of cannabis is largely unacceptable. For more information, *see p48*.
Foreigners found with harder drugs should expect prosecution. Organisations offering advice can do little to assist foreigners with drug-related problems, though the Drugs Prevention Centre is happy to provide help in several languages, including English. Its helpline (408 7774, 3-5pm Mon-Thur) offers advice and information on drugs and alcohol abuse. There's also a 24-hour Crisis/Detox emergency number: 408 7777.

Electricity

The voltage here is 220, 50-cycle AC and compatible with British equipment, but because the Netherlands uses two-pin continental plugs you'll need an adaptor. American visitors may need a transformer.

Embassies

American Consulate General
Museumplein 19, 1071 DJ (575 5309/visas 0900 872 8472 premium rate/www.usemb.nl). Tram 3, 5, 12, 16. **Open** *US citizens services* 8.30-11.30am Mon-Fri; *immigrant visas* 1.30-3pm. **Map** p314 D6.

Australian Embassy
Carnegielaan 4, 2517 KH, The Hague (070 310 8200/0800 0224 794 Australian citizen emergency phone/www.australian-embassy.nl). **Open** 8.30am-4.55pm Mon-Fri. *Visa and immigration* 10am-12.30pm at counter, telephone enquiries 3-4.30pm Mon-Fri.

British Consulate General
Koningslaan 44, 1075 AE (676 4343/www.britain.nl). Tram 2. **Open** *British citizens* 9am-noon, 2-5.30pm Mon-Fri. *Visa enquiries* 9am-noon Mon-Fri.

Directory

British Embassy

Lange Voorhout 10, 2514 ED, The Hague (070 427 0427/www.britain. nl). **Open** 9am-5.30pm Mon-Fri. For visa and tourist information, contact the Consulate (*see p287*).

Canadian Embassy

Sophialaan 7, 2514 JP, The Hague (070 311 1600/www.canada.nl). **Open** 10am-5.30pm Mon-Fri. *Consular and passport section* 10am-1pm, 2-4.30pm Mon-Fri.

Irish Embassy

Dr Kuyperstraat 9, 2514 BA, The Hague (070 363 0993/www. irishembassy.nl). **Open** 10am-12.30pm, 2.30-5pm Mon-Fri. *Visa enquires* 10am-noon Mon-Fri.

New Zealand Embassy

Carnegielaan 10, 2517 KH, The Hague (070 365 8037/visas 070 365 8037/www.immigration.govt.nz/ Branch/TheHagueBranchHome/). **Open** 9am-12.30pm, 1.30-5.30pm Mon-Fri.

Emergencies

In an emergency, call **112**, free from any phone (mobiles included), and specify police, ambulance or fire service. For helplines, *see p289*; for hospitals, *see below*; for police stations, *see p292*.

Gay & lesbian

Help & information

COC Amsterdam

Rozenstraat 14, the Jordaan (626 3087/www.cocamsterdam.nl). Tram 13, 14, 17. **Open** *Telephone enquiries* noon-5pm Mon, Tue, Thur, Fri; noon-8pm Wed. *Info-Coffeeshop* 1-5pm Sat. **Map** p309 B3.
The Amsterdam branch of COC deals with the social side of gay life. The coffeeshop's a good place to enquire about the gay scene in general.

COC National

Rozenstraat 8, the Jordaan (623 4596/textphone 620 7541/www. coc.nl). Tram 13, 14, 17. **Open** 9.30am-5pm Mon, Tue, Wed, Fri; 9.30am-1pm Wed. **Map** p310 C3.
COC's head office deals with all matters relating to gays and lesbians.

Gay & Lesbian Switchboard

Postbus 11573, 1001 GN (623 6565/ www.switchboard.nl). **Open** noon-8pm daily.

Whether it's information or safe-sex advice, the friendly English-speakers here are well informed.

Homodok-Lesbisch Archief Amsterdam (Gay and Lesbian Archives)

Nieuwpoortkade 2a, Westerpark (606 0712/fax 606 0713/ www.ihlia.nl). Tram 10, 12, 14. **Open** 10am-4pm Mon-Fri.
A non-lending library of books, journals, articles and a large video collection. Call before visiting.

IIAV

Obiplein 4, Oost (665 0820/ www.iiav.nl). Tram 3, 7, 10, 14/ bus 15, 22. **Open** noon-5pm Mon; 10am-5pm Tue-Fri.
This women's archive was removed to Berlin during World War II, where it vanished. In 1992, it was found in Moscow, but the Russians are still refusing to return it. The current collection, started after the war, is officially an archive, but there are a lot of other resources, including several online databases.

Het Vrouwenhuis (the Women's House)

Nieuwe Herengracht 95, Southern Canal Belt (625 2066/fax 538 9185/www.akantes.nl). Tram 7, 9, 14/Metro Waterlooplein. **Open** *Office* 10am-5pm Mon-Fri. *Library, internet café* noon-5pm Wed, Thur. **Map** p311 F3.
There's a well-stocked library here (membership is €12.50 a year), free internet facilities (noon-5pm Wed, Thur), courses (mostly in Dutch) and women's events (check website).

Other groups & organisations

Dikke Maatjes

Kantershof 583, 1104 HG (www.dikkemaatjes.nl).
'Dikke Maatjes' means 'close friends', though its literal translation is 'fat friends'. That's exactly what this gay club is for: chubbies and admirers.

Mama Cash

PO Box 15686, 1001 ND (689 3634/fax 683 4647/www.mama cash.nl). **Open** 9am-5pm Mon-Fri.
This group funds women's groups and women-run businesses, and has sponsored many lesbian organisations and events in the city.

Netherbears

Postbus 15495, 1001 ML (www.netherbears.nl).
A hairy men's club. Check website.

Sportclub Tijgertje

Postbus 10521, 1001 EM (673 2458/www.tijgertje.nl).
Tijgertje organises a wide variety of sports activities, from yoga to wrestling, for gays and lesbians, including an HIV swimming group.

Wild Side

c/o COC Amsterdam, Rozenstraat 14, the Jordaan (071 512 8632/ www.wildside.dds.nl).
A group for woman-to-woman SM, which holds workshops, meetings and parties, and publishes a free bi-monthly, bilingual newsletter.

Yang Club

PO Box 218, 3430 AE Nieuwegein (06 453 88270/www.longyang clubholland.nl).
The Dutch branch of this worldwide organisation for Asian and oriental gays and their friends meets every 4th Sunday at COC (*see p215*)

Health

As with any trip abroad, it's of course advisable to take out medical insurance before you leave. If you're a UK citizen, you should also get hold of an E111 form (*see p290*) to facilitate reciprocal cover. For emergency services, medical or dental referral agencies and AIDS/HIV information, *see p289*.

Afdeling Inlichtingen Apotheken

694 8709.
A 24-hour service that can direct you to your nearest chemist.

Centraal Doktorsdienst/Atacom

592 3333/www.atacom.nl.
A 24-hour English-speaking line for advice about medical symptoms.

Accident & emergency

In the case of minor accidents, try the outpatient departments at the following hospitals (*ziekenhuis*), all open 24 hours a day year-round.

Academisch Medisch Centrum

Meibergdreef 9, Zuid (566 9111/first aid 566 3232). Metro Holendrechp/ bus 59, 60, 120, 126, 158.

Boven IJ Ziekenhuis

Statenjachtstraat 1, Noord (634 6346/first aid 634 6200). Bus 34, 36, 37, 39, 171, 172.

Onze Lieve Vrouwe Gasthuis

's Gravesandeplein 16, Oost (599 9111/first aid 599 3016). Tram 3, 6, 10/Metro Weesperplein or Wibautstraat. **Map** p316 G4.

St Lucas Andreas Ziekenhuis

Jan Tooropstraat 164, West (510 8911/first aid 510 8161). Tram 13/bus 19, 47, 80, 82, 97.

VU Ziekenhuis

De Boelelaan 1117, Zuid (444 4444/first aid 444 3636). Metro Amstelveenseweg/bus 142, 147, 148, 149, 170, 171, 172.

Contraception & abortion

Amsterdams Centrum voor seksueele gezondheid

Sarphatistraat 618-26, the Plantage (624 5426). Tram 6, 9, 10, 14/bus 22. **Open** 9am-4pm Mon-Fri. **Map** p316 G3.
An abortion clinic. Besides giving information on health, the staff at this family-planning centre can help visitors with prescriptions for contraceptive pills, morning-after pills (also available Sat/Sun between 5 and 6pm: €32.50, cash only), condoms, IUD fitting and cervical smears. Prescription charges vary.

Polikliniek Oosterpark

Oosterpark 59, Oost (693 2151). Tram 3, 6, 9. **Open** *Advice services* 9am-5pm daily. **Map** p316 H4.
Advice on contraception and abortion. Non-residents will be charged a fee for an abortion based on the term of the pregnancy.

Dentists

For a dentist (*tandarts*), call 0900 821 2230. Operators can put you in touch with your nearest dentist; lines are open 24 hours. Alternatively, make an appointment at one of the clinics listed below.

AOC

Wilhelmina Gasthuisplein 167, Oud West (616 1234). Tram 1, 2, 3, 5, 6, 12. **Open** 9am-noon, 1-4pm Mon-Fri. **Map** p313 B5.

Emergency dental treatment. They also have a Dutch language recorded service on 686 1109 that tells you where a walk-in clinic will be open at 11.30am and 9.30pm that day. Ask staff at your hotel to call if you're not confident of understanding Dutch.

TBB

570 9595.
A 24-hour service that can refer callers to a dentist. Operators can also give details of chemists open outside normal hours.

Opticians

For details of opticians and optometrists in Amsterdam, *see p165* or look under 'Opticiens' in the *Gouden Gids*.

Pharmacies

For pharmacy hours, *see below*. For pharmacies, *see p182*.

Prescriptions

Chemists (*drogists*) sell toiletries and non-prescription drugs and are usually open from 9.30am to 5.30pm, Monday to Saturday. For prescription drugs, go to a pharmacy (*apotheek*), usually open from 9.30am to 5.30pm Monday to Friday. Outside these hours, phone Afdeling Inlichtingen Apotheken (*see p288*) or consult the daily *Het Parool*, which publishes details of which *apotheken* are open late that week. Details are posted at local *apotheken*.

STDs, HIV & AIDS

The Netherlands was one of the first countries to pour money into research once the HIV virus was recognised. But though the country was swift to take action and promote safe sex, condoms are still not distributed free in clubs and bars as they are in the UK.

As well as the groups listed below, the AIDS Helpline (689 2577; open 2-10pm Mon-Fri), part of HIV Vereniging (*see below*), offers advice and can put you in contact with every department you need. Also the

city's health department, the GG&GD, runs free and anonymous STD clinics.

GG&GD

Groenburgwal 44 (555 5822/ www.soa.nl). Tram 9,14/Metro Waterlooplein. **Open** 8.30-10.30am, 1.30-3.30pm Mon-Fri; 7-10.30pm Tue, Thur. **Map** p311 E3.
Examinations and treatment of STDs, including an HIV test, are free. Walk-in or call for an appointment.

HIV Vereniging

1e Helmersstraat 17 B-3, Oud West (689 3915/www.hivnet.org). Tram 1, 2, 3, 5, 6, 12. **Open** 9am-5pm Mon-Fri. **Map** p314 C5.
The Netherlands HIV Association supports the interests of those who are HIV positive, including offering legal help, and produces a bi-monthly Dutch magazine, *HIV Nieuws* (€38 per year). There's an HIV café every Sun (4-8pm), a buffet on the first Sun of the month (5.30pm, call by Fri to reserve, cost €5),Tue dinners (from 6pm, cost €5); and Wed lunch (from 12.30pm, cost €2.50).
Checkpoint is located here. You can get HIV test results in one hour. Call 689 2577 (2-6pm Mon-Fri) to make an appointment for the Friday evening clinic or walk-in any Friday between 7pm and 9pm. The cost for the test is €15.

Schorer Gay and Lesbian Health

Sarphatistraat 35, Southern Canal Belt (573 9444/664 6069/www. schorer.nl). Tram 7, 10. **Open** 9am-5pm Mon-Fri. **Map** p315 F4.
This state-funded agency offers psycho-social support, education and HIV prevention advice for gays and lesbians. Staff speak English.

Stichting AIDS Fonds

Keizersgracht 390-392, Western Canal Belt (626 2669/fax 627 5221/ www.aidsfonds.nl). Tram 1, 2, 5. **Open** 9am-5pm Mon-Fri. **Map** p314 C4.
This group runs fundraisers and channels money into research and safe sex promotion. It also runs a AIDS/STD infoline for gay and lesbian-specific health questions (0900 204 2040, 2-10pm Mon-Fri) and organises workshops on anal sex. Parts of its website are in English.

Helplines

Alcoholics Anonymous

625 6057/www.aa-netherlands.org. **Open** 24hr answerphone.
A lengthy but informative message in English/Dutch details times and

Directory

dates of meetings, and contact numbers for counsellors. The website is in English and you can locate meetings per day or per town.

Narcotics Anonymous
662 6307. **Open** 24hr answerphone in English/Dutch with phone numbers of counsellors.

SOS Telephone Helpline
675 7575. **Open** 24hrs daily.
A counselling service – comparable to the Samaritans in the UK and Lifeline in the US – for anyone with emotional problems, run by volunteers. English isn't always understood at first, but keep trying and someone will be able to help you.

ID

Everyone is required to carry some sort of identification when opening accounts at banks or other financial institutions, job seeking, applying for benefits, if found on public transport without a ticket or when going to a professional football match. You have to register with the local council, which is in the same building as the Aliens' Police (*see p295*).

Insurance

EU countries have reciprocal medical arrangements with the Netherlands. British citizens will need form E111, which can be found in leaflet T6 at UK post offices or obtained by filling in the application form in leaflet SA30, available from the Dutch Post Office. Read the small print so you know how to get treatment at a reduced charge: you may have to explain this to the Dutch doctor or dentist who treats you. If you need treatment, photocopy your insurance form and leave it with the doctor or dentist concerned. Not all treatments are covered by the E111, so take out private travel insurance covering both health and personal belongings. Citizens of other EU countries should

make sure they have obtained one of the forms E110, E111 or E112; citizens of all other countries should take out insurance before their visit.

Internet

Among Amsterdam's ISPs are Xs4all (www.xs4all.nl) and Chello (www.chello.nl). All global ISPs have a presence here (check websites for a local number). Local hotels are increasingly well equipped, whether with dataports in the rooms or a terminal in the lobby. For a selection of websites, *see p297*.

Internet cafés

Easy Internet Café
Reguliersbreestraat 22, Southern Canal Belt (no phone/www. easyeverything.com). Tram 16, 24, 25. **Open** 9am-10pm daily. **Rates** from €2.50/unit. **No credit cards.** **Map** p315 D4.
The amount of time one unit buys depends on how busy the place is: it can be as little as a half-hour or as much as six hours. Passes for one to 30 days are also available. Branches at Damrak 33 and Leidsestraat 24.

Freeworld
Nieuwendijk 30, Old Centre: New Side (620 0902/www.freeworld-internetcafe.nl). Tram 1, 2, 5, 13, 17, 20. **Open** 9am-1am Mon-Thur, Sun; 9am-3am Fri, Sat. **Rates** €1/30 min. **No credit cards.** **Map** p310 D2.
You surf, you drink: refreshments are compulsory.

Internet Cafe
Martelaarsgracht 11, Old Centre: New Side (no phone/www. internetcafe.nl). Tram 4, 9, 16, 20, 24, 25. **Open** 9am-1am Mon-Thur, Sun; 9am-3am Fri, Sat. **Rates** around €1/30min. **No credit cards.** **Map** p310 D2.
Compulsory drinks: offered frequently by the staff.

Left luggage

There is a staffed left-luggage counter at Schiphol Airport (601 2443/www.schiphol.nl) where you can store luggage for up to one month, open from 7am to 10.45pm daily, (€5/item/24hrs, €3/item/each

24hrs after). There are also lockers in the arrival and departure halls, while in Amsterdam there are lockers at Centraal Station with 24-hour access (from €3/24 hrs).

Legal help

ACCESS
Plein 24, 2511 CS, The Hague (070 346 2525/www.access-nl.org). **Open** 10am-4pm Mon-Fri.
The Administrative Committee to Coordinate English Speaking Services provides assistance in English through an information line, workshops and counselling.

Bureau Voor Rechtshulp
Spuistraat 10, Old Centre: New Side (520 5100/www.bureaurechtshulp.nl). Tram 1, 2, 5. **Open** *Telephone enquiries* 9am-1pm; 2-5pm Mon-Fri. *By appointment* 9am-1pm Mon-Fri. **Map** p310 C3.
Qualified lawyers give free or low-cost legal advice. Other location at 2e Oosterparkstraat 274.

Legal Advice Line
444 6333. **Open** *Telephone enquiries* 9pm-5pm Mon-Thur. Free advice from student lawyers.

Libraries

You'll need to show proof of residence in Amsterdam and ID to join a library (*bibliotheek*) and borrow books. It costs €21 (23s-64s) or €12.50 (19s-22s, over-65s) per year and is free for under-18s. However, in public libraries (*openbare bibliotheek*) you can read books, papers and magazines without membership. For university libraries, *see p294*.

Centrale Bibliotheek
Prinsengracht 587, Western Canal Belt (523 0800/www.oba.nl). Tram 1, 2, 5. **Open** 1-9pm Mon; 10am-9pm Tue-Thur; 10am-5pm Fri, Sat; *Oct-Mar* 10am-5pm Sun. **Map** p314 C4.
Anyone can use the main public library for reference purposes. There's a variety of English-language books.

Lost property

Report lost property to the police immediately; *see p292*. If you lose your passport, inform your embassy or consulate as well. For anything lost at the Hoek van Holland ferry terminal or Schiphol Airport, contact the company you're travelling with. For lost credit cards, *see p292*.

Centraal Station

Stationsplein 15, Old Centre: Old Side (0900 202 1163). Tram 1, 2, 4, 5, 9, 13, 16, 17, 24, 25. **Open** 8am-6pm Mon-Fri; 7am-5pm Sat. **Map** p310 D1. Items found on trains are kept here for three days (it's easiest to just go to any window where they sell tickets and ask) and then sent to Centraal Bureau Gevonden Voorwerpen (Central Lost Property Office), 2e Daalsedijk 4, 3551 EJ Utrecht (030 235 3923, 8am-5pm Mon-Fri). Items are held for three months. If you pick it up it costs €10, posting costs €15 and up.

GVB Lost Property

Prins Hendrikkade 108-14, Old Centre: New Side (0900 8011). Tram 1, 2, 4, 5, 9, 13, 16, 17, 24, 25. **Open** 9am-4.30pm Mon-Fri. **Map** p310 C1. Ring before 10pm, describe what you lost on bus, metro or tram, and leave a number. They will call you back within three days if it is found.

Police Lost Property

Stephensonstraat 18, Zuid (559 3005). Tram 12/Metro Amstel Station/bus 14. **Open** *In person* 9.30am-3.30pm Mon-Fri. *By phone* noon-3.30pm Mon-Fri. Before contacting here, check the local police station.

Media

Newspapers & magazines

De Telegraaf is the country's biggest-selling paper, the nearest it has to a tabloid. *Het Parool* is a hip afternoon rag and rates as the Amsterdam paper (its Saturday *PS* supplement also has easily decipherable entertainment listings). *De Volkskrant*'s readers are young liberals while *NRC Handelsblad* is the highbrow national.

For Anglophones, the Amsterdam Tourist Board publishes the monthly *Day by Day*, a basic listings guide available at VVV Tourist

offices (€1.50). For more on local English-language listing magazines *see p286* **'Bloids of Amsterdam.**

Foreign magazines and papers are widely available, but pricey; British papers are around €2 for a daily, €4 for a Sunday. Athenaeum is a browser's dream; 100 metres away, Waterstone's stocks UK publications, and the American Book Center is nearby. For all, *see p161*.

Broadcast media

Besides the national basics (Ned 1, Ned 2 and Ned 3), Amsterdam also has its own 'city CNN' – the really quite cool AT5 (its site www.at5.nl has some English) – as well as Salto, that broadcasts typically local and low-budget culture/cult stuff. There's also about a dozen national commercial stations; they include Yorin and Veronica (both painfully commercial); and NET5, RTL4 and RTL5 (mostly series and films from the US). There are now about 30 extra channels on cable, including stations in German, French, Italian and Belgian, various local channels, and multinationals such as BBC World, CNN and National Geographic. The basic deal also includes BBC1 and 2, so there's no need to miss out on an episode of *EastEnders*. The wall-to-wall porn is largely an urban myth, so don't expect any late-night thrills unless your hotel has the 'extended service', which usually also features film channels, Discovery, Eurosport and other cable stalwarts. Dutch radio is generally as bland as the TV, but at least Radio Netherlands (www.rnw.nl) often has some interesting stuff in English.

Money

Since January 2002 the Dutch currency has been the Euro.

ATMs

Cash machines are only found at banks here: as yet, no bank has been resourceful enough to set any up in shops or bars, as is increasingly the case in the UK and parts of the US. If your cashcard carries the Maestro or Cirrus symbols you should be able to withdraw cash from ATMs, though it's worth checking with your bank a) that it's possible and b) what the charging structure is.

Banks

There's usually little difference between the rates of exchange offered by banks and bureaux de change, but banks tend to charge less commission. Most banks are open 9am to 5pm, Monday to Friday, with the Postbank opening on Saturday mornings as well. Dutch banks will buy and sell foreign currency and exchange travellers' cheques, but few of them will give cash advances against credit cards. For a list of banks, *see p285*, or check *Gouden Gids* under 'Banken'.

Bureaux de change

A number of bureaux de change can be found in the city centre. The ones listed offer reasonable rates, though they usually charge more than banks. Hotel and tourist bureaus cost more.

American Express

Damrak 66, Old Centre: New Side (504 8777/www.americanexpress. com). Tram 4, 9, 14, 16, 24, 25. **Open** 9am-5pm Mon-Fri; 9am-noon Sat. **Map** p310 D2.

GWK Travelex

Centraal Station, Old Centre: Old Side (0900-0566 €0.25/min/ www.gwktravelex.nl). Tram 1, 2, 4, 5, 9, 13, 16, 17, 24, 25. **Open** 8am-10pm daily (Sun from 9am). *Telephone enquiries* 8am-11pm daily. **Map** p310 D1. **Other locations:** Leidseplein 1-3 (8.30am-10pm daily); Schiphol Airport (7am-10pm daily); Damrak 86 (10am-10pm daily); Dam 23-5

Directory

(9.15am-7pm Mon-Fri, 10.15am-5.45pm Sun); Damrak 1-5 (9am-8pm daily); Leidseplein 31a (10.15am-5.45pm Mon-Fri, 10.30am-6pm Sat, 10.30am-6pm Sun).

Credit cards

Credit cards are widely used. The majority of restaurants will take at least one type of card; they're less popular in bars and shops, so always carry some cash. **Chip and pin** is upcoming. The most popular cards, in descending order, are Visa, Mastercard (aka Eurocard), American Express and Diners Club. If you lose your card, call the relevant 24-hour number immediately.

American Express 504 8666.
Diners Club 654 5511.
Mastercard/Eurocard 030 283 5555 if card was issued in the Netherlands; otherwise, freephone 0800 022 5821.
Visa 660 0611 if card was issued in the Netherlands; otherwise, freephone 0800 022 4176.

Tax

Sales tax (aka VAT) – 19 per cent on most items, six per cent on goods such as books and food, more on alcohol, tobacco and petrol – will be included in the prices quoted in shops. If you live outside the EU, you are entitled to a tax refund on purchases of up to €137 from one shop on any one day. At shops with the Global Refund TAX FREE SHOPPING sign get the assistant to give you a Global Refund Cheque (export certificate), and then, as you leave the country, present it to a customs official who'll stamp it; you can then collect your cash at the ABN-AMRO bank at Schiphol Airport or via post at a later date (ask the official for information).

Opening hours

For all our listings in this guide we give full opening times, but as a general rule, shops are open from 1pm to 6pm on Monday (if they're open at all; many shops are closed Mondays); 10am to 6pm Tuesday to Friday, with some open until 9pm on Thursdays; and 9am to 5pm on Saturdays. Smaller shops are more erratic; if in doubt, phone. For shops that open late, *see p175*.

The city's bars open at various times during the day and close at around 1am throughout the week, except for Fridays and Saturdays, when they stay open until 2am or 3am. Restaurants generally open in the evening from 5pm until 11pm (though some close as early as 9pm); many are closed on Sunday and Monday.

Police stations

Dutch police, (www.politie-amsterdam-amstelland.nl, some English), are under no obligation to grant a phone call to those they detain – they can hold people for up to six hours for questioning if the alleged crime is not serious, 24 hours for major matters – but they'll phone the relevant consulate on behalf of a foreign detainee. If you are a victim of a crime, need practical or medical support, have lost your documents – anything really that might go wrong as a tourist – the Police Station on Nieuwezijds Voorburgwal has a special Amsterdam Tourist Assistance Service (ATAS, *see below*). For emergencies, *see p288*. There is also a 24-hour police service line 0900 8844 for the Amsterdam area.

Hoofdbureau van Politie (Police Headquarters)

Elandsgracht 117, the Jordaan (0900 8844). Tram 7, 10. **Open** 24hrs daily. **Map** p314 C4.

Amsterdam Tourist Assistance Service (ATAS)

Nieuwezijds Voorburgwal 104-108 (625 3246). Tram 1, 2, 5, 6, 13, 17. **Open** 10am-10pm daily. **Map** p310 C2.

Postal services

For post destined for outside Amsterdam, use the *overige bestemmingen* slot in letter boxes. The logo for the national postal service is TPG Post (white letters on a red oblong). Most post offices – recognisable by their red and blue signs – are open 9am to 5pm, Monday to Friday. In 2006, they plan to change their name to TNT Post and orange will become their main branding colour for logo and postboxes alike. The postal information phoneline is 058 233 3333. Housed in every post office is Postbank, a money-changing facility. It costs €0.61 to send a postcard to anywhere in Europe, and €0.77 beyond. Apart from in post offices, stamps (*postzegels*) can be bought from tobacconists and souvenir shops.

Post offices

For all the post offices in the region, look in *Gouden Gids* under 'postkantoren'. Two handy branches are at Waterlooplein 10 (Jodenbuurt, 620 3081, 9am-6pm Mon-Fri, 10am-1.30pm Sat) and Albert Cuypstraat 151/155 (the Pijp, 662 2635, 9am-5pm Mon-Fri, 10am-1.30pm Sat).

Main Post Office

Singel 250, Old Centre: New Side (330 0555). Tram 1, 2, 5, 13, 14, 17. **Open** 9am-6pm Mon-Wed, Fri; 9am-8pm Thur; 10am-1.30pm Sat. **Map** p310 C3.

Post restante/ general delivery

Post Restante

Hoofdpostkantoor, Singel 250, 1016 AB Amsterdam. **Map** p310 C3.
If you're not sure where you're going to end up staying in Amsterdam – and some visitors remain unsure throughout their visit – people can send post to the above address. You'll be able to collect it from the main post office (*see above*); take along some picture ID when you're collecting your mail.

Tickets please

Though the Amsterdam Tourist board and the GWK sell tickets for concerts, plays and other events, the main ticket retailer in Amsterdam is the AUB. Its services run from online sales to personal service at its Leidseplein shop. AUB also has a new ticketpoint in Lloyd Hotel (*see p70* **Cooking culture with Lloyd**).

Before you buy tickets, it helps to know what's on, when. For this, pick up an English language listing mag like *Amsterdam Weekly* (for more *see p286* '**Bloids of Amsterdam**') or the AUB's free monthly magazine *Uitkrant*, both available in many theatres and bookshops (as is *Uitgids*, an annual publication offering details of subscription series and the like). It's only in Dutch – as is the online version (*see below*) – but it's easy to decipher. *Uitkrant* (pronounced 'out-krant') can also be had at the AUB Ticketshop in

Leidseplein, which is open from 10am to 6pm daily except Thursday, when it closes at 9pm and Sundays when it opens at noon. Expect to pay 2 commission per ticket. It's also the place to go if you want to browse through the different flyers and other listings mags. The Leidseplein location also acts as a last-minute ticketshop, when that night's unsold tickets for theatre and concerts are on sale for half the face price (plus 1 service charge). The tickets go on sale at noon.

You can also buy tickets by phone, though the commission is about 50 per cent higher and you'll be paying premium phone rates. The *Uitlijn* ('out-line') service is on 0900 0191 (+31 20 621 1288 from abroad), and is open 9am to 8pm daily. Finally, for a commission of around 2.50 per ticket, you can book online at www.uitlijn.nl.

Religion

Catholic
St John and St Ursula Begijnhof 30, Old Centre: New Side (622 1918/www.begijnhofamsterdam.nl). Tram 1, 2, 4, 5, 16, 24, 25. **Open** *Chapel* 1-6.30pm Mon; 9am-6.30pm Tue-Fri; 9am-6pm Sat, Sun. *Adoration of the Eucharist* 4-5pm, 5.30-6.30pm Mon-Fri; 5-6pm Sat, Sun. *Services* 9am, 5pm Mon-Fri, 9am Sat; 10am (in Dutch), 11.15am (in French) Sun. Phone for details. **Map** p310 D3. Check out also the Begijnhof Shop for tourist information and religious books and souvenirs.

Dutch Reformed Church
Oude Kerk, Oudekerksplein, Old Centre: Old Side (625 8284/www.oudekerk.nl). Tram 4, 9, 16, 24, 25. **Open** 11am-5pm Mon-Sat; 1-5pm Sun. *Services* in Dutch; 11am Sun. **Map** p310 D2.

Jewish
Liberal Jewish Community Amsterdam *Jacob Soetendorpstraat 8, Zuid (642 3562/office rabbinate 644 2619). Tram 4.* **Open** *Rabbi's office* 10am-3pm Mon-Thur; 10am-1pm Fri. *Services* 8pm Fri; 10am Sat. **Orthodox Jewish Community Amsterdam** *Postbus 7967, Van der Boechorststraat 26, Zuid (646 0046). Bus 69, 169.* **Open** 9am-5pm Mon-Fri by appointment only. Information on orthodox synagogues and Jewish facilities.

Muslim
THAIBA Islamic Cultural Centre Kraaiennest 125, Zuid (698 2526). Metro Gaasperplas. Phone for details of mosques, prayer times and cultural activities.

Reformed Church
English Reformed Church, Begijnhof 48, Old Centre: New Side (624 9665/www.ercadam.nl). Tram 1, 2, 4, 5, 9, 16, 24, 25. **Services** in English 10.30am Sun. **Map** p310 D3. The main place of worship for the local English-speaking community.

Safety & security

Amsterdam is a relatively safe city, but that's not to say you shouldn't take care. The Red Light District is rife with undesirables who, if not violent, are expert pickpockets; be vigilant, especially on or around bridges, and try to avoid making eye contact with anyone who looks like they may be up to no good.

Take care on the train to Schiphol, where there has been a recent spate of thefts, and, if you cycle, lock your bike. Otherwise, just use common sense, keeping valuables in a safe place, not leaving bags unattended, and so on.

Smoking

Smoking is common, though an impending law that aims to guarantee a smoke-free work environment may change that. But meanwhile, you'll have no problems sparking up. For smoking dope, *see p48*.

Study

Amsterdam's two major universities are the UvA (Universiteit van Amsterdam), which has around 27,000 students, and the VU (Vrije Universiteit), with 14,000. Many UvA buildings across town are historic and listed (recognise them by their red and black plaques), whereas the VU has just one big building at de Boelelaan, in the south of Amsterdam.

Students are often entitled to discounts; presenting an ISIC card is usually enough.

Courses
A number of UvA departments offer international courses and programmes at all levels. Details are available from the

Directory

Office of Foreign Relations (Binnengasthuisstraat 9, 1012 ZA, 525 8080).

Amsterdam-Maastricht Summer University

Felix Meritis Building, Keizersgracht 324, Southern Canal Belt (620 0225/ www.amsu.edu). Tram 1, 2, 5. **Courses** mid July-early Sept. **Map** p314 C4.
AMSU offers a summer programme of courses, workshops and seminars in the arts, economics, politics, sciences, European studies, plus classes in Maastricht.

Crea

Turfdraagsterpad 17, Old Centre: Old Side (525 1400/www.crea.uva. nl). Tram 4, 9, 14, 16, 24, 25. **Open** 10am-11pm Mon-Fri; 10am-5pm Sat; 11am-5pm Sun. *Mid-July-mid-Aug* 10am-5pm Mon-Fri. **Map** p310 D3.
Inexpensive creative courses, lectures and performances, covering theatre, radio, video, media, dance, music, photography and fine art. Courses are not in English. They've also got a new second branch to expand their offerings: Crea II Vendelstraat 2, (525 4889). Open 10am-11pm Mon-Fri; 10am-5pm Sat; 11am-5pm Sun.

UvA Service & Information Centre

Binnengasthuisstraat 9, Old Centre: Old Side (525 8080/www.english. uva.nl). Tram 4, 9, 16, 24, 25. **Open** *In person* 10am-5pm Mon-Wed, Fri; 10am-7pm Thur. *Telephone enquiries* 9am-10am Tue-Thur; *free appointment* 11am-noon Tue-Thur. **Map** p310 D3.
Personal advice on studying and everything that goes with it.

VU Student Information

De Boelelaan 1105 (Office 444 7777/ direct line 444 5000/www.english. vu.nl). **Open** 9am-5pm Mon-Fri.
Help on courses and accommodation. Foreign students call 444 5030.

Student bookshop

VU Boekhandel

De Boelelaan 1105, Zuid (644 4355/ www.vuboekhandel.nl). Tram 5/Metro 51. **Open** 9am-7pm Mon-Fri; 10am-3.30pm Sat. **Credit** AmEx, MC, V.

Students' unions

AEGEE

Vendelsstraat 2, Old Centre: Old Side (525 2496/www.aegee-amsterdam. nl). Tram 4, 6, 9, 24, 25. **Open** 2-5pm Mon-Fri. **Map** p310 D3.

The Association des Etats Généraux des Etudiants de l'Europe organises seminars, workshops, summer courses and sporting events.

SRVU

De Boelelaan 1083a, Zuid (444 9424/www.srvu.org). Tram 5/Metro 51. **Open** 11am-4pm Mon-Fri.
SRVU is the union for VU students. It can help foreign students find a place to stay, and offer general advice. Membership is €10 per year.

University libraries

Both libraries below hold many academic titles and also provide access to the internet. There is also an Adam Netpas that allows you to use the UvA, VU libraries and public libraries of Amsterdam (*openbare bibliotheek*), €32.50 a year with passport ID.

UvA Main Library

Singel 425, Old Centre: New Side (525 2326/www.uba.uva.nl). Tram 1, 2, 5. **Open** *Study* 8.30am-midnight Mon-Fri; 9.30am-5pm Sat; 11am-5pm Sun. *Borrowing* 9.30am-6pm Mon-Thur; 9.30am-5pm Fri; 9.30am-1pm Sat. **Map** p314 D4.
To borrow books you need a UB (*Universiteit Bibliotheek*, University Library) card (€22.50): foreign students can get one if they're in Amsterdam for three months or more. Cards can be issued for one day, one month or one year. Day €3 and week €7.50 cards enable you to read books but not withdraw them.

VU Main Library

De Boelelaan 1105, Zuid (598 5200/ www.ubvu.vu.nl). Tram 5/Metro 51. **Open** *Study* 7am-11pm Mon-Fri; 8.15am-4pm Sat; *July-Aug* 8.15am-11pm Mon-Fri. *Borrowing* 9am-6pm Mon-Thur; 9am-5pm Fri.
Membership (€20/year) is open to foreign students.

Telephones

We list all Amsterdam numbers without the city code, which is 020. To call within the city, you don't need the code: just dial the seven-digit number. To call Amsterdam from elsewhere in the Netherlands, add 020 at the start of the listed number. Numbers in the Netherlands outside Amsterdam are listed with their code.

In addition to the standard city codes, three other types of numbers appear from time to time in this book. 0800 numbers are freephone numbers; those prefixed 0900 are charged at premium rates (€0.20 a minute or more); and 06 numbers are for mobile phones. If you're in doubt, call directory enquiries (0900 8008).

Dialling & codes

From the Netherlands

Dial the following code, then the number:
To Australia: 00 61
To Irish Republic: 00 353
To UK: 00 44, plus number (drop first '0' from area code)
To USA & Canada: 00 1

To the Netherlands

Dial the relevant international access code listed below, then the Dutch country code 31, then the number; drop the first '0' of the area code, so for Amsterdam use 20 rather than 020. To call 06 (mobile) numbers from abroad, there is no city code: just drop the first '0' from the 06 and dial the number as it appears. However, 0800 (freephone) and 0900 (premium rate) numbers cannot be reached from abroad.
From Australia: 00 11
From Irish Republic: 00
From UK: 00
From USA: 011

Within the Netherlands

National directory enquiries: 0900 8008 (€1.15/call)
International directory enquiries: 0900 8418 (€1.15/call)
Local operator: 0800 0101
International operator: 0800 0410

Making a call

Listen for the dialling tone (a hum), insert a phonecard or money, dial the code (none for calls within Amsterdam), then the number. A digital display on public phones shows credit remaining, but only those coins that are wholly unused are returned. Phoning from a hotel is pricey.

International calls

International calls can be made from all phone boxes. For more information on rates, phone international directory enquiries (costs €1.15) 0900 8418.

Directory

Telephone directories

Found in post offices (see p292). When phoning information services, taxis or train stations you may hear the recorded message, 'Er zijn nog drie [3]/twee [2]/een [1] wachtende(n) voor u.' This tells you how many people are ahead of you in the telephone queuing system.

Public phones

Public phone boxes are mainly glass with a green trim. There are also telephone 'poles', identifiable by the KPN logo. Most phones take cards rather than coins, available from the Amsterdam Tourist Board, stations, post offices and tobacconists. You can use credit cards in many phones.

Mobile phones

Amsterdam's mobile network is run on a mix of the 900 and 1800 GSM bands, which means all dual-band UK handsets should work here. However, it's always best to check with your service provider that it has an arrangement with a Dutch provider. US phone users should always contact their provider before departure to check compatibility.

Time

Amsterdam is an hour ahead of Greenwich Mean Time (GMT). All clocks on Central European Time (CET) now go back and forward on the same dates as GMT.

Tipping

Though a service charge will be included in hotel, taxi, bar, café and restaurant bills, it's polite to round your payment up to the nearest Euro for small bills and to the nearest five Euros for larger sums – though a standard 10% is becoming more and more common – leaving the extra in change rather than filling in the blank on a credit card slip. In taxis, most people tip ten per cent.

Toilets

For men there are the historic green metal urinals and additional weekend conveniences at places like Leidseplein. For the ladies, it's a sadder story: public loos are rare, and you may be forced to buy something in a bar or café.

Tourist information

Amsterdam Tourist Board (VVV)

Stationsplein 10, Old Centre: New Side (0900 400 4040/www.visit amsterdam.nl). Tram 1, 2, 4, 5, 9, 13, 16, 17, 24, 25. **Open** 9am-5pm daily. **Map** p310 D1.
The main office of the VVV is right outside Centraal Station. English-speaking staff can change money and provide details on transport, entertainment, exhibitions and day-trips in the Netherlands. They also arrange hotel bookings for a fee of €14 by phone (see p54) or €3 at a VVV office, excursions or car hire for free. There is a good range of brochures for sale detailing walks and cycling tours, as well as cassette tours, maps and, for €1.50, a monthly listings magazine Day by Day.
The info line features an English-language service (€0.40/min).
Other locations: Leidseplein 1 (9.15am-5pm Mon-Thur, Sun; 9.15am-7pm Fri, Sat); Centraal Station, platform 2B 15 (8am-8pm Mon-Sat; 9am-5pm Sun); Schiphol Airport, arrivals hall 2 (7am-10pm daily).

Visas & immigration

Citizens from the rest of the EU, the USA, Canada, Australia and New Zealand only need a valid passport for a stay up to three months. Citizens of other countries should apply in advance for a tourist visa. Confirm visa requirements well before you plan to travel, with your local Dutch embassy or consult www.immigratiedienst.nl.

For stays longer than three months, apply for a residents' permit (MVV visa), generally easier to get if you're from one of the countries listed above. (Technically, EU citizens don't need a residents' permit, but they will be required for all sorts of bureaucratic functions.)

When you have an address, take your birth certificate to Dienst Vreemdelingenpolitie (Aliens' Police; Johan Huizingalaan 757, Slotervaart; 559 6300/www.immigratie dienst.nl), pick up a form and wait for an interview.

When to go

Climate

Amsterdam's climate is changeable. January and February are cold, with summer humid. If you know Dutch, try the weather line on 0900 8003 (€0.60/min). For mean temperatures, see p285 **Weather report**.

Public holidays

Called 'Nationale Feestdagen' in Dutch, they are as follows: New Year's Day; Good Friday; Easter Sunday and Monday; Koninginnedag (Queen's Day, 30 April); Remembrance Day (4 May); Liberation Day (5 May); Ascension Day; Whit (Pentecost) Sunday and Monday; Christmas Day, and Boxing Day.

Women

Aside from some pockets of the Red Light District late at night, central Amsterdam is fairly safe for women, as long as usual common-sense safety precautions are observed.

De Eerstelijn and Meldpunt Vrouwenopvang

611 6022. **Open** 24hrs.
Call this number for support if you have been a victim of rape, assault, sexual harassment or threats. In cases of immediate threat or violence you will be referred to a safe house.

Working in Amsterdam

EU nationals with a resident's permit can work here; non-EU citizens will find it difficult to get a visa without a job in place. Jobs are hard to come by; more so with no visa.

Directory

Vocabulary

The vast majority of people you'll meet in Amsterdam will speak good English, and you'll probably be able to get by without a word of Dutch during your stay. However, a little effort goes a long way, and the locals are appreciative of those visitors polite enough to take five minutes and learn some basic phrases. Here are a few that might help.

PRONUNCIATION GUIDE

ch – as in 'loch'
ee – as in 'hay'
g – similar to 'ch'
ie – as in 'lean'
ei – as in 'line'
j – as in 'yes' except when preceded by 'i', when it should be said as 'ay' (*see below, 'y'*).
oe – as in 'loon'
oo – as in 'no'
ou, au, ui – as in 'cow'
tie – as in 'itsy bitsy'
tje – as in 'church'
v – as in 'for'
w – as in 'which', with a hint of 'v'
y, ij – a cross between the 'i' (as used in 'hide') and the 'ay' (as used in 'way')

WORDS

hello – hallo (*hullo*) or dag (*daarg*)
goodbye – tot ziens (*tot zeens*)
bye – dag (*daarg*)
yes – ja (*yah*)
yes please – ja, graag
no – nee (*nay*)
no thanks – nee, dank je (*nay, dank ye*)
please – alstublieft (*als-too-bleeft*); which is also used to mean 'there you are' when exchanging items with others
thank you – dank u (*dank-oo*)
thanks – bedankt
excuse me – pardon
good – goed
bad – slecht
big – groot
small – klein (*kline*)
waiter – ober
nice – mooi (*moy*)
tasty – lekker (*lecker*)
open – open
closed – gesloten/dicht
inside – binnen
outside – buiten (*bowten*)
left – links
right – rechts (*reks*)
straight on – rechtdoor
far – ver (*fair*)
near – dichtbij (*dikt-bye*)
entrance – ingang
exit – uitgang (*owtgang*)

car – auto
bus – bus
train – trein
ticket/s – kaart/kaarten
postcard – briefkaart
stamp – postzegel
glass – glas
coffee – koffie
tea – thee
water – water
wine – wijn
beer – bier
booking – reservering
the bill – rekening

PLACES

street – straat (*straart*)
square – plein (*pline*)
canal – gracht
shop – winkel
bank – bank
post office – postkantoor
pharmacy – apotheek
hotel – hotel
hotel room – hotelkamer
single/twin/double bedroom – eenpersoonskamer/tweepersoonskamer met aparte bedden/tweepersoonskamer
bar – bar
restaurant – restaurant
hospital – ziekenhuis
bus stop – bushalte
station – station

DAYS

Monday – Maandag
Tuesday – Dinsdag
Wednesday – Woensdag
Thursday – Donderdag
Friday – Vrijdag
Saturday – Zaterdag
Sunday – Zondag
today – vandaag
yesterday – gisteren
tomorrow – morgen
morning – ochtend
afternoon – middag
evening – avond
night – nacht
weekend – weekeinde

PHRASES

Excuse me, do you speak English?
– sorry, spreekt u Engels? (*sorry, spraykt oo Engels?*)
Sorry, I don't speak Dutch
– het spijt me, ik spreek geen Nederlands (*et spite meh, ik spraykhane nayderlants*)
I don't understand
– Ik begrijp het niet (*ik begripe et neet*)
What is that?
– wat is dat? (*vot is dat?*)
Where is…?
– waar is…?
What's the time?
– hoe laat is het?

My name is…
– mijn naam is… (*mine naam is…*)
I want…
– Ik wil graag…
how much is…?
– wat kost…?
Could I have a receipt?
– mag ik een bonnetje alstublieft?
Do you accept credit cards?
– Nemen jullie/u krediet kaarten?
How far is it to…?
– hoe ver is het naar…?
I would like a ticket to…
– Ik wil graag een kaart naar…
Do you have a light?
– Hebt je/u een vuurtje?
What's your name?
– Hoe heet jij/u?
Would you like a drink?
– Wil je/u iets te drinken?
I don't smoke
– Ik rook niet
I'm tired
– Ik ben moe
I disapprove of drugs
– Ik heb een afkeur voor drugs
I am sick
– Ik ben ziek
I think I ate too much spacecake
– Ik denk dat ik te veel spacecake heb opgegeten

INSULTS

fuck! – kut (female private parts)
bloody lunatic! – boer (literally 'farmer' – used by cyclists against car drivers)
arsehole! – lul (male private parts)
motherfucker! – moederneuker
beanpole! – volgeschieten palingvel (literally 'shit-filled eel-skin' – directed towards skinny person)

NUMBERS

0 nul
1 een
2 twee
3 drie
4 vier
5 vijf
6 zes
7 zeven
8 acht
9 negen
10 tien
11 elf; 12 twaalf; 13 dertien; 14 veertien; 15 vijftien; 16 zestien; 17 zeventien; 18 achttien; 19 negentien; 20 twintig; 21 eenentwintig; 22 twee'ntwintig; 30 dertig; 31 eenendertig; 32 twee'ndertig; 40 veertig; 50 vijftig; 60 zestig; 70 zeventig; 80 tachtig; 90 negentig; 100 honderd; 101 honderd een; 200 tweehonderd; 1,000 duizend; 2,000 twee duizend; 100,000 honderd duizend; 1,000,000 een miljoen.

Directory

Further Reference

Books

Fiction

Baantjer *De Cock* series
This ex-Amsterdam cop used his experiences to write a series of crime novels set in town. Also a TV series.
Albert Camus *The Fall*
Man recalls his Parisian past while in Amsterdam's 'circles of hell'.
Arnon Grunberg *Blue Mondays*
Philip Roth's *Goodbye Columbus* goes Dutch in this 1994 bestseller.
Harry Mulisch *The Assault*
A boy's perspective on World War II. Also classic film.
Multatuli *Max Havelaar or the Coffee Auctions of the Dutch Trading Company*
The story of a colonial officer and his clash with the corrupt government.
Janwillem van der Wetering *The Japanese Corpse*
An off-the-wall police procedural set in Amsterdam.
Manfred Wolf (ed) *Amsterdam: A Traveller's Literary Companion*
The country's best writers tell tales of the city.

Non-fiction

Kathy Batista & Florian Migsch *A Guide to Recent Architecture: The Netherlands*
Part of the excellent pocket series, with great pictures.
Sean Condon *My 'Dam Life*
Offbeat insights by Australian wit.
Anne Frank *The Diary of Anne Frank*
The still-shocking wartime diary of the young Frank.
RH Fuchs *Dutch Painting*
A comprehensive guide.
Zbigniew Herbert *Still Life with a Bridle*
The Polish poet and essayist meditates on the Golden Age.
Etty Hillesum *An Interrupted Life: The Diaries and Letters 1941-1943*
The moving wartime experiences of a young Amsterdam Jewish woman who died in Auschwitz.
Geert Mak *Amsterdam: A Brief Life of the City*
The city's history told through the stories of its people.
Simon Schama *The Embarrassment of Riches*
A lively social and cultural history of the Netherlands.
David Winners *Brilliant Orange: the Neurotic Genius of Dutch Football*
Excellent delve into the Dutch psyche that takes in much more than just football.

Wim de Wit *The Amsterdam School: Dutch Expressionist Architecture*
Early 20th-century architecture.

Music

Albums

Arling & Cameron *Music for Imaginary Films* (2000)
Showered with acclaim, eclectic duo reinvent the history of film soundtracks.
Chet Baker *Live at Nick's* (1978)
Accompanied by his favourite rhythm section, Chet soars in one of his best live recordings.
The Beach Boys *Holland* (1973)
Californians hole up in Holland and start recording.
The Ex *Starters Alternators* (1998)
Anarcho squat punks/improv-jazzsters team up with Steve Albini.
Human Alert *Ego Ego* (2005)
Hysterically funny punk legends go orchestral.
Osdorp Posse *Origineel Amsterdams* (2000)
Nederhop maestros offer a primer in local street talk for *moederneukers*.

Films

Amsterdam Global Village
dir. Johan van der Keuken (1996)
A meditative and very long arty cruise through Amsterdam's streets and peoples.
Amsterdamned
dir. Dick Maas (1987)
Thriller with psychotic frogman and lots of canal chase scenes, made only slightly worse by continuity problems that result in characters turning an Amsterdam corner and ending up in Utrecht.
The Fourth Man
dir. Paul Verhoeven (1983)
Mr *Basic Instinct* films Gerard Reve novel with Jeroen Krabbe seething with homoerotic desire.
Hufters en Hofdames (Bastards and Bridesmaids)
dir. Eddy Terstall (1997)
Twentysomethings use Amsterdam as backdrop against which to have relationship trouble.
Karacter (Character)
dir. Mike van Diem (1997)
An impeccable father-son drama.
De Noorderlingen (The Northerners)
dir. Alex van Warmerdam (1992)
Absurdity and angst in a lonely Dutch subdivision.
Turks Fruit (Turkish Delight)
dir. Paul Verhoeven (1973)

Sculptor Rutger Hauer witnesses his babe's brain tumour.
Yes Nurse! No Nurse!
Dir. Pieter Kramer (2002)
Musical cult classic for connoisseurs of camp.
Zusje (Little Sister)
dir. Robert Jan Westdijk (1995)
A family affair with voyeuristic overtones.

Websites

www.amsterdam.nl
An accessible site with advice on living in and visiting Amsterdam. The searchable maps are terrific.
www.amsterdamhotspots.nl
An upbeat review-based site of, er, Amsterdam hotspots.
www.amsterdam-webcams.com
Some personal, some public, all in Amsterdam.
www.archined.nl
News and reviews of Dutch architecture, in both Dutch and English. Informative and interesting.
www.bmz.amsterdam.nl/adam
Fantastically detailed site devoted to Amsterdam's architectural heritage. Some pages in English.
www.channels.nl
Takes you, virtually, through Amsterdam's streets with reviews of their hotels, restaurants and clubs.
www.expatica.com
English news and reviews aimed at the expat in the Netherlands.
www.gayamsterdamlinks.com
What you'd expect.
www.panoramsterdam.nl
Over three hundred 360-degree shots of Amsterdam
gemeentearchief.amsterdam.nl
Dutch-only site of city archive.
www.nobodyhere.com
Winner of the 2003 Webby Award for best personal website. Weird and beautiful.
www.simplyamsterdam.nl
Aimed at the 'independent traveller'.
www.squat.net
The lowdown on the squat scene.
www.uitlijn.nl
Event listings for Amsterdam, in Dutch but fairly easy to navigate.
www.underwateramsterdam.com
An alternative listings e-mag in whose shallows several *Time Out* writers lurk.
www.urbanguide.nl
A guide to clubs, restaurants etc geared to the urban trendy hipster.
www.visitamsterdam.nl
The tourist board site which has gotten a tad hipper recently.
www.xs4all.nl/~4david
Drug techniques you never even knew existed.

Directory

Advertisers' Index

Please refer to the relevant page for contact details

Selected House Number	*463*
Place of Interest and/or Entertainment	
Hospital or College	
Pedestrianised street	
Railway Station	
Metro Station	Ⓜ
Area Name	**LEIDSEPLEIN**

0   250 m   500 m

© Copyright Time Out Group 2005   1/4 mile

Maps

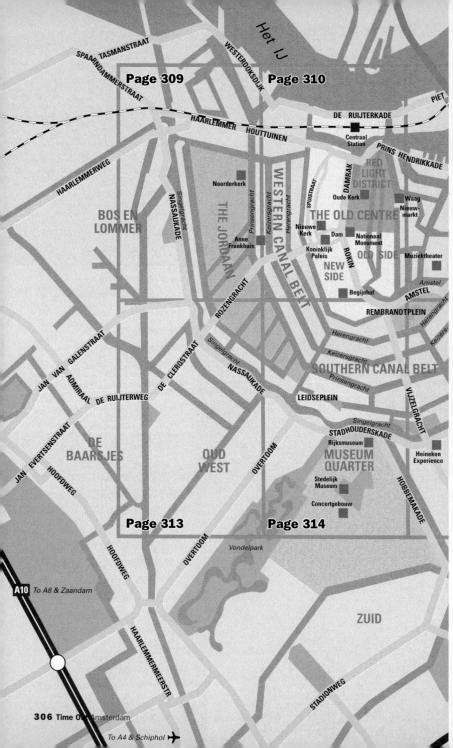

Page 309

Page 310

Het IJ

SPAARNDAMMERSTRAAT
TASMANSTRAAT
WESTERDOKSDIJK
PIET

DE RUIJTERKADE

HAARLEMMER HOUTTUINEN

Centraal
Station

PRINS HENDRIKKADE

HAARLEMMERWEG

RED
LIGHT
DISTRICT

DAMRAK

SPUISTRAAT

Noorderkerk

Oude Kerk

Waag

BOS EN
LOMMER

Singelgracht
NASSAUKADE

THE JORDAAN

Prinsengracht

Keizersgracht

Herengracht

WESTERN CANAL BELT

THE OLD CENTRE

Nieuw-
markt

Nieuwe
Kerk

Dam

Nationaal
Monument

OLD SIDE

Muziektheater

Anne
Frankhuis

Koninklijk
Paleis

ROKIN

NEW
SIDE

ROZENGRACHT

Amstel

Begijnhof

AMSTEL

REMBRANDTPLEIN

Singelgracht

DE CLERCQSTRAAT

NASSAUKADE

SOUTHERN CANAL BELT

Herengracht

Herengracht

Keizersgracht

Keizers

JAN VAN GALENSTRAAT

ADMIRAAL DE RUIJTERWEG

Prinsengracht

VIJZELGRACHT

LEIDSEPLEIN

JAN EVERTSENSTRAAT

Singelgracht

DE BAARSJES

HOOFDWEG

STADHOUDERSKADE

OUD
WEST

OVERTOOM

Rijksmuseum

MUSEUM
QUARTER

Heineken
Experience

HOBBEMAKADE

Page 313

Page 314

Stedelijk
Museum

Concertgebouw

OVERTOOM

Vondelpark

HOOFDWEG

A10 To A8 & Zaandam

ZUID

HAARLEMMERMEERSTR

STADIONWEG

To A4 & Schiphol ✈

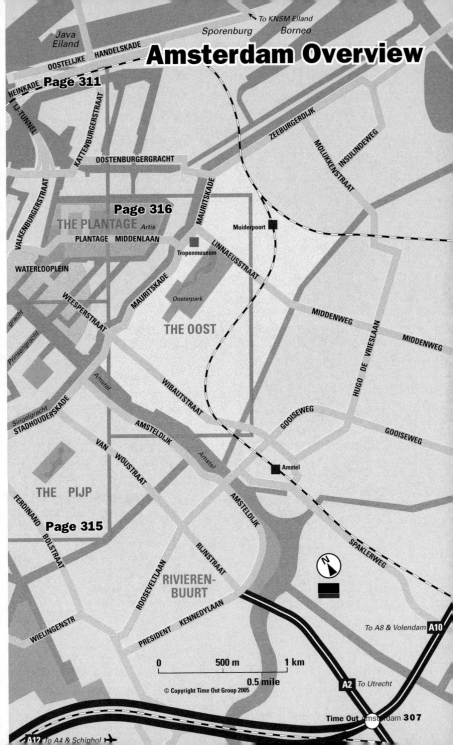

Amsterdam Overview

Java Eiland

To KNSM Eiland

Sporenburg   Borneo

OOSTELIJKE HANDELSKADE

HEINKADE **Page 311**

IJ-TUNNEL

KATTENBURGERSTRAAT

ZEEBURGERDIJK

MOLUKKENSTRAAT

INSULINDEWEG

OOSTENBURGERGRACHT

VALKENBURGERSTRAAT

MAURITSKADE

Page 316

THE PLANTAGE Artis

Muiderpoort

PLANTAGE MIDDENLAAN

LINNAEUSSTRAAT

Tropenmuseum

WATERLOOPLEIN

MAURITSKADE

gracht

WEESPERSTRAAT

Oosterpark

MIDDENWEG

MIDDENWEG

Prinsengracht

THE OOST

HUGO DE VRIESLAAN

Amstel

WIBAUTSTRAAT

Singelgracht

STADHOUDERSKADE

GOOISEWEG

AMSTELDIJK

GOOISEWEG

VAN WOUSTRAAT

Amstel

Amstel

FERDINAND BOLSTRAAT

THE PIJP

Amstel

Page 315

AMSTELDIJK

SPAKLERWEG

ROOSEVELTLAAN

RIJNSTRAAT

RIVIEREN-BUURT

N

WIELINGENSTR

PRESIDENT KENNEDYLAAN

To A8 & Volendam **A10**

0   500 m   1 km

0.5 mile

A2 To Utrecht

© Copyright Time Out Group 2005

A12 To A4 & Schiphol

The Netherlands

© Copyright Time Out Group 2005

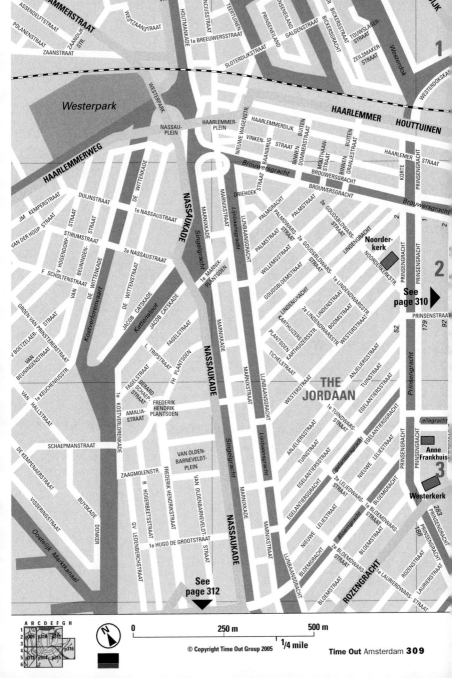

The Jordaan

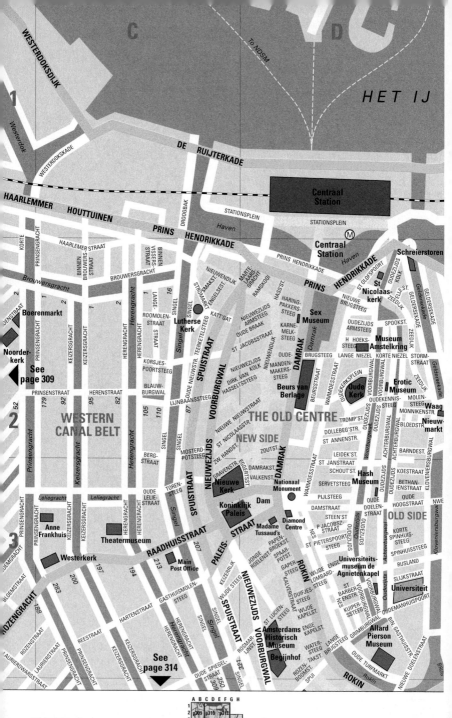

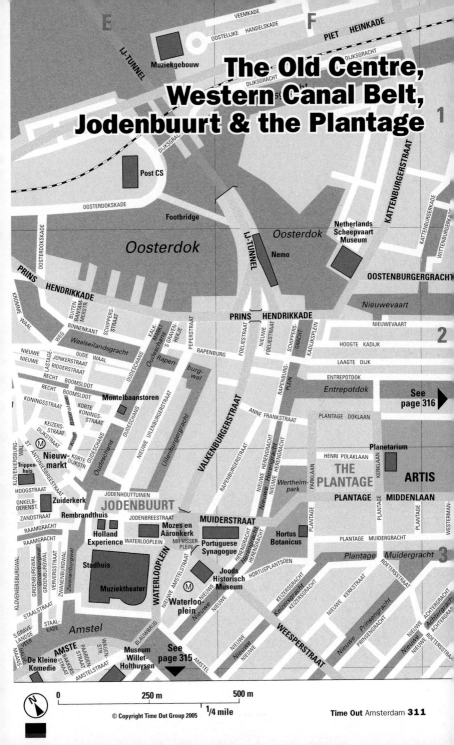

The Old Centre, Western Canal Belt, Jodenbuurt & the Plantage

VEEMKADE
OOSTELIJKE HANDELSKADE
PIET HEINKADE

IJ-TUNNEL
Muziekgebouw

DIJKSGRACHT

KATTENBURGERSTRAAT
KATTENBURGERKADE
WITTENBURGERK...

1

Post CS
OOSTERDOKSKADE

Footbridge

Oosterdok

Netherlands
Scheepvaart
Museum

OOSTENBURGERGRACH...

Oosterdok

IJ-TUNNEL
Nemo

OOSTERDOKSKADE

PRINS
HENDRIKKADE

KROMME WAAL

BUITEN BANTAM MERSTR
BINNENKANT
SCHIPPERS-STRAAT

KALK-MARKT
'S GRAVEN-HEKJE
PEPERSTRAAT

PRINS HENDRIKKADE

FOELIESTRAAT
NIEUWE FOELIESTRAAT
SCHIPPERSGRACHT
KADIJKSPLEIN

Nieuwevaart

NIEUWEVAART

2

Waalseilandsgracht

NIEUWE
NIEUWE
LASTAGE
RECHT BOOMSSLOOT
RECHT BOOMSSLOOT
KONINGSSTRAAT
KEIZERS-STRAAT
DIJKSTRAAT

OUDE WAAL
JONKERSTRAAT
RIDDERSTRAAT

Rapen
burg-
wal

Montelbaanstoren

OUDESCHANS
KORTE KONINGS-STRAAT
OUDESCHANS

NIEUWE UILENBURGERSTRAAT

RAPENBURG

VALKENBURGERSTRAAT

ANNE FRANKSTRAAT

RAPENBURGERSTRAAT

RAPENBURG PLEIN

Entrepotdok

RAPENBURG

HOOGTE KADIJK

LAAGTE DIJK

ENTREPOTDOK

PLANTAGE DOKLAAN

See
page 316

Planetarium

HENRI POLAKLAAN

KERKLAAN

ARTIS

KLOVENIERSBURG...
ST ANTONIESBREESTRAAT
Trippen
huis

Nieuw-
markt

KORTE
OUDEDIJKSTR
OUDESCHANS

Uilenburgergracht

Wertheim-
park

THE
PLANTAGE

NIEUWE HERENGRACHT
NIEUWE HERENGRACHT

PARKLAAN

PLANTAGE

PLANTAGE MIDDENLAAN

PLANTAGE

WESTERMAN-

HOOGSTRAAT
ONKELB-OERENST.
ZANDSTRAAT
RAAMGRACHT
RAAMGRACHT

Zuiderkerk

Rembrandthuis

JODENHOUTTUINEN

JODENBUURT

JODENBREESTRAAT

MUIDERSTRAAT

Hortus
Botanicus

PLANTAGE MUIDERGRACHT

S GRAVE-LANDSE VEER
STAALSTRAAT

KLOVENIERSBURGWAL
GROENBURGWAL
GROENBURGWAL
VERVERSSTRAAT
ZWANENBURGWAL

STAAL-KADE

Holland
Experience
Stadhuis

WATERLOOPLEIN
Mozes en
Aäronkerk

MR VISSER-PLEIN
Portuguese
Synagogue

Muziektheater

WATERLOOPLEIN

Joods
Historisch
Museum

Waterloo-
plein

NIEUWE AMSTELSTRAAT

HERENGRACHT
NIEUWE HERENGRACHT

HORTUSPLANTSOEN

KEIZERSGRACHT
KEIZERSGRACHT

Plantage Muidergracht

NIEUWE KERKSTRAAT

ROETERSSTRAAT

NIEUWE ACHTERGRACHT
ACHTERGRA...
NIEUWE ACHTERGRA...

3

Amstel

WAGENAAR
PAARDEN STR.
STRAAT

BLAUWBRUG

NIEUWE
NIEUWE

Nieuwe Prinsengracht
NIEUWE PRINSENGRACHT

NIEUWE ROETERSSTRAAT

De Kleine
Komedie

AMSTE
S GRAVE-LANDSE VEER
NANNIE-MAANS-

PAARDEN
BAKKERS STRAAT
AMSTELSTRAAT

Museum
Willet-
Holthuysen

See
page 315

NIEUWE
NIEUWE
WEESPERSTRAAT

AMSTEL

0   250 m   500 m
1/4 mile

© Copyright Time Out Group 2005

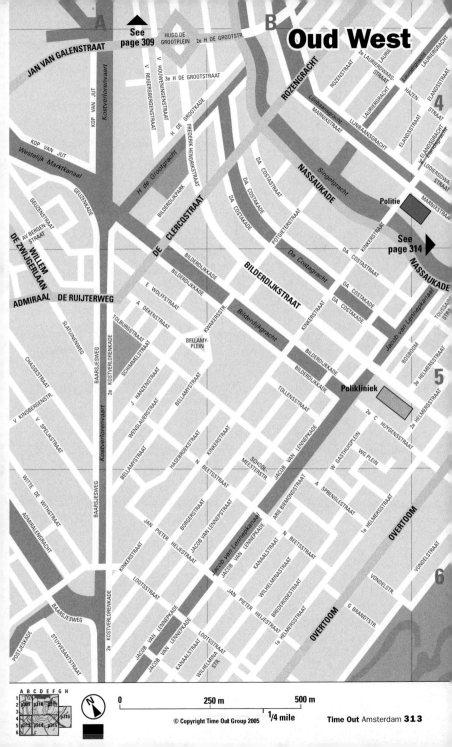

Oud West

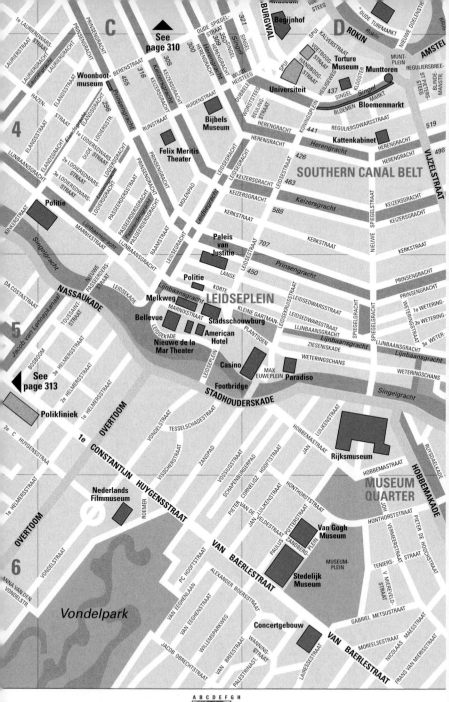

See page 310

See page 313

C

BURGWAL

Begijnhof

D ROKIN

Oude Turfmarkt

AMSTEL

Torture Museum

Munttoren

Universiteit

Woonboot-museum

Bloemenmarkt

Bijbels Museum

Kattenkabinet

SOUTHERN CANAL BELT

Felix Meritis Theater

VIJZELSTRAAT

Politie

Paleis van Justitie

Politie

LEIDSEPLEIN

Melkweg

Bellevue

Stadsschouwburg

Nieuwe de la Mar Theater

American Hotel

Casino

Paradiso

Footbridge

STADHOUDERSKADE

Polikliniek

OVERTOOM

Rijksmuseum

MUSEUM QUARTER

HOBBEMAKADE

Nederlands Filmmuseum

1e CONSTANTIJN HUYGENSSTRAAT

VAN BAERLESTRAAT

Van Gogh Museum

Stedelijk Museum

OVERTOOM

Vondelpark

Concertgebouw

VAN BAERLESTRAAT

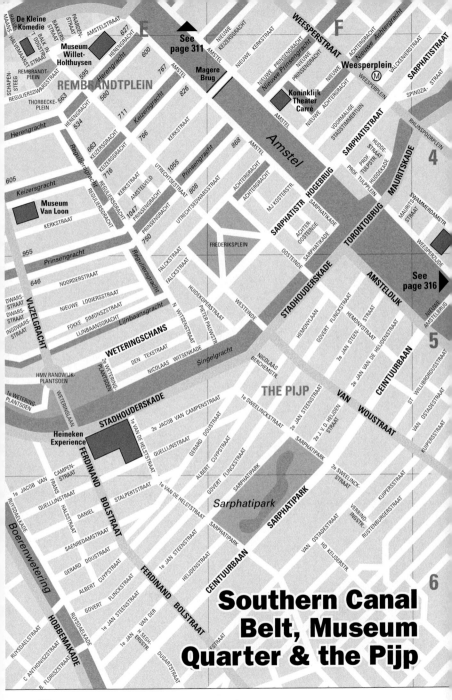

Southern Canal Belt, Museum Quarter & the Pijp

© Copyright Time Out Group 2005

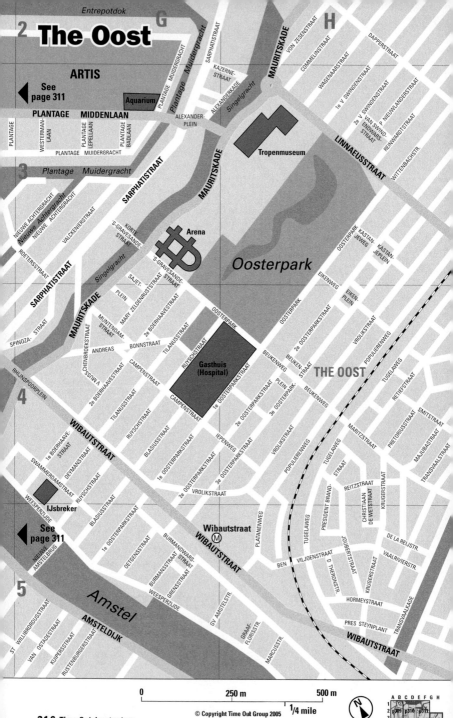

The Oost

G Entrepotdok

H

ARTIS

See page 311

PLANTAGE MIDDENLAAN

Aquarium

Tropenmuseum

Plantage Muidergracht

SARPHATISTRAAT

Arena

Oosterpark

MAURITSKADE

LINNAEUSSTRAAT

Gasthuis (Hospital)

THE OOST

WIBAUTSTRAAT

IJsbreker

See page 311

Wibautstraat Ⓜ

WIBAUTSTRAAT

Amstel

AMSTELDIJK

WIBAUTSTRAAT

| 0 | 250 m | 500 m |

1/4 mile

© Copyright Time Out Group 2005

Street Index

About the maps

This index has been designed to tie in with other available maps of Amsterdam, and certain principles of the Dutch language have been followed for reasons of consistency and ease of use:
● Where a street is named after a person – Albert Cuypstraat, for example – it is alphabetised by surname. Albert Cuypstraat, therefore, is listed under 'C'.
● Where a street takes a number as a prefix, it has been listed under the name of the street, rather than the number. 1e Bloemdwarsstraat, then, is alphabetised under 'B'.

● The following prefixes have been ignored for the purposes of alphabetisation: Da, De, Den, 's, Sint (St), 't, Van, Van der. Where street names contain one of these prefixes, they have been alphabetised under the subsequent word. For example, Da Costakade can be found under 'C', and Van Breestraat is listed under 'B'.
● In Dutch, 'ij' is essentially the same as 'y'. Street names containing 'ij' – Vijzelstraat, for example – have been alphabetised as if 'ij' were a 'y'.

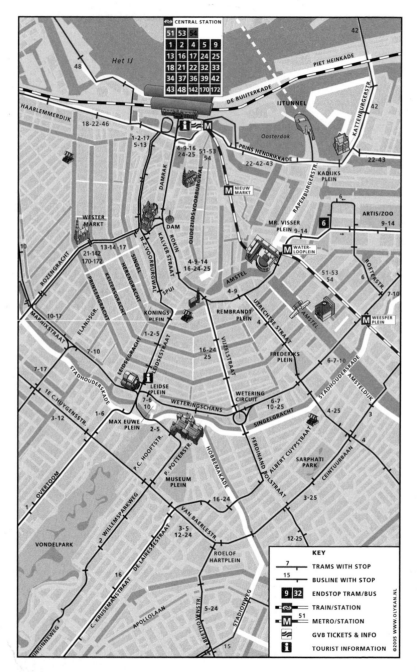